EATCS
Monographs on Theoretical Computer Science
Volume 25

Editors: W. Brauer G. Rozenberg A. Salomaa

Advisory Board: G. Ausiello M. Broy S. Even
J. Hartmanis N. Jones T. Leighton M. Nivat
C. Papadimitriou D. Scott

Wolfgang Wechler

Universal Algebra for Computer Scientists

Springer-Verlag
Berlin Heidelberg New York
London Paris Tokyo
Hong Kong Barcelona Budapest

Author

Prof. Dr. Wolfgang Wechler †
Universität Würzburg, Institut für Informatik
Am Hubland, W-8700 Würzburg, Germany

Editors

Prof. Dr. Wilfried Brauer
Institut für Informatik, Technische Universität München
Arcisstr. 21, W-8000 München 2, Germany

Prof. Dr. Grzegorz Rozenberg
Institute of Applied Mathematics and Computer Science
University of Leiden, Niels-Bohr-Weg 1, P.O. Box 9512
NL-2300 RA Leiden, The Netherlands

Prof. Dr. Arto Salomaa
Department of Mathematics, University of Turku
SF-20500 Turku 50, Finland

ISBN 3-540-54280-9 Springer-Verlag Berlin Heidelberg NewYork
ISBN 0-387-54280-9 Springer-Verlag NewYork Berlin Heidelberg

Typesetting: Data conversion by author
Offsetprinting: Color-Druck Dorfi GmbH, Berlin. Binding: Lüderitz & Bauer, Berlin
45/3020-543210 – Printed on acid-free paper

Wolfgang Wechler in Memoriam

It is very unusual that the series editors begin a book with a memorial notice. The sad news of Wolfgang Wechler's untimely death reached us during the final production stage in September. The author wrote the preface in July. He seemed to have recovered from his serious illness.

Wolfgang Wechler's work was very well known in the computer science community. Until 1989 he could be met personally only in conferences in eastern Europe. We know how happy he was about the opening of the western borders.

As a scientist Wolfgang Wechler was an algebraist and a logician with a broad view on possible applications. The present book shows his excellent style.

Wilfried Brauer, Grzegorz Rozenberg, Arto Salomaa

To my family

and

to my friends

Preface

In the last two decades universal algebra has become useful and important in theoretical computer science. In particular, structural aspects such as syntax and semantics, data abstraction, etc., are mainly investigated by methods of universal algebra. To describe, for instance, the semantics of data types or program schemes, algebras are generally needed as models in which all syntactic symbols involved in the considered objects are interpreted.

One of the fundamental ideas of universal algebra is the representation of logical notions in nonlogical terms. The famous Birkhoff Variety Theorem states that a class of algebras is equationally definable if and only if it is closed under subalgebras, images and products; such a class is called a variety. This characterization result was the starting point of universal algebra. Similar results are obtainable for other classes of algebras defined by more general formulas like implications, finitary implications and universal Horn clauses. Besides axiomatic classes, theories are studied and characterized algebraically. For instance, a set E of equations is an equational theory if and only if E, considered as a relation, is a fully invariant congruence. Again this result can be generalized for the other kinds of formula mentioned above.

Before we study universal algebra, basic concepts are introduced in Chapter 1. These are the notions of generation, structural induction, algebraic recursion and deduction as well as equivalence relations, partial orders and terminating relations. In particular, terminating relations are shown to be equivalent to well-founded or Noetherian relations. Therefore, we can use Noetherian induction to prove properties of terminating relations. Furthermore, trees are dealt within the framework of well-founded partially ordered sets. Finally, ω-complete ordered sets and fixpoint methods are investigated as a prerequisite of semantics for recursive program schemes.

Chapter 2 deals with reduction systems. Symbolic manipulations on syntactic objects are based upon their providing models for computation in an operational setting. Our motivation for reduction systems, especically for term rewriting systems, results from solving the word problem for (fully invariant) congruences. Confluence and termination are the basic properties. A reduction system is called complete if it is confluent and terminating. Both properties are undecidable in general. Hence, special techniques are developed to prove confluence as well as termination. When dealing with term rewriting systems, which are defined by a finite set of reduction rules, the test of confluence can be localized provided the system is terminating. Local confluence, in turn, is testable via critical pairs. This leads to a completion procedure, known as Knuth-Bendix Completion. For term rewriting systems several termination proofs are presented based on polynomial ordering, Knuth-Bendix ordering and recursive path ordering.

The main topic of Chapter 3 about universal algebra is the algebraic characterization of equational and implicational classes of algebras and their theories. In the case of implications we distinguish three subcases: (1) implications with an infinite number of variables and an infinite number of premises; (2) implications with a finite number of variables but an infinite number of premises; and (3) implications with a finite number of variables as well as a finite number of premises. Implications of the second kind are called finitary implications, while implications of the third kind are called universal Horn clauses.

Chapter 4 presents two applications of universal algebra in theoretical computer science. First, we deal with data type specifications. For that purpose, the concept of an algebra has to be generalized to that of a many-sorted algebra which consists of finitely many carrier sets. The theory of many-sorted algebras is a straightforward gerneralization of usual (one-sorted) algebras. There are only a few subtle differences caused by the fact that some of the carrier sets of a many-sorted algebra may be empty. Secondly, we consider the algebraic semantics of recursive program schemes which are finite sets of recursive definitions of unknown functions. To assign a meaning to a recursive definition we use fixpoint techniques. Therefore, algebras have to be equipped with an ω-complete order. The theory of ω-complete ordered algebras is developed so far that we are able to derive a variety theorem for classes of ω-complete ordered algebras which are defined by inequalities of terms. But there is no related logic. For that purpose, we have to introduce inequalities of infinite trees.

In the appendices, two short reviews are given, one about sets and classes, and the other about algebraic structures as a means to deal with ordered algebras in a more general framework.

Although this book is mostly self-contained, the reader is assumed to have some familiarity with the mathematical formulation of problems in theoretical computer science. The level of the presentation is of graduate work; some is at advanced undergraduated level. The material in the book can be used for different courses: Term Rewriting Systems (Sects. 1.1 – 1.4, 2.1, 2.2); Abstract Data Type Specification (Sects. 1.1 – 1.3, 3.1, 3.2, 4.1); and Fixpoint–Semantics (Sects. 1.1 – 1.5, 4.2).

I would like to acknowledge the help of many colleagues and friends. Some of them suggested major changes and improvements; others found small but dangerous errors. I thank them all and hope that the list below doesn't leave too many of them unmentioned: Jiri Adamek, Wiktor Bartol, Jürgen Brunner, Peter Burmeister, Ingo Dahn, Hans-Dieter Ehrich, Heinrich Hussmann, Gregorz Jarzembski, Werner Kuich, Alex Pelin, Heinrich Seidel and Magnus Steinby, who read the final version very carefully. Mainly in discussions with Jiri Adamek, Wiktor Bartol and Gregorz Jarzembski, I found a way of presenting universal algebra using some methods of category theory which are not explicitly mentioned. Special thanks are due to Klaus Wagner for his steady encouragement especially in the last period of writing this book. Thomas Feilhauer and Manfred Rossdeutsch did a good job in producing the final TEXversion of the book. Finally, I wish to thank Andrew Ross from Springer–Verlag for his editorial help.

Würzburg, July 1991 Wolfgang Wechler

Contents

1 Preliminaries

Basic notions and results are presented in this chapter. We start with elementary concepts of set theory and algebra in Section 1.1. Closure systems are the key tool in Section 1.2. The fundamental concepts of generation, induction, recursion and deduction are based upon them. Section 1.3 deals with relations. Union, product and star of relations are called regular operations. It turns out that they are essential for our development. Furthermore, equivalence relations and partial orders are studied. Terminating relations will be needed, in particular, for proving termination of term rewriting systems later. Because termination is generally an undecidable property, special proof techniques are required. Well-founded and well-behaved relations provide such methods. In Section 1.4, trees and labelled trees are considered within the framework of well-founded partially ordered sets. Finally, ω-complete partially ordered sets and fixpoint methods are studied in Section 1.5 as a prerequisite of semantics for recursive program schemes.

1.1 Basic Notions

We are going to recall some basic notions from set theory in Section 1.1.1. The reader is assumed to be familiar with non-formalized set theory. A more detailed introduction is given in Appendix 1. Section 1.1.2 presents elementary notions from algebra.

1.1.1 Sets

A ***set*** is a collection of objects. The objects composing a set are its ***elements***. The statement that an object x is an element of a set A is written $x \in A$. The notation $x \notin A$ signifies that x is not an element of A.

The equality of sets is defined by extensionality. Two sets A and B are ***equal***, in symbols $A = B$, if they have exactly the same elements, i.e., $x \in A$ iff [1] $x \in B$ for all x. A set is therefore uniquely determined by its elements. We call a set ***finite*** if it contains a finite number of elements; otherwise it is called ***infinite***. To specify a finite set, we merely have to list all its elements. The set whose elements are $x_1, x_2, \ldots, x_n$ is denoted by

$$\{x_1, x_2, \ldots, x_n\}.$$

Sometimes this notation is also used for infinite sets like $\{x_1, x_2, \ldots\}$ provided that all elements are known by some rule. A one-element set $\{x\}$ is also called ***singleton***.

The ***empty set***, which by definition has no elements, is designated by $\emptyset$. Observe that all sets containing no element are equal by definition so that we can speak of the empty set.

---

[1] "iff" abbreviates "if and only if"

Besides listing elements there is another way to describe sets. For any set A and any property $\mathcal{P}$ [2], there is a set B such that $x \in B$ iff $x \in A$ and x has the property $\mathcal{P}$. This set B is unique by extensionality. We denote it by $\{x \in A \,|\, \mathcal{P}(x)\}$ or simply by

$$\{x \,|\, \mathcal{P}(x)\}$$

when A is understood from the context.

A set A is said to be a ***subset*** of a set B, in symbols $A \subseteq B$, if each element of A is an element of B. Trivial subsets of B are B itself and the empty set $\emptyset$. Any subset A of B differing from B is called ***proper***.

The set of all subsets of a given set A is called the ***power set*** of A, denoted by $\wp(A)$. Now, by definition, a subset of $\wp(A)$ is a set of subsets of A, which is often called a ***system***, or more precisely, a system over A.

Union and ***intersection*** have their usual meaning. They are also definable for a system $\mathcal{A}$ over a given set A:

$$\bigcup \mathcal{A} = \{x \in A \,|\, x \in X \text{ for some } X \text{ in } \mathcal{A}\},$$
$$\bigcap \mathcal{A} = \{x \in A \,|\, x \in X \text{ for all } X \text{ in } \mathcal{A}\}.$$

We call two sets ***disjoint*** if their intersection is empty. The ***difference*** of sets A and B, denoted by $A - B$, is the set of all those elements in A that are not in B. If B is a subset of A, the difference $A - B$ is also called the (relative) ***complement*** of B with respect to A. Whenever the set A is fixed in advance, we shall simply speak of the complement of B.

The ***direct product*** of two sets A and B consists of all ordered pairs (x, y) with their first component x in A and their second component y in B, in symbols,

$$A \times B = \{(x, y) \,|\, x \in A \text{ and } y \in B\}.$$

This notion is extended to finitely many sets, say $A_1, \ldots, A_n$, in a straightforward manner:

$$A_1 \times \ldots \times A_n \;=\; \{(x_1, \ldots, x_n) \,|\, x_i \in A_i \text{ for } i = 1, \ldots, n\}.$$

In the case that $A_1, \ldots, A_n$ are equal, say, $A_1 = \ldots = A_n = A$, we put

$$A^n = A_1 \times \ldots \times A_n.$$

Moreover, we define A^0 to be $\{\emptyset\}$.

---

[2] A convenient notation for the statement "x has the property $\mathcal{P}$" is $\mathcal{P}(x)$. The phrase "x has the property $\mathcal{P}$" is known as a predicate and therefore $\mathcal{P}$ is sometimes called a predicate symbol.

A subset of a direct product $A \times B$ of arbitrarily given sets A and B is said to be a ***relation*** from A to B. In particular, a relation f from A to B is called a ***partial mapping*** if, for all x in A and all y, z in B, $(x,y) \in f$ and $(x,z) \in f$ imply $y = z$. The ***domain*** of f, denoted by $Dom(f)$, is the set of all elements x in A such that there is an element y in B with $(x,y) \in f$. If x belongs to $Dom(f)$, then there is exactly one element y in B with $(x,y) \in f$. This is expressed by writing $y = f(x)$ or $f : x \mapsto y$; and y is called the ***image*** of x under f. The notion of image is extended to subsets as follows: $f(X) = \{f(x) | x \in X\}$ for $X \subseteq A$ where $f(A)$ is also called the ***range*** of f. If $y = f(x)$, then x is said to be an ***inverse image*** of y. Notice that the set of all inverse images of elements in B is the domain of f. A partial mapping f from A to B is called a (total) ***mapping*** if the domain of f equals A. When f is a mapping from A to B, we write $f : A \rightarrow B$.

Let $f : A \rightarrow B$ and $g : B \rightarrow C$ be mappings. The ***composition*** (or ***product***) of f and g, denoted by $f \cdot g$, is a mapping from A to C defined as follows:

$$(f \cdot g)(x) = g(f(x)) \qquad \text{for all } x \text{ in } A.$$

Sometimes it is convenient to express the composition of mappings by a diagram. When, for instance, a mapping h equals a composition $f \cdot g$ we say that the diagram in Fig. 1.1 commutes.

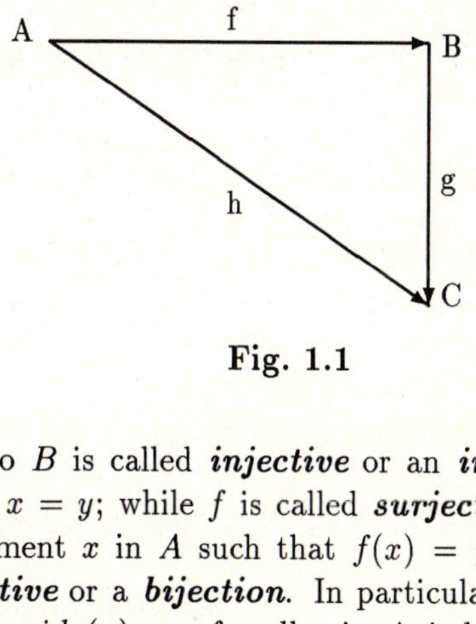

Fig. 1.1

A mapping f from A to B is called ***injective*** or an ***injection*** if, for all x and y in A, $f(x) = f(y)$ implies $x = y$; while f is called ***surjective*** or a ***surjection*** if, for all y in B, there is an element x in A such that $f(x) = y$. An injective and surjective mapping is called ***bijective*** or a ***bijection***. In particular, the ***identity mapping*** id_A on A, which is defined by $id_A(x) = x$ for all x in A, is bijective. Consider an arbitrary bijective mapping f from A to B. Then f determines a mapping g from B to A by the rule: $g(x) = y$ iff $f(y) = x$ for all x in B and all y in A. Obviously, g is bijective, too. We call g the ***inverse mapping*** of f and denote it by f^{-1}. Note that $(f^{-1})^{-1} = f$. If $f : A \rightarrow B$ is a surjection, then, by the Axiom of Choice (see Appendix 1), there is a mapping $g : B \rightarrow A$ such that $g \cdot f = id_B$. Given mappings $f : A \rightarrow B$ and $g : B \rightarrow A$, then f is injective and g is surjective whenever $f \cdot g = id_A$. This follows from the fact that f is injective if $f \cdot g$ is so and g is surjective if $f \cdot g$ is so. Now we have that

$f : A \to B$ is bijective iff there is a mapping $g : B \to A$ such that $f \cdot g = id_A$ and $g \cdot f = id_B$.

Let $f : B \to C$ be a mapping. If A is a subset of B, then the mapping $g : A \to C$, defined by $g(x) = f(x)$ for all x in A, is called the ***restriction*** of f to A; and we write $f|A$ instead of g. Similarly, if D is a subset of C and $f(B) \subseteq D$, then f may be ***cut down*** to a mapping $h : B \to D$ by restricting the target. We shall not use any special notation for this mapping.

Given two mappings $f : A \to B$ and $g : A' \to B$, where A' is a subset of A, if $g = f|A'$, then f is said to be an ***extension*** of g. Thus, e.g., if $f : A \to B$ is any mapping and $A' \subseteq A$, then f is an extension of $f|A'$, but of course, in general, f is not determined uniquely by $f|A'$.

With each set A we associate its ***cardinality***, denoted by $card(A)$, so that $card(A) = card(B)$ iff there exists a bijective mapping from A onto B. The empty set is assigned cardinality 0. For any finite set, say $\{a_1, \ldots, a_n\}$, the cardinality equals the number n of (distinct) elements. Two sets A and B are said to be ***equipotent*** if they have the same cardinality. For convenience, equipotent sets will often be identified.

We denote by $I\!N$ the set of ***natural numbers*** $0, 1, 2, \ldots$. They may be represented as finite sets as follows: 0 stands for the empty set $\emptyset$, 1 for $\{\emptyset\}$, 2 for $\{\emptyset, \{\emptyset\}\}$, 3 for $\{\emptyset, \{\emptyset, \{\emptyset\}\}\}$ and so on. Expressed in a more readable way, this means that $0 = \emptyset$ and $n = \{0, 1, \ldots, n-1\}$ for $n \geq 1$. A set A is called ***countably infinite*** if it is equipotent to $I\!N$, while A is said to be ***countable*** if A is finite or countably infinite.

Let A and I be sets. A ***family*** of elements in A indexed by I is a mapping f from I to A. Instead of f we write $(a_i \mid i \in I)$, where $a_i = f(i)$ for all indices $i \in I$, or simply (a_i) when no doubt about the index set I may arise; a_i is called the i-coordinate. If a family is indexed by natural numbers, then we prefer to speak of a ***sequence***. This is a general usage whenever the index set is an ordinal. For a family $(A_i \mid i \in I)$ of sets (subsets of a fixed set), union and intersection are defined as follows:

$$\bigcup(A_i \mid i \in I) = \{x \mid x \in A_i \text{ for some } i \in I\},$$
$$\bigcap(A_i \mid i \in I) = \{x \mid x \in A_i \text{ for all } i \in I\}.$$

In case I is a finite index set, say $I = \{1, 2, \ldots, n\}$, we may also use the infix notations $A_1 \cup A_2 \cup \ldots \cup A_n$ and $A_1 \cap A_2 \cap \ldots \cap A_n$. These notations are meaningful since union and intersection are associative. Moreover, the direct product of sets can be generalized by setting

$$\prod (A_i \mid i \in I) = \{(x_i) \mid x_i \in A_i \text{ for all } i \in I\}.$$

For a finite index set, say $I = \{1, 2, \ldots, n\}$, we will identify the equipotent sets $A_1 \times A_2 \times \ldots \times A_n$ and $\Pi\ (A_i|\ i = 1, 2, \ldots, n)$. Given a family $(A_i \mid i \in I)$ of equal sets, say, $A_i = A$ for all $i \in I$, we write A^I instead of $\Pi\ (A_i \mid i \in I)$. In fact, A^I is the set of all mappings from I to A. Thus, $A^\emptyset = \{\emptyset\}$ because there is exactly one mapping, namely the empty mapping (set) $\emptyset$, from the empty set to any set A. However, there is no mapping from any nonempty set to the empty set. Hence $\emptyset^I = \emptyset$ provided I is nonempty.

The following are important examples of mappings which will occur frequently in the sequel. If A is a set and B is a set containing A as a subset, then the identity mapping on A can be regarded as a mapping from A to B, which is called the inclusion mapping or simply the ***inclusion*** from A to B, often denoted by $in_A : A \to B$. For instance, if B is the union over a family $(A_i \mid i \in I)$ of sets A_i, we write $in_j : A_j \to \bigcup(A_i \mid i \in I)$ for the inclusion of the j-th component A_j in $\bigcup(A_i \mid i \in I)$, i.e., $in_j(x) = x$ for all $x \in A_j$.

Given a direct product $A = \Pi\ (A_i \mid i \in I)$, then for any fixed element $j \in I$, the mapping which assigns to each x of A its j-coordinate defines a mapping $pr_j : \Pi\ (A_i \mid i \in I) \to A_j$ called the ***projection*** of $\Pi\ (A_i \mid i \in I)$ on the j-th factor A_j, i.e., $pr_j(x) = x_j$ for all $x = (x_i \mid i \in I)$ in A.

In universal algebra, which is the topic of Chapter 3, we have to deal with very large collections of algebras. To prevent the well-known set theoretic difficulties, which may arise, we must know how to manipulate large collections safely. Therefore the concept of a set will intuitively be generalized by introducing ***classes***. We require the following:

(1) Every set is a class; and
(2) For every property $\mathcal{P}$ ranging over sets, there exists a class $\mathcal{A}$ such that X belongs to $\mathcal{A}$ iff X satisfies $\mathcal{P}$.

According to the set-building principle the shorthand notation $\{X \mid \mathcal{P}(X)\}$ will also be used to denote the class required in condition (2) assuming that X ranges over sets only.

A more detailed discussion about sets and classes may be found in Appendix 1.

1.1.2 Algebras

Let A be a set and n be any natural number. An ***n-ary operation*** on A is a mapping from A^n to A. Specifically, a nullary operation on A is a mapping $f : \{\emptyset\} \to A$, which is fully determined by $f(\emptyset)$. Hence nullary operations may be identified with elements from A and they are then called ***constants***. We call $f : A \to A$ a ***unary*** operation, while $f : A^2 \to A$ is said to be ***binary***.

An ***algebra*** is a set together with a family of finitary operations. Consider an algebra (A, f) with one binary operation f. Instead of $f(x, y)$ we write more commonly $x \cdot y$ or even xy when f is assumed to be subject to ***associativity***, i.e., $(x \cdot y) \cdot z = x \cdot (y \cdot z)$ for all $x, y, z \in A$. In this case, f is called multiplication. A ***semigroup*** is now an algebra with an associative binary operation.

In order to specify the arity of the operations in a proper way we introduce the following concept. A ***signature*** is a set Σ, whose elements are called ***operation symbols***, together with a mapping $ar : \Sigma \to \mathbb{N}$, called the ***arity function***, assigning to each operation symbol its finite ***arity***. When we speak of a signature the arity function is usually not mentioned explicitly. If the operation symbols are grouped into subsets according to their arity: $\Sigma_n = \{\sigma \in \Sigma \mid ar(\sigma) = n\}$, then the signature is uniquely determined by the family $(\Sigma_n \mid n \in \mathbb{N})$. Often we make no distinction between the signature Σ and the associated family $(\Sigma_n \mid n \in \mathbb{N})$.

A ***realization*** of an n-ary operation symbol in a set A is an n-ary operation on A. Given a signature Σ, a ***Σ-algebra*** $\boldsymbol{A}$ is a pair $\boldsymbol{A} = (A, \Sigma^A)$ consisting of a set A, called the ***carrier*** of $\boldsymbol{A}$, and a family $\Sigma^A = (\sigma^A | \sigma \in \Sigma)$ of realizations σ^A of operation symbols σ from Σ.

Frequently we say that A carries the structure of a Σ-algebra. Following custom, the Σ-algebra and its carrier set as well as the operations and the corresponding operation symbols are notationally identified when no confusion results. Furthermore, if the operations are unspecified or a specification is unemphasized, we simply speak of an algebra instead of a Σ-algebra.

Next, let us present some examples of algebras all of which have a finite signature. In general, if Σ is a finite signature, say $\Sigma = \{\sigma_1, \ldots, \sigma_k\}$, we often write $(A, \sigma_1^A, \ldots, \sigma_k^A)$ for (A, Σ^A), usually adopting the convention $ar(\sigma_1) \geq ar(\sigma_2) \geq \ldots \geq ar(\sigma_k)$.

A ***group*** is an algebra $(G, \cdot, i, e)$ with a binary, a unary and a nullary operation subject to the following conditions:

(G1) $(x \cdot y) \cdot z = x \cdot (y \cdot z)$,

(G2) $i(x) \cdot x = e$,

(G3) $e \cdot x = x$

for all $x, y, z \in G$. Instead of $i(x)$ we usually write x^{-1} and call it the ***inverse*** of x.

The reader may verify that the additional equations

(G2′) $x \cdot i(x) = e$,

(G3′) $x \cdot e = x$

are valid in each group. A group is said to be ***commutative*** (or ***abelian***) if $x \cdot y = y \cdot x$ for all $x, y \in G$.

Groups are generalized to monoids. A ***monoid*** is an algebra $(M, \cdot, e)$ with an associative binary operation $\cdot$ and a constant e, which is a ***unit*** (or ***neutral element***), i.e., $e \cdot x = x$ and $x \cdot e = x$ for all $x \in M$.

A ***ring*** is an algebra $(R, +, \cdot, -, 0)$ such that $(R, +, -, 0)$ is a commutative group, where $-$ is unary, but instead of $x + (-y)$ we write $x - y$ as usual, $(R, \cdot)$ is a semigroup, and addition and multiplication are related by the ***distributive laws***:

$$x \cdot (y + z) = (x \cdot y) + (x \cdot z),$$
$$(x + y) \cdot z = (x \cdot z) + (y \cdot z).$$

If, moreover, there is a constant, say 1, which acts as unit with respect to multiplication: $1 \cdot x = x = x \cdot 1$, we speak of a ***ring with unit***. Evidently, the set $\mathbb{Z}$ of all ***integers***, the set $\mathbb{Q}$ of all ***rationals*** and the set $\mathbb{R}$ of all ***reals*** are rings with unit under the common operations. In these number rings the product of several elements can only be equal to zero if at least one of the factors equals zero. If in a certain ring $a \cdot b = 0$ and $a \neq 0$, $b \neq 0$, then a and b are called ***divisors of zero***. An arbitrary ring is said to be ***zero divisor free*** if there are no such elements. The number rings $\mathbb{Z}, \mathbb{Q}$, and $\mathbb{R}$ are zero divisor free rings. Note that $0 \neq 1$ holds in all these rings and, in particular, in $\mathbb{Q}$ and $\mathbb{R}$ every nonzero element x has a (multiplicative) inverse x^{-1} such that $x \cdot x^{-1} = 1 = x^{-1} \cdot x$. Such rings are called ***fields***; the rationals and reals form fields.

Rings with unit are generalized to semirings. A ***semiring*** is an algebra $(S, +, \cdot, 0, 1)$ such that $(S, +, 0)$ is a commutative monoid, $(S, \cdot, 1)$ is a monoid, multiplication is distributive over addition, and 0 acts as a ***zero element***: $0 \cdot x = 0 = x \cdot 0$. Every ring with unit is a semiring. Moreover, the set $\mathbb{N}$ of all natural numbers is a semiring with respect to the usual operations.

Besides associativity and commutativity of a binary operation $*$ on a set A, we often need the following property: $x * x = x$ for all $x \in A$. Such an operation is called ***idempotent***. An idempotent and commutative semigroup is also called a ***semilattice***, while a ***lattice*** is an algebra $(L, \vee, \wedge)$ with two binary operations $\vee$ (called ***join***) and $\wedge$ (called ***meet***) such that $(L, \vee)$ and $(L, \wedge)$ are semilattices and join and meet are connected by the ***absorption laws***:

$$x \wedge (x \vee y) = x,$$
$$x \vee (x \wedge y) = x.$$

A lattice $(L, \vee, \wedge)$ is said to be ***distributive*** if it satisfies the laws:

$$x \wedge (y \vee z) = (x \wedge y) \vee (x \wedge z),$$
$$x \vee (y \wedge z) = (x \vee y) \wedge (x \vee z).$$

Actually it is enough to assume that one of the two equations holds; this implies that the other holds, too.

Any power set is a distributive lattice with respect to union and intersection.

1.2 Generation, Structural Induction, Algebraic Recursion and Deductive Systems

The mathematical concepts and methods in theoretical computer science mainly belong to constructive mathematics, and here constructivity is to be understood quite literally. Of course, one has to deal with infinite sets without enumerating their elements, but even infinite sets have to be specified in a finitistic manner. This means that every object is built up from a given finite set of atomic objects by finitely many applications of rules from a given finite set of rules. Such inductive definitions are studied in Section 1.2.1. In Section 1.2.2 we show that to each such definition there corresponds an inductive method of proving assertions about the defined elements. Section 1.2.3 deals with algebraic recursion in order to provide a preview of the important notion of freeness which will be studied thoroughly in Chap. 3. Finally, in Section 1.2.4 deductive systems are considered. We show that deductive systems can be thought of as algebraic closure systems.

1.2.1 Generation

The syntactic generation of objects from a given set of atomic objects using certain rules is described here on an abstract level. We illustrate such a generation by an example.

Nondeterministic while-programs are built up from a given set S of atomic programs (statements) using (nondeterministic) branching, sequencing and (nondeterministic) looping. These construction rules, also called ***control structures***, are depicted in Figs. 1.2–1.4.

Branching :

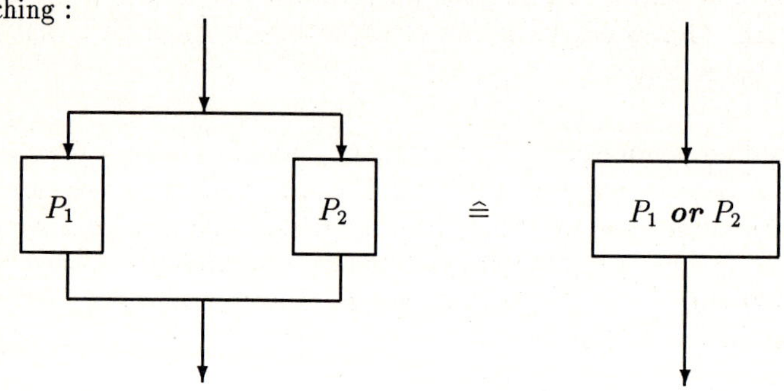

Fig. 1.2

Sequencing :

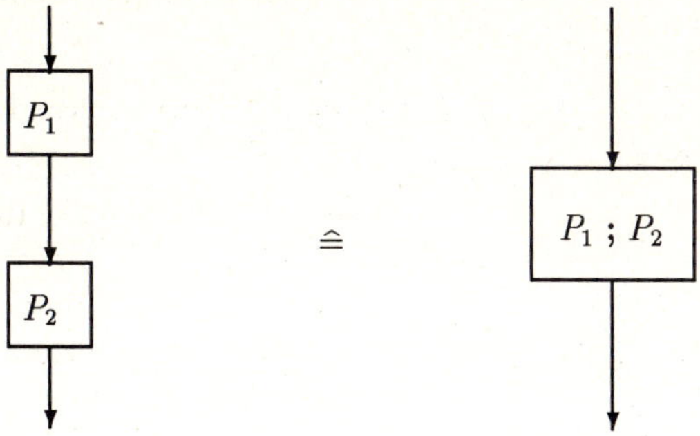

Fig. 1.3

Looping :

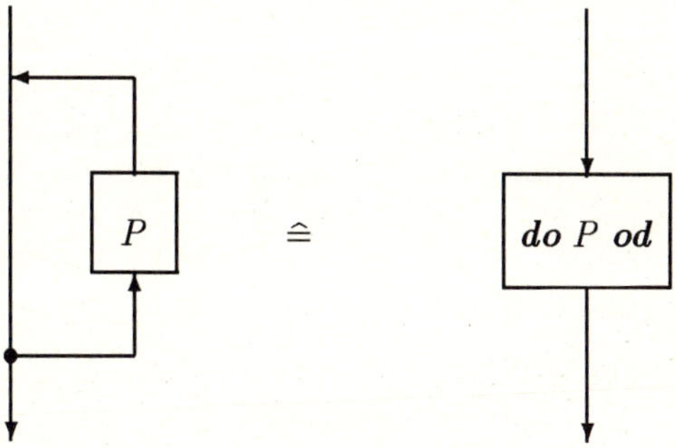

Fig. 1.4

We say that a set W is ***closed*** with respect to these control structures if W satisfies the three conditions below:

If $P_1, P_2 \in W$, then $(P_1 \textbf{\textit{ or }} P_2) \in W$.

If $P_1, P_2 \in W$, then $(P_1 \; ; \; P_2) \in W$.

If $P \in W$, then $(\textbf{do } P \textbf{ od}) \in W$.

The set of ***nondeterministic while-programs*** over S, denoted by $WP(S)$, is the least closed set containing S.

It should be mentioned that we prefer the nondeterministic version of while-programs because of their simple construction rules. To define deterministic while-programs, tests have to be introduced and branching as well as looping must be replaced by the ***if-then-else*** and ***while*** control structures, respectively.

In order to understand the general idea of such a definition we first ask the following question: what does it mean that $WP(S)$ is the **least** closed set containing S? If there is another closed set W containing S, then $WP(S)$ must be a subset of W. The existence of a unique least closed set containing S is guaranteed by the fact that the intersection of closed sets is again closed. Hence $WP(S)$ is well-defined.

This example suggests the following definition.

Definition 1. *Let U be a set (called the universe). A set $\mathcal{C}$ of subsets of U is called a* ***closure system*** *over U if U belongs to $\mathcal{C}$ and the intersection of any nonempty subsystem of $\mathcal{C}$ is also in $\mathcal{C}$.*

Note. $\mathcal{C}$ is a closure system iff the intersection of any subsystem of $\mathcal{C}$ belongs to $\mathcal{C}$. Take into consideration that the intersection of the empty subsystem equals U. ■

Example 1. The power set of any set U is a closure system. ■

Example 2. Consider the direct product $A \times B$ of two sets A and B as a universe. The set of all partial mappings from A to B is not a closure system because $A \times B$ is not a partial mapping. However, the set of all relations from A to B is evidently a closure system over $A \times B$. ■

Let $\mathcal{C}$ be a closure system over U. Its elements are called ***closed*** sets. Given a subset X of U, the least closed set containing X is called the ***closure*** of X, denoted by $cl_{\mathcal{C}}(X)$. We have $cl_{\mathcal{C}}(X) = X$ iff $X \in \mathcal{C}$.

Now we are going to study several closures of a relation. First, let us agree upon some standard notation. If R is a given (binary) relation from A to B, we shall write xRy or $x\overline{R}y$ instead of $(x, y) \in R$ or $(x, y) \notin R$, respectively.

Example 3. A relation R on a set A is called ***reflexive*** if each element of A is related to itself, i.e., xRx for all $x \in A$. Obviously, the set of all reflexive relations on A is a closure system over $A \times A$. If R is an arbitrary relation on A, then

$$ref(R) = \{(x, y) \in A \times A \mid x = y \text{ or } xRy\}$$

is the ***reflexive closure*** of R. A relation R on A is called ***irreflexive*** if $x\overline{R}x$ for all $x \in A$. The set of all irreflexive relations on A does not form a closure system. ■

Example 4. A relation R on a set A is called ***symmetric*** if, for all $x, y \in A$, xRy whenever yRx. The set of all symmetric relations on A is a closure system. Given an arbitrary relation R on A,

$$sym(R) = \{(x, y) \in A \times A \mid xRy \text{ or } yRx\}$$

is the ***symmetric closure*** of R. A relation R is called ***antisymmetric*** if, for all $x, y \in A$, xRy and yRx imply $x = y$; R is called ***asymmetric*** if, for all $x, y \in A$, xRy implies $y\overline{R}x$. The sets of all antisymmetric or asymmetric relations are not closure systems, respectively. ■

Example 5. A relation R on a set A is called ***transitive*** if, for all $x, y, z \in A$, xRy and yRz imply xRz. The set of all transitive relations on A is a closure system. To construct the transitive closure of a given relation R on A we have to introduce the notion of an R-path. Let x and z be elements of A. An R-path from x to z is a finite sequence $(y_0, y_1, \ldots, y_n)$ in A such that $x = y_0$, $y_n = z$ and $y_{i-1} R y_i$ for $i = 1, 2, \ldots, n$. We claim that

$$tra(R) = \{(x, z) \in A \times A \mid \text{there is an } R\text{-path from } x \text{ to } z\}$$

is the ***transitive closure*** of R. It follows from this definition that $tra(R)$ is a transitive relation including R. Assume that S is another transitive relation on A such that $R \subseteq S$. Using the Principle of Finite Induction we may show that the initial and final point of any R-path are in relation S, i.e., $tra(R) \subseteq S$. Hence $tra(R)$ is the least transitive relation including R. ■

Definition 2. *Let $\mathcal{C}$ be a closure system over U and let $C \in \mathcal{C}$. A subset X of U is called a* ***generating system*** *(more precisely a $\mathcal{C}$-generating system) for C if the closure of X is C, i.e., $cl_{\mathcal{C}}(X) = C$. In this case, C is said to be* ***generated*** *(more precisely $\mathcal{C}$-generated) by X.*

Example 6. Let M be a monoid with unit element e. The multiplication of M is extended to subsets as follows: $X \cdot Y = \{x \cdot y \mid x \in X \text{ and } y \in Y\}$ for $X, Y \subseteq M$. Given a subset X of M we define

$$X^{(0)} = \{e\} \quad \text{and} \quad X^{(n)} = X^{(n-1)} \cdot X \quad \text{for} \quad n \geq 1.$$

Note that $X^{(1)} = X$. Now we put

$$X^* = \bigcup (X^{(n)} \mid n \in \mathbb{N}).$$

It is an easy exercise to verify that X^* is the submonoid generated by X. ■

Often we need combined closures like the reflexive and transitive closure of a given relation. To construct such combined closures in an appropriate way we first associate to any closure system $\mathcal{C}$ over U a mapping from the power set $\wp(U)$ into itself, which associates the closure $cl_{\mathcal{C}}(X)$ to each X of $\wp(U)$. The following properties are easily checked:

(1) Extensivity: $X \subseteq cl_{\mathcal{C}}(X)$,

(2) Idempotency: $cl_{\mathcal{C}}(cl_{\mathcal{C}}(X)) = cl_{\mathcal{C}}(X)$,

(3) Monotonicity: $X \subseteq Y$ implies $cl_{\mathcal{C}}(X) \subseteq cl_{\mathcal{C}}(Y)$

for all subsets X, Y in U.

Definition 3. *Let U be a set. An extensive, idempotent and monotone mapping from $\wp(U)$ into itself is called a* ***closure operator*** *on U.*

Note that an extensive and monotone mapping $f : \wp(U) \to \wp(U)$ is already idempotent if $f(f(X)) \subseteq f(X)$ for all subsets X in U.

Given a closure system $\mathcal{C}$ over U the associated mapping $cl_{\mathcal{C}}$ is evidently a closure operator on U. Conversely, every closure operator cl on U determines a closure system

$$\mathcal{C}_{cl} = \{X \mid X \subseteq U \text{ and } cl(X) = X\}$$

over U such that

$$\mathcal{C} = \mathcal{C}_{cl_{\mathcal{C}}} \qquad \text{and} \qquad cl = cl_{\mathcal{C}_{cl}}.$$

Hence closure systems and closure operators are in a one-to-one correspondence.

Let cl_1 and cl_2 be closure operators on U. We put

$$cl_1 \leq cl_2 \quad \text{iff} \quad cl_1(X) \subseteq cl_2(X) \text{ for all } X \subseteq U.$$

Proposition 1. *Let cl_1 and cl_2 be closure operators on a given set U. If $cl_2 \cdot cl_1 \leq cl_1 \cdot cl_2$, then $cl_1 \cdot cl_2$ is a closure operator on U, too.*

Proof. The composition of two closure operators is obviously extensive and monotone. Therefore, it remains to show that $cl_1 \cdot cl_2$ is idempotent:

$$\begin{aligned}(cl_1 \cdot cl_2) \cdot (cl_1 \cdot cl_2) &= cl_1 \cdot (cl_2 \cdot cl_1) \cdot cl_2\\ &\leq cl_1 \cdot (cl_1 \cdot cl_2) \cdot cl_2\\ &= cl_1 \cdot cl_2.\end{aligned}$$

■

Let us now apply this method to construct combined closures of relations. We know that ref, sym and tra are closure operators. Because of

$$\begin{aligned}ref(sym(R)) &= sym(ref(R)),\\ ref(tra(R)) &= tra(ref(R)),\\ sym(tra(R)) &\subseteq tra(sym(R))\end{aligned}$$

we conclude that $ref \cdot sym$, $ref \cdot tra$ and $sym \cdot tra$ are closure operators. Of course, $sym \cdot ref$ and $tra \cdot ref$ are also closure operators.

Finally we present a method for defining closure operators, which will be of importance in Chap. 3. Let A and B be sets. Given a relation R from A to B. For any subset X of A we define a subset $fml(X)$ of B by the rule

$$fml(X) = \{y \in B \mid (x, y) \in R \text{ for all } x \in X\},$$

and similarly, for any subset Y of B, we define a subset $mod(Y)$ [3] of A by

$$mod(Y) = \{x \in A \mid (x, y) \in R \text{ for all } y \text{ in } Y\}.$$

---

[3] In Chap. 3 such subsets will be used. There fml abbreviates "formulas" (e.g., equations, implications or universal Horn clauses), whereas mod abbreviates "models".

Thus we have two mappings

$$fml:\ \wp(A) \rightarrow \wp(B) \quad \text{and} \quad mod:\ \wp(B) \rightarrow \wp(A)$$

with the properties

(1) $X \subseteq mod(fml(X))$ and $Y \subseteq fml(mod(Y))$;

(2) if $X_1 \subseteq X_2$, then $fml(X_2) \subseteq fml(X_1)$; and
if $Y_1 \subseteq Y_2$, then $mod(Y_2) \subseteq mod(Y_1)$;

(3) $fml(mod(fml(X))) = fml(X)$ and
$mod(fml(mod(Y))) = mod(Y)$.

Conditions (1) and (2) follow immediately from the definition; if (2) is applied to (1), we get $fml(mod(fml(X))) \subseteq X$ and $mod(fml(mod(Y))) \subseteq Y$, while (1) applied to $mod(Y)$ and $fml(X)$, respectively, gives the reverse inequalities. Thus any mappings which satisfy (1) and (2) also satisfy (3).

A pair of mappings between $\wp(A)$ and $\wp(B)$ is called a ***Galois connection*** if it satisfies (1) and (2), and hence (3).

To establish the link with closure systems we observe that in any Galois connection the mapping $mod \cdot fml$ is a closure operator on A and $fml \cdot mod$ is a closure operator on B. Moreover, the mappings fml and mod give bijections between these two closure systems.

1.2.2 Structural Induction

In this section we exhibit proof principles related to generation processes.

Let $\mathcal{C}$ be a closure system over a set U. Our aim is to determine a method for proving a property $\mathcal{P}$ for all elements of a set A of $\mathcal{C}$. If A is generated by X, it suffices to show that

(1) $\mathcal{P}$ holds for all elements in X; and

(2) The set of all elements of A, for which $\mathcal{P}$ holds, is closed.

By definition, A is the least closed set containing X. Hence $\mathcal{P}$ holds for all elements in A.

Of course, this proof scheme has the disadvantage that condition (2) may be hard to verify unless sufficient information about the closure system is given.

To overcome this difficulty let us consider special closure systems associated with algebras. Given a Σ-algebra $\boldsymbol{A}$, a subset B of A is said to be ***closed*** (under the operations of $\boldsymbol{A}$) if, for each n-ary operation symbol σ of Σ and all $x_1, \dots, x_n$ in A,

$$\sigma^A(x_1, \dots, x_n) \in B \quad \text{whenever} \quad x_1, \dots, x_n \in B.$$

Restricting the operations on A to a closed subset B we get a Σ-algebra $\boldsymbol{B}$ with B as its carrier. $\boldsymbol{B}$ is called a ***subalgebra*** of $\boldsymbol{A}$. Indeed, the set of all (carriers of) subalgebras of $\boldsymbol{A}$ is a closure system.

Definition 4. *A closure system $\mathcal{C}$ is called* ***algebraic*** *if there is an algebra such that $\mathcal{C}$ equals the set of all its subalgebras.*

Let $\boldsymbol{A}$ be a Σ-algebra and let X be a subset A. Then the ***algebra generated*** by X is the least subalgebra of $\boldsymbol{A}$ which includes X. We denote the (carrier of the) generated algebra by $\langle X \rangle$. Hence, $\langle X \rangle = \bigcap\{B | X \subseteq B \text{ and } \boldsymbol{B} \text{ is a subalgebra of } \boldsymbol{A}\}$.

Theorem 2 (Principle of Structural Induction). *Let $\boldsymbol{A}$ be a Σ-algebra generated by X. To prove that a property $\mathcal{P}$ holds for all elements in A, it suffices to show the validity of (1) and (2) below:*

(1) Induction basis. $\mathcal{P}$ holds for all elements in X.

(2) Induction step. If $\mathcal{P}$ holds for any $a_1, \dots, a_n$ in A (induction hypothesis), then $\mathcal{P}$ holds for $\sigma^A(a_1, \dots, a_n)$ for all $\sigma \in \Sigma_n$, $n \in \mathbb{N}$.

Proof. Let $A_\mathcal{P}$ denote the set of all elements in A, for which $\mathcal{P}$ holds: $A_\mathcal{P} = \{a \in A | \mathcal{P}(a)\}$. We have to show that $A_\mathcal{P}$ equals A. Of course, $A_\mathcal{P} \subseteq A$. By the induction basis, $X \subseteq A_\mathcal{P}$ and, by the induction step, $A_\mathcal{P}$ is closed. Since A is assumed to be the least closed set including X we derive $A \subseteq A_\mathcal{P}$. Hence, $A = A_\mathcal{P}$. That is, $\mathcal{P}$ holds for all elements in A. ■

The induction step is a refinement of condition (2) above rendered possible by the choice of an algebraic closure system.

The external description of the generation process for algebras is the basis of the Principle of Structural Induction. But, in contrast to such a "top-down description", there exists also an internal description, which may be viewed as a "bottom-up construction".

Given a subset X of a Σ-algebra $\boldsymbol{A}$, we denote by $\Sigma^A(X)$ the set of all elements generated in one step from X. Formally,

$$\Sigma^A(X) = \{\sigma^A(x_1, \dots, x_n) | \, \sigma \in \Sigma_n, \, n \in \mathbb{N} \text{ and } x_1, \dots, x_n \in X\}.$$

The algebra generated by X can now be described internally.

Define a mapping g from the powerset of A into itself by $g(X) = X \cup \Sigma^A(X)$ and then its finite powers as follows

$$g^0(X) = X \quad \text{and} \quad g^n(X) = g(g^{n-1}(X)) \quad \text{for} \quad n \geq 1 .$$

Note that $g^1(X) = g(X)$. Evidently, $X \subseteq g(X) \subseteq g^2(X) \subseteq \ldots$.

Proposition 3. *Let* $\boldsymbol{A}$ *be a* Σ*-algebra. For any subset* X *of* A,

$$\langle X \rangle = \bigcup (g^n(X) \mid n \in \mathbb{N}).$$

Proof. If we put $B = \bigcup (g^n(X) \mid n \in \mathbb{N})$, then, of course, $X \subseteq B$. Moreover, B is closed under the operations of $\boldsymbol{A}$. For if $x_1, \ldots, x_n \in B$, where $x_i \in g^{k_i}(X)$ $(i = 1, \ldots, n)$, then if $m = \max\{k_1, \ldots, k_n\}$, $x_1, \ldots, x_n \in g^m(X)$, whence $\sigma^A(x_1, \ldots, x_n) \in g^{m+1}(X)$ and consequently $\sigma^A(x_1, \ldots, x_n) \in B$. Hence $\langle X \rangle \subseteq B$ since $\langle X \rangle$ is the least subalgebra including X.

On the other hand, $g^n(X) \subseteq \langle X \rangle$ for all $n \in \mathbb{N}$ as we may show by induction over n. Thus $B \subseteq \langle X \rangle$ and so $B = \langle X \rangle$. That is,

$$\langle X \rangle = \bigcup (g^n(X) \mid n \in \mathbb{N}).$$

■

1.2.3 Terms and Algebraic Recursion

In this section we are concerned with the syntactic generation which yields the notion of a term. As we will see, terms always have a unique representation by generators. A main consequence is then that every homomorphism on terms is already uniquely determined by the images of the generators. This fact allows algebraic recursion.

Let us reconsider the definition of nondeterministic while-programs from Section 1.2.1. In order to say that these objects are generated a suitable closure system has to be defined. But what is the underlying universe? The syntactic description of a nondeterministic while-program is a formal expression, which is nothing but a finite sequence of symbols.

Given any set A, the ***word monoid*** $W(A)$ over A is defined as follows: The elements of $W(A)$ are the n-tuples $w = (x_1, \ldots, x_n)$ with $n \geq 0$ of elements from A. The product of two elements $u = (x_1, \ldots, x_m)$ and $v = (y_1, \ldots, y_n)$ is defined as the concatenation $uv = (x_1, \ldots, x_m, y_1, \ldots, y_n)$. This produces a monoid with $e = ()$ as unit. We shall agree to write x instead of the 1-tuple (x). Similarly, $w = (x_1, \ldots, x_n)$ may be written $w = x_1 \ldots x_n$ if $n \geq 1$. Because of this, w is called a ***word***, $x \in A$ is called a ***letter*** and A itself is called an ***alphabet*** [4)].

---

4) The elements of A are assumed to be indivisible symbols.

Evidently, each word has a unique representation by letters because two words $u = x_1 \dots x_m$ and $v = y_1 \dots y_n$ are equal iff $m = n$ and $x_i = y_i$ for $i = 1, \dots, m$. The ***length*** of a word w, in symbols $|w|$, is the number of occurrences of the letters in w. Thus

$$|e| = 0 \quad \text{and} \quad |uv| = |u| + |v|$$

for all words u and v over A.

A can be regarded as a subset of $W(A)$ by the convention $x = (x)$. Consider the submonoid A^* generated by A. By definition, A^* equals $W(A)$, which means that $W(A)$ is generated by A. Because of the unique representation of words by letters A is also called a ***basis*** or a ***free generating system*** of $W(A)$.

Now all symbols occuring in nondeterministic while-programs are joined together to form an alphabet $A = S \cup \{\textbf{\textit{or}},\ ;, \textbf{\textit{do}},\ \textbf{\textit{od}}\} \cup \{(,)\}$, where S is a given set of atomic programs. Then the word

$$(((\textbf{\textit{do}}\, P_1\ \textbf{\textit{od}})\,;P_2)\,\textbf{\textit{or}}\,(P_3\,;P_4))$$

with P_1, P_2, P_3, P_4 atomic programs is a nondeterministic while-program, whereas the word ***or do*** P_1 **;** ***do*** is not a nondeterministic while-program. We must be able to select well-formed expressions among the words. For that reason the control structures are regarded as operation symbols.

Let Σ be a signature and X be a set (of variables). A **Σ-*word*** over X is defined to be a word over the union of Σ and X. Througout this section we always assume for convenience that Σ and X are disjoint.

Definition 5. *Let Σ be a signature and X be a set of variables. A* **Σ-*term*** *over X is a Σ-word over X which can be derived by finitely many applications of (1) and (2) below:*

(1) Each x of X is a Σ-term over X.

(2) If $\sigma \in \Sigma_n$, $n \in \mathbb{N}$, and $t_1, \dots, t_n$ are Σ-terms over X, then $\sigma\, t_1 \dots t_n$ is a Σ-term over X.

The set of all Σ-terms over X is denoted by $T_\Sigma(X)$.

When X or/and Σ are unspecified or unemphasized we shall simply speak about Σ-terms or terms.

For any term t of $T_\Sigma(X)$ there exists a finite subset Y of X such that t belongs to $T_\Sigma(Y)$. Thus

$$T_\Sigma(X) = \bigcup \{T_\Sigma(Y) |\ Y \subseteq X \text{ and Y is finite.}\}$$

The finite set $var(t)$ of variables occuring in a term t is defined as follows:

(1) $var(x) \;=\; \{x\}$ for all x in X; and

(2) $var(\sigma\, t_1 \dots t_n) = var(t_1) \cup \dots \cup var(t_n)$ for every n-ary operation symbol σ of Σ and all $t_1, \dots, t_n$ in $T_\Sigma(X)$.

Notice that $var(\sigma) = \emptyset$ if σ is a nullary operation symbol. We say that t is a ***ground term*** if $var(t) = \emptyset$. The set of all ground terms is denoted by T_Σ. Hence $T_\Sigma = T_\Sigma(\emptyset)$. In particular, $T_\Sigma = \emptyset$ if $\Sigma_0 \;=\; \emptyset$.

Example 1. Consider the signature of nondeterministic while-programs consisting of a unary operation symbol ***do*** – ***od*** and two binary operation symbols ***or*** and ;. For instance

$$\textbf{\textit{or}}\ ;\ \textbf{\textit{do}} - \textbf{\textit{od}}\ P_1\ P_2\ ;\ P_3\ P_4$$

is a term over S. In infix-notation this term reads as follows

$$((\textbf{\textit{do}}\ P_1\ \textbf{\textit{od}}\ )\ ;\ P_2)\ \textbf{\textit{or}}\ (P_3\ ;\ P_4).$$

where the pair of outermost parentheses is omitted. ∎

Convention. We shall agree to use the most readable notation for terms. This permits us to represent terms on an extended alphabet with parentheses and commas, which is closer to standard mathematical practice. Also, infix notation and indentation is permitted to keep some of the term structure more apparent in the Σ-word. ∎

The set $T_\Sigma(X)$ can be made into an algebra if the construction of a new term from n given terms and an n-ary operation symbol is thought of as an operation:

$$\sigma^{T_\Sigma(X)}(t_1, \dots, t_n) = \sigma\, t_1 \dots t_n$$

for any n-ary operation symbol σ of Σ and all $t_1, \dots, t_n$ in $T_\Sigma(X)$.

Definition 6. *Let Σ be a signature and X be a set of variables. The algebra $\mathbf{T}_\Sigma(X)$ with carrier $T_\Sigma(X)$ and operations defined as above is called the Σ-term algebra over X or, shortly, the **term algebra**.*

According to our terminology, X is a generating system for the term algebra over X. Moreover, for each term t of $T_\Sigma(X)$ of word length greater than 1 there exist a unique natural number n greater than 0, a unique n-ary operation symbol σ of Σ and a unique n-tuple $(t_1, \dots, t_n)$ of terms $t_1, \dots, t_n$ in $T_\Sigma(X)$ such that $t \;=\; \sigma\, t_1 \dots t_n$. Thus each term has a unique representation by generators (variables).

As a consequence we will derive that any interpretation of the variables from X in an arbitrary algebra can be uniquely extended to an interpretation of the syntactically generated terms. To formalize this principle, which is fundamental for semantics, we need a further notion. Given Σ-algebras $\boldsymbol{A}$ and $\boldsymbol{B}$, a mapping f from A to B is called a ***homomorphism***, or more precisely a Σ-homomorphism, if f is compatible with the operations, i.e.,

$$f(\sigma^A(x_1,\ldots,x_n)) = \sigma^B(f(x_1),\ldots,f(x_n))$$

for every n-ary operation symbol σ of Σ and all $x_1,\ldots,x_n$ in A. We use the notation $f:\boldsymbol{A}\to\boldsymbol{B}$ to indicate that f is a homomorphism from $\boldsymbol{A}$ to $\boldsymbol{B}$. A homomorphism from an algebra $\boldsymbol{A}$ into itself is called an ***endomorphism*** of $\boldsymbol{A}$.

When h is a homomorphism from an algebra $\boldsymbol{A}$ into an algebra $\boldsymbol{B}$ and f is a mapping from a subset X of A to B such that the restriction of h to X is equal to f, h is said to be a ***homomorphic extension*** of f.

Theorem 4 (Principle of Finitary Algebraic Recursion). *Let Σ be a signature and X be a set of variables. Every mapping f from X to any Σ-algebra $\boldsymbol{A}$ admits a unique homomorphic extension $f^\sharp$ from the Σ-term algebra $\boldsymbol{T}_\Sigma(X)$ over X to $\boldsymbol{A}$.*

Proof. The required mapping $f^\sharp : T_\Sigma(X)\to A$ is defined by the rules:

(1) $f^\sharp(x)=f(x)$ for all x in X; and

(2) $f^\sharp(\sigma\, t_1\ldots t_n)=\sigma^A(f^\sharp(t_1),\ldots,f^\sharp(t_n))$ for every n-ary operation symbol σ of Σ and all terms $t_1,\ldots,t_n$ in $T_\Sigma(X)$.

Notice that, by the rule (2), $f^\sharp(\sigma)=\sigma^A$ for all nullary operation symbols σ.

Obviously, $f^\sharp$ is well-defined in the sense that each term $\sigma t_1\ldots t_n$ has a unique image under $f^\sharp$. By condition (1), $f^\sharp$ extends f. In the term algebra $\boldsymbol{T}_\Sigma(X)$ we have $\sigma^{T_\Sigma(X)}(t_1,\ldots,t_n) = \sigma\, t_1\ldots t_n$. Hence condition (2) can be transformed as follows: $f^\sharp(\sigma\, t_1\ldots t_n)=\sigma^A(f^\sharp(t_1),\ldots,f^\sharp(t_n))$ which means that $f^\sharp$ is a homomorphism.

Therefore, it remains to show that $f^\sharp$ is unique as an homomorphic extension. Assume that g is another homomorphism from $\boldsymbol{T}_\Sigma(X)$ to $\boldsymbol{A}$ such that $g(x) = f(x)$ for all x in X. Using the Principle of Structural Induction we are going to prove $g=f^\sharp$. The property $\mathcal{P}$ is defined so that for each t of $T_\Sigma(X)$, $\mathcal{P}(t)$ means $g(t) = f^\sharp(t)$.

Evidently, the induction basis is valid because of $g(x) = f^\sharp(x)$ for all x in X, by assumption. Now, let $t_1,\ldots,t_n \in T_\Sigma(X)$. If we assume that $g(t_i) = f^\sharp(t_i)$ for $i = 1,\ldots,n$ (induction hypothesis), then

$$\begin{aligned} g(\sigma^{T_\Sigma(X)}(t_1,\ldots,t_n)) &= \sigma^A(g(t_1),\ldots,g(t_n)) && \text{g is a homomorphism}\\ &= \sigma^A(f^\sharp(t_1),\ldots,f^\sharp(t_n)) && \text{induction hypothesis}\\ &= f^\sharp(\sigma^{T_\Sigma(X)}(t_1,\ldots,t_n)) && f^\sharp \text{ is a homomorphism.}\end{aligned}$$

Hence, by the Principle of Structural Induction, $g(t) = f^\sharp(t)$ for all terms t in $T_\Sigma(X)$. That is, $g = f^\sharp$. ■

Using the Principle of Finitary Algebraic Recursion, the ***height*** $hg(t)$ of a term t is defined as follows:

(1) $hg(x) = 0$ for all x in X;

(2a) $hg(\sigma) = 0$ for all nullary operation symbols; and

(2b) $hg(\sigma t_1 \ldots t_n) = 1 + \max\{hg(t_1), \ldots, hg(t_n)\}$ for every n-ary operation symbol σ and all terms $t_1, \ldots, t_n$.

The set $T_\Sigma(X)$ of all terms over X can be partitioned into "stages" $T_\Sigma(X)_k$, defined by $T_\Sigma(X)_k = \{t \in T_\Sigma(X) | \; hg(t) = k\}$ for all $k \in \mathbb{N}$. Hence

$$T_\Sigma(X) = \bigcup \{T_\Sigma(X)_k | \; k \in \mathbb{N}\}.$$

The Principle of Structural Induction simplifies now to an induction over the height of terms, which is often called the ***Principle of Term Induction.*** It reads as follows: To prove that a property $\mathcal{P}$ holds for all terms in $T_\Sigma(X)$, it suffices to show the validity of (1) and (2) below:

(1) Induction basis. $\mathcal{P}$ holds for all variables and constants.

(2) Induction step. If $\mathcal{P}$ holds for any terms $t_1, \ldots, t_n$ in $T_\Sigma(X)$ (induction hypothesis), then $\mathcal{P}$ holds for $\sigma \, t_1 \ldots t_n$ for all $\sigma \in \Sigma_n$ with $n \geq 1$.

We close the section by considering the semantics of nondeterministic while-programs. The set $WP(S)$ of all nondeterministic while-programs over S is identical with the set of all Σ-terms over S, where Σ is the signature given by $\Sigma_1 = \{\textbf{do} - \textbf{od}\}$, $\Sigma_2 = \{\textbf{or}, \textbf{;}\}$ and $\Sigma_n = \emptyset$ otherwise. An interpretation of nondeterministic while-programs is a mapping from $WP(S)$ to a suitable domain A. First, all atomic programs have to be interpreted. Therefore a mapping m from S to A is assumed to be given. By the Principle of Finitary Algebraic Recursion, m admits a unique extension to a homomorphism $m^\sharp : WP(S) \to A$ when A is equipped with operations corresponding to the program constructs. Let us denote them by $+, \cdot$ and $*$, where $+$ is the realization of ***or*** in A, $\cdot$ is the realization of ; in A and $*$ is the realization of ***do – od*** in A. Hence the defining rules for the semantics of nondeterministic while-programs are now the following:

(1) $m^\sharp(P_1 \; \textbf{or} \; P_2) \;=\; m^\sharp(P_1) \;+\; m^\sharp(P_2)$,

(2) $m^\sharp(P_1 \; ; P_2) \;=\; m^\sharp(P_1) \;\cdot\; m^\sharp(P_2)$,

(3) $m^\sharp(\textbf{do} \; P \; \textbf{od}) \;=\; (m^\sharp(P))^*$.

These rules express the requirement that a semantics should obey the principle of compositionality: the meaning of a composite program is a composition of the meanings of its components.

1.2.4 Deductive Systems

In this section we intend to show that algebraic closure systems are closely related to logical calculi. First, let us illustrate this connection by means of propositional logic. We choose a signature consisting of a unary operation symbol $\neg$ (called ***negation***) and a binary operation symbol $\Rightarrow$ (called ***implication***). Terms over a given (countably infinite) set of variables are called ***propositional sentences*** in this context. Deduction is based on the inference rule: from p and $p \Rightarrow q$, infer q. This rule is the well-known ***modus ponens.***

A formal proof system is given by the following axiom schemes:

(A1) $p \Rightarrow (q \Rightarrow p)$,

(A2) $(p \Rightarrow (q \Rightarrow r)) \Rightarrow ((p \Rightarrow q) \Rightarrow (p \Rightarrow r))$,

(A3) $(\neg p \Rightarrow \neg q) \Rightarrow (q \Rightarrow p)$

and modus ponens as inference rule.

For example, a formal proof for the deduction of $p \Rightarrow p$ is the following sequence:

$$p_1 = p \Rightarrow ((p \Rightarrow p) \Rightarrow p),$$

$$p_2 = (p \Rightarrow ((p \Rightarrow p) \Rightarrow p)) \Rightarrow ((p \Rightarrow (p \Rightarrow p)) \Rightarrow (p \Rightarrow p)),$$

$$p_3 = (p \Rightarrow (p \Rightarrow p)) \Rightarrow (p \Rightarrow p),$$

$$p_4 = p \Rightarrow (p \Rightarrow p),$$

$$p_5 = p \Rightarrow p,$$

where p_1 is an instance of the axiom scheme (A1) with $q = p \Rightarrow p$; p_2 is the axiom (A2) with $q = p \Rightarrow p$ and $r = p$; p_3 is inferred by modus ponens; p_4 is the axiom (A1) with $q = p$ and p_5 is inferred by modus ponens.

A set X of propositional sentences is said to be ***closed*** (with respect to formal proofs) if p belongs to X whenever p is provable from X. It turns out that all closed sets form an algebraic closure system.

Let S be a set (whose elements may be called sentences). An n-ary ***inference rule*** R on S is a subset of $S^n \times S$, where n is an arbitrary natural number. Note that a nullary inference rule is a subset of S. Adopting the usual notation for inference rules we write

$$\frac{p_1, \ldots, p_n}{p} \quad \text{via } R$$

instead of $(p_1, \ldots, p_n, p) \in R$; $p_1, \ldots, p_n$ are called the ***premises*** and p is called the ***conclusion*** of the inference rule R. When R is known from the context we skip "via R". Moreover, we shall agree upon the following convention. If R is a nullary inference rule, then R is said to be an ***axiom***. But, as before, any p of R is usually called an axiom (scheme).

Let $\mathcal{R}$ be a set of inference rules over S. Given a subset X of S and an element p of S, we say "p is provable from X using $\mathcal{R}$" if there is a finite sequence $p_1, \ldots, p_k$ of elements of S such that p_k is p and, for each $i = 1, \ldots, k$, either $p_i \in X$ or there is an n-ary inference rule R in $\mathcal{R}$ (for some $n \geq 0$) and $j_1, \ldots, j_n < i$ such that $(p_{j_1}, \ldots, p_{j_n}, p) \in R$. The sequence $p_1, \ldots, p_k$ is said to be a ***formal proof*** of p from X.

We write

$$X \vdash_{\mathcal{R}} p$$

when p is provable from X using $\mathcal{R}$. In case X is empty, we simply write $\vdash_{\mathcal{R}} p$ instead of $\emptyset \vdash_{\mathcal{R}} p$. Frequently, the subscript $\mathcal{R}$ is omitted.

Definition 7. *Let S be a set and $\mathcal{R}$ be a set of inference rules on S. The triple $(S, \mathcal{R}, \vdash_{\mathcal{R}})$ is called a **formal proof system**.*

Often, $\mathcal{R}$ itself is said to be a formal proof system.

Let $(S, \mathcal{R}, \vdash_{\mathcal{R}})$ be a formal proof system. A subset X of S is called ***deductively closed*** if, for each $p \in S$, $X \vdash_{\mathcal{R}} p$ implies $p \in X$.

Definition 8. *A closure system $\mathcal{C}$ is called **deductive** if there is a formal proof system such that $\mathcal{C}$ consists of all deductively closed sets.*

Every algebraic closure system is deductive since the operations of an algebra can be thought of as inference rules of a formal proof system. For the converse we need the following criterion.

Lemma 5 (Birkhoff-Frink Theorem). *A closure system $\mathcal{C}$ over U is algebraic iff its closure operator satisfies the following finiteness condition:*

$$cl_{\mathcal{C}}(X) = \bigcup \{cl_{\mathcal{C}}(Y) | Y \subseteq X \text{ and } Y \text{ is finite}\}$$

for all subsets X of U.

Proof. (1) Necessity: Assume $\mathcal{C}$ is an algebraic closure system. By definition, there is an algebra $\boldsymbol{A}$ such that $\mathcal{C}$ consists of all subalgebras of $\boldsymbol{A}$. Hence $cl_{\mathcal{C}}(X)$ is the subalgebra generated by a subset X of A. Now, it follows from Proposition 3 that

$$cl_{\mathcal{C}}(X) = \bigcup (g^n(X) | n \in \mathbb{N}).$$

Clearly, $\bigcup\{cl_{\mathcal{C}}(Y) | Y \subseteq X \text{ and } Y \text{ is finite}\} \subseteq cl_{\mathcal{C}}(X)$ for all subsets X of A. To show the opposite inclusion we assume that a is an arbitrary element in $cl_{\mathcal{C}}(X)$. Then $a \in g^n(X)$

for some $n \geq 0$. Hence $a \in g^n(Y)$ for some finite subset Y of X as may be shown by the Principle of Finite Induction; and so $a \in cl_{\mathcal{C}}(Y)$. That is,

$$cl_{\mathcal{C}}(X) \subseteq \bigcup\{cl_{\mathcal{C}}(Y) \mid Y \subseteq X \text{ and } Y \text{ is finite}\}.$$

(2) Sufficiency: Let $\mathcal{C}$ be a closure system over U such that its closure operator satisfies the finiteness condition: $cl_{\mathcal{C}}(X) = \bigcup\{cl_{\mathcal{C}}(Y) \mid Y \subseteq X \text{ and } Y \text{ is finite}\}$. For each finite subset Z of U and each $a \in cl_{\mathcal{C}}(Z)$ define an n-ary operation $f_{Z,a} : U^n \to U$, where $n = card(Z)$, by

$$f_{Z,a}(x_1, \ldots, x_n) = \begin{cases} a & \text{if } Z = \{x_1, \ldots, x_n\}, \\ x_1 & \text{otherwise.} \end{cases}$$

Let $\boldsymbol{A}$ denote the resulting algebra. It remains to show that $cl_{\mathcal{C}}(X) = \langle X \rangle$ for all subsets X in U. Then $\mathcal{C}$ is algebraic.

Evidently, $\langle X \rangle \subseteq cl_{\mathcal{C}}(X)$ since $f_{Z,a}(x_1, \ldots, x_n) \in cl_{\mathcal{C}}(\{x_1, \ldots, x_n\})$. On the other hand, $cl_{\mathcal{C}}(X) = \bigcup\{cl_{\mathcal{C}}(Y) \mid Y \subseteq X \text{ and } Y \text{ is finite}\}$ and, for $Y = \{x_1, \ldots, x_n\}$ finite, $cl_{\mathcal{C}}(Y) = \{f_{Y,a}(x_1, \ldots, x_n) \mid a \in cl_{\mathcal{C}}(Y)\} \subseteq \langle Y \rangle$, which implies $cl_{\mathcal{C}}(X) \subseteq \langle X \rangle$. Thus $\mathcal{C}$ consists of all subalgebras of $\boldsymbol{A}$. That is, $\mathcal{C}$ is an algebraic closure system. ■

Theorem 6. *A closure system is deductive if and only if it is algebraic.*

Proof. It suffices to show that every deductive closure system $\mathcal{C}$ is algebraic. By definition, there is a formal proof system $(S, \mathcal{R}, \vdash_{\mathcal{R}})$ such that $\mathcal{C}$ consists of all deductively closed sets and its closure operator is defined by

$$cl_{\mathcal{C}}(X) = \{p \in S \mid X \vdash_{\mathcal{R}} p\}$$

for all subsets X of U.

If p is provable from X, then there is a finite subset Y of X such that p is already provable from Y. This yields

$$cl_{\mathcal{C}}(X) = \bigcup\{cl_{\mathcal{C}}(Y) \mid Y \subseteq X \text{ and } Y \text{ is finite}\}.$$

Hence $\mathcal{C}$ is an algebraic closure system by Lemma 5. ■

1.3 Relations

In this section some more or less well-known properties of relations are summarized. A special emphasis is laid on the calculus of relations.

First, let us recall some basic notions. A (binary) relation from a set A to another set B is a subset of $A \times B$. The set of all such relations is denoted by $Rel(A, B)$. In case B

equals A, we will speak of a relation on A. The set of all relations on A is denoted by $Rel(A)$. When R is a relation we mostly use the infix notation xRy instead of $(x,y) \in R$.

There is the following possibility to picture a (finite) relation R on a set A. Each element of A is represented by a point and two points corresponding to elements x and y are connected by an arrow, $x \to y$, whenever xRy holds. For example, if $A = \{1,2,3,4\}$ and $R = \{(1,2),(1,4),(2,1),(3,3)\}$, then R is depicted in Fig. 1.5.

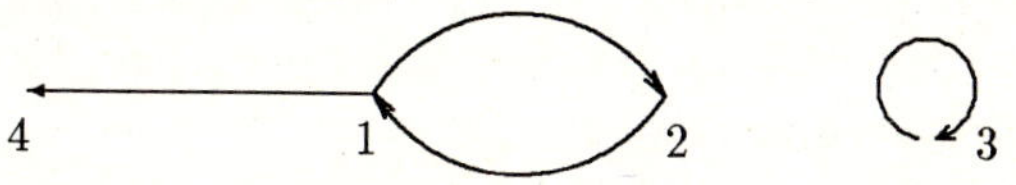

Fig. 1.5

Because of this graphical representation, a preferable notation for an arbitrary relation is the arrow $\to$ itself.

Since relations are sets by definition, the set theoretic operations on relations are defined as for sets in general. The ***complement*** of a relation R from A to B is denoted by $\overline{R}$; that is, for any $(x,y) \in A \times B$, $x\overline{R}y$ iff xRy does not hold. When a special symbol is used the complementary relation is designated by a stroke. Thus $\not\to$ is the complement of $\to$. Let R be a relation from A to B. The ***converse*** (***inverse***) ***relation*** R^{-1} is a relation from B to A defined by $xR^{-1}y$ iff yRx for all x in B and all y in A. We shall agree upon the following notational convention. If a relation is denoted by a special symbol, which is somehow directed, then the reversed symbol denotes the converse relation. For instance, $\leftarrow$ is the converse of $\to$.

Any (partial) mapping is a particular relation. The identity mapping id_A on a set A is therefore also called ***identity relation*** on A.

1.3.1 Regular Operations

In the relational approach to program semantics the regular operations play an important role. We intend to illustrate this fact by establishing a simple semantic domain for the nondeterministic while-programs.

If we think of a nondeterministic while-program as a device which produces an output for any input, then the set of all possible input-output pairs describes the meaning of a program. Without loss of generality we assume that all inputs and outputs belong to a common set A. Then an interpretation assigns to each nondeterministic while-program a relation on A. According to the Principle of Finitary Algebraic Recursion (Theorem 4 in Section 1.2.3), such an interpretation is completely determined when all atomic programs are interpreted and there is an operation on $Rel(A)$ corresponding to each control structure used.

The meaning of nondeterministic branching is to be understood as a nondeterministic choice. Hence it is intuitively clear that union should be the operation corresponding to ***or***.

Sequencing has the meaning of a consecutive execution of two programs. If we receive y as an output when we input x into $P_1\,;P_2$, then there must be an output z of P_1 which is at the same time an input of P_2 to which P_2 responds by producing y as an output. This leads to the product of relations defined below. Consequently, sequencing is represented by the product of relations.

Definition 1. *Let A, B and C be sets. The **(relational) product** of a relation $R \in Rel(A,B)$ and a relation $S \in Rel(B,C)$, denoted by $R \cdot S$, is a relation from A to C defined as follows. For all x in A and all y in C, $x(R \cdot S)y$ iff there is $z \in B$ such that xRz and zSy.*

Note that $Rel(A)$ forms a monoid with respect to (relational) multiplication and identity relation id_A as unit.

The iterative execution of a program P is the "looping" of P a certain finite (possibly zero) number of times: (x,y) is an input-output pair of ***do*** P ***od*** iff either $x = y$ (P is skipped) or (x,y) is an input-output pair of P ***;*** ***do*** P ***od*** (after evaluating P the loop is reentered). Let R be a relation defining the meaning of P. Then any relation satisfying the equation $X = id_A \cup R \cdot X$ could be taken as the meaning of ***do*** P ***od***. Subsequently, we will see that this equation always has a least solution which is the most appropriate relation for describing the meaning of ***do*** P ***od***.

Now we introduce the unary operation star and show that R^* is the least solution of the equation $X = id_A \cup R \cdot X$. Star together with union and product are usually referred as the ***regular operations***.

For any relation R on a given set A the powers $R^{(n)}$, $n \in \mathbb{N}$, are recursively defined as follows:

$$R^{(0)} = id_A \quad \text{and} \quad R^{(n)} = R \cdot R^{(n-1)} \text{ for } n \geq 1.$$

Definition 2. *For any relation R on a set A the **star** R^* is defined by*

$$R^* = \bigcup (R^{(n)} \mid n \in \mathbb{N}).$$

We will also use the notation $R^+ = \bigcup(R^{(n)} \mid n \geq 1)$.

An easy calculation yields $R^* = id_A \cup R \cdot R^*$. Hence R^* is a solution of the equation $X = id_A \cup R \cdot X$. The next lemma shows that R^* is indeed the least solution.

Lemma 1. *For any two relations R and X on a set A,*

$$X = id_A \cup R \cdot X \quad \textit{implies} \quad R^* \subseteq X.$$

Proof. If $X = id_A \cup R \cdot X$, then $id_A \subseteq X$ and $R \cdot X \subseteq X$. By the Principle of Finite Induction, we may prove that $R^{(n)} \subseteq X$ for all natural numbers n. Hence $\bigcup(R^{(n)} | n \in \mathbb{N}) \subseteq X$. ■

Let us return to the meaning of nondeterministic looping. If we unfold the loop ***do** P **od*** presented in Fig. 1.6, we get the infinite diagram depicted in Fig. 1.7.

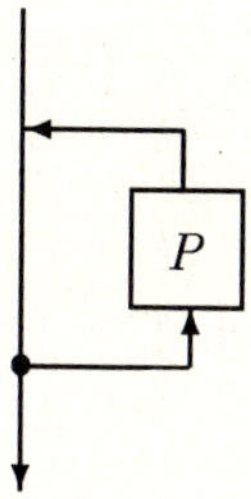

Fig. 1.6

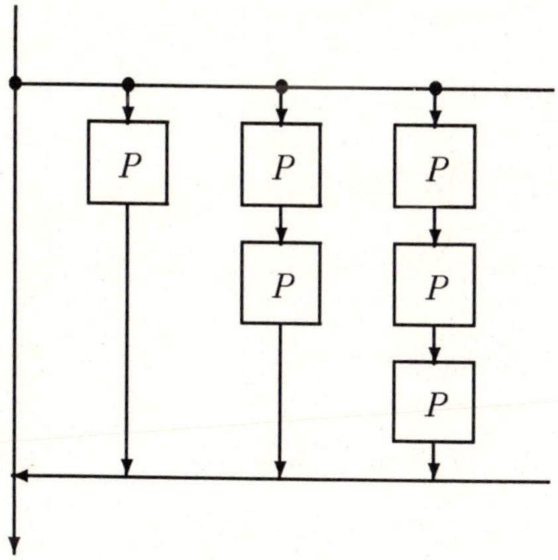

Fig. 1.7

Hence unfolding can be considered to be merely an infinite branching of the iterated program P, and informally we have the equality

$$\textbf{\textit{do}}\ P\ \textbf{\textit{od}} = \text{skip}\ \textbf{\textit{or}}\ P\ \textbf{\textit{or}}\ P;\ P\ \textbf{\textit{or}}\ P;\ P;\ P\ \textbf{\textit{or}} \ldots$$

(the infinite expression on the right-hand side of the equality is not a syntactically valid program). This intuitive argument suggests that the star operation should be related to nondeterministic looping.

Having assigned an operation on $Rel(A)$ to each control structure we are in a position to define the relational (or input-output) semantics of nondeterministic while-programs. By the Principle of Finitary Algebraic Recursion (Theorem 4 in Section 1.2.3), every mapping $m : S \to Rel(A)$, which interprets the atomic programs, can be uniquely extended by the rules:

(1) $m^\sharp(P_1\ \textbf{\textit{or}}\ P_2) = m^\sharp(P_1) \cup m^\sharp(P_2)$,

(2) $m^\sharp(P_1\,;P_2) = m^\sharp(P_1) \cdot m^\sharp(P_2)$,

(3) $m^\sharp(\textbf{\textit{do}}\ P\ \textbf{\textit{od}}) = (m^\sharp(P))^*$,

to a homomorphism $m^\sharp : WP(S) \to Rel(A)$, which defines the meaning of each program in $WP(S)$.

Example 1. Consider the nondeterministic while-program

$$P = (\textbf{\textit{do}}\ S_1\ \textbf{\textit{od}})\ ;\ S_2$$

where S_1 and S_2 are given atomic programs, which are interpreted as relations R_1 and R_2 over the natural numbers with

$$\begin{aligned} R_1 &= \{\,(x, x-5) | x \geq 5\,\} \quad \text{and} \\ R_2 &= \{\,(0,0), \ldots, (4,4)\,\}. \end{aligned}$$

That is, $m(S_1) = R_1$ and $m(S_2) = R_2$.

Then $m^\sharp(P) = m^\sharp(S_1)^* \cdot m^\sharp(S_2) = m(S_1)^* \cdot m(S_2) = R_1^* \cdot R_2 = \bigcup_{n \in \mathbb{N}} (R_1^n \cdot R_2)$.

Now, by induction over n, we get

$$R_1^n = \{\,(x, x-5n) | x \geq 5\,\}.$$

Hence, $R_1^n \cdot R_2 = \{\,(5n, 0), \ldots, (5n+4, 4)\,\}$ which results

$$R_1^* \cdot R_2 = \{\,(x,y) | x \equiv y(5), 0 \leq y < 5\,\},$$

where $x \equiv y(5)$ iff $x = 5n + y$ for some $n \in \mathbb{N}$; x is called congruent to y modulo 5. When we input a natural number x, the program P computes as output a natural number $0 \leq y < 5$, which is congruent to x modulo 5. For instance, input $x = 28$ results $y = 3$. ■

We conclude this section by presenting some useful properties of the star operation.

Proposition 2. *If R and S are relations on a set A, then*

$$(R \cup S)^* = R^* \cdot (S \cdot R^*)^*.$$

Proof. Claim: $(R \cup S)^* \subseteq R^* \cdot (S \cdot R^*)^*$.

By Lemma 1, it suffices to show that $R^* \cdot (S \cdot R^*)^*$ satisfies the equation

$$X = id_A \cup (R \cup S) \cdot X.$$

This assertion is verified by the following computation:

$$\begin{aligned} R^* \cdot (S \cdot R^*)^* &= (S \cdot R^*)^* \cup R \cdot R^* \cdot (S \cdot R^*)^* \\ &= id_A \cup S \cdot R^* \cdot (S \cdot R^*)^* \cup R \cdot R^* \cdot (S \cdot R^*)^* \\ &= id_A \cup (R \cup S) \cdot R^* \cdot (S \cdot R^*)^*. \end{aligned}$$

Claim: $R^* \cdot (S \cdot R^*)^* \subseteq (R \cup S)^*$.

We have to show that $R^{(m)} \cdot (S \cdot R^*)^{(n)} \subseteq (R \cup S)^*$ for all $m, n \in \mathbb{N}$, or equivalently, that $R^{(m)} \subseteq (R \cup S)^*$ and $R^{(m)} \cdot (S \cdot R^{(l_1)}) \cdot \ldots \cdot (S \cdot R^{(l_n)}) \subseteq (R \cup S)^*$ for all $m, l_1, \ldots, l_n \in \mathbb{N}$ and $n \geq 1$. But these assertions follow from the definition of $(R \cup S)^*$. ■

By Proposition 2, the inclusion

$$R^* \cdot S^* \subseteq (R \cup S)^*$$

always holds. Next, we are going to exhibit conditions under which the opposite inclusion is valid, too.

It follows immediately from the definition that star is a monotone operation: $R \subseteq S$ implies $R^* \subseteq S^*$; and that $R^* \cdot R^* = R^*$. Furthermore, star is idempotent: $(R^*)^* = R^*$. By induction over n, we may prove the following condition:

$$S \cdot R^* \subseteq R^* \cdot S^* \text{ implies } (S \cdot R^*)^{(n)} \subseteq R^* \cdot S^* \text{ for all } n \in \mathbb{N},$$

which yields the result below.

Lemma 3. *Given relations R and S, then*

$$S \cdot R^* \subseteq R^* \cdot S^* \quad \textit{implies} \quad (S \cdot R^*)^* \subseteq R^* \cdot S^*.$$ ■

Now the conditions mentioned above can be presented.

Proposition 4. *For any relations R and S on a set A, the following conditions are equivalent:*

(1) $S \cdot R^* \subseteq R^* \cdot S^*$,

(2) $S^* \cdot R^* \subseteq R^* \cdot S^*$,

(3) $(R \cup S)^* \subseteq R^* \cdot S^*$.

Proof. It is easily seen that conditions (1) and (2) are equivalent. Therefore, we only prove the equivalence of conditions (1) and (3).

Claim: (1) $\Rightarrow$ (3). If (1) holds, then $(S \cdot R^*)^* \subseteq R^* \cdot S^*$ by Lemma 3. Now, by Proposition 2, $(R \cup S)^* = R^* \cdot (S \cdot R^*)^*$. Hence

$$(R \cup S)^* \subseteq R^* \cdot R^* \cdot S^* = R^* \cdot S^*.$$

Claim: (3) $\Rightarrow$ (1). Taking into account that $S \cdot R^* \subseteq R^* \cdot (S \cdot R^*)^*$, we get $S \cdot R^* \subseteq (R \cup S)^*$ which implies

$$S \cdot R^* \subseteq R^* \cdot S^*$$

by the assumed condition (3). ■

1.3.2 Equivalence Relations

Mathematical abstractions are based on equivalence relations. If we want to ignore some inessential attributes of the objects in a certain set, then all objects with the same essential attributes have to be identified. Such an identification is a reflexive, symmetric and transitive relation. This motivates the following definition.

Definition 3. *A reflexive, symmetric and transitive relation is called an* ***equivalence relation*** *or simply an* ***equivalence****.*

In the sequel the following notation will be used. If R is an equivalence relation on a set A, then instead of xRy we will write $x \sim y\,(R)$ or simply $x \sim y$. (Some typographical relatives of $\sim$ may also be used). When $x \sim y\,(R)$, x is said to be ***equivalent*** to y (***modulo*** R).

Let a be an element of A. The set of all elements equivalent to a modulo R,

$$[a]_R = \{x \in A \,|\, x \sim a\,(R)\}\,,$$

is called the ***equivalence class*** [5] ***modulo*** R with a as its ***representative***. The subscript R is frequently omitted.

[5] Unfortunately, the term "class" is traditionally unavoidable in this context. Of course, equivalence classes are sets.

The set of all equivalence classes of A modulo R, denoted by A/R, is called the ***quotient set*** of A ***modulo*** R. If with each x of A we associate $[x]_R$, we obtain a mapping from A to A/R, called the ***natural mapping*** or ***identification*** related to R and denoted nat_R or simply nat. Clearly, nat_R is surjective.

In order to formalize the abstraction processes mentioned above we have to decompose a given set into subsets. Let A be a set. A set P of pairwise disjoint nonempty subsets of A is called a ***partition*** of A whenever $A = \bigcup P$. Obviously, each element of A belongs to exactly one subset. The subsets forming a partition are also called ***blocks***.

We may say that abstraction on a set A is formalized by the concept of partition. There is a one-to-one correspondence between partitions and equivalence relations. If P is a partition on A, an equivalence $\sim$ is defined by the rule: $x \sim y$ iff x and y are in the same block of the partition. Conversely, any equivalence relation on A induces a partition on A consisting of its equivalence classes. Hence, abstraction is based on equivalence relations.

Our next goal is the generation of equivalence relations. Since the set of all equivalences on a set A is a closure system an equivalence relation on A can be generated by an arbitrary relation on A. Using the method of combining closures according to Proposition 1 in Section 1.2.1 we are going to present a generation principle.

Given a relation $\rightarrow$, $ref(\rightarrow)$, $sym(\rightarrow)$ and $tra(\rightarrow)$ are the reflexive, symmetric and transitive closure of $\rightarrow$, respectively.

Lemma 5. *For a relation* $\rightarrow$ *on a set* A *the following holds:*

(1) $ref(\rightarrow) \;=\; id_A \cup \rightarrow,$

(2) $sym(\rightarrow) \;= \leftarrow \cup \rightarrow,$

(3) $tra(\rightarrow) \;= \rightarrow^+.$

Proof. (1) and (2) are trivial.

(3) By definition, $\rightarrow^+ = \rightarrow \cup \rightarrow^2 \cup \ldots$. Evidently, $\rightarrow^+$ is a transitive relation including $\rightarrow$. Thus $tra(\rightarrow) \subseteq \rightarrow^+$. On the other hand, $\rightarrow^n \subseteq tra(\rightarrow)$ for all $n \geq 1$, which may be proved by induction over n. Hence, $\rightarrow^+ \subseteq tra(\rightarrow)$ and consequently, $\rightarrow^+$ is the transitive closure of $\rightarrow$. ∎

We abbreviate $id_A \cup \rightarrow$ by $\rightarrow^=$ and $\leftarrow \cup \rightarrow$ by $\leftrightarrow$. Similarly, $\leftrightarrow^=$ denotes $id_A \cup \leftrightarrow$. Note that $\leftrightarrow^= \;=\; ref(sym(\rightarrow)) \;=\; sym(ref(\rightarrow))$. So $\leftrightarrow^=$ is the reflexive and symmetric closure of $\rightarrow$. Since $\rightarrow^* \;=\; (id_A \cup \rightarrow)^+ \;=\; tra(ref(\rightarrow)) \;=\; ref(tra(\rightarrow))$, $\rightarrow^*$ is the reflexive and transitive closure of $\rightarrow$.

Furthermore, $\leftrightarrow^+ = tra(sym(\rightarrow))$. Because $sym(tra(\rightarrow)) \subseteq tra(sym(\rightarrow))$, we get that $\leftrightarrow^+$ is the symmetric and transitive closure of $\rightarrow$.

The different closures of a given relation $\rightarrow$ are listed below:

$\rightarrow^=$ is the reflexive closure of $\rightarrow$;

$\leftrightarrow$ is the symmetric closure of $\rightarrow$;

$\rightarrow^+$ is the transitive closure of $\rightarrow$;

$\leftrightarrow^=$ is the reflexive and symmetric closure of $\rightarrow$;

$\rightarrow^*$ is the reflexive and transitive closure of $\rightarrow$; and

$\leftrightarrow^+$ is the symmetric and transitive closure of $\rightarrow$.

Theorem 6. *If $\rightarrow$ is a relation, then $\leftrightarrow^*$ is the equivalence relation it generates.*

Proof. First, $tra(sym(\rightarrow))$ is symmetric since transitivity carries a symmetric relation into a symmetric relation. Together with the commutativity of ref with tra and sym we have the fact that $ref(tra(sym(\rightarrow)))$ is reflexive, symmetric and transitive. That is, $ref(tra(sym(\rightarrow))) = \leftrightarrow^*$ is the equivalence closure of $\rightarrow$. ■

Theorem 6 produces an explicit description of a generated equivalence. Let $\rightarrow$ be a relation on a set A. Two elements a and b of A are equivalent modulo the equivalence generated by $\rightarrow$ iff there exist a natural number m and a sequence $a_0, a_1, \ldots, a_m$ of elements from A such that $a = a_0, a_m = b$ and $a_{i-1} \rightarrow a_i$ or $a_i \rightarrow a_{i-1}$ for $i = 1, \ldots, m$, which is illustrated (for $m = 5$) in Fig. 1.8:

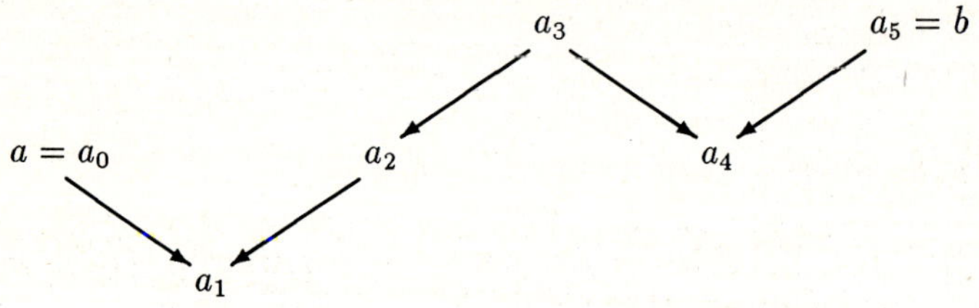

Fig. 1.8

1.3.3 Partial Orders

We shall need a few facts about partial orders, and these are surveyed here.

Definition 4. *A reflexive, transitive and antisymmetric relation on a set A is called a* ***partial order*** *on A.*

It is customary to use the symbol $\leq$ (or some typographical relative of it) for any partial order. A set together with a partial order on it is called a ***partially ordered set***, hereafter abbreviated ***poset***. We shall simply say that a set A is a poset without explicit mentioning the partial order on A.

If $\leq$ is a partial order on A, the ***proper part*** of $\leq$, usually denoted by $<$, is defined as follows: $x < y$ iff $x \leq y$ and $x \neq y$. Since the proper part of a partial order is evidently irreflexive, transitive and asymmetric we call a relation a ***proper order*** if it possesses these properties [6]. Observe that the reflexive closure of a proper order $<$, denoted by $\leq$, is again a partial order.

Two elements x and y of a given poset A are called ***comparable*** if $x \leq y$ or $y \leq x$; otherwise, x and y are said to be ***incomparable***. A subset of pairwise comparable (incomparable) elements is called a ***chain*** (***antichain***). A poset that is itself a chain is called ***totally ordered***. At the other extreme, any set A may be regarded as ***totally unordered*** if the identity relation on A is taken as the partial order; thus no two distinct elements are comparable or, in other words, A is an antichain; often A is called a ***discrete poset***.

Given a poset A and a nonempty subset X of A, an element $m \in X$ is said to be ***minimal*** in X if, for all $x \in A, x < m$ implies $x \notin X$. Note that the converse $\geq$ of any partial order $\leq$ is also a partial order, which yields a certain duality of notions. Hence, $m \in X$ is called ***maximal*** in X if, for all $x \in A, x > m$ implies $x \notin X$. An element $a \in X$ is called the ***least element*** in X if $a \leq x$ for all $x \in X$; dually, a is called the ***greatest element*** in X if $a \geq x$ for all $x \in X$.

According to our terminology above, a partial order $\leq$ on a set A is called a ***total order*** (or a ***linear order***) if $x \leq y$ or $x \geq y$ for all $x, y \in A$. Now it is surprising that total orders are characterizable as maximal partial orders in the following sense. Denote by PO the set of all partial orders on A. PO itself is partially ordered with respect to set inclusion; and PO is nonempty since the identity relation id_A belongs to PO.

Suppose that $R \in PO$ is a total order and let S be an arbitrary partial order in PO such that $R \subseteq S$. If R is properly included in S, then there is a pair $(x, y) \in S - R$, where necessarily $x \neq y$. Now, by the assumption that R is total, $(y, x) \in R$ and hence $(y, x) \in S$. But this leads to a contradiction since $x = y$, by the antisymmetry of S.

---

[6] Asymmetry of a proper order follows already from irreflexivity and transitivity.

Conversely, assume that $R \in PO$ is maximal. If R is not total, there must be a pair (a,b) of distinct elements in A such that $(a,b) \notin R \cup R^{-1}$. Consider the reflexive and transitive closure of $R \cup \{(a,b)\}$, say $S = (R \cup \{(a,b)\})^* = R \cup R \cdot \{(a,b)\} \cdot R$. It is easily checked that S is also antisymmetric and hence a partial order including R properly. But this contradicts the maximality of R. Therefore we have proved the following statement: A partial order is total iff it is maximal.

Example 1. For any set A, its power set $\wp(A)$ is a poset with respect to set inclusion. The least element is the empty set and the greatest element is A. ∎

Example 2. Let A be any set and $\perp$ be a new element ($\perp \notin A$). Put $A_\perp = A \cup \{\perp\}$. Then $A_\perp$ is a poset with respect to the following partial order:

$$x \leq y \quad \text{iff} \quad x = \perp \text{ or } x = y$$

for all x and y in $A_\perp$. It is called a ***flat poset*** with the least element $\perp$. When A has more than one element there is no greatest element but all elements of A are maximal. Furthermore, $A_\perp$ has only finite chains. Actually, every chain contains at most two elements. The set A is an antichain. ∎

Example 3. Consider the word monoid $W(A)$ over a given set A. The relation $\leq_{pre}$ on $W(A)$, defined by $u \leq_{pre} v$ iff $v = uw$ for some $w \in W(A)$, is a partial order on $W(A)$. It is called the ***prefix-order*** on $W(A)$. The empty word is the least element. However, there is no greatest element. ∎

Let A be a poset. Given any subset X of A, an element $a \in A$ with the property $x \leq a$ for all x in X is called an ***upper bound*** for X in A. When such an element exists, we say that X is ***bounded from above in*** A. A lower bound of X is defined dually. A subset X of a poset is called ***directed*** (***upwards***) if any pair of elements in X has an upper bound in X; formally, for all $x, y \in X$, there is $z \in X$ such that $x \leq z$ and $y \leq z$. A subset X is directed downwards if any pair of elements in X has a lower bound in X; when nothing to the contrary is said, "directed" will always mean "directed upwards".

If a subset X has a least upper bound, this is called the ***supremum*** of X and written $\sup X$. Similarly, the greatest lower bound, if it exists, is called the ***infimum*** of X and written $\inf X$. In particular, the supremum of the empty subset exists iff the poset has a least element. Similarly, the infimum of the empty subset exists iff the poset has a greatest element.

Example 4. In any poset, every finite nonempty chain has a supremum and an infimum. ∎

Example 5. In a flat poset, any chain has a supremum and every nonempty chain has an infimum. ∎

Example 6. Consider the poset $(\wp(A), \subseteq)$, where A is an arbitrary set. Every subset of $\wp(A)$ has a supremum and an infimum. ∎

Any poset A with the property that the supremum and the infimum of each two-element subset exist can be regarded as an algebra $(A, \vee, \wedge)$, where $x \vee y = \sup\{x, y\}$ and $x \wedge y = \inf\{x, y\}$. It is easy to show that $(A, \vee, \wedge)$ is a lattice.

Conversely, if $(A, \vee, \wedge)$ is a given lattice, we can define a partial order $\leq$ on A by the rule: $x \leq y$ iff $x \wedge y = x$. It is easily seen that $\sup\{x, y\} = x \vee y$ and $\inf\{x, y\} = x \wedge y$ for all $x, y \in A$.

Because of this one-to-one correspondence between lattices and posets for which suprema and infima of all two-element subsets exist, we often call a poset with this property a lattice, too. A poset in which every subset has a supremum and an infimum is said to be a ***complete lattice***. Every complete lattice $(A, \vee, \wedge)$ has a closure operator cl on A, where $cl(X) = \{x \in A \mid x \leq \sup X\}$ for any subset X of A. On the other hand, every closure system $\mathcal{C}$ is a complete lattice, partially ordered by set inclusion, where

$$\sup \mathcal{A} = cl_{\mathcal{C}}(\bigcup \mathcal{A}) \quad \text{and} \quad \inf \mathcal{A} = \bigcap \mathcal{A}$$

for each subsystem $\mathcal{A}$ of $\mathcal{C}$.

It should be mentioned that closure operators provide a powerful technique for constructing complete lattices. They allow us to enlarge any poset to a complete lattice. Given a poset A, we define

$$(X] = \{a \in A \mid a \leq x \text{ for some } x \text{ in } X\}$$

for each subset X of A. Evidently, the mapping $X \mapsto (X]$ is a closure operator; and the corresponding closure system, denoted by $\mathcal{C}(A)$, is a complete lattice. Notice that $\mathcal{C}(A)$ is even an algebraic closure system. The closure operator induces a mapping $m : A \to \mathcal{C}(A)$ by $m(x) = (x]$ for all $x \in A$; instead of $(\{x\}]$ we simply write $(x]$. It is easily seen that $x \leq y$ iff $(x] \subseteq (y]$. Hence m is an order-preserving injection. Moreover, the image $m(A)$ is isomorphic to A. Identifying $m(A)$ with A, we have shown that any poset can be enlarged to a complete lattice.

Definition 5. *Let A and B be posets. A mapping f from A to B is called* ***monotone*** *(or* ***order-preserving****) if, for all $x, y \in A$, $x \leq y$ implies $f(x) \leq f(y)$. In particular, a monotone mapping $f : A \to B$ is called* ***full*** *if, for all $x, y \in A$, $x \leq y$ whenever $f(x) \leq f(y)$.*

Two posets A and B are said to be ***isomorphic*** if there is a bijection f from A to B such that f and f^{-1} are monotone; f is called an ***isomorphism***.

Given a poset A, a poset B is called an ***ordered image*** of A if there is a monotone surjection from A to B.

Example 7. Consider the poset $W(A)$, where A is any set, under prefix-order (see Example 3). The mapping f from $W(A)$ to the natural numbers which assigns the length to each word of $W(A)$ is a monotone surjection. Hence the poset of natural numbers (with respect to the usual ordering) is an ordered image of $W(A)$. ■

To make ordered images internally describable the notion of partial order has to be generalized.

Definition 6. *A reflexive and transitive relation is called a* ***quasi-order*** *(or* ***preorder****).*

Any quasi-order $\lesssim$ on a set A induces an equivalence relation on A: $x \sim y$ iff $x \lesssim y$ and $x \gtrsim y$ for all $x, y \in A$. The ***proper part*** of a quasi-order $\lesssim$, also denoted by $<$, is defined as $\lesssim$ but not $\sim$. A quasi-order $\lesssim$ on A is said to be ***total*** if $x \lesssim y$ or $x \gtrsim y$ for all $x, y \in A$.

If A is a given set and $\lesssim$ a quasi-order on A, then the quotient set $A/\sim$ can be partially ordered: $[x] \leq [y]$ iff $x \lesssim y$ for all $x, y \in A$. In order to indicate that $A/\sim$ is a poset we denote it by $A/\lesssim$.

Now let A be a poset with partial order $\leq$ on it. A quasi-order $\lesssim$ on A is called ***admissible*** if, for all $x, y \in A$, $x \leq y$ implies $x \lesssim y$.

Definition 7. *Let A be a poset. If $\lesssim$ is an admissible quasi-order on A, then $A/\lesssim$ is called the* ***quotient poset*** *of A modulo $\lesssim$.*

It is important to observe that every quotient poset $A/\lesssim$ is an ordered image of A because the associated natural mapping $nat : A \to A/\lesssim$, which assigns the equivalence class $[x]$ to each x of A, is a monotone surjection.

Let A and B be posets. To every monotone mapping $f : A \to B$ we associate a quasi-order: $x \lesssim y$ iff $f(x) \leq f(y)$ for all $x, y \in A$; $\lesssim$ is called the ***order kernel*** of f and written $ker_{\leq} f$. In fact, $ker_{\leq} f$ is an admissible quasi-order on A. If $\lesssim$ is any admissible quasi-order on a given poset A, then $ker_{\leq} nat = \lesssim$.

Proposition 7. *Every ordered image of a poset A is isomorphic to a quotient poset of A.*

Proof. Assume that B is an ordered image of a given poset A. Then, by definition, there is a monotone surjection $f : A \to B$. Consider the quotient poset $A/ker_{\leq} f$ and define a mapping, say $g : A/ker_{\leq} f \to B$, such that $g([x]) = f(x)$ for all $x \in A$. In fact, g is well-defined. For if $[x] = [y]$, then $(x, y) \in ker_{\leq} f$ and $(y, x) \in ker_{\leq} f$. That is, $f(x) \leq f(y)$ and $f(y) \leq f(x)$, hence $f(x) = f(y)$. Obviously, $f = nat \cdot g$, where $nat : A \to A/ker_{\leq} f$. Thus g is a surjection since f is so. Moreover, it follows directly from the observation above that g is also injective, and hence g is a bijection.

It remains to show that g and g^{-1} are monotone. If $[x] \leq [y]$, then $(x,y) \in ker_{\leq}f$, by definition, and therefore $f(x) \leq f(y)$, which implies $g([x]) \leq g([y])$. Since g is even full monotone, g^{-1} is monotone, too. ■

We finish this section by mentioning an important proof method.

Zorn's Lemma. *A poset in which every chain has an upper bound, has a maximal element.* ■

Observe that a poset is nonempty iff the empty set, which is a chain trivially, has an upper bound. This leads to an equivalent formulation of Zorn's Lemma: A nonempty poset in which every nonempty chain has an upper bound, has a maximal element.

It should be mentioned that Zorn's Lemma is equivalent to the Axiom of Choice (see, e.g., /Halmos-74/, /Stoll-61/).

Using Zorn's Lemma we are able to prove that every partial order is embeddable into a total order. Given a poset $(A, \leq)$, we consider the set $PO(\leq)$ of all partial orders on A, which include $\leq$. Evidently, $PO(\leq)$ is a nonempty poset with respect to set inclusion. In order to apply Zorn's Lemma we have to show that every nonempty chain has an upper bound. Let $(R_i | i \in I)$ be a chain in $PO(\leq)$. Put $R = \bigcup(R_i | i \in I)$. We claim that $R \in PO(\leq)$. Of course, $\leq$ is included in R. R is evidently reflexive. R is transitive, for if xRy and yRz, then xR_iy and yR_jz for some $i,j \in I$. Since $(R_i | i \in I)$ is a chain, $R_i \subseteq R_j$ or $R_i \supseteq R_j$. Let $R_i \subseteq R_j$ without loss of generality. Thus xR_jy and yR_jz and so xR_jz, by the transitivity of R_j, whence xRz. R is also antisymmetric. Now, by Zorn's Lemma, $PO(\leq)$ has a maximal element, say M. As we know, M is a total order, which includes $\leq$ by construction. Thus we have proved the following statement:

Lemma 8. *Every partial order on a set A is embeddable into a total order on A.* ■

1.3.4 Terminating Relations

Termination is one of the basic concepts in theoretical computer science, which expresses in a certain way a finiteness condition. It should be intuitively clear that such conditions are necessary for any constructive proof method.

First, we are going to introduce ***well-founded*** or ***Noetherian*** relations and prove afterwards that they coincide with the terminating ones. Therefore the notion of a minimal element has to be generalized. Let $\rightarrow$ be a relation on a set A and let B be a nonempty subset of A. An element m of B is said to be $\rightarrow$***–minimal*** if, for all x in $A, m \rightarrow x$ impies $x \notin B$. Consider any partial order $\leq$ on A. An element m of B is minimal (in the usual sense) iff m is $>$–minimal. In the sequel we will only speak of minimal elements when no confusion may arise.

Definition 8. *A relation on a set A is called **well-founded** (or **Noetherian**) if every nonempty subset of A has a minimal element.*

Observe that a well-founded relation $\rightarrow$ on a set A is necessarily ***acyclic***, i.e., there is no element a of A such that $a \rightarrow^* a$ holds. Hence the relation $\rightarrow$ on $A = \{a, b, c\}$ determined by the following picture

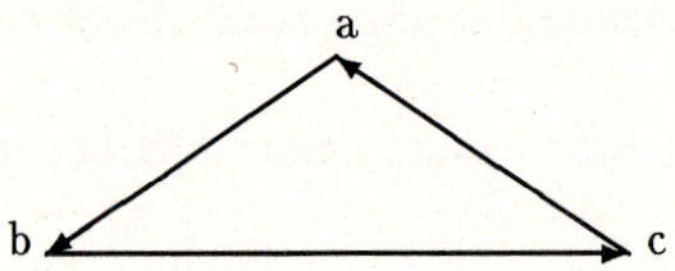

is not well-founded since it is not acyclic. Note that the set A itself has no minimal element.

Theorem 9 (Principle of Noetherian Induction). *Let $\rightarrow$ be a well-founded relation on a set A. A property $\mathcal{P}$ holds for any element a of A if $\mathcal{P}$ holds for all x in A with $a \rightarrow x$. Formally, if*

$$\forall a \in A(\,\forall x \in A(\, a \rightarrow x \Rightarrow \mathcal{P}(x)\,) \Rightarrow \mathcal{P}(a)\,), \qquad (*)$$

then $\mathcal{P}$ holds for all a in A.

Proof. Let $A_{\mathcal{P}}$ denote the set of all elements in A for which $\mathcal{P}$ holds. We have to show that $A_{\mathcal{P}}$ equals A whenever the induction formula $(*)$ is valid. Let us indirectly assume that $A_{\mathcal{P}}$ is a proper subset of A but $(*)$ is valid. Then put $B = A - A_{\mathcal{P}}$. Since B is a nonempty subset, it contains a minimal element, say m. Hence no element x of A with $m \rightarrow x$ belongs to B. That is, $\mathcal{P}(x)$ holds for all $x \in A$ with $m \rightarrow x$. Thus, $\mathcal{P}$ holds for m because of $(*)$, which contradicts $m \notin A_{\mathcal{P}}$. ■

To introduce terminating relations we need some more notions. Let $\rightarrow$ be an arbitrary relation on a set A. Given elements a and b of A, we say that a is ***reduced to b in one step*** if $a \rightarrow b$, and b is called an (immediate) ***reduct*** of a. An element a of A is called ***reducible*** if a has any reduct. Otherwise, a is called ***irreducible***. Furthermore, we say that an element a of A has a ***terminating reduction*** if there are elements $x_0, x_1, \ldots, x_m$ of A such that $a = x_0, x_i \rightarrow x_{i+1}$ for $i = 0, 1, \ldots, m-1$ and x_m is irreducible. This will be written

$$a = x_0 \rightarrow x_1 \rightarrow \ldots \rightarrow x_m \downarrow .$$

Consider the relation depicted in Fig. 1.9:

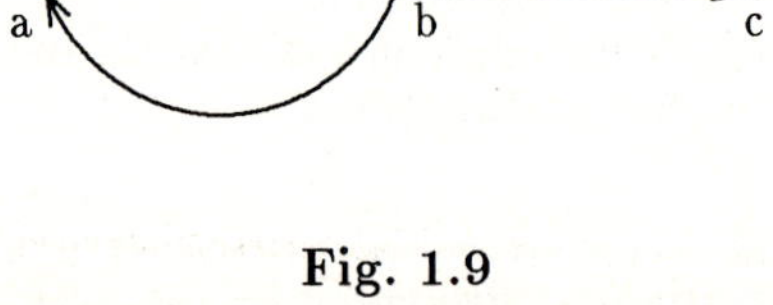

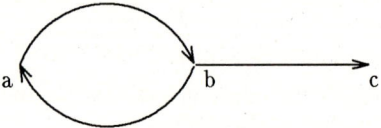

Fig. 1.9

Obviously, every element a, b and c has a terminating reduction. Note, however, that the relation is not well-founded since it is not acyclic.

A relation is called ***weakly terminating*** if every element has a terminating reduction. It is easy to see that any well-founded relation is weakly terminating. Assume $\to$ is a well-founded relation on a set A. Take an arbitrary element a of A and set $B_a = \{x \in A | a \to^* x\}$. Since B_a is a nonempty subset of A, B_a has a minimal element, say m. Note $a \to^* m$. We claim that m is irreducible. For if m were reducible, then $m \to b$ for some element b of A. That is, $a \to^* m \to b$ and hence b belongs to B_a. But this contradicts the minimality of m. Hence, $\to$ is weakly terminating.

We say that an element a of A has a ***nonterminating reduction*** if there is an infinite sequence $(x_n | n \in \mathbb{N})$ in A such that $a = x_0$ and $x_n \to x_{n+1}$ for all $n \in \mathbb{N}$, which will be written

$$a = x_0 \to x_1 \to x_2 \to \dots \quad .$$

Definition 9. *A relation $\to$ on a set A is called **terminating** if every element of A has only terminating reductions. That is, $\to$ is terminating if there is no infinite sequence $(x_n | n \in \mathbb{N})$ in A such that $x_n \to x_{n+1}$ for all $n \in \mathbb{N}$.*

A terminating relation is weakly terminating and no element has a nonterminating reduction.

Theorem 10. *A relation is well-founded (Noetherian) if and only if it is terminating.*

Proof. To prove necessity we assume that $\to$ is a well-founded relation on a set A. Note that $\to$ is then weakly terminating. We are going to show that $\to$ is even terminating by excluding all nonterminating reductions. If there were a nonterminating reduction, say $a = x_0 \to x_1 \to x_2 \to \dots$, then $\{x_n | n \in \mathbb{N}\}$ is a nonempty subset of A. Hence there is a minimal element, say x_m, in $\{x_n | n \in \mathbb{N}\}$. But $x_m \to x_{m+1}$ contradicts the minimality of x_m. Thus no element of A has a nonterminating reduction.

To prove sufficiency we assume that $\to$ is a terminating relation on a nonempty set A. Let B be a nonempty subset of A. We have to show that B has a minimal element. Take any element b of B. If already b is minimal, then we are done. Therefore consider the case where b is not minimal in B. Then there is an element x_1 in B such that $b \to x_1$. Now, either x_1 is minimal in B or x_1 is not. In the first case the proof is finished. But otherwise, we iterate our procedure to get $x_2, x_3, \dots$ (note that we have to use the Axiom of Choice to select the sequence). Now, by assumption, this sequence is terminating:

$$b \to x_1 \to x_2 \to \dots \to x_m \downarrow,$$

where x_m is irreducible in B, i.e., there is no reduct of x_m in B. In other words, x_m is minimal. ■

Well-foundedness and termination are hence equivalent notions. But the Principle of Noetherian Induction is also equivalent to them in the following sense. Let $\to$ be an arbitrary relation on a set A. We say that a property $\mathcal{P}$ is ***inductive*** (with respect to $\rightarrow$) if the induction formula

$$\forall a \in A(\ \forall x \in A(\ a \rightarrow x \ \Rightarrow\ \mathcal{P}(x)\ )\ \Rightarrow\ \mathcal{P}(a)\ )$$

is valid in A.

Proposition 11. *For any relation $\rightarrow$ on a set A the following three conditions are equivalent:*

(1) $\rightarrow$ is well-founded (Noetherian).

(2) Every inductive property $\mathcal{P}$ on A holds for all $x \in A$.

(3) $\rightarrow$ is terminating.

Proof. The implication (1) $\Rightarrow$ (2) is a reformulation of the Principle of Noetherian Induction. To prove that (3) follows from (2) we define a property $\mathcal{P}$ on A by setting: $\mathcal{P}(a)$ iff every reduction starting from a is terminating. Obviously, $\mathcal{P}$ is inductive. Now, by (2), every reduction in A is terminating. That is, $\rightarrow$ is terminating. Finally, (1) follows from (3) by Theorem 10. In fact, (1) and (3) are equivalent. ■

We close this section by studying some further notions related to termination. A relation $\rightarrow$ on a set A is called ***finitely branching*** (or ***locally finite***) if for each a of A the set of all reducts of a is finite, i.e., $\{x \in A | a \rightarrow x\}$ is finite for all $a \in A$. We say that $\rightarrow$ is ***finitary*** (or ***globally finite***) if its transitive closure $\rightarrow^*$ is finitely branching, i.e., $\{x \in A | a \rightarrow^* x\}$ is finite for all $a \in A$.

Lemma 12. *A finitely branching relation is finitary whenever it is terminating.*

Proof. Assume $\rightarrow$ is a terminating relation on a set A. Define a mapping Δ from A into the power set of A by $\Delta(a) = \{x \in A | a \rightarrow^* x\}$. Then

$$\Delta(a) = \bigcup\{\Delta(x) | a \rightarrow x\} \quad \text{for all} \quad a \in A \quad .$$

In order to use Noetherian Induction we introduce a property $\mathcal{P}$ on A as follows: $\mathcal{P}(a)$ iff $\Delta(a)$ is finite. If $\rightarrow$ is finitely branching, then $\Delta(a)$ is finite whenever $\Delta(x)$ is finite for all x in A with $a \rightarrow x$. That is, $\mathcal{P}$ is an inductive property. Hence $\mathcal{P}$ holds for all a in A, which means that $\rightarrow$ is finitary. ■

A relation on a set A is called ***bounded*** if the length of the reductions of every element in A is bounded. Thus any bounded relation is terminating but not vice versa. Consider the relation on the natural numbers defined by $0 \rightarrow n$ and $n + 1 \rightarrow n$ for $n \geq 1$ as depicted in Fig. 1.10.

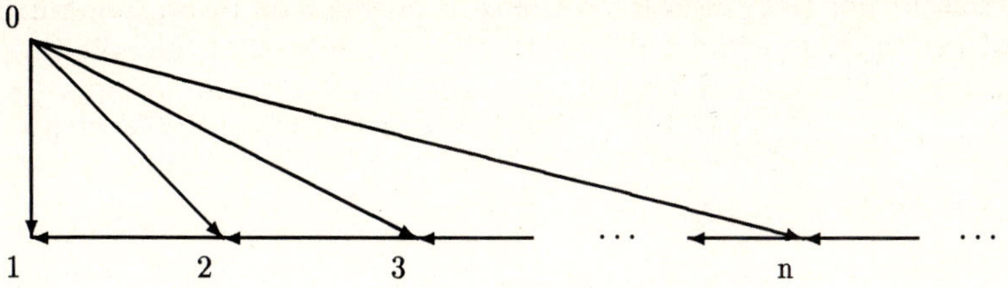

Fig. 1.10

Certainly, $\rightarrow$ is terminating but a terminating reduction starting with 0 can be arbitarily long. Thus $\rightarrow$ is unbounded.

Proposition 13. *A finitely branching relation is terminating if it is bounded.*

Proof. Let $\rightarrow$ be a finitely branching relation on a set A. If $\rightarrow$ is assumed to be terminating, then $\rightarrow$ is finitary by Lemma 12. Hence $\Delta(a) = \{x \in A \mid a \rightarrow^* x\}$ is finite for each a of A. Now observe that any terminating relation is acyclic, i.e., there is no element a of A with $a \rightarrow^* a$. Therefore every reduction starting from a is bounded by the cardinality of $\Delta(a)$. ■

1.3.5 Well-Quasi-Orders

In this section we demonstrate the usefulness of quasi-orders or partial orders for termination proofs. Consider, for instance, the length ordering of words. Let A be a set. We define for any two words w and w' of $W(A)$: $w \lesssim w'$ iff $|w| \leq |w'|$. Obviously, $\lesssim$ is a quasi-order and there is no infinite strictly descending chain

$$w_0 > w_1 > w_2 > \ldots$$

Hence $>$ is well-founded.

For the sake of convenience we shall adopt the usual convention of calling a quasi-order $\lesssim$ itself ***well-founded*** if its associated proper order $>$ is well-founded.

One of the main techniques in termination proofs is to construct extensions of a given quasi-order which preserve well-foundedness. This is a non-trivial property. For instance, when the usual ordering of natural numbers is extended to integers, well-foundedness is not preserved.

Example 1. If $\leq$ is a partial order on a set A, then the word monoid $W(A)$ generated by A can be ***lexicographically ordered*** as follows. Given any two words w and w' over A, we define $w <_{lex} w'$ iff either

(1) $w = e$ and $w' \neq e$; or

(2) $w = a_1 a_2 \ldots a_m, w' = b_1 b_2 \ldots b_n$ and there is an integer j with $1 \leq j \leq \min\{m, n\}$ such that $a_i = b_i$ for $i = 1, \ldots, j-1$ and $a_j < b_j$.

It is easily seen that the reflexive closure of $<_{lex}$, denoted by $\leq_{lex}$ and called ***lexicographical order***, is a partial order on $W(A)$ extending $\leq$ in the following sense. For all letters $a, b \in A, a \leq b$ implies $a \leq_{lex} b$. But this extension does not preserve well-foundedness. Take, e.g., a two-letter alphabet $A = \{a, b\}$ with $a < b$. Then

$$b >_{lex} ab >_{lex} aab >_{lex} \cdots$$

is an infinite strictly descending chain. Though $\leq$ is well-founded its extension $\leq_{lex}$ is not. ■

Example 2. Consider another possibility to extend a partial order $\leq$ on a set A to the word monoid $W(A)$ generated by A. Given any two words w and w' of $W(A)$, we define $w \ll_{lex} w'$ iff either

(1) $|w| < |w'|$; or

(2) $|w| = |w'|$ and $w <_{lex} w'$,

where $\leq_{lex}$ is defined in Example 1.

Let $\lll_{lex}$ be the reflexive closure of $\ll_{lex}$. We call $\lll_{lex}$ the ***lexical order*** on $W(A)$. Obviously, $\lll_{lex}$ is a partial order on $W(A)$ extending $\leq$. Note that the lexical order is the intersection of the length ordering and the lexicographical order, which are both partial orders on $W(A)$ extending the given partial order. The restriction of the lexicographical order to words of equal length preserves well-foundedness. If $\leq$ is well-founded, then $\lll_{lex}$ is also well-founded. ■

In what follows we introduce a stronger notion than that of well-foundedness. Let $\lesssim$ be a quasi-order on a set A. An infinite sequence $(x_n | n \in I\!N)$ in A is called ***good*** if there are indices i and j such that $i < j$ and $x_i \lesssim x_j$, otherwise it is termed a ***bad*** sequence. We say that $\lesssim$ is ***well-behaved*** if every infinite sequence is good.

Definition 10. *A well-behaved quasi-order is called a* ***well-quasi-order***.

In fact, well-behavedness is stronger than well-foundedness.

Proposition 14. *Every well-quasi-order is well-founded.*

Proof. Let $\lesssim$ be a well-quasi-order on a set A. Consider an infinite sequence $(x_n | n \in I\!N)$ in A such that $x_n > x_{n+1}$ for all $n \in I\!N$. Hence for every $m, n \in I\!N$,

$$x_n \gtrsim x_{n+m} \quad \text{and} \quad x_n \not\lesssim x_{n+m} \, . \qquad (*)$$

by the transitivity of $\lesssim$. Since $\lesssim$ is assumed to be well-behaved, there exist some indices $i, j \geq 0$ such that $i < j$ and $x_i \lesssim x_j$. But this contradicts $(*)$. Thus $\lesssim$ is well-founded. ■

As a consequence we get the following

Corollary. *A quasi-order on a set A is well-behaved iff it is well-founded and every antichain in A is finite.*

Proof. Let $\lesssim$ be a quasi-order on a set A. If we assume that $\lesssim$ is a well-quasi-order, then $\lesssim$ is well-founded, by Proposition 14, and it remains to show that every antichain in A is finite. Let us indirectly assume that $(x_n | n \in \mathbb{N})$ is an infinite antichain. That is, there is no pair of distinct elements which are comparable. Since $\lesssim$ is assumed to be well-behaved, however, there must be a pair of distinct elements which are comparable. Hence there is no infinite antichain in A.

Conversely, let $\lesssim$ be a well-founded quasi-order on A such that every antichain in A is finite. If we indirectly assume that $\lesssim$ is not well-behaved, then a bad sequence, say $(x_n | n \in \mathbb{N})$, must exist in A, which means that, for all $i, j \in \mathbb{N}, i < j$ implies $x_i \not\lesssim x_j$. Since $\lesssim$ is well-founded, there exists an integer m such that $x_m \not> x_n$ for all $n > m$. Hence $\{x_n | n > m\}$ is an infinite antichain. Thus $\lesssim$ is well-behaved. ∎

To characterize well-quasi-orders we need the notion of a subsequence. Given an infinite sequence $(x_n | n \in \mathbb{N})$ in A, an infinite ***subsequence*** of it is any infinite sequence $(y_n | n \in \mathbb{N})$ such that there is an injective monotone mapping f from $\mathbb{N}$ into $\mathbb{N}$ such that $y_n = x_{f(n)}$ for all $n \in \mathbb{N}$.

Proposition 15. *A quasi-order $\lesssim$ on a set A is a well-quasi-order if and only if every infinite sequence $(x_n | n \in \mathbb{N})$ in A contains an infinite subsequence $(x_{f(n)} | n \in \mathbb{N})$ such that $x_{f(n)} \lesssim x_{f(n+1)}$ for all $n \in \mathbb{N}$.*

Proof. Sufficiency is evident by the definition of a well-quasi-order. To prove necessity we assume that $\lesssim$ is a well-quasi-order on a set A. Let $(x_n | n \in \mathbb{N})$ be an infinite sequence in A. We say that x_i is ***terminal*** iff there is no $j > i$ such that $x_i \lesssim x_j$. We claim that the number of terminal elements is finite in the given sequence. Otherwise, the infinite sequence of terminal elements in it is a bad sequence (because if the sequence of terminal elements were good, then we would have $x_i \lesssim x_j$ for two terminal elements, which contradicts the fact that x_i is terminal), and this contradicts the fact that $\lesssim$ is a well-quasi-order. Hence there is some $m > 0$ such that x_i is not terminal for every $i \geq m$. Define an injective monotone mapping f inductively as follows. Let $f(0) = m$, and for any $n \geq 0$, let $f(n+1)$ be the least integer such that $x_{f(n)} \lesssim x_{f(n+1)}$ and $f(n+1) > f(n)$. Note that such an element exists since every element $x_{f(n)}$ is not terminal by the choice of m and the definition of f. The infinite subsequence $(x_{f(n)} | n \in \mathbb{N})$ has the required property. ∎

Example 3. Now we consider an extension of a well-quasi-order. Let $\lesssim$ be a quasi-order on A. First we are going to extend $\lesssim$ to the word monoid $W(A)$ generated by A. Given any two words w and w' we define $w \sqsubset w'$ iff either

(1) $w = e$ and $w' \neq e$; or

(2) there exist elements $a_1, \ldots, a_m, b_1, \ldots, b_n$ of A with $w = a_1 \ldots a_m$, $w' = b_1 \ldots b_n$ such that $a_i \lesssim b_{j_i}$ for $i = 1, \ldots, m$ and some $j_1, j_2, \ldots, j_m$ with $1 \leq j_1 < j_2 < \ldots < j_m \leq n$.

Evidently, the reflexive closure $\sqsubseteq\!\!\!\sim$ of $\sqsubset$ is a quasi-order on $W(A)$ extending $\lesssim$. Observe that the extension $\sqsubseteq\!\!\!\sim$ has the following property. Let $a, b \in A$ and $u, v \in W(A)$. If $a \lesssim b$ and $u \sqsubseteq\!\!\!\sim v$, then $au \sqsubseteq\!\!\!\sim bv$.

Claim: *If $\lesssim$ is a well-quasi-order on A, then $\sqsubseteq\!\!\!\sim$ is a well-quasi-order on $W(A)$.*

Let us indirectly assume that $\sqsubseteq\!\!\!\sim$ is not, but $\lesssim$ is, a well-quasi-order. Then there exists at least one bad sequence in $W(A)$. Take a minimal bad sequence $(w_n | n \in I\!N)$ satisfying the following properties:

(i) $|w_0| < |v_0|$ for all bad sequences $(v_n | n \in I\!N)$;

(ii) $|w_m| < |v_m|$ for all bad sequences $(v_n | n \in I\!N)$ such that $v_i = w_i$ for $i = 0, 1, \ldots, m-1$.

In any minimal bad sequences $(w_n | n \in I\!N)$ all words w_n are nonempty, i.e., $w_n = a_n v_n$ for some $a_n \in A$ and $v_n \in W(A)$. Therefore two new infinite sequences can be determined: (1) the sequence $(a_n | n \in I\!N)$ of the first letters of the words w_n; and (2) the sequence $(v_n | n \in I\!N)$ of words obtained by removing the first letter of w_n.

Consider the infinite sequence $(a_n | n \in I\!N)$ in A. Since $\lesssim$ is assumed to be a well-quasi-order there exists an infinite ascending subsequence of $(a_n | n \in I\!N)$, say $a_{n_0} \lesssim a_{n_1} \lesssim a_{n_2} \lesssim \ldots$ for natural numbers $n_0 < n_1 < n_2 < \ldots$.

The related infinite subsequence $(v_{n_i} | i \geq 0)$ of $(v_n | n \in I\!N)$ is a good sequence. Otherwise, if this subsequence were bad, there are two cases.

Case 1: $n_0 = 0$. Then $(v_{n_i} | i \geq 0)$ is a bad sequence with $|v_0| < |w_0|$, contradicting the minimality of $(w_n | n \in I\!N)$.

Case 2: $n_0 > 0$. Then, the infinite sequence $(w_0, w_1, \ldots, w_{n_0 - 1}, v_{n_0}, v_{n_1}, \ldots)$ is also bad with $|v_{n_0}| < |w_{n_0}|$, contradicting the minimality of $(w_n | n \in I\!N)$.

Since $(v_{n_i} | i \geq 0)$ is a good sequence, there are some positive integers i, j such that $n_i < n_j$ and $v_{n_i} \sqsubseteq\!\!\!\sim v_{n_j}$. Take into account that $a_{n_i} \lesssim a_{n_j}$. Thus we get

$$a_{n_i} v_{n_i} \sqsubseteq\!\!\!\sim a_{n_j} v_{n_j},$$

that is, $w_{n_i} \sqsubsetsim w_{n_j}$ but this shows that $(w_n | n \in I\!N)$ is a good sequence, contradicting the initial assumption. ■

An important method for preserving well-foundedness under extension is Higman's Theorem, which is derived below. A special version is already presented in the example above, where the well-quasi-order on a set A is extended to a well-quasi-order on the word monoid generated by A. The general case deals with an algebra that is generated by a set.

Let $\boldsymbol{A}$ be an algebra over a signature Σ. A given quasi-order $\lesssim$ on Σ is often called a ***precedence ordering*** of operation symbols. Now we consider a certain type of quasi-order on the carrier of the algebra.

Definition 11. *Let $\boldsymbol{A}$ be a Σ-algebra and $\lesssim$ a precedence ordering on Σ. A quasi-order $\sqsubsetsim$ on A is called a **divisibility order based on** $\lesssim$ if, for all operation symbols σ, τ and all elements $a, a_1, \ldots, a_m, b_1, \ldots, b_n$ in A, the following two conditions are satisfied:*

(1) If $a \sqsubsetsim a_i$ for some $i = 1, \ldots, m$, then $a \sqsubsetsim \sigma^A(a_1, \ldots, a_m)$; and

(2) If $\sigma \lesssim \tau$ and $a_i \sqsubsetsim b_{j_i}$ for $i = 1, \ldots, m$ and some $j_1, j_2, \ldots, j_m$ with $1 \leq j_1 < j_2 < \ldots < j_m \leq n$, then $\sigma^A(a_1, \ldots, a_m) \sqsubsetsim \tau^A(b_1, \ldots, b_n)$.

The clause (2) of the definition above can be written in simpler form if we use vector-like notations. Therefore, let us introduce words over A. When we denote $(a_1, \ldots, a_m)$ by $\overline{a}$ and $(b_1, \ldots, b_n)$ by $\overline{b}$, we have the following formulation instead of (2):

(2′) If $\sigma \lesssim \tau$ and $\overline{a} \sqsubsetsim \overline{b}$, then $\sigma^A(\overline{a}) \sqsubsetsim \tau^A(\overline{b})$,

where the extension of $\lesssim$ to words over A is also denoted by $\sqsubsetsim$.

Divisibility orders have a very important property. An algebra is already well-quasi-ordered if some generating set is so.

Theorem 16 (Higman's Theorem). *Let $\boldsymbol{A}$ be an algebra over a signature Σ. Assume that A is equipped with a divisibility order which is based on a well-quasi-order on Σ. If the divisibility order restricted to any generating set of $\boldsymbol{A}$ is a well-quasi-order, then the divisibility order on $\boldsymbol{A}$ is already a well-quasi-order.*

Proof. Let $\boldsymbol{A}$ be a Σ-algebra which is equipped with a divisibility order $\sqsubsetsim$ based on a well-quasi-order $\lesssim$ on Σ. Assume that $\boldsymbol{A}$ is generated by a set X. Then $A = \bigcup(A_k | k \in I\!N)$, where $A_0 = X$ and $A_k = A_{k-1} \cup \Sigma^A(A_{k-1})$ (cf. Proposition 3 in Section 1.2.2). Now we define the ***rank*** of each element a of A, denoted by $|a|$, to be the least natural number k such that $a \in A_k$.

We indirectly assume that $\sqsubseteq$ is not a well-quasi-order on A but its restriction to X is a well-quasi-order. Then there exists at least one bad sequence in A. We define a minimal bad sequence $(a_n | n \in \mathbb{N})$ satisfying the following properties:

(i) $|a_0| < |a'_0|$ for all bad sequences $(a'_n | n \in \mathbb{N})$ in A;

(ii) $|a_m| < |a'_m|$ for all bad sequences $(a'_n | n \in \mathbb{N})$ such that $a'_i = a_i$ for $i = 0, 1, \ldots, m-1$.

Obviously, $|a_n| \geq 1$ for infinitely many $n \geq 0$. Otherwise, the sequence would contain an infinite subsequence of elements from X. Then, by assumption, there are $i, j \geq 0$ such that $i < j$ and $a_i \sqsubseteq a_j$ contradicting the fact that $(a_n | n \in \mathbb{N})$ is bad.

Without loss of generality we assume that $|a_n| \geq 1$ for all $n \in \mathbb{N}$. That is, $a_n = \sigma_n^A(b_{n1}, \ldots, b_{nm_n})$ of A for some m_n-ary operation symbol σ_n and some elements $b_{n1}, \ldots, b_{nm_n}$ of A. For the sake of convenience let us consider $b_{n1}, \ldots, b_{nm_n}$ as a word and denote it by $\overline{b}_n$. Then we will simply write $a_n = \sigma_n^A(\overline{b}_n)$. Furthermore, the set of all elements b_{nm_j} will be denoted by B. That is, $\overline{b}_n$ is a word over B.

We claim that $\sqsubseteq$ is a well-quasi-order over B. Otherwise, let $(b_n | n \in \mathbb{N})$ be a bad sequence over B. First, assume that $b_0 = b_{0j}$ for some j. Then $|b_0| < |a_0|$ contradicts the fact that $(a_n | n \in \mathbb{N})$ is a minimal bad sequence. Secondly, assume that $b_0 = b_{mj}$ for some m and j. Then the sequence

$$(a_0, a_1, \ldots, a_{m-1}, b_0, b_1, \ldots)$$

is bad. Note that $a_i \sqsubseteq b_j$ would imply $a_i \sqsubseteq a_k$ for some a_k and l such that $b_j = b_{kl}$. But since $|b_0| < |a_m|$, this contradicts the fact that $(a_n | n \in \mathbb{N})$ is a minimal bad sequence. Hence $\sqsubseteq$ is a well-quasi-order on B. As we have seen in Example 3, the extension of $\sqsubseteq$ to $W(B)$ is also a well-quasi-order. Let us also denote this extension by $\sqsubseteq$.

Now consider the infinite sequence $(\sigma_n | n \in \mathbb{N})$ related to $(a_n | n \in \mathbb{N})$. Since $\lesssim$ is assumed to a well-quasi-order on Σ, there is an infinite ascending subsequence

$$\sigma_{n_0} \lesssim \sigma_{n_1} \lesssim \sigma_{n_2} \lesssim \ldots$$

for natural numbers $n_0 < n_1 < n_2 \ldots$. Next , consider the infinite sequence $(\overline{b}_{n_i} | i \geq 0)$ of words over B such that $a_{n_i} = \sigma_{n_i}^A(\overline{b}_{n_i})$. Since $\sqsubseteq$ is a well-quasi-order on $W(B)$, there exist $i, j \geq 0$ such that $n_i < n_j$ and $\overline{b}_{n_i} \sqsubseteq \overline{b}_{n_j}$. By the definition of $\sqsubseteq$, it follows that $a_{n_i} \sqsubseteq a_{n_j}$, which contradicts the initial assumption that $(a_n | n \in \mathbb{N})$ is a bad sequence. ■

At the end of this section we study partial orders which are well-behaved.

Definition 12. *A well-behaved partial order is called a* ***partial well-order.***

Recall that any partial well-order on a set A is well-founded. Thus, by definition, every nonempty subset of A has minimal elements. It turns out that partial well-orders are characterizable by strengthening this condition as follows.

Proposition 17. *A partial order on a set A is a partial well-order if and only if every nonempty subset of A has minimal elements, but only a finite number of them.*

Proof. Assume $\leq$ is a partial well-order on a set A. Then $\leq$ is well-founded and hence every nonempty subset of A has minimal elements. If there were a nonempty subset B with infinitely many pairwise distinct minimal elements, we could choose an infinite sequence, say $(m_n | n \in \mathbb{N})$. By assumption, there exist indices i and j such that $i < j$ and $m_i \leq m_j$. But this contradicts the minimality of m_j. Thus, every nonempty subset of A has only a finite number of minimal elements.

If $\leq$ is supposed to be a partial order on a set A such that every nonempty subset of A has minimal elements, but only a finite number of them, then $\leq$ is well-founded. It remains to show that $\leq$ is indeed well-behaved. Therefore assume that A is infinite. If $\leq$ were not well-behaved, then a bad sequence, say $(x_n | n \in \mathbb{N})$, would exist in A. That is, for all $i, j \in \mathbb{N}, i < j$ implies $x_i \not\leq x_j$. Since $\leq$ is well-founded there exists $m \in \mathbb{N}$ such that $x_m \not\geq x_n$ for all $n > m$. Hence $\{x_n | n > m\}$ is an infinite set of minimal elements, which is a contradiction. Thus $\leq$ is well-behaved. ■

Let us recall that a partial order $\leq$ on a set A is total iff every two elements of A are comparable. Hence the empty set is the only antichain in a total order. Thus a total partial order is well-behaved iff it is well-founded.

Definition 13. *A well-founded total order is called a* ***well-order.***

A typical example of a well-order is the usual ordering of natural numbers.

Proposition 18. *A partial order on a set A is a well-order if and only if every nonempty subset of A has a unique minimal element.*

Proof. If we assume that $\leq$ is a well-order on a set A, then every nonempty subset B of A has minimal elements. Since $\leq$ is total, any two elements are comparable. Hence B has a unique minimal element. Conversely, assume that $\leq$ is a partial order on A such that every nonempty subset B has a unique minimal element, which is, in fact, the least element of B. In particular, any two-element subset $\{x, y\}$ has a least element. That is, $x \leq y$ or $y \leq x$. Hence $\leq$ is a total partial order. On the other hand, $\leq$ is well-founded. ■

Notice that a unique minimal element in a nonempty subset B is the same as the least element in B.

Example 4 (cf. Appendix 1). Any ordinal α is a well-ordered set under the ordering:

$$\beta \sqsubseteq \gamma \quad \text{iff} \quad \beta = \gamma \text{ or } \beta \in \gamma$$

for all $\beta, \gamma \in \alpha$. Indeed, every well-ordered set is isomorphic, as a poset, to an ordinal. ■

Recall that every partial order can be embedded into a total order. But, if additionally the given partial order on a set A is well-founded, the embedding total order becomes a well-order. This generalization requires, however, quite another proof, not merely a modification of the first one. Its main idea is to index all elements of A by ordinals. Then the well-order on any ordinal induces a well-order of A, which happens, by construction, to include the given partial order.

Proposition 19. *Every well-founded partial order on a nonempty set A is embeddable into a well-order on A.*

Proof. Let $\leq$ be a well-founded partial order on A. By definition, every nonempty subset of A has minimal elements. First, choose a minimal element of A, say a_0. Given an ordinal β, we assume that a_α is already defined for all $\alpha \in \beta$. Then put $A_\beta = A - \{a_\alpha | \alpha \in \beta\}$. When A_β is empty we are done, since all elements of A are indexed. Otherwise, if A_β is nonempty, take a minimal element of A_β, say a_β. In this manner we get $A = \{a_\alpha | \alpha \in \gamma\}$ for some ordinal γ. Evidently, the well-order on γ induces a well-order on A:

$$a_\alpha \sqsubseteq a_\beta \quad \text{iff} \quad \alpha = \beta \text{ or } \alpha \in \beta$$

for all $\alpha, \beta \in \gamma$. It remains to show that $\sqsubseteq$ embeds $\leq$. Therefore assume that $a_\alpha \leq a_\beta$. If $a_\alpha = a_\beta$, then, of course, $a_\alpha \sqsubseteq a_\beta$. In case $a_\alpha < a_\beta$, a_α does not belong to A_β, by the minimality of a_β in A_β. Hence $\alpha \in \beta$ and so $a_\alpha \sqsubset a_\beta$. ■

As a particular case of Proposition 19, when the partial order on A is the identity relation, we obtain the so-called ***Principle of Well-Ordering***: Any set can be well-ordered. Note that the identity relation on any set is always well-founded.

1.3.6 Cofinality, Multiset Ordering and Polynomial Ordering

In this section we study extensions of a quasi-order on a set A to all subsets of A, all multisets of A and all polynomials over A. These are important extensions used in many termination proofs.

Let $\lesssim$ be a quasi-order on a set A. Given any two subsets X and Y of A, we define

$$X \sqsubseteq Y \quad \text{iff} \quad \forall x \in X \, \exists \, y \in Y (x \lesssim y).$$

Clearly, $\sqsubseteq\!\!\!\!\sim$ is a quasi-order on the power set $\wp(A)$ of A extending $\lesssim$ in the following sense. For all $x, y \in A$, if $x \lesssim y$ then $\{x\} \sqsubseteq\!\!\!\!\sim \{y\}$. When $X \sqsubseteq\!\!\!\!\sim Y$, we say that Y is ***cofinal in*** X. If $X \sim Y$, i.e., $X \sqsubseteq\!\!\!\!\sim Y$ and $Y \sqsubseteq\!\!\!\!\sim X$, then X and Y are called ***mutually cofinal.***

Example 1. Consider the usual partial order $\leq$ on natural numbers. Every infinite subset X of $\mathbb{N}$ is mutually cofinal with $\mathbb{N}$ because $X \subseteq \mathbb{N}$ implies $X \sqsubseteq\!\!\!\!\sim \mathbb{N}$ and, on the other hand, $\mathbb{N} \sqsubseteq\!\!\!\!\sim X$ since for all $n \in \mathbb{N}$ there is an element x in X with $n \leq x$, by the infinity of X. Two finite subsets X and Y of $\mathbb{N}$ are mutually cofinal iff their greatest elements are the same. In particular, X is mutually cofinal with $\{n\}$ iff n is the greatest element in X. ■

Observe that antisymmetry is not preserved under cofinality ordering. Hence, if we start with a partial order on A, its extension is only a quasi-order in general.

Now we are going to define a finer extension than cofinality so that antisymmetry is eventually preserved under some natural restrictions.

Let $\lesssim$ be a given quasi-order on a set A. For any two subsets X and Y of A we define $X \lll\!\!\!\!\sim Y$ iff $(Y - X)$ is cofinal in $(X - Y)$. Formally,

$$X \lll\!\!\!\!\sim Y \quad \text{iff} \quad \forall\, x \in (X - Y)\, \exists\, y \in (Y - X) (x \lesssim y)\,.$$

Certainly, $\lll\!\!\!\!\sim$ is reflexive. But $\lll\!\!\!\!\sim$ is not transitve in general. Consider the set $\mathbb{N}$ of natural numbers equipped with the usual ordering. Let $X = \{2n | n \in \mathbb{N}\}, Y = \{3n | n \in \mathbb{N}\}$, and $Z = \{4n | n \in \mathbb{N}\}$. Then $X \lll\!\!\!\!\sim Y$ and $Y \lll\!\!\!\!\sim Z$, but not $X \lll\!\!\!\!\sim Z$. However, if we restrict $\lll\!\!\!\!\sim$ to finite subsets, transitivity is then preserved.

We denote by $\wp_\omega(A)$ the set of all finite subsets of A. For the sake of simplicity the restriction of $\lll\!\!\!\!\sim$ to $\wp_\omega(A)$ is also denoted by $\lll\!\!\!\!\sim$ and it is called the extension of $\lesssim$ to $\wp_\omega(A)$.

Proposition 20. *If $\lesssim$ is a quasi-order on A, then so is its extension $\lll\!\!\!\!\sim$ to the set $\wp_\omega(A)$ of all finite subsets of A. In particular, antisymmetry is preserved. That is, if $\lesssim$ is a partial order on A, then so is its $\lll\!\!\!\!\sim$ extension to $\wp_\omega(A)$. Furthermore, the extension is a total order whenever $\lesssim$ is total.*

Proof. Assume that $\lesssim$ is a quasi-order on A. First, we show that its extension $\lll\!\!\!\!\sim$ to the set of all finite subsets of A is also a quasi-order. By definition, $\lll\!\!\!\!\sim$ is reflexive. Therefore, it remains to prove that $\lll\!\!\!\!\sim$ is transitive. Let X, Y and Z be finite subsets of A such that $X \lll\!\!\!\!\sim Y$ and $Y \lll\!\!\!\!\sim Z$. Without loss of generality we suppose that X, Y and Y, Z are pairwise inequivalent. That is, $X \lll Y$ and $Y \lll Z$. In order to show that then $X \lll Z$ follows, we take an arbitrary element $x \in X - Z$. Now we distinguish two cases with respect to Y: (1) $x \in Y$; or (2) $x \notin Y$. First, if $x \in Y$, then there is an element

$z \in Z - Y$ with $x < z$, by the assumption $Y \ll Z$. Secondly, if $x \notin Y$, then there is an element $y \in Y - X$ with $x < y$, by the assumption $X \ll Y$. Observe that there are the following two possibilities: (i) $y \in Z$; or (ii) $y \notin Z$. Consider the second case. Let $y \notin Z$. Then there is an element $z \in Z - Y$ with $y < z$, by the assumption $Y \ll Z$. Thus $x < z$. Hence, we have that for all $x \in X - Z$ there is an element $z \in Z - Y$ such that $x < z$. If z does not belong to X, we are done.

Now consider the case where $z \in X$. Then there is an element $y_1 \in Y - X$ with $z < y_1$, by the assumption $X \ll Y$. When $y_1 \in Z$, we are done. But $y_1 \notin Z$ implies that there is an element $z_1 \in Z - Y$ with $y_1 < z_1$, by the assumption $Y \ll Z$. Again, when $z_1 \in X$, we are done. Otherwise we iterate our procedure and obtain a chain $z < y_1 < z_1 < y_2 < \dots$. Since X, Y and Z are assumed to be finite sets, the chain must stop after finitely many steps with an element of $Z - X$. Hence we get

$$\forall\, x \in (X - Z)\, \exists\, z \in (Z - X)\, (x < z).$$

That is, $X \ll Z$.

Two finite subsets X and Y are equivalent if they are the same up to replacement of individual elements with equivalent ones under the given quasi-order $\lesssim$. Hence, if $\lesssim$ is additionally antisymmetric, then X and Y are equivalent iff $X = Y$. That is, if $\lesssim$ is a partial order on A, then so is its extension $\lesssim\!\!\!\lesssim$ to all finite subsets of A.

If $\lesssim$ is total, then any finite set has maximal elements, which are all equivalent. Given finite sets X and Y, we can compare the maximal elements of $X - Y$ and $Y - X$. Hence X and Y are comparable with respect to $\lesssim\!\!\!\lesssim$. That is, $\lesssim\!\!\!\lesssim$ is total. ■

The well-foundedness of an extension will now be studied. Let us first search for a suitable tool to do that.

Example 2. Consider the following strictly descending chain of finite subsets of natural numbers

$$\{5,8\} \gg \{1,3,5,7\} \gg \{1,5,7\} \gg \{5,6\} \gg \{5\} \gg \{2,3\}.$$

Now we assign an acyclic relation to it, which may be represented as a ***tree*** [7] in Fig. 1.11. We start with a root and connect it with the elements 5 and 8 of the first set. Then edges from 8 to 1, 3 and 7 are constructed. This indicates the relation of the second set to the first one: 8 is replaced by the smaller elements 1, 3 and 7. In the third step the element 3 is removed from the second set to obtain the third one. This is pointed out by an edge from 3 to a special symbol $\perp$. Next, 1 is removed and 7 is replaced by 6. Hence, edges from 1 to $\perp$ and 7 to 6 are constructed in the fourth step. In the fifth step, 6 is removed, which means an edge from 6 to $\perp$. Finally, edges from 5 to 2 and 3 are constructed. ■

[7] The concept of a (rooted) tree will be introduced in the next section. Here it is sufficient to think of a tree as an acyclic relation.

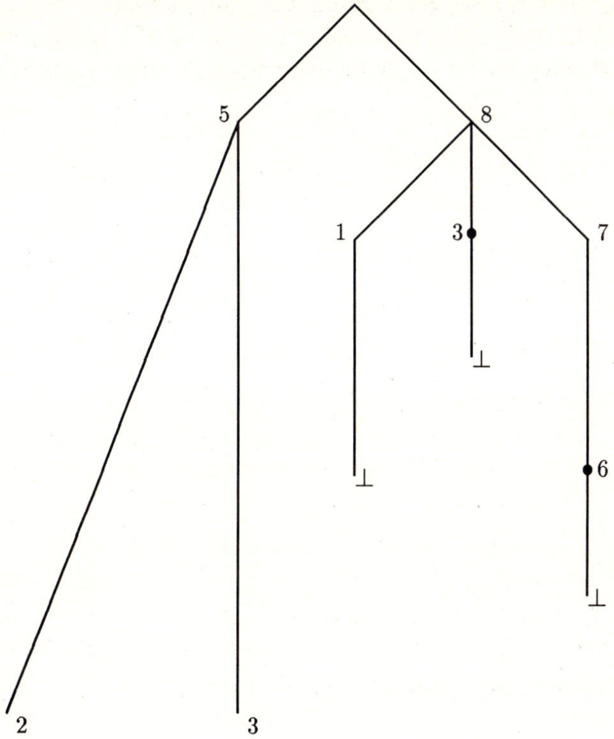

Fig. 1.11

Associating a tree with an infinite strictly descending chain of finite subsets, as indicated in the example above, at least one edge is constructed in each step. Thus the tree becomes infinite but finitely branching because all subsets in the chain are supposed to be finite. Using the following theorem, which is the crucial point in our consideration, an infinite strictly descending chain of elements can be constructed.

Theorem 21 (König's Infinity Lemma). *Let A be an infinite set and $\rightarrow$ be a relation on A. If A can be partitioned into finite nonempty subsets A_n, $n \in \mathbb{N}$, such that for all $n \geq 0$ and all y in A_{n+1}, there is an element x of A_n with $x \rightarrow y$, then there exists an infinite chain*

$$a_0 \rightarrow a_1 \rightarrow a_2 \rightarrow \ldots$$

Proof. Let $\rightarrow$ be a relation on an infinite set A. Assume that $(A_n | n \in \mathbb{N})$ is a partition of A into finite nonempty subsets fulfilling the assumption of the theorem. We define a new relation $\Rightarrow$ on A by

$$x \Rightarrow y \quad \text{iff} \quad x \rightarrow y \text{ and } x \in A_n,\ y \in A_{n+1} \text{ for some } n \geq 0.$$

Because $\Rightarrow$ is included in $\rightarrow$, it suffices to show that $\Rightarrow$ is nonterminating.

If we indirectly assume that $\Rightarrow$ is terminating, then, by Lemma 12, $\Rightarrow$ is finitary since $\Rightarrow$ is finitely branching, by definition. Hence, the set $\Delta(a) = \{x \in A \mid a \Rightarrow^* x\}$ is finite for each a of A. Let $\Delta(A_0)$ denote the union over all $\Delta(a)$, where a runs over A_0. That is,

$$\Delta(A_0) = \{x \in A | a \Rightarrow^* x \text{ for some } a \in A_0\}.$$

Observe that $\Delta(A_0)$ is finite.

Next, we are going to show that $\Delta(A_0)$ equals A, which leads to a contradiction. By induction over n we will prove that

$$A_n = \{x \in A | a \Rightarrow^n x \text{ for some } a \in A_0\}.$$

The induction basis is trivially true for $n = 0$. Now assume the induction hypothesis is true for n. Since

$$A_{n+1} = \{y \in A | x \Rightarrow y \text{ for some } x \in A_n\},$$

we get

$$A_{n+1} = \{y \in A | a \Rightarrow^{n+1} y \text{ for some } a \in A_0\}.$$

Hence, $A = \bigcup(A_n | n \in I\!N) = \{y \in A | a \Rightarrow^* y \text{ for some } a \in A_0\}$. That is, $A = \Delta(A_0)$, which is contradiction. Thus $\Rightarrow$ is not terminating. ■

Now we are ready to obtain our desired result.

Theorem 22. *A quasi-order $\lesssim$ on a set A is well-founded if and only if its extension $\lll$ to the set $\wp_\omega(A)$ of all finite subsets of A is well-founded.*

Proof. Of course, only necessity has to be shown. We indirectly assume that $\lesssim$ is a well-founded quasi-order on A, but its extension $\lll$ to $\wp_\omega(A)$ is not well-founded. Then, by definition, there is an infinite strictly descending chain $X_0 \gg X_1 \gg X_2 \gg \ldots$. Now we associate with it an infinite but finitely branching tree, which contains an infinite strictly descending chain of elements, by König's Infinity Lemma. Hence $\lll$ is not well-founded, so we get a contradiction. ■

Such extensions will be used for termination proofs, but often, however, they will appear in a more general setting. For instance, to prove termination of term rewriting systems, sequences of subterms have to be investigated. Here we are confronted with the problem that in a given term a certain subterm may occur finitely many times. This motivates the following generalization of the notion of set.

A ***multiset*** (or ***bag***) of a given set A is an unordered collection of elements of A, with possible multiple occurrences of elements. By abuse of set building notation, we also denote multisets by braces. For instance, $\{a, a, b, b, b, c\}$ is a multiset. More precisely, a multiset M of A is a mapping $M : A \to I\!N$; and the image $M(x)$ of $x \in A$ under M is called the ***multiplicity*** of x in M. Thus, the multiset $\{a, a, b, b, b, c\}$ is actually the mapping M from $\{a, b, c\}$ to $I\!N$ defined by $M(a) = 2$, $M(b) = 3$ and $M(c) = 1$.

Any subset of A is a particular case of a multiset, where each element of A has at most multiplicity 1. For any multiset M of A and $x \in A$ we will write $x \in M$ if $M(x) > 0$; and $x \notin M$ if $M(x) = 0$.

Let M and N be multisets of A. We say that M is ***included*** in N, in symbols $M \subseteq N$, if $M(x) \leq N(x)$ for all x in A. The ***complement*** $N - M$ is defined by $(N - M)(x) = \max\{0, N(x) - M(x)\}$ for all x in A. The ***sum*** of M and N, denoted by $M + N$, is defined as follows: $(M + N)(x) = M(x) + N(x)$ for all x in A. The ***union*** $M \cup N$ and ***intersection*** $M \cap N$ are defined by $(M \cup N)(x) = \max\{M(x), N(x)\}$ and $(M \cap N)(x) = \min\{M(x), N(x)\}$ for all x in A.

A multiset M of A is said to be ***finite*** if its support, $\{x \in A \mid M(x) \neq 0\}$, is finite. The set of all finite multisets of A is denoted by $\mathcal{M}_\omega(A)$.

A quasi-order $\lesssim$ on A may be extended to multisets of A. For multisets M and N of A we define

$$M \lesssim\!\!\!\!\lesssim_{multi} N \quad \text{iff} \quad \forall\, x \in (M - N)\, \exists\, y \in (N - M)\; (x \lesssim y).$$

If $M \subseteq N$, then $M - N = \emptyset$ and hence $M \lesssim\!\!\!\!\lesssim_{multi} N$. If M and N are incomparable as multisets, i.e., $M \not\subseteq N$ and $N \not\subseteq M$, then $M \lesssim\!\!\!\!\lesssim_{multi} N$ iff for all x whose multiplicity in M is greater than its multiplicity in N, there is an element y whose multiplicity in N is greater than its multiplicity in M such that $x \lesssim y$. That is, an element of N can be replaced by any finite number of smaller elements in M to obtain $M \ll_{multi} N$. Let us introduce an auxiliary relation between M and N to express the fact that a single element of N, say a, is replaced by zero or more smaller elements in M, say $x_1, \ldots, x_k$. We define $M <_{multi} N$ iff there is an element a in N such that (1) $M = N - \{a\}$; or (2) there are elements $x_1, \ldots, x_k$ with $x_i < a$ for $i = 1, \ldots, k$ such that $M(a) = N(a) - 1$ and $M(x_i) > N(x_i)$ for $i = 1, \ldots, k$. Note that for finite multisets M and N the proper multiset ordering $\ll_{multi}$ is the transitve closure of the relation $<_{multi}$. It follows that $\ll_{multi}$ is transitive.

Proposition 23. *If $\lesssim$ is a quasi-order on a set A, then so is its extension $\lesssim\!\!\!\!\lesssim_{multi}$ to the set $\mathcal{M}_\omega(A)$ of all finite multisets of A. In particular, antisymmetry is preserved. That is, if $\lesssim$ is a partial order on A, then so its extension $\lesssim\!\!\!\!\lesssim_{multi}$ to $\mathcal{M}_\omega(A)$. Furthermore, the extension is a total order whenever $\lesssim$ is total.*

Proof. Assume that $\lesssim$ is a quasi-order on A. Evidently, the multiset ordering $\lesssim\!\!\!\!\lesssim_{multi}$ is reflexive. As we have seen above, $\lesssim\!\!\!\!\lesssim_{multi}$ is transitive as a relation on $\mathcal{M}_\omega(A)$. Thus the extension $\lesssim\!\!\!\!\lesssim_{multi}$ of $\lesssim$ to finite multisets is also a quasi-order. Two finite multisets M and N are equivalent, i.e., $M \sim_{multi} N$, iff M and N are the same multiset up to replacement of individual elements by equivalent ones with possibly different multiplicities. For instance, $\{a, a, a, b\} \sim_{multi} \{a, b, b\}$ iff $a \sim b$. If $\lesssim$ is a partial order, then $M \sim_{multi} N$ iff $M = N$. That is, $\lesssim\!\!\!\!\lesssim_{multi}$ is then a partial order, too. Now, assume that $\lesssim$ is a total quasi-order on A. Let M and N be finite multisets. Consider the following sets

$X = \{x|M(x) > N(x)\}$ and $Y = \{y|N(y) > M(y)\}$. Both sets have maximal elements. The maximal elements of X or Y are pairwise equivalent. Since $\lesssim$ is total, the maximal elements of X and Y are comparable. Then, by definition, the multisets M and N are comparable. Hence, $\lll_{multi}$ is total whenever $\lesssim$ is total. ■

Generalizing the tree construction introduced above, Dershowitz and Manna (/Dershowitz-Manna-79/) were the first to prove the following result.

Theorem 24. *A quasi-order $\lesssim$ on a set A is well-founded if and only if its extension $\lll_{multi}$ to the set $\mathcal{M}_\omega(A)$ of all finite multisets of A is well-founded.*

Proof. Assume that $\lesssim$ is a well-founded relation on A. Let $A_\bot = A \cup \{\bot\}$, where $\bot \notin A$. We define $\bot < x$ for all $x \in A$ and extend the given quasi-order to $A_\bot$. Clearly, $\lesssim$ is well-founded on $A_\bot$. If we indirectly suppose that $\lll_{multi}$ is not well-founded, then there exists an infinite strictly descending chain $M_0 \gg_{multi} M_1 \gg_{multi} M_2 \gg_{multi} \ldots$ of finite multisets. We derive a contradiction by constructing the following tree. Each node in the tree is labelled with some element of $A_\bot$; at each stage of the construction, the set of all leaf nodes in the tree forms a finite multiset of A. Begin with a root with successors corresponding to each element of M_0. Since $M_0 \gg_{multi} M_1$, there must exist finite multisets X and Y, such that X is not empty and $X \subseteq M_0, M_1 = (M_0 - X) + Y$, and $\forall y \in Y\ \exists x \in X (y < x)$. Then for each $y \in Y$, add a successor labelled y to the corresponding x. In addition, grow a successor $\bot$ from each of the elements of X. (Since X is nonempty, growing $\bot$ ensures that even if Y is empty, at least one node is added to the tree. Since Y is finite, the nodes corresponding to X each have a finite number of successors.) Repeat the process for $M_1 \gg_{multi} M_2, M_2 \gg_{multi} M_3$, and so on.

Since at least one node is added for each finite multiset M_i in the chain, were the chain infinite, the tree corresponding to the chain would also be infinite. By König's Infinity Lemma, an infinite finitely branching tree must have an infinite path. On the other hand, by our construction, all paths in the tree are strictly descending sequences with respect to the well-founded quasi-order $\lesssim$ on $A_\bot$, and must be finite. Thus we have derived a contradiction, implying that the strictly descending chain $M_0 \gg_{multi} M_1 \gg_{multi} M_2 \gg_{multi} \ldots$ cannot be infinite. Hence, $\lll_{multi}$ is well-founded on the set of all finite multisets.

Conversely, assume that $\lll_{multi}$ is well-founded on $\mathcal{M}_\omega(A)$ but $\lesssim$ is not well-founded on A. Then there exists an infinite strictly descending chain $x_0 > x_1 > x_2 > \ldots$ of elements in A. The corresponding sequence of singletons $\{x_0\} \gg_{multi} \{x_1\} \gg_{multi} \{x_2\} \gg_{multi} \ldots$ forms an infinite strictly descending chain of elements in $\mathcal{M}_\omega(A)$, and $\lll_{multi}$ is therefore not well-founded, which contradicts the assumption. ■

Finite multisets specialize to polynomials with natural number coefficients when the underlying set is a word monoid. Given a set X (of variables), we consider the word monoid $W(X)$ over X. Instead of $\mathcal{M}_\omega(W(X))$ we write $\mathbb{N}\langle X\rangle$ as usual, and call its elements ***polynomials*** in (noncommuting) variables from X with coefficients in $\mathbb{N}$.

Recall that any p of $\mathbb{N}\langle X\rangle$ is, by definition, a mapping $p : W(X) \to \mathbb{N}$ such that $p(w) \neq 0$ for finitely many words w in $W(X)$ only. It is convenient to use the following notation for $p \in \mathbb{N}\langle X\rangle$:

$$p = \sum_{w \in W(X)} (p, w)w,$$

where (p, w) is the image $p(w)$ of $w \in W(X)$ under p, called the ***w-coefficient***. Frequently, the summation index $w \in W(X)$ is omitted. For instance, $p = 2x^2y + 3x$ is such a polynomial in which terms with 0-coefficients are omitted. Note that we agree to write x^n instead of the word $x \dots x$ consisting of n times x.

In $\mathbb{N}\langle X\rangle$, ***addition*** and ***multiplication*** are defined as follows. Given $p, q \in \mathbb{N}\langle X\rangle$,

$$p + q = \sum_{w \in W(X)} ((p, w) + (q, w))w$$

and

$$p \cdot q = \sum_{w \in W(X)} \left(\sum_{uv=w} (p, u) \cdot (q, v) \right) w.$$

It is easily seen that $\mathbb{N}\langle X\rangle$ forms a semiring with respect to these operations. $\mathbb{N}$ is a subsemiring under the identification of natural numbers with (constant) polynomials. Let n be any natural number. Then n is regarded as a polynomial, say $\boldsymbol{n}$, defined by $(\boldsymbol{n}, e) = n$ and $(\boldsymbol{n}, w) = 0$ for all nonempty words w.

Any polynomial p contains only a finite number of different variables. That is, p is an element of $\mathbb{N}\langle\{x_1, \dots, x_n\}\rangle$ for some $x_1, \dots, x_n$ of X. To designate that the variables occurring in p are $x_1, \dots, x_n$, one often writes $p = p(x_1, \dots, x_n)$. Variables can be substituted by polynomials. A mapping $S : X \to \mathbb{N}\langle X\rangle$ is called a (polynomial) ***substitution***. Every substitution extends uniquely to a semiring homomorphism S^* from $\mathbb{N}\langle X\rangle$ into itself by $S^*(p) = \sum(p, w)S^{\S}(w)$ with $S^{\S}(e) = 1$ and $S^{\S}(xw) = S(x) \cdot S^{\S}(w)$ for all $x \in X$ and $w \in W(X)$, where $S^{\S}$ is the unique extension of S to a monoid homomorphism from $W(X)$ to the multiplicative monoid $\mathbb{N}\langle X\rangle$. Given a polynomial p in n variables, say $p = p(x_1, \dots, x_n)$, we shall write $p(p_1, \dots, p_n)$ instead of $S^*(p)$ if S is given by $S(x_i) = p_i$ for $i = 1, \dots, n$; $p(p_1, \dots, p_n)$ is said to be an ***instantiation*** of p. In particular, if $p(a_1, \dots, a_n)$ is an instantiation of p by natural numbers $a_1, \dots, a_n$ (regarded as polynomials), then $p(a_1, \dots, a_n)$ is itself a natural number.

Now, for two polynomials $p = p(x_1, \dots, x_m)$ and $p' = p'(x_1, \dots, x_n)$ with $m \leq n$, we define $p \lesssim p'$ iff

$$p(a_1, \dots, a_m) \leq p'(a_1, \dots, a_n) \text{ for all positive natural numbers } a_1, \dots, a_n.$$

Evidently, $\lesssim$ is a quasi-order on $\mathbb{N}\langle X\rangle$. The use of this polynomial order for termination proofs has, however, the disadvantage that it is undecidable whether $p \lesssim p'$ holds true or not for any two polynomials p and p' (/Lankford-79/).

Let $\equiv$ denote the equivalence relation associated with $\lesssim$. It is easily seen that two polynomials p and p' are equivalent, $p \equiv p'$, iff p and p' are the same polynomials in commuting variables. For instance, $p = 2xyx + x^2y$ and $p' = 3x^2y$ are equivalent. It is an easy exercise to show that $\equiv$ is a semiring congruence. Hence the quotient algebra $\mathbb{N}\langle X\rangle/\equiv$ is also a semiring, denoted by $\mathbb{N}[X]$. Its elements are called polynomials in commuting variables from X with coefficients in $\mathbb{N}$. Specifically, $\lesssim$ determines a partial order on $\mathbb{N}[X]$.

Theorem 25. *Polynomial order is well-founded.*

Proof. If polynomial order $\lesssim$ were not well-founded, an infinite strictly descending chain $p_0 > p_1 > p_2 > \ldots$ of polynomials would exist, which by instantiation would produce an infinite strictly descending chain of natural numbers. ■

The following properties are direct consequences of the fact that addition and multiplication of polynomials are strictly increasing operations: $p < p'$ implies $p + q < p' + q$, $p \cdot q < p' \cdot q$ and $q \cdot p < q \cdot p'$. Let p, p' and q be polynomials such that $q = q(x_1, \ldots, x_n)$.

(1) If $p < p'$, then $q(x_1, \ldots, x_{i-1}, p, x_{i+1}, \ldots, x_n) < q(x_1, \ldots, x_{i-1}, p', x_{i+1}, \ldots, x_n)$.

Consider, e.g., polynomials $p = x$, $p' = 2xy$ and $q = 3x + 2xy^2$. Obviously, $p < p'$. Now take $q(x,p) = 3x + 2x^3$ and $q(x,p') = 3x + 8x^2yxy$. Then $q(x,p) < q(x,p')$. Let $p = p(x_1, \ldots, x_m)$ and $p' = p'(x_1, \ldots, x_n)$ be polynomials with $m \leq n$.

(2) If $p < p'$, then $p(p_1, \ldots, p_m) < p'(p_1, \ldots, p_n)$ for all polynomials $p_1, \ldots, p_n$.

For example, take $p = 2x + y$ and $p' = 3xy^2 + y$; of course, $p < p'$. Now, for $p_1 = xy$ and $p_2 = y + z$, we get $p(p_1, p_2) = 2p_1 + p_2 = 2xy + y + z$ and $p'(p_1, p_2) = 3p_1p_2^2 + p_2 = 3xy(y+z)^2 + y + z = 3xy^3 + 3xy^2z + 3xyzy + 3xyz^2 + y + z$. Evidently, $p(p_1, p_2) < p'(p_1, p_2)$.

1.4 Trees

Trees are used in many branches of mathematics and computer science. It is therefore not surprising that their definitions vary depending on the specific purpose. We shall introduce trees within the framework of well-founded partially ordered sets. This general setting has in our opinion the advantage that the connection with other concepts is more explicit.

In Section 1.4.1, trees are introduced as special well-founded posets. Moreover, two fundamental tools for reasoning about trees, König's Infinity Lemma for Trees and Kruskal's Tree Theorem, are mentioned.

Section 1.4.2 deals with labelled trees. Finite labelled trees are regarded as (graphical) representations of terms. However, we also need infinite labelled trees. For them an ordering called syntactic order is introduced which will be the basis for a suitable approximation theory in semantics. Finally, the homeomorphic embedding of trees is studied to provide a method in termination proofs.

1.4.1 Trees and Well-Founded Partially Ordered Sets

For the sake of convenience some basic notions are recalled. A partial order $\leq$ on a set A is a reflexive, antisymmetric and transitive relation on A. A set equipped with a partial order is called a partially ordered set or simply a poset. A partial order $\leq$ on A is well-founded iff there is no infinite strictly descending chain

$$x_0 > x_1 > x_2 > \dots$$

of elements in A.

A well-founded chain is also well-ordered since each of its nonempty subsets has a least element.

Recall that our intention is to try to find out the characteristic features of a tree as a special well-founded poset. Intuitively, a ***tree*** consists of a set of ***nodes*** and a set of ***edges*** with the property that, first, there is a distinguished node, called the ***root***, into which no edge enters, and second, from the root there is a unique path to every node.

Finite trees may be visualized as directed graphs. In Fig. 1.12 a finite tree is depicted, where the direction of edges is always top-down; we will generally adopt this convention.

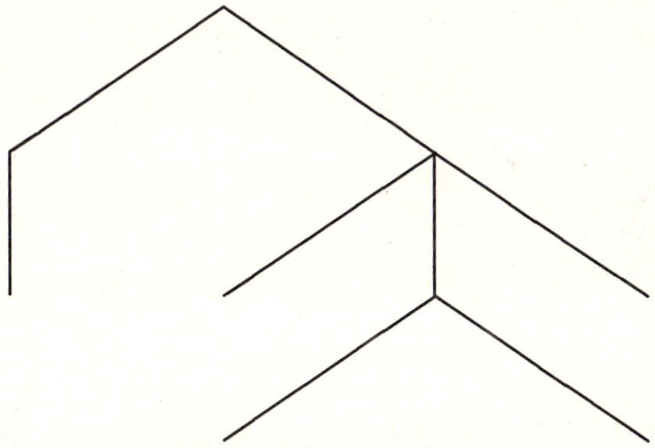

Fig. 1.12

Thinking of a tree as a poset we require that a least element exists and the predecessors of any node form a chain, where x is called a ***predecessor*** of a given element a if $x \leq a$, while a predecessor distinct from a is said to be ***proper***. Dually, x is called a (***proper***) ***successor*** of a if $a \leq x$ $(a < x)$.

Definition 1. *A well-founded poset with a least element is called a* ***tree*** *if the predecessors of each of its elements form a chain.*

Now we are going to present a certain kind of standard tree. Let A be a set. Given two words v and w over A, we say that v is a ***prefix*** of w if there is some word u over A such that $vu = w$. This leads to the prefix-order on $W(A)$:

$$v \leq_{pre} w \quad \text{iff } v \text{ is a prefix of } w,$$

which was already introduced in Section 1.3.3. A subset W of $W(A)$ is called ***prefix-closed*** if all prefixes of words in W belong to W, too.

Proposition 1. *Let A be a set. Any nonempty prefix-closed set of words over A is a tree with respect to prefix-order.*

Proof. Let $W \neq \emptyset$ be a prefix-closed subset of $W(A)$. Since the empty word e is a prefix of any word, e belongs to W. Evidently, e is the least element of W.

Given an arbitrary word w of W we have to show that the set of all its predecessors is a chain. Therefore assume that v and v' are predecessors of w, that is, $v \leq_{pre} w$ and $v' \leq_{pre} w$. Then, by definition, there are words u and u' over A such that $vu = w$ and $v'u' = w$. Because of the unique representation of a word by letters, either v must be a prefix of v' or, vice versa, v' must be a prefix of v. Hence, v and v' are comparable and, consequently, all predecessors of w form a chain. ∎

In particular, the set of all words over A is a tree. When A is an n-element set, $W(A)$ is said to be the ***full n-ary tree***.

Example 1. Let $A = \{1, 2\}$. Then, for instance,

$$\{e, 1, 2, 11, 12, 21, 22, 121, 221, 222, 2211, 22112\}$$

is a prefix-closed subset of $W(A)$ and hence a tree. It has the graphical representation shown in Fig. 1.13. ∎

Any prefix-closed subset W of $W(A)$ admits a decomposition into "levels":

$$W_n = \{w \in W \mid |w| = n\} \quad \text{for } n \geq 0,$$

so that a node at level n has exactly n proper predecessors. In general, however, the sets of predecessors in a tree are not finite. To define the notion of level we first introduce the rank of a node.

It is known from (axiomatic) set theory that every well-ordered set can be identified with an ordinal number. Taking this for granted we associate with each node of a tree the ordinal number corresponding to the set of all its predecessors. It is called the ***rank*** of the node considered.

Now, the subsets of nodes in a tree with equal rank are said to be ***levels***. If, in particular, the rank is finite, then we speak of a ***finite level***. Of course, the level of rank zero consists of the root only. The levels of a tree are singletons iff the tree is a chain.

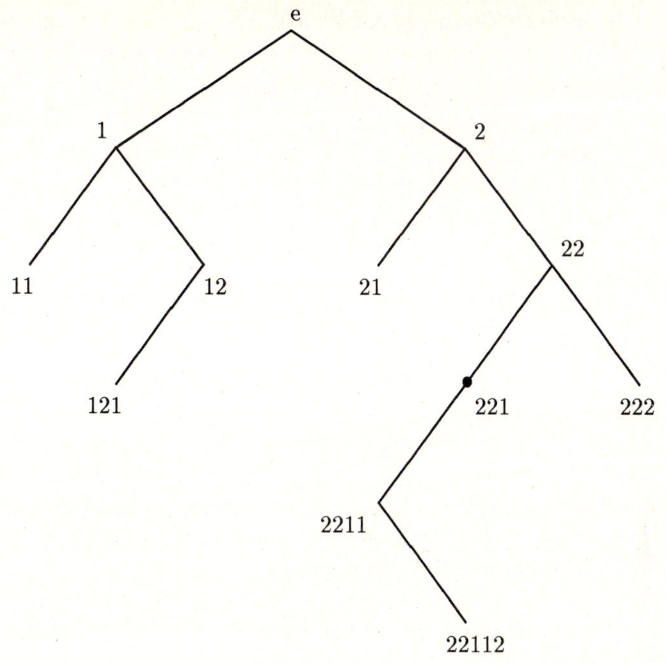

Fig. 1.13

Note. It should be mentioned that the notion of rank allows us to use induction. When the rank ranges over infinite ordinals the Principle of Transfinite Induction (Appendix 1) must be applied. Induction over the rank is often called the ***Principle of Tree Induction.*** ■

If a tree A has only finite levels, then the set of all predecessors of each node is finite. Let a_0 be the root of A, i.e., a_0 is the least element of A. The finite sequence $a_0 < a_1 < \ldots < a_n$ of all predecessors of an element $a = a_n$ can be taken as an "address" of a. In this way we get an injective mapping f from A to the set of all words over $A - \{a_0\}$, where f maps a_0 onto the empty word. Hence $f(A)$ can be regarded as a representation of the given tree. By definition, $f(A)$ is a prefix-closed set of words. Therefore, prefix-closed sets of words can be treated as ***standard trees*** in the class of all trees with finite levels only.

When, in particular, A is a countable tree there is a special addressing. Denote by $\mathbb{N}_+$ the set of all positive integers. Each node of A will be assigned a word over $\mathbb{N}_+$ as an ***address*** by the following rules. The root of A is addressed by the empty word. The elements of rank 1, that constitute the first level, are enumerated by positive integers in an arbitrary but fixed manner. Assume that already all nodes with rank less than n $(n \geq 1)$ are addressed by words over $\mathbb{N}_+$, where the address of any node with rank k is a word of length k. The n-th level consisting of all elements from A with rank n is partitioned into disjoint subsets: two elements belong to the same subset iff they have the same predecessor of rank $n-1$. Then, each such subset is again enumerated by positive integers in an arbitrary but fixed manner. Now, the address of an element a of rank n is a word wm, where w is the address of the immediate predecessor of a and m is the positive integer assigned to a. For better readability we sometimes write $w.m$ instead of wm, where dots may be generally used to separate natural numbers as letters in words to make the notation unambiguous. For instance, 1.1.2 is different from 11.2; the first word is of length 3 and the second one is of length 2.

Since this addressing is unique up to isomorphism of posets we derive the following result.

Proposition 2. *Every countable tree is isomorphic to a prefix-closed set of words over* $\mathbb{N}_+$. ■

We close the section by mentioning two interesting results on trees. Neither result is directly applied in our further development, but some other versions are applied which will then be proved.

To formulate a version of König's Infinity Lemma suitable for trees we have to introduce an additional notion. A chain B of a tree A is said to be a ***branch*** if B is a maximal chain, that is, for any chain C of A, $B \subseteq C$ implies $B = C$.

König's Infinity Lemma for Trees. *Any infinite tree, all of whose finite levels are finite, has an infinite branch.* ■

The proof follows from Theorem 21 in Section 1.3.6.

Let A and B be trees. We say that A is ***homeomorphically embedded*** into B if there is an injective mapping h from A to B such that for each node a of A, the images of the immediate successors of a under h are successors of distinct successors of $h(a)$.

Example 2. Consider the finite trees in Fig. 1.14.

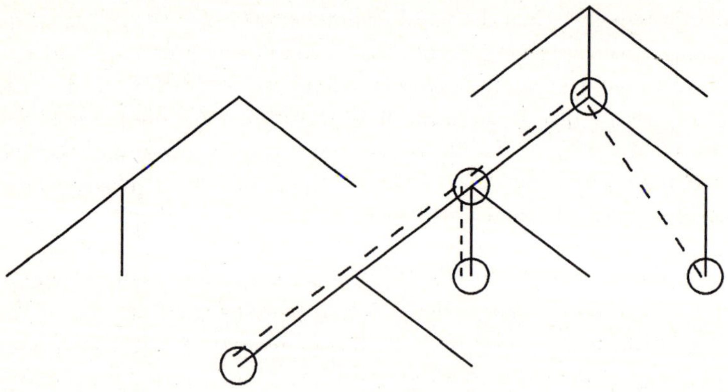

Fig. 1.14

The tree on the left-hand side is homeomorphically embedded into the tree on the right-hand side. ■

To construct a homeomorphic embedding from a tree A into a tree B, we first map the root of A onto some node of B, say b, and then all other nodes of A are injectively mapped into successors of b such that, informally speaking, it is possible to rebuild A in the subtree of B with root b by considering paths as new edges.

On finite trees homeomorphic embedding has an important property.

Kruskal's Tree Theorem. *The homeomorphic embedding is a partial well-order on any set of finite trees.* ■

A proof is given in /Nash-Williams-63/. In the literature, Kruskal's Tree Theorem and its generalizations are intensively studied; see, e.g., /Dershowitz-87/, /Dershowitz-Jouannaud-90/, /Kruskal-72/, /Puel-85/, /Raoult-88/, /Simpson-85/.

1.4.2 Labelled Trees

Labelled trees arise naturally as representation of terms. For instance, the term $(a + b) *(-a + c)$ has the tree representation depicted in Fig. 1.15.

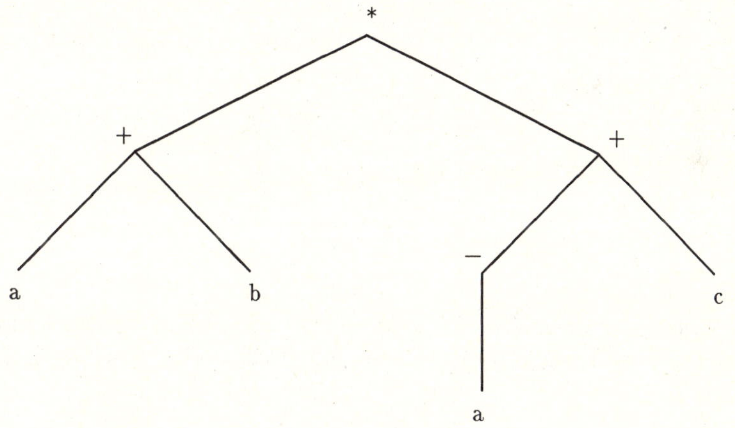

Fig. 1.15

When a labelled tree is thought of as a graphical representation of a term we would imagine that the class of underlying trees can be restricted to the finite ones. However, for our applications in semantics we need infinite labelled trees, as the example below should show.

Example 1. Consider the flowchart scheme in Fig. 1.16.

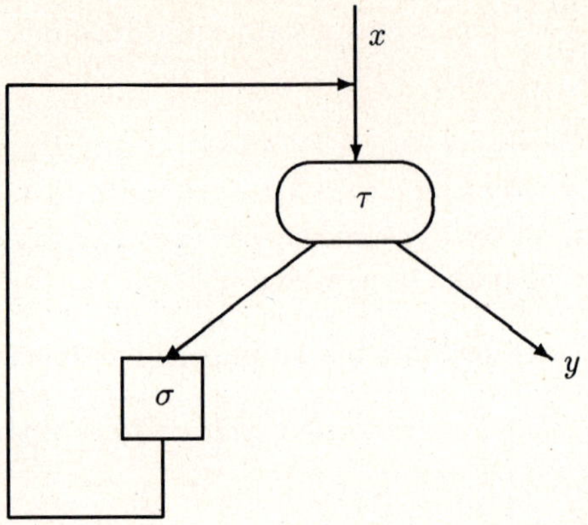

Fig. 1.16

This may be syntactically described by the equation

$$x = \tau(\sigma(x), y)$$

in a self-explanatory way. The term on the right-hand side has the representation shown in Fig. 1.17.

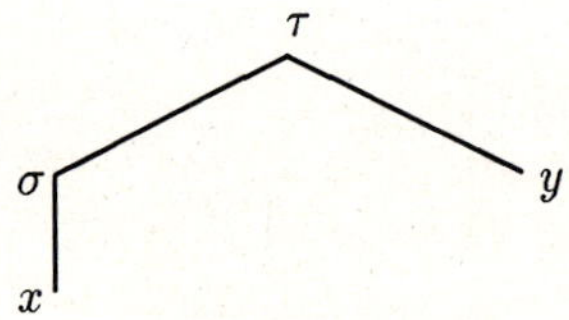

Fig. 1.17

Solving the equation means replacing x by $\tau(\sigma(x), y)$ as many times as possible. This method is called ***unfolding***. It results in the infinite labelled tree shown in Fig. 1.18.

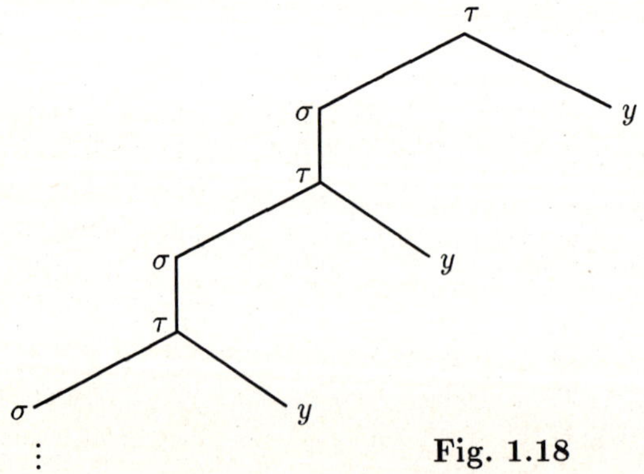

Fig. 1.18

Example 1 shows that we will need infinite labelled trees, but still only countably infinite ones. Therefore, by Proposition 2, we assume, without loss of generality, that the underlying trees are prefix-closed subsets of $W(\mathbb{N}_+)$. A labelled tree is then a pair consisting of a prefix-closed subset of $W(\mathbb{N}_+)$ and a labelling function assigning either an operation symbol of a signature Σ or a variable of a set X to each node. As previously, we always assume that Σ and X are disjoint.

Since the underlying tree is known implicitly whenever a labelling function is given as a partial mapping from $W(\mathbb{N}_+)$ to $\Sigma \cup X$, we shall identify a labelled tree with its labelling function for simplicity. This suggests the following definition.

Definition 2. *Let Σ be a signature and X be a set of variables. A partial mapping T from $W(\mathbb{N}_+)$ into $\Sigma \cup X$ is called a **partial Σ-tree over** X if $Dom(T)$ is prefix-closed and, for all $w \in Dom(T)$,*

(1) $T(w) \in \Sigma_0 \cup X$ if w is a leaf in $Dom(T)$ (i.e., w is maximal in $Dom(T)$); and
(2) $T(w) \in \Sigma_n$ if w is not a leaf and there is a natural number n such that $\max\{k \in \mathbb{N}_+ \mid w.k \in Dom(T)\} \leq n$.

A partial Σ-tree over X with a finite domain is said to be ***finite***. The set of all partial Σ-trees over X is denoted by $Tr_\Sigma(X)$, while $FTr_\Sigma(X)$ designates the subset of all finite partial Σ-trees over X. If X is empty, we simply write Tr_Σ and FTr_Σ instead of $Tr_\Sigma(\emptyset)$ and $FTr_\Sigma(\emptyset)$, respectively.

To avoid misunderstandings some clarifying remarks are necessary. It may happen that a node in a partial Σ-tree is labelled by an n-ary operation symbol ($n \geq 1$) but less than n edges leave the node. That is precisely why we speak of partial Σ-trees.

A prefix-closed subset D of $W(\mathbb{N}_+)$ is said to be a ***tree domain*** if, for all w in $W(\mathbb{N}_+)$ and all n in $\mathbb{N}_+$, $w.n \in D$ implies $w.k \in D$ for $k = 1, \ldots, n-1$. Now we call $T \in Tr_\Sigma(X)$ a ***total Σ-tree*** over X if $Dom(T)$ is a tree domain and, for all $w \in Dom(T)$,

(1) $T(w) \in \Sigma_0 \cup X$ if w is a leaf in $Dom(T)$; and

(2) $T(w) \in \Sigma_n$ if w is not a leaf and $n = \max\{k \in \mathbb{N}_+ \mid w.k \in Dom(T)\}$.

Any partial Σ-tree can be regarded as a total one if the signature is enlarged by a special symbol, say $\perp$, which is treated as a new nullary operation symbol. Formally, the enlarged signature $\Sigma_\perp$ is defined by: $(\Sigma_\perp)_0 = \Sigma_0 \cup \{\perp\}$, where $\perp \notin \Sigma_0$, and $(\Sigma_\perp)_n = \Sigma_n$ for all $n \geq 1$. To any partial Σ-tree T we associate a total $\Sigma_\perp$-tree $\overline{T}$ as follows: its domain $Dom(\overline{T})$ is the least tree domain including $Dom(T)$ such that $w.n \in Dom(\overline{T})$ whenever $T(w) \in \Sigma_n$ and, for all w in $Dom(\overline{T})$, $\overline{T}(w) = T(w)$ if $w \in Dom(T)$, and $\overline{T}(w) = \perp$ if $w \notin Dom(T)$. In $\overline{T}$, exactly n edges leave each node labelled by an n-ary operation symbol; however, some of the successor nodes may be labelled by $\perp$. Since it is then easily visible whether a Σ-tree (considered as $\Sigma_\perp$-tree) is partial or total depending on the occurence of $\bot$, we will simply speak of Σ-trees. Sometimes we may emphasize that a given Σ-tree is partial or total.

Definition 3. *The partial order $\sqsubseteq$ on $Tr_\Sigma(X)$, defined by $T \sqsubseteq T'$ iff $Dom(T) \subseteq Dom(T')$ and $T(w) = T'(w)$ for all w in $Dom(T)$, is called the* ***syntactic order.***

The following statement is easy to check.

Lemma 3. *$(Tr_\Sigma(X), \sqsubseteq)$ is a poset with a least element.* ∎

The least element is the nowhere defined partial mapping. According to our convention it is the trivial tree consisting of the root only, which is labelled by $\bot$. For simplicity we denote the least element itself by $\bot$.

Our next aim is a characterization of the syntactic order. For that reason the replacement of a subtree in a given tree by another one must be introduced. First, however, the notion of a subtree has to be defined.

Definition 4. *Let T be a Σ-tree over X. Given any address u of T, the* ***subtree*** *of T at the address u is a Σ-tree over X, denoted by T/u, which is defined as follows:*

$$Dom(T/u) = \{w \in W(\mathbb{N}_+) \mid uw \in Dom(T)\}$$

and

$$(T/u)(w) = T(uw)$$

for all $w \in Dom(T/u)$.

Definition 5. *Let T and T' be Σ-trees over X. Given any address u of T, the* ***replacement*** *of the subtree of T at the address u by T' is a Σ-tree over X, denoted by $T[u/T']$, which is defined as follows:*

$$Dom(T[u/T']) = \{uv \mid v \in Dom(T')\} \bigcup \{w \in Dom(T) \mid u \not\leq_{pre} w\}$$

and

$$T[u/T'](w) = \begin{cases} T'(w) & \text{if } w = uv \text{ for some } v \in Dom(T'), \\ T(w) & \text{if } w \in Dom(T) \text{ and } u \text{ is not a prefix of } w, \end{cases}$$

for all $w \in Dom(T[u/T'])$.

The two cases of Definition 5 are visualized in Fig. 1.19.

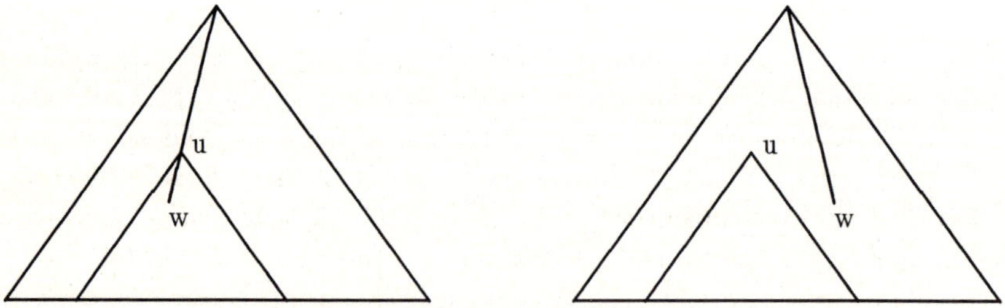

Fig. 1.19

Selecting and replacing subtrees often have to be done successively. Thus, their compatibility must be studied. To do so, observe that the choice of two addresses u and v in a given Σ-tree gives rise to three cases: (1) u and v are incomparable, in symbols $u|v$; (2) u is a prefix of v; and (3) v is a prefix of u. By a straightforward calculation we derive

Lemma 4. *Let $T, T_1, T_2 \in Tr_\Sigma(X)$ and $u, v \in Dom(T)$, $w \in Dom(T_1)$ and $w' \in Dom(T/v)$. Then*

$$T[u/T_1]/v = \begin{cases} T/v & \text{if } u|v, \\ T_1/w & \text{if } v = uw, \\ (T/v)[w'/T_1] & \text{if } u = vw'; \end{cases}$$

and

$$T[u/T_1][v/T_2] = \begin{cases} T[v/T_2][u/T_1] & \text{if } u|v, \\ T[u/T_1[w/T_2]] & \text{if } v = uw, \\ T[v/T_2] & \text{if } u = vw'. \end{cases}$$

■

Selection and replacement of subtrees are fundamental operations for solving term equations in the framework of algebraic semantics. Here, only a first glance at this is given in the example below.

Example 2. Let Σ be a signature with a unary operation symbol σ and a binary operation symbol τ. The term equation

$$x = t(x, y)$$

with $t = \tau(\sigma(x), y)$, which describes syntactically the flowchart in Fig. 1.16, defines a mapping f from $Tr_\Sigma(\{y\})$ into itself by

$$f(T') = t[1.1/T'] \quad \text{for all } T' \in Tr_\Sigma(\{y\}).$$

Consider the Σ-tree T depicted in Fig. 1.18. Its addresses are all words of the form 1^k or $(1.1)^k.2$ with $k \in I\!N$. Here we use the usual power notation: $m^0 = e$ and $m^k = m.m^{k-1}$ for $k, m \in I\!N_+$. T is defined by

$$T(w) = \begin{cases} \tau & \text{if } w = 1^{2k},\ k \in I\!N, \\ \sigma & \text{if } w = 1^{2k+1},\ k \in I\!N, \\ y & \text{if } w = 1^{2k}.2,\ k \in I\!N, \end{cases}$$

for all $w \in Dom(T)$.

It is easy to see that

$$T = f(T)$$

since $Dom(T) = Dom(f(T)) = Dom(t[1.1/T])$ and $T(w) = (f(T))(w) = t[1.1/T](w)$ for all $w \in Dom(T)$.

It is also clear intuitively that T is a fixpoint of f as indicated in Fig. 1.20.

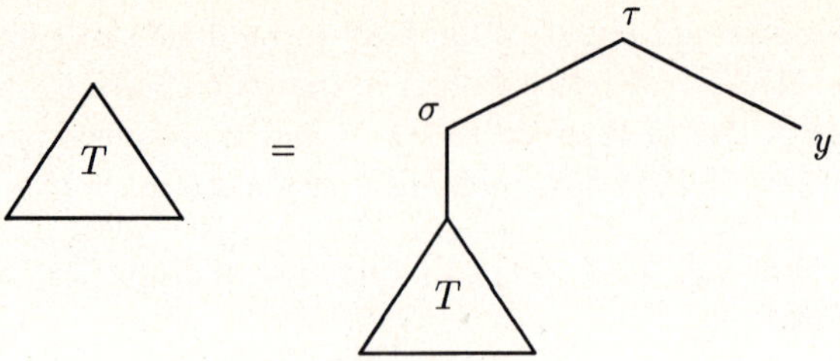

Fig. 1.20

The iterative process of computing T yields an infinite ascending chain of approximations:

$$T_0 \sqsubseteq T_1 \sqsubseteq T_2 \ldots$$

where

$$T_0 = \perp \quad \text{and} \quad T_n = t[1.1/T_{n-1}] \text{ for } n \geq 1. \qquad \blacksquare$$

In principle, it is not an easy task to solve tree equations or to find fixpoints of the associated mappings, as one might infer from the previous example. Therefore a suitable approximation theory based on $\sqsubseteq$ will be developed later, using fixpoint techniques. Computing the approximations we always start with the least element $\perp$, which expresses the fact that nothing is known about the result at the beginning. During the iterative computation process approximations are obtained but still not everything is known about the result in any of them. This may be indicated by labelling the corresponding addresses by $\perp$. In other words, in the result, which is an infinite Σ-tree, some of its subtrees are not yet computed. They are represented by $\perp$.

Informally speaking, approximations should obey the following compatibility with replacement. If T' is a "better" approximation than T, then replacing a subtree by T' at some address in a given Σ-tree should also yield a better approximation than replacing the same subtree by T. This motivates the notion of invariance.

A relation $\rightarrow$ on $Tr_\Sigma(X)$ is called ***invariant*** if, for all T, T_1 and T_2 in $Tr_\Sigma(X)$ and all $u \in Dom(T)$,

$$T_1 \rightarrow T_2 \quad \text{implies} \quad T[u/T_1] \rightarrow T[u/T_2].$$

The desired characterization of the approximation order can now be derived.

Proposition 5. *The syntactic order $\sqsubseteq$ is the least invariant partial order on the set of all Σ-trees over X with $\perp$ as the least element.*

Proof. It is not difficult to verify that $\sqsubseteq$ is an invariant partial order on $Tr_\Sigma(X)$ and $\perp \sqsubseteq T$ for all T in $Tr_\Sigma(X)$.

Let $\leq$ be an arbitrary invariant partial order on $Tr_\Sigma(X)$ such that $\perp \leq T$ for all T in $Tr_\Sigma(X)$. For any two Σ-trees $T, T' \in Tr_\Sigma(X)$ we have to show that $T \sqsubseteq T'$ implies $T \leq T'$.

If $T \sqsubseteq T'$, then $Dom(T) \subseteq Dom(T')$ by definition. Put $D = Dom(T') - Dom(T)$. When D is empty, T equals T' and, consequently, $T \leq T'$. Assume now that D is not empty. Then D contains finitely many minimal elements (with respect to the prefix-order), say $u_1, \ldots, u_k$. The corresponding subtrees of T' are denoted by $T_1, \ldots, T_k$, i.e., $T_i = T'/u_i$ for $i = 1, \ldots, k$. Because $u_1, \ldots, u_k$ do not belong to $Dom(T)$, we have $T(u_i) = \perp$ for $i = 1, \ldots, k$. Hence

$$T = T'[u_1/\perp] \ldots [u_k/\perp].$$

By assumption, $\perp \leq T_i$ for $i = 1, \ldots, k$. Thus

$$T'[u_1/\perp] \ldots [u_k/\perp] \leq T'[u_1/T_1] \ldots [u_k/T_k],$$

by the invariance and transitivity of $\leq$, and consequently

$$T \leq T'[u_1/T_1] \ldots [u_k/T_k],$$

which yields $T \leq T'$. ■

In what follows we focus our attention on finite total Σ-trees, which can be thought of as Σ-terms as we already know. But let us first establish this one-to-one correspondence. By analogy with Σ-trees the set of addresses of any $t \in T_\Sigma(X)$ is a subset of $W(I\!N_+)$, also denoted by $Dom(t)$, which is recursively defined as follows:

(1) If $t \in \Sigma_0 \cup X$, then $Dom(t) = \{e\}$;

(2) If $t = \sigma\, t_1 \ldots t_n$, then $Dom(t) = \{e\} \cup \{iu \mid i = 1, \ldots, n \text{ and } u \in Dom(t_i)\}$.

Now we associate with t a total finite Σ-tree $t^\bullet$ over X by the rules:

(1) $Dom(t^\bullet) = Dom(t)$;

(2a) If $t \in \Sigma_0 \cup X$, then $t^\bullet(e) = t$; and

(2b) If $t = \sigma\, t_1 \ldots t_n$, then for all w in $Dom(t)$

$$t^\bullet(w) = \begin{cases} \sigma & \text{if } w = e, \\ t_k^\bullet(v) & \text{if } w = k.v \text{ for } k = 1, \ldots, n. \end{cases}$$

In the sequel, we identify t with $t^\bullet$; and the set $T_\Sigma(X)$ of all Σ-terms over X will be identified as the set of all total finite Σ-trees over X. Similarly, T_Σ stands for the set of all total finite Σ-trees (over $\emptyset$).

Example 3. Let Σ be a signature with two nullary operation symbols 0 and 1, a unary operation symbol $\neg$ and two binary operation symbols $\vee$ and $\wedge$. The term $t = \neg(\neg 0 \vee 1)$ has the tree representation shown in Fig. 1.21. ■

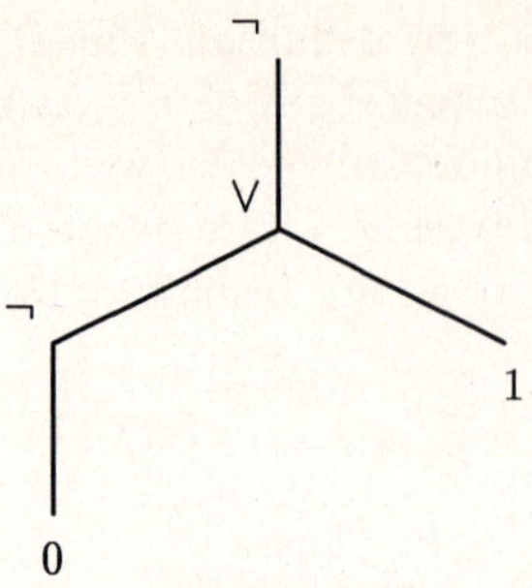

Fig. 1.21

Because of this identification all concepts introduced for Σ-trees carry over to Σ-terms. Although it is therefore not really necessary to define the notions of subterm and replacement of terms, we will, nevertheless, redefine them in an alternative way.

Let t be a Σ-term over X. The ***subterm*** of t at an address u of t, denoted by t/u, is inductively defined as follows:

(1) If $t \in \Sigma_0 \cup X$, then $t/e = t$; and

(2) If $t = \sigma\, t_1 \ldots t_n$, then $t/e = t$ and $t/iu = t_i/u$ for $i = 1, \ldots, n$ and $u \in Dom(t_i)$.

The term obtained by ***replacement*** of the subterm at address u in t by another term t', denoted by $t[u/t']$, is inductively defined as follows:

(1) $t[e/t'] = t'$; and

(2) $(\sigma\, t_1 \ldots t_n)[iu/t'] = \sigma\, t_1 \ldots t_{i-1} t_i[u/t'] t_{i+1} \ldots t_n$ for $i = 1, \ldots, n$ and $u \in Dom(t_i)$.

The reader may convince her/himself that these notions coincide with those given in Definitions 4 and 5 (up to identification).

Example 4. Consider the signature introduced in Example 3. The term $t = (0 \vee (x \wedge 1)) \vee y$ possesses the following addresses: $e, 1, 2, 1.1, 1.2, 1.2.1, 1.2.2$; as we may directly derive from the tree representation given in Fig. 1.22.

The replacement of the subterm at the address 1.2 by the term $t' = \neg x \vee (1 \wedge y)$ represented in Fig. 1.23 yields

$$t[1.2/t'] = (0 \vee (\neg x \vee (1 \wedge y))) \vee y.$$

This result has the tree representation shown in Fig. 1.24. ■

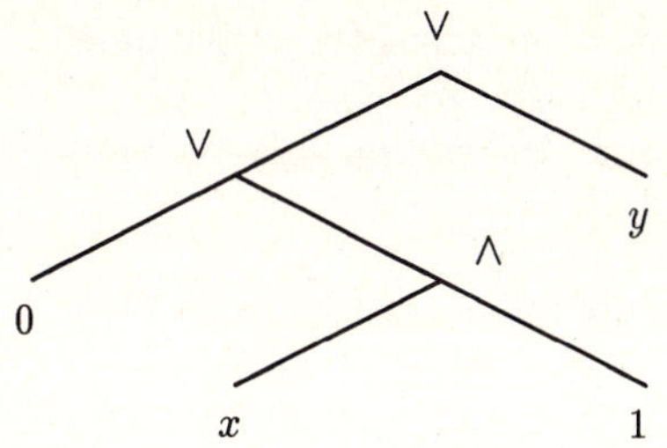

Fig. 1.22

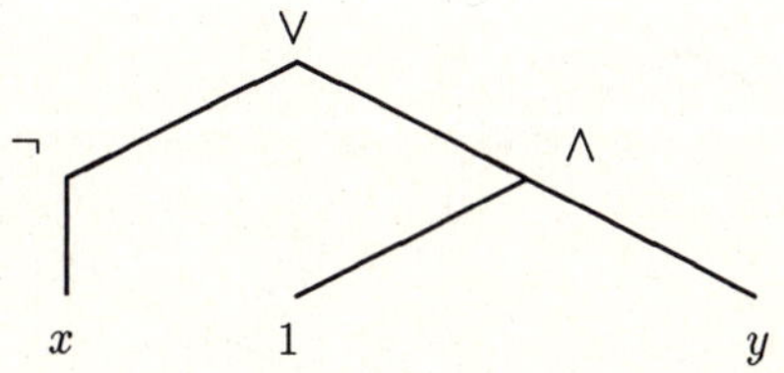

Fig. 1.23

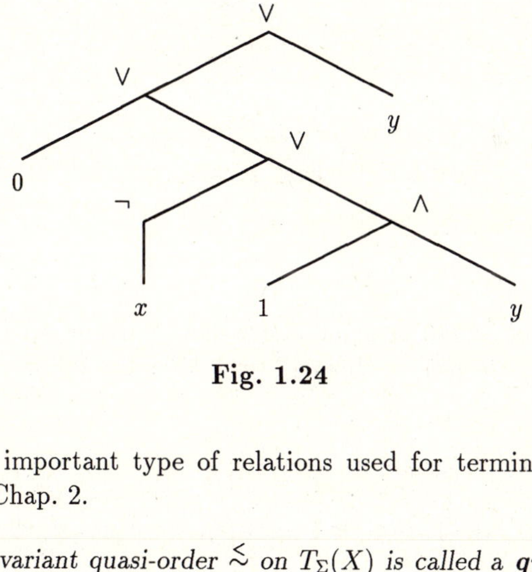

Fig. 1.24

Finally we study an important type of relations used for termination proofs of term rewriting systems in Chap. 2.

Definition 6. *An invariant quasi-order* $\precsim$ *on* $T_\Sigma(X)$ *is called a* ***quasi-simplification order*** *if, for all* $t, t' \in T_\Sigma(X), t \precsim t'$ *whenever* t *is a subterm of* t'*. In particular, a quasi-simplification order is said to be a* ***simplification order*** *if it is antisymmetric.*

We now explain the main idea for using quasi-simplification orders. Given a quasi-order $\precsim$ on $T_\Sigma(X)$, we first search for the least quasi-simplification order on $T_\Sigma(X)$ extending $\precsim$. It happens that such a least quasi-simplification order, say $\overset{\triangleleft}{\sim}$, exists with the additional property that $\overset{\triangleleft}{\sim}$ is well-behaved, i.e., $\overset{\triangleleft}{\sim}$ is a well-quasi-order. Since any relation including a well-behaved one is also well-behaved, we conclude that every quasi-simplification order extending $\lesssim$ is a well-quasi-order and consequently well-founded.

Next we generalize the homeomorphic embedding of trees. Let us consider an example in order to get a hint as to how to do it.

Example 5. Let Σ be the signature introduced in Example 3. Consider the Σ-terms t and t' represented as trees in Fig. 1.25.

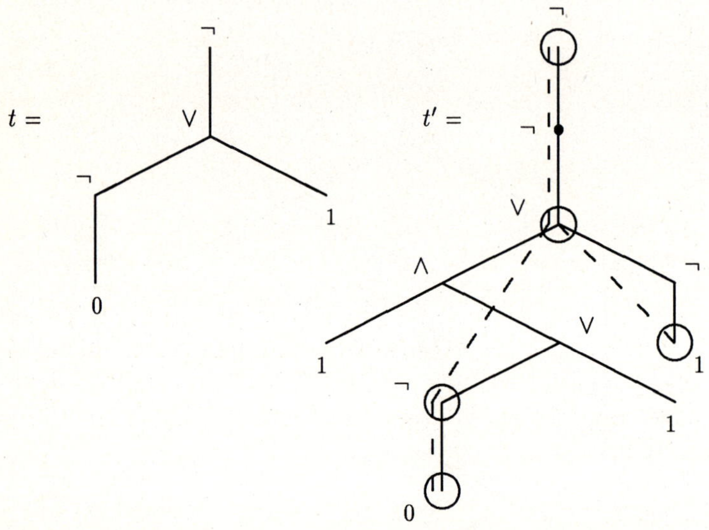

Fig. 1.25

We may regard t' as homeomorphically embedding t, as the dashed edges indicate. ■

The intuitive argument in the example above can be expressed formally. There is an injective mapping $h : \mathit{Dom}(t) \to \mathit{Dom}(t')$ such that the following two conditions are fulfilled:

(1) $t(w) = t'(h(w))$ for all $w \in \mathit{Dom}(t)$; and

(2) $h(w)k \leq_{pre} h(wk)$ for all $w \in \mathit{Dom}(t)$, $k = 1, \ldots, n$, where $t(w) \in \Sigma_n$.

Observe that h is monotone with respect to prefix-order:

$$u \leq_{pre} v \quad \text{implies} \quad h(u) \leq_{pre} h(v) \quad \text{for all } u, v \in \mathit{Dom}(t).$$

Inspecting condition (1) we recognize the possibility to use a precedence order $\lesssim$ on operation symbols by requiring $t(w) \lesssim t'(h(w))$ for all $w \in \mathit{Dom}(t)$. This leads to the following generalization.

Definition 7. *Let Σ be a signature and X be a set of variables. Given a quasi-order $\lesssim$ on $\Sigma \cup X$, we say that the relation $\stackrel{\triangleleft}{\sim}$ on $T_\Sigma(X)$ determined by the rule: $t \stackrel{\triangleleft}{\sim} t'$ iff there is an injective mapping $h : Dom(t) \to Dom(t')$ such that the two conditions below are fulfilled:*

(1) $t(w) \lesssim t'(h(w))$ for all $w \in Dom(t)$; and

(2) $h(w)k \leq_{pre} h(wk)$ for all $w \in Dom(t)$, $k = 1, \ldots, n$, where $t(w) \in \Sigma_n$,

is a ***homeomorphic embedding based on*** $\lesssim$.

Note that the homeomorphic embedding based on the identity relation is a straightforward generalization of the homeomorphic embedding of (finite) trees introduced in the previous section.

Lemma 6. *If $\lesssim$ is a quasi-order on $\Sigma \cup X$, then the homeomorphic embedding based on $\lesssim$ is a quasi-order on $T_\Sigma(X)$.*

Proof. Let $\lesssim$ be a quasi-order on $\Sigma \cup X$ and denote by $\stackrel{\triangleleft}{\sim}$ the homeomorphic embedding based on $\lesssim$. Obviously, $\stackrel{\triangleleft}{\sim}$ is reflexive. It remains to prove that $\stackrel{\triangleleft}{\sim}$ is transitive. Therefore assume that t, t', t'' are terms in $T_\Sigma(X)$ such that $t \stackrel{\triangleleft}{\sim} t'$ and $t' \stackrel{\triangleleft}{\sim} t''$. By definition, there are injective mappings $h : Dom(t) \to Dom(t')$ and $g : Dom(t') \to Dom(t'')$ satisfying conditions (1) and (2) of Definition 7.

We claim that the composition $f = h \cdot g$, which is certainly injective, fulfills conditions (1) and (2), too. First, $t''(f(w)) = t''(g(h(w))) \lesssim t'(h(w)) \lesssim t(w)$ for all $w \in Dom(t)$, and hence condition (1) is fulfilled. To verify the second condition we proceed as follows:

$$\begin{aligned} f(w)k &= g(h(w))k \leq_{pre} g(h(w)k) && \text{since } g \text{ fulfills (2)} \\ &\leq_{pre} g(h(wk)) = f(wk) && \text{since } h \text{ fulfills (2) and } g \text{ is monotone} \end{aligned}$$

for all $w \in Dom(t)$, $k = 1, \ldots, n$, where $t(w) \in \Sigma_n$. Now, by definition, $t \stackrel{\triangleleft}{\sim} t''$. That is, $\stackrel{\triangleleft}{\sim}$ is transitive. ■

To apply Higman's Theorem for showing that homeomorphic embedding is well-behaved we need the following characterization.

Lemma 7. *If $\stackrel{\triangleleft}{\sim}$ is a homeomorphic embedding based on a quasi-order $\lesssim$ on $\Sigma \cup X$, then, for all terms t and t' in $T_\Sigma(X)$, $t \stackrel{\triangleleft}{\sim} t'$ iff either*

(i) $t = \sigma t_1 \ldots t_m$, $t' = \sigma' t'_1 \ldots t'_n$ with $\sigma \lesssim \sigma'$ and $t_i \stackrel{\triangleleft}{\sim} t'_{j_i}$ for all $i = 1, \ldots, m$ and some $j_1, \ldots, j_m$ with $1 \leq j_1 < j_2 < \ldots < j_m \leq n$; or

(ii) $t' = \sigma' t'_1 \ldots t'_n$ and $t \stackrel{\triangleleft}{\sim} t'_j$ for some $j = 1, \ldots, n$; or

(iii) $t \lesssim t'$ if $t, t' \in \Sigma_0 \cup X$.

Proof. Assume that $t \overset{\triangleleft}{\sim} t'$. By definition, there is an injective mapping $h : Dom(t) \rightarrow Dom(t')$ such that conditions (1) and (2) of Definition 7 are fulfilled. Now we distinguish two cases.

Case 1: $h(e) = e$ (where e is the empty word).

Then $t(e) \lesssim t'(e)$. If $t(e) = t$ and $t'(e) = t'$ are in $\Sigma_0 \cup X$, then $t \lesssim t'$, and hence *(iii)* holds. If $t(e) \in \Sigma_m$ and $t'(e) \in \Sigma_n$, then $t = \sigma\, t_1 \ldots t_m$, $t' = \sigma'\, t'_1 \ldots t'_n$ with $\sigma \lesssim \sigma'$. Note that h induces m injective mappings $h_i : Dom(t_i) \rightarrow Dom(t'_{j_i})$ defined by $h_i(w) = h(iw)$ for all $w \in Dom(t_i)$, $i = 1, \ldots, m$, where $1 \leq j_1 < j_2 < \ldots < j_m \leq n$.

It is easy to see that $t_i(w) \lesssim t'_{j_i}(h_i(w))$ for all $w \in Dom(t_i)$. Furthermore, $h_i(w)k \leq_{pre} h_i(wk)$ for all $w \in Dom(t_i)$, $k = 1, \ldots, n_i$, where $t_i(w)$ belongs to Σ_{n_i}. Hence $t_i \overset{\triangleleft}{\sim} t'_{j_i}$ for all $i = 1, \ldots, m$, where $1 \leq j_1 < j_2 < \ldots < j_m \leq n$; and so *(i)* holds.

Case 2: $h(e) = ju$ for some $j \in \mathbb{N}_+$ and $u \in W(\mathbb{N}_+)$.

If $t' = \sigma'\, t'_1 \ldots t'_n$, then h determines an injective mapping $h' : Dom(t) \rightarrow Dom(t'_j)$ by the rule: $h'(w) = v$ iff $h(w) = jv$ for all $w \in Dom(t)$. Since

$$t(w) \lesssim t'(h(w)) = t'(jh'(w)) = t'_j(h'(w))$$

for all $w \in Dom(t)$ and

$$h(w)k \leq_{pre} h(wk) = jh'(wk) \quad \text{implies} \quad h'(w)k \leq_{pre} h'(wk)$$

for all $w \in Dom(t)$, $k = 1, \ldots, m$, where $t(w) \in \Sigma_n$, we derive $t \overset{\triangleleft}{\sim} t'_j$, which means that *(ii)* is valid.

Conversely, $t \overset{\triangleleft}{\sim} t'$ whenever one of the conditions *(i)* -- *(iii)* is fulfilled. The easy proof is left to the reader. ■

Now we are ready to obtain our main result which may be considered as a version of Kruskal's Tree Theorem for labelled finite trees.

Theorem 8. *Let Σ be a signature and X a set of variables. If $\lesssim$ is a well-quasi-order on $\Sigma \cup X$, then the homeomorphic embedding $\overset{\triangleleft}{\sim}$ based on $\lesssim$ is a well-quasi-order on $T_\Sigma(X)$.*

Proof. By Lemma 7, $\overset{\triangleleft}{\sim}$ is a divisibility order on the term algebra $\boldsymbol{T}_\Sigma(X)$. Since $\boldsymbol{T}_\Sigma(X)$ is generated by X we conclude, by Higman's Theorem (Theorem 16 in Sect. 1.3.5), that $\overset{\triangleleft}{\sim}$ is a well-quasi-order because Σ and X are well-quasi-ordered. ■

Given a quasi-order $\lesssim$ on $\Sigma \cup X$, we say that a quasi-order $\overset{\sqsubset}{\sim}$ on $T_\Sigma(X)$ ***prolongs*** $\lesssim$ if $\lesssim$ and $\overset{\sqsubset}{\sim}$ coincide on $\Sigma_0 \cup X$ and, for all operation symbols $\sigma \in \Sigma_m$ and $\sigma' \in \Sigma_n$,

$$\sigma \lesssim \sigma' \text{ implies } \sigma\, t_{j_1} \ldots t_{j_m} \overset{\sqsubset}{\sim} \sigma'\, t_1 \ldots t_n \text{ for all terms } t_1, \ldots, t_n \text{ in } T_\Sigma(X), \text{ and some indices such that } 1 \leq j_1 < j_2 < \ldots < j_m \leq n.$$

Our next goal is to show that the homeomorphic embedding based on a given quasi-order $\lesssim$ is the least quasi-simplification order prolonging $\lesssim$.

Lemma 9. *The homeomorphic embedding based on a quasi-order on $\Sigma \cup X$ is a quasi-simplification order on $T_\Sigma(X)$.*

Proof. Let $\lesssim$ be a quasi-order on $\Sigma \cup X$ and denote by $\overset{\triangleleft}{\sim}$ the homeomorphic embedding based on $\lesssim$.

Claim 1: $\overset{\triangleleft}{\sim}$ is invariant.

If t_1 and t_2 are terms in $T_\Sigma(X)$ such that $t_1 \overset{\triangleleft}{\sim} t_2$, we have to show that $t[u/t_1] \overset{\triangleleft}{\sim} t[u/t_2]$ for all $t \in T_\Sigma(X)$ and $u \in Dom(t)$. Assume $t_1 \overset{\triangleleft}{\sim} t_2$. By definition, there is an injective mapping $h : Dom(t_1) \to Dom(t_2)$ satisfying the conditions (1) and (2) of Definition 7.

Define a mapping $f : Dom(t[u/t_1]) \to Dom(t[u/t_2])$ as follows:

$$f(w) = \begin{cases} uh(v) & \text{if } w = uv \text{ for some } v \in Dom(t_1), \\ w & \text{if } u \text{ is not a prefix of } w \end{cases}$$

for all $w \in Dom(t[/t_1])$.

Evidently, f is injective. Now we have to verify both conditions of Definition 7. Let us start with condition (1). Therefore take $w \in Dom(t[u/t_1])$. Suppose that u is a prefix of w, i.e., $w = uv$ for some $v \in Dom(t_1)$. Hence

$$\begin{aligned} t[u/t_1](w) &= t[u/t_1](uv) = t_1(v) \lesssim t_2(h(v)) = \\ &= t[u/t_2](uh(v)) = t[u/t_2](f(uv)) = t[u/t_2](f(w)). \end{aligned}$$

If we assume that u is not a prefix of w, then

$$t[u/t_1](w) = t(w) = t(f(w)) = t[u/t_2](f(w)).$$

Hence, condition (1) is fulfilled.

To prove condition (2) we proceed analogously. Suppose u is a prefix of w. Then

$$f(w)k = uh(v)k \leq_{pre} uh(vk) = f(wk).$$

In the other case, where u is not a prefix of w, we have

$$f(w)k = wk = f(wk), \quad \text{and hence} \quad f(w)k \leq_{pre} f(wk).$$

Claim 2: $t \overset{\triangleleft}{\sim} t'$ whenever t is a subterm of t'.

If t is a subterm of t', then $t = t'/u$ for some $u \in Dom(t')$. The mapping $h : Dom(t) \to Dom(t')$ defined by $h(w) = uw$ for all $w \in Dom(t)$ fulfills the required conditions of Definition 7. Thus $t \overset{\triangleleft}{\sim} t'$. ∎

Before we prove the desired property of homeomorphic embeddings being the least one among all quasi-simplification orders prolonging a given quasi-order, we illustrate this property by the following example.

Example 6. Let Σ be the signature introduced in Example 3. For the Σ-terms t and t' from Example 5 we assert that $t \leq t'$, where $\leq$ is any given simplification order on T_Σ. Searching for common subterms in t and t', we get

$$t/1.1 = t'/1.1.1.2.1 \quad \text{and} \quad t/1.2 = t'/1.1.2.1.$$

Since $\leq$ is consistent with the subterm relation, it follows that

$$t'/1.1.1.2.1 \leq t'/1.1.1 \quad \text{and} \quad t'/1.1.2.1 \leq t'/1.1.2$$

and therefore

$$t/1.1 \leq t'/1.1.1 \quad \text{and} \quad t/1.2 \leq t'/1.1.2.$$

Because of $t/1 = t/1[1/(t/1.1)][2/(t/1.2)]$ we derive

$$t/1 \leq t/1[1(t'/1.1.1)][2/(t'/1.1.2)]$$

by the invariance of $\leq$. On the other hand, the right-hand side equals $t'/1.1$, which implies $t/1 \leq t'/1.1$. By the subterm property, $t'/1.1 \leq t'/1$. Hence $t/1 \leq t'/1$ and so

$$t = t[1/(t/1)] \leq t[1/(t'/1)] = t'. \qquad \blacksquare$$

Proposition 10. *Let Σ be a signature and X be a set of variables. Given a quasi-order $\lesssim$ on $\Sigma \cup X$, the homeomorphic embedding based on $\lesssim$ is the least quasi-simplification order on $T_\Sigma(X)$ prolonging $\lesssim$.*

Proof. Let $\lesssim$ be a quasi-order on $\Sigma \cup X$. Consider an arbitrary quasi-simplification order $\mathrel{\overset{\sqsubset}{\sim}}$ on $T_\Sigma(X)$ and assume that $\mathrel{\overset{\sqsubset}{\sim}}$ prolongs $\lesssim$. We have to show that $t \mathrel{\overset{\sqsubset}{\sim}} t'$ whenever $t \mathrel{\overset{\triangleleft}{\sim}} t'$ for all terms t and t' in $T_\Sigma(X)$. This will be done by using the Principle of Term Induction over t'. Suppose $t \mathrel{\overset{\triangleleft}{\sim}} t'$.

(1) Induction basis: If $t' \in \Sigma_0 \cup X$, then t must also belong to $\Sigma_0 \cup X$ and hence $t \lesssim t'$. Now, by the assumption that $\mathrel{\overset{\sqsubset}{\sim}}$ prolongs $\lesssim$, $t \mathrel{\overset{\sqsubset}{\sim}} t'$.

(2) Induction step: Suppose $t' = \sigma' t'_1 \ldots t'_n$. By Lemma 7, there are two possibilities, either *(i)* $t = \sigma t_1 \ldots t_m$ and $\sigma \lesssim \sigma'$, $t_i \mathrel{\overset{\triangleleft}{\sim}} t'_{j_i}$ for $i = 1, \ldots, m$, where $1 \leq j_1 < j_2 < \ldots < j_m \leq n$; or *(ii)* $t \mathrel{\overset{\triangleleft}{\sim}} t'_j$ for some $j = 1, \ldots, n$.
In case *(i)* we proceed as follows. By induction hypothesis, $t_i \mathrel{\overset{\sqsubset}{\sim}} t'_{j_i}$ for $i = 1, \ldots, m$ and hence, by the invariance of $\mathrel{\overset{\sqsubset}{\sim}}$, $\sigma t_1 \ldots t_m \mathrel{\overset{\sqsubset}{\sim}} \sigma t'_{j_1} \ldots t'_{j_m}$, whence $t \mathrel{\overset{\sqsubset}{\sim}} t'$ since $\mathrel{\overset{\sqsubset}{\sim}}$ prolongs $\lesssim$.
In case *(ii)*, $t \mathrel{\overset{\sqsubset}{\sim}} t'_j$ by the induction hypothesis. Since $\mathrel{\overset{\sqsubset}{\sim}}$ is assumed to be consistent with the subterm relation, we obtain $t \mathrel{\overset{\sqsubset}{\sim}} t'$. $\blacksquare$

As an immediate consequence of Proposition 10 in conjunction with Theorem 8 we derive our main result, due to Dershowitz /Dershowitz-79/, /Dershowitz-82/.

Theorem 11. *Let Σ be a signature and X be a set of variables. Any quasi-simplification order on $T_\Sigma(X)$ prolonging a well-quasi-order on $\Sigma_0 \cup X$ is a well-quasi-order, too.* $\blacksquare$

Since any quasi-order on a finite set is well-behaved we get the following conclusion.

Corollary. *If Σ is a finite signature and X is a finite set of variables, then any quasi-simplification order on $T_\Sigma(X)$ is a well-quasi-order.* $\blacksquare$

1.5 ω-Complete Posets and Fixpoint Theorem

This section presents the order theoretic foundation of fixpoint semantics for recursive program schemes based on a suitable approximation theory due to Scott /Scott-Strachey-71/. Informally speaking, when a stepwise computation delivers approximations, say $a_0, a_1, a_2, \ldots$, they can be arranged as an ascending chain such that its supremum represents the result of the computation. Therefore posets are needed, in which every countable chain has a supremum. This kind of completeness is investigated in Section 1.5.1.

In Section 1.5.2, a fixpoint theorem and related methods are established. It will turn out later that every mapping associated with a recursive program scheme, sometimes called a procedure body, has a least fixpoint. Hence we may say that the meaning of a recursive program scheme is the least fixpoint of its procedure body. This subject will be studied thoroughly in Section 4.2.4.

Finally, a method of completing a given poset is presented in Section 1.5.3.

1.5.1 ω-Complete Posets

A first glance at fixpoint semantics for recursive program schemes, which are syntactically described by term equations, was already given in the preceding section. In any stepwise computation the approximations may be arranged as an ascending chain $a_0 \leq a_1 \leq a_2 \leq \ldots$ under an appropriate partial order comparing the "amount of information" about the result. The result of the computation should be its limit. It is intuitively clear that the supremum of the chain is suitable for such a limit. Hence we have to require that every countable chain has a supremum. This leads to the definition below.

Definition 1. *A poset in which every countable chain has a supremum is called* ***ω-complete****.*

Note that any ω-complete poset A has a least element, usually denoted by $\perp$ (read "bottom"), which is the supremum of the empty chain in A.

Example 1. Every finite poset with a least element is ω-complete. ■

Example 2. Any flat poset is ω-complete. ■

Example 3. Every complete lattice is trivially an ω-complete poset. In particular, every power set (with respect to set inclusion) is ω-complete. ■

One of our motivating example is the poset of all partial mappings from a set A to a set B, denoted $(Par(A, B), \subseteq)$, partially ordered by set inclusion. That is, $f \subseteq g$ iff

$Dom(f) \subseteq Dom(g)$ and $f(x) = g(x)$ for all $x \in Dom(f)$. To prove ω-completeness of $(Par(A,B), \subseteq)$ it is more convenient to use an equivalent characterization of ω-completeness by means of directed subsets.

Recall that a subset X of a poset A is directed iff every two elements $x, y \in X$ have an upper bound in X, i.e., $x \leq z$ and $y \leq z$ for some $z \in X$. First, we ask the question whether, for each directed subset X of A such that its supremum exists, there is a chain Y in A whose supremum exists and $\sup X = \sup Y$.

Lemma 1. *Let X and Y be subsets of a given poset. If X and Y are mutually cofinal and the supremum of X exists then the supremum of Y exists too, and $\sup X = \sup Y$.* ■

The proof is left to the reader as an exercise.

Lemma 2. *Given a poset A, every countable directed subset of A is mutually cofinal with a countable chain in A.*

Proof. Let A be a poset. Of course, the empty set is a directed subset of A as well as a chain in A. Therefore, consider a nonempty subset X of A and assume X is directed. If X is finite, then the supremum of X exists and, evidently, X is mutually cofinal to the one-element chain consisting of $\sup X$. Now suppose X is countably infinite, i.e., $X = \{x_n \mid n \in I\!N\}$. Define a sequence $(y_n \mid n \in I\!N)$ as follows: $y_0 = x_0$ and y_n is an upper bound of $\{x_0, x_1, \ldots, x_n\} \cup \{y_1, y_2, \ldots, y_{n-1}\}$ for $n \geq 1$. By definition, $y_n \leq y_{n+1}$ and $x_n \leq y_n$ for all $n \in I\!N$. Hence $Y = (y_n \mid n \in I\!N)$ is a chain which is cofinal in X. For Y is a subset of X, X is also cofinal in Y and so X and Y are mutually cofinal. ■

Observe that the Y constructed in the proof above is a special countably infinite chain. We call $(a_n \mid n \in I\!N)$ an ***ω-chain*** if $a_n \leq a_{n+1}$ for all $n \in I\!N$. Of course, not every countably infinite chain is an ω-chain.

Corollary. *Every nonempty countable directed subset of a given poset is mutually cofinal with an ω-chain in A; and hence, every nonempty countable chain in A is mutually cofinal with an ω-chain in A.* ■

In conjunction with Lemma 1 we obtain

Proposition 3. *For any poset A the following conditions are equivalent:*

(1) Every nonempty countable chain in A has a supremum in A.

(2) Every nonempty countable directed subset in A has a supremum in A.

(3) Every ω-chain in A has a supremum in A. ■

This leads to three equivalent definitions of ω-completeness, which we will use freely in the sequel.

Lemma 4. *$(Par(A, B), \subseteq)$ is an ω-complete poset.*

Proof. Evidently, $(Par(A, B), \subseteq)$ is a poset with least element. Let $\mathcal{D}$ be any directed subset of $Par(A, B)$. Since $\bigcup \mathcal{D}$ is a partial mapping from A to B, $\bigcup \mathcal{D}$ is the supremum of $\mathcal{D}$. Hence $Par(A, B)$ is ω-complete. ■

Note that no restriction on the cardinality of $\mathcal{D}$ is needed in the proof above. Usually, a poset is said to be ***Δ-complete*** if each of its directed subsets has a supremum. Thus $(Par(A, B), \subseteq)$ is, in fact, Δ-complete.

An intuitive explanation in Section 1.4.2 motivates the idea that Σ-trees may serve as a basis for symbolic computations. Therefore, ω-completeness has to be examined for the poset of all Σ-trees in order to develop a precise formalism for such computations.

Theorem 5. *Let Σ be a signature and X be a set of variables. The poset $(Tr_\Sigma(X), \sqsubseteq)$ of all Σ-trees over X is ω-complete.*

Proof. Clearly, $(Tr_\Sigma(X), \sqsubseteq)$ is a poset under syntactic order as shown in Lemma 3 in Section 1.4.2. Recall that every Σ-tree T over X is a particular partial mapping from $W(\mathbb{N}_+)$ to $\Sigma \cup X$. Hence, by Lemma 4, each directed subset $\mathcal{D}$ of $Tr_\Sigma(X)$ has a supremum, say $S = \sup \mathcal{D} = \bigcup \mathcal{D}$, which is again a partial mapping from $W(\mathbb{N}_+)$ to $\Sigma \cup X$ such that $Dom(S) = \bigcup\{Dom(T) \mid T \in \mathcal{D}\}$ and, for all w in $Dom(S)$, $S(w) = T(w)$ if $w \in Dom(T)$ for some $T \in \mathcal{D}$.

By definition, $Dom(T)$ is prefix-closed for all T. But, of course, $Dom(S)$ is also prefix-closed as a union of prefix-closed subsets. So, it remains to show that S is compatible as required in Definition 2 of Section 1.4.2. Suppose w is maximal in $Dom(S)$. Then w is maximal in $Dom(T)$ for some $T \in \mathcal{D}$ and hence $T(w) \in \Sigma_0 \cup X$, whence $S(w) \in \Sigma_0 \cup X$. Now consider a word $w \in W(\mathbb{N}_+)$ and $k \in \mathbb{N}_+$ such that $w.k \in Dom(S)$. Since $w.k \in Dom(T)$ for some $T \in \mathcal{D}$, $T(w) \in \Sigma_n$ for some $n \geq k$, and consequently $S(w) \in \Sigma_n$. Thus T is a Σ-tree. ■

Again we remark that $(Tr_\Sigma(X), \sqsubseteq)$ is shown to be Δ-complete.

Example 4. Consider the ω-chain of trees

$$T_0 \sqsubseteq T_1 \sqsubseteq T_2 \sqsubseteq \ldots$$

presented in Example 2 of Section 1.4.2, where $T_0 = \bot$ and $T_n = t[1.1/T_{n-1}]$ for $n \geq 1$ with $t = \tau(\sigma(x), y)$. As a partial mapping T_n is defined by $Dom(T_n) = \{1^{2k} \mid k < n\} \cup \{1^{2k+1} \mid k < n\} \cup \{1^{2k}.2 \mid k < n\}$ and

$$T_n(w) = \begin{cases} \tau & \text{if } w = 1^{2k},\ k < n, \\ \sigma & \text{if } w = 1^{2k+1},\ k < n, \\ y & \text{if } w = 1^{2k}.2,\ k < n, \end{cases}$$

for all $w \in Dom(T_n)$, $n \in \mathbb{N}$. Let T be the supremum of $\{T_n \mid n \in \mathbb{N}\}$. As we know, T is determined by $Dom(T) = \bigcup\{Dom(T_n) \mid n \in \mathbb{N}\}$ and, for all $w \in Dom(T)$, $T(w) =$

$T_n(w)$ if $w \in Dom(T_n)$ for some $n \in I\!N$. Thus $Dom(T) = \{1^k \mid k \in I\!N\} \cup \{1^{2k}.2 \mid k \in I\!N\}$ and

$$T(w) = \begin{cases} \tau & \text{if } w = 1^{2k},\ k \in I\!N, \\ \sigma & \text{if } w = 1^{2k+1},\ k \in I\!N, \\ y & \text{if } w = 1^{2k}.2,\ k \in I\!N, \end{cases}$$

for all $w \in Dom(T)$. Hence T is the tree depicted in Fig. 1.18. ■

1.5.2 Fixpoint Theorem

Consider the recursive procedure for computing factorials:

$$fac(x) \;=\; \textbf{\textit{if}}\ x = 0\ \textbf{\textit{then}}\ 1\ \textbf{\textit{else}}\ x \cdot fac(x-1).$$

It determines a mapping f from $Par(I\!N, I\!N)$ into itself as follows:

$$f(\varphi)(x) = \begin{cases} 1 & \text{if } x = 0, \\ x \cdot \varphi(x-1) & \text{if } x - 1 \in Dom(\varphi) \end{cases}$$

for all partial mappings φ from $I\!N$ into $I\!N$ and all $x \in I\!N$.

Starting with the nowhere defined partial mapping $\varphi_0 = \emptyset$, we get $\varphi_1 = f(\varphi_0) = \{(0,1)\}$ as a first approximation, $\varphi_2 = f(\varphi_1) = \{(0,1),(1,1)\}$ as a second approximation, and $\varphi_n = f(\varphi_{n-1}) = \{(m, m!) \mid m < n\}$ as an n-th approximation, where $0! = 1$ and $m! = 1\cdot 2\cdot\ldots(m-1)\cdot m$ for $m \geq 1$. Obviously the approximations of fac form an ω-chain $\varphi_0 \subseteq \varphi_1 \subseteq \varphi_2 \subseteq \ldots$. Since $Par(I\!N, I\!N)$ is ω-complete the supremum of $(\varphi_n \mid n \in I\!N)$ exists. Put $fac = \sup(\varphi_n \mid n \in I\!N)$. Then $Dom(fac) = \bigcup\{Dom(\varphi_n) \mid n \in I\!N\} = I\!N$ and $fac(x) = x!$ for all $x \in I\!N$.

It is intuitively clear that the computation of factorials stops after ω steps. But what is the general reason for that? Given a mapping f from an ω-complete poset A into itself; we think of f as determined by a recursive procedure like fac. Starting with the last element, f defines a sequence $a_0, a_1, a_2, \ldots$ in A:

$$a_0 = \bot, \text{where } \bot \text{ is the least element of } A\text{; and}$$
$$a_n = f(a_{n-1}) \text{ for } n \geq 1.$$

Let us assume that f is monotone so that $a_0 \leq a_1 \leq a_2 \leq \ldots$ becomes an ω-chain. Computation stops after ω many steps provided the "result" $a = \sup(a_n \mid n \in I\!N)$ is a fixpoint of f. Since $\sup(a_n \mid n \in I\!N) = \sup(f(a_n) \mid n \in I\!N)$, a is a fixpoint of f, i.e., $f(a) = a$, if

$$f(\sup(a_n \mid n \in I\!N)) \;=\; \sup(f(a_n) \mid n \in I\!N).$$

This important compatibility condition should be given a name.

Definition 2. *Let A and B be posets. A mapping f from A to B is called **ω-continuous** if, for every nonempty countable chain X in A that has a supremum, the supremum of $f(X)$ exists and $f(\sup X) = \sup f(X)$.*

Note that we could also use nonempty countable directed subsets or ω-chains in the definition above.

Any ω-continuous mapping $f : A \to B$ is monotone. For if $x \leq y$, then $f(y)$ is the supremum of $\{f(x), f(y)\}$ and so $f(x) \leq f(y)$. If A and B have least elements, we do not require that an ω-continuous mapping $f : A \to B$ preserves them. Let us call any mapping f from A to B ***strict*** if $f(\bot) = \bot$. In case f is a strict ω-continuous mapping, then $f(\sup X) = \sup f(X)$ for every countable chain X (including the empty chain). Two ω-complete posets A and B are called ***isomorphic*** if there is a bijection f from A to B such that f and f^{-1} are strict ω-continuous; f is called an ***isomorphism***.

Example 1. The mapping $f : Par(\mathbb{N}, \mathbb{N}) \to Par(\mathbb{N}, \mathbb{N})$, defined by

$$f(\varphi)(x) = \begin{cases} 1 & \text{if x} = 0, \\ x \cdot \varphi(x-1) & \text{if } x - 1 \in Dom(\varphi) \end{cases}$$

for all $\varphi \in Par(\mathbb{N}, \mathbb{N})$ and all $x \in \mathbb{N}$, is ω-continuous. ∎

An important class of ω-continuous mappings is established in the next lemma.

Lemma 6. *Let T be a Σ-tree over X. Given any address u of T, the mapping $f : Tr_\Sigma(X) \to Tr_\Sigma(X)$ defined by $f(T') = T[u/T']$ for all $T' \in Tr_\Sigma(X)$, is ω-continuous.*

Proof. Evidently, f is monotone. For if $T' \sqsubseteq T''$, then $T[u/T'] \sqsubseteq T[u/T'']$, by the invariance of $\sqsubseteq$ as shown in Proposition 5 in Section 1.4.2, and so $f(T') \sqsubseteq f(T'')$. Consider any ω-chain $T_0 \sqsubseteq T_1 \sqsubseteq T_2 \sqsubseteq \ldots$ in $Tr_\Sigma(X)$. We have to prove that $f(\sup T_n \mid n \in \mathbb{N})$ is the supremum of $f(T_0) \sqsubseteq f(T_1) \sqsubseteq f(T_2) \sqsubseteq \ldots$ or, equivalently,

$$T[u/\sup(T_n \mid n \in \mathbb{N})] = \sup(T[u/T_n] \mid n \in \mathbb{N}).$$

First, the domains of both sides of the equation are equal because $Dom(T[u/\sup(T_n \mid n \in \mathbb{N})]) = \{uv \mid v \in Dom(\sup(T_n \mid n \in \mathbb{N}))\} \cup \{w \in Dom(T) \mid u \not\leq_{pre} w\} = \{uv \mid v \in Dom(T_n) \text{ for some } n \in \mathbb{N}\} \cup \{w \in Dom(T) \mid u \not\leq_{pre} w\} = \bigcup\{Dom(T[u/T_n]) \mid n \in \mathbb{N}\} = Dom(\sup(T[u/T_n] \mid n \in \mathbb{N}))$. Now it remains to verify

$$T[u/\sup(T_n \mid n \in \mathbb{N})](w) = (\sup(T[u/T_n] \mid n \in \mathbb{N}))(w) \qquad (*)$$

for every word w of the common domain of both sides. Suppose u is not a prefix of w. Then, obviously, equation $(*)$ holds. If $w = uv$ for some $v \in Dom(\sup(T_n \mid n \in \mathbb{N}))$, then there is a natural number n such that $w = uv$ for some $v \in Dom(T_n)$. Hence $T[u/\sup(T_n \mid n \in \mathbb{N})](w) = T_n(v) = (\sup(T[u/T_n] \mid n \in \mathbb{N}))(w)$. ∎

Let f be a mapping from a set A into itself. We say that an element x of A is a ***fixpoint*** of f if $f(x) = x$. The set of all fixpoints of f is denoted by $Fix(f)$. In the sequel we will show that any ω-continuous mapping f from an ω-complete poset A into itself has fixpoints, in particular, $Fix(f)$ is a nonempty subposet of A and has a least element, called the ***least fixpoint*** of f and denoted by $fix(f)$. To compute the least fixpoint of f

we start with the least element $\bot$ of A and take $f(\bot)$ as first approximation. Evidently, $\bot \leq f(\bot)$. From this follows $f(\bot) \leq f(f(\bot))$ by the monotonicity of f. Iterating this step we obtain an ω-chain of approximations:

$$\bot \;=\; f^0(\bot) \;\leq\; f^1(\bot) \;\leq\; f^2(\bot) \;\leq\; \ldots\,.$$

Here the common power notation is used: $f^0(x) = x$ and $f^n(x) = f(f^{n-1}(x))$ for $n \geq 1$. (Note that $f^n(\bot) \leq f^{n+1}(\bot)$ for all $n \in \mathbb{N}$ must be proved by induction over n.) The supremum of $(f^n(\bot) \mid n \in \mathbb{N})$ is certainly a fixpoint of f since

$$f(\sup(f^n(\bot) \mid n \in \mathbb{N})) \;=\; \sup(f^n(\bot) \mid n \in \mathbb{N})$$

by the ω-continuity of f. Hence f has fixpoints.

Theorem 7 (Fixpoint Theorem). *Every ω-continuous mapping f from an ω-complete poset A into itself has a least fixpoint; specifically, $fix(f) = \sup(f^n(\bot) \mid n \in \mathbb{N})$ where $\bot$ is the least element of A.*

Proof. By the observation above, $\sup(f^n(\bot) \mid n \in \mathbb{N})$ is a fixpoint of f. Now assume that a is an arbitrary fixpoint of f. Because $\bot \leq a$ we derive $f^n(\bot) \leq a$ for all $n \in \mathbb{N}$, by induction over n. Thus $\sup(f^n(\bot) \mid n \in \mathbb{N}) \leq a$. That is, $\sup(f^n(\bot) \mid n \in \mathbb{N})$ is the least fixpoint of f. ■

For a short review of various variants of the Fixpoint Theorem the interested reader is referred to /Lassez-Nguyen-Sonenberg-82/.

Example 2. Reconsider the term equation $x = t(x, y)$ with $t = \tau(\sigma(x), y)$ of Example 2 in Section 1.4.2. There, a mapping f from $Tr_\Sigma(\{y\})$ into itself was defined by $f(T') = t[1.1/T']$ for all $T' \in Tr_\Sigma(\{y\})$. By Lemma 6, f is ω-continuous.

In order to construct the least fixpoint of f, we have to compute the approximations $f^n(\bot)$ for all $n \in \mathbb{N}$. Evidently, $T_n = f^n(\bot)$, where T_n was already introduced in Example 4 in Section 1.5.1. Furthermore, it was shown that the supremum of $(T_n \mid n \in \mathbb{N})$ is the tree T determined by $Dom(T) = \{1^k \mid k \in \mathbb{N}\} \cup \{1^{2k}.2 \mid k \in \mathbb{N}\}$ and

$$T(w) \;=\; \begin{cases} \tau & \text{if } w = 1^{2k},\; k \in \mathbb{N}, \\ \sigma & \text{if } w = 1^{2k+1},\; k \in \mathbb{N}, \\ y & \text{if } w = 1^{2k}.2,\; k \in \mathbb{N}, \end{cases}$$

for all $w \in Dom(T)$. This is visualized in Fig. 1.18. ■

The special construction of the least fixpoint as the supremum of an ω-chain suggests the following induction principle. Let $\mathcal{P}$ be a property on an ω-complete poset A. We want to show that $\mathcal{P}$ holds for the least fixpoint of an ω-continuous mapping $f : A \to A$. It is enough to prove that, first, $\mathcal{P}$ holds for the least element $\bot$ of A; and, second, $\mathcal{P}$ holds for $f^{n+1}(\bot)$ whenever $\mathcal{P}$ holds for $f^n(\bot)$. The induction from the chain $(f^n(\bot) \mid n \in \mathbb{N})$ to its supremum requires, however, that $\mathcal{P}$ fulfills the following condition: If $\mathcal{P}$ holds for each element of an ω-chain $(a_n \mid n \in \mathbb{N})$, then $\mathcal{P}$ holds for $\sup(a_n \mid n \in \mathbb{N})$. Such a property is said to be ***admissible***.

Theorem 8 (Principle of Fixpoint Induction). *Let f be an ω-continuous mapping from an ω-complete poset A into itself. To prove that an admissible property $\mathcal{P}$ on A holds for the least fixpoint of f it suffices to show the validity of (1) and (2) below:*

(1) Induction basis. $\mathcal{P}$ holds for the least element.

(2) Induction step. If $\mathcal{P}$ holds for any element a of A (induction hypothesis), then $\mathcal{P}$ holds for $f(a)$.

Proof. By induction over n, we can derive from (1) and (2) that $\mathcal{P}$ holds for all elements of the ω-chain $(f^n(\bot) \mid n \in \mathbb{N})$. Since $\mathcal{P}$ is assumed to be admissible, $\mathcal{P}$ holds for $\sup(f^n(\bot) \mid n \in \mathbb{N})$ and so, by the Fixpoint Theorem, $\mathcal{P}$ holds for the least fixpoint of f. ■

It should be mentioned that in place of (2) a weaker condition would suffice, namely: If $\mathcal{P}$ holds for $f^n(\bot)$, then $\mathcal{P}$ holds for $f^{n+1}(\bot)$, for all $n \in \mathbb{N}$.

Remark. An interesting logic, called Logic for Computable Functions (abbreviated LCF), is based on ω-complete posets and ω-continuous mappings, where the Principle of Fixpoint Induction appears as an inference rule. LCF is used in program verification. For an overview of the subject the interested reader is referred to /Loeckx-Sieber-84/; a complete treatment is found in /Milner-79/. ■

Proposition 9 (Park's Theorem). *Let f be an ω-continuous mapping from an ω-complete poset A into itself. If a is an element of A such that $f(a) \leq a$, then $fix(f) \leq a$.*

Proof. Let A be an ω-complete poset. To any element a of A a property $\mathcal{P}_a$ on A is assigned as follows: $\mathcal{P}_a(x)$ iff $x \leq a$. Obviously, $\mathcal{P}_a$ is admissible. Assume that $f : A \to A$ is ω-continuous such that $f(a) \leq a$. Then $\mathcal{P}_a$ holds for $f(x)$ whenever $\mathcal{P}_a$ holds for x. Of course, $\mathcal{P}_a$ holds for the least element. Hence, by the Principle of Fixpoint Induction, $\mathcal{P}_a$ holds for the least fixpoint of f. That is, $fix(f) \leq a$. ■

We close the section with another view of the Fixpoint Theorem. Let A be an ω-complete poset. To each ω-continuous mapping $f : A \to A$ an element of A, the least fixpoint $fix(f)$, is associated. Denote by $[A \to B]$ the set of all ω-continuous mappings $f : A \to B$. The correspondence $f \mapsto fix(f)$ defines a mapping from $[A \to A]$ to A, denoted by fix; fix is called ***fixpoint operator***. Note that $[A \to B]$ is a poset with respect to pointwise order: $f \leq g$ iff $f(x) \leq g(x)$ for all $x \in A$.

Lemma 10. *If A and B are ω-complete posets, then so is $[A \to B]$.*

Proof. Let X be a countable chain in $[A \to B]$. It is easily seen that $(\sup X)(a) = \sup(f(a) \mid f \in X)$ for each a of A. We have to show that $\sup X$ is an ω-continuous mapping from A into itself. Therefore, assume $(a_n \mid n \in \mathbb{N})$ is a countable chain in A. Then

$$\begin{aligned}(\sup X)(\sup(a_n \mid n \in \mathbb{N})) &= \sup(f(\sup(a_n \mid n \in \mathbb{N})) \mid f \in X) \\ &= \sup(\sup(f(a_n) \mid n \in \mathbb{N}) \mid f \in X) \\ &= \sup(\sup(X)(a_n) \mid n \in \mathbb{N}).\end{aligned}$$

The second step is valid because each f of X is ω-continuous. Thus $\sup X$ belongs to $[A \to B]$ and $\sup X$ is, indeed, the supremum of X. ∎

Our aim is to show the ω-continuity of the fixpoint operator $fix : [A \to A] \to A$. For that reason mappings $fix_n : [A \to A] \to A$ are introduced by $fix_n(f) = f^n(\bot)$ for all $n \in \mathbb{N}$. Now, by the Fixpoint Theorem,

$$fix(f) = \sup(fix_n(f) \mid n \in \mathbb{N}).$$

Lemma 11. *For each f of $[A \to A]$,*

$$\sup(fix_n(f) \mid n \in \mathbb{N}) = (\sup(fix_n \mid n \in \mathbb{N}))(f).$$ ∎

The proof is omitted and left to the reader as an exercise. Hence fix is the supremum of $(fix_n \mid n \in \mathbb{N})$. With this prerequisite we readily achieve our goal.

Proposition 12. *The fixpoint operator is ω-continuous.*

Proof. Combining Lemmas 10 and 11, we see that the fixpoint operator fix is ω-continuous if all derived mappings $fix_n, n \in \mathbb{N}$, are so. But this is easily proved using the Principle of Finite Induction. ∎

1.5.3. Free ω-Completion

First, we study the embedding of a given poset into a complete lattice, for which some preparations are needed. A downward closed subset C of a poset A is called a ***cone***. That is, C is a cone of A iff, for all x and y in A, $x \in C$ whenever $x \leq y$ and $y \in C$. $\mathcal{C}$(A) denotes the set of all cones in A. Evidently, $\mathcal{C}(A)$ is a closure system with its associated closure operator cl determined by $cl(X) = (X]$, where $(X] = \{a \in A \mid a \leq x$ for some x of $X\}$ for each subset X of A (see Section 1.3.3); $(X]$ is the cone generated by X. A cone is said to be ***principal*** if it can be generated by a single element. Keep in mind that $(X] \subseteq (Y]$ iff X is cofinal in Y. In particular, $(x] = (y]$ iff $x \leq y$.

As a closure system $\mathcal{C}(A)$ is a complete lattice (with respect to subset inclusion) in which A is embeddable by the full monotone mapping $m : A \to \mathcal{C}(A)$ assigning the principal cone $(x]$ to each x of A. In other words, A can be identified with the subposet of all principal cones in $\mathcal{C}(A)$.

Example 1. Consider the poset of all natural numbers. There are only two nonprincipal cones in $\mathcal{C}(\mathbb{N})$, namely $(\emptyset]$ and $(\mathbb{N}]$. If we identify each principal cone $(n]$ with n, $\mathcal{C}(\mathbb{N})$ becomes the ω-chain

$$\bot < 0 < 1 < \ldots < \omega,$$

where $\bot = (\emptyset]$ is the least element and $\omega = (\mathbb{N}]$ is the greatest element in $\mathcal{C}(\mathbb{N})$. Note that the least element of $\mathbb{N}$ is not preserved by the embedding. Hence m is not strict.■

In $\mathcal{C}(A)$, all existing suprema in A are generally destroyed, not only the least element as supremum of the empty chain. Suppose X is a subset of A whose supremum $\sup_A X$ exists in A. Since $x \leq \sup_A X$ for all x in X, X is cofinal in $\{\sup_A X\}$, hence $(X] \subseteq (\sup_A X]$. If $\sup_A X$ does not belong to X, $(X]$ is even properly included in $(\sup_A X]$. In $\mathcal{C}(A)$, $(X]$ is the supemum of $\{(x] \mid x \in X\}$. After identifying each principal cone $(x]$ with $x \in X$, we get a new supremum of X in $\mathcal{C}(A)$ that is different from $\sup_A X$; that is, $\sup_A X \neq \sup_{\mathcal{C}(A)} X$ provided $\sup_A X$ exists and $\sup_A X$ is not in X. If $\sup_A X$ belongs to X, then $\sup_A X = \sup_{\mathcal{C}(A)} X$.

Consider now a ***strict poset***, that is a poset A with a least element $\bot$. Its embedding $m : A \to \mathcal{C}(A)$ is not strict as long as $(\emptyset]$ is not excluded from $\mathcal{C}(A)$. Let $\mathcal{C}'(A)$ denote the set of all cones in A which are generated by nonempty sets, i.e., $\mathcal{C}'(A) = \{(X] \mid X \text{ is a nonempty subset of } A\}$. It is easy to see that $\mathcal{C}'(A)$ is also a closure system if A is a strict poset. In this case $m : A \to \mathcal{C}'(A)$ is a strict full monotone mapping from A into the complete lattice $\mathcal{C}'(A)$.

Next, we want to select the smallest ω-complete subposet of $\mathcal{C}'(A)$ containing all principal cones in A. By Proposition 3 in Section 1.5.1, only countable directed subsets of $\mathcal{C}'(A)$ must have suprema.

Definition 3. *Let A be a poset. A nonempty cone C in A is called an **ideal** if C is directed.*

Let $\mathcal{I}(A)$ denote the set of all ideals in A. Since the union over a directed set of directed subsets of A is also a directed subset of A, any directed set D of ideals has a supremum, namely $\sup D = \bigcup D$. Hence $(\mathcal{I}(A), \subseteq)$ is an ω-complete poset, but still too "large" for an ω-completion of A. The key to our construction is the following property of ideals.

Lemma 13. *A subset I of a given poset A is an ideal iff $I = (X]$ for some nonempty directed subset X of A.* ■

The simple proof is omitted.

We are now in a position to restrict $\mathcal{I}(A)$ in an appropriate way to get the desired ω-complete poset. Let $\mathcal{D}_\omega(A)$ denote the set of all nonempty countable directed subsets of A, and set $A_\omega = \{(X] \mid X \in \mathcal{D}_\omega(A)\}$.

Lemma 14. *If A is a strict poset, then A_ω is an ω-complete poset with respect to subset inclusion.*

Proof. Let A be a strict poset. It is obvious that A_ω is a strict poset, too. To prove ω-completeness take any nonempty countable directed subset D of A_ω. Since $\bigcup D$ is in $\mathcal{D}_\omega(A)$, $(\bigcup D]$ belongs to A_ω. However, $\bigcup D$ is already a cone. That is, $(\bigcup D] = \bigcup D$ and consequently, $\bigcup D$ is the supremum of D in A_ω. ∎

Our aim is to complete a given strict poset in a universal way as required in the following definition.

Definition 4. *Let A be a strict poset. An ω-complete poset $\overline{A}$ is called a* ***free ω-completion*** *of A if there is a strict full monotone mapping $m : A \to \overline{A}$ such that the universal property (C) below holds:*

> *(C) Every strict monotone mapping f from A to any ω-complete poset B admits a unique (strict) ω-continuous extension $f_\omega : \overline{A} \to B$ with $f = m \cdot f_\omega$.*

It is easy to see that any two free ω-completions of a strict poset A are isomorphic. Therefore, we speak of the free ω-completion of A denoted by $\mathbf{C}_\omega(A)$.

Theorem 15. *Any strict poset has a free ω-completion.*

Proof. Let A be a strict poset. We assert that A_ω is the free ω-completion of A. The embedding $m : A \to A_\omega$, defined by $m(x) = (x]$ for all x in A, is clearly a strict full monotone mapping. Let f be an arbitrary strict monotone mapping from A to any ω-complete poset B. Define the extension $f_\omega : A_\omega \to B$ as follows:

$$f_\omega(I) \;=\; \sup f(X)$$

for each I of A_ω such that $I = (X]$ for some $X \in \mathcal{D}_\omega(A)$. First, f_ω is well-defined. For if $(X] = (Y]$, then X and Y are mutually cofinal and so are $f(X)$ and $f(Y)$; hence $\sup f(X) = \sup f(Y)$ by Lemma 1 in Section 1.5.1. Second, f_ω extends f because $f_\omega(m(x)) = f_\omega((x]) = \sup\{f(x)\} = f(x)$ for all x in A. Since f and m are strict, so is f_ω.

Claim: f_ω is ω-continuous.

It is easy to see that f_ω is monotone. Let D be a nonempty countable directed subset of A_ω. Then $\sup f_\omega(D) \leq f_\omega(\sup D)$ by the monotonicity of f_ω. That is, $f_\omega(\sup D)$ is an upper bound of $f_\omega(D)$. If b is another upper bound of $f_\omega(D)$, then $f_\omega(\bigcup D) \leq b$. Recall that $\bigcup D = \sup D$. Thus $f_\omega(\sup D)$ is, in fact, the least upper bound of f_ω, i.e., $\sup f_\omega(D) = f_\omega(\sup D)$. Hence f_ω is ω- continuous.

Claim: f_ω is unique.

Suppose g and h are strict ω-continuous mappings from A to B such that $m \cdot g = f = m \cdot h$. We have to show $g = h$. Let I be any element of A_ω. By definition, $I = (X]$ for some $X \in \mathcal{D}_\omega(A)$. The crucial point in showing the equality of g and h is the fact that $I = \sup\{(x] \mid x \in X\} = \bigcup\{(x] \mid x \in X\}$. Now we proceed as follows:

$$\begin{aligned} g(I) &= g(\sup\{(x] \mid x \in X\}) \\ &= \sup\{g((x]) \mid x \in X\} \text{ since } g \text{ is } \omega\text{-continuous} \\ &= \sup\{h((x]) \mid x \in X\} \text{ since } g((x]) = h((x]) \\ &= h(\sup\{(x] \mid x \in X\}) \text{ since } h \text{ is } \omega\text{-continuous} \\ &= h(I). \end{aligned}$$

Thus $g = h$, which proves the claim. ■

Example 2. Let $\mathcal{N}$ be the ω-chain of natural numbers equipped with a greatest element, say $\top$. That is, $\mathcal{N} = I\!N \cup \{\top\}$ with $n \leq n+1$ and $n \leq \top$ for all n in $I\!N$. The free ω-completion $\mathbf{C}_\omega(\mathcal{N})$ of $\mathcal{N}$ is the following ω-chain:

$$0 < 1 < \ldots < \omega < \top.$$

In $\mathcal{N}$, $\top$ is the supremum of $I\!N$ but $\top$ is not preserved in $\mathbf{C}_\omega(\mathcal{N})$; there is a new supremum of $I\!N$, namely ω.

Of course, $\mathcal{N}$ is embedded into $\mathbf{C}_\omega(\mathcal{N})$ by inclusion. Now consider an ω-complete poset B. If $f : \mathcal{N} \to B$ is a strict monotone mapping, its extension $f_\omega : \mathbf{C}_\omega(\mathcal{N}) \to B$ is determined as follows: $f_\omega(x) = f(x)$ for all x in $\mathcal{N}$ and $f_\omega(\omega) = \sup_B f(I\!N)$. Clearly, f_ω is a strict ω-continuous mapping which is unique. ■

By analogy with the completion by cones the free ω-completion of a strict poset A destroys all existing suprema of nonempty countable chains in A. In particular, if $\sup_A X$ exists for any nonempty countable chain X in A, then $\sup_{\mathbf{C}_\omega(A)} X < \sup_A X$.

There is, however, a possibility to remedy this fact by constructing another kind of ω-completion. Given a strict poset A, an ω-complete poset $\overline{A}$ is called a ***conservative ω-completion*** of A if there is a strict ω-continuous mapping $m : A \to \overline{A}$ such that every strict ω-continuous mapping f from A to any ω-complete poset B admits a unique strict ω-continuous extension $\overline{f}$ from $\overline{A}$ to B with $f = m \cdot \overline{f}$. A conservative ω-completion of A is obtainable if we choose a suitable subposet of A_ω. We call an ideal I of A closed under suprema of countable chains if, for each countable chain X in I whose supremum $\sup_A X$ exists in A, $\sup_A X$ belongs to I. Take the subset A'_ω of A_ω consisting of all ideals closed under suprema of countable chains. Then it can be shown that A'_ω is the conservative ω-completion of A. In a more general setting such completions are investigated in /Markowsky-76/, /Banaschewski-Nelson-82/.

In what follows we shall explain how every element of a free ω- completion is "finitely approximated" in a certain sense. Let A be an ω-complete poset. An element a of A is said to be ***ω-compact*** if, for each ω-chain $(x_n \mid n \in I\!N)$ in A, $a \leq \sup(x_n \mid n \in I\!N)$ implies $a \leq x_k$ for some k in $I\!N$. Observe that the least element of a strict poset is always ω-compact. Here we prefer to use ω-chains. It is easily shown that a is ω-compact iff, for all (nonempty) countable chains or directed subsets X in A, $a \leq \sup X$ implies $a \leq x$ for some $x \in X$.

Proposition 16. *A Σ-tree is ω-compact if and only if it is finite.*

Proof. First, we indirectly assume that a given Σ-tree T over X is ω-compact but not finite. Take the ω-chain $(T_n \mid n \in \mathbb{N})$ of finite "cuts" T_n of T defined as follows: $Dom(T_n) = \{w \in Dom(T) \mid |w| \leq n\}$ and $T_n(w) = T(w)$ for all $w \in Dom(T_n), n \in \mathbb{N}$. Then $T = \sup(T_n \mid n \in \mathbb{N})$. If T were infinite, there would be no natural number k such that $T \sqsubseteq T_k$, i.e., T would not be ω-compact.

Second, suppose T is finite. Consider any ω-chain $(T_n \mid n \in \mathbb{N})$ in $Tr_\Sigma(X)$. If $T \sqsubseteq \sup(T_n \mid n \in \mathbb{N})$, then $Dom(T) \subseteq \bigcup(Dom(T_n) \mid n \in \mathbb{N})$ and for all $w \in Dom(T)$, $T(w) = T_n(w)$ if $w \in Dom(T_n)$. Since $Dom(T)$ is finite and all $Dom(T_n)$, $n \in \mathbb{N}$, form an ω-chain, $Dom(T_0) \subseteq Dom(T_1) \subseteq \ldots$; by assumption, $Dom(T)$ is a subset of $Dom(T_k)$ for some $k \in \mathbb{N}$; hence $T \sqsubseteq T_k$ because $T(w) = T_k(w)$ for all $w \in Dom(T)$. That is, T is ω-compact. ■

This result is in accordance with our experience of approximation. We suggest therefore the following notion. Let A be an ω-complete poset. Given an element a of A, any compact element x of A with $x \leq a$ is called a ***finite approximation*** of a. We put

$$Fin(a) \;=\; \{x \in A \mid x \leq a \text{ and } x \text{ is } \omega\text{-compact}\}.$$

This notion is extended to subsets: $Fin(X) = \bigcup\{Fin(x) \mid x \in X\}$ for each subset X of A. Then $Fin(A)$ is the set of all compact elements of A.

Example 3. Consider the set $Par(\mathbb{N}, \mathbb{N})$ of all partial mappings from $\mathbb{N}$ into itself. We know that $(Par(\mathbb{N}, \mathbb{N}), \subseteq)$ is an ω-complete poset with respect to subset inclusion. It is easily seen that a partial mapping is ω-compact iff its domain is finite. Now take the factorial function fac defined by $fac(x) = x!$ for all $x \in \mathbb{N}$. Then

$$Fin(fac) \;=\; \{g \mid Dom(g) \text{ is finite and } g(x) = x! \text{ for all } x \in Dom(g)\}.$$

Evidently, $Fin(fac)$ is directed. Since $(Par(\mathbb{N}, \mathbb{N}), \subseteq)$ is even Δ-complete, $Fin(fac)$ has a supremum. Of course,

$$fac \;=\; \sup Fin(fac).$$

So, the factorial function is finitely approximated in some sense. ■

In our opinion such approximations are only meaningful when we are able to select an ω-chain of finite approximations such that its supremum yields the result desired.

Definition 5. *An ω-complete poset A is called **ω-inductive** if, for each element a of A, there is an ω-chain $(a_n \mid n \in \mathbb{N})$ of ω-compact elements with $a = \sup(a_n \mid n \in \mathbb{N})$.*

Again we could use (nonempty) countable chains or directed subsets instead of ω-chains in the previous definition.

Example 4. The poset $(Tr_\Sigma(X), \sqsubseteq)$ of all Σ-trees over X is ω-inductive. For every $T \in Tr_\Sigma(X)$ we have

$$T = \sup(T_n \mid n \in I\!N)$$

with T_n the finite cuts of T as defined above. Obviously, $(T_n \mid n \in I\!N)$ is an ω-chain of finite Σ-trees over X. By Proposition 16, all T_n are ω-compact. ∎

Lemma 17. *Every element of an ω-inductive poset is the supremum of all its finite approximations.*

Proof. Let A be an ω-inductive poset. Given an element a of A, there is an ω-chain $(a_n \mid n \in I\!N)$ with $a_n \in Fin(a)$ such that $a = \sup(a_n \mid n \in I\!N)$. By Lemma 1 in Section 1.5.1, it is enough to show that $Fin(a)$ is mutually cofinal to $(a_n \mid n \in I\!N)$. But this is simply done. ∎

In order to prove the main property of ω-inductive posets, we need the following lemma, which states that the converse of Lemma 1 in Section 1.5.1 holds under an additional assumption.

Lemma 18. *Let X and Y be countable chains of a given ω-complete poset. If X consists of ω-compact elements only, then X is cofinal in Y whenever $\sup X \leq \sup Y$.*

Proof. Let A be an ω-complete poset. If X and Y are countable chains such that $\sup X \leq \sup Y$, then $x \leq \sup Y$ for all $x \in X$. Since each x of X is supposed to be ω-compact, $x \leq y$ for some $y \in Y$. So, for all x in A, there is an element y in Y with $x \leq y$. That is, by definition, X is cofinal in Y. ∎

In an ω-inductive poset A, ω-compact elements form a "basis" in the sense that any ω-continuous mapping from A to another ω-complete poset is already uniquely specified on the ω-compact elements of A.

Theorem 19. *Let A be an ω-inductive poset and B be an ω-complete poset. Every (strict) monotone mapping f from the set $Fin(A)$ of all ω-compact elements of A to B admits a unique extension to a (strict) ω-continuous mapping f^c from A to B such that $f^c(x) = f(x)$ for all $x \in Fin(A)$.*

Proof. Define a mapping $f^c : A \to B$ by

$$f^c(a) = \sup f(Fin(a))$$

for all $a \in A$. We have to guarantee that the supremum of $f(Fin(a))$ exists. By the defintion of ω-inductivity, for each element a of A, there is an ω-chain $X = (a_n \mid n \in I\!N)$ such that $a = \sup X$ and $X \subseteq Fin(a)$. On the other hand, we have $a = \sup Fin(a)$, by Lemma 17. Hence $\sup X = \sup Fin(a)$. Using Lemma 18, we derive that

$Fin(a)$ is mutually cofinal to X. From this follows that $f(Fin(a))$ and $f(X)$ are also mutually cofinal because f is assumed to be monotone. By Lemma 1 in Section 1.5.1, the supremum of $f(Fin(a))$ exists.

Claim: f^c is ω-continuous.

Let X be a nonempty countable chain in A. The monotonicity of f^c yields $\sup f^c(X) \leq f^c(\sup X)$. Now, it remains to show the converse relation. Since $Fin(\sup X) = Fin(X)$, we get $f^c(\sup X) = \sup f(Fin(X))$. Observe that X is cofinal in $Fin(X)$. Hence $f(Fin(X))$ is cofinal in $f(X)$ because f is monotone. From this follows $\sup f(Fin(X)) \leq \sup f(X)$. Thus $f^c(\sup X) \leq \sup f(X)$. Since $f(X)$ is cofinal in $f^c(X)$, we have $\sup f(X) \leq \sup f^c(X)$. Hence $f^c(\sup X) \leq \sup f(X)$.

Claim: $f^c(x) = f(x)$ for all $x \in Fin(A)$.

Let x be an arbitrary ω-compact element of A. Then, by definition, $x \in Fin(x)$. It follows easily that $f(x)$ is the least upper bound of $f(Fin(x))$, i.e., $f(x) = \sup f(Fin(x))$. Hence $f^c(x) = f(x)$ for all $x \in Fin(A)$.

Claim: f^c is the unique extension of f.

Suppose $g : A \to B$ is ω-continuous with $g(x) = f(x)$ for all $x \in Fin(A)$. We have to show that $g = f^c$. Let a be any element of A. Then we conclude as follows:

$$\begin{aligned} f^c(a) &= \sup f(Fin(a)) \text{ by definition} \\ &= \sup g(Fin(a)) \text{ since } g(x) = f(x) \text{ for each } x \in Fin(A) \\ &= g(\sup Fin(a)) \text{ since } g \text{ is } \omega\text{-continuous} \\ &= g(a). \end{aligned}$$

The last equation holds by Lemma 17. ∎

We close the section with a characterization of ω-inductive posets as free ω-completions.

Proposition 20. *Any free ω-completion is an ω-inductive poset.*

Proof. Let A be a strict poset. First, we determine the ω-compact elements of its free ω-completion A_ω. Let I be any element of A_ω. By definition, $I = (X]$ for some $X \in \mathcal{D}_\omega(A)$. Suppose I is ω-compact. Because $I = \bigcup\{(x] \mid x \in X\} = \sup\{(x] \mid x \in X\}$ we obtain $I = \sup((x_n] \mid n \in \mathbb{N})$ by choosing an ω-chain $((x_n] \mid n \in \mathbb{N})$ of principal ideals mutually cofinal with the nonempty countable directed set $\{(x] \mid x \in X\}$. Hence $I \subseteq (x_k]$ for some k in $\mathbb{N}$ by the ω-compactness of I. That is, I is principal. Conversely, every principal ideal is an ω-compact element of A_ω.

Since any ideal $I \in A_\omega$ is the supremum of an ω-chain $((x_n] \mid n \in \mathbb{N})$, whose elements are ω-compact as we have shown, A_ω is ω-inductive. ∎

Corollary. *The ω-compact elements of the free ω-completion $\mathbf{C}_\omega(A)$ of a given strict poset A are exactly the images of elements from A under the embedding $m : A \to \mathbf{C}_\omega(A)$. Specifically, $m(A)$ is the set of ω-compact elements of $\mathbf{C}_\omega(A)$. That is, $Fin\ (\mathbf{C}_\omega(A)) = m(A)$.* ■

The converse statement of Proposition 20 holds up to isomorphism.

Proposition 21. *Every ω-inductive poset is isomorphic to the free ω-completion of its ω-compact elements.*

Proof. Let A be an ω-inductive poset. The set of all its ω-compact elements, $Fin(A)$, is a strict subposet. We assert that the free ω-completion $\mathbf{C}_\omega(Fin(A))$ of $Fin(A)$ is isomorphic to A as ω-complete posets. Therefore, we have to establish a bijection f from A to $\mathbf{C}_\omega(Fin(A))$ such that f and f^{-1} are strict ω-continuous. Define f as follows:

$$f(x) \;=\; Fin(x) \text{ for all } x \text{ in } A.$$

Claim: f is a bijection.

First, f is injective. For if $f(x) = f(y)$, then $Fin(x) = Fin(y)$ and so $\sup Fin(x) = \sup Fin(y)$; hence $x = y$ by Lemma 18. Second, f is surjective. Take an arbitrary element of $\mathbf{C}_\omega(Fin(A))$, say I. Without loss of generality we may assume that $\mathbf{C}_\omega(Fin(A))$ consists of all $(X]$ with $X \in \mathcal{D}_\omega(Fin(A))$. Since the supremum of X exists in A we obtain $Fin(\sup X) = (X]$. Actually, f is surjective since $I = f(\sup X)$ for some X in $\mathcal{D}_\omega(Fin(A))$ such that $I = (X]$.

Claim: f is strict ω-continuous.

If X is a countable chain in A, then $f(\sup X) = Fin(\sup X) = \bigcup\{Fin(x) \mid x \in X\} = \sup f(X)$. In particular, $f(\bot) = Fin(\bot) = (\bot]$.

Claim: f^{-1} is strict ω-continuous.

The inverse mapping f^{-1} is determined by $f^{-1}(I) = \sup X$ for all I in $\mathbf{C}_\omega(Fin(A))$ with $I = (X]$. Evidently, f^{-1} is strict since $f^{-1}((\bot]) = \sup\{\bot\} = \bot$.

Let $((X_n] \mid n \in \mathbb{N})$ be an ω-chain in $\mathbf{C}_\omega(Fin(A))$. Recall that $\sup((X_n] \mid n \in \mathbb{N}) = \bigcup((X_n] \mid n \in \mathbb{N})$. Set $X = \bigcup(X_n \mid n \in \mathbb{N})$ and $a_n = \sup X_n$ for all $n \in \mathbb{N}$. We have $f^{-1}(\sup((X_n] \mid n \in \mathbb{N})) = \sup X$. On the other hand, $f^{-1}((X_n] \mid n \in \mathbb{N}) = (a_n \mid n \in \mathbb{N})$. So, it remains to show $\sup(a_n \mid n \in \mathbb{N}) = \sup X$. Obviously, $\sup X$ is an upper bound of $(a_n \mid n \in \mathbb{N})$. If b is another upper bound of $(a_n \mid n \in \mathbb{N})$, then $x \leq b$ for all $x \in X$. That is, $\sup X \leq b$; hence $\sup X$ is the supremum of $(a_n \mid n \in \mathbb{N})$ and consequently, $f^{-1}(\sup((X_n] \mid n \in \mathbb{N})) = \sup f^{-1}((X_n] \mid n \in \mathbb{N})$, which proves the claim. ■

As an immediate consequence we get the following result.

Theorem 22. *The ω-complete poset of all Σ-trees over X is isomorphic to the free ω-completion of the strict poset of all finite Σ-trees over X.*

Proof. Let Σ be a signature and let X be a set of variables. The set $Tr_\Sigma(X)$ of all Σ-trees over X forms an ω-complete poset with respect to the syntactic order $\sqsubseteq$ as shown in Theorem 5 in Section 1.5.1. By Proposition 16, a Σ-tree T of $Tr_\Sigma(X)$ is ω-compact iff T is finite. That is, $Fin(Tr_\Sigma(X)) = FTr_\Sigma(X)$. Note that $(FTr_\Sigma(X), \sqsubseteq)$ is a strict poset. Since $(Tr_\Sigma(X), \sqsubseteq)$ is an ω-inductive poset (cf. Example 4), $(Tr_\Sigma(X), \sqsubseteq)$ is isomorphic to the free ω-completion of $(FTr_\Sigma(X), \sqsubseteq)$, by Proposition 21. ■

Dealing with infinite trees we are always able to approximate them by finite trees in the following sense. For any tree $T \in Tr_\Sigma(X)$, there exists an ω-chain $(T_n \mid n \in \mathbb{N})$ of finite trees $T_n \in FTr_\Sigma(X)$ such that

$$T = \sup(T_n \mid n \in \mathbb{N}).$$

As we know (cf. Example 4), each T_n is a finite cut of T.

Let us consider the set of all finite approximations of T, $Fin(T) = \{t \in FTr_\Sigma(X) \mid t \sqsubseteq T\}$. It is easily seen that $Fin(T)$ is directed. Hence the supremum of $Fin(T)$ exists. By definition, $\sup Fin(T) \sqsubseteq T$. Since the ω-chain $(T_n \mid n \in \mathbb{N})$ of finite cuts of T is a subset of $Fin(T)$, we get $\sup(T_n \mid n \in \mathbb{N}) \sqsubseteq \sup Fin(T)$. Thus, $T \sqsubseteq \sup Fin(T)$ and consequently

$$T = \sup Fin(T)$$

as another version of an approximation of a given tree.

2 Reductions

Reduction systems are widely used in theoretical computer science. Symbolic manipulations on syntactic objects are based upon their providing models for computation in an operational setting.

In Section 2.1, the word problem is explained and its possible solution by the confluence method is studied. Section 2.2 deals with reduction systems.

2.1 Word Problem

Quotient structures, which appear very often in our applications, are considered here too but now from a constructive point of view. Given an arbitrary set A and an equivalence relation $\sim$ on A, the quotient $A/\sim$ consists of all equivalence classes. Each class is represented by an element of A which is, of course, not determined uniquely; nevertheless, operating with equivalence classes is always done through representatives. Consequently, for an effective computation in $A/\sim$ we must be able to check the equivalence:

Is it decidable for any two elements a and b of A whether $a \sim b$ holds true or not ?

This is the well-known ***word problem*** for the equivalence $\sim$.

In Section 2.1.1, the word problem is solved for a simple example using the confluence method. Section 2.1.2 is devoted to the word problem for congruences.

2.1.1 Confluence Method

The word problem is said to be ***solvable*** (or ***decidable***) if there is an algorithm for deciding whether two given elements are equivalent or not. Only in cases where the word problem is solvable can computations be carried out using representatives. This accentuates the fundamental significance of the word problem. In general, the word problem is unsolvable /Davis-58/. Analysing a simple example of a solvable word problem, we shall elaborate a useful solution method.

Considering the data type stack, we shall study the word problem of semantical equality. A ***stack*** is a list in which elements of a finite nonempty set V (vocabulary) can be written and erased by means of the operations *push* and *pop*: *push* writes an element of V at the first empty place counted from left to right and *pop* erases the leftmost element. In order to indicate which element of V is written by *push* we use the elements of V as subscripts: $push_x$ means the operation of writing the element x of V. Besides this family of unary operations we also have a nullary operation *nil* representing the empty list.

If we define a signature Σ as follows: $\Sigma_0 = \{nil\}$, $\Sigma_1 = \{pop\} \cup \{push_x \mid x \in V\}$ and $\Sigma_n = \emptyset$ for $n \geq 2$, then each ground term of T_Σ represents the contents of a stack. For instance, $push_a\ pop\ push_b\ push_b\ nil$ represents the stack containing *ab*. But the same stack is also represented by $push_a push_b nil$. That is, both ground terms are semantically equal.

Applying *pop* after having applied $push_x$ for some x of V is equivalent to doing nothing. Moreover, if we apply *pop* on the empty list, then the result is *nil*. This leads to the following reduction relation $\rightarrow$ on T_Σ defined so that, for all ground terms t and $t', t \rightarrow t'$ iff

(1) $t = w\ pop\ nil$ and $t' = w\ nil$ for some word w over Σ_1; or

(2) $t = w\ pop\ push_x\ w'\ nil$ and $t' = w\ w'\ nil$ for some words w and w' over Σ_1 and some x of V.

Two ground terms are said to be ***semantically equal*** if they are equivalent modulo the equivalence generated by $\rightarrow$. Note that $t \leftrightarrow^* t'$ iff t and t' represent the same stack.

The word problem for this equivalence is hence the problem of finding an algorithm to decide whether two ground terms represent the same stack. How can we solve this problem?

First, assume that two given ground terms t and t' are semantically equal, i.e., $t \leftrightarrow^* t'$. According to the generation principle for equivalences (Theorem 6 in Section 1.3.2) there is a sequence $t_0, t_1, ..., t_m$ of ground terms such that $t = t_0$, $t_m = t'$ and $t_{i-1} \rightarrow t_i$ or $t_i \rightarrow t_{i-1}$ for $i = 1, ..., m$, which is illustrated (for $m = 5$) in Fig. 2.1.

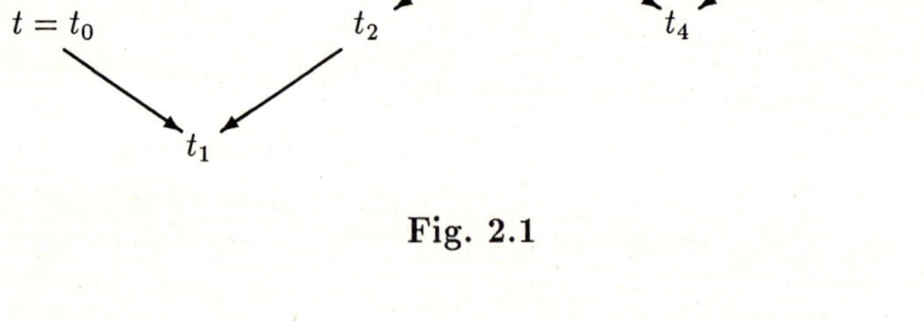

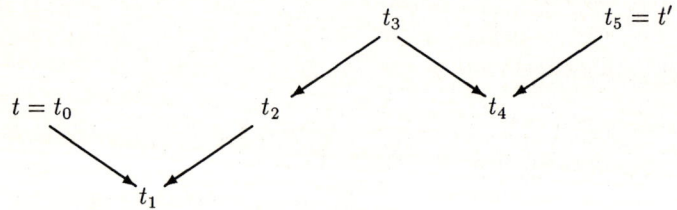

Fig. 2.1

Now, consider the ground terms t_1 and t_4, which are both reducible from t_3 (see Fig. 2.2.)

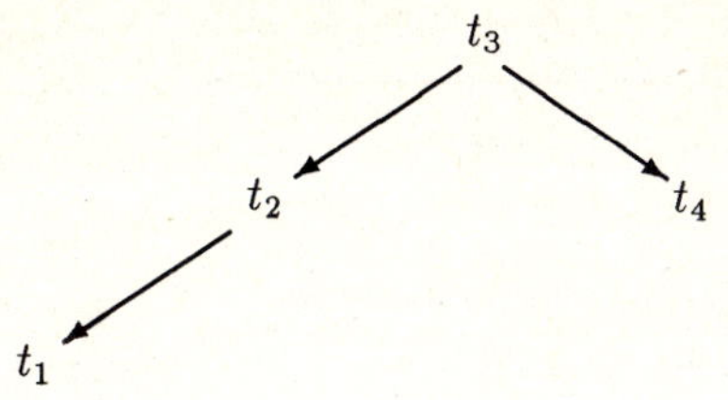

Fig. 2.2

Next, assume that t_1 and t_4 can be reduced to a common ground term (Fig. 2.3). When such a ground term, say $\bar{t}$, exists with $t_1 \rightarrow^* \bar{t}$ and $t_4 \rightarrow^* \bar{t}$, t_1 and t_4 are said to be convergent.

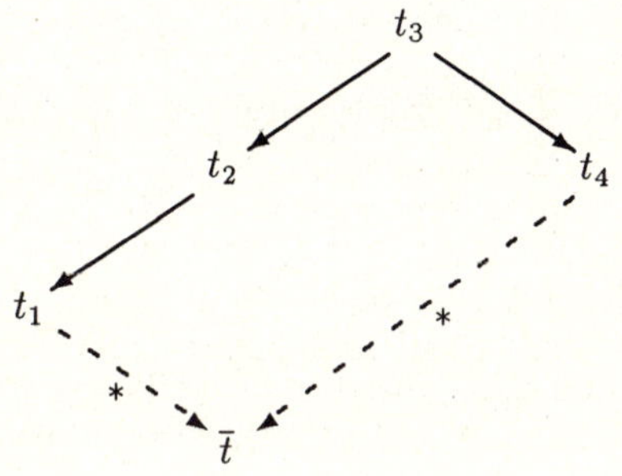

Fig. 2.3

If t_1 and t_4 are convergent, then so are t and t'. Evidently, convergent ground terms are always semantically equal. But does the opposite implication also hold true? To answer this question affirmatively for our example we need some more notions which we are going to introduce on an abstract level.

Let $\rightarrow$ be an arbitrary relation on a set A. Two elements x and y of A are called ***convergent***, in symbols $x \downarrow y$, if there is an element z of A such that $x \rightarrow^* z$ and $y \rightarrow^* z$; while x and y are said to be ***convertible*** if $x \leftrightarrow^* y$. Note that $\downarrow$ is a relation defined by $\downarrow = \rightarrow^* \cdot \leftarrow^*$, where $\leftarrow$ is the converse of $\rightarrow$.

Definition 1. *A relation $\rightarrow$ on a set A has the **Church-Rosser property** (hereafter abbreviated **CR-property**) if any two elements are convergent whenever they are convertible.*

The CR-property may be expressed by a diagram (Fig. 2.4),

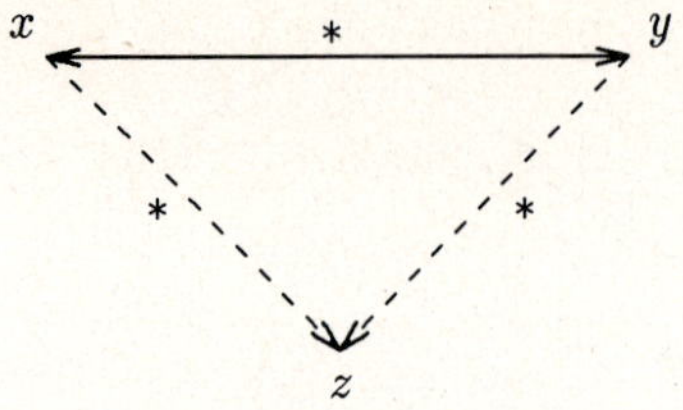

Fig. 2.4

where the dashed arrows indicate that the existence of an element z is required. Formally, for all $x, y \in A$, $x \leftrightarrow^* y$ implies that there exists an element z such that $x \to^* z$ and $y \to^* z$. This is equivalent to the inclusion $\leftrightarrow^* \subseteq \downarrow$.

Lemma 1. *A relation $\to$ has the CR-property iff $\leftrightarrow^* = \downarrow$.*

Proof. It is enough to show $\downarrow \subseteq \leftrightarrow^*$. By Proposition 2 in Section 1.3.1, we have

$$\leftrightarrow^* = \to^* \cdot (\leftarrow \cdot \to^*)^*.$$

Because of $\leftarrow^* \subseteq (\leftarrow \cdot \to^*)^*$ it follows that $\to^* \cdot \leftarrow^* \subseteq \leftrightarrow^*$, i.e., $\downarrow \subseteq \leftrightarrow^*$. ■

Can the CR-property be reduced to another property easier to recognize? Let $\to$ be a relation on a set A. Two elements x and y are said to be ***divergent***, in symbols $x \uparrow y$, if there is an element z of A such that $z \to^* x$ and $z \to^* y$ holds. Dually to $\downarrow$, the relation $\uparrow$ is defined by $\uparrow = \leftarrow^* \cdot \to^*$.

Definition 2. *A relation on a set A is called **confluent** if all pairs of divergent elements of A are convergent. That is, $\uparrow \subseteq \downarrow$.*

Confluence can also be visualized by a diagram (Fig. 2.5),

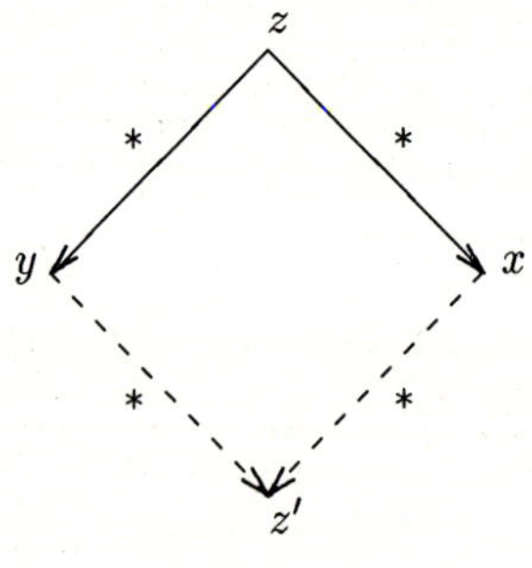

Fig. 2.5

where our convention about the dashed arrows is used. Formally, for all $x, y, z \in A$, $z \rightarrow^* x$ and $z \rightarrow^* y$ imply that there exists an element z' in A such that $x \rightarrow^* z'$ and $y \rightarrow^* z'$.

Theorem 2 (Church-Rosser Theorem). *A relation has the Church-Rosser property if and only if it is confluent.*

Proof. Let $\rightarrow$ be a relation on a set A.

(1) To prove necessity we assume that $\rightarrow$ has the CR-property. Then $\rightarrow^* \cdot \leftarrow^* = \leftrightarrow^*$ by Lemma 1. Because of $\leftarrow^* \cdot \rightarrow^* \subseteq \leftrightarrow^*$, by Proposition 2 in Section 1.3.1, we get

$$\leftarrow^* \cdot \rightarrow^* \subseteq \rightarrow^* \cdot \leftarrow^*,$$

which means that $\rightarrow$ is confluent.

(2) To prove sufficiency we assume that $\rightarrow$ is confluent. Using Proposition 2 in Section 1.3.1 again we derive

$$\leftrightarrow^* = \rightarrow^* \cdot \bigcup((\leftarrow \cdot \rightarrow^*)^n \mid n \in \mathbb{N}).$$

By induction over n we show that $(\leftarrow \cdot \rightarrow^*)^n \subseteq \rightarrow^* \cdot \leftarrow^*$ for all $n \in \mathbb{N}$.

(i) Induction basis: The assertion holds trivially for $n = 0$.

(ii) Induction step: If $(\leftarrow \cdot \rightarrow^*)^n \subseteq \rightarrow^* \cdot \leftarrow^*$ (induction hypothesis), then

$$\begin{aligned}
(\leftarrow \cdot \rightarrow^*)^{n+1} &= \leftarrow \cdot \rightarrow^* \cdot (\leftarrow \cdot \rightarrow^*)^n & \\
&\subseteq \leftarrow \cdot \rightarrow^* \cdot \rightarrow^* \cdot \leftarrow^* & \text{by induction hypothesis} \\
&= \leftarrow \cdot \rightarrow^* \cdot \leftarrow^* & \text{because } \rightarrow^* \cdot \rightarrow^* = \rightarrow^* \\
&\subseteq \rightarrow^* \cdot \leftarrow^* \cdot \leftarrow^* & \text{by confluence} \\
&= \rightarrow^* \cdot \leftarrow^* & \text{because } \leftarrow^* \cdot \leftarrow^* = \leftarrow^* .
\end{aligned}$$

Hence, $\bigcup((\leftarrow \cdot \rightarrow^*)^n \mid n \in \mathbb{N}) \subseteq \rightarrow^* \cdot \leftarrow^*$ and consequently

$$\leftrightarrow^* \subseteq \rightarrow^* \cdot \leftarrow^*,$$

which means that $\rightarrow$ has the CR-property. ■

The Church-Rosser Theorem is the basis of the ***confluence method*** explained below. Let $\rightarrow$ be a confluent and terminating relation on a set A. Given an element x of A, any reduction starting from x terminates after finitely many steps with an element, say $\overline{x}$. By the confluence of $\rightarrow$, $\overline{x}$ is uniquely determined. For if x were reducible to two irreducible elements y and z, then these elements would be convergent and, hence, equal. So x is always reducible to a unique element $\overline{x}$, which is called the (***canonical***) ***normal form*** of x, usually denoted by $nf(x)$. To compute normal forms effectively the following two problems have to be decidable:

(1) Is any given element of A irreducible with respect to $\rightarrow$?

(2) Does $x \rightarrow y$ hold for any two elements x and y of A?

Now let $\sim$ be an equivalence relation on a set A such that $\sim$ is generated by a confluent and terminating relation $\rightarrow$ on A. Assume the two problems (1) and (2) from above are decidable for $\rightarrow$. Then the word problem for $\sim$ is solvable since

$$x \sim y \text{ iff } nf(x) = nf(y)$$

for all x and y in A. Normally, it must be assumed that the equality of elements can be tested. In our subsequent applications this is always the case as the elements of A will be terms (or words) for which equality means simply syntactic equality.

Now, let us come back to our motivating example of stacks. Observe that a ground term is reducible iff it contains the *pop* symbol. After the reduction is performed in one step one *pop* symbol is erased. Thus, any reduction sequence terminates. That is, $\rightarrow$ is terminating. On the other hand, it is easily seen that $\rightarrow$ is confluent. Hence, semantical equality of stack ground terms is generated by a confluent and terminating reduction relation $\rightarrow$. Since irreducibility of a stack ground term as well as the question whether for two stack ground terms t and t' the relation $t \rightarrow t'$ holds are decidable, the word problem of semantical equality is solvable via equality of normal forms.

2.1.2 Word Problem for Congruences

In the previous section, stacks were syntactically described by ground terms over the stack signature. In fact, stacks are equivalence classes. Therefore the question arises how to manipulate them using representatives. If two ground terms t and t' represent the same stack, then *pop* t and *pop* t' as well as $push_x t$ and $push_x t'$ must be semantically equal, too. Informally speaking, the equivalence must be compatible with the operations.

A relation $\rightarrow$ on a Σ-algebra $\boldsymbol{A}$ is called ***compatible*** if, for all n-ary operation symbols σ in Σ and all elements $x_1, \ldots, x_n, y_1, \ldots, y_n$ in A,

$$x_1 \rightarrow y_1, ..., x_n \rightarrow y_n \text{ implies } \sigma^A(x_1, \ldots, x_n) \rightarrow \sigma^A(y_1, \ldots, y_n).$$

Definition 3. *A compatible equivalence relation on* $\boldsymbol{A}$ *is called a* ***congruence*** *on* $\boldsymbol{A}$.

Example 1. Consider the stack again. It is easily seen that the reduction relation $\rightarrow$ introduced in the previous section is compatible. Since the generated equivalence $\leftrightarrow^*$ is also compatible the semantical equality is a congruence on the algebra of ground terms. ■

Example 2. Take the additive monoid of natural numbers. The relation $\rightarrow$ defined by $m \rightarrow n$ iff $n = 3m$ for all m and n in $I\!N$ is certainly compatible. However, the generated equivalence $\leftrightarrow^*$ is not so. For instance, $2 \leftrightarrow^* 6$ and $3 \leftrightarrow^* 27$, but $2+3$ is not equivalent to $6+27$. ■

Let $\boldsymbol{A}$ be a Σ-algebra and $\sim$ be a congruence on $\boldsymbol{A}$. Then the quotient set $A/\!\sim$ becomes a Σ-algebra if the operations are defined by representatives as follows. For each n-ary operation symbol σ in Σ and all $x_1, \ldots, x_n \in A$ we put

$$\sigma^{A/\sim}([x_1], ..., [x_n]) = [\sigma^A(x_1, \ldots, x_n)].$$

However, this definition must be justified. Let $y_1, \ldots, y_n \in A$ such that $[x_i] = [y_i]$ for $i = 1, ..., n$. We have to show that $\sigma^A(y_1, \ldots, y_n)$ represents the same equivalence class as $\sigma^A(x_1, \ldots, x_n)$. Note $[x_i] = [y_i]$ iff $x_i \sim y_i$. Since $\sim$ is supposed to be compatible with the operations it follows that both results are equivalent: $\sigma^A(x_1, \ldots, x_n) \sim \sigma^A(y_1, \ldots, y_n)$; hence they represent the same equivalence class, i.e., $[\sigma^A(x_1, \ldots, x_n)] = [\sigma^A(y_1, \ldots, y_n)]$. In other words, the operation $\sigma^{A/\sim}$ is well-defined.

Definition 4. *Let $\boldsymbol{A}$ be a Σ-algebra and $\sim$ be a congruence on $\boldsymbol{A}$. The Σ-algebra with carrier set $A/\!\sim$ and operations $\sigma^{A/\sim}$ as defined above is called the* ***quotient algebra*** *of $\boldsymbol{A}$ modulo $\sim$, and it is denoted by $\boldsymbol{A}/\!\sim$.* ■

Example 3. Let Σ be the stack signature. By Example 1 we know that the equivalence generated by the reduction relation is a congruence. Consider the quotient set $T_\Sigma/\!\leftrightarrow^*$. Each ground term t can be reduced to its normal form which does not contain any *pop* symbol. Hence a canonical form is uniquely determined by a finite sequence of elements from V. This yields a bijective mapping from the quotient set $T_\Sigma/\!\leftrightarrow^*$ to the set $W(V)$ of all words over V, where *nil* is mapped onto the empty word. Now, it is easy to see that the quotient algebra of stacks is isomorphic to the algebra

$$(W(V), pop^{W(V)}, (push_x^{W(V)} \mid v \in V), nil^{W(V)})$$

with its operations given by

$$pop^{W(V)}(w) = \begin{cases} e & \text{if} \quad w = e \text{ (e is the empty word),} \\ w' & \text{if} \quad w = xw' \text{ for some } x \in V, w' \in W(V); \end{cases}$$

$push_x^{W(V)}(w) = xw$ ($x \in V$); and

$nil^{W(V)} = e.$ ■

Our aim is to solve the word problem for congruences using the confluence method. This requires a special generation of congruences, namely as the equivalence closure of a certain "reduction relation". Of course, all congruences on a given algebra form a closure system so that they can be generated by relations in general. But the equivalence closure of a compatible relation need not to be compatible as shown in Example 2. Therefore the congruence generated by a relation $\rightarrow$ on an algebra $\boldsymbol{A}$, which is denoted by $con(\rightarrow)$, cannot be obtained as an equivalence closure of the compatible relation generated by $\rightarrow$, which is denoted by $com(\rightarrow)$. We may only prove that $con(\rightarrow) = com(\longleftrightarrow^=)^+$.

How can we render it possible that a generated congruence is an equivalence closure of a reduction relation? First, let us investigate a simple case. A relation $\rightarrow$ on a monoid M is called ***invariant*** if, for all $x, y, a, b \in M$,

$$x \rightarrow y \text{ implies } a \cdot x \cdot b \rightarrow a \cdot y \cdot b.$$

The set of all invariant relations on M is surely a closure system so that we can generate an invariant relation by an arbitrary relation on M. The invariant relation generated by $\rightarrow$ is denoted by $\overset{\bullet}{\rightarrow}$.

An easy calculation shows that the monoid congruence generated by $\rightarrow$ is the equivalence closure of the invariant relation generated by $\rightarrow$:

$$con(\rightarrow) \ = \overset{\bullet}{\longleftrightarrow}{}^*.$$

This generation principle is suitable for transforming the word problem of monoid congruences to the decision problem of invariant relations.

The generation process for monoid congruences explained above gives us a hint for the general case of algebras. We try to generalize the notion of invariance. By definition, a congruence is an equivalence relation compatible with the operations:

$$(x_1, \ldots, x_n) \mapsto \sigma^A(x_1, \ldots, x_n).$$

By giving fixed values in A to some of the arguments, we obtain k-ary operations for $k \leq n$; in particular, if we fix all the x_i except one, we obtain for any $n-1$ elements $a_1, ..., a_{n-1}$ of A and any $i = 1, ..., n$, a unary operation

$$x \mapsto \sigma^A(a_1, ..., a_{i-1}, x, a_i, ..., a_{n-1}).$$

We shall say that this operation is an ***elementary translation*** derived from σ^A by specialization in A. Generally, a mapping from A into itself is said to be a ***translation*** if it is either the identity mapping or it can be expressed as a product of a finite number of elementary translations. The unary operations are a special case of translations.

Lemma 3. *An equivalence relation on an algebra is a congruence iff it admits all translations; more precisely, a congruence admits all translations, while an equivalence admitting all elementary translations is a congruence.*

Proof. If $\sim$ is a congruence on an algebra $\boldsymbol{A}$, then for any n-ary operation symbol σ and any $x, y_1, ..., y_n \in A$, if $x \sim y_i$, then

$$\sigma^A(y_1, \ldots, y_n) \sim \sigma^A(y_1, ..., y_{i-1}, x, y_{i+1}, ..., y_n).$$

Hence $\sim$ admits all elementary translations and so, by an easy induction, $\sim$ admits all translations.

Conversely, assume that an equivalence $\sim$ on $\boldsymbol{A}$ admits all elementary translations. Let $x_1, ..., x_n, y_1, ..., y_n \in A$. If $x_i \sim y_i$ for $i = 1, ..., n$, then we have for any n-ary operation σ^A:

$$\begin{aligned}\sigma^A(x_1, \ldots, x_n) &\sim \sigma^A(y_1, x_2, x_3, ..., x_n)\\ &\sim \sigma^A(y_1, y_2, x_3, ..., x_n)\\ &\cdots\\ &\sim \sigma^A(y_1, y_2, y_3, ..., y_n).\end{aligned}$$

Thus $\sim$ is compatible with the operations and hence a congruence. ■

Translations of term algebras are easily described. A mapping $\tau : \boldsymbol{T}_\Sigma(X) \to \boldsymbol{T}_\Sigma(X)$ is a translation iff there are a term $t \in T_\Sigma(X)$ and an address $u \in Dom(t)$ such that

$$\tau(t') = t[u/t']$$

for all t' in $T_\Sigma(X)$.

Recall that a relation $\to$ on the term algebra $\boldsymbol{T}_\Sigma(X)$ is invariant iff, for all $t_1, t_2, t \in T_\Sigma(X)$ and all $u \in Dom(t)$, $t_1 \to t_2$ implies $t[u/t_1] \to t[u/t_2]$. This can now be expressed as follows: A relation on $\boldsymbol{T}_\Sigma(X)$ is invariant iff it admits all translations; which leads to our concept of invariance.

Definition 5. *A relation on an algebra is called* ***invariant*** *if it admits all translations.*

The elementary translations on a monoid M are the left and right multiplications with an arbitrary element, while the translations are mapping $\tau_{a,b} : M \to M$, where $a, b \in M$, defined by $\tau_{a,b}(x) = a \cdot x \cdot b$ for all x in M.

Hence the general notion of an invariant relation specializes to invariant relations on monoids.

As a corollary of Lemma 3 we get:

Proposition 4. *An equivalence on an algebra is a congruence if and only if it is invariant.* ■

The essential remark that all invariant relations on an algebra form a closure system permits us to generate them. Given a relation $\to$ on an algebra, $\xrightarrow{\bullet}$ denotes the invariant relation it generates.

Lemma 5. *If $\to$ is a relation on an algebra $\boldsymbol{A}$, then, for all a and b in A, $a \xrightarrow{\bullet} b$ iff there exists a translation τ on $\boldsymbol{A}$ and elements x, y of A such that $a = \tau(x)$, $b = \tau(y)$ and $x \to y$.*

Proof. Denote by $inv(\to)$ the relation on A consisting of all pairs (a, b) such that $a = \tau(x)$, $b = \tau(y)$ with $x \to y$ for some translation τ on $\boldsymbol{A}$ and some elements x and y

of A. Since, by definition, the identity mapping is a translation on $\boldsymbol{A}$, $\to$ is a subset of $inv(\to)$. Furthermore, the product of translations is again a translation, which implies that $inv(\to)$ is an invariant relation. Hence, $\stackrel{\bullet}{\to} \subseteq inv(\to)$ because $\stackrel{\bullet}{\to}$ is supposed to be the least invariant relation including $\to$. On the other hand, the opposite inclusion is trivially true. Thus $\stackrel{\bullet}{\to} = inv(\to)$. ∎

From this characterization it follows that the invariant closure of a symmetric relation is symmetric and therefore $\stackrel{\bullet}{\longleftrightarrow}$ designates unambiguously the invariant and symmetric relation generated by $\to$.

Theorem 6. *If $\to$ is a relation on an algebra $\boldsymbol{A}$, then the congruence it generates is the equivalence closure of the invariant relation generated by $\to$. That is,*

$$con(\to) = \stackrel{\bullet}{\longleftrightarrow}^*.$$

Proof. It remains to show that $\stackrel{\bullet}{\longleftrightarrow}^*$ is invariant. Take two arbitrary elements a and b from A. Then $a \stackrel{\bullet}{\longleftrightarrow}^* b$ iff there is a sequence of elements $a_0, a_1, ..., a_m$ of A such that $a = a_0, a_m = b$ and $a_{i-1} \stackrel{\bullet}{\longleftrightarrow} a_i$ for $i = 1, ..., m$. Since $\stackrel{\bullet}{\longleftrightarrow}$ is invariant, $\tau(a_{i-1}) \stackrel{\bullet}{\longleftrightarrow} \tau(a_i)$ for all $i = 1, \ldots, m$ and all translations τ on $\boldsymbol{A}$. It follows readily that

$$\tau(a) \stackrel{\bullet}{\longleftrightarrow}^* \tau(b)$$

for all translations τ on A. Hence $\stackrel{\bullet}{\longleftrightarrow}^*$ is invariant. ∎

Now we have achieved the following explicit description of a generated congruence. Let $\to$ be a relation on an algebra $\boldsymbol{A}$. Two elements a and b of A are equivalent modulo the generated congruence iff there exist a natural number m, a sequence $a = a_0, a_1, \ldots, a_m = b$ and pairs $(x_1, y_1), ..., (x_m, y_m)$ of elements from A, and translations $\tau_1, \ldots, \tau_m$ on $\boldsymbol{A}$ such that either

$$a_{i-1} = \tau_i(x_i) \text{ and } a_i = \tau_i(y_i); \text{ or}$$
$$a_i = \tau_i(x_i) \text{ and } a_{i-1} = \tau_i(y_i)$$

and $x_i \to y_i$ for $i = 1, ..., m$. This is illustrated (for $m = 5$) in Fig. 2.6,

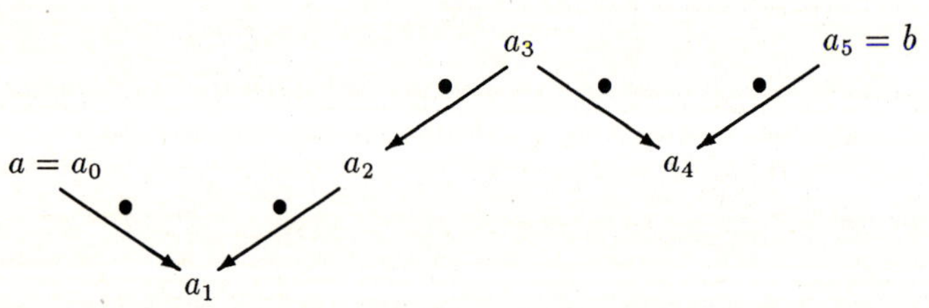

Fig. 2.6

where

$$\begin{aligned}
a_0 &= \tau_1(x_1),\ a_1 = \tau_1(y_1) \text{ and } x_1 \to y_1;\\
a_2 &= \tau_2(x_2),\ a_1 = \tau_2(y_2) \text{ and } x_2 \to y_2;\\
a_3 &= \tau_3(x_3),\ a_2 = \tau_3(y_3) \text{ and } x_3 \to y_3;\\
a_3 &= \tau_4(x_4),\ a_4 = \tau_4(y_4) \text{ and } x_4 \to y_4;\\
a_5 &= \tau_5(x_5),\ a_4 = \tau_5(y_5) \text{ and } x_5 \to y_5.
\end{aligned}$$

Note. A useful formula is the following

$$con(\to) = \bigcup\{con(\{(x,y)\}|x \to y \text{ and } x,y \in A\},$$

which says that a congruence generated by a relation $\to$ on a given algebra $\boldsymbol{A}$ is the union over all congruences generated by single pairs (x, y) of elements such that $x \to y$. These congruences are usually called principal. The Birkhoff-Frink Theorem (Lemma 5 in Section 1.2.4) ensures us that the congruences on an algebra form an algebraic closure system. ■

By Theorem 6, the word problem for congruences can be transformed into a decision problem for invariant relations. It will turn out that congruences, and hence especially invariant relations on term algebras, play an important role in our development.

Theorem 7. *If $\to$ is a relation on the term algebra $\boldsymbol{T}_\Sigma(X)$, then, for all terms t and t' in $T_\Sigma(X)$, $t \xrightarrow{\bullet} t'$ iff there exist an address u of t and terms t_1, t_2 of $T_\Sigma(X)$ such that $t/u = t_1$, $t' = t[u/t_2]$ and $t_1 \to t_2$.*

Proof. Denote by $inv(\to)$ the set of all pairs (t, t') of terms such that there exist an address u of t and terms t_1, t_2 of $T_\Sigma(X)$ with $t/u = t_1, t' = t[u/t_2]$ and $t_1 \to t_2$. When u is in particular the empty word, the pair (t, t') specializes to (t_1, t_2). Hence $\to$ is included in $inv(\to)$.

Claim: $inv(\to)$ is invariant.

Take $(t, t') \in inv(\to)$. By definition, $t/u = t_1, t' = t[u/t_2]$ and $t_1 \to t_2$ for some address $u \in Dom(t)$ and some terms $t_1, t_2 \in T_\Sigma(X)$. We have to show $(\tau(t), \tau(t')) \in inv(\to)$ for all translations τ on $\boldsymbol{T}_\Sigma(X)$. Recall that any translation τ is determined by a term $\bar{t} \in T_\Sigma(X)$ and an address $v \in Dom(\bar{t})$ such that $\tau(t) = \bar{t}[v/t]$ and $\tau(t') = \bar{t}[v/t']$.

Using Lemma 4 in Section 1.4.2 for terms, we get

$$\bar{t}[v/t]/vu = t/u = t_1 \text{ and } \bar{t}[v/t'] = \bar{t}[v/t[u/t_2]] = \bar{t}[v/t][vu/t_2].$$

Hence $\tau(t)/w = t_1$, $\tau(t') = \tau(t)[w/t_2]$ and $t_1 \to t_2$, where $w = vu$. That is, $(\tau(t), \tau(t')) \in inv(\to)$. Hence, $inv(\to)$ is invariant, which proves the claim.

Now, by definition, $\stackrel{\bullet}{\to}$ is the least invariant relation including $\to$. Thus $\stackrel{\bullet}{\to} \subseteq inv(\to)$. It remains to show that $inv(\to)$ is included in $\stackrel{\bullet}{\to}$. Observe that

$$inv(\to) = \{(\tau(t_1), \tau(t_2)) \mid t_1 \to t_2 \text{ and } \tau \text{ is a translation on } \boldsymbol{T}_\Sigma(X)\}.$$

Because of $\to \subseteq \stackrel{\bullet}{\to}$ we get $inv(\to) \subseteq \stackrel{\bullet}{\to}$ since $\stackrel{\bullet}{\to}$ is invariant. Hence $\stackrel{\bullet}{\to} = inv(\to)$. ■

Subsequently we turn to a special class of congruences.

Definition 6. *A relation $\to$ on an algebra $\boldsymbol{A}$ is called **stable** if, for all endomorphisms h of $\boldsymbol{A}$ and all $x, y \in A$,*

$$x \to y \text{ implies } h(x) \to h(y).$$

*A stable and invariant relation is called **fully invariant**.*

Stable relations on term algebras are characterizable by substitutions. Let X be a set. A mapping from X into the set of terms over X is called a (term) ***substitution***. Observe that every endomorphism of a term algebra is uniquely determined by a suitable substitution. If h is a given endomorphism of $\boldsymbol{T}_\Sigma(X)$, then $h = s^\sharp$ where $s : X \to T_\Sigma(X)$ is a substitution defined by $s(x) = h(x)$ for all x in X. Often, a substitution $s : X \to T_\Sigma(X)$ is required to satisfy the condition $s(x) = x$ for all except finitely many x in X. Hence, $D(s) = \{x \in X \mid s(x) \neq x\}$ is then a finite subset of X. But we will not require this condition. However, when $D(S)$ is finite, say $D(s) = \{x_1, ..., x_n\}$, the following notation shall be used :

$$s = \{x_1 \mapsto t_1, ..., x_n \mapsto t_n\}$$

where $t_i = s(x_i)$ for $i = 1, ..., n$.

Lemma 8. *A relation $\to$ on the term algebra $\boldsymbol{T}_\Sigma(X)$ is stable iff, for all substitutions $s : X \to T_\Sigma(X)$ and all terms $t_1, t_2 \in T_\Sigma(X), t_1 \to t_2$ implies $s^\sharp(t_1) \to s^\sharp(t_2)$.* ■

The set of all stable relations on an algebra is certainly a closure system. So, stable relations can be generated by arbitrary ones. Let $\to$ be a relation on an algebra A. Its stable closure is denoted by $\Rightarrow$.

Lemma 9. *The fully invariant closure of a relation $\to$ on an algebra $\boldsymbol{A}$ is the invariant closure of $\Rightarrow$.*

Proof. By Proposition 1 in Section 1.2.1 we have to show that the invariant closure of a stable relation is stable. It suffices to prove this property for elementary invariance. The rest is done by a simple induction.

Let $\to$ be a stable relation on A and denote by $\stackrel{e}{\to}$ its closure under elementary translations. Then, for any elements $a, b \in A, a \stackrel{e}{\to} b$ iff there are an operation symbol σ and elements $a_1, ..., a_{n-1}, x, y \in A$ such that $a = \sigma^A(a_1, ..., a_{i-1}, x, a_i, ..., a_{n-1})$, $b = \sigma^A(a_1, ..., a_{i-1}, y, a_i, ..., a_{n-1})$ and $x \to y$. If h is an arbitrary endomorphism of $\boldsymbol{A}$, then $h(x) \to h(y)$, by assumption, and hence $h(a) \stackrel{e}{\to} h(b)$ because

$$h(a) = \sigma^A(h(a_1), ..., h(a_{i-1}), h(x), h(a_i), ..., h(a_{n-1})), \text{ and}$$

$$h(b) = \sigma^A(h(a_1), ..., h(a_{i-1}), h(y), h(a_i), ..., h(a_{n-1})).$$

Thus $\xrightarrow{e}$ is stable. By induction we can show that the invariant closure of a stable relation is again stable. ■

Let us denote the fully invariant closure of an arbitrary relation $\rightarrow$ by $\overset{\bullet}{\Longrightarrow}$.

Lemma 10. *If $\rightarrow$ is a relation on an algebra $\boldsymbol{A}$, then, for all a and b in A, $a \overset{\bullet}{\Longrightarrow} b$ iff there exist a translation τ on $\boldsymbol{A}$, an endomorphism h of $\boldsymbol{A}$ and elements $x, y \in A$ such that $a = \tau(h(x)), b = \tau(h(y))$ and $x \rightarrow y$.*

Proof. By Lemma 5, $a \overset{\bullet}{\Longrightarrow} b$ iff there is a translation τ on $\boldsymbol{A}$ and elements $x', y' \in A$ such that $a = \tau(x'), b = \tau(y')$ and $x' \Rightarrow y'$. Furthermore, $x' \Rightarrow y'$ iff there are an endomorphism h of $\boldsymbol{A}$ and elements $x, y \in A$ such that $x' = h(x), y' = h(y)$ and $x \rightarrow y$. Combining both criteria yields the assertion. ■

Theorem 11. *If $\rightarrow$ is a relation on the term algebra $\boldsymbol{T}_\Sigma(X)$, then, for all terms t and t' in $T_\Sigma(X)$, $t \overset{\bullet}{\Longrightarrow} t'$ iff there exist a substitution $s : X \rightarrow T_\Sigma(X)$, an address u of t an terms t_1, t_2 of $T_\Sigma(X)$ such that $t/u = s^\sharp(t_1)$, $t' = t[u/s^\sharp(t_2)]$ and $t_1 \rightarrow t_2$.* ■

Now we focus our attention on the generation of fully invariant congruences. Note that a congruence is fully invariant iff it is stable.

Theorem 12. *If $\rightarrow$ is a relation on an algebra $\boldsymbol{A}$, the fully invariant congruence $con_f(\rightarrow)$ it generates is the equivalence closure of the relation $\overset{\bullet}{\Longrightarrow}$ generated by $\rightarrow$. That is,*

$$con_f(\rightarrow) = \overset{\bullet}{\Longleftrightarrow}{}^*.$$

Proof. By Theorem 6, $\overset{\bullet}{\Longleftrightarrow}{}^*$ is the congruence generated by the stable closure $\Rightarrow$ of $\rightarrow$. So, it remains to show that $\overset{\bullet}{\Longleftrightarrow}{}^*$ is stable. But this follows readily from the fact that the reflexive, transitive and symmetric closure of a stable relation is stable. ■

Let us explain this generation principle in case of term algebras only. Given a relation $\rightarrow$ on the term algebra $\boldsymbol{T}_\Sigma(X)$, two terms t and t' are equivalent modulo the generated fully invariant congruence iff there exist a natural number m, a sequence $t = t_0, t_1, ..., t_m = t'$ and pairs $(t'_1, t''_1), ..., (t'_m, t''_m)$ of terms from $T_\Sigma(X)$, addresses $u_1, \ldots, u_m$ and substitutions $s_1, \ldots, s_m$ such that either

$$t_{i-1}/u_i = s_i^\sharp(t'_i) \text{ and } t_i = t_{i-1}[u_i/s_i^\sharp(t''_i)], \text{ where } u_i \in Dom(t_i); \text{ or}$$

$$t_i/u_i = s_i^\sharp(t'_i) \text{ and } t_{i-1} = t_i[u_i/s_i^\sharp(t''_i)], \text{ where } u_i \in Dom(t_i)$$

and $t'_i \rightarrow t''_i$ for $i = 1, ..., m$. This is illustrated (for $m = 5$) in Fig. 2.7,

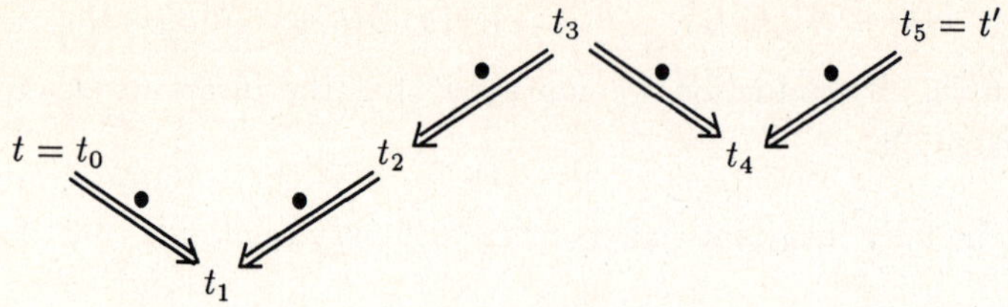

Fig. 2.7

where

$$t_0/u_1 = s_1^\sharp(t_1'), t_1 = t_0[u_1/s_1^\sharp(t_1'')] \text{ and } t_1' \to t_1'';$$

$$t_2/u_2 = s_2^\sharp(t_2'), t_1 = t_2[u_2/s_2^\sharp(t_2'')] \text{ and } t_2' \to t_2'';$$

$$t_3/u_3 = s_3^\sharp(t_3'), t_2 = t_3[u_3/s_3^\sharp(t_3'')] \text{ and } t_3' \to t_3'';$$

$$t_3/u_4 = s_4^\sharp(t_4'), t_4 = t_3[u_4/s_4^\sharp(t_4'')] \text{ and } t_4' \to t_4'';$$

$$t_5/u_5 = s_5^\sharp(t_5'), t_4 = t_5[u_5/s_5^\sharp(t_5'')] \text{ and } t_5' \to t_5''.$$

Note. Similarly as for congruences the following formula holds

$$con_f(\to) = \bigcup\{con_f(\{(x,y)\}|x \to y \text{ for some } x, y \in A\}$$

which implies that all fully invariant congruences on an algebra form an algebraic closure system. ■

We conclude the section with an important remark. The foregoing investigations suggest the following concept as a means of transforming the word problem for fully invariant congruences on term algebras into a reduction problem. A pair $(\boldsymbol{T}_\Sigma(X), \to)$ is called a term reduction system if $\to$ is a fully invariant relation on $\boldsymbol{T}_\Sigma(X)$. Then, by Theorem 12, the equivalence closure of $\to$ is a fully invariant congruence on $\boldsymbol{T}_\Sigma(X)$. Such term reduction systems will be studied in Section 2.2.2.

2.2 Reduction Systems

Here, our motivation for reduction systems stems from solving the word problem for congruences. First, we introduce abstract reduction systems in order to develop as far as possible the properties common to all reduction systems. This will be done in Section 2.2.1. It will be shown how the important test of confluence can be reduced to the test of local confluence.

Section 2.2.2 deals with term reduction systems. Besides localization, the use of critical pairs is here one of the main ideas concerning the confluence test.

In Section 2.2.3, termination of term rewriting systems is studied.

2.2.1 Abstract Reduction Systems

A pair $(A, \to)$ consisting of a set A and a relation $\to$ on it is called an (abstract) ***reduction system***. We say that a reduction system $(A, \to)$ has a property (e.g., it is terminating, confluent, etc.) if the relation $\to$ has the property. In this context, $\to$ is called a ***reduction relation***, while the generated equivalence $\leftrightarrow^*$ is called a ***convertibility relation***.

Definition 1. *A confluent and terminating reduction system is called* ***complete***.

Example 1. Consider the reduction system $(A, \to)$ given by $A = \{a, b, c\}$ and $\to$ as depicted in Fig. 2.8. Then $(A, \to)$ is certainly terminating but not confluent.

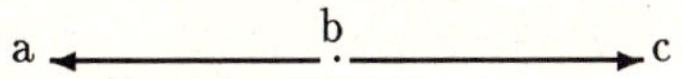

Fig. 2.8

We are now going to characterize complete reduction systems. Let $(A, \to)$ be an arbitrary reduction system. An element x of A admits a ***normal form*** if there is an irreducible element, say y, in A such that $x \to^* y$. In Example 1, a and c are normal forms of b.

If $(A, \to)$ is a confluent reduction system, each element of A has at most one normal form. When $(A, \to)$ is a terminating reduction system, each element of A has at least one normal form. Hence, in a compete reduction system every element has exactly one normal form, often called the ***canonical normal form***.

The test for confluence can often be carried out in an algorithmic way using two important ideas:

(1) localization; and

(2) critical pairs.

Localization is generally applicable and is studied in the sequel. The method of critical pairs will be explained for term reduction systems in the next section.

Definition 2. *A reduction system $(A, \to)$ is called* ***locally confluent*** *if all pairs of elements x and y in A are convergent whenever $z \to x$ and $z \to y$ for some element z of A.*

Local confluence is visualized in Fig. 2.9.

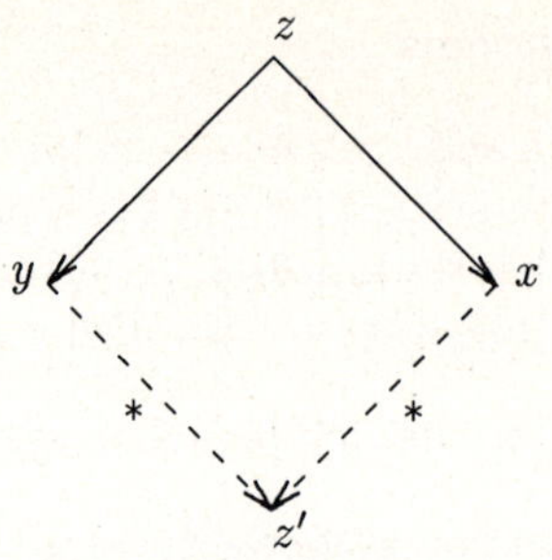

Fig. 2.9

Evidently, every confluent reduction system is locally confluent. The converse, however, is not true, as the following example indicates.

Example 2. The reduction system depicted in Fig. 2.10 is locally confluent, but not confluent.

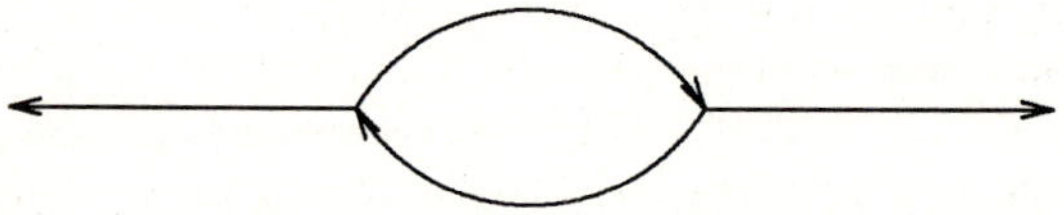

Fig. 2.10

Observe that the reduction system is not terminating. ■

Proposition 1 (Newman's Lemma). *A terminating reduction system is confluent if and only if it is locally confluent.*

Proof. It suffices to show that local confluence implies confluence provided the reduction system is terminating. Therefore assume that $(A, \rightarrow)$ is a locally confluent and terminating reduction system. We shall use the Principle of Noetherian Induction. For that purpose a suitable property $\mathcal{P}$ has to be found. Let us define

$$\mathcal{P}(a) \quad \text{iff} \quad \forall x, y(a \rightarrow^* x \wedge a \rightarrow^* y \Rightarrow x \downarrow y).$$

Now, we have to verify that

$$\forall a \in A(\forall x \in A(a \rightarrow x \Rightarrow \mathcal{P}(x)) \Rightarrow \mathcal{P}(a)) \qquad (*)$$

holds. Take an arbitrary element a of A. First, if a is irreducible, then $\mathcal{P}$ holds for a trivially. Hence, the induction formula $(*)$ is valid. Secondly, suppose a is reducible. To show that $\mathcal{P}$ holds for a, we have to show that for all $x, y \in A, a \rightarrow^* x$ and $a \rightarrow^* y$

imply $x \downarrow y$. By assumption there are elements b and c in A such that $a \to b \to^* x$ and $a \to c \to^* y$. Since $(A, \to)$ is supposed to be locally confluent, b and c must be convergent. That is, $b \to^* d$ and $c \to^* d$ for some element d of A. By induction hypothesis, $\mathcal{P}$ holds for b and c. Thus d and x are convergent resulting an element z, i.e., $d \to^* z$ and $x \to^* z$. The same argument is applied once more, namely y and z are convergent, by the induction hypothesis as well. There must be an element z' such that $y \to^* z'$ and $z \to^* z'$. But, then x and y are convergent, too, which means that $\mathcal{P}$ holds for a. ■

As a corollary we get an important criterion for completeness.

Theorem 2. *A reduction system is complete if and only if it is locally confluent and terminating.* ■

As already mentioned, reduction systems were introduced to solve word problems. For a given equivalence relation $\sim$ we have to find a complete reduction relation $\to$ so that $\to$ generates $\sim$. In fact, we will actually deal with congruences or even fully invariant congruences. Taking into account that different relations on a set A can generate the same equivalence we are led to the following definition.

Definition 3. *Two reduction systems are called* ***equivalent*** *if their corresponding convertibility relations coincide.*

Given a reduction system $(A, \to)$, any complete reduction system equivalent to it is called a ***completion*** of $(A, \to)$. Our main goal is an algorithmic construction of such a completion when it is possible. Therefore the question arises whether every reduction system has a completion.

Consider an arbitrary reduction system $(A, \to)$. Assume that S is a mapping from A into itself such that, for all x in A, $S(x) \leftrightarrow^* x$ and, for all x, x' in A, $S(x) = S(x')$ whenever $x \leftrightarrow^* x'$. By the Axiom of Choice such a mapping does always exist. S selects (in a unique manner) a representative for each equivalence class. Dealing with these selected representatives we are able to define a complete reduction system $(A, \Rightarrow)$ equivalent to $(A, \to)$ by setting

$$x \Rightarrow y \text{ iff } x \neq y \text{ and } y = S(x)$$

for all x and y in A.

Although every reduction system has a completion we are, in general, unable to construct it algorithmically. The idea of a possible algorithmic construction is based on Theorem 2. Given a terminating reduction system $(A, \to)$ we try to construct a completion $(A, \Rightarrow)$ by locating all situation in which local confluence is injured. This suggests the following procedure. Start with the relation $\to$ and compute the set $CP(\to)$ of "critical pairs" of $\to$, where $(x, y) \in A \times A$ is called ***critical*** if there is an element z of A such that $z \to x$ and $z \to y$, but x and y are not convergent. If $CP(\to)$ is empty, the reduction relation $\rightarrow$ is locally confluent and hence confluent, which means that $(A, \rightarrow)$ is already complete. In case there exists at least one critical pair (x, y) we remedy the violation of local confluence by allowing that either x is reducible to y or, vica versa, y is reducible to x depending on the analysis whether adjoining (x, y) or (y, x) to the reduction relation $\rightarrow$ leaves the termination property untouched. When both possibilities destroy the termination property the procedure stops with "failure". After adjoining a critical pair to $\rightarrow$ we get a new relation. Again its critical pairs are computed and eventually added. If the procedure terminates with a relation $\Rightarrow$, then there is no critical pair left. Consequently, $(A, \Rightarrow)$ is a completion of $(A, \rightarrow)$. By construction, $(A, \Rightarrow)$ is a compete reduction system. But, it should also be clear that $(A, \Rightarrow)$ and $(A, \rightarrow)$ are equivalent.

In general, however, there are infinitely many critical pairs. So, the procedure above is not algorithmic. Even in case we start with a finite relation infinitely many critical pairs may occur during the completion process. An improvement can be expected only if the given reduction relation is generated by finitely many rules, as we will see in the next section. Let us illustrate this situation by the following example.

Example 3. Consider the reduction system $(W(X), \rightarrow)$, where $W(X)$ is the word monoid over the two-letter alphabet $X = \{x, y\}$ and the reduction relation is defined as follows. Let w and w' be words over X. We define

$w \rightarrow w'$ iff there are words $w_1, w_2 \in W(X)$ such that $w = w_1 xxyx w_2$ and $w' = w_1 w_2$.

It is worth noticing that $\rightarrow$ is an invariant relation.

In general, a reduction system over a word monoid with an invariant reduction relation is called a ***semi-Thue system.***

Evidently, the reduction system is terminating since any reduction step decreases the length of the word involved. But it is not confluent because the following critical pair exists:

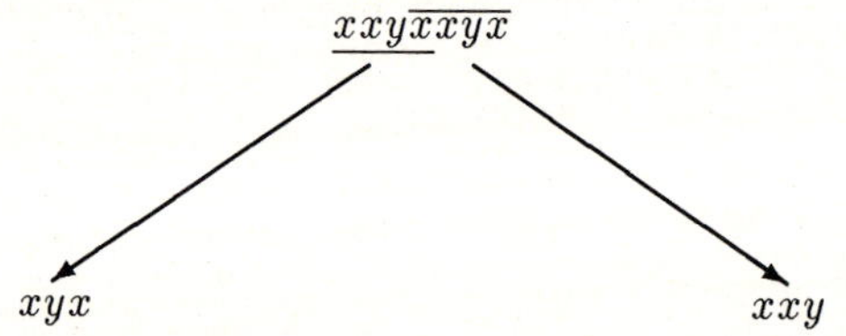

Take into account that the reduction relation is generated as an invariant relation by the single rule $xxyx \rightarrow e$. Therefore, it suffices to study all possible "overlappings" of its left-hand side $xxyx$. But there is only one such possibility, namely $xxyxxyx$ with the indicated overlapping $\underline{xxyx}\overline{}\!\!\!\overline{xyx}$.

Next, we have to analyse the critical pair (xyx, xxy) to see whether $xyx \rightarrow xxy$ or $xxy \rightarrow xyx$ should be added as a new rule. Since the left- and right-hand sides of each rule have the same length we need a termination relation on $W(X)$ as an additional input such that $\rightarrow$ is a subrelation of it.

Taking the lexical order on $W(X)$ induced by $x < y$, we have to add $xyx \rightarrow xxy$ since $xyx \gg_{lex} xxy$. Let $\rightarrow_1$ be the invariant relation on $W(X)$ generated by $\{xxyx \rightarrow e, xyx \rightarrow xxy\}$. Hence, for all $w, w' \in W(X)$, $w \rightarrow_1 w'$ iff there are $w_1, w_2 \in W(X)$ such that either

(1) $w = w_1 xxyx w_2$ and $w' = w_1 w_2$; or

(2) $w = w_1 xyx w_2$ and $w' = w_1 xxy w_2$.

The reduction system $(W(X), \rightarrow_1)$ is terminating by construction and, moreover, equivalent to $(W(X), \rightarrow)$. Indeed, since $\rightarrow$ is a subset of $\rightarrow_1$ we have $\leftrightarrow^* \subseteq \leftrightarrow_1^*$. On the other hand, two words forming a critical pair with respect to $\rightarrow$ are always equivalent modulo $\leftrightarrow^*$. Thus $\rightarrow_1 \subseteq \leftrightarrow^*$, which implies the opposite inclusion $\leftrightarrow_1^* \subseteq \leftrightarrow^*$.

But $(W(X), \rightarrow_1)$ is still not confluent. The overlapping of the left-hand sides of both rules yields new critical pairs. Let us derive all situations in a systematic manner. For that reason we denote the first rule by r_0:

$$r_0 = xxyx \rightarrow e;$$

and the second rule by r_1:

$$r_1 = xyx \rightarrow xxy.$$

Now all possible overlappings will be examined. The overlapping of the left-hand side of r_0 with itself was already considered in the first step, and it gave the rule r_1.

As a first case we study the overlapping of the left-hand side of r_0 with that of r_1.

Case 1:

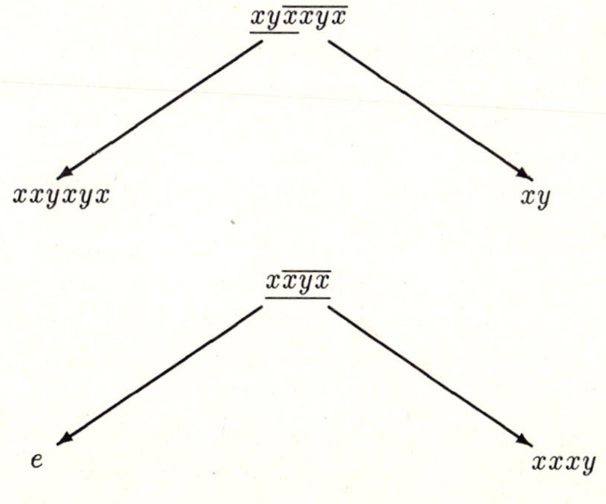

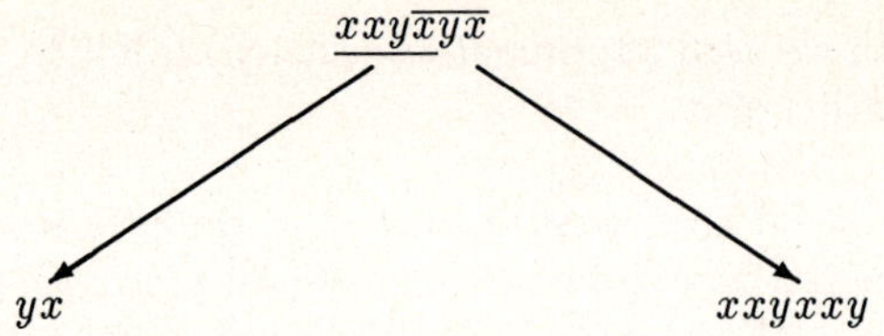

As the next case we study the overlapping of the left-hand side of r_1 with itself.

Case 2:

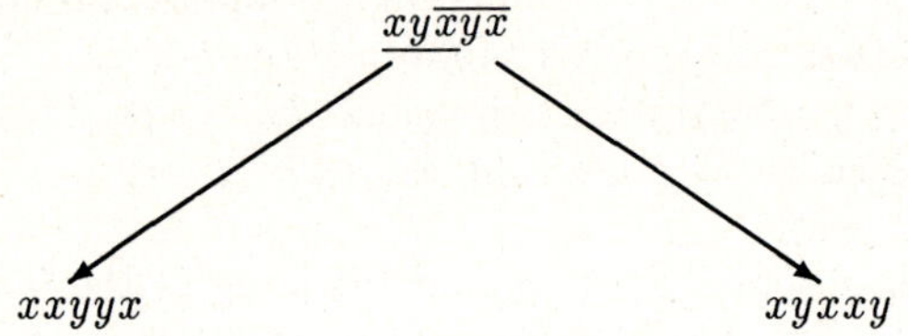

According to the chosen terminating criterion we adjoin the following new rules:

$$xxyxyx \to xy, \ xxxy \to e, \ xxyxxy \to yx, \ xyxxy \to xxyyx.$$

Let $\to_2$ be the invariant relation on $W(X)$ generated r_0, r_1 and the rules above. Then $(W(X), \to_2)$ is certainly terminating and equivalent to $(W(X), \to)$ but not yet confluent.

For instance, the overlapping of the left-hand sides of $r_0 = xxyx \to e$ with the left-hand side of the rule $xxyxyx \to xy$:

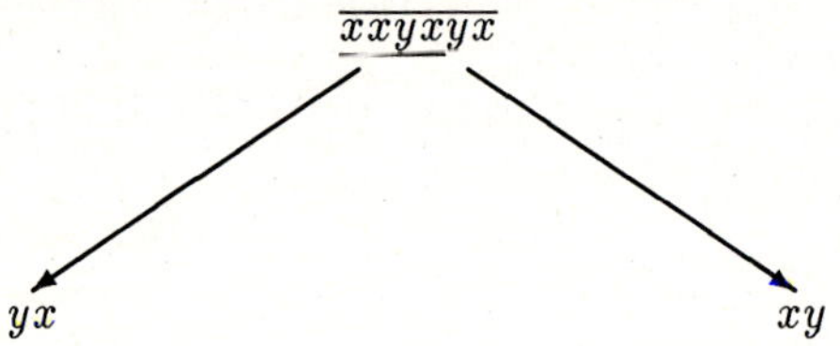

results in the critical pair (yx, xy). But after adjoining the new rule $yx \to xy$ no other overlappings produce critical pairs.

Therefore we achieve a completion $(W(X), \to_3)$ of $(W(X), \to)$, where $\to_3$ is the invariant relation on $W(X)$ generated by the rules:

$$\begin{aligned} xxyx &\to e, \\ xyx &\to xxy, \\ xxyxyx &\to xy, \\ xxxy &\to e, \end{aligned}$$

$$xxyxxy \to yx,$$
$$xyxxy \to xxyyx,$$
$$yx \to xy.$$

It is easily seen that $(W(X), \to_3)$ is equivalent to the complete reduction system $(W(X), \Rightarrow)$, where $\Rightarrow$ is generated by the rules:

$$xxxy \to e,$$
$$yx \to xy$$

(all redundant rules are cancelled). Hence, $(W(X), \Rightarrow)$ is also a completion of $(W(X), \to)$. ■

2.2.2 Term Rewriting Systems

Symbolic manipulations of syntactic objects are based on reductions of terms and they provide models of computation in an operational setting. These models have the useful property of being directly applicable to obtain decision procedures for the word problems of fully invariant congruences.

Here we shall present a short introduction to term rewriting systems. For further information the reader is referred to the literature (see, e.g., /Dershowitz-Jouaunaud-90/, /Drosten-89/, /Huet-Oppen-80/, /Jouaunaud-Lescanne-87/, /Klop-87/).

Recall that the word problem of fully invariant congruences can be transformed into a reduction problem of fully invariant relations. For that reason, a fully invariant relation on a term algebra is called a ***term reduction***. By definition, a relation $\to$ on $\boldsymbol{T}_\Sigma(X)$ is a term reduction iff, for all terms $t, t', t'' \in T_\Sigma(X)$, all addresses u of t'' and all substitutions $s : X \to T_\Sigma(X)$,

(1) $t \to t'$ implies $t''[u/t] \to t''[u/t']$; and

(2) $t \to t'$ implies $s^\sharp(t) \to s^\sharp(t')$,

where (1) is the condition of invariance and (2) is that of stability. To apply the confluence method for solving the word problem, term reduction must be terminating and confluent. But both properties are undecidable in general /Benninghofen-Kemmerich-Richter-87/, /Huet-Lankford-78/. However, when a term reduction is terminating and finitely generated, confluence becomes decidable, as we will see later.

There is a necessary condition for termination.

Lemma 3. *If $\to$ is a terminating term reduction on $\boldsymbol{T}_\Sigma(X)$, then, for all terms t and t' in $T_\Sigma(X)$, $t \to t'$ implies $var(t') \subseteq var(t)$.*

Proof. Let $\rightarrow$ be a terminating term reduction on $\boldsymbol{T}_\Sigma(X)$. If we indirectly assume that there are terms $t, t' \in T_\Sigma(X)$ with $t \rightarrow t'$ and $var(t') \not\subseteq var(t)$, then there is a variable z of X such that z occurs in t' but not in t. Define a substitution $s : X \rightarrow T_\Sigma(X)$ by

$$s(x) = \begin{cases} x & \text{if} \quad x \neq z, \\ t & \text{if} \quad x = z. \end{cases}$$

Put $t_0 = t$ and $t_1 = s^\sharp(t')$. Because of $t = s^\sharp(t)$ and $t \rightarrow t'$ we get, by the stability of $\rightarrow$,

$$t_0 \rightarrow t_1.$$

For $z \in var(t')$, there is an address u of t' such that $t'/u = z$. Hence $t_1/u = s^\sharp(t')/u = s^\sharp(t_1/u) = s(z) = t$ and $t_1 = t_1[u/t]$. Now we put $t_2 = t_1[u/t_1]$ so that $t_1 \rightarrow t_2$, by the invariance of $\rightarrow$. Again t_1 is a subterm of t_2, namely $t_2/u = t_1$. Proceeding in this way we define a nonterminating reduction sequence

$$t_0 \rightarrow t_1 \rightarrow t_2 \rightarrow \ldots$$

contradicting the assumption that $\rightarrow$ is terminating. ■

In accordance with the necessary condition of termination derived above we say that $(T_\Sigma(X), \rightarrow)$ is a ***term reduction system*** if $\rightarrow$ is a term reduction such that $var(t') \subseteq var(t)$ whenever $t \rightarrow t'$ for $t, t' \in T_\Sigma(X)$. A pair (t, t') of terms $t, t' \in T_\Sigma(X)$ is called a ***reduction rule*** if $t \rightarrow t'$ and every variable that occurs in t' occurs also in t.

Since all term reductions on $\boldsymbol{T}_\Sigma(X)$ form a closure system they can be generated by sets of reduction rules. This leads to a simple syntactic description of term reduction.

Definition 4. *A **term rewriting system** (hereafter abbreviated **TRS**) is a set of reduction rules.*

In the sequel we employ the following notational convention. Given a TRS R, we assume that $R \subseteq T_\Sigma(X) \times T_\Sigma(X)$ for some set X. Each rule (t_1, t_2) of R is written as $t_1 \rightarrow t_2$; while the term reduction generated by R is denoted by $\rightarrow_R$. Using the explicit description of the fully invariant closure presented in Theorem 12 in Section 2.1.2, we get $t \rightarrow_R t'$ iff there exist a substitution $s : X \rightarrow T_\Sigma(X)$, an address u of t and a reduction rule $t_1 \rightarrow t_2$ of R such that $t/u = s^\sharp(t_1)$ and $t' = t[u/s^\sharp(t_2)]$.

Reducing t to t' in one step causes the following algorithmic problem called matching. Given two terms t and t', a substitution s is called a ***match*** of t to t' when t' is obtained from t by s, i.e., $t' = s^\sharp(t)$; t' is then said to be an ***instance*** of t.

In other words, $t \rightarrow_R t'$ holds if we find a match s of a subterm of t to the left-hand side t_1 of some reduction rule $t_1 \rightarrow t_2$ of R such that t' is obtained from t by replacing the subterm by the instance $s^\sharp(t_2)$ of the right-hand side t_2 of the reduction rule.

Let R be a TRS. The term reduction $\rightarrow_R$ it generates will be thought of as its semantics. Via this generated term reduction all notions for reduction systems carry over to term rewriting systems. For example, we say that a TRS R is terminating if $\rightarrow_R$ is so.

Now we turn to our main problem, to complete a terminating term rewriting system by the Knuth-Bendix method. To illustrate the underlying idea we use a "naive" attempt in the following example: all critical pairs have to be transformed into reduction rules. Historical and basic features of the critical-pair completion procedure are given in /Buchberger-87/.

Example 1 (after /Klop-87/). Consider the group signature consisting of a binary operation symbol $\cdot$, a unary operation symbol i and a nullary operation symbol e. We start by giving the axioms for groups a "sensible" orientation:

(1) $(x \cdot y) \cdot z \;\rightarrow\; x \cdot (y \cdot z)$,

(2) $i(x) \cdot x \;\rightarrow\; e$,

(3) $e \cdot x \;\rightarrow\; x$.

The TRS R defined by these three reduction rules is terminating but not confluent. The termination of R will not be discussed here. It will be studied in the next section. Confluence is violated, as can be seen by superposition of, e.g., (1) and (2) with result $(i(x) \cdot x) \cdot z$. In a certain sense $(i(x) \cdot x) \cdot z$ is the most general term subject to the two possible reductions: $(i(x) \cdot x) \cdot z \rightarrow_R e \cdot z$ by (2) and $(i(x) \cdot x) \cdot z \rightarrow_R i(x) \cdot (x \cdot z)$ by (1). The pair $(e \cdot z, i(x) \cdot (x \cdot z))$ is called critical. After the reduction $e \cdot z \rightarrow_R z$ we have the problematic pair of terms z and $i(x) \cdot (x \cdot z)$; problematic because their equality is derivable from the group axioms, but they are not convergent with respect to the reduction rules available so far. Therefore we adopt a new reduction rule

(4) $i(x) \cdot (x \cdot z) \rightarrow z$.

Now we have a superposition of reduction rules (4) and (2): $i(i(y)) \cdot (i(y) \cdot y) \rightarrow_R y$ and $i(i(y)) \cdot (i(y) \cdot y) \rightarrow_R i(i(y)) \cdot e$. This yields the critical pair $(y, i(i(y)) \cdot e)$ which cannot be further reduced. We adopt the new reduction rule

(5) $i(i(y)) \cdot e \rightarrow y$.

As it turns out, at a later stage, this last reduction rule will become superfluous. We go on searching for critical pairs. Superposition of (4) and (3): $i(e) \cdot (e \cdot z) \rightarrow_R z$ and $i(e) \cdot (e \cdot z) \rightarrow_R i(e) \cdot z$.

We adopt the new reduction rule

(6) $i(e) \cdot z \rightarrow z$

which will be deleted later.

Superposition of (1) and (5): $(i(i(y))\cdot e)\cdot x \rightarrow_R i(i(y))\cdot(e\cdot x)$ and $(i(i(y))\cdot e)\cdot x \rightarrow_R y\cdot x$.

We adopt the new reduction rule

$$(7)\ \ i(i(y)) \cdot x \rightarrow y \cdot x$$

which will be deleted later.

Superposition of (5) and (7): $i(i(y)) \cdot e \rightarrow_R y$ and $i(i(y)) \cdot e \rightarrow_R y \cdot e$.

We adopt the new reduction rule

$$(8)\ \ y \cdot e \rightarrow y.$$

Superposition of (5) and (8): $i(i(y)) \cdot e \rightarrow_R y$ and $i(i(y)) \cdot e \rightarrow_R i(i(y))$.

We adopt the new reduction rule

$$(9)\ \ i(i(y)) \rightarrow y.$$

Notice that reduction rules (5) and (7) can be deleted by means of (9) since the critical pairs $(i(i(y)) \cdot e, y)$ and $(i(i(y)) \cdot x, y \cdot x)$ are now convergent.

Superposition of (6) and (8): $i(e) \cdot e \rightarrow_R e$ and $i(e) \cdot e \rightarrow_R i(e)$.

We adopt the new reduction rule

$$(10)\ \ i(e) \rightarrow e$$

which makes (6) superfluous.

Superposition of (2) and (9): $i(i(y)) \cdot i(y) \rightarrow_R e$ and $i(i(y)) \cdot i(y) \rightarrow_R y \cdot i(y)$.

We adopt the new reduction rule

$$(11)\ \ y \cdot i(y) \rightarrow e.$$

Superposition of (1) and (11): $(y \cdot i(y)) \cdot x \rightarrow_R y \cdot (i(y) \cdot x)$ and $(y \cdot i(y)) \cdot x \rightarrow_R e \cdot x$.

We adopt the new reduction rule

$$(12)\ \ y \cdot (i(y) \cdot x) \rightarrow x,$$

where the right-hand side is obtained from $e \cdot x$ by (3). Superposition (again) of (1) and (11): $(x \cdot y) \cdot i(x \cdot y) \rightarrow_R x \cdot (y \cdot i(x \cdot y))$ and $(x \cdot y) \cdot i(x \cdot y) \rightarrow_R e$.

We adopt the new reduction rule

(13) $x \cdot (y \cdot i(x \cdot y)) \rightarrow e$

which will be deleted by the next reduction rule.

Superposition of (13) and (4): $i(x) \cdot (x \cdot (y \cdot i(x \cdot y))) \rightarrow_R i(x) \cdot e$ and $i(x) \cdot (x \cdot (y \cdot i(x \cdot y))) \rightarrow_R y \cdot i(x \cdot y)$.

We adopt the new reduction rule

(14) $y \cdot i(x \cdot y) \rightarrow i(x)$

which becomes superfluous by the next reduction rule.

Superposition of (4) and (14): $i(y) \cdot (y \cdot i(x \cdot y)) \rightarrow_R i(x \cdot y)$ and $i(y) \cdot (y \cdot i(x \cdot y)) \rightarrow_R i(y) \cdot i(x)$.

We adopt the new reduction rule

(15) $i(x \cdot y) \rightarrow i(y) \cdot i(x)$.

The TRS is complete now:

$$
\begin{array}{lrcl}
\text{(TG1)} & (x \cdot y) \cdot z & \rightarrow & x \cdot (y \cdot z), \\
\text{(TG2)} & i(x) \cdot x & \rightarrow & e, \\
\text{(TG3)} & e \cdot x & \rightarrow & x, \\
\text{(TG4)} & i(x) \cdot (x \cdot z) & \rightarrow & z, \\
\text{(TG5)} & y \cdot e & \rightarrow & y, \\
\text{(TG6)} & i(i(y)) & \rightarrow & y, \\
\text{(TG7)} & i(e) & \rightarrow & e, \\
\text{(TG8)} & y \cdot i(y) & \rightarrow & e, \\
\text{(TG9)} & y \cdot (i(y) \cdot x) & \rightarrow & x, \\
\text{(TG10)} & i(x \cdot y) & \rightarrow & i(y) \cdot i(x).
\end{array}
$$

This completion procedure by hand was naive, since we were not very systematic in searching for critical pairs, and especially since we were guided by an intuitive sense only of what direction to take when generating a new reduction rule. In most cases there was no other possibility, but in case (TG10) the other direction was at least as plausible, as it is even length-decreasing. However, the other direction $i(y) \cdot i(x) \to i(x \cdot y)$ would have led to disastrous complications (described in /Knuth-Bendix-70/). ■

The main feature of the Knuth-Bendix method demonstrated in the previous example is, intuitively speaking, the resolution of all critical situations with respect to local confluence. To develop this method formally we have to clarify when such situations arise. Let R be a TRS. In checking its local confluence, any two "diverging" one-step reductions (see Fig. 2.11) must be inspected for a common reduct $\bar{t}$ so that t' and t'' are convergent (see Fig. 2.12).

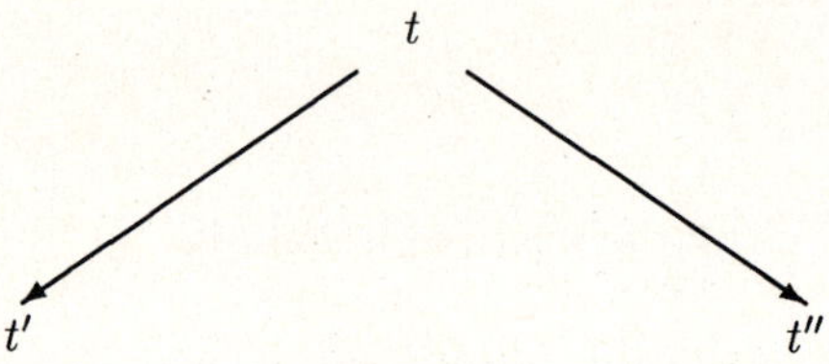

Fig. 2.11

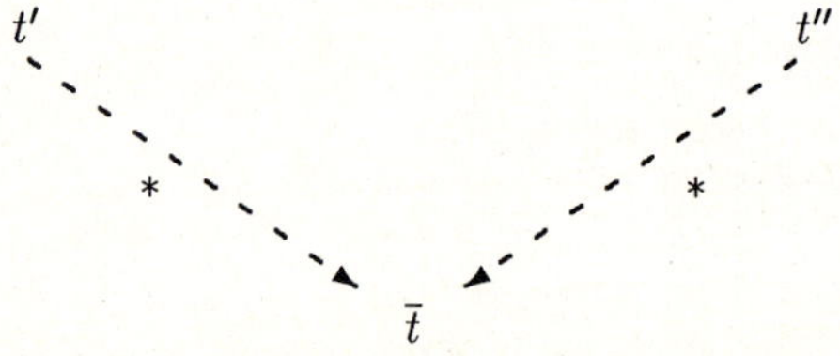

Fig. 2.12

The two one-step reductions are induced by two reduction rules of R, say $t_1 \to t_1'$ and $t_2 \to t_2'$, so that t possesses two addresses u_1 and u_2 with

$$t/u_1 = s_1^\sharp(t_1) \text{ and } t' = t[u_1/s_1^\sharp(t_1')] \text{ for some match } s_1; \text{ and}$$

$$t/u_2 = s_2^\sharp(t_2) \text{ and } t'' = t[u_2/s_2^\sharp(t_2')] \text{ for some match } s_2.$$

According to prefix-order on addresses there are two cases to be distinguished: either both addresses are incomparable or one address is a prefix of the other one.

Case (1). If u_1 and u_2 are incomparable, then $t'/u_2 = t/u_2 = s_2^\sharp(t_2)$ and $t''/u_1 = t/u_1 = s_1^\sharp(t_1)$ and hence, by definition, $t' \to_R t'[u_2/s_2^\sharp(t_2')]$ and $t'' \to_R t''[u_1/s_1^\sharp(t_1')]$. Because of $t'[u_2/s_2^\sharp(t_2')] = t[u_1/s_1^\sharp(t_1')][u_2/s_2^\sharp(t_2')] = t[u_2/s_2^\sharp(t_2')][u_1/s_1^\sharp(t_1')] = t''[u_1/s_1^\sharp(t_1')]$, we get

$$t' \to_R \bar{t} \text{ and } t'' \to_R \bar{t}$$

with $\bar{t} = t'[u_2/s_2^\sharp(t_2')] = t''[u_1/s_1^\sharp(t_1')]$.

If the addresses are incomparable, the reductions can be carried out independently without one interfering with the other so that no critical situation is caused.

Case (2). Assume, without loss of generality, that u_1 is a prefix of u_2, i.e., $u_2 = u_1 v$ for some word v. In this case it suffices to check whether $s_1^\sharp(t_1')$ and t''/u_1 have a common reduct, say $\hat{t}$. By the invariance of $\rightarrow_R^*$, t' and t'' have then also a common reduct:

$$t' = t[u_1/s_1^\sharp(t_1')] \rightarrow_R^* t[u_1/\hat{t}] \text{ and } t'' = t[u_1/(t''/u_1)] \rightarrow_R^* t[u_1/\hat{t}].$$

Note that $t/u_1 = t''/u_1$ since $t'' = t[u_2/s_2^\sharp(t_2')]$ and u_1 is assumed to be a prefix of u_2.

Subcase (2i). Assume that $v = v_1 v_2$ for some words v_1 and v_2 such that t_1/v_1 is a variable, say $t_1/v_1 = z$. Then $s_1(z)/v_2 = s_1^\sharp(t_1)/v = (t/u_1)/v = t/u_2 = s_2^\sharp(t_2)$ and, consequently, $s_1(z) \rightarrow_R s_1(z)[v_2/s_2^\sharp(t_2')]$. This leads to a new substitution s defined by

$$s(x) = \begin{cases} s_1(x) & \text{if } x \neq z, \\ s_1(z)[v_2/s_2^\sharp(t_2')] & \text{if } x = z, \end{cases}$$

for all x in X.

Using the Principle of Term Induction one may easily prove that $s_1^\sharp(t) \rightarrow_R^* s^\sharp(t)$ holds for all $t \in T_\Sigma(X)$. In particular, $s_1^\sharp(t_1') \rightarrow_R^* s^\sharp(t_1')$. Now, it suffices to show that $t''/u_1 \rightarrow_R^* s^\sharp(t_1')$. Observe that $t''/u_1 = t[u_2/s_2^\sharp(t_2')]/u_1 = (t/u_1)[v/s_2^\sharp(t_2')] = s_1^\sharp(t_1)[v/s_2^\sharp(t_2')]$ and $s_1^\sharp(t_1)[v/s_2^\sharp(t_2')] = s^\sharp(t_1')$. Thus $t''/u_1 = s^\sharp(t_1)$ and so $t''/u_1 \rightarrow_R^* s^\sharp(t_1')$ because of $s^\sharp(t_1) \rightarrow_R^* s^\sharp(t_1')$, by the stability of $\rightarrow_R^*$. Hence, t' and t'' are convergent, $t' \rightarrow_R^* \bar{t}$ and $t'' \rightarrow_R^* \bar{t}$, where $\bar{t} = t[u_1/s^\sharp(t_1')]$. Thus, subcase (2i) does also not lead to a critical situation of local confluence.

Finally, we turn to the case where local confluence is injured.

Subcase (2ii). Assume that t_1/v is a nonvariable subterm of t_1. Then

$$s_1^\sharp(t_1/v) = s_1^\sharp(t_1)/v = (t/u_1)/v = t/u_2 = s_2^\sharp(t_2).$$

Consider the TRS for groups derived in Example 1. For instance, the term $t = (i(x)\cdot x)\cdot z$ is reducible to $t' = i(x) \cdot (x \cdot z)$, by the reduction rule $(x \cdot y) \cdot z \rightarrow x \cdot (y \cdot z)$, as well as to $t'' = e \cdot z$, by the reduction rule $i(x) \cdot x \rightarrow e$. According to our notation, $t_1 = (x \cdot y) \cdot z$, $t_1' = x \cdot (y \cdot z)$, $t_2 = i(x) \cdot x$ and $t_2' = e$. The corresponding matches (substitutions) are $s_1 = \{x \mapsto i(x), y \mapsto x\}$ and $s_2 = \emptyset$ (hence $s_2^\sharp$ is the identity mapping) such that $t = s_1^\sharp(t_1)$ and $t/1 = s_2^\sharp(t_2) = t_2$. Furthermore, $u_1 = e$ (empty word), $u_2 = 1$ and so $v = 1$. Note that $t_1/v = x \cdot y$ is a nonvariable subterm of t_1. Recall that $s_1^\sharp(t_1') = i(x) \cdot (x \cdot z)$ and $t''/u_1 = e \cdot z$ are not convergent with respect to the first three reduction rules for groups.

In general $s_1^\sharp(t_1')$ and t''/u_1 must be considered as a critical pair for local confluence. But, as in the example above, we may always assume, that u_1 is the empty word. Then $t'' = t[v/s_2^\sharp(t_2')] = s_1^\sharp(t_1)[v/s_2^\sharp(t_2')]$ since $t = s_1^\sharp(t_1)$ and hence $s_1^\sharp(t_1')$ and $s_1^\sharp(t_1)[v/s_2^\sharp(t_2')]$ form a critical pair for local confluence.

In the foregoing investigations we have seen how left-hand sides of reduction rules overlap each other, producing critical pairs to be checked for confluence. Let us try to find the most general way that such overlapping occurs.

Lemma 4. *Let t_1 and t_2 be terms with disjoint variables. Assume v is an address of t_1 with t_1/v a nonvariable subterm. If s_1 and s_2 are substitutions such that*

$$s_1^\sharp(t_1/v) = s_2^\sharp(t_2),$$

then there is a substitution s with the property

$$s^\sharp(t_1/v) = s^\sharp(t_2).$$

Proof. Define a substitution s by

$$s(x) = \begin{cases} s_1(x) & \text{if} \quad x \in var(t_1), \\ s_2(x) & \text{if} \quad x \in var(t_2). \end{cases}$$

Then

$$s^\sharp(t_1/v) = s_1^\sharp(t_1/v) = s_2^\sharp(t_2) = s^\sharp(t_2).$$ ■

Now we are in a position to define most general overlappings by means of the important concept of "unification". Two terms t and t' of $T_\Sigma(X)$ are said to be ***unifiable*** if there is a substitution $s : X \to T_\Sigma(X)$ such that $s^\sharp(t) = s^\sharp(t')$; s is called a ***unifier***. Consider, for example, the terms

$$t = f(x_1, g(x_2)) \quad \text{and} \quad t' = f(h(x_3), x_4).$$

It is easily seen that t and t' are unifiable and

$$s_1 = \{x_1 \mapsto h(x_3), x_4 \mapsto g(x_2)\}$$

as well as

$$s_2 = \{x_1 \mapsto h(g(t')), x_3 \mapsto g(t'), x_4 \mapsto g(x_2)\}$$

are unifiers. Intuitively, s_1 is more general than s_2.

On the set of all unifiers of t and t' we introduce a quasi-order. Let s_1 and s_2 be unifiers of t and t'. We say that s_1 is ***more general*** than s_2, in symbols $s_1 \lesssim s_2$, if there is a substitution $s : X \to T_\Sigma(X)$ such that

$$s_2(x) = s^\sharp(s_1(x)) \quad \text{for all} \quad x \in X.$$

A unifier m of t and t' is called a ***most general unifier*** (mgu) of t and t' if $m \lesssim s$ holds for all unifiers s of t and t'. Note that a most general unifier is only unique up to renaming of variables.

Definition 5. *Let $t_1 \to t_1'$ and $t_2 \to t_2'$ be two reduction rules of a given TRS R. We assume that the variables are renamed appropriately so that t_1 and t_2 share no variables. If v is an address of t_1 such that t_1/v is a nonvariable subterm and*

$$s^\sharp(t_1/v) = s^\sharp(t_2)$$

for a mgu s of t_1/v and t_2, then $(s^\sharp(t_1'), s^\sharp(t_1)[v/s^\sharp(t_2')])$ is called a ***critical pair*** *in R.*

Both components of a critical pair $(s^\sharp(t_1'), s^\sharp(t_1)[v/s^\sharp(t_2')])$ are the two outcomes of reducing $s^\sharp(t_1)$ by $t_1 \to t_1'$ and $t_2 \to t_2'$, respectively.

Example 2. Consider the reduction rules (4) and (13) from Example 1:

$$i(x) \cdot (x \cdot z) \to z \text{ and } x \cdot (y \cdot i(x \cdot y)) \to e.$$

Let us rename the variables of the first reduction rule so that we have $t_1 = i(x') \cdot (x' \cdot z)$ and $t_2 = x \cdot (y \cdot i(x \cdot y))$. Then

(1) $t_1/2 = x' \cdot z$ is a nonvariable subterm; and

(2) $t_1/2$ and t_2 are unifiable with a mgu $s = \{x' \mapsto x, z \mapsto y \cdot i(x \cdot y)\}$.

Now we obtain

$$s^\sharp(t_1') = s^\sharp(z) = y \cdot i(x \cdot y) \text{ and } s^\sharp(t_1)[2/s^\sharp(t_2')] = (i(x) \cdot (x \cdot z))[2/e] = i(x) \cdot e.$$

Thus $(y \cdot i(x \cdot y), i(x) \cdot e)$ is a critical pair. ■

The next lemma shows that all critical situations, which one may arrive at by checking local confluence, are instances of critical pairs. In other words, the concept of critical pairs describes a critical situation in a most general way.

Lemma 5. *Let $t_1 \to t_1'$ and $t_2 \to t_2'$ be two reduction rules of a given TRS R. Assume that v is an address of t_1 with t_1/v is a nonvariable subterm. If there are substitutions s_1 and s_2 such that*

$$s_1^\sharp(t_1/v) = s_2^\sharp(t_2),$$

then there exists a critical pair (t', t'') in R and a substitution s such that

$$s^\sharp(t') = s_1^\sharp(t_1') \quad \text{and} \quad s^\sharp(t'') = s_1^\sharp(t_1)[v/s_2^\sharp(t_2')].$$

Proof. Given a TRS $R \subseteq T_\Sigma(X) \times T_\Sigma(X)$ and let $r : X \to X$ be a bijection (called a variable renaming) such that $var(t_1) \cap var(r^\sharp(t_2)) = \emptyset$. By Lemma 4, t_1/v and $r^\sharp(t_2)$ are unifiable. That is,

$$\overline{s}^\sharp(t_1/v) = \overline{s}^\sharp(r^\sharp(t_2))$$

for some substitutions $\overline{s}$, where

$$\overline{s}(x) = \begin{cases} s_1(x) & \text{if} \quad x \in var(t_1), \\ s_2(r^{-1}(x)) & \text{if} \quad x \in var(r^\sharp(t_2)). \end{cases}$$

Because of the assumption $var(t_1') \subseteq var(t_1)$ and $var(t_2') \subseteq var(t_2)$, we get $\overline{s}^\sharp(t_1') = s_1^\sharp(t_1')$ and $\overline{s}^\sharp(r^\sharp(t_2')) = s_2^\sharp(t_2')$. Suppose m is a mgu of t_1/v and $r^\sharp(t_2)$. Then $m \lesssim \overline{s}$, i.e., $\overline{s}^\sharp(t) = s^\sharp(m^\sharp(t))$ for all terms t, where s is some substitution. Define a critical pair (t', t'') as follows:

$$t' = m^\sharp(t_1') \text{ and } t'' = m^\sharp(t_1[v/r^\sharp(t_2')]).$$

Now we have to show

$$s^\sharp(t') = s_1^\sharp(t_1') \text{ and } s^\sharp(t'') = s_1^\sharp(t_1)[v/s_2^\sharp(t_2')].$$

First, $s_1^\sharp(t_1') = \overline{s}^\sharp(t_1') = s^\sharp(m^\sharp(t_1')) = s^\sharp(t')$ and, secondly, $s_1^\sharp(t_1)[v/s_2^\sharp(t_2')] = \overline{s}^\sharp(t_1)[v/\overline{s}^\sharp(r^\sharp(t_2'))] = \overline{s}^\sharp(t_1[v/r^\sharp(t_2')]) = s^\sharp(m^\sharp(t_1[v/r^\sharp(t_2')])) = s^\sharp(t'')$. ∎

The test of local confluence can now be restricted to critical pairs.

Theorem 6 (Huet's Test for Local Confluence). *A TRS is locally confluent if and only if all its critical pairs are convergent.* ∎

If a TRS is finite, then the set of all its critical pairs is finite. Hence local confluence is a decidable property for finite TRSs. Using Newman's Lemma (Proposition 1 in Section 2.2.1), we conclude that confluence is decidable for any terminating finite TRS.

In case of terminating TRSs we obtain an algorithm for testing confluence. Suppose R is a terminating TRS. Then, as we know, any term admits normal forms. When a certain strategy is chosen to compute a normal form of t, we denote the result by $NF(t)$.

Theorem 7 (Knuth-Bendix Theorem). *A terminating TRS R is confluent if and only if $NF(t') = NF(t'')$ for all critical pairs (t', t'') in R.*

Proof. Let $R \subseteq T_\Sigma(X) \times T_\Sigma(X)$ be a terminating TRS. We denote by $CP(R)$ the set of all critical pairs in R. If $(t', t'') \in CP(R)$, then, by definition, $t \to_R t'$ and $t \to_R t''$ for some term t in $T_\Sigma(X)$. Assume that R is confluent. Then every term has a unique normal form. Consequently, $NF(t') = NF(t'')$.

Sufficiency follows easily from Theorem 6. For if $NF(t') = NF(t'')$ for all $(t', t'') \in CP(R)$, then R is locally confluent. Now, since R is supposed to be terminating, R is confluent by Newman's Lemma (Proposition 1 in Section 2.2.1). ∎

In what follows we shall explain a completion procedure based on Theorem 7, which is called the ***Knuth-Bendix Completion Procedure*** (hereafter abbreviated ***KB-procedure***). Let R be a terminating finite TRS. Analysing the construction applied in

Example 1 we may generally say that the KB-procedure computes a sequence $(R_n|n \in \mathbb{N})$ of finite sets of reduction rules so that the following conditions are satisfied:

(1) R_n is terminating and equivalent to R; and

(2) Any critical pair in R_n is convergent in R_{n+1}.

Preserving termination is the crucial point in that construction. A critical pair in R_n becomes convergent in R_{n+1} only if the corresponding reduction rule preserves termination. How to make this problem manageable?

Lemma 8. *Let R be a TRS. If $>$ is a terminating fully invariant relation on $\boldsymbol{T}_\Sigma(X)$, then R is terminating whenever $t > t'$ for each reduction rule $t \to t'$ of R.*

Proof. Let R be a TRS such that $R \subseteq T_\Sigma(X) \times T_\Sigma(X)$. By definition, $\to_R$ is the least fully invariant relation on $\boldsymbol{T}_\Sigma(X)$ which includes R. If we assume that R is included in $>$, then $\to_R$ is also included in $>$. But any relation included in a terminating one is terminating, too. ∎

Lemma 8 gives the following termination proof technique. A terminating fully invariant relation is used as an additional input for the KB-procedure. Of course, we have to require implicitly that any such relation, say $>$, is recursive. That is, for each pair of terms t and t', it is decidable whether $t > t'$ holds or not. But there is an obstacle to be mentioned. When a critical pair arises during the completion process such that its two components are incomparable with respect to $>$, the KB-procedure aborts with an error message, which indicates that $>$ fails to prove termination. Then we may restart the KB-procedure with another terminating fully invariant relation.

KB-procedure

Input: finite TRS $R = \{(t_1, t_1'), ..., (t_m, t_m')\}$,
terminating fully invariant relation $>$.

Output: complete TRS $\overline{R}$, which is equivalent to R,
or error message.

Method: a sequence $(R_n|n \in \mathbb{N})$ of finite TRSs is
computed iteratively, if possible, as follows:

begin $R_{-1} := \emptyset; R_0 := \emptyset; n := 0;$
    for $i = 1, ..., m$ ***do***
        if t_i, t_i' are incomparable ***then*** stop with error message
        else if $t_i > t_i'$ ***then*** add $t_i \to t_i'$ to R_0
                        else add $t_i' \to t_i$ to R_0;
    while $R_n \neq R_{n-1}$ ***do***
    begin $R_{n+1} := R_n$; compute $NF(t)$ and $NF(t')$ for any

critical pair (t, t') in R_n;
if $NF(t), NF(t')$ are incomparable ***then*** stop with error message
else if $NF(t) > NF(t')$ ***then*** add $NF(t) \to NF(t')$ to R_{n+1}
else add $NF(t') \to NF(t)$ to R_{n+1};

$n := n + 1$

end

end.

The correctness of the KB-procedure was first completely proved by Huet /Huet-81/.

Theorem 9 (Correctness of the KB-Procedure). *Let R be a finite TRS. If the KB-procedure computes a sequence $(R_n | n \in \mathbb{N})$ of finite TRSs without error message, then the union over all R_n is a completion of R.*

Proof. Assume that the KB-procedure computes a sequence $(R_n | n \in \mathbb{N})$ of finite TRSs. Let us denote the union over all R_n by $\overline{R}$. By construction, $\overline{R}$ is confluent and, moreover, all R_n are terminating. Indeed, R_0 is terminating and the termination of R_{n-1} implies the termination of R_n, by Lemma 8. Then $\overline{R}$ is terminating, too.

It remains to show that $\overline{R}$ is equivalent to R. That is to say, $\overline{R}$ and R generate the same fully invariant congruence. First, we prove that every R_n is equivalent to R. (1) Trivially, R_0 is equivalent to R. (2) Since $R_{n-1} \subseteq R_n$, the fully invariant congruence generated by R_{n-1} is included in the fully invariant congruence generated by R_n. By construction, a reduction rule (t, t') of R_n, which is not in R_{n-1}, is a critical pair in R_{n-1}. Thus, R_n is a subset of the fully invariant congruence generated by R_{n-1} and, consequently, R_{n-1} and R_n are equivalent. Now, by induction over n, every R_n is equivalent to R.

Evidently, the fully invariant congruence generated by R is included in the fully invariant congruence generated by $\overline{R}$. On the other hand, every reduction rule (t, t') of $\overline{R}$ belongs to some R_n. Hence $\overline{R}$ is a subset of the fully invariant congruence generated by R. Thus, $\overline{R}$ is a completion of R. ■

Let us comment on the KB-procedure once more. Besides abortion there are two other possibilities, namely the KB-procedure either stops successfully or does not terminate at all. If the KB-procedure stops after finitely many steps, then $R_k = R_{k+1} = R_{k+2} = ...$ for some $k \geq 0$. In this case, R_k is the completion of R. Otherwise, when the KB-procedure does not terminate, the completion of R exists but needs infinitely many computation steps.

2.2.3 Termination of Term Rewriting Systems

Termination is a fundamental property of term rewriting systems. Specifically, the successful use of the KB-procedure depends upon our ability to prove the termination of the term rewriting systems that are generated during the process of completion. In general, as already noted, termination is an undecidable property. Therefore various termination proof methods have been developed to show that special systems terminate. Some of these techniques that are most often used in practice are presented in the sequel.

First, we make a simple but useful observation. A relation $\rightarrow$ on a set A is terminating iff its transitive closure $\rightarrow^+$ is so. That is why we always assume, without loss of generality, that our relations are transitive. Moreover, it is necessary that a terminating relation is irreflexive. This leads immediately to proper orders which are, by definition, irreflexive and transitive relations.

Definition 6. *A terminating proper order on $\boldsymbol{T}_\Sigma(X)$ is called a* ***reduction order*** *if it is fully invariant.*

A reformulation of Lemma 8 in Section 2.2.2 yields our first termination criterion. Throughout this section, the TRS R is defined over $T_\Sigma(X)$, i.e., $R \subseteq T_\Sigma(X) \times T_\Sigma(X)$.

Theorem 10 (First Termination Criterion). *A TRS R is terminating if there is a reduction order $>$ on $\boldsymbol{T}_\Sigma(X)$ such that $t > t'$ for all reduction rules $t \rightarrow t'$ in R.* ■

A construction of reduction orders is explained subsequently. Let A and B be sets. If a mapping $h : A \rightarrow B$ is given, then any terminating proper order $>$ on B induces a terminating proper order $\gg$ on A by the rule

$$x \gg y \text{ iff } h(x) > h(y)$$

for all $x, y \in A$. Note that $\gg$ may be regarded as the inverse image of $>$ under h. The problem arises: How can full invariance be preserved under inverse image? Of course, when we deal with fully invariant relations, A and B must be algebras.

Lemma 11. *If $h : \boldsymbol{A} \rightarrow \boldsymbol{B}$ is a homomorphism, then $\gg$ is invariant whenever $>$ is so.*

Proof. Assume that $>$ is an invariant proper order on $\boldsymbol{B}$. We have to show that, for all $x, y \in A, x \gg y$ implies $\tau(x) \gg \tau(y)$ for all translations τ on $\boldsymbol{A}$. Recall that a translation is either the identity mapping or a finite product of elementary translations. It is easily seen that a transitive relation is invariant iff it admits all elementary translations. So, by the transitivity of $\gg$, it is enough to prove that $x \gg y$ implies $\tau(x) \gg \tau(y)$ for all elementary translations τ on $\boldsymbol{A}$. Consider such an elementary translation τ on $\boldsymbol{A}$. By definition, $\tau(x) = \sigma^A(a_1, ..., a_{i-1}, x, a_i, ..., a_{n-1})$ for some n-ary operation σ^A and fixed elements $a_1, ..., a_{n-1}$ of A. Hence $h(\tau(x)) = h(\sigma^A(a_1, ..., a_{i-1}, x, a_i, ..., a_{n-1})) = \sigma^B(h(a_1), ..., h(a_{i-1}), h(x), h(a_i), ..., h(a_{n-1})) = \tau'(h(x))$, where τ' is an elementary translation of $\boldsymbol{B}$. Suppose $x \gg y$. Then $h(x) > h(y)$, by definition, and hence $\tau'(h(x)) > \tau'(h(y))$ for all (elementary) translations τ' on $\boldsymbol{B}$, since $>$ is assumed to be invariant. Thus $h(\tau(x)) > h(\tau(y))$. That is, $x \gg y$ implies $\tau(x) \gg \tau(y)$ for all elementary translations τ on $\boldsymbol{A}$. ■

In order to preserve stability under inverse image of a homomorphism $h : \boldsymbol{A} \rightarrow \boldsymbol{B}$, we must require that h fulfills the following condition: For every endomorphism f of $\boldsymbol{A}$

there is an endomorphism g of $\boldsymbol{B}$ such that $f \cdot h = h \cdot g$ holds. In this case, h is said to be ***stable***.

Lemma 12. *If $h : \boldsymbol{A} \to \boldsymbol{B}$ is a stable homomorphism, then $\gg$ is fully invariant whenever $>$ is so.*

Proof. Assume that $>$ is a fully invariant proper order on $\boldsymbol{B}$. By Lemma 11, $\gg$ is then invariant. So, it remains to prove that $\gg$ is stable. That is, $x \gg y$ implies $f(x) \gg f(y)$ for all endomorphisms f of $\boldsymbol{A}$. Since h is assumed to be stable, $h(f(x)) = g(h(x))$ as well as $h(f(y)) = g(h(y))$ for some endomorphism g of $\boldsymbol{B}$. Now, $h(x) > h(y)$ implies $g(h(x)) > g(h(y))$ for all endomorphisms g of $\boldsymbol{B}$, by the stability of $>$. Hence, $x \gg y$ implies $f(x) \gg f(y)$ for all endomorphisms f of $\boldsymbol{A}$. ■

To apply this method we need at least a set A with a terminating proper order $>$ on A. Then we have to define a Σ-algebra on A so that $>$ becomes fully invariant. When we succeed to find a stable homomorphism h from $\boldsymbol{T}_\Sigma(X)$ to $\boldsymbol{A}$, the inverse image of $>$ is a reduction order on $\boldsymbol{T}_\Sigma(X)$, by Lemma 12.

In what follows we consider the well-founded quasi-order of polynomials. Therefore, a Σ-algebra has to be defined on the set $\mathbb{N}\langle X\rangle$ of all polynomials with variables from X and coefficients in $\mathbb{N}$. Given a mapping I from Σ to $\mathbb{N}\langle X\rangle$ such that $I(\sigma)$ is a polynomial in n variables for every n-ary operation symbol σ of Σ, a realization of σ is defined as follows:

$$\sigma^{\mathbb{N}\langle X\rangle}(p_1, \ldots, p_n) = p(p_1, \ldots, p_n),$$

where $p = p(x_1, \ldots, x_n)$ is the polynomial associated with σ, i.e., $I(\sigma) = p$; and $p(p_1, \ldots, p_n)$ means the substitution of x_i by p_i in p. In this context, I is called a ***polynomial interpretation*** of Σ.

Furthermore, every polynomial interpretation I of Σ determines uniquely a homomorphism $I^* : \boldsymbol{T}_\Sigma(X) \to \mathbb{N}\langle X\rangle$ by the conditions (1) and (2) below:

(1) $I^*(x) = x$ for all $x \in X$; and

(2) $I^*(\sigma t_1 \ldots t_n) = I(\sigma)(I^*(t_1), \ldots, I^*(t_n))$ for every n-ary operation symbol σ of Σ and all terms $t_1, \ldots, t_n \in T_\Sigma(X)$.

In fact, I^* is the homomorphic extension of the inclusion mapping $in : X \to \mathbb{N}\langle X\rangle$, defined by $in(x) = x$ for all $x \in X$, which exists uniquely by the Principle of Finitary Recursion (Theorem 4 in Section 1.2.3); formally, $I^* = in^\sharp$.

Lemma 13. *If I is a polynomial interpretation of Σ, then I^* is a stable homomorphism.*

Proof. It suffices to show that, for every term substitution $s : X \to T_\Sigma(X)$, there is a polynomial substitution, say $S : X \to \mathbb{N}\langle X\rangle$, such that

$$I^*(s^\sharp(t)) = S^*(I^*(t)) \text{ for all } t \in T_\Sigma(X). \tag{$*$}$$

Let $s : X \to T_\Sigma(X)$ be an arbitrary term substitution. Define the polynomial substitution $S : X \to I\!N\langle X\rangle$ as follows: $S(x) = I^*(s(x))$ for all $x \in X$. Using the Principle of Term Induction we are going to prove the equation above.

(1) Basic step. Equation $(*)$ holds for all $x \in X$ because

$$I^*(s^\sharp(x)) = I^*(s(x)) = S(x) = S(I^*(x)) = S^*(I^*(x)).$$

Equation $(*)$ holds for all nullary operation symbols σ:

$$I^*(s^\sharp(\sigma)) = I^*(\sigma) = I(\sigma) = S^*(I(\sigma)) = S^*(I^*(\sigma)).$$

(2) Induction step. If $I^*(s^\sharp(t_i)) = S^*(I^*(t_i))$ for terms $t_i \in T_\Sigma(X), i = 1, \ldots, n$ (induction hypothesis), then

$$\begin{aligned} I^*(s^\sharp(\sigma t_1 \ldots t_n)) &= I^*(\sigma s^\sharp(t_1) \ldots s^\sharp(t_n)) = I(\sigma)(I^*(s^\sharp(t_1)), \ldots, I^*(s^\sharp(t_n))) \\ &= I(\sigma)(S^*(I^*(t_1)), \ldots, S^*(I^*(t_n))) = S^*(I^*(\sigma t_1 \ldots t_n)) \end{aligned}$$

for all n-ary operation symbols σ. Hence equation $(*)$ holds for all terms t in $T_\Sigma(X)$. ■

The stability of I^* can be expressed as follows:

$$I^*(t(t_1, \ldots, t_n)) = I^*(t)(I^*(t_1), \ldots, I^*(t_n))$$

for all terms $t, t_1, \ldots, t_n \in T_\Sigma(X)$, where $t(t_1, \ldots, t_n)$ means the result of substituting t_i for x_i in $t = t(x_1, \ldots, x_n)$, while $I^*(t)(I^*(t_1), \ldots, I^*(t_n))$ is the result of substituting the polynomials $I^*(t_i)$ for x_i in $I^*(t)$.

Definition 7. *Let Σ be a signature. If I is a polynomial interpretation of Σ, the proper order $>_I$ on $\mathbf{T}_\Sigma(X)$, defined by*

$$t >_I t' \text{ iff } I^*(t) > I^*(t')$$

for all $t, t' \in T_\Sigma(X)$, is called the ***polynomial interpretation order*** *based on I.*

Now we are ready to achieve our goal.

Proposition 14. *Every polynomial interpretation order is a reduction order.*

Proof. Let I be a given polynomial interpretation of Σ. Evidently, the polynomial interpretation order $>_I$ based on I is a terminating proper order on $T_\Sigma(X)$ since any polynomial order is well-founded by Theorem 25 in Section 1.3.6. Observe that the proper polynomial order is fully invariant. Hence, by Lemma 12, $>_I$ is also fully invariant because I^* is a stable homomorphism as shown in Lemma 13. That is, $>_I$ is a reduction order. ■

Although polynomial interpretation orders are a powerful tool for proving termination, the problem is to find appropriate polynomials associated with the operation symbols, a task which can be quite tedious; hopefully, computer experiments will lead to some heuristics. An implementation is described in /Ben Cherifa-Lescanne-86/.

Example 1. Consider a signature consisting of two binary operation symbols, say $+$ and $\cdot$. A polynomial interpretation is defined by associating the polynomial $x + y$ with $+$ and xy^2 with $\cdot$. Hence

$$I^*(x + y) = x + y \text{ and } I^*(x \cdot y) = xy^2.$$

Then, e.g., $I^*(x \cdot (y + z)) = x \cdot I^*(y + z)^2 = xy^2 + xz^2 + xyz + xzy$ and $I^*((x \cdot y) + (x \cdot z)) = I^*(x \cdot y) + I^*(x \cdot z) = xy^2 + xz^2$. Thus

$$x \cdot (y + z) >_I (x \cdot y) + (x \cdot z).$$ ■

Example 2. Using the First Termination Criterion (Theorem 10) we can prove that the TRS for groups, derived in Example 1 in the previous section, is terminating. Let us choose the following polynomial interpretation I determined by

$$\begin{aligned} I^*(e) &= 2, \\ I^*(i(x)) &= x^2, \\ I^*(x \cdot y) &= 2xy + x. \end{aligned}$$

For instance, $I^*((x \cdot y) \cdot z) = 4xyz + 2xz + 2xy + x$, while $I^*(x \cdot (y \cdot z)) = 4xyz + 2xy + x$. That is,

(1) $(x \cdot y) \cdot z >_I x \cdot (y \cdot z)$.

The next inequality:

(2) $i(x) \cdot x >_I e$

holds because of $I^*(i(x) \cdot x) = 2x^3 + x^2 > 2 = I^*(e)$.
Similarly, we derive

(3) $e \cdot x >_I x$,

(4) $i(x) \cdot (x \cdot z) >_I z$,

(5) $y \cdot e >_I y$,

(6) $i(i(y)) >_I y$,

(7) $i(e) >_I e$,

(8) $y \cdot i(y) >_I e$,

(9) $y \cdot (i(y) \cdot x) >_I x$,

(10) $i(x \cdot y) >_I i(y) \cdot i(x)$.

The last inequality, which is perhaps surprising, is necessary for termination. The special choice of the polynomials above results in this inequality. ■

Example 3. Given a signature with a unary operation symbol f and a binary operation symbol $*$, we take the following three polynomial interpretations I_1, I_2 and I_3 determined by

$$I_1^*(f(x)) = 2x \quad \text{and} \quad I_1^*(x * y) = xy,$$

$$I_2^*(f(x)) = x^2 \quad \text{and} \quad I_2^*(x * y) = xy + y,$$

$$I_3^*(f(x)) = x^2 \quad \text{and} \quad I_3^*(x * y) = xy + x.$$

Their different effect is visible as follows:

$$f(x) * f(y) >_{I_1} f(x * y),$$

$$f(x * y) >_{I_2} f(x) * f(y),$$

$$f(x * y) >_{I_3} f(y) * f(x).$$

■

In their pioneering paper /Knuth-Bendix-70/, Knuth and Bendix first presented a reduction order. Let Σ be an arbitrary signature with at least one nullary operation symbol. We assume that Σ is equipped with a total order $\leq$, called ***precedence order***, and a so-called ***weight function*** $w : \Sigma \to \mathbb{N}$ satisfying the following two conditions: (i) The weight of every nullary operation symbol is positive; and (ii) If the weight of a unary operation symbol σ is zero, then σ is the greatest element in Σ. That is, every unary operation symbol has positive weight, with the possible exception of the greatest element provided it is unary.

The weight function can be extended to a mapping $w^\sharp$ from $T_\Sigma(X)$ to $\mathbb{N}$ by the rules

$$w^\sharp(x) = min\{w(\sigma) | \sigma \in \Sigma_0\} \text{ for all } x \in X; \text{ and}$$

$$w^\sharp(\sigma t_1 \ldots t_n) = w(\sigma) + w^\sharp(t_1) + \ldots + w^\sharp(t_n)$$

for every n-ary operation symbol σ of Σ and all terms $t_1, \ldots, t_n$ in $T_\Sigma(X)$. For any term t, let $|t|_x$ be the number of occurences of x in t.

Definition 8. *Let Σ be a signature. If $\leq$ is a total order on Σ and $w : \Sigma \to \mathbb{N}$ is a weight function, then the induced **Knuth-Bendix order** $>_{KB}$ on $T_\Sigma(X)$ is defined as follows. For any two terms t and t', $t >_{KB} t'$ iff either*

(1) $w^\sharp(t) > w^\sharp(t')$ *and* $|t|_x > |t'|_x$ *for all* $x \in X$*; or*

(2) $w^\sharp(t) = w^\sharp(t')$ *and* $|t|_x = |t'|_x$ *for all* $x \in X$ *and either*

(2a) $t = \sigma ... \sigma t'$ *and* σ *is the greatest element in* Σ*; or*

(2b) $t = \sigma t_1 \dots t_m, t' = \sigma' t'_1 \dots t'_n$ *and either (i)* $\sigma > \sigma'$*; or (ii)* $\sigma = \sigma'$ *and* $t_1 = t'_1, ..., t_{i-1} = t'_{i-1}, t_i >_{KB} t'_i$ *for some* $i = 1, ..., n$*, where* $m = n$*.*

Proposition 15. *Every Knuth-Bendix order is a reduction order.*

Proof. Let $\leq$ be a total order on a given signature Σ and let $w : \Sigma \to I\!N$ be a weight function. Evidently, the induced Knuth-Bendix order $>_{KB}$ is a proper order on $T_\Sigma(X)$. To show that $>_{KB}$ is invariant we assume $t_1 >_{KB} t_2$ for any two terms $t_1, t_2 \in T_\Sigma(X)$. Consider an arbitrary term $t \in T_\Sigma(X)$. Then we have to prove $t[u/t_1] >_{KB} t[u/t_2]$ for every address u of t. But, by the transitivity of $>_{KB}$, it suffices to quantify over all addresses u of t with $u \in I\!N_+$. First, we suppose $w^\sharp(t_1) > w^\sharp(t_2)$ and $|t_1|_x > |t_2|_x$ for all $x \in X$. Obviously, $w^\sharp(t[u/t_1]) > w^\sharp(t[u/t_2])$ and $|t[u/t_1]|_x > |t[u/t_2]|_x$ for all $x \in X$. Hence, by condition (1) of the definition above, $t[u/t_1] >_{KB} t[u/t_2]$. Secondly, suppose $w^\sharp(t_1) = w^\sharp(t_2)$ and $|t_1|_x = |t_2|_x$ for all $x \in X$. Then, of course, $w^\sharp(t[u/t_1]) = w^\sharp(t[u/t_2])$ and $|t[u/t_1]|_x = |t[u/t_2]|_x$ for all $x \in X$. Now, by condition (2b) subcase (ii) of the definition above, we conclude $t[u/t_1] >_{KB} t[u/t_2]$. Thus $>_{KB}$ is indeed invariant. Similarly, one shows that $>_{KB}$ is stable and hence fully invariant.

So it remains to prove that $>_{KB}$ is terminating. If $>_{KB}$ were not terminating, an infinite chain $t_0 >_{KB} t_1 >_{KB} t_2 >_{KB} ...$ of terms would exist. By definition, $var(t_n) \subseteq var(t_0)$ for all $n \geq 1$. Therefore, we can take a ground substitution $s : X \to T_\Sigma$ such that, by the stability of $>_{KB}$, $s^\sharp(t_0) >_{KB} s^\sharp(t_1) >_{KB} s^\sharp(t_2) >_{KB} ...$ becomes an infinite chain of ground terms. Furthermore, without loss of generality, we can assume that all these ground terms have the same weight w.

Now let t be a ground term with k_n operation symbols of arity n. It is easy to prove inductively that

$$k_0 = 1 + k_2 + 2k_3 + 3k_4 + ...$$

Since each nullary operation symbol has positive weight, we have $w \geq k_0$; so there are only a finite number of choices for $k_0, k_2, k_3, ...$, if we are to have a ground term of weight w. Furthermore, if each unary operation symbol has a positive weight, we have $w \geq k_1$, so there would be only finitely many ground terms of weight w. Therefore an infinite chain $t_0 >_{KB} t_1 >_{KB} t_2 >_{KB} ...$ is impossible unless there is a unary operation symbol of weight zero.

Assume there is a unary operation symbol σ with weight zero. Define a mapping h from T_Σ into itself by $h(t)$ to be the ground term obtained from t by erasing all occurences of σ. Clearly, if t is a ground term of weight w, so is $h(t)$. By the observation above, only finitely many ground terms $h(t)$ exist of weight w. To complete the proof of the proposition, we will show there is no infinite chain $t_0 >_{KB} t_1 >_{KB} t_2 >_{KB} ...$ of ground terms such that $h(t_0) = h(t_1) = h(t_2) = ...$ Observe that each ground term t of T_Σ may be regarded as a word over Σ. That is, $t = \sigma^{r_1}\alpha_1\sigma^{r_2}\alpha_2...\sigma^{r_n}\alpha_n$, where $r_1, \ldots, r_n \in \mathbb{N}$ and $\alpha_1, \ldots, \alpha_n$ are words over $\Sigma - \{\sigma\}$. Define $r(t) = (r_1, \ldots, r_n)$, an n-tuple of natural numbers. It is now easy to verify that, if $h(t) = h(t')$, we have $t >_{KB} t'$ iff $r(t) >_{lex} r(t')$ in lexicographic order. Since $>_{lex}$ is terminating (on words of equal length), the proof of Proposition 15 is complete. ■

Note that if σ were a unary operation symbol of weight zero such that $\sigma < \tau$ for some $\tau \in \Sigma$, $>_{KB}$ would not be terminating since there would be an infinite chain of ground terms of the form $\tau\alpha >_{KB} \sigma\tau\alpha >_{KB} \sigma\sigma\tau\alpha >_{KB} ....$ And if we have nullary operation symbols of weight zero, other counterexamples arise; for example, if σ is nullary and τ is binary, both of weight zero, then $\tau\tau\sigma\sigma\sigma >_{KB} \tau\sigma\tau\tau\sigma\sigma\sigma >_{KB} \tau\sigma\tau\sigma\tau\tau\sigma\sigma\sigma >_{KB} ....$ This accounts for the restrictions we have imposed on the arities and weights.

Example 4. Consider the group signature with precedence $e < \cdot < i$ and weights: $w(e) = 1, w(i) = 0$ and $w(\cdot) = 1$. Then, for instance,

$$(x \cdot y) \cdot z >_{KB} x \cdot (y \cdot z)$$

by condition (2b) subcase (ii) since $x \cdot y >_{KB} x$; or

$$i(x \cdot y) >_{KB} i(y) \cdot i(x)$$

by condition (2b) subcase (i) because $i > e$; or

$$i(i(y)) >_{KB} y$$

by condition (2a).

Knuth and Bendix /Knuth-Bendix-70/ have used this order to prove the termination of the term rewriting system for groups. ■

We are now going to generalize the First Termination Criterion. The following result /Manna-Ness-70/ serves as a basis.

Proposition 16. *A TRS R is terminating if there is a terminating invariant proper order $>$ on $T_\Sigma(X)$ such that $s^\sharp(t) > s^\sharp(t')$ for all reduction rules $t \to t'$ in R and every substitution $s : X \to T_\Sigma(X)$.*

Proof. Given a TRS R, the associated term reduction $\to_R$ is defined to be the fully invariant relation generated by R. Using Lemma 9 in Section 2.1.2, $\to_R$ is then the invariant closure of $sta(R)$, where $sta(R)$ denotes the stable closure of R. Note that $sta(R) = \{(s^\sharp(t), s^\sharp(t')) | t \to t'$ in R and $s : X \to T_\Sigma(X)$ is a substitution$\}$.

If we assume that $>$ is a terminating invariant proper order on $T_\Sigma(X)$ such that $s^\sharp(t) > s^\sharp(t')$ for all $t \to t'$ in R and every substitution $s : X \to T_\Sigma(X)$, then $sta(R) \subseteq >$ and hence $\to_R \subseteq >$, since $>$ is invariant. Thus $\to_R$ is terminating. ■

In proving the termination of a finite TRS R we can even weaken the assumption of the preceding proposition by requiring a proper order $>$ on $T_\Sigma(X)$ which is terminating only over all terms that could appear in any one reduction sequence; formally, $\rightarrow_R^+ \cap >$ must be terminating. Following /Dershowitz-82/ we call a proper order $>$ on $T_\Sigma(X)$ for which $\rightarrow_R^+ \cap >$ is terminating for any finite R, ***terminating for reductions***, the advantage being that a reduction sequence for a finite TRS R can only involve a finite number of operation symbols and finitely many variables. /Dershowitz-82/ has first recognized the usefulness of quasi-simplification orders in this context.

Proposition 17. *If $\lesssim$ is any quasi-simplification order on $T_\Sigma(X)$, then $>$ is terminating for reductions.* ■

The proof follows directly from Theorem 11 in Section 1.4.2.

As an immediate consequence we derive the following termination proof method.

Corollary. *A finite TRS R is terminating if there is a simplification order $\leq$ on $T_\Sigma(X)$ such that $s^\sharp(t) > s^\sharp(t')$ for all reduction rules $t \rightarrow t'$ in R and every substitution $s : X \rightarrow T_\Sigma(X)$.*

Proof. If $\leq$ is a given simplification order on $T_\Sigma(X)$, then, by definition, $\leq$ is invariant and hence $>$ is invariant, too. Since $>$ is terminating for reductions, by Proposition 17, we obtain a terminating invariant proper order, namely $\rightarrow_R^+ \cap >$. Now, it follows from Proposition 16 that R is terminating. ■

To apply quasi-simplification orders causes the following problem. In contrast to partial orders, invariance of a quasi-order does not necessarily imply the invariance of its proper part. But, in spite of this difficulty, the termination proof method presented above can be generalized so that quasi-simplification orders are applicable.

Theorem 18 (Second Termination Criterion). *A finite TRS R is terminating if there is a quasi-simplification order $\lesssim$ on $T_\Sigma(X)$ such that $s^\sharp(t) > s^\sharp(t')$ for all reduction rules $t \rightarrow t'$ in R and every substitution $s : X \rightarrow T_\Sigma(X)$.*

Proof. Let $\lesssim$ be a given quasi-simplification order on $T_\Sigma(X)$. If R were not terminating, then an infinite reduction sequence $t_0 \rightarrow_R t_1 \rightarrow_R t_2 \rightarrow_R \ldots$ would exist and hence, under the assumption of the theorem, $t_0 \gtrsim t_1 \gtrsim t_2 \gtrsim \ldots$. Now we intend to select an infinite strictly descending subsequence, which leads then to a contradiction since $>$ is terminating for reductions by Proposition 17.

Observe that $t_i > t_{i+1}$ holds whenever t_i can be matched with a left-hand side of some reduction rule in R. Now we can suppose, without loss of generality, that this happens because, otherwise, we choose a subterm of t_0 so that in its initiated reduction sequence such a situation appears for some index i. By transitivity, we obtain $t_0 > t_i$; put $t_i = t_i'$. Continuing with the sequence we find a term, say t_2', such that $t_1' > t_2'$. In this manner, an infinite strictly descending chain $t_0 > t'_1 > t'_2 > \ldots$ is constructed. This yields a contradiction. ■

Now we turn to quasi-simplification orders on the set of ground terms T_Σ, which is therefore tacitily assumed to be nonempty. A mapping $s : X \to T_\Sigma$ is called a ***ground substitution***.

Theorem 19 (Dershowitz's Termination Criterion). *A finite TRS R is terminating if there is a quasi-simplification order $\lesssim$ on T_Σ such that $s^\sharp(t) > s^\sharp(t')$ for all reduction rules $t \to t'$ in R and every ground substitution $s : X \to T_\Sigma$.*

Proof. Let $\lesssim$ be a given quasi-simplification order on T_Σ. Take a fixed but arbitrary ground substitution $s_0 : X \to T_\Sigma$ and consider the inverse image of $\lesssim$ under $s_0^\sharp$: $t \sqsubseteq t'$ iff $s_0^\sharp(t) \lesssim s_0^\sharp(t')$ for all terms $t, t' \in T_\Sigma(X)$. By Lemma 11, $\sqsubseteq$ is a quasi-simplification order on $T_\Sigma(X)$. By Theorem 18, it suffices to show $s_0^\sharp(s^\sharp(t)) > s_0^\sharp(s^\sharp(t'))$ for all reduction rules $t \to t'$ in R and every substitution $s : X \to T_\Sigma(X)$. But this is obviously true since the product of any substitution s with s_0 is a ground substitution. ■

An important class of quasi-simplification orders is obtainable by comparing paths through terms. In the literature, such ***path orders*** have been intensively studied (cf. /Bachmair-Plaisted-85/, /Dershowitz-82/, /Jouannaud-Lescanne-Reinig-82/, /Kapur-Narendran-Sivakumar-85/, /Lescanne-84/, /Rusinowitch-87/).

Definition 9. *Let Σ be a signature. If $\lesssim$ is a quasi-order on Σ, the induced **recursive path order** $\lesssim_{rpo}$ on T_Σ is defined as follows. For any two ground terms t and t' such that $t = \sigma t_1 \ldots t_m$ and $t' = \sigma' t'_1 \ldots t'_n$, $t \lesssim_{rpo} t'$ iff either*

(1) $\sigma < \sigma'$ and $\{t_1, \ldots, t_m\} \ll_{rpo} \{t'\}$; or

(2) $\sigma \sim \sigma'$ and $\{t_1, \ldots, t_m\} \lll_{rpo} \{t'_1, \ldots, t'_n\}$; or

(3) $\sigma \not\lesssim \sigma'$ and $\{t\} \lll_{rpo} \{t'_1, \ldots, t'_n\}$,

where $\lll_{rpo}$ is the multiset order induced by $\lesssim_{rpo}$.

The order, as given above, is defined on ground terms, but can be extended to nonground terms by including the following clause: $x \lesssim_{rpo} t$ iff $x \in var(t)$.

Proposition 20. *Every recursive path order (on ground terms) is a quasi-simplification order.*

Proof. Let $\lesssim$ be a quasi-order on a given signature Σ. The induced recursive path order on T_Σ is denoted by $\lesssim_{rpo}$. We have to show that (i) $\lesssim_{rpo}$ is a quasi-order; (ii) $\lesssim_{rpo}$ is invariant; and (iii) $\lesssim_{rpo}$ has the subterm property, i.e., $t \lesssim_{rpo} t'$ whenever t is a subterm of t'.

Claim: If $t \lesssim_{rpo} t'$ for two terms t and t', then

(a) $t_i \lesssim_{rpo} t'$ for any immediate subterm t_i of t; and

(b) $t \lesssim_{rpo} t''$ for any term t'' such that t' is an immediate subterm of t'' (t'' is an immediate superterm of t').

Let $t = \sigma t_1 \ldots t_m$ and $t' = \sigma' t'_1 \ldots t'_n$ and assume that $t \lesssim_{rpo} t'$. We prove (a) and (b) simultaneously by term induction. For (a), consider the three cases of the definition.

(1) If $\sigma < \sigma'$, then $\{t_1, \ldots, t_m\} \lll_{rpo} \{t'\}$. By the definition of $\lll_{rpo}$, $t_i \lesssim_{rpo} t'$ for $i = 1, \ldots, m$.

(2) If $\sigma \sim \sigma'$, then $\{t_1, \ldots, t_m\} \lll_{rpo} \{t'_1, \ldots, t'_n\}$. By the definition of $\lll_{rpo}$, for each $i = 1, \ldots, m$ there is an index j with $j = 1, \ldots, n$ such that $t_i \lesssim_{rpo} t'_j$. By the induction hypothesis (b) it follows that $t_i \lesssim_{rpo} t'$.

(3) If $\sigma \not\lesssim \sigma'$, then $\{t\} \lll_{rpo} \{t'_1, \ldots, t'_n\}$. By the definition of $\lll_{rpo}, t \lesssim_{rpo} t'_j$ for some $j = 1, \ldots, n$. By the induction hypothesis (a), $t_i \lesssim_{rpo} t'_j$ for all $i = 1, \ldots, m$, and by the induction hypothesis (b), we get $t_i \lesssim_{rpo} t'$.

For (b), let $t'' = \sigma'' t''_1 \ldots t''_p$ and suppose $t' = t''_j$ for some $j = 1, \ldots, n$. We again consider the three cases of the definition. Note that $t_i \lesssim_{rpo} t'$ for all $i = 1, \ldots, m$.

(1) Let $\sigma < \sigma''$. It follows from the induction hypothesis (b) that $t_i \lesssim_{rpo} t''$, and therefore $\{t_1, \ldots, t_m\} \lll_{rpo} \{t''\}$. Thus, by the definition of $\lesssim_{rpo}, t \lesssim_{rpo} t''$.

(2) Let $\sigma \sim \sigma''$. We already know (a) that $t_i \lesssim_{rpo} t'$ for all $i = 1, \ldots, m$. Thus, by the definition of $\lll_{rpo}$, $\{t_1, \ldots, t_m\} \lll_{rpo} \{t''_1, \ldots, t''_p\}$ since $t' = t''_j$ for some $j = 1, \ldots, p$ by assumption. Hence, by the definition of $\lesssim_{rpo}, t \lesssim_{rpo} t''$.

(3) Let $\sigma \not\lesssim \sigma''$. We are given that $t \lesssim_{rpo} t'$. It follows from the definition of $\lll_{rpo}$ that $\{t\} \lll_{rpo} \{t''_1, \ldots, t''_p\}$ since $t' = t''_j$ for some $j = 1, \ldots, p$ by assumption. Hence, by the definition of $\lesssim_{rpo}, t \lesssim_{rpo} t''$. This proves the claim.

Now we are going to show the required properties of $\lesssim_{rpo}$.

(i) $\lesssim_{rpo}$ is a quasi-order. Observe that $\lesssim_{rpo}$ is reflexive. Thus, it remains to show transitivity. Let $t = \sigma t_1 \ldots t_m, t' = \sigma' t'_1 \ldots t'_n$ and $t'' = \sigma'' t''_1 \ldots t''_p$. We assume that

$t \lesssim_{rpo} t'$ and $t' \lesssim_{rpo} t''$. By term induction we show $t \lesssim_{rpo} t''$. Here we have to consider five cases.

(1) Let $\sigma < \sigma''$. By the definition of $\lesssim_{rpo}, t \lesssim_{rpo} t''$ if $\{t_1, \ldots, t_m\} \lll_{rpo} \{t''\}$. That is, we have to show that $t_i \lesssim_{rpo} t''$ for $i = 1, \ldots, m$. By the claim (a), $t_i \lesssim_{rpo} t'$ for $i = 1, \ldots, m$. Together with $t' \lesssim_{rpo} t''$ we conclude $t_i \lesssim_{rpo} t''$ by the induction hypothesis.

(2) Let $\sigma \sim \sigma''$. We must show that $\{t_1, \ldots, t_m\} \lll_{rpo} \{t''_1, \ldots, t''_p\}$. To proceed we distinguish two subcases.

(2a) If $\sigma \sim \sigma' \sim \sigma''$, then $\{t_1, \ldots, t_m\} \lll_{rpo} \{t'_1, \ldots, t'_n\}$, by the assumption $t \lesssim_{rpo} t'$, and $\{t'_1, \ldots, t'_n\} \lll_{rpo} \{t''_1 \ldots t''_p\}$, by the assumption $t' \lesssim_{rpo} t''$. That is, for all $i = 1, \ldots, m$ there exists an index j with $j = 1, \ldots, n$ such that $t_i \lesssim_{rpo} t'_j$, and for all $j = 1, \ldots, n$ there exists an index k with $k = 1, \ldots, p$ such that $t'_j \lesssim_{rpo} t''_k$. By the induction hypothesis, for all $i = 1, \ldots, m$ there exists an index k with $k = 1, \ldots, p$ such that $t_i \lesssim_{rpo} t''_k$. Hence $\{t_1, \ldots, t_m\} \lll_{rpo} \{t''_1, \ldots, t''_p\}$.

(2b) If $\sigma' \not\lesssim \sigma''$, then $\{t'\} \lll_{rpo} \{t''_1, \ldots, t''_p\}$, by the assumption $t' \lesssim_{rpo} t''$. That is, $t' \lesssim_{rpo} t''_j$ for some j with $j = 1, \ldots, p$. By the claim (a), we have $t_i \lesssim_{rpo} t'$ for all $i = 1, \ldots, m$. Hence, by the induction hypothesis, $t_i \lesssim_{rpo} t''_j$ for all $i = 1, \ldots, m$. Thus, $\{t_1, \ldots, t_m\} \lll_{rpo} \{t''_1, \ldots, t''_p\}$.

(3) Let $\sigma \not\lesssim \sigma''$. We must show that $\{t\} \lll_{rpo} \{t''_1, \ldots, t''_p\}$. Assume that $\sigma' \not\lesssim \sigma''$. Then $\{t'\} \lll_{rpo} \{t''_1, \ldots, t''_p\}$ by the assumption $t' \lesssim_{rpo} t''$. That is, $t' \lesssim_{rpo} t''_j$ for some j with $j = 1, \ldots, p$. Together with the assumption $t \lesssim_{rpo} t'$ we get $t \lesssim_{rpo} t''_j$ by the induction hypothesis. Hence $\{t\} \lll_{rpo} \{t''_1, \ldots, t''_p\}$.

(4) Let $\sigma \not\lesssim \sigma'$. Then $\{t\} \lll_{rpo} \{t'_1, \ldots, t'_n\}$ by the assumption $t \lesssim_{rpo} t'$. That is, $t \lesssim_{rpo} t'_j$ for some j with $j = 1, \ldots, n$. By the claim (a), $t'_i \lesssim_{rpo} t''$ for all $i = 1, \ldots, n$ follows from $t' \lesssim_{rpo} t''$. Now, we have $t \lesssim_{rpo} t'_j$ and $t'_j \lesssim_{rpo} t''$. It follows that $t \lesssim_{rpo} t''$ by the induction hypothesis.

These five cases cover all possible relations between σ, σ' and σ''. Thus, transitivity is proved.

(ii) $\lesssim_{rpo}$ is invariant. Since $\lesssim_{rpo}$ is transitive it suffices to show that $\lesssim_{rpo}$ admits all elementary translation, i.e., for all terms t and t', $t \lesssim_{rpo} t'$ implies $\tau(t) \lesssim_{rpo} \tau(t')$, where τ is an arbitrary elementary translation. Note that $\tau(x) = \sigma t_1 \ldots t_{i-1} x t_{i+1} \ldots t_n$ for some n-ary operation symbol σ and fixed terms $t_1, \ldots, t_{i-1}, t_{i+1}, \ldots, t_n$. If $t \lesssim_{rpo} t'$, then $\{t_1, \ldots, t_{i-1}, t, t_{i+1}, \ldots, t_n\} \lessapprox_{rpo} \{t_1, \ldots, t_{i-1}, t', t_{i+1}, \ldots, t_n\}$. Hence, by clause (2) of the Definition 10, $\tau(t) \lesssim_{rpo} \tau(t')$.

(iii) $\lesssim_{rpo}$ has the subterm property. Since $\lesssim_{rpo}$ is transitive it suffices to show that $t \lesssim_{rpo} t'$ whenever t is an immediate subterm of t'. Therefore, assume that t is such an immediate subterm of given term t'. By the reflexivity of $\lesssim_{rpo}$, we have $t \lesssim_{rpo} t$. Now, by claim (b), $t \lesssim_{rpo} t'$. ■

An advantageous feature of recursive path orders should be mentioned here. We can always start with a discrete precedence of operation symbols, and add to it only as necessary to satisfy given inequalities between terms. That is to say a recursive path order is ***incremental***; a property useful for its implementation.

Example 5 (after /Dershowitz-87/). Let Σ be a signature with an unary operation symbol $\neg$ and two binary operation symbols $\vee$ and $\wedge$ ordered by the following precedence: $\neg > \wedge > \vee$. Consider the TRS R consisting of the reduction rules (R1) to (R5) below:

$$
\begin{array}{lrcl}
\text{(R1)} & \neg\neg x & \rightarrow & x, \\
\text{(R2)} & \neg(x \vee y) & \rightarrow & \neg x \wedge \neg y, \\
\text{(R3)} & \neg(x \wedge y) & \rightarrow & \neg x \vee \neg y, \\
\text{(R4)} & x \wedge (y \vee z) & \rightarrow & (x \wedge y) \vee (x \wedge z), \\
\text{(R5)} & (x \vee y) \wedge z & \rightarrow & (x \wedge z) \vee (y \wedge z).
\end{array}
$$

To show that R is terminating, by Theorem 19, we have to verify the following inequalities:

$$
\begin{array}{lrcl}
(1) & \neg\neg t & >_{rpo} & t, \\
(2) & \neg(t \vee t') & >_{rpo} & \neg t \wedge \neg t', \\
(3) & \neg(t \wedge t') & >_{rpo} & \neg t \vee \neg t', \\
(4) & t \wedge (t' \vee t'') & >_{rpo} & (t \wedge t') \vee (t \wedge t''), \\
(5) & (t \vee t') \wedge t'' & >_{rpo} & (t \wedge t'') \vee (t' \wedge t''),
\end{array}
$$

for any ground terms t, t' and t''.

The first inequality (1) follows from the subterm condition of simplification orderings. By the definition of $>_{rpo}$, to show that the second inequality (2) holds, we must prove that $\neg(t \vee t') >_{rpo} \neg t$ and $\neg(t \vee t') >_{rpo} \neg t'$. Now, since the outermost operation symbols are the same, namely $\neg$, in both cases one must show that $t \vee t' >_{rpo} t$ and $t \vee t' >_{rpo}$

t'. But this is true by the subterm condition. By an analogous argument, the third inequality (3) holds. For the fourth inequality (4), we must show $t \wedge (t' \vee t'') >_{rpo} t \wedge t'$ and $t \wedge (t' \vee t'') >_{rpo} t \wedge t''$. Again the outermost operation symbols are the same, namly $\wedge$, so we have to show that $\{t, t' \vee t''\} \gg_{rpo} \{t, t'\}$ and $\{t, t' \vee t''\} \gg_{rpo} \{t, t''\}$. These two inequalities between multisets hold, since the element $t' \vee t''$ is greater than both t' and t'' with which it is replaced. Similarly, the fifth inequality (5) may be shown to hold. Therefore, this TRS R is indeed terminating. ∎

3 Universal Algebra

In the last two decades universal algebra has become useful and important in theoretical computer science. In particular, structural aspects such as syntax and semantics, data abstraction, etc., are mainly investigated by methods of universal algebra. To describe, for example, the semantics of abstract data types or program schemes, algebras are generally needed as models in which all syntactic symbols involved in the considered objects are interpreted. In this approach, classes of algebras have to be manipulated in a suitable way.

For that reason some set theoretic constructions must be carried over to algebras by which algebras can be composed and decomposed. Section 3.1 introduces some basic constructions.

In Section 3.2, Birkhoff's characterization of equationally defined classes of algebras is presented. A logical concept (equationally defined class of algebras) is characterized in terms of nonlogical notions. A class of algebras is said to be a variety if it is closed under subalgebras, images and direct products. Then the famous Birkhoff Variety Theorem states that a class of algebras is equationally definable if and only if it is a variety. Analogously, the logical notion of consequence is algebraically characterizable by means of fully invariant congruences. This leads naturally to a related proof system called equational logic. The second main result is Birkhoff's Completeness Theorem for Equational Logic.

Along the same line implicationally defined classes of algebras are studied in Section 3.3. But here we have to distinguish three subcases: (1) implications with an infinite number of variables and an infinite number of premises; (2) implications with a finite number of variables but an infinite number of premises; and (3) implications with a finite number of variables as well as a finite number of premises. Implications of the second kind are called finitary implications, while implications of the third kind are called universal Horn clauses.

3.1 Basic Constructions

First, we deal with subalgebras and (homomorphic) images. If we want to know something about a given algebra we may try to get the information by studying its subalgebras or images provided the algebra can be rebuilt by them. The related composition principles are directed union and direct limit. We are especially interested in composing algebras from "simpler" ones, where simple refers to some finiteness condition.

Section 3.1.1 deals with subalgebras and generation. The main result states that every algebra is the directed union of its finitely generated subalgebras.

In Section 3.1.2, images of an algebra are considered. In this case generation has to be replaced by presentation and, on the other hand, direct limits are the corresponding compositions. Similarly, every algebra is isomorphic to a direct limit of finitely presented algebras.

Section 3.1.3 studies a third kind of composition based on direct products. However, it turns out that no useful decompositions of algebras are derivable by means of direct products. Therefore, subdirect products are introduced as a more general notion. As a main result we get that every algebra is isomorphic to a subdirect product of subdirectly irreducible algebras.

Reduced products and ultraproducts are briefly surveyed in Section 3.1.4.

3.1.1 Subalgebras and Generation

The notion of an algebra has already been introduced as a set together with a family of finitary operations. It is often advantageous to specify operations by a signature Σ. Recall that a Σ-algebra $\boldsymbol{A}$ is a pair (A, Σ^A) consisting of a set A called the carrier of $\boldsymbol{A}$ and a family $\Sigma^A = (\sigma^A \mid \sigma \in \Sigma)$ of operations σ^A on A, where σ^A is the realization of the operation symbol σ of Σ. Whenever a collection $\mathcal{K}$ of algebras is considered in the sequel we shall tacitly assume that all algebras in $\mathcal{K}$ are Σ-algebras for a fixed signature Σ. To emphasize this assumption we may, more precisely, speak of a collection of ***similar*** algebras.

Now we introduce our first concept of a finite description based on the generation of an algebra $\boldsymbol{A}$. Let $\langle X \rangle$ denote the subalgebra of $\boldsymbol{A}$ generated by a subset X of A. By definition, $\langle X \rangle$ is the least subalgebra of $\boldsymbol{A}$ (with respect to set inclusion) containing X. An algebra $\boldsymbol{A}$ is called ***finitely generated*** if $A = \langle X \rangle$ for some finite subset X of A. If $X = \{x_1, \ldots, x_n\}$, we simply write $\langle x_1, \ldots, x_n \rangle$ instead of $\langle \{x_1, \ldots, x_n\} \rangle$. In particular, we say that an algebra is ***cyclic*** if it can be generated by a single element.

Example 1. Consider a group G. We want to exhibit all cyclic subgroups. Let $x \in G$. The finite powers x^n, $n \in \mathbb{N}$, of x are defined as follows:

$$x^0 = e \ (e \text{ is the unit element of } G) \quad \text{and} \quad x^n = x^{n-1} \cdot x \quad \text{for } n \geq 1.$$

Powers can be extended to integers by the rule: x^{-n} is the inverse of x^n for all $n \in \mathbb{N}$. The least positive integer n such that $x^n = e$ is called the ***order*** of x.

If x has finite order n, then all powers $x^0 = e$, $x^1 = x$, $x^2, \ldots, x^{n-1}$ are pairwise distinct. It is easy to show that $\{x^k \mid k = 0, 1, \ldots, n-1\}$ is a subgroup since it is closed under the operations. In particular, multiplication and inverses of these powers are given by

$$x^k \cdot x^l = \begin{cases} x^{k+l} & \text{if } k + l < n, \\ x^{(k+l)-n} & \text{if } k + l \geq n; \end{cases}$$

and $x^{-k} = x^{n-k}$ for all $k, l = 0, 1, \ldots, n-1$. On the other hand, every subgroup containing x includes $\{x^k \mid k = 0, 1, \ldots, n-1\}$. Hence $\{x^k \mid k = 0, 1, \ldots, n-1\}$ is the least subgroup containing x. That is, $\langle x \rangle = \{x^k \mid k = 0, 1, \ldots, n-1\}$.

We say that x has infinite order if, for all $n \in \mathbb{N}$, $x^n = e$ implies $n = 0$. In this case we derive $\langle x \rangle = \{x^p \mid p \in \mathbb{Z}\}$. Note that all powers x^p, $p \in \mathbb{Z}$, are pairwise distinct.

Two cyclic subgroups $\langle x \rangle$ and $\langle y \rangle$ are isomorphic iff either x and y have the same finite order or x and y have infinite order. ■

Let $\boldsymbol{A}$ be an arbitrarily given algebra. Recall that the closure system of all subalgebras of $\boldsymbol{A}$ is algebraic by definition. According to the Birkhoff-Frink Theorem (Lemma 5 in Section 1.2.4) the corresponding closure operator $\langle\ \rangle$ satisfies the finiteness condition

$$\langle X \rangle = \bigcup \{\langle Y \rangle \mid Y \subseteq X \text{ and } Y \text{ is finite}\}$$

for all subsets X of A. Hence $\boldsymbol{A}$ is the union over all its finitely generated subalgebras.

Here the question arises whether the union over a set of similar algebras is again an algebra. In general, however, this is not true. Consider, e.g., the algebras $(\mathbb{N}, +)$ and $(\mathbb{N}, \cdot)$, where $+$ and $\cdot$ are addition and multiplication of natural numbers, respectively. Of course, there is no algebra $(\mathbb{N}, *)$, where $*$ is a binary operation, such that $(\mathbb{N}, +)$ and $(\mathbb{N}, \cdot)$ are subalgebras of $(\mathbb{N}, *)$. Therefore a necessary condition has to be required so that the union over a set $\mathcal{K}$ of algebras is again an algebra: for each two algebras $\boldsymbol{A}$ and $\boldsymbol{B}$ of $\mathcal{K}$ there must be an algebra $\boldsymbol{C}$ in $\mathcal{K}$ such that $\boldsymbol{A}$ and $\boldsymbol{B}$ are subalgebras of $\boldsymbol{C}$. This is what we will call a directed set. But we prefer to formulate this condition for a family of algebras indexed by a directed poset I, i.e., for all pairs of indices $i, j \in I$ there is an upper bound k in I with $i, j \leq k$.

We say that a family $(\boldsymbol{A}_i \mid i \in I)$ of similar algebras is ***directed*** if, for all $i, j \in I$, $\boldsymbol{A}_i$ is a subalgebra of $\boldsymbol{A}_j$ whenever $i \leq j$.

When $(\boldsymbol{A}_i \mid i \in I)$ is a directed family of algebras [1)], the union A over all carriers A_i, $A = \bigcup(A_i \mid i \in I)$, can be made into an algebra. Let $x_1, \ldots, x_n$ be elements of A. Then $x_1 \in A_{i_1}, \ldots, x_n \in A_{i_n}$ for some indices $i_1, \ldots, i_n$ of I. Since I is directed there is an upper bound k such that $i_1, \ldots, i_n \leq k$ and hence $x_1, \ldots, x_n \in A_k$. For each n-ary operation symbol σ of Σ we put

$$\sigma^A(x_1, \ldots, x_n) = \sigma^{A_k}(x_1, \ldots, x_n).$$

It is essential to observe that the definition of σ^A is independent of the special choice of k as an upper bound. Thus σ^A is well-defined. Evidently, each σ^{A_i}, $i \in I$, can be regarded as a partial mapping from A^n to A with $Dom(\sigma^{A_i}) = A^n$. Since $(\sigma^{A_i} \mid i \in I)$ is directed its supremum exists and equals σ^A, i.e., $\sigma^A = \bigcup(\sigma^{A_i} \mid i \in I)$.

[1)] A directed family of algebras always means a directed family of similar algebras.

Definition 1. *Let* $(\boldsymbol{A}_i | i \in I)$ *be a directed family of algebras. The algebra* $\boldsymbol{A}$ *with carrier* $A = \bigcup(A_i | i \in I)$ *and operations* $\sigma^A = \bigcup(\sigma^{A_i} | i \in I)$ *is called the* ***directed union*** *of* $(\boldsymbol{A}_i | i \in I)$*; written* $\bigcup(\boldsymbol{A}_i | i \in I)$.

The conclusion of the Birkhoff-Frink Theorem stated above can now be reformulated.

Theorem 1. *Every algebra is the directed union over all its finitely generated subalgebras.* ∎

Although this result seems to be rather general it may happen that the finitely generated subalgebras are "simpler" than the given algebra. This possibility is illustrated by the following example.

Example 2. We equip the set $A = \{x \in \mathbb{Q} | 0 \leq x < 1\}$ with a binary operation $*$ and a unary operation i. For $x, y \in A$ we set

$$x * y = \begin{cases} x + y & \text{if } x + y < 1, \\ x + y - 1 & \text{if } x + y \geq 1; \end{cases}$$

and

$$i(x) = \begin{cases} 1 - x & \text{if } x \neq 0, \\ 0 & \text{if } x = 0. \end{cases}$$

Obviously, $(A, *, i, 0)$ is an abelian group and each of its elements has a finite order.

What are the finitely generated subgroups? Given a finite subset X of A, say $X = \{x_1, \ldots, x_n\}$, we have $x_i = p_i/q_i$ for some positive integers p_i and q_i $(i = 1, \ldots, n)$. If q denotes the least common multiple of $q_1, \ldots, q_n$, then $x_i = m_i p_i / q$ for some positive integer m_i $(i = 1, \ldots, n)$. Hence $x_1, \ldots, x_n$ are elements of the cyclic subgroup generated by $1/q$ and consequently $\langle X \rangle$ is a subgroup of $\langle 1/q \rangle$. Therefore every finitely generated subgroup is finite.

As we will see all finite subgroups are cyclic. Let U be a finite subgroup. If $U = \{a_1, \ldots, a_n\}$, then $a_i^n = 0$ for all $i = 1, \ldots, n$, which is a general property of any finite subgroup of a given group, as the reader may convince her/himself. Hence, $a_i = p_i/n$ for some positive integer p_i $(i = 1, \ldots, n)$, whence $U \subseteq \langle 1/n \rangle$. Since $\langle 1/n \rangle$ has exactly n elements it follows that $U = \langle 1/n \rangle$. Thus every finite subgroup of n elements is generated by $1/n$. Let us denote the cyclic subgroup $\langle 1/n \rangle$ by $\boldsymbol{Z}_n$ for $n \in \mathbb{N}$.

If m is a divisor of n, then $\boldsymbol{Z}_m$ is a subgroup of $\boldsymbol{Z}_n$. This leads to a partial order on the index set $\mathbb{N}$: $m \leq n$ iff m is a divisor of n. Observe that $\mathbb{N}$ is directed with respect to this partial order. Therefore $(\boldsymbol{Z}_n | n \in \mathbb{N})$ is a directed family of subalgebras. By Theorem 1, we have $\boldsymbol{A} = \bigcup(\boldsymbol{Z}_n | n \in \mathbb{N})$, which says that the abelian group $\boldsymbol{A}$ is the directed union over all its finite cyclic subgroups. ∎

The generation of an algebra has a certain influence on homomorphisms. Let $\boldsymbol{A}$ be an algebra generated by X. Every homomorphism h from $\boldsymbol{A}$ to another algebra $\boldsymbol{B}$ can be cut down to a homomorphism from $\boldsymbol{A}$ to the subalgebra of $\boldsymbol{B}$ generated by $f(X)$

since $f(\langle X \rangle) = \langle f(X) \rangle$, which follows from the "bottom-up construction" of $\boldsymbol{A}$ (see Proposition 3 in Section 1.1.2) using the Principle of Structural Induction. Similarly, we can prove that two homomorphisms from $\boldsymbol{A}$ to $\boldsymbol{B}$ are equal if their restrictions on X are so. In other words, a homomorphism from $\boldsymbol{A}$ to $\boldsymbol{B}$ is already uniquely determined by its restriction to the generators of $\boldsymbol{A}$.

Now consider the particular case where h is a homomorphism from $\boldsymbol{A}$ to the directed union over a directed family $(\boldsymbol{A}_i | i \in I)$ of algebras. Let in_i, $i \in I$, denote the inclusion of $\boldsymbol{A}_i$ into the directed union $\bigcup(\boldsymbol{A}_i | i \in I)$. If $\boldsymbol{A}$ is finitely generated, then h factorizes through some component. Assume $X = \{x_1, \ldots, x_n\}$ is a finite generating set of $\boldsymbol{A}$. Then $h(x_1) \in A_{i_1}, \ldots, h(x_n) \in A_{i_n}$ and so $h(x_1) \in A_k, \ldots, h(x_n) \in A_k$ for some k, by the assumption that $(\boldsymbol{A}_i | i \in I)$ is a directed set. Hence h can be cut down to a homomorphism from $\boldsymbol{A}$ to $\boldsymbol{A}_k$, say $g : \boldsymbol{A} \to \boldsymbol{A}_k$; and, of course, $h = g \cdot in_k$ as shown in Fig. 3.1.

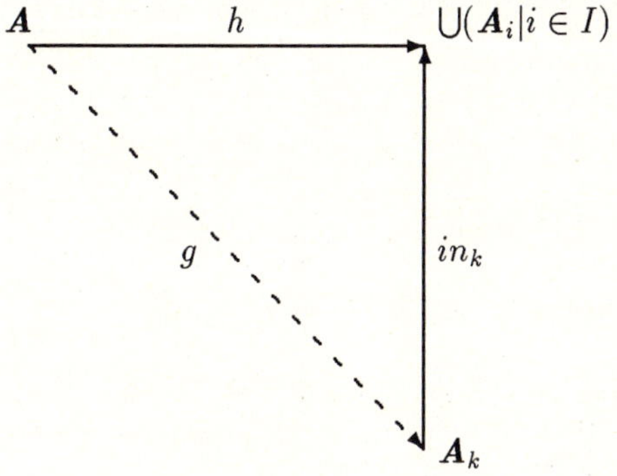

Fig. 3.1

Let us mention a further important property, which may be considered as the universal property of directed unions. Given a directed family $(\boldsymbol{A}_i | i \in I)$ of algebras. If $(h_i | i \in I)$ is a family of homomorphisms $h_i : \boldsymbol{A}_i \to \boldsymbol{B}$, $i \in I$, such that h_i equals the restriction of h_j to A_i whenever $i \leq j$, then there exists a unique homomorphism h from the directed union $\bigcup(\boldsymbol{A}_i | i \in I)$ to $\boldsymbol{B}$ with $h_i = in_i \cdot h$ for all $i \in I$.

3.1.2 Images and Presentation

In this section we study algebras by their images. Let $\boldsymbol{A}$ and $\boldsymbol{B}$ be similar algebras. Recall that a homomorphism h from $\boldsymbol{A}$ to $\boldsymbol{B}$ is a structure preserving mapping from A to B. We say that $\boldsymbol{B}$ is a homomorphic image or ***image***, for short, of $\boldsymbol{A}$ if there is a surjective homomorphism from $\boldsymbol{A}$ to $\boldsymbol{B}$.

Contrary to subalgebras we run here into a set theoretic problem. The collection of all images of a given algebra $\boldsymbol{A}$ is a proper class, while the collection of all subalgebras of $\boldsymbol{A}$ is certainly a set, namely a subset of the power set of A. This leads to the following question:

Is there any **set** of representatives among all images of $\boldsymbol{A}$?

What are typical representatives for images? Every quotient $\boldsymbol{A}/R$ of $\boldsymbol{A}$ is an image, where R is any congruence of $\boldsymbol{A}$, since the natural mapping $nat_R : A \to A/R$, defined by $nat_R(x) = [x]_R$, is a surjective homomorphism. Of course, all quotients of $\boldsymbol{A}$ form a set because there is only a set of congruences on $\boldsymbol{A}$. Specifically, all congruences on $\boldsymbol{A}$ build a subset of the power set of $A \times A$. Our question may now be reformulated: Is any image isomorphic to a quotient?

Two similar algebras $\boldsymbol{A}$ and $\boldsymbol{B}$ are called ***isomorphic***, in symbols $\boldsymbol{A} \cong \boldsymbol{B}$, if there is a bijective homomorphism f from $\boldsymbol{A}$ to $\boldsymbol{B}$; f itself is called an ***isomorphism***. Observe that f^{-1} is then also an isomorphism.

To solve this problem a congruence $\sim$ is associated with any homomorphism h from $\boldsymbol{A}$ to $\boldsymbol{B}$ by the rule: $x \sim y$ iff $h(x) = h(y)$, called the ***kernel*** of h and written $ker\ h$.

Theorem 2 (Homomorphism Theorem). *If h is a surjective homomorphism from an algebra $\boldsymbol{A}$ to a similar algebra $\boldsymbol{B}$, then $\boldsymbol{B}$ is isomorphic to $\boldsymbol{A}/ker\ h$.*

Proof. Let h be a surjective homomorphism from $\boldsymbol{A}$ to $\boldsymbol{B}$. We define a mapping $f : A/ker\ h \to B$ by

$$f([x]) = h(x) \quad \text{for all } x \in A.$$

In fact, f is well-defined. For if $[x] = [y]$, then $h(x) = h(y)$, by the definition of $ker\ h$. Moreover, f is injective since $f([x]) = f([y])$ implies $h(x) = h(y)$; and hence $[x] = [y]$. Since h is assumed to be surjective, so f is surjective, too. It is easily seen that f is a homomorphism. Thus f is an isomorphism. ∎

Based on the Homomorphism Theorem the class of all images of an algebra $\boldsymbol{A}$ is representable by the set of all quotient algebras of $\boldsymbol{A}$. In other words, the concept of a surjective homomorphism can be replaced by that of a congruence.

The compatibility of the subalgebra and quotient constructions is expressible as follows. Let $\boldsymbol{A}$ be an algebra and $\boldsymbol{B}$ be a subalgebra of $\boldsymbol{A}$. If R is a congruence on $\boldsymbol{A}$, then $R \cap (B \times B)$, denoted by R_B, is a congruence of $\boldsymbol{B}$. We frequently omit the subscript B if no confusion may arise. Consider the subset B_R of A defined by $B_R = \{a \in A | B \cap [a]_R \neq \emptyset\}$. Since B_R is closed under the operations, $\boldsymbol{B}_R$ is a subalgebra of $\boldsymbol{A}$. By a straightforward proof we get: $\boldsymbol{B}/R$ is isomorphic to $\boldsymbol{B}_R/R$. This statement is usually called the ***First Isomorphism Theorem***. Now let us consider the iteration of quotient construction. Given two congruences R and S on an algebra $\boldsymbol{A}$ such that $S \subseteq R$, we define R/S by the rule: $[x]_S(R/S)[y]_S$ iff xRy. It is left to the reader to show that R/S is a congruence on $\boldsymbol{A}/S$. Now we have: $(\boldsymbol{A}/S)/(R/S)$ is isomorphic to $\boldsymbol{A}/R$. This property is usually called the ***Second Isomorphism Theorem***, which says that every iterated quotient construction is already obtainable in one step.

Although the essence of the relationship between homomorphisms and congruences seems to be the intrinsic characterization of "all images" by the Homomorphism Theorem, the following basic properties are often used:

(1) Every homomorphism h induces a congruence, namely its kernel $ker\ h$.

(2) Every congruence R is induced by a surjective homomorphism, namely by the natural homomorphism nat_R.

Let $\boldsymbol{A}$, $\boldsymbol{B}$ and $\boldsymbol{C}$ be similar algebras. If $f : \boldsymbol{A} \to \boldsymbol{B}$ and $g : \boldsymbol{A} \to \boldsymbol{C}$ are homomorphisms such that f is a surjection, then there is a, necessarily unique, homomorphism $h : \boldsymbol{B} \to \boldsymbol{C}$ iff $kerf \subseteq kerg$ (see Fig. 3.2).

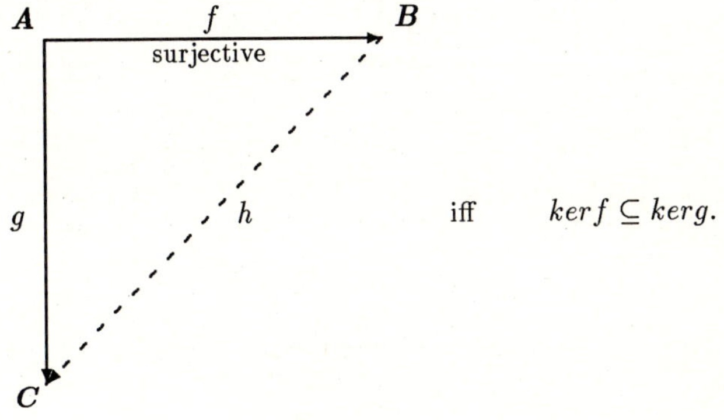

Fig. 3.2

In case g is also a surjective homomorphism we write $g \precsim f$ if there is a homomorphism h such that $g = f \cdot h$. Clearly, $\precsim$ is a quasi-order on all surjective homomorphisms starting from $\boldsymbol{A}$. The induced equivalence is denoted by $\cong$. We say that f and g are ***isomorphic*** if $f \cong g$. Note that $f \cong g$ iff $g = f \cdot h$ for a unique isomorphism h.

Now a one-to-one correspondence between surjective homomorphisms and congruences can be established. If $f : \boldsymbol{A} \to \boldsymbol{B}$ is a surjective homomorphism, then f is isomorphic to the natural homomorphism $nat_{kerf} : \boldsymbol{A} \to \boldsymbol{A}/kerf$, i.e.,

$$f \cong nat_{kerf}.$$

Conversely, if R is a congruence on $\boldsymbol{A}$, then the kernel of $nat_R : \boldsymbol{A} \to \boldsymbol{A}/R$ coincides with R, i.e.,

$$R = ker\ nat_R.$$

Proposition 3 (Image Factorization). *Every homomorphism h admits a factorization $h = g \cdot f$, where f is a surjective and g is an injective homomorphism. This factorization is unique in the following sense. If $h = f' \cdot g'$ is another factorization with f' a surjective* *and g' an injective homomorphism, then there exists a unique homomorphism d such that $f \cdot d = f'$ and $d \cdot g' = g$.*

Proof. Let h be a homomorphism from an algebra $\boldsymbol{A}$ to an algebra $\boldsymbol{B}$.

(1) Existence of a factorization:

It is easily seen that the set theoretic image $h(A)$ is closed with respect to the operations in $\boldsymbol{B}$. Hence $h(A)$ is a subalgebra of $\boldsymbol{B}$. Now we define two mappings f and g as follows: f is h cut down to $h(A)$, i.e.,

$$f : A \to h(A) \quad \text{with } f(a) = h(a) \text{ for all } a \text{ in } A$$

and g is the inclusion of $h(A)$ into B, i.e.,

$$g : h(A) \to B \quad \text{with } g(c) = c \quad \text{for all } c \text{ in } h(A).$$

Evidently, f is a surjective and g is an injective homomorphism. By definition, $h = f \cdot g$.

(2) Uniqueness of the factorization:

Assume that f, f' are surjective and g, g' are injective homomorphisms such that $f \cdot g = f' \cdot g'$ (see Fig. 3.3).

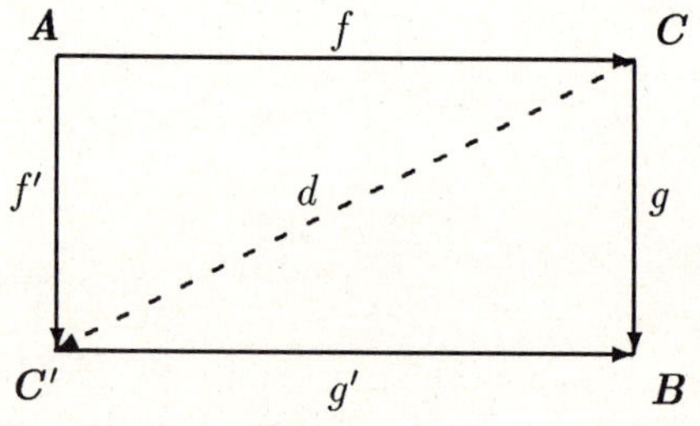

Fig. 3.3

Claim: There exists exactly one homomorphism d such that $f \cdot d = f'$ and $d \cdot g' = g$.

We define $d : \boldsymbol{C} \to \boldsymbol{C}'$ as follows:

$$d(c) = f'(a) \text{ whenever } f(a) = c.$$

Indeed, d is defined for all c in C since f is surjective. But we have to ensure more, namely that d is well-defined. If we assume $f(a) = f(a')$ for some $a, a' \in A$, then we have to show that $f'(a) = f'(a')$. Now, $f(a) = f'(a)$ implies $g(f(a)) = g(f(a'))$. Because of $f \cdot g = f' \cdot g'$, we get $g'(f'(a)) = g'(f'(a'))$ which implies $f'(a) = f'(a')$ by the injectivity of g'.

It remains to show that d is unique. If $d' : \boldsymbol{C} \to \boldsymbol{C}'$ is a homomorphism with $f \cdot d' = f'$ and $d' \cdot g' = g$, then $d' \cdot g' = g = d \cdot g'$, which means $g'(d'(c)) = g'(d(c))$ for all c in C. Since g' is injective we conclude that $d'(c) = d(c)$ for all c in C, i.e., $d' = d$. ■

Note. The homomorphism d is always an isomorphism. It is sometimes called the ***diagonal fill-in***. ■

Our second concept of a finite description will be based on the fact that every algebra is representable as an image.

Proposition 4. *Every algebra is an image of a term algebra.*

Proof. Let $\boldsymbol{A}$ be an algebra generated by a set X. Consider the inclusion mapping $f : X \to A$ defined by $f(x) = x$ for all $x \in X$. By the Principle of Finitary Algebraic Recursion (Theorem 4 in Section 1.2.3), f admits a unique homomorphic extension $f^\sharp : \boldsymbol{T}_\Sigma(X) \to \boldsymbol{A}$ such that $f^\sharp(x) = f(x)$ for all x in X. The set theoretic image $f^\sharp(T_\Sigma(X))$ of $T_\Sigma(X)$ under $f^\sharp$ is a subalgebra of $\boldsymbol{A}$, say $\boldsymbol{B}$. X is a subset of B because $X = f(X) = f^\sharp(X)$. By assumption, $\boldsymbol{A}$ is the least subalgebra of itself containing X. Thus $\boldsymbol{B}$ equals $\boldsymbol{A}$ and so $f^\sharp$ is surjective, which proves the assertion. ■

As a conclusion we get that any algebra $\boldsymbol{A}$ is isomorphic to $\boldsymbol{T}_\Sigma(G)/\sim$ where G is a suitable set and $\sim$ is a congruence on $\boldsymbol{T}_\Sigma(G)$. Since all congruences on $\boldsymbol{T}_\Sigma(G)$ form a closure system, $\sim$ can be generated by a relation R on $T_\Sigma(G)$; often elements of G are called ***generators***, while elements of R are called ***relators***. The pair (G, R) is said to be a ***presentation*** of $\boldsymbol{A}$. Conversely, any pair (G, R) consisting of a set G and a relation R on $T_\Sigma(G)$ presents an algebra, namely the quotient of $\boldsymbol{T}_\Sigma(G)$ modulo the congruence generated by R. Let us denote this quotient by $\langle G; R\rangle$. A presentation (G, R) is ***finite*** if G and R are finite. Now we are in a position to introduce a second concept of a finite description. An algebra $\boldsymbol{A}$ is called ***finitely presented*** if $\boldsymbol{A}$ is isomorphic to $\langle G; R\rangle$ for some finite presentation (G, R).

Remark. Any presentation (G, R) of an algebra leads to a word problem (cf. Section 2.1.2):

> Is it decidable whether two terms of $T_\Sigma(G)$ are equivalent modulo the congruence generated by R?

In general, even for finite presentations the word problem is unsolvable. In spite of the fact that a finite presentation seems to be optimal as a finite description of an (infinite) algebra $\boldsymbol{A}$ we must therefore be aware that $\boldsymbol{A}$ need not be manageable from the algorithmic point of view. ■

Example 1. Let Σ be the stack signature introduced by a nullary operation symbol *nil* and unary operation symbols *pop* and $push_x$ with $x \in V$, where V is a given finite alphabet. Consider the Σ-algebra

$$\boldsymbol{A} = (A, pop^A, (push_x^A \mid x \in V), nil^A)$$

where the carrier A is the set of all words over V and, for $w \in A$,

$pop^A(e) = e$ and $pop^A(w) = w'$ if $w = xw'$ for some $x \in V$;

$push_x^A(w) = xw$ for $x \in V$; and

$nil^A = e$ (empty word).

We claim that $\boldsymbol{A}$ is presented by the empty set of generators and the set R of the following relators:

$(pop\ nil, nil)$ and

$(pop\ push_x\ t, t)$ for all ground terms t and all $x \in V$.

The ground terms of T_Σ can be identified with strings since only unary operation symbols are applied on the single nullary operation symbol *nil*; to each ground term t a word $\bar{t}$ over $\{p\} \cup V$ is uniquely assigned when *pop* is mapped onto p; $push_x$ is mapped onto x for $x \in V$; and *nil* is mapped onto the empty word e. For instance, $t = push_x\ pop\ push_y\ push_z\ nil$ is mapped onto the word $\bar{t} = xpyz$. In the sequel t and $\bar{t}$ are identified.

Denote by $\sim$ the Σ-congruence on $W(\{p\} \cup V)$ generated by R. Then

$$t_1 \sim t_2 \text{ iff } (t_1 = wp \text{ and } t_2 = w) \text{ or } (t_1 = wpxw' \text{ and } t_2 = ww').$$

Observe that to each word w over $\{p\} \cup V$ there exists a unique word w' over V such that $w \sim w'$. Hence $\boldsymbol{A} = W(\{p\} \cup V)/\sim$. (Without the identification we would have that $\boldsymbol{A}$ is isomorphic to $W(\{p\} \cup V)/\sim$).

Define a family $(R_n | n \in \mathbb{N})$ of a subset R_n of R as follows

$$R_0 = \{(pop\ nil\ , nil)\}$$

and

$$R_n = R_0 \cup \{(pop\ push_x\ t, t) | \, x \in V \text{ and } |t| < n\} \quad \text{for } n \geq 1.$$

What arc the finitely presented algebras $\boldsymbol{A}_n = \langle \emptyset; R_n \rangle$? The carrier of $\boldsymbol{A}_n$ is the set of all words w over $\{p\} \cup V$ with the property that p occurs in w only if there is a suffix $w' \in W(V)$ with length greater than n.

Formally, $A_n = W(V) \cup W(\{p\} \cup V) \cdot V^{n+1}$ for $n \in \mathbb{N}$.

The algebras $\boldsymbol{A}_n$ are given by

$$\boldsymbol{A}_n = (A_n, pop^{A_n}, (push_x^{A_n} | \, x \in V), nil^{A_n}),$$

where

$$pop^{A_n}(w) = \begin{cases} pop^A(w) & \text{if } |w| \leq n,\ w \in A_n, \\ pw & \text{if } |w| > n,\ w \in A_n; \end{cases}$$

$$push_x^{A_n}(w) = xw \qquad \text{for } x \in V,\ w \in A_n; \text{ and}$$

$$nil^{A_n} = e.$$

We see that the pushdown principle is not generally satisfied in $\boldsymbol{A}_n$. Only for words w of length less than n do we have

$$pop^{A_n}(push_x^{A_n}(w)) = w$$

for each x of V. ■

Now we turn to the question:

How can an algebra be composed from finitely presented algebras?

Let $\boldsymbol{A}$ be an algebra presented by (G, R). Let I be the set of all finite presentations (X, P), where X is a finite subset of G and P is a finite relation included in the restriction of the congruence $con(R)$ generated by R to $T_\Sigma(X)$. A partial order $\leq$ is defined as follows:

$$(X, P) \leq (Y, Q) \quad \text{iff} \quad X \subseteq Y \text{ and } P \subseteq Q.$$

Evidently, I is directed. Each $i = (X, P)$ of I presents an algebra $\boldsymbol{A}_i = \langle X; P \rangle$. Furthermore, for all $i, j \in I$ with $i \leq j$ there are homomorphisms

$$h_{ij} : \boldsymbol{A}_i \to \boldsymbol{A}_j$$

defined by $h_{ij}([t]_{con(P)}) = [t]_{con(Q)}$, where $i = (X, P)$ and $j = (Y, Q)$. By $con(P)$ and $con(Q)$ we denote the congruences generated by P and Q, respectively. The family $(h_{ij} | i, j \in I)$ of homomorphisms fulfills the following conditions:

(1) $h_{ii} = id_{A_i}$ for all $i \in I$; and

(2) $h_{ij} \cdot h_{jk} = h_{ik}$ for all $i \leq j \leq k$ in I.

This motivates the following definition. Let $(I, \leq)$ be a directed poset. We say that a family $(\boldsymbol{A}_i | i \in I)$ of similar algebras is a ***direct family*** if there are homomorphisms h_{ij} from $\boldsymbol{A}_i$ to $\boldsymbol{A}_j$ such that the conditions (1) and (2) above are satisfied. Often the family of homomorphisms $h_{ij} : \boldsymbol{A}_i \to \boldsymbol{A}_j$ itself is called a direct family. For notational convenience, when referring to direct families we will omit explicit mention of I, and we usually write $(h_{ij} : \boldsymbol{A}_i \to \boldsymbol{A}_j)$.

Example 2. Take the family $(\boldsymbol{A}_n | n \in \mathbb{N})$ of the finitely presented algebras $\boldsymbol{A}_n$ from Example 1. For all $m \leq n$ we define homomorphisms $h_{m,n}$ from $\boldsymbol{A}_m$ to $\boldsymbol{A}_n$ by

$$h_{m,n}(w) = \begin{cases} w & \text{if } |w| \leq m+1, \\ w' & \text{if } |w| > m+1 \text{ and there is } w' \in A_n \text{ such that } (w, w') \in con(R_n) \end{cases}$$

for all w in A_m. Note that w' is uniquely determined. It is easy to show that these homomorphisms form a direct family. ■

Given a direct family $(h_{ij} : \boldsymbol{A}_i \to \boldsymbol{A}_j)$, a new algebra may be constructed in a canonical way. We build the quotient, denoted by A_∞, of the union over all carrier sets A_i modulo the equivalence relation $\sim$ defined by $x \sim y$ iff

$x \in A_i$, $y \in A_j$ and there exists $z \in A_k$ such that $i, j \leq k$ and $h_{ik}(x) = z = h_{jk}(y)$.

Without loss of generality we assume that the carrier sets A_i are pairwise disjoint.

Now let us define operations on the set A_∞. Given n elements of A_∞, say $[x_1], \ldots, [x_n]$, there are indices $i_1, \ldots, i_n$ in I such that $x_1 \in A_{i_1}, \ldots, x_n \in A_{i_n}$. By the definition of the equivalence $\sim$, there are elements $y_1, \ldots, y_n$ in A_k for some k such that $x_i \sim y_i$ for $i = 1, \ldots, n$. For any n-ary operation symbol σ we set

$$\sigma^{A_\infty}([x_1], \ldots, [x_n]) = [\sigma^{A_k}(y_1, \ldots, y_n)].$$

It is easy to check that σ^A is well-defined.

Moreover, each carrier set A_i can be mapped into A_∞. The related mappings

$$h_i : A_i \to A_\infty \quad \text{defined by } h_i(x) = [x] \text{ for } x \in A_i$$

are, in fact, homomorphisms satisfying the condition

$$h_i = h_{ij} \cdot h_j \quad \text{for all } i \leq j \text{ of } I.$$

Definition 2. *Let $(h_{ij} : \boldsymbol{A}_i \to \boldsymbol{A}_j)$ be a direct family of algebras. The algebra with carrier set A_∞ and operations as defined above is called the* ***direct limit*** *of $(h_{ij} : \boldsymbol{A}_i \to \boldsymbol{A}_j)$. The associated family $(h_i : \boldsymbol{A}_i \to \boldsymbol{A}_\infty)$ is called the* ***limit cone****.*

Note. Direct limits are also called inductive limits or colimits and the associated limit cones are then called limit cocones. ■

Lemma 5. *The limit cone $(h_i : \boldsymbol{A}_i \to \boldsymbol{A}_\infty)$ has the following universal property:*

(L) For every family $(f_i : \boldsymbol{A}_i \to \boldsymbol{B})$ of homomorphisms with $f_i = h_{ij} \cdot f_j$ for all $i \leq j$ there exists a unique homomorphism $f : \boldsymbol{A}_\infty \to \boldsymbol{B}$ such that $f_i = h_i \cdot f$ for all $i \in I$ (see Fig. 3.4).

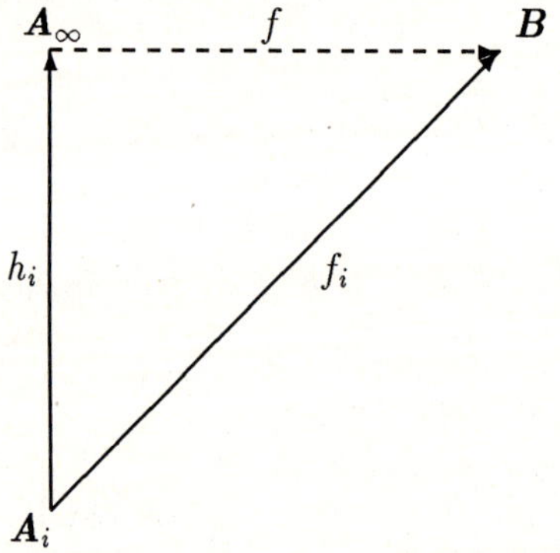

Fig. 3.4

Proof. (1) Existence of f:

For any element $[x]$ of A_∞ there is an index i of I such that x belongs to A_i. Then the mapping

$$f : A_\infty \to B \quad \text{determined by } f([x]) = f_i(x)$$

is certainly well-defined. Suppose $[x] = [y]$ for some $x \in A_i$ and $y \in A_j$. Since I is directed we have $i, j \leq k$ for some k of I such that there is an element z in A_k with $h_{ik}(x) = z = h_{jk}(y)$. Thus $f_i(x) = f_k(h_{ik}(x)) = f_k(z) = f_k(h_{jk}(y)) = f_j(y)$.

It is an easy exercise to check that f is a homomorphism.

(2) Uniqueness of f:

Assume that $g : \boldsymbol{A}_\infty \to \boldsymbol{B}$ is a homomorphism with $f_i = h_i \cdot g$ for all $i \in I$. Then $g([x]) = g(h_i(x)) = f_i(x) = f([x])$ for all x in A_i and all $i \in I$. Hence g equals f. ∎

Direct limits are uniquely determined, up to isomorphism, by the associated limit cone as stated subsequently.

Proposition 6. *Let $(h_{ij} : \boldsymbol{A}_i \to \boldsymbol{A}_j)$ be a direct family of algebras. A family $(f_i : \boldsymbol{A}_i \to \boldsymbol{A})$ of homomorphisms has the universal property (L) if and only if $\boldsymbol{A}$ is isomorphic to the direct limit of $(h_{ij} : \boldsymbol{A}_i \to \boldsymbol{A}_j)$.*

Proof. It suffices to show that for any two families $(f_i : \boldsymbol{A}_i \to \boldsymbol{A})$ and $(g_i : \boldsymbol{A}_i \to \boldsymbol{B})$, which have the universal property (L), the algebras $\boldsymbol{A}$ and $\boldsymbol{B}$ are isomorphic. By definition, there are exactly one homomorphism $f : \boldsymbol{B} \to \boldsymbol{A}$ and one homomorphism $g : \boldsymbol{A} \to \boldsymbol{B}$ such that $f_i = g_i \cdot f$ and $g_i = f_i \cdot g$ for all $i \in I$. Hence $f_i = f_i \cdot (g \cdot f)$ and $g_i = g_i \cdot (f \cdot g)$ for all $i \in I$. Because id_A and id_B are the only homomorphisms with $f_i = f_i \cdot id_A$ and $g_i = g_i \cdot id_B$, respectively, we conclude $g \cdot f = id_A$ and $f \cdot g = id_B$, which implies that f and g are isomorphisms with $g = f^{-1}$. Thus $\boldsymbol{A}$ and $\boldsymbol{B}$ are isomorphic. ∎

As a rule we will use the following notation in the sequel. If $(h_{ij} : \boldsymbol{A}_i \to \boldsymbol{A}_j)$ is a direct family of algebras, its direct limit will be denoted by $\lim(\boldsymbol{A}_i | i \in I)$. Furthermore, the uniquely determined homomorphism f in the universal property (L) is often denoted by $\lim(f_i | i \in I)$.

Example 3. Reconsider the stack algebras of Example 1. We assert that $\boldsymbol{A}$ is isomorphic to the direct limit of the finitely presented algebras $\boldsymbol{A}_n$. Using Proposition 6, a family $(h_n : \boldsymbol{A}_n \to \boldsymbol{A})$ of homomorphisms with the universal property (L) must be found. Define

$$h_n(w) = \begin{cases} w & \text{if } |w| \leq n+1 \\ w' & \text{if } |w| > n+1 \text{ and there is } w' \in A \text{ such that } w \sim w' \end{cases}$$

for all w in A_n, where $\sim$ is the congruence generated by R. It is left to the reader to verify the properties required. ∎

The direct limit is an appropriate composition principle for building up algebras from finitely presented ones.

Theorem 7. *Every algebra is isomorphic to a direct limit of finitely presented algebras.*

Proof. Let $\boldsymbol{A}$ be an arbitrary algebra presented by (G, R). As previously explained the index poset for the direct family, by which the direct limit will be constructed, is defined by

$$I = \{(X, P) | X \subseteq G,\ P \subseteq con(R) \cap (T_\Sigma(X) \times T_\Sigma(X)) \text{ and } X, P \text{ finite}\}.$$

The direct family of finitely presented algebras is given by $(h_{ij} : \boldsymbol{A}_i \rightarrow \boldsymbol{A}_j)$ where $\boldsymbol{A}_i = \langle X; P\rangle$ and $h_{ij}([t]_{con(P)}) = [t]_{con(Q)}$ for $i \leq j$ with $i = (X, P)$ and $j = (Y, Q)$. Similarly, we define a family $(h_i : \boldsymbol{A}_i \rightarrow \boldsymbol{A})$ of homomorphisms as follows

$$h_i([t]_{con(P)}) = [t]_{con(R)} \quad \text{for all } i = (X, P).$$

Claim: $(h_i : \boldsymbol{A}_i \rightarrow \boldsymbol{A})$ has the universal property (L).

By definition, $h_i = h_{ij} \cdot h_j$ for all $i \leq j$ of I.

Assume that $(f_i : \boldsymbol{A}_i \rightarrow \boldsymbol{B})$ is a family of homomorphisms such that $f_i = h_{ij} \cdot f_j$ for all $i \leq j$ of I. We have to show that there is exactly one homomorphism $f : \boldsymbol{A} \rightarrow \boldsymbol{B}$ with $f_i = h_i \cdot f$ for all $i \in I$.

(1) Existence of f:

Since $\boldsymbol{A}$ is assumed to be presented by (G, R), there is an isomorphism from $\boldsymbol{A}$ onto $\boldsymbol{T}_\Sigma(G)/con(R)$ associating a congruence class $[t]_{con(R)}$ to each a of A. Taking into account that every term has only finitely many variables from G we deduce that a finite subset X of G exists such that t belongs to $T_\Sigma(X)$. Choose an arbitrary but finite subset P of $con(R)$ restricted on $T_\Sigma(X)$. Then we get

$$h_i([t]_{con(P)}) = a \quad \text{for } i = (X, P),$$

which means that every element a of A has an inverse image in some $\boldsymbol{A}_i$. Therefore we define $f : \boldsymbol{A} \rightarrow \boldsymbol{B}$ by

$$f(a) = f_i([t]_{con(P)}) \quad \text{for all } a \text{ in } A$$

provided $h_i([t]_{con(P)}) = a$. Obviously, f is well-defined. It is clear that f is a homomorphism with the property required:

$$f_i = h_i \cdot f \quad \text{for all } i \in I.$$

(2) Uniqueness of f:

If $g : \boldsymbol{A} \to \boldsymbol{B}$ is a homomorphism with $f_i = h_i \cdot g$ for all $i \in I$, then

$$g(a) = g(h_i([t]_{con(P)})) = f_i([t]_{con(P)}) = f(h_i([t]_{con(P)})) = f(a)$$

for all a in A assuming that $h_i([t]_{con(P)}) = a$. Hence g equals f. ■

Finally, we are going to show that every direct limit $\lim(\boldsymbol{A}_i | i \in I)$ is isomorphic to a directed union $\bigcup(\boldsymbol{B}_i | i \in I)$ over images $\boldsymbol{B}_i$ of $\boldsymbol{A}_i$, $i \in I$.

Therefore consider any direct family $(h_{ij} : \boldsymbol{A}_i \to \boldsymbol{A}_j)$ of algebras. Denote its direct limit by $\boldsymbol{A}$ and its limit cone by $(h_i : \boldsymbol{A}_i \to \boldsymbol{A})$. For all i in I define the quotient algebras $\boldsymbol{A}_i/ker\ h_i$. It is essential to observe that $ker\ h_i = \bigcup\{ker\ h_{ij} | i \leq j\}$, which implies $ker(h_{ij} \cdot nat_j) = ker\ h_i$ for all $i \leq j$. Hence, there exist homomorphisms f_{ij} from $\boldsymbol{A}_i/ker\ h_i$ to $\boldsymbol{A}_j/ker\ h_j$ such that $h_{ij} \cdot nat_j = nat_i \cdot f_{ij}$ for all $i \leq j$. In fact,

$$(f_{ij} : \boldsymbol{A}_i/ker\ h_i \to \boldsymbol{A}_j/ker\ h_j)$$

is a direct family of algebras. Let $\boldsymbol{B}$ denote its direct limit with limit cone $(f_i : \boldsymbol{A}_i/ker\ h_i \to \boldsymbol{B})$. Using Lemma 5 we may prove that there are homomorphisms $f : \boldsymbol{A} \to \boldsymbol{B}$ and $g : \boldsymbol{B} \to \boldsymbol{A}$, both uniquely determined, such that $f \cdot g = id_A$ and $g \cdot f = id_B$. Hence $\boldsymbol{A}$ and $\boldsymbol{B}$ are isomorphic. That is,

$$\lim(\boldsymbol{A}_i | i \in I) \cong \lim(\boldsymbol{A}_i/ker\ h_i | i \in I).$$

Next, we assert that all f_{ij}, $i \leq j$, are injections. For if $f_{ij}([a]_i) = f_{ij}([b]_i)$ for $i \leq j$ and $[a]_i = nat_i(a)$, $[b]_i = nat_i(b)$ with $a, b \in A_i$, then $nat_j(h_{ij}(a)) = nat_j(h_{ij}(b))$ and consequently $[a]_i = [b]_i$ because of $ker\ h_i = \bigcup\{ker\ h_{ij} | i \leq j\}$. Evidently, the limit cone $(f_i : \boldsymbol{A}_i/ker\ h_i \to \boldsymbol{B})$ consists of injections, too. Thus $\boldsymbol{B}_i = f_i(\boldsymbol{A}_i/ker\ h_i)$ is a subalgebra of $\boldsymbol{B}$ for each i of I and $(\boldsymbol{B}_i | i \in I)$ is a directed family of algebras. It follows easily that

$$\lim(\boldsymbol{A}_i | i \in I) \cong \bigcup(\boldsymbol{B}_i | i \in I)$$

and each $\boldsymbol{B}_i$ is an image of $\boldsymbol{A}_i$. In other words, direct limits can be constructed by means of directed unions and images.

One of the main features of finitely presented algebras with respect to direct limits is the fact that every homomorphism from such an algebra to a direct limit factorizes through some component. This is analogous to the factorization of a homomorphism from a finitely generated algebra to a direct union of algebras through a certain component.

Proposition 8. *Let $(h_{ij} : \boldsymbol{A}_i \to \boldsymbol{A}_j)$ be a direct family of algebras. Every homomorphism h from a finitely presented algebra $\boldsymbol{A}$ to $\lim(\boldsymbol{A}_i | i \in I)$ factorizes through some component $\boldsymbol{A}_k$, i.e., there exists a homomorphism $g : \boldsymbol{A} \to \boldsymbol{A}_k$ such that $f = g \cdot h_k$, where $h_k : \boldsymbol{A}_k \to \lim(\boldsymbol{A}_i | i \in I)$ belongs to the associated limit cone (see Fig. 3.5).*

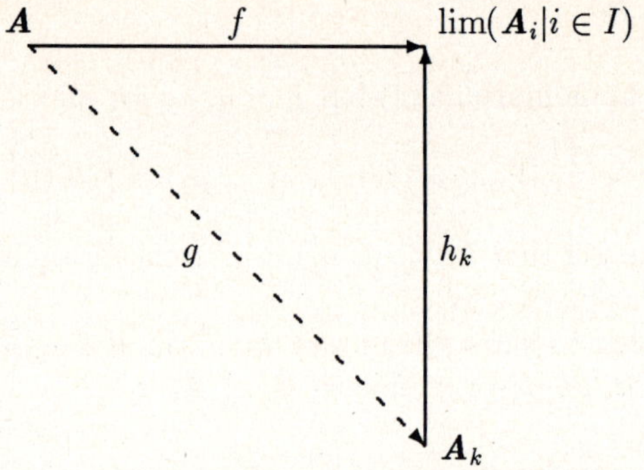

Fig. 3.5

Proof. Given a finitely presented algebra $\boldsymbol{A}$, there are a finite set X and a finite relation P on $T_\Sigma(X)$ such that $\boldsymbol{A}$ is isomorphic to the quotient $\boldsymbol{T}_\Sigma(X)/con(P)$. For simplicity we identify $\boldsymbol{A}$ with $\boldsymbol{T}_\Sigma(X)/con(P)$. Let f be any homomorphism from $\boldsymbol{A}$ to $\lim(\boldsymbol{A}_i| i \in I)$. By the finiteness of X and the fact that the index set I is directed, we get

$$f(nat(X)) = h_j(A_j)$$

for some index j of I.

Define a mapping $\alpha : X \to A_j$ by the rule:

$$h_j(\alpha(x)) = f(nat(x)) \quad \text{for all } x \text{ in } X.$$

By the Principle of Finitary Algebraic Recursion (Theorem 4 in Section 1.2.3), α admits a unique homomorphic extension $\alpha^\sharp : \boldsymbol{T}_\Sigma(X) \to \boldsymbol{A}_j$ such that $\alpha^\sharp \cdot h_j = nat \cdot f$ (see Fig. 3.6).

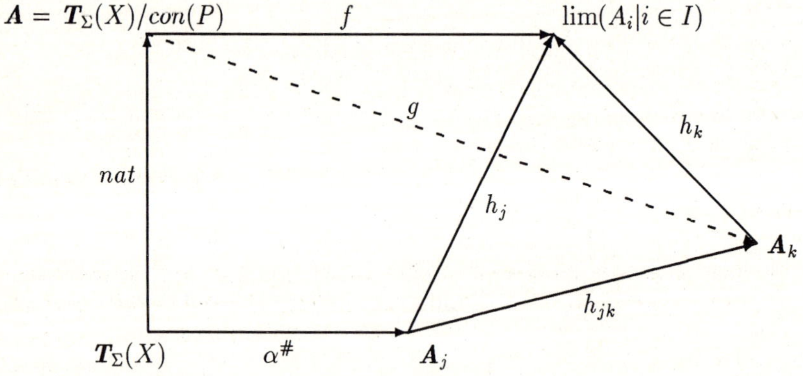

Fig. 3.6

Now we can claim that there is a homomorphism $g : \boldsymbol{A} \to \boldsymbol{A}_k$ with the property $nat \cdot g = \alpha^\sharp \cdot h_{jk}$. For that purpose we have to show that $con(P) \subseteq ker(\alpha^\sharp \cdot h_{jk})$.

P is finite, by assumption, say $P = \{(t_i, t'_i) | i = 1, \dots, n\}$. Since $f(nat(t_i)) = f(nat(t'_i))$ for $i = 1, \dots, n$, we have $h_j(\alpha^\sharp(t_i)) = h_j(\alpha^\sharp(t'_i))$ for $i = 1, \dots, n$. Hence P is a subset of $ker(\alpha^\sharp \cdot h_j)$ and so $con(P) \subseteq ker(\alpha^\sharp \cdot h_j)$. Because of $h_j = h_{jk} \cdot h_k$, we have

$$con(P) \subseteq ker(\alpha^\sharp \cdot h_{jk} \cdot h_k) \subseteq ker(\alpha^\sharp \cdot h_{jk}).$$

Thus, in fact, g exists so that $nat \cdot g = \alpha^\sharp \cdot h_{jk}$. Using the defining property of the limit cone, $h_j = h_{jk} \cdot h_k$, again we get

$$nat \cdot f = \alpha^\sharp \cdot h_j = \alpha^\sharp \cdot h_{jk} \cdot h_k = nat \cdot (g \cdot h_k),$$

which implies $f = g \cdot h_k$, by the surjectivity of nat. ∎

3.1.3 Direct Products and Subdirect Decompositions

This section presents another way of composing algebras. Let $(\boldsymbol{A}_i | i \in I)$ be a family of similar algebras. The direct product of all carrier sets, $A = \prod(A_i | i \in I)$, becomes an algebra if operations are defined coordinatewise. Recall that a family $(pr_i | i \in I)$ of projections is associated with the direct product such that any element a of A is completely determined by its coordinates $pr_i(a)$, and any choice of elements $a_i \in A_i$ defines a unique element a of A by $pr_i(a) = a_i$ for all $i \in I$.

Definition 3. *Let $(\boldsymbol{A}_i | i \in I)$ be a family of algebras* [2]. *The algebra $\boldsymbol{A}$ with carrier $A = \prod(A_i | i \in I)$ and with operations σ^A, where σ is any n-ary operation symbol and $a_1, \dots, a_n \in A$, defined by the equation*

$$pr_i(\sigma^A(a_1, \dots, a_n)) = \sigma^{A_i}(pr_i(a_1), \dots, pr_i(a_n))$$

for all $i \in I$, is called the ***direct product*** *of $(\boldsymbol{A}_i | i \in I)$; we use the notation $\prod(\boldsymbol{A}_i | i \in I)$.*

If the index set I is finite, say $I = \{1, \dots, n\}$, we write

$$\boldsymbol{A}_1 \times \dots \times \boldsymbol{A}_n$$

instead of $\prod(\boldsymbol{A}_i | i = 1, \dots, n)$.

Observe that the projections are homomorphisms, actually surjective homomorphisms.

Like direct limits, direct products can be characterized by the associated families of projections.

Lemma 9. *Let $\boldsymbol{A} = \prod(\boldsymbol{A}_i | i \in I)$ be the direct product of a given family $(\boldsymbol{A}_i | i \in I)$ of algebras. The associated family $(pr_i : \boldsymbol{A} \to \boldsymbol{A}_i)$ of projections has the following universal property:*

> *(P) For every family $(f_i : \boldsymbol{B} \to \boldsymbol{A}_i)$ of homomorphisms there exists a unique homomorphism $f : \boldsymbol{B} \to \boldsymbol{A}$ such that $f \cdot pr_i = f_i$ for all $i \in I$ (see Fig. 3.7).*

[2] A family of algebras always means a family of similar algebras.

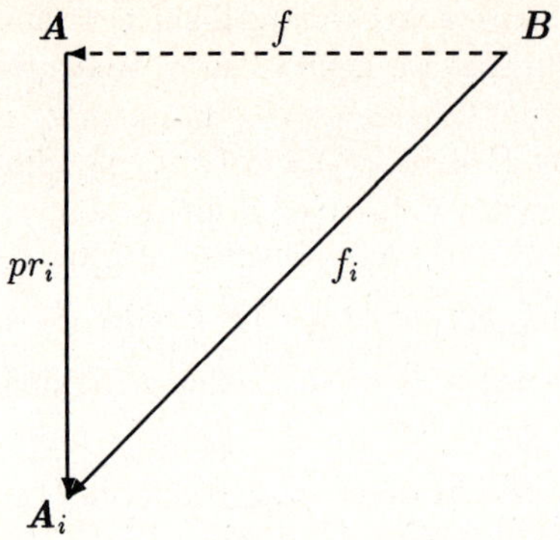

Fig. 3.7

Proof. First, we define a mapping f from B to A by

$$f(b) = (f_i(b) | i \in I) \quad \text{for all } b \text{ in } B.$$

Evidently,

$$f \cdot pr_i = f_i \quad \text{for all } i \in I.$$

It is easily seen that f is indeed a homomorphism.

So, it remains to prove that f is uniquely determined. Assume g is a homomorphism from $\boldsymbol{B}$ to $\boldsymbol{A}$ with $g \cdot pr_i = f_i$ for all $i \in I$. But then

$$g \cdot pr_i = f_i = f \cdot pr_i \quad \text{for all } i \in I,$$

which implies $g = f$. For if $g(b) = (a_i | i \in I)$ and $f(b) = (b_i | i \in I)$ were different for some $b \in B$, then $a_j \neq b_j$ for some index j; hence $pr_j(g(b)) \neq pr_j(f(b))$ is a contradiction. Thus $g(b) = f(b)$ for all $b \in B$, i.e., $g = f$. ■

The uniquely determined homomorphism f in the universal property (P) is usually denoted by $\prod(f_i | i \in I)$.

As a simple conclusion we get the characterization of direct products mentioned above.

Proposition 10. *For any given family $(\boldsymbol{A}_i | i \in I)$ of algebras, a family $(p_i : \boldsymbol{A} \to \boldsymbol{A}_i)$ of homomorphisms has the universal property (P) if and only if $\boldsymbol{A}$ is isomorphic to the direct product $\prod(\boldsymbol{A}_i | i \in I)$.*

Proof. It suffices to show that for any two families $(p_i : \boldsymbol{A} \to \boldsymbol{A}_i)$ and $(q_i : \boldsymbol{B} \to \boldsymbol{A}_i)$ of homomorphisms which have the universal property (P), the algebras $\boldsymbol{A}$ and $\boldsymbol{B}$ are isomorphic. By definition, there is exactly one homomorphism $p : \boldsymbol{A} \to \boldsymbol{B}$ and one homomorphism $q : \boldsymbol{B} \to \boldsymbol{A}$ such that $p \cdot q_i = p_i$ and $q \cdot p_i = q_i$ for all $i \in I$. Hence $(p \cdot q) \cdot p_i = p_i$ and $(q \cdot p) \cdot q_i = q_i$ for all $i \in I$. Because id_A and id_B are the only homomorphisms with $id_A \cdot p_i = p_i$ and $id_B \cdot q_i = q_i$, respectively, we conclude that $p \cdot q = id_A$ and $q \cdot p = id_B$, which implies that p and q are isomorphisms with $q = p^{-1}$. Thus $\boldsymbol{A}$ and $\boldsymbol{B}$ are isomorphic. ■

We want to compose algebras as direct products of "simpler" algebras. Therefore undecomposable algebras will be given a name. We say that a nontrivial algebra $\boldsymbol{A}$ (i.e., A contains more than one element) is ***directly irreducible*** if $\boldsymbol{A}$ is not isomorphic to a direct product of two nontrivial algebras. Using the Principle of Finite Induction we can prove that every finite algebra is isomorphic to a direct product of directly irreducible algebras. This result is, however, not extendable to infinite algebras in general. In order to get a meaningful decomposition of infinite algebras the composition principle must be generalized.

Definition 4. *Let $(\boldsymbol{A}_i|i \in I)$ be a family of algebras. A subalgebra $\boldsymbol{A}$ of $\prod(\boldsymbol{A}_i|i \in I)$ is called a* ***subdirect product*** *of $(\boldsymbol{A}_i|i \in I)$ if each $\boldsymbol{A}_i$ is an image of $\boldsymbol{A}$ under the i-th projection, that is, $\boldsymbol{A}_i = pr_i(\boldsymbol{A})$ for all $i \in I$.*

Since a subdirect product is not uniquely determined by a given family of algebras we use the more appropriate notion of a ***subdirect representation*** of an algebra $\boldsymbol{A}$, which is an injective homomorphism (embedding) $h : \boldsymbol{A} \to \prod(\boldsymbol{A}_i|i \in I)$ such that each algebra $\boldsymbol{A}_i$ is an image of $\boldsymbol{A}$, i.e., $h \cdot pr_i$ is surjective for each $i \in I$. It can happen that an algebra $\boldsymbol{A}$ with more than one element has only trivial subdirect representations in the sense that for every subdirect representation $h : \boldsymbol{A} \to \prod(\boldsymbol{A}_i|i \in I)$ there is at least an index $i \in I$ such that $h \cdot pr_i$ is an isomorphism. Such algebras are said to be ***subdirectly irreducible***. Of use to us is the following alternative formulation of this concept.

Lemma 11. *$\boldsymbol{A}$ is subdirectly irreducible iff there exist two distinct elements x and y in A such that $x \sim y$ for every nontrivial congruence $\sim$ on $\boldsymbol{A}$.*

Proof. Let $\boldsymbol{A}$ be a nontrivial algebra.

(1) Necessity: We indirectly assume that for any pair of distinct elements x and y of A there is a nontrivial congruence, say $R_{x,y}$ (i.e., $R_{x,y}$ is different from id_A) such that $(x, y) \notin R_{x,y}$. Denote by I the set of all these congruences on $\boldsymbol{A}$. Now we define a homomorphism $h : \boldsymbol{A} \to \prod(\boldsymbol{A}/R|\, R \in I)$ by $h(a) = ([a]_R|\, R \in I)$ for all a in A. Note that h is injective. For if $h(a) = h(b)$, then $[a]_R = [b]_R$ for all R in I, whence $a = b$ since the intersection over all R in I is id_A. Since no homomorphism $h \cdot pr_R$, given by $(h \cdot pr_R)(a) = [a]_R$, is injective, by the assumption that each R of I is nontrivial, $\boldsymbol{A}$ admits a nontrivial subdirect representation. Hence $\boldsymbol{A}$ is not subdirectly irreducible.

(2) Sufficiency: Assume that there are two distinct elements x and y in A such that $x \sim y$ for every nontrivial congruence $\sim$ on $\boldsymbol{A}$. Given an arbitrary subdirect representation $h : \boldsymbol{A} \to \prod(\boldsymbol{A}_i|i \in I)$ of $\boldsymbol{A}$, we have to show that for at least one index $i \in I$, $h \cdot pr_i$ is injective or, equivalently, $ker(h \cdot pr_i) = id_A$. By definition, h is injective. Hence $h(x) \neq h(y)$. If $h(x) = (a_i|\, i \in I)$ and $h(y) = (b_i|\, i \in I)$, then $a_i \neq b_i$ for some $i \in I$. Thus $(x, y) \notin ker(h \cdot pr_i)$ and so $ker(h \cdot pr_i)$ is the trivial congruence id_A, by assumption. $\boldsymbol{A}$ admits only trivial subdirect representations. Thus $\boldsymbol{A}$ is subdirectly irreducible. ■

Using Lemma 11, we can readily list some subdirectly irreducible algebras.

Example 1. Any two-element algebra is subdirectly irreducible. ■

Example 2. Every cyclic group with a prime number of elements is subdirectly irreducible. ■

Example 3. The subdirectly irreducible distributive lattices are particularly easy to describe. Recall that a lattice $(L, \vee, \wedge)$ is distributive if it satisfies the identity

$$x \wedge (y \vee z) = (x \wedge y) \vee (x \wedge z) \quad \text{for all } x, y, z \text{ in } L.$$

Furthermore, keep in mind that any lattice defines a partial order by the rule: $x \leq y$ iff $x \wedge y = x$.

We shall show that a distributive lattice L is subdirectly irreducible iff L has two elements. Since any two-element algebra is subdirectly irreducible we have only to show that every distributive lattice with more than two elements is subdirectly reducible. Given a distributive lattice L with at least three elements, it is essential to observe that there exists a chain $a < b < c$ in L. Let R and S be the congruences on L generated by the pairs (a, b) and (b, c), respectively. By definition, R and S are nontrivial congruences. Therefore it suffices to prove that their intersection is the trivial congruence id_L. For that purpose we use the fact: xRy iff $x \wedge a = y \wedge a$ and $x \vee b = y \vee b$ as well as xSy iff $x \wedge b = y \wedge b$ and $x \vee c = y \vee c$. Hence $x(R \cap S)y$ implies $x \vee b = y \vee b$ and $x \wedge b = y \wedge b$, thus $x = y$. ■

Theorem 12 (Birkhoff's Subdirect Representation Theorem). *Every algebra is isomorphic to a subdirect product of subdirectly irreducible algebras.*

Proof. As the assertion is trivially true for algebras with one element as well as for subdirectly irreducible algebras we assume that $\boldsymbol{A}$ is a nontrivial algebra which is not subdirectly irreducible.

To each pair of distinct elements x and y of A we assign the set $C_{x,y}$ of all congruences R on $\boldsymbol{A}$ with $(x, y) \notin R$. As $\boldsymbol{A}$ is supposed to be subdirectly reducible, by Lemma 11, $C_{x,y}$ is nonempty. Furthermore, the union of every chain in $C_{x,y}$ is again a congruence not containing (x, y); hence every chain has an upper bound in $C_{x,y}$. Thus, by Zorn's Lemma, $C_{x,y}$ has a maximal element. Let I denote the set of all these maximal congruences: $I = \{M | M$ is maximal in $C_{x,y}$ for some pair of distinct elements x and y of $A\}$. Since the intersection over all congruences in I is the trivial congruence id_A, a subdirect representation of $\boldsymbol{A}$ is definable by

$$h : \boldsymbol{A} \to \prod(\boldsymbol{A}/M | M \in I)$$

where $h(a) = ([a]_M | M \in I)$. Note that $h \cdot pr_M$ is surjective for each M of I.

Now it remains to prove that $\boldsymbol{A}/M$ is subdirectly irreducible for each M of I. By definition, there are distinct elements x and y of A such that $(x, y) \notin M$ and $(x, y) \in R$

for every congruence R on $\boldsymbol{A}$, which properly includes M. Hence $[x]_M$ and $[y]_M$ are distinct elements in $\boldsymbol{A}/M$. Using Lemma 11 we have to show that $([x]_M, [y]_M) \in S$ for every nontrivial congruence S on $\boldsymbol{A}/M$. According to the Second Isomorphism Theorem (Section 3.1.2) the congruences on $\boldsymbol{A}/M$ are in a one-to-one correspondence with those of $\boldsymbol{A}$ which include M. Define a mapping f from the set of all congruences R on $\boldsymbol{A}$ with $M \subseteq R$ to the set of all congruences on $\boldsymbol{A}/M$ by

$$f(R) = \{([a]_M, [b]_M) \mid a, b \in A \text{ and } (a,b) \in R\}.$$

The reader may verify that f is bijective. Instead of proving $([x]_M, [y]_M) \in S$ for every nontrivial congruence S it suffices to show that $(x, y) \in R$ for all congruences R on $\boldsymbol{A}$ such that $M \subseteq R$ and $M \neq R$. But this follows readily by the maximality of M. ■

As an application of this result a useful characterization of distributive lattices will be inferred. In conjunction with Example 3 we derive from Theorem 12 that every distributive lattice is isomorphic to a subdirect product of $(\boldsymbol{A}_i | i \in I)$, where $A_i = \{0, 1\}$ for each i of I. Take into account that then the direct product is equipotent to the power set of I. We call a nonempty subset A of any power set a ***ring of sets*** if $X, Y \in A$ implies $X \cup Y \in A$ and $X \cap Y \in A$. Evidently any ring of sets is a distributive lattice with respect to union and intersection. Hence every distributive lattice is isomorphic to a ring of sets. This special case of Birkhoff's Subdirect Representation Theorem is often called ***Stone's Representation Theorem for Distributive Lattices.***

We conclude this section by investigating an important subclass of distributive lattices. A ***bounded*** lattice is one with a least element 0 and a greatest element 1 with respect to the induced partial order. In a bounded lattice L, an element $a \in L$ is called a ***complement*** of $b \in L$ if $a \wedge b = 0$ and $a \vee b = 1$. As an exercise the reader may prove that in a bounded distributive lattice, an element can have only one complement. A ***complemented lattice*** is a bounded lattice in which every element has a complement. The unique complement of an element a of a complemented distributive lattice, also called a ***Boolean lattice***, is denoted by a'. When complementation $'$ and constants 0,1 are regarded as operations we speak of a ***Boolean algebra***, which can be defined in an alternative way: $(B, \vee, \wedge, ', 0, 1)$ is a Boolean algebra iff $(B, \vee, \wedge)$ is a distributive lattice such that the following identities hold

$$x' \wedge x = 0 \quad \text{and} \quad x' \vee x = 1;$$
$$0 \wedge x = 0 \quad \text{and} \quad 1 \wedge x = x.$$

$\mathbb{B}$ will denote the two-element Boolean algebra.

Lemma 13. *$\mathbb{B}$ is, up to isomorphism, the only directly irreducible Boolean algebra.*

Proof. Of course, $\mathbb{B}$ is directly irreducible as a two-element algebra. If $\boldsymbol{B}$ is assumed to be a Boolean algebra with more than two elements, we have to show that $\boldsymbol{B}$ is isomorphic to a direct product of two nontrivial Boolean algebras. In this case, B contains an element a with $0 < a < 1$. Set $B_1 = \{x \in B | 0 \leq x \leq a\}$ and $B_2 = \{x \in B |$

$0 \leq x \leq a'\}$. Both subsets of B can be made into Boolean algebras: $(B_1, \vee, \wedge, c_1, 0, a)$ and $(B_2, \vee, \wedge, c_2, 0, a')$, where $\vee$ and $\wedge$ in B_1 and B_2 are the same operations as in B except restricted to B_1 and B_2, respectively, and the complementations c_1 in B_1 and c_2 in B_2 are defined by $c_1(x) = a \wedge x'$ an $c_2(x) = a' \wedge x'$.

Claim: $\boldsymbol{B} \cong \boldsymbol{B}_1 \times \boldsymbol{B}_2$.

Let f be a mapping from B to $B_1 \times B_2$ determined by $f(x) = (a \wedge x, a' \wedge x)$. It is easily seen that f is a homomorphism. Therefore it remains to show that f is bijective. In fact, f is injective. For if $f(x) = f(y)$, then $a \wedge x = a \wedge y$ and $a' \wedge x = a' \wedge y$, whence $(a \wedge x) \vee (a' \wedge x) = (a \wedge y) \vee (a' \wedge y)$. Hence, by distributivity, $(a \vee a') \wedge x = (a \vee a') \wedge y$, which implies $x = y$. To prove the surjectivity of f, we take an arbitrary element (b_1, b_2) of $B_1 \times B_2$. Then $a \wedge b_1 = b_1$ and $a' \wedge b_2 = b_2$ as well as $a \wedge b_2 = 0$ and $a' \wedge b_1 = 0$. Hence we have

$$\begin{aligned} f(b_1 \vee b_2) &= (a \wedge (b_1 \vee b_2), a' \wedge (b_1 \vee b_2)) = \\ &= ((a \wedge b_1) \vee (a \wedge b_2), (a' \wedge b_1) \vee (a' \wedge b_2)) = \\ &= (b_1, b_2). \end{aligned}$$

Thus f is surjective.

Since $\boldsymbol{B}_1$ and $\boldsymbol{B}_2$ are nontrivial Boolean algebras, $\boldsymbol{B}$ is not directly irreducible. ■

Hence every finite Boolean algebra is completely determined as being isomorphic to a (finite) direct product $\mathbb{B} \times \ldots \times \mathbb{B}$. The n-fold direct product $\mathbb{B} \times \ldots \times \mathbb{B}$ is equipotent to the power set of an n-element set. Obviously, any power set $\wp(A)$ can be regarded as a Boolean algebra $(\wp(A), \cup, \cap, {}', \emptyset, A)$, where $X' = A - X$ is the set-complement of $X \subseteq A$. As an alternative characterization we obtain that every finite Boolean algebra is isomorphic to the Boolean algebra of all subsets of a finite set. A subalgebra of the Boolean algebra of all subsets of an arbitrary set is usually called a ***field of sets***. Now Theorem 12 yields ***Stone's Representation Theorem for Boolean Algebras***: every Boolean algebra is isomorphic to a field of sets.

3.1.4 Reduced Products and Ultraproducts

Reduced products and ultraproducts play a significant role in the connection of universal algebra with model theory. Ultraproducts are special cases of reduced products, which in turn are certain quotients of direct products, while subdirect products were certain subalgebras of direct products. In this section we only present basic definitions and some elementary results.

Let $(\boldsymbol{A}_i | i \in I)$ be a family of algebras, where I is an infinite index set. Consider two elements of the direct product $\prod(\boldsymbol{A}_i | i \in I)$, say $a = (a_i | i \in I)$ and $b = (b_i | i \in I)$. We say a and b are ***almost equal*** if $a_i = b_i$ for all except finitely many indices $i \in I$.

What are the formal properties of the concept "almost equal"? A subset X of I is called ***cofinite*** if $I - X$ is finite. Let F_I denote the set of all cofinite subsets of I. Then F_I fulfills the following conditions:

(1) F_I is nonempty;

(2) $X \cap Y \in F_I$ whenever $X, Y \in F_I$;

(3) If $X \in F_I$ and $X \subseteq Y$, then $Y \in F_I$; and

(4) $\emptyset$ is not in F_I.

This leads to the following definition. A ***filter*** over a set I is any set F of subsets of I such that F satisfies the conditions (1) – (3) above. F is called a ***proper filter*** if condition (4) is additionally fulfilled. Observe that a filter F is a proper filter iff $F \neq \wp(I)$. If we simply speak of a filter, we shall tacitly assume that F is a filter over the set $I = \bigcup F$.

Example 1. Given an infinite set I, the set F_I of all cofinite subsets of I is evidently a filter, called the ***Fréchet filter*** over I. ■

Example 2. Let I be a set. Then the singleton $\{I\}$ is the ***trivial filter*** over I. ■

The set of all filters over a set I is a closure system. Hence filters can be generated by any system over I. If M is a subset of $\wp(I)$, then

$$F(M) = \{X \in \wp(I) | X_1 \cap \ldots \cap X_n \subseteq X \text{ for some } X_1, \ldots, X_n \in M\} \cup \{I\}$$

is the filter generated by M.

Example 3. Consider an infinite set M. We denote by I the set of all finite subsets of M, $I = \wp_\omega(M)$. To each m of M we associate the set $\hat{m}$ of all finite subsets of M, which contain m,

$$\hat{m} = \{X \in I | m \in X\}.$$

If we put $\hat{M} = \{\hat{m} | m \in M\}$, then $\hat{M}$ is a subset of $\wp(I)$ and we can form the filter generated by $\hat{M}$. $F(\hat{M})$ is just the set of all subsets X of I such that for some $i \in I$, every $j \in I$ which includes i belongs to X. Moreover, $F(\hat{M})$ is a proper filter. ■

A filter F over I is said to be an ***ultrafilter*** if, for all subsets X of I,

$$X \in F \quad \text{iff} \quad I - X \notin F.$$

Any ultrafilter is proper. For if F is a filter, $F \neq \emptyset$ and hence $I \in F$. Thus $I - I = \emptyset$ does not belong to F since F is an ultrafilter.

Reduced products will be introduced next as certain quotients of direct products. For that reason, a congruence on the direct product $\prod(\boldsymbol{A}_i|i \in I)$ is associated with each filter over I.

Let $(\boldsymbol{A}_i|i \in I)$ be a family of algebras. To any filter F over I we associate a relation $=_F$ on $\prod(A_i|\, i \in I)$ as follows. For all x, y in $\prod(A_i|\, i \in I)$,

$$x =_F y \quad \text{iff} \quad \{i \in I|\, pr_i(x) = pr_i(y)\} \in F.$$

Lemma 14. *$=_F$ is a congruence on $\prod(\boldsymbol{A}_i|i \in I)$.*

Proof. First, we show that $=_F$ is an equivalence. Since $I \in F$, $=_F$ is reflexive. By definition, $=_F$ is symmetric. To prove transitivity suppose $x =_F y$ and $y =_F z$. Then $\{i \in I|\, pr_i(x) = pr_i(y)\} \in F$ and $\{i \in I|\, pr_i(y) = pr_i(z)\} \in F$. Hence, the intersection of both sets belongs to F, too. That is, $\{i \in I|\, pr_i(x) = pr_i(y) \text{ and } pr_i(y) = pr_i(z)\} \in F$ and so $\{i \in I|\, pr_i(x) = pr_i(z)\} \in F$. Now, by definition, $x =_F z$. Thus, $=_F$ is an equivalence on $A = \prod(A_i|\, i \in I)$.

It remains to show that $=_F$ is compatible with the operations. Let σ be any n-ary operation symbol and consider arbitrary elements $x_1, \ldots, x_n, y_1, \ldots, y_n$ in A. If $x_k =_F y_k$ for $k = 1, \ldots, n$, then $\{i \in I|\, pr_i(x_k) = pr_i(y_k)\} \in F$, by the condition (2) for a filter F. Now, by the condition (3) for a filter F, $\{i \in I|\, pr_i(\sigma^A(x_1, \ldots, x_n)) = pr_i(\sigma^A(y_1, \ldots, y_n))\} \in F$. Thus $\sigma^A(x_1, \ldots, x_n) =_F \sigma^A(y_1, \ldots, y_n)$ and $=_F$ is, in fact, a congruence on $\boldsymbol{A} = \prod(\boldsymbol{A}_i|i \in I)$. ∎

Definition 5. *Let $(\boldsymbol{A}_i|i \in I)$ be a family of algebras. If F is a filter over I, the quotient algebra $\prod(\boldsymbol{A}_i|i \in I)/{=_F}$ is called the **reduced product** of $(\boldsymbol{A}_i|i \in I)$ modulo F, denoted by $\prod(\boldsymbol{A}_i|i \in I)/F$. In particular, if F is an ultrafilter, $\prod(\boldsymbol{A}_i|i \in I)/F$ is called the **ultraproduct** of $(\boldsymbol{A}_i|i \in I)$ modulo F.*

Notice that the reduced product $\prod(\boldsymbol{A}_i|i \in I)/F$ modulo the trivial filter $F = \{I\}$ coincides with the direct product since, in this case, $=_F$ is the identity relation.

In general, reduced products can be constructed by means of direct limits and direct products. Let $(\boldsymbol{A}_i|i \in I)$ be a family of algebras. Given a filter F over I, we define

$$\boldsymbol{A}_X = \prod(\boldsymbol{A}_i|\, i \in X)$$

for each X of F; and for each $X, Y \in F$ with $X \supseteq Y$, a homomorphism

$$h_{X,Y} : \boldsymbol{A}_X \to \boldsymbol{A}_Y \quad \text{by} \quad h_{X,Y} = \prod(pr_i^X\,|\, i \in Y),$$

where pr_i^X are the associated projections of $\boldsymbol{A}_X$. It is important to observe that any filter is a downward directed poset. Hence

$$(h_{X,Y}|\, X, Y \in F)$$

is a direct family of homomorphisms.

Proposition 15. *Let* $(\boldsymbol{A}_i|i \in I)$ *be a family of algebras with nonempty carriers. For any filter* F *over* I *the reduced product* $\prod(\boldsymbol{A}_i|i \in I)/F$ *is isomorphic to the direct limit of* $(h_{X,Y} : \boldsymbol{A}_X \to \boldsymbol{A}_Y| X, Y \in F)$.

Proof. Let $\boldsymbol{A} = \prod(\boldsymbol{A}_i|i \in I)/F$. By Proposition 6 in Section 3.1.2, we have to exhibit a family $(h_X : \boldsymbol{A}_X \to \boldsymbol{A})$ of homomorphisms, which has the universal property (L). Denote by p_X the homomorphism from $\prod(\boldsymbol{A}_i|i \in I)$ to $\boldsymbol{A}_X$ defined by

$$p_X = \prod(pr_i| i \in X).$$

Let us consider the following diagram of homomorphisms in Fig. 3.8.

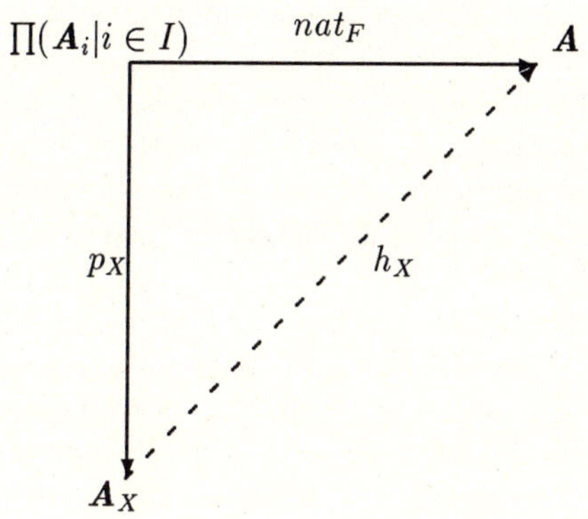

Fig. 3.8

Since p_X is surjective the existence of h_X follows from the fact that $ker\ p_X \subseteq ker\ nat_F$. Note that $ker\ nat_F$ coincides with $=_F$. By definition of $h_{X,Y}$, we have $p_X \cdot h_{X,Y} = p_Y$; hence $nat_F = p_Y \cdot h_Y = p_X \cdot h_{X,Y} \cdot h_Y = p_X \cdot h_X$, which implies

$$h_X = h_{X,Y} \cdot h_Y$$

for all X, Y with $Y \subseteq X$.

It remains to show that the family $(h_X| X \in F)$ has the universal property (L) of direct limits. Assume that $(f_X : \boldsymbol{A}_X \to \boldsymbol{B}| X \in F)$ is a family of homomorphisms such that $f_X = h_{X,Y} \cdot f_Y$ for all X, Y with $Y \subseteq X$. Since, in particular, I belongs to F, we have a homomorphism f_I from $\prod(\boldsymbol{A}_i|i \in I)$ to $\boldsymbol{B}$. It is easily seen that f_I factorizes through $\boldsymbol{A}$:

$$f_I = nat_F \cdot f$$

for some homomorphism $f : \boldsymbol{A} \to \boldsymbol{B}$. Let $a = (a_i| i \in I)$ and $b = (b_i| i \in I)$. Suppose $a =_F b$. Then $\{i \in I| a_i = b_i\} \in F$. Put $X = \{i \in I| a_i = b_i\}$ and abbreviate $(a_i| i \in X)$ and $(b_i| i \in X)$ by a_X and b_X, respectively. Hence $f_X(a_X) = f_X(b_X)$; consequently

$h_{I,X} \cdot f_X = f_I$ and so $ker\ f_I \subseteq ker\ h_{I,X}$ for all X in F, which implies $ker\ f_I \subseteq \bigcap\{ker\ h_{I,X} | X \in F\}$. Since this intersection equals $=_F$ and nat_F is surjective, we obtain the factorization stated above. Observe that f is uniquely determined by f_I. Taking into consideration that $nat_F = h_{I,X} \cdot h_X$, we derive $h_{I,X} \cdot h_X \cdot f = nat_F \cdot f = f_I$. On the other hand, $f_I = h_{I,X} \cdot f_X$ by assumption. Thus $h_{I,X} \cdot (h_X \cdot f) = h_{I,X} \cdot f_X$ for all X in F. Because $h_{I,X}$ is surjective, it follows that

$$h_X \cdot f = f_X$$

for all X in F, which proves that $(h_X | X \in F)$ has the universal property (L). ■

3.2 Equationally Defined Classes of Algebras

Universal algebra has its origin in Birkhoff's ingenious characterization of equationally defined classes of algebras. A class of algebras is said to be equationally definable if there is a set E of universally quantified term equations such that exactly the algebras of the class validate every equation of E. For instance, all semigroups form such a class. In 1935, Birkhoff proved the following result: A class $\mathcal{K}$ of algebras is equationally definable if and only if $\mathcal{K}$ is closed under subalgebras, images and direct products.

In Section 3.2.1, equations and equationally defined classes of algebras are introduced. For that reason the concept of validation of an equation in an algebra has to be defined. We search for "typical" algebras with respect to validation in Section 3.2.2. Such algebras are called free in a given class $\mathcal{K}$. The word "free" indicates that these algebras validate exactly those equations which are valid in every algebra of $\mathcal{K}$; they are free of other additional equations. Section 3.2.3 exhibits the characterization mentioned above known as Birkhoff's Variety Theorem. Equational theories and their connection with equational logic are studied in Section 3.2.4. Finally, Section 3.2.5 presents term rewriting as an algorithmic tool for equational theories.

3.2.1 Equations

Equations were already used intuitively to axiomatize algebras. For instance, a semigroup is an algebra $(A, \cdot)$ with one binary operation subject to the associativity law: $(a \cdot b) \cdot c = a \cdot (b \cdot c)$ for all a, b, c in A.

In this section, we first formalize the notion of equation. Afterwards satisfaction and validation of an equation in an algebra has to be defined. Finally, preservation properties for equations with respect to algebra constructions will be investigated.

Definition 1. *Let V be a countably infinite set (of "variables"). Given a signature Σ, an* ***equation****, more precisely, Σ-equation, denoted by*

$$\forall X(t = t'),$$

is a triple (X, t, t') with X a finite subset of V and t, t' terms in $T_\Sigma(X)$. If X is empty, we speak of a ***ground equation****, denoted by $\forall\emptyset(t = t')$.*

Instead of $\forall X(t = t')$ we also write $\forall\, x_1, \ldots, x_n(t = t')$ if $X = \{x_1, \ldots, x_n\}$.

What does it mean that an equation $\forall X(t = t')$ is valid in an algebra $\boldsymbol{A}$? Consider, for example, a signature with one binary operation symbol only. In the algebra $(\mathbb{N}, \cdot)$ with carrier $\mathbb{N}$ and common multiplication as operation the equation $\forall\, x, y, z\ ((x \cdot y) \cdot z = x \cdot (y \cdot z))$ is valid since every valuation of the variables x, y, z by natural numbers yields identity of both sides of the equation in $\mathbb{N}$. To define validation generally we need to evaluate variables, by a so-called assignment. In general, validation is based on the valuation of variables occurring in the given equation.

A mapping α from X into an algebra $\boldsymbol{A}$ is usually called an ***assignment*** from X to $\boldsymbol{A}$. By the Principle of Finitary Algebraic Recursion (Theorem 4 in Section 1.2.3), α admits a unique homomorphic extension $\alpha^\sharp : \boldsymbol{T}_\Sigma(X) \to \boldsymbol{A}$.

Definition 2. *An equation $\forall X(t = t')$ is* ***valid*** *in an algebra $\boldsymbol{A}$, in symbols*

$$\boldsymbol{A} \models \forall X(t = t'),$$

if $\alpha^\sharp(t) = \alpha^\sharp(t')$ for all assignments α from X to $\boldsymbol{A}$.

The formal use of a universal quantifier $\forall$ in our notation for an equation, $\forall X(t = t')$, just expresses that validation means quantification over all assignments, as required in the definition above. Recall that an equation is precisely a triple (X, t, t'). Usually, an equation (X, t, t') is said to be ***satisfied*** by an assignment α from X to $\boldsymbol{A}$ if $\alpha^\sharp(t) = \alpha^\sharp(t')$; this is denoted by

$$(\boldsymbol{A}, \alpha) \models t = t'.$$

Thus, $\boldsymbol{A} \models \forall X(t = t')$ iff $(\boldsymbol{A}\ , \alpha) \models t = t'$ for all assignments α from X to A.

We now study preservation properties with respect to certain algebraic constructions, such as subalgebra, image, direct product, etc.

Proposition 1. *Every equation valid in an algebra $\boldsymbol{A}$ is also valid in each subalgebra of $\boldsymbol{A}$.*

Proof. Let $\forall X(t = t')$ be an equation valid in a given algebra $\boldsymbol{A}$. Consider any subalgebra $\boldsymbol{B}$ of $\boldsymbol{A}$. Every assignment β from X to $\boldsymbol{B}$ determines an assignment α from X to A, namely $\alpha = \beta \cdot in_B$, where $in_B : \boldsymbol{B} \to \boldsymbol{A}$ is the inclusion of $\boldsymbol{B}$ into $\boldsymbol{A}$. Using the Principle of Finitary Algebraic Recursion (Theorem 4 in Section 1.2.3) one may prove $\alpha^\sharp = (\beta \cdot in_B)^\sharp = \beta^\sharp \cdot in_B$. Now, by the assumption $\boldsymbol{A} \models \forall X(t = t')$, we derive $in_B(\beta^\sharp(t)) = in_B(\beta^\sharp(t'))$. Hence $\beta^\sharp(t) = \beta^\sharp(t')$, since in_B is injective. That is, $\forall X(t = t')$ is valid in $\boldsymbol{B}$. ■

Proposition 2. *Every equation valid in an algebra $\boldsymbol{A}$ is also valid in each image of $\boldsymbol{A}$.*

Proof. If $\boldsymbol{B}$ is an image of $\boldsymbol{A}$, then there is a surjective homomorphism $h : \boldsymbol{A} \to \boldsymbol{B}$. By the Axiom of Choice, there is a mapping from $\boldsymbol{B}$ to $\boldsymbol{A}$, say g, such that $g \cdot h = id_B$. Let

$\forall X(t = t')$ be an equation valid in $\boldsymbol{A}$. To every assignment β from X to $\boldsymbol{B}$ we associate an assignment α from X to $\boldsymbol{A}$ by $\alpha = \beta \cdot g$. Because

$$h(\alpha^\sharp(x)) = h(\alpha(x)) = h(g(\beta(x))) = \beta(x) = \beta^\sharp(x)$$

for all x in X, we derive $\beta^\sharp = \alpha^\sharp \cdot h$, by the Principle of Finitary Algebraic Recursion (Theorem 4 in Section 1.2.3). Now, by the assumption $\boldsymbol{A} \models \forall X(t = t')$, we get $\beta^\sharp(t) = \beta^\sharp(t')$. Hence $\boldsymbol{B} \models \forall X(t = t')$. ■

Proposition 3. *Let $(\boldsymbol{A}_i | i \in I)$ be a family of algebras. Every equation valid in each $\boldsymbol{A}_i$, $i \in I$, is also valid in the direct product $\prod(\boldsymbol{A}_i | i \in I)$.*

Proof. Let $\forall X(t = t')$ be an equation valid in each $\boldsymbol{A}_i$, $i \in I$. If α_i is an assignment from X to $\boldsymbol{A}_i$, then $\prod(\alpha_i | i \in I)$ is an assignment from X to $\prod(\boldsymbol{A}_i | i \in I)$. By the Principle of Finitary Algebraic Recursion (Theorem 4 in Section 1.2.3), the unique homomorphic extension $\alpha^\sharp$ fulfills the condition $\alpha^\sharp(t) = (\alpha_i^\sharp(t) | i \in I)$ for all terms t in $T_\Sigma(X)$, i.e., $\alpha^\sharp = \prod(\alpha_i^\sharp | i \in I)$. Therefore the assumption $\boldsymbol{A}_i \models \forall X(t = t')$ for all $i \in I$ implies $\prod(\boldsymbol{A}_i | i \in I) \models \forall X(t = t')$. ■

Although these preservation properties derived so far are sufficient for our further development we will additionally study preservation of equations under other algebra constructions like directed union, direct limit, subdirect product and reduced product.

Proposition 4. *Let $(\boldsymbol{A}_i | i \in I)$ be a directed family of algebras. Every equation valid in each algebra $\boldsymbol{A}_i$, $i \in I$, is also valid in the directed union $\bigcup(\boldsymbol{A}_i | i \in I)$.*

Proof. Given an equation $\forall X(t = t')$, we indirectly assume that $\boldsymbol{A}_i \models \forall X(t = t')$ for all $i \in I$, but $\forall X(t = t')$ is not valid in $\bigcup \boldsymbol{A}_i | i \in I$. Then there is at least one assignment α from X to $\bigcup(\boldsymbol{A}_i | i \in I)$ such that $\alpha^\sharp(t) \neq \alpha^\sharp(t')$. Since X is a finite set, α factorizes through some algebra, say $\boldsymbol{A}_k$, $\alpha = \beta \cdot h_k$ with $\beta : X \to A_k$ and $h_k : \boldsymbol{A}_k \to \bigcup(\boldsymbol{A}_i | i \in I)$ is the embedding $h_k(a) = a$ for all a in A_k. Using the Principle of Finitary Algebraic Recursion (Theorem 4 in Section 1.2.3) we get $\alpha^\sharp = (\beta \cdot h_k)^\sharp = \beta^\sharp \cdot h_k$. Hence $h_k(\beta^\sharp(t)) \neq h_k(\beta^\sharp(t'))$, which implies $\beta^\sharp(t) \neq \beta^\sharp(t')$ by the injectivity of h_k. But this is a contradiction. ■

Since direct limits can be constructed by means of directed unions and quotients it follows, by Proposition 2 and Proposition 4, that equations are preserved under direct limits.

Proposition 5. *Let $(h_{ij} : \boldsymbol{A}_i \to \boldsymbol{A}_j)$ be a direct family of algebras. Every equation valid in each $\boldsymbol{A}_i$, $i \in I$, is also valid in the direct limit* $\lim(\boldsymbol{A}_i | i \in I)$. ■

By definition, subdirect products are special subalgebras of direct products. Hence, by Propositions 1 and 3, equations are preserved under subdirect products.

Proposition 6. *Let $(\boldsymbol{A}_i | i \in I)$ be a family of algebras. Every equation valid in each $\boldsymbol{A}_i$, $i \in I$, is also valid in a subdirect product of $(\boldsymbol{A}_i | i \in I)$.* ■

Similarly, preservation under reduced products follows from Propositions 2 and 3.

Proposition 7. *Let $(\boldsymbol{A}_i | i \in I)$ be a family of algebras and let F be any filter over I. Every equation valid in each $\boldsymbol{A}_i$, $i \in I$, is also valid in the reduced product $\prod(\boldsymbol{A}_i | i \in I)/F$.* ■

Altogether we have shown that an equation is preserved under the formation of subalgebras, images, direct products, directed unions, direct limits, subdirect products and reduced products.

An algebra $\boldsymbol{A}$ is said to be a ***model*** of a set E of equations if $\boldsymbol{A}$ validates each equation of E. The class of all models of E, denoted by $Mod\ E$, is also called the ***model class*** of E. For two sets E and E' of equations we have

$$Mod\ E \subseteq Mod\ E' \quad \text{whenever} \quad E' \subseteq E.$$

A class $\mathcal{K}$ of similar algebras is called ***abstract*** if $\mathcal{K}$ is closed under isomorphic algebras, i.e., $\boldsymbol{A}$ belongs to $\mathcal{K}$ whenever $\boldsymbol{A}$ is isomorphic to an algebra in $\mathcal{K}$. Observe that a model class of any set E of equations is always abstract. Dealing with abstract classes of algebras, we will often identify isomorphic algebras for notational simplicity.

Definition 3. *An abstract class $\mathcal{K}$ of algebras is called an **equational class** (or **equationally definable**) if $\mathcal{K}$ is the model class of some set of equations.*

Example 1. The class of all semigroups is evidently an equational class. ■

Using the preservations derived above we get immediately the following closure properties of any equational class.

Theorem 8. *Let $\mathcal{K}$ be an equational class. An algebra $\boldsymbol{A}$ belongs to $\mathcal{K}$ whenever one of the following conditions (1) – (7) below is fulfilled:*

(1) $\boldsymbol{A}$ is a subalgebra of an algebra in $\mathcal{K}$;

(2) $\boldsymbol{A}$ is an image of an algebra in $\mathcal{K}$;

(3) $\boldsymbol{A}$ is the direct product of a family of algebras in $\mathcal{K}$;

(4) $\boldsymbol{A}$ is the directed union of a directed family of algebras in $\mathcal{K}$;

(5) $\boldsymbol{A}$ is the direct limit of a direct family of algebras in $\mathcal{K}$;

(6) $\boldsymbol{A}$ is a subdirect product of a family of algebras in $\mathcal{K}$;

(7) $\boldsymbol{A}$ is a reduced product of a family of algebras in $\mathcal{K}$. ■

3.2.2 Free Algebras

In this section we solve the following question: For which class $\mathcal{K}$ of algebras can we find an algebra in $\mathcal{K}$, say $\boldsymbol{F}$, such that an equation is valid in $\mathcal{K}$ iff it is valid in $\boldsymbol{F}$? We say that an equation $\forall X(t = t')$ is valid in a class $\mathcal{K}$ of algebras, denoted by $\mathcal{K} \models \forall X(t = t')$, if each algebra of $\mathcal{K}$ validates $\forall X(t = t')$.

Our question is now the following: Is it possible to find an algebra in $\mathcal{K}$, say $\boldsymbol{F}$, and an assignment φ from X to $\boldsymbol{F}$ such that

$$\mathcal{K} \models \forall X(t = t') \quad \text{iff} \quad (\boldsymbol{F}, \varphi) \models t = t' \;?$$

Supposing that $\boldsymbol{F}$ and φ exist, we have to exhibit their defining features. If $\mathcal{K} \models \forall X(t = t')$, then of course $(\boldsymbol{F}, \varphi) \models t = t'$, by definition. Consider an arbitrary algebra $\boldsymbol{A}$ of $\mathcal{K}$ and any assignment α from X to $\boldsymbol{A}$. Then $\alpha^\sharp(t) = \alpha^\sharp(t')$, i.e., $(t, t') \in \mathit{ker}\ \alpha^\sharp$. We depict this situation in Fig. 3.9.

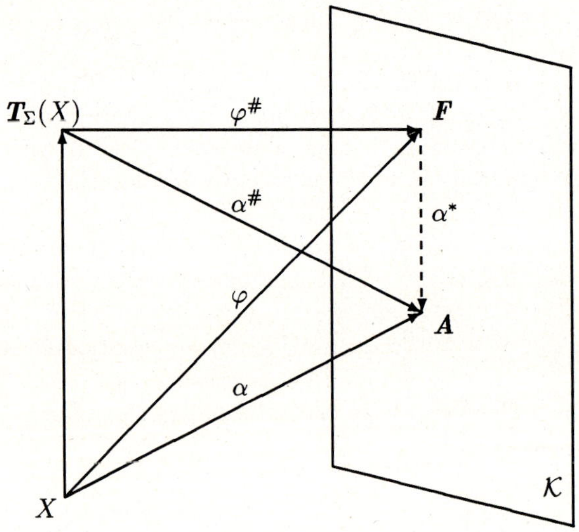

Fig. 3.9

Our crucial assumption is now the following: $\alpha^\sharp$ factorizes uniquely through $\varphi^\sharp$. Under this assumption $\mathit{ker}\ \varphi^\sharp \subseteq \mathit{ker}\ \alpha^\sharp$ for all assignments α. Hence $\mathit{ker}\ \varphi^\sharp$ coincides with the intersection over all $\mathit{ker}\ \alpha^\sharp$, where α is any assignment from X to an arbitrary algebra $\boldsymbol{A}$. Thus $(\boldsymbol{F}, \varphi) \models t = t'$ implies $\mathcal{K} \models \forall X(t = t')$. This leads to one of our main concepts.

Definition 4. *Let $\mathcal{K}$ be a class of algebras. Given a set X, an algebra $\boldsymbol{F}$ of $\mathcal{K}$ is called* ***free in $\mathcal{K}$ relative to a mapping*** *$\varphi : X \to F$ if, for every mapping α from X to any algebra $\boldsymbol{A}$ of $\mathcal{K}$, there is a unique homomorphism $\alpha^* : \boldsymbol{F} \to \boldsymbol{A}$ such that $\alpha = \varphi \cdot \alpha^*$. When X is the empty set, $\boldsymbol{F}$ is called* ***initial*** *in $\mathcal{K}$. In this case, there is a unique homomorphism from $\boldsymbol{F}$ to $\boldsymbol{A}$.*

Note. Assume that $\boldsymbol{F}$ is free in $\mathcal{K}$ relative to $\varphi : X \to F$ and that $\boldsymbol{G}$ is free in $\mathcal{K}$ relative to $\psi : X \to G$. Then, by definition, the homomorphisms φ^* and ψ^* exist uniquely such that $\varphi = \psi \cdot \varphi^*$ and $\psi = \varphi \cdot \psi^*$, which imply that $\varphi = \varphi \cdot (\psi^* \cdot \varphi^*)$ and $\psi = \psi \cdot (\varphi^* \cdot \psi^*)$. Since $\varphi = \varphi \cdot id_F$ and $\psi = \psi \cdot id_G$ trivially hold, we get $\psi^* \cdot \varphi^* = id_F$ and $\varphi^* \cdot \psi^* = id_G$, by the requirement of uniqueness. Hence φ^* and ψ^* are bijective and, in particular, $\psi^* = \varphi^{*^{-1}}$. Consequently $\boldsymbol{F}$ and $\boldsymbol{G}$ are isomorphic. If $\boldsymbol{F}$ and $\boldsymbol{G}$ are initial in $\mathcal{K}$, then there are unique homomorphisms $h_G : \boldsymbol{F} \to \boldsymbol{G}$ and $h_F : \boldsymbol{G} \to \boldsymbol{F}$. Consider $h_G \cdot h_F$ and $h_F \cdot h_G$. Then $h_G \cdot h_F = id_F$ and $h_F \cdot h_G = id_G$ since id_F and id_G are the unique homomorphisms from $\boldsymbol{F}$ into $\boldsymbol{F}$ and $\boldsymbol{G}$ into $\boldsymbol{G}$, respectively. Hence h_F and h_G are isomorphisms. That is, $\boldsymbol{F}$ and $\boldsymbol{G}$ are isomorphic. ■

In the foregoing investigation we proved the important fact that free algebras are typical in the sense mentioned above.

Theorem 9. *Let $\mathcal{K}$ be a class of algebras. If a free algebra $\boldsymbol{F}$ in $\mathcal{K}$ relative to $\varphi : X \to F$ exists, then*

$$\mathcal{K} \models \forall X(t = t') \quad \textit{iff} \quad (\boldsymbol{F}, \varphi) \models t = t'.$$ ■

Subsequently some useful properties of free algebras will be exhibited. A class of algebras is said to be ***nontrivial*** if it contains a nontrivial algebra with at least two elements.

Lemma 10. *Let $\mathcal{K}$ be a nontrivial class of algebras. If there is a free algebra in $\mathcal{K}$ relative to $\varphi : X \to F$, then φ is injective.*

Proof. We indirectly assume that φ is not injective. Then there are two distinct elements x and y in X such that $\varphi(x) = \varphi(y)$. Let $\boldsymbol{A}$ be an algebra in $\mathcal{K}$ with at least two elements, say a and b. If we choose a mapping α from X to A such that $\alpha(x) = a$ and $\alpha(y) = b$, then $\alpha(x) = \alpha^*(\varphi(x)) = \alpha^*(\varphi(y)) = \alpha(y)$ yields a contradiction. ■

In the sequel we will agree upon the following convention. Let $\mathcal{K}$ be a class of algebras. If $\boldsymbol{F}$ is free in $\mathcal{K}$ relative to an injective mapping $\varphi : X \to F$, then X is always regarded as a subset of F (by an appropriate identification). In this case, $\boldsymbol{F}$ is called ***free in*** $\mathcal{K}$ over X, and we write $\boldsymbol{F}_{\mathcal{K}}(X)$ instead of $\boldsymbol{F}$. Notice that $\boldsymbol{F}_{\mathcal{K}}(X)$ is determined only up to isomorphism. When X is unemphasized, we simply speak of a free algebra.

Lemma 11. *Let $\mathcal{K}$ be an abstract class of algebras such that $\mathcal{K}$ is closed under subalgebras. The free algebra in $\mathcal{K}$ over X, if it exists, is generated by X.*

Proof. Given a set X, we suppose that $\boldsymbol{F}_{\mathcal{K}}(X)$ exists. Let us consider the subalgebra of $\boldsymbol{F}_{\mathcal{K}}(X)$ generated by X, say $\boldsymbol{A}$. Evidently, there is an injective homomorphism $h : \boldsymbol{A} \to \boldsymbol{F}_{\mathcal{K}}(X)$ such that $h(a) = a$ for all a in A. We have to show that h is also surjective. Consider the inclusion mapping $in_X : X \to A$. By definition, there is a unique homomorphism, in_X^* from $\boldsymbol{F}_{\mathcal{K}}(X)$ to $\boldsymbol{A}$, such that $in_X = \varphi \cdot in_X^*$, where $\varphi : X \to \boldsymbol{F}_{\mathcal{K}}(X)$. By the uniqueness of *, $(in_X \cdot h)^* = in_X^* \cdot h$ since $\varphi \cdot (in_X \cdot h)^* = in_X \cdot h$ and $\varphi \cdot (in_X^* \cdot h) = in_x \cdot h$. On the other hand, $(in_x \cdot h)^* = id_{\boldsymbol{F}_{\mathcal{K}}(X)}$. Hence, $in_x^* \cdot h = id_{\boldsymbol{F}_{\mathcal{K}}(X)}$ and consequently h is surjective. ■

When X is a generating system for the free algebra $\boldsymbol{F}_{\mathcal{K}}(X)$ in $\mathcal{K}$ over X, we also say that X is a ***free generating system*** or a ***basis*** of $\boldsymbol{F}_{\mathcal{K}}(X)$; and $\boldsymbol{F}_{\mathcal{K}}(X)$ is said to be ***freely generated*** by X.

We speak of ***absolutely free algebras*** instead of free algebras in $\mathcal{K}$ if $\mathcal{K}$ is the class of all similar algebras. A reformulation of the Principle of Finitary Algebraic Recursion (Theorem 4 in Section 1.2.3) yields

Theorem 12. *Term algebras are absolutely free algebras, which are freely generated.* ■

The construction of free algebras is generally a complicated task. In the sequel we will list some examples. If $\mathcal{K}$ is a fixed class of algebras, e.g., the class of all monoids, then we will speak of a free monoid instead of a free algebra in $\mathcal{K}$.

Example 1. It is easy to show that the word monoid $W(X)$ over a set X is the free monoid over X. ■

Example 2. Consider the class of all commutative monoids. Given a set X, the set $\mathcal{M}_\omega(X)$ of all finite multisets over X forms a commutative monoid if the binary operation, denoted by $+$, is defined as follows. Let M and N be finite multisets over X:

$$(M+N)(x) = M(x) + N(x) \quad \text{for all } x \text{ in } X.$$

The empty multiset is the unit.

We assert that $\mathcal{M}_\omega(X)$ is the free commutative monoid. Let A be an arbitrary commutative monoid. Then every mapping α from X to A has a unique homomorphic extension $\alpha^* : \mathcal{M}_\omega(X) \to A$ by

$$\alpha^*(M) = \sum_{x \in X} M(x) \cdot \alpha(x) \quad \text{for all } M \text{ in } \mathcal{M}_\omega(X),$$

where for every natural number n and each a of A, $n \cdot a$ means the n-fold sum of a. Observe that the sum over X is well-defined since it is always finite.

As a by-product we get that the commutative monoid of natural numbers with respect to addition is initial in the class of all commutative monoids. ■

Example 3. The semiring $\mathbb{N}\langle X\rangle$ of all polynomials in (noncommuting) variables from X with coefficients in $\mathbb{N}$ is free in the class of all semirings. For if R is an arbitrary semiring, then every mapping α from X to R admits a unique homomorphic extension $\alpha^* : \mathbb{N}\langle X\rangle \to R$ by

$$\alpha^*(p) = \sum_{w \in W(X)} (p, w) \cdot \alpha^{\S}(w)$$

for all $p \in \mathbb{N}\langle X\rangle$, where $\alpha^{\S} : W(X) \to R$ is the unique extension of α to a monoid homomorphism from the word monoid to $(R, \cdot, 1)$: $\alpha^{\S}(w) = \alpha(x_1) \cdot \ldots \cdot \alpha(x_n)$ for

$w = x_1 \dots x_n$. The semiring of natural numbers under the common operations is initial in the class of all semirings. ■

3.2.3 Varieties

Equational classes of algebras are "closed" under subalgebras, images and direct products as shown in the previous section. Here we shall prove the converse. Therefore we have to define the closures of an abstract class of algebras under the constructions mentioned above.

To every abstract class $\mathcal{K}$ of algebras we associate new abstract classes, denoted by $\mathbf{S}\mathcal{K}$, $\mathbf{H}\mathcal{K}$ and $\mathbf{P}\mathcal{K}$, as follows:

$\boldsymbol{A} \in \mathbf{S}\mathcal{K}$ iff $\boldsymbol{A}$ is a subalgebra of an algebra in $\mathcal{K}$;
$\boldsymbol{A} \in \mathbf{H}\mathcal{K}$ iff $\boldsymbol{A}$ is an image of an algebra in $\mathcal{K}$; and
$\boldsymbol{A} \in \mathbf{P}\mathcal{K}$ iff $\boldsymbol{A}$ is the direct product of a family of algebras in $\mathcal{K}$.

Let $\mathbf{F}$ stand for $\mathbf{S}, \mathbf{H}$ or $\mathbf{P}$. We say that an abstract class $\mathcal{K}$ is ***closed*** under $\mathbf{F}$ if $\mathbf{F}\mathcal{K} \subseteq \mathcal{K}$. In general, $\mathbf{F}$ is called an ***operator*** on abstract classes of algebras. If $\mathbf{S}\mathcal{K} \subseteq \mathcal{K}$, we also say that $\mathcal{K}$ is closed under subalgebras. Similarly, the same convention is made for other concrete operators such as $\mathbf{H}$ and $\mathbf{P}$.

Example 1. Consider a signature consisting of two nullary operation symbols 0 and 1, a unary operation symbol $-$ and two binary operation symbols $+$ and

(i) The class of all rings, where not necessarily $0 \neq 1$, is closed under $\mathbf{S}, \mathbf{H}$ and $\mathbf{P}$.

(ii) The class of all rings, where $0 \neq 1$, is only closed under $\mathbf{S}$. It is not closed under $\mathbf{H}$ since the ***zero ring*** $\{0\}$ is an image of any ring, but the zero ring does not satisfy $0 \neq 1$. The same argument is true when we consider all possible direct products. The direct product of an empty family is a singleton (trivial algebra). Notice, however, that the class of all rings with $0 \neq 1$ is closed under all nonempty direct products.

(iii) The class of all zero divisor free rings is only closed under $\mathbf{S}$. It is not even closed under nonempty direct products. The direct product $\mathbb{Z} \times \mathbb{Z}$ is not zero divisor free although $\mathbb{Z}$ is so.

(iv) The class of all fields is closed neither under $\mathbf{S}$ nor $\mathbf{H}$ nor $\mathbf{P}$. The field of all rationals has $\mathbb{Z}$ as a subring, which is not a field. ■

For our investigation we need various combinations of $\mathbf{S}, \mathbf{H}$ and $\mathbf{P}$. It is customary to write the compositions of these operations as follows. If $\mathbf{F}$ and $\mathbf{G}$ are operators, we set

$$\mathbf{FG}\mathcal{K} = \mathbf{F}(\mathbf{G}\mathcal{K})$$

for every abstract class $\mathcal{K}$. By analogy with mappings, $\mathbf{F}$ is called a ***closure operator*** if for all abstract classes $\mathcal{K}$ and $\mathcal{K}'$ the following conditions are fulfilled:

(1) Extensivity: $\mathcal{K} \subseteq \mathbf{F}\mathcal{K}$;

(2) Idempotency: $\mathbf{FF}\mathcal{K} = \mathbf{F}\mathcal{K}$; and

(3) Monotonicity: $\mathcal{K} \subseteq \mathcal{K}'$ implies $\mathbf{F}\mathcal{K} \subseteq \mathbf{F}\mathcal{K}'$.

It is easily seen that $\mathbf{S}, \mathbf{H}$ and $\mathbf{P}$ are closure operators. Given operators $\mathbf{F}$ and $\mathbf{G}$ we define

$$\mathbf{F} \leq \mathbf{G} \quad \text{iff} \quad \mathbf{F}\mathcal{K} \subseteq \mathbf{G}\mathcal{K} \text{ for all abstract classes } \mathcal{K}.$$

Similarly as for Proposition 1 in Section 1.2.1 we may prove the fact that if $\mathbf{F}$ and $\mathbf{G}$ are closure operators such that $\mathbf{GF} \leq \mathbf{FG}$, then $\mathbf{FG}$ is a closure operator, too.

Lemma 13. *The following holds:*

(1) $\mathbf{SH} \leq \mathbf{HS}$*;*

(2) $\mathbf{PS} \leq \mathbf{SP}$*;*

(3) $\mathbf{PH} \leq \mathbf{HP}$.

Proof. Let $\mathcal{K}$ be an abstract class of algebras.

(1) Assume that $\boldsymbol{A} \in \mathbf{SH}\mathcal{K}$. Then there is an algebra $\boldsymbol{C} \in \mathcal{K}$ and an image $\boldsymbol{B}$ of $\boldsymbol{C}$ such that $\boldsymbol{A}$ is a subalgebra of $\boldsymbol{B}$. Let h be a surjective homomorphism from $\boldsymbol{C}$ to $\boldsymbol{B}$. Since $h^{-1}(A)$ is a subalgebra of $\boldsymbol{C}$, one gets $h^{-1}(A) \in \mathbf{S}\mathcal{K}$. Because of $A = h(h^{-1}(A))$ we derive $\boldsymbol{A} \in \mathbf{HS}\mathcal{K}$.

(2) Assume that $\boldsymbol{A} \in \mathbf{PS}\mathcal{K}$. Then $\boldsymbol{A}$ is either a trivial algebra or there is a nonempty family $(\boldsymbol{A}_i \mid i \in I)$ with $\boldsymbol{A}_i \in \mathbf{S}\mathcal{K}$ such that $\boldsymbol{A} = \prod(\boldsymbol{A}_i \mid i \in I)$. If $\boldsymbol{A}$ is trivial, then $\boldsymbol{A} \in \mathbf{SP}\mathcal{K}$. So it remains to consider the second case. Since $\boldsymbol{A}_i \in \mathbf{S}\mathcal{K}$, there are algebras $\boldsymbol{B}_i \in \mathcal{K}$ for all $i \in I$ such that $\boldsymbol{A}_i$ is a subalgebra of $\boldsymbol{B}_i$. Obviously, $\boldsymbol{A}$ is then a subalgebra of $\prod(\boldsymbol{B}_i \mid i \in I)$, i.e., $A \in \mathbf{SP}\mathcal{K}$.

(3) Assume that $\boldsymbol{A} \in \mathbf{PH}\mathcal{K}$. Then there is a family $(\boldsymbol{A}_i \mid i \in I)$ of algebras $\boldsymbol{A}_i \in \mathbf{H}\mathcal{K}$ such that $\boldsymbol{A} = \prod(\boldsymbol{A}_i \mid i \in I)$. Without loss of generality we can suppose that I is nonempty. By definition, there are algebras $\boldsymbol{B}_i$ such that $\boldsymbol{A}_i$ is an image of $\boldsymbol{B}_i$ for all i in I. Let $h_i : \boldsymbol{B}_i \to \boldsymbol{A}_i$ be a surjective homomorphism for each i of I. Put $\boldsymbol{B} = \prod(\boldsymbol{B}_i \mid i \in I)$. Then there is exactly one homomorphism $h : \boldsymbol{B} \to \boldsymbol{A}$ such that $h \cdot pr_i^A = pr_i^B \cdot h_i$ for all $i \in I$. Evidently, h is surjective and consequently, $\boldsymbol{A} \in \mathbf{HP}\mathcal{K}$. ■

By Lemma 13, $\mathbf{HS}$, $\mathbf{PS}$ and $\mathbf{HP}$ are closure operators.

Definition 5. *An abstract class of algebras is called a **variety** if it is closed under subalgebras, images and products.*

Note. Every variety contains all trivial algebras. Hence the abstract class of all trivial algebras is the least variety, called ***trivial variety***, while a variety $\mathcal{K}$ is said to be ***nontrivial*** if $\mathcal{K}$ contains an algebra with at least two elements. ∎

Example 2. Among the class of algebras considered in Example 1, only the class of all rings is a variety. ∎

The intersection of any class of varieties of similar algebras is again a variety. That is to say, varieties form a closure system. According to our terminology we say that a variety $\mathcal{V}$ is ***generated*** by a given abstract class $\mathcal{K}$ of algebras if $\mathcal{V}$ is the least variety such that $\mathcal{K} \subseteq \mathcal{V}$. Surprisingly, the variety generated by $\mathcal{K}$ can be constructed in a single step.

Theorem 14 (Tarski's Theorem). *If $\mathcal{K}$ is any abstract class of algebras, then* $\mathbf{HSP}\mathcal{K}$ *is the variety generated by $\mathcal{K}$.*

Proof. That $\mathbf{HSP}\mathcal{K}$ is a variety follows from Lemma 13 and the idempotence of each operator:

$$\mathbf{H}(\mathbf{HSP}\mathcal{K}) \subseteq \mathbf{HSP}\mathcal{K};$$
$$\mathbf{S}(\mathbf{HSP}\mathcal{K}) \subseteq \mathbf{HSSP}\mathcal{K} \subseteq \mathbf{HSP}\mathcal{K};$$
$$\mathbf{P}(\mathbf{HSP}\mathcal{K}) \subseteq \mathbf{HPSP}\mathcal{K} \subseteq \mathbf{HSPP}\mathcal{K} \subseteq \mathbf{HSP}\mathcal{K}.$$

Obviously, $\mathcal{K} \subseteq \mathbf{HSP}\mathcal{K}$. On the other hand, if $\mathcal{V}$ is a variety with $\mathcal{K} \subseteq \mathcal{V}$, then $\mathbf{HSP}\mathcal{K} \subseteq \mathcal{V}$. Hence $\mathbf{HSP}\mathcal{K}$ is the least variety including $\mathcal{K}$. ∎

Our aim is to show that both notions, equational class and variety, are logically equivalent. By Theorem 8, every equational class is a variety. To prove the converse some properties of free algebras are needed.

Theorem 15 (Existence of Free Algebras). *Let $\mathcal{K}$ be a nontrivial abstract class of algebras. If $\mathcal{K}$ is closed under subalgebras and direct products, the free algebras exist in $\mathcal{K}$.*

Proof. Assume that $\mathcal{K}$ is a nontrivial abstract class of algebras closed under $\mathbf{S}$ and $\mathbf{P}$. Denote by I the set of all congruences R on $\boldsymbol{T}_\Sigma(X)$ such that $\boldsymbol{T}_\Sigma(X)/R$ is in $\mathcal{K}$, where X is an arbitrarily given set. I is nonempty since the entire relation $T_\Sigma(X) \times T_\Sigma(X)$ belongs to I.

Now define an algebra $\boldsymbol{F}$ as quotient of $\boldsymbol{T}_\Sigma(X)$ modulo the intersection R_0 of I. It is easily seen that $\boldsymbol{F}$ is isomorphic to the subdirect product $\{([t]_R \mid R \in I) \mid t \in T_\Sigma(X)\}$ of the family $(\boldsymbol{T}_\Sigma(X)/R \mid R \in I)$. By assumption, $\boldsymbol{F}$ is contained in $\mathcal{K}$.

Let $\boldsymbol{A}$ be an arbitrary algebra in $\mathcal{K}$. For any mapping $\alpha : X \to A$ we have to exhibit a unique homomorphism $\alpha^* : \boldsymbol{F} \to \boldsymbol{A}$ such that $\alpha = \varphi \cdot \alpha^*$, where $\varphi : X \to F$ is given by $\varphi(x) = [x]_{R_0}$ for all x in X.

Consider the unique homomorphic extension $\alpha^\sharp : \boldsymbol{T}_\Sigma(X) \to \boldsymbol{A}$ of α, which exists by the Principle of Finitary Algebraic Recursion (Theorem 4 in Section 1.2.3). Note that

$\boldsymbol{T}_\Sigma(X)/ker\ \alpha^\sharp$ is isomorphic to a subalgebra of $\boldsymbol{A}$; hence $\boldsymbol{T}_\Sigma(X)/ker\ \alpha^\sharp$ is in $\mathcal{K}$ and so $ker\ \alpha^\sharp$ belongs to I. Since $R_0 \subseteq ker\ \alpha^\sharp$, we can define α^* so that

$$\alpha^*([t]_{R_0}) = \alpha^\sharp(t)$$

for all $t \in T_\Sigma(X)$. ■

Concerning varieties the existence of free algebras is guaranteed by Theorem 15.

Theorem 16. *Every nontrivial variety admits free algebras.* ■

To continue, another technical lemma is necessary.

Lemma 17. *An algebra* $\boldsymbol{A}$ *belongs to a variety* $\mathcal{K}$ *whenever all its finitely generated subalgebras are in* $\mathcal{K}$.

Proof. Let $\mathcal{K}$ be a variety. It suffices to show that $\mathcal{K}$ is closed under directed unions. By Theorem 1 in Section 3.3.1, any algebra $\boldsymbol{A}$ is the directed union of its finitely generated subalgebras; hence the assertion follows directly.

Now assume that $(\boldsymbol{A}_i | i \in I)$ is a directed family of algebras in $\mathcal{K}$. We shall prove that $\boldsymbol{A} = \bigcup(\boldsymbol{A}_i | i \in I)$ is also in $\mathcal{K}$. First, the direct product $\prod(\boldsymbol{A}_i | i \in I)$ is certainly in $\mathcal{K}$ since $\mathbf{P}\mathcal{K} \subseteq \mathcal{K}$. Second, define a subalgebra $\boldsymbol{B}$ the carrier of which consists of all families $(a_i | i \in I)$ with the property that there is an index $k \in I$ such that $a_i = a_k$ for all $i \geq k$. Evidently, the subset of all those families is closed under operations and so $\boldsymbol{B}$ is, indeed, a subalgebra. Of course, $\boldsymbol{B}$ belongs to $\mathcal{K}$ since $\mathbf{S}\mathcal{K} \subseteq \mathcal{K}$. Third, a quotient algebra of $\boldsymbol{B}$ is defined by means of the following congruence $\sim$ on $\boldsymbol{B}$: $(a_i | i \in I) \sim (b_i | i \in I)$ iff there is an index $k \in I$ such that $a_i = b_i$ for all $i \geq k$. Since $\mathbf{H}\mathcal{K} \subseteq \mathcal{K}$, $\boldsymbol{B}/\sim$ belongs to $\mathcal{K}$.

Claim: $\boldsymbol{A}$ is isomorphic to $\boldsymbol{B}/\sim$.

Define a family $(h_i | i \in I)$ of homomorphisms $h_i : \boldsymbol{A}_i \to \boldsymbol{B}/\sim$ by $h_i(a) = [(a_j | j \in I)]$ for all $a \in A_i$, where $a_j = a$ if $i \leq j$. Observe that h_i is a well-defined homomorphism. Moreover, h_i is the restriction of h_j to $\boldsymbol{A}_i$ whenever $i \leq j$. Hence, there exists a unique homomorphism $h : \boldsymbol{A} \to \boldsymbol{B}/\sim$ such that $h_i = in_i \cdot h$ for all $i \in I$, where $in_i : \boldsymbol{A}_i \to \boldsymbol{A}$ is the inclusion of $\boldsymbol{A}_i$ into $\boldsymbol{A}$. It is easily seen that h is a bijection. Thus $\boldsymbol{A}$ is isomorphic to $\boldsymbol{B}/\sim$.

Therefore we have shown that $\bigcup(\boldsymbol{A}_i | i \in I)$ belongs to $\mathcal{K}$. ■

Corollary. *Every variety is closed under directed unions.* ■

Any variety is generated by its free algebras. This characteristic feature is closely related to the defining property of free algebras with respect to validation (cf. Theorem 9).

Theorem 18. *If $\mathcal{K}$ is a nontrivial variety, then*

$$\mathcal{K} = \mathbf{HSP}\{\boldsymbol{F}_{\mathcal{K}}(X) \mid X \text{ is a finite set}\}.$$

Proof. Let $\mathcal{K}$ be a nontrivial variety. Denote by $\mathcal{F}_{\mathcal{K}}$ the class of all free algebras in $\mathcal{K}$ over finite sets. Clearly, $\mathcal{F}_{\mathcal{K}} \subseteq \mathcal{K}$ for $\mathcal{K}$ is a variety. Using Tarski's Theorem (Theorem 14) we obtain $\mathbf{HSP}\mathcal{F}_{\mathcal{K}} \subseteq \mathcal{K}$. To prove the opposite inclusion it suffices to show that every finitely generated algebra of $\mathcal{K}$ belongs to $\mathbf{HSP}\mathcal{F}_{\mathcal{K}}$, by Lemma 17. If we suppose that an algebra $\boldsymbol{A} \in \mathcal{K}$ is generated by a finite set X, then $\boldsymbol{A}$ is an image of $\boldsymbol{F}_{\mathcal{K}}(X)$. Hence $\boldsymbol{A} \in \mathbf{HSP}\mathcal{F}_{\mathcal{K}}$ and consequently $\mathcal{K} \subseteq \mathbf{HSP}\mathcal{F}_{\mathcal{K}}$, which completes the proof. ■

Corollary 1. *If $\mathcal{K}$ is a nontrivial variety, then* (1) $\mathcal{K} = \mathbf{HSP}\{\boldsymbol{F}_{\mathcal{K}}(V)\}$ *where V is a countably infinite set; and* (2) $\mathcal{K} = \mathbf{HSP}\{\boldsymbol{F}_{\mathcal{K}}(Z)\}$ *where Z is any infinite set.*

Proof. (1) follows directly from Theorem 18. To prove (2), let $\mathcal{K}$ be a nontrivial variety and let Z be any infinite set. Evidently, $\mathbf{HSP}\{\boldsymbol{F}_{\mathcal{K}}(Z)\} \subseteq \mathcal{K}$ since $\boldsymbol{F}_{\mathcal{K}}(Z)$ is in $\mathcal{K}$. On the other hand, $\boldsymbol{F}_{\mathcal{K}}(V)$ is a subalgebra of $\boldsymbol{F}_{\mathcal{K}}(Z)$. That is, $\boldsymbol{F}_{\mathcal{K}}(V) \in \mathbf{S}\boldsymbol{F}_{\mathcal{K}}(Z)$ and so $\mathbf{HSP}\{\boldsymbol{F}_{\mathcal{K}}(V)\} \subseteq \mathbf{HSP}\{\boldsymbol{F}_{\mathcal{K}}(Z)\}$. Thus $\mathbf{HSP}\{\boldsymbol{F}_{\mathcal{K}}(Z)\} = \mathcal{K}$. ■

The generation of varieties by their free algebras gives a useful criterion for comparison.

Corollary 2. *For nontrivial varieties $\mathcal{K}$ and $\mathcal{K}'$ the following conditions are equivalent:*

(1) $\mathcal{K} \subseteq \mathcal{K}'$,

(2) $\boldsymbol{F}_{\mathcal{K}}(X) \in \mathcal{K}'$ *for all finite sets X,*

(3) $\boldsymbol{F}_{\mathcal{K}}(V) \in \mathcal{K}'$.

(4) $\boldsymbol{F}_{\mathcal{K}}(Z) \in \mathcal{K}'$ *for any infinite set Z.* ■

Any nontrivial variety is fully determined either by all free algebras over finite sets or by the free algebra over a countably infinite set. In the sequel we shall fix a countably infinite set, say V, and refer to it as the "standard alphabet" of variables.

When we try to prove that every variety is equationally definable, we must find a suitable set of equations. In a first attempt we would take all equations valid in the variety. But this leads to a proper class of equations, whereas the restriction to equations with variables from V prevents this difficulty.

Given an abstract class $\mathcal{K}$ of algebras, $Eq\ \mathcal{K}$ denotes the set of all equations $\forall X(t = t')$ such that $X \subseteq V$ and $\mathcal{K} \models \forall X(t = t')$. $Eq\ \mathcal{K}$ is called the ***equational theory*** of $\mathcal{K}$.

If $\mathcal{K}$ and $\mathcal{K}'$ are abstract classes of algebras, then

$$Eq\ \mathcal{K} \subseteq Eq\ \mathcal{K}' \quad \text{whenever} \quad \mathcal{K}' \subseteq \mathcal{K}.$$

It is easy to see that the equational theory of a variety coincides with that of any of its generating class. That is, $Eq\ \mathcal{K} = Eq\ \mathbf{HSP}\mathcal{K}$ for any abstract class of algebras. Using

Theorem 18 we derive

$$\begin{aligned} Eq\ \mathcal{K} &= Eq\ \{\boldsymbol{F}_{\mathcal{K}}(X) \mid X \text{ is a finite set}\} \\ &= Eq\ \{\boldsymbol{F}_{\mathcal{K}}(V)\} \end{aligned}$$

for every nontrivial variety $\mathcal{K}$. This is another version of the typicality of free algebras with respect to validation. The reader may prove that, in addition, $Eq\ \mathcal{K} = Eq\ \{\boldsymbol{F}_{\mathcal{K}}(Z)\}$ for every nontrivial variety and any infinite set Z. In other words, an equation $\forall X(t = t')$ is valid in a nontrivial variety $\mathcal{K}$ iff $\boldsymbol{F}_{\mathcal{K}}(X) \models \forall X(t = t')$ iff $\boldsymbol{F}_{\mathcal{K}}(V) \models \forall X(t = t')$ iff $\boldsymbol{F}_{\mathcal{K}}(Z) \models \forall X(t = t')$, where Z is any infinite set.

The importance of this result lies mainly in its theoretical aspect; it is not so much of practical use since the construction of free algebras is rather complicated in general. On the other hand, in simple cases when we know the free algebras, there is no deep insight concerning its equational theory.

Sometimes the application of suitable decomposition principles is more advantageous. Let $\mathcal{K}$ be a variety. If $Gen_\omega \mathcal{K}$ denotes the subclass of all its finitely generated algebras, then

$$Eq\ \mathcal{K} = Eq\ Gen_\omega \mathcal{K}$$

as the reader may verify by means of Theorem 1 in Section 3.1.1. Thus an equation is valid in $\mathcal{K}$ iff it is valid in all finitely generated algebras in $\mathcal{K}$.

Example 3. An idempotent semigroup is usually called a ***band***. It is known from the literature that every finitely generated band is finite. Hence an equation is valid in all bands iff it is valid in all finite bands. ∎

Birkhoff's Subdirect Representation Theorem (Theorem 12 in Section 3.1.3) may also be applied. Given a variety $\mathcal{K}$, if $Irr\ \mathcal{K}$ denotes the subclass of all subdirectly irreducible algebras in $\mathcal{K}$, then

$$Eq\ \mathcal{K} = Eq\ Irr\ \mathcal{K};$$

an equation is valid in $\mathcal{K}$ iff it is valid in all subdirectly irreducible algebras in $\mathcal{K}$.

Example 4. Consider the variety of distributive lattices. In Example 3 in Section 3.1.3 we have shown that a distributive lattice is subdirectly irreducible iff it is a two-element chain. Hence an equation is valid in all distributive lattices iff it is valid in a two-element chain. The same is true for Boolean algebras. ∎

Now we turn again to the axiomatization of varieties by equations.

Lemma 19. *If $\mathcal{K}$ is a nontrivial variety, then the free algebras in $Mod\ Eq\ \mathcal{K}$ belong to $\mathcal{K}$.*

Proof. Let $\mathcal{K}$ be a nontrivial variety. We set $\mathcal{K}' = Mod\ Eq\ \mathcal{K}$. Evidently, $\mathcal{K}'$ is also a nontrivial variety. Consider now the free algebras in $\mathcal{K}$ and $\mathcal{K}'$. Note that $\mathcal{K}$ is included in $\mathcal{K}'$. Hence $\boldsymbol{F}_{\mathcal{K}}(X) \in \mathcal{K}'$.

Since $\boldsymbol{F}_{\mathcal{K}}(V)$ is in $\mathcal{K}'$, φ admits a unique homomorphic extension φ^* from $\boldsymbol{F}_{\mathcal{K}'}(V)$ to $\boldsymbol{F}_{\mathcal{K}}(V)$ such that $\varphi = \psi \cdot \varphi^*$. Moreover, φ and ψ have homomorphic extensions $\varphi^\sharp$ and $\psi^\sharp$ from $\boldsymbol{T}_\Sigma(V)$ to $\boldsymbol{F}_{\mathcal{K}}(V)$ and $\boldsymbol{F}_{\mathcal{K}'}(V)$, respectively, with $\varphi = in_V \cdot \varphi^\sharp$ and $\psi = in_V \cdot \psi^\sharp$, where $in_V : V \to T_\Sigma(V)$ is the inclusion. It follows that $\varphi^\sharp = \psi^\sharp \cdot \varphi^*$ (see Fig. 3.10)

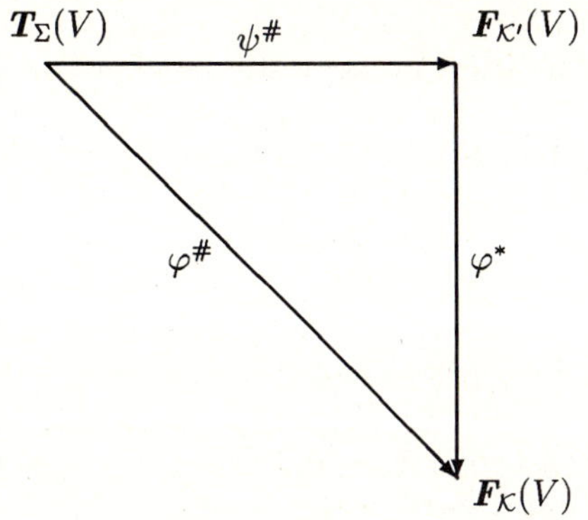

Fig. 3.10

Claim: φ^* is injective.

Let a and b be any elements of $\boldsymbol{F}_{\mathcal{K}'}(V)$. Since $\psi^\sharp$ is surjective there are terms t and t' in $T_\Sigma(V)$ such that $\psi^\sharp(t) = a$ and $\psi^\sharp(t') = b$. Let $X = var(t) \cup var(t')$. If $\varphi^*(a) = \varphi^*(b)$, then $\varphi^\sharp(t) = \varphi^\sharp(t')$. That is, $\forall X(t = t')$ is in $Eq\ \mathcal{K}$. But, then $\forall X(t = t')$ is also valid in $\boldsymbol{F}_{\mathcal{K}'}(V)$ and so $\psi^\sharp(t) = \psi^\sharp(t')$, hence $a = b$. Indeed, φ^* is an injective homomorphism. Thus $\boldsymbol{F}_{\mathcal{K}'}(V)$ belongs to $\mathbf{S}\mathcal{K}$. Since $\mathbf{S}\mathcal{K} \subseteq \mathcal{K}$, $\boldsymbol{F}_{\mathcal{K}'}(V)$ is in $\mathcal{K}$. ■

Proposition 20. *If $\mathcal{K}$ is a variety, then $\mathcal{K} = Mod\ Eq\ \mathcal{K}$.*

Proof. We have only to show that $Mod\ Eq\ \mathcal{K}$ is included in $\mathcal{K}$ since the converse inclusion holds trivially. Let $\mathcal{K}'$ abbreviate $Mod\ Eq\ \mathcal{K}$. By Theorem 8 in Section 3.2.1, $\mathcal{K}'$ is a variety. If $\mathcal{K}$ is trivial, then so is $\mathcal{K}'$. Assume $\mathcal{K}$ is a nontrivial variety, then $\mathcal{K}'$ is nontrivial, too. By Lemma 19, $\boldsymbol{F}_{\mathcal{K}'}(V)$ belongs to $\mathcal{K}$, where V is a countably infinite set. Hence $\mathcal{K}'$ is included in $\mathcal{K}$, by Corollary 2 to Theorem 18. ■

Now we are ready to prove our main result.

Theorem 21 (Birkhoff's Variety Theorem). *Let $\mathcal{K}$ be an abstract class of algebras. Then $\mathcal{K}$ is an equational class if and only if $\mathcal{K}$ is a variety.*

The proof follows from Theorem 8 in Section 3.2.1 and Proposition 20. ■

Using Birkhoff's Variety Theorem we can deduce further closure properties. Let $\mathcal{K}$ be any variety. Since $\mathcal{K}$ is an equational class, $\mathcal{K}$ is closed under directed unions, direct limits, subdirect products and reduced products.

Let us formally introduce operators related to these closure properties. Given an abstract class $\mathcal{K}$ of algebras, we define operators $\mathbf{U}$, $\mathbf{L}$, $\mathbf{P}_{sub}$ and $\mathbf{P}_{red}$ as follows:

$\boldsymbol{A} \in \mathbf{U}\mathcal{K}$ iff $\boldsymbol{A}$ is a directed union of a directed family of algebras in $\mathcal{K}$.

$\boldsymbol{A} \in \mathbf{L}\mathcal{K}$ iff $\boldsymbol{A}$ is a direct limit of a direct family of algebras in $\mathcal{K}$.

$\boldsymbol{A} \in \mathbf{P}_{sub}\mathcal{K}$ iff $\boldsymbol{A}$ is a subdirect product of a family of algebras in $\mathcal{K}$.

$\boldsymbol{A} \in \mathbf{P}_{red}\mathcal{K}$ iff $\boldsymbol{A}$ is a reduced product of a family of algebras in $\mathcal{K}$.

The observation above immediately yields the following.

Proposition 22. *If $\mathcal{K}$ is a variety, then $\mathcal{K}$ is closed under directed unions, direct limits, subdirect products and reduced products.* ■

We shall only mention here that $\mathbf{U}$ and $\mathbf{L}$ are not closure operators, while $\mathbf{P}_{sub}$ and $\mathbf{P}_{red}$ are indeed closure operators. Of course, all operators are extensive and monotone. But idempotency is not satisfied for $\mathbf{U}$ and $\mathbf{L}$ (see /Kruse-67/, /Platt-71/). It is easily seen that $\mathbf{P}_{sub}$ is idempotent, whereas the idempotency of $\mathbf{P}_{red}$ is not obvious (see /Burris-Sankappanavar-81/).

The fact that varieties are closed under directed unions, direct limits, subdirect products and reduced products can also be expressed by the following inequalities of the related operators:

$$\mathbf{U}, \mathbf{L}, \mathbf{P}_{sub}, \mathbf{P}_{red} \leq \mathbf{HSP}.$$

Furthermore, we have

$$\mathbf{L} \leq \mathbf{UH} \quad \text{and} \quad \mathbf{P}_{red} \leq \mathbf{LP}$$

since direct limits can be constructed by means of directed unions and quotients as shown in Section 3.1.2 and, on the other hand, reduced products are representable as direct limits of certain direct products, by Proposition 15 in Section 3.1.4. By definition,

$$\mathbf{P}_{sub} \leq \mathbf{SP} \quad \text{and} \quad \mathbf{P}_{red} \leq \mathbf{HP}.$$

Kogalovskii /Kogalovskii-65/ proved that, in particular,

$$\mathbf{HP}_{sub} = \mathbf{HSP}.$$

The different characterizations of equational classes will now be summarized.

Corollary. *For any abstract class $\mathcal{K}$ of algebras the following are equivalent:*

(1) $\mathcal{K}$ is an equational class.

(2) $\mathcal{K}$ is a variety.

(3) $\mathcal{K}$ is closed under $\mathbf{S}$, $\mathbf{H}$ *and* $\mathbf{P}$.

(4) $\mathcal{K} = Mod\ Eq\ \mathcal{K}$.

(5) $\mathcal{K} = Mod\ Eq\ \mathcal{K}'$ *for some abstract class* $\mathcal{K}'$.

(6) $\mathcal{K} = \mathbf{HSP}\mathcal{K}$.

(7) $\mathcal{K} = \mathbf{HSP}\mathcal{K}'$ *for some abstract class* $\mathcal{K}'$.

(8) $\mathcal{K} = \mathbf{HP}_{sub}\mathcal{K}$.

(9) $\mathcal{K} = \mathbf{HP}_{sub}\mathcal{K}'$ *for some abstract class* $\mathcal{K}'$.

(10) $\mathcal{K}$ *is generated as a variety by a single algebra.* ■

The proof of the equivalences follows from Birkhoff's Variety Theorem, Proposition 20, Tarski's Theorem, Kogalovskii's result and Theorem 18.

Finally, we will focus our attention on another aspect of equational classes. The validity relation gives rise to a Galois connection (see Section 1.2.1) between Eq and Mod, considered as mappings, since we have

$$\mathcal{K} \subseteq Mod\ Eq\ \mathcal{K} \quad \text{and} \quad E \subseteq Eq\ Mod\ E;$$

and

$$Eq\ \mathcal{K} \subseteq Eq\ \mathcal{K}' \quad \text{whenever} \quad \mathcal{K}' \subseteq \mathcal{K};$$
$$Mod\ E \subseteq Mod\ E' \quad \text{whenever} \quad E' \subseteq E.$$

Hence $Mod\ Eq$ and $Eq\ Mod$ are closure operators.

By Proposition 20, varieties are closed classes of algebras with respect to $Mod\ Eq$. Thus $Mod\ Eq = \mathbf{HSP}$, by Tarski's Theorem.

In the next section, the closed sets of equations with respect to the other closure operator, $Eq\ Mod$, will be studied.

3.2.4 Equational Theories

By analogy with Birkhoff's Variety Theorem, which characterizes a logical concept (equational class) in terms of algebraic notions (closure under **S**, **H** and **P**), our second main logical concept, equational theory, will be characterized algebraically in this section.

Throughout the sequel a countably infinite set V is fixed as a "standard alphabet" of variables; and we will always assume that for any equation $\forall X(t = t')$ its set X of variables is a subset of V.

Definition 6. *A set E of equations is called an* ***equational theory*** *if E is the equational theory of some abstract class of algebras.*

Using the fact that Eq and Mod form a Galois connection we have $Eq\ Mod\ Eq\ \mathcal{K} = Eq\ \mathcal{K}$. Thus, E is an equational theory iff

$$E = Eq\ Mod\ E.$$

Any set E of equations can be thought of as a relation $\overline{E}$ on $T_\Sigma(V)$ where $\overline{E} = \{(t,t')|\forall X(t = t') \in E\}$. Frequently, E is written instead of $\overline{E}$ if no ambiguity is caused. Let $=_E$ denote the fully invariant congruence on $\boldsymbol{T}_\Sigma(V)$ generated by $\overline{E}$. That is, $=_E$ is the congruence generated by the stable closure $sta(\overline{E})$ of $\overline{E}$. By definition, $sta(\overline{E})$ is the closure of $\overline{E}$ under all endomorphisms of $\boldsymbol{T}_\Sigma(V)$. Hence, $sta(\overline{E}) = \{(s^\sharp(t), s^\sharp(t'))|\forall X(t = t') \in E \text{ and } s : X \to T_\Sigma(V)\}$. Observe that we can restrict the substitutions on subsets of V. Henceforth, a mapping $s : X \to T_\Sigma(V)$ is also called a ***substitution*** provided X is a subset of V.

Proposition 23. *If E is an equational theory, then $\overline{E}$ is a fully invariant congruence on $\boldsymbol{T}_\Sigma(V)$. That is, $=_E = \overline{E}$.* ■

The simple proof is left to the reader as an exercise.

Lemma 24. *Given a set E of equations, $\boldsymbol{T}_\Sigma(V)/{=_E}$ is a model for E.*

Proof. Let E be any set of equations. For each equation $\forall X(t = t')$ of E we have to show $\boldsymbol{T}_\Sigma(V)/{=_E} \models \forall X(t = t')$. Therefore, consider an assignment α from X to $T_\Sigma(V)/{=_E}$. Now, it is important to observe that every assignment α is definable by a substitution $s : X \to T_\Sigma(V)$ as follows:

$$\alpha = s \cdot nat \text{ with } nat : T_\Sigma(V) \to T_\Sigma(V)/{=_E}\,.$$

By the Principle of Finitary Algebraic Recursion (Theorem 4 in Section 1.2.3) we derive $\alpha^\sharp = s^\sharp \cdot nat$. Thus $\forall X(t = t')$ is valid in $\boldsymbol{T}_\Sigma(V)/{=_E}$ iff $nat(s^\sharp(t)) = nat(s^\sharp(t'))$. In other terms, $\forall X(t = t')$ is valid in $\boldsymbol{T}_\Sigma(V)/{=_E}$ iff $s^\sharp(t) =_E s^\sharp(t')$ for all substitutions $s : X \to T_\Sigma(V)$.

By definition, $=_E$ is the fully invariant congruence on $\boldsymbol{T}_\Sigma(V)$ generated by $\overline{E}$. Hence $s^\sharp(t) =_E s^\sharp(t')$ for all substitutions $s : X \to T_\Sigma(V)$ and each equation $\forall X(t = t')$ of E. Consequently, $\boldsymbol{T}_\Sigma(V)/{=_E}$ is a model for E. ■

Corollary 1. *If R is a fully invariant congruence on $\boldsymbol{T}_\Sigma(V)$, then, for every equation $\forall X(t = t')$,*

$$\boldsymbol{T}_\Sigma(V)/R \models \forall X(t = t') \quad \textit{iff} \quad (t,t') \in R.$$ ■

For the moment, a set E of equations is called ***nontrivial*** if E does not contain $\forall x, y\, (x = y)$ for any pair of different variables x and y in V. Observe that $Mod\ E$ is a nontrivial variety iff E is nontrivial.

Corollary 2. *If E is a nontrivial set of equations, then $\boldsymbol{T}_\Sigma(V)/=_E$ is the free algebra over V in $Mod\ E$.* ■

Proposition 25. *Given a set E of equations, the equational theory of $Mod\ E$ is the fully invariant congruence generated by E. Specifically, $=_E = Eq\ Mod\ E$.*

Proof. By Proposition 23, $Eq\ Mod\ E$ is a fully invariant congruence. Obviously, $E \subseteq Eq\ Mod\ E$. So it remains to show that $Eq\ Mod\ E$ is the least fully invariant congruence with this property.

Assume R is a fully invariant congruence on $\boldsymbol{T}_\Sigma(V)$ such that $\overline{E} \subseteq R$. By Corollary 1 to Lemma 24, $\boldsymbol{T}_\Sigma(V)/R$ is a model for E, hence $Eq\ Mod\ E \subseteq Eq\ \{\boldsymbol{T}_\Sigma(V)/R\} = R$, hence $Eq\ Mod\ E$ is the least fully invariant congruence on $\boldsymbol{T}_\Sigma(V)$ including E. ■

For our purpose the crucial property of fully invariant congruences is the following.

Proposition 26. *If E is a set of equations such that $\overline{E}$ is a fully invariant congruence on $\boldsymbol{T}_\Sigma(V)$, then*

$$E = Eq\ Mod\ E.$$

Proof. By Proposition 25, $=_E = Eq\ Mod\ E$. Recall that $=_E$ is the least fully invariant congruence on $\boldsymbol{T}_\Sigma(V)$, which includes $\overline{E}$. If $\overline{E}$ is assumed to be a fully invariant congruence, then, of course, $=_E = \overline{E}$ and so $E = Eq\ Mod\ E$. ■

We are now in a position to derive our second main result.

Theorem 27 (Birkhoff's Criterion for Equational Theories). *Let E be a set of equations. Then E is an equational theory if and only if $\overline{E}$ is a fully invariant congruence on $\boldsymbol{T}_\Sigma(V)$.*

Proof. If E is an equational theory, then $\overline{E}$ is a fully invariant congruence on $\boldsymbol{T}_\Sigma(V)$, by Proposition 23. Conversely, if E is a set of equations such that $\overline{E}$ is a fully invariant congruence on $\boldsymbol{T}_\Sigma(V)$, then $E = Eq\ Mod\ E$, by Proposition 26; hence E is an equational theory. ■

Birkhoff's Criterion for Equational Theories can be presented in another version.

Definition 7. *An equation $\forall X(t = t')$ is said to be a* ***logical consequence*** *of a given set E of equations, in symbols*

$$E \models \forall X(t = t'),$$

if $\forall X(t = t')$ is valid in all models of E.

By Proposition 25, $E \models \forall X(t = t')$ iff $t =_E t'$. An equational theory is a set of equations closed under logical consequences.

Corollary. *A set E of equations is an equational theory iff an equation $\forall X(t = t')$ belongs to E whenever $E \models \forall X(t = t')$.* ∎

Fully invariant congruences constitute, so to speak, an algebraic description of equational theories. Since all fully invariant congruences on $\boldsymbol{T}_\Sigma(V)$ form an algebraic closure system (see the note to Theorem 12 in Section 2.1.2) there exists a formal proof system such that equational theories are deductively closed sets. In other words, corresponding to the logical consequence relation $\models$ there exists a syntactical consequence relation $\vdash$.

Definition 8. *Let us denote by EL the following set of inference rules of* ***equational logic****.*

(I) Rules of congruence

(EL1) $\forall X(t = t)$;

(EL2) $$\frac{\forall X(t = t')}{\forall X(t' = t)};$$

(EL3) $$\frac{\forall X(t = t'), \forall X(t' = t'')}{\forall X(t = t'')};$$

(EL4) $$\frac{\forall X_1(t_1 = t_1'), \ldots, \forall X_n(t_n = t_n')}{\forall X(\sigma\, t_1 \ldots t_n = \sigma\, t_1' \ldots t_n')}$$
for every n-ary operation symbol σ, where $X = X_1 \cup \ldots \cup X_n$.

(II) Rule of full invariance

(EL5) $$\frac{\forall X(t = t')}{\forall Y(s^\sharp(t) = s^\sharp(t'))}$$
for all substitutions $s : X \to T_\Sigma(V)$ where $Y = \bigcup\{var(s(x)) | x \in X\}$.

(III) Rule of abstraction

(EL6) $$\frac{\forall X(t = t')}{\forall Y(t = t')}$$
where $Y = X \cup \{y\}$ for some $y \in V - X$.

(IV) Rule of concretion

(EL7) $$\frac{\forall X(t = t')}{\forall Y(t = t')}$$
where $Y = X - \{x\}$ for some $x \in V - (var(t) \cup var(t'))$.

The inference rules are obtained by transforming the defining properties of a fully invariant congruence: reflexivity ($EL1$), symmetry ($EL2$), transitivity ($EL3$), compatibility

$(EL4)$; and stability $(EL5)$. Since quantification is expressed explicitly the two additional rules of abstraction and concretion are required.

Deductions are finite sequences of equations called ***formal proofs*** leading from a given set E of equations, the premises of the deduction, to another equation $\forall X(t = t')$, the conclusion of the deduction. Equations occurring in a formal proof are either in E or else can be inferred from earlier equations of the sequence by one of the inference rules $(EL1)$ – $(EL7)$. We say that $\forall X(t = t')$ is ***deducible*** from E if there is a deduction from E whose last equation is $\forall X(t = t')$. Notation: we write

$$E \vdash_{EL} \forall X(t = t')$$

to indicate that $\forall X(t = t')$ is deducible from E. Frequently, the subscript EL is omitted when no confusion can arise.

Remark. According to Definition 8 in Section 1.2.4 a formal proof system consists of a set of inference rules together with a notion of formal proof expressed by $\vdash$. Our definition above is to be understood in such a way. ■

Example 1. Consider the signature of groups with a nullary operation symbol e, a unary operation symbol i and a binary operation symbol . Let E be the axiom system consisting of the following equations:

(G1) $\forall x, y, z\,((x \cdot y) \cdot z = x \cdot (y \cdot z))$;

(G2) $\forall x\,(i(x) \cdot x = e)$; and

(G3) $\forall x\,(e \cdot x = x)$.

For instance, the equation

$$\forall x\ (x \cdot i(x) = e)$$

is deducible from E by the following formal proof:

(1) $\forall x\,(i(i(x)) \cdot i(x) = e)$ from (G2) by $(EL5)$ for $s = \{x \mapsto i(x)\}$

(2) $\forall x\,((i(i(x)) \cdot i(x)) \cdot x = e \cdot x)$ from (1) and $(EL1)$ for $t = x$ by $(EL4)$ for $\cdot$

(3) $\forall x\,((i(i(x)) \cdot i(x)) \cdot x = x)$ from (2) and (G3) by $(EL3)$

(4) $\forall x\,(i(x) = i(x))$ from $(EL1)$ for $t = x$ by $(EL4)$ for i

(5) $\forall x\,(((i(i(x)) \cdot i(x)) \cdot x) \cdot i(x) = x \cdot i(x))$ from (3) and (4) by $(EL4)$ for $\cdot$

(6) $\forall x\,((i(i(x)) \cdot i(x)) \cdot x = i(i(x)) \cdot (i(x) \cdot x))$
from (G1) by $(EL5)$ for $s = \{x \mapsto i(i(x)), y \mapsto i(x), z \mapsto x\}$

(7) $\forall x\,((i(i(x)) \cdot i(x)) \cdot x = i(i(x)) \cdot e)$ from (6) and (G2) by $(EL3)$

(8) $\forall x\, (((i(i(x)) \cdot i(x)) \cdot x) \cdot i(x) = (i(i(x)) \cdot e) \cdot i(x))$
from (7) and (4) by $(EL4)$ for $\cdot$

(9) $\forall x\, (x \cdot i(x) = (i(i(x)) \cdot e) \cdot i(x))$ from (5) and (8) by $(EL3)$

(10) $\forall x\, ((i(i(x)) \cdot e) \cdot i(x) = i(i(x)) \cdot (e \cdot i(x)))$
from (G1) by $(EL5)$ for $s = \{x \mapsto i(i(x)),\ y \mapsto e,\ z \mapsto i(x)\}$

(11) $\forall x\, ((i(i(x)) \cdot e) \cdot i(x) = i(i(x)) \cdot i(x))$ from (10) and (G3) by $(EL3)$

(12) $\forall x\, (i(i(x)) \cdot i(x) = e)$ from (G2) by $(EL5)$ for $s = \{x \mapsto i(x)\}$

(13) $\forall x\, ((i(i(x)) \cdot e) \cdot i(x) = e)$ from (11) and (12) by $(EL3)$

(14) $\forall x\, (x \cdot i(x) = e)$ from (9) and (13) by $(EL3)$.

(Note that (7), (9), (11) and (13) are not derivable in a single step as mentioned; but the missing intermediate steps are obvious and therefore they are omitted.)

Hence

$$E \vdash_{EL} \forall x\ (x \cdot i(x) = e).$$

The reader may prove similarly that $\forall x\ (x \cdot e = x)$ is also deducible from the group axioms. ■

Informally speaking, our formal proof system is ***sound*** (or ***correct***): the inference rules $(EL1)$ – $(EL7)$ never lead us from premises which are logical consequences of a given set E of equations to conclusions which are not logical conesquences of E. For example, consider $(EL4)$. If we assume that $E \models \forall X_i(t_i = t_i')$ for $i = 1, \ldots, n$, then $t_i =_E t_i'$, hence $\sigma\, t_1 \ldots t_n =_E \sigma\, t_1' \ldots t_n'$ since $=_E$ is a (fully invariant) congruence on $\boldsymbol{T}_\Sigma(V)$. Thus $E \models \forall X(\sigma\, t_1 \ldots t_n = \sigma\, t_1' \ldots t_n')$, and $(EL4)$ is sound. The soundness of the remaining inference rules can be shown similarly.

Proposition 28 (Soundness of Equational Logic). *Given a set E of equations, every equation which is deducible from E is a logical consequence of E.* ■

Now we can take up the question whether every equation which is a logical consequence of a given set E of equations is also deducible from E.

Theorem 29 (Birkhoff's Completeness Theorem for Equational Logic). *Let E be a set of equations. An arbitrary equation $\forall X(t = t')$ is a logical consequence of E if and only if $\forall X(t = t')$ is deducible from E. Formally,*

$$E \models \forall X(t = t') \quad \textit{iff} \quad E \vdash_{EL} \forall X(t = t').$$

Proof. By Proposition 28, it is enough to show that

$$E \models \forall X(t = t') \quad \text{implies} \quad E \vdash_{EL} \forall X(t = t').$$

Recall that $E \models \forall X(t = t')$ iff $t =_E t'$, where $=_E$ is the fully invariant congruence on $\boldsymbol{T}_\Sigma(V)$ generated be $\overline{E}$. Denote by $ded(E)$ the relation $\{(t,t') | E \vdash_{EL} \forall X(t = t')\}$. Using the inference rules $(EL1)$ – $(EL7)$ we can easily show that $ded(E)$ is a fully invariant congruence on $\boldsymbol{T}_\Sigma(V)$. By definition, $E \vdash_{EL} \forall X(t = t')$ for each equation $\forall X(t = t')$ of E, i.e., $\overline{E} \subseteq ded(E)$. Hence $=_E \subseteq ded(E)$, which proves the implication above. ∎

By the completeness result, the semantical notion of logical consequence is in a one-to-one correspondence with the syntactic notion of formal proof (deducibility). To study logical consequences of a set E of equations we have either to look at all models of E for validation of a certain equation or, on the other hand, when working with deducibility we can use induction arguments on the length of a formal proofs.

Finally, we present another version of Birkhoff's Completeness Theorem for Equational Logic. Taking into consideration that an equation $\forall X(t = t')$ is a logical consequence of a set E of equations iff $\forall X(t = t')$ is valid in the free algebra over X in $Mod\ E$, we have that $\forall X(t = t')$ is deducible from E iff $\boldsymbol{F}_{Mod\ E}(X) \models \forall X(t = t')$. Let $=_{E,X}$ denote the restriction of $=_E$ to $\boldsymbol{T}_\Sigma(X)$, i.e., $=_{E,X} \; = \; =_E \cap (T_\Sigma(X) \times T_\Sigma(X))$. Since $\boldsymbol{T}_\Sigma(X)/{=_{E,X}}$ is isomorphic to $\boldsymbol{F}_{Mod\ E}(X)$ (from Corollary 2 to Lemma 24), it follows that

$$E \vdash_{EL} \forall X(t = t') \quad \text{iff} \quad \boldsymbol{T}_\Sigma(X)/{=_{E,X}} \models \forall X(t = t').$$

In particular,

$$E \vdash_{EL} \forall\, \emptyset(t = t') \quad \text{iff} \quad \boldsymbol{T}_\Sigma/{=_{G(E)}} \models \forall\, \emptyset(t = t'),$$

where $=_{G(E)}$ is written instead of $=_{E,\emptyset}$. Note that $=_{G(E)}$ is the congruence on $\boldsymbol{T}_\Sigma$ generated by all ground instances of equations in E. That is, $=_{G(E)}$ is generated by $G(E) = \{(g^\sharp(t), g^\sharp(t')) | \forall X(t = t') \in E \text{ and } g : X \to T_\Sigma\}$ as a congruence.

The initial algebra $\boldsymbol{T}_\Sigma/{=_{G(E)}}$ in $Mod\ E$ is often called an ***abstract data type*** (see Section 4.1.2); and its equational theory $Eq\ \{\boldsymbol{T}_\Sigma/{=_{G(E)}}\}$ is also called the ***inductive theory*** of E, sometimes abbreviated $Ind\ E$.

Here the following question arises: Is it possible to enlarge equational logic so that it becomes complete for $Ind\ E$?

Structural induction could be taken as an additional inference rule. But Nourani /Nourani-81/ has proved that equational logic with structural induction on terms as an additional inference rule is not complete. This follows from Matijasevic's Theorem (see /Davis-Matijasevic-Robinson-76/) which states that the set of all equations valid in the standard model of natural numbers is not recursively enumerable.

Example 2. Let Σ be a signature with two nullary operation symbols a and b and a binary operation symbol $*$. Consider the following set E of equations:

$$\forall x, y, z\ ((x * y) * z = x * (y * z)) \quad \text{and} \quad \forall \emptyset\ (a * b = b * a).$$

Define an algebra $\boldsymbol{F}$ with carrier $F = I\!N \times I\!N - \{(0,0)\}$ and operations realized as follows: $a^F = (1,0)$, $b^F = (0,1)$ and $(k,l) * (m,n) = (k+m, l+n)$. It is easily seen that $\boldsymbol{F}$ is initial in $Mod\,E$. Now we have $\boldsymbol{F} \models \forall x\,(a * x = x * a)$, i.e., $\forall x\,(a * x = x * a)$ belongs to $Ind\,E$. But $\forall x\,(a * x = x * a)$ is not deducible from E. ■

We close the section with a summary of the different characterizations of equational theories.

Corollary. *For any set E of equations the following are equivalent:*

(1) E is an equational theory.

(2) $\overline{E}$ *is a fully invariant congruence on* $\boldsymbol{T}_\Sigma(V)$.

(3) $E = Eq\,Mod\,E$.

(4) $E = Eq\,Mod\,E'$ *for some set* E' *of equations.*

(5) If $E \models \forall X(t = t')$, *then* $\forall X(t = t') \in E$.

(6) If $E \vdash_{EL} \forall X(t = t')$, *then* $\forall X(t = t') \in E$.

(7) $E = Eq\,\{\boldsymbol{T}_\Sigma(V)/{=_E}\}$. ■

The proof of these equivalences follows from Birkhoff's Criterion for Equational Theories, Proposition 26 and Birkhoff's Completeness Theorem for Equational Logic.

If we consider *Eq Mod* as a closure operator on $\boldsymbol{T}_\Sigma(V)$ by identifying any set E of equations with the associated relation $\overline{E}$ on $T_\Sigma(V)$, then the closed sets are exactly the fully invariant congruences on $\boldsymbol{T}_\Sigma(V)$.

Starting with the Galois connection between *Mod* and *Eq*, we can say that our two main problems investigated previously are the following:

(1) Which abstract classes of algebras are *Mod Eq*-closed?

(2) Which sets of equations are *Eq Mod*-closed?

Both problems were solved; in case (1), we know that varieties are just the *Mod Eq*-closed classes, while, in case (2), the fully invariant congruences on $\boldsymbol{T}_\Sigma(V)$ are *Eq Mod*-closed.

Keep in mind that *Mod* as well as *Eq* are bijections between the related closure systems. This one-to-one correspondence between varieties and fully invariant congruences on $\boldsymbol{T}_\Sigma(V)$ was first discovered by B.H. Neumann /Neumann-62/. Recall that any closure system is a (complete) lattice. So we may speak of the lattice of varieties and the lattice of fully invariant congruences. Neumann's correspondence is now expressible formally as follows. All fully invariant congruences on $\boldsymbol{T}_\Sigma(V)$ form a (complete) algebraic lattice which is anti-isomorphic to the lattice of all varieties. Note that for fully invariant congruences E and E', $E \subseteq E'$ implies $Mod\ E' \subseteq Mod\ E$, which is to say that Mod is antitone.

3.2.5 Term Rewriting as an Algorithmic Tool for Equational Theories

This section deals with the validity problem for equational theories. Given a set E of equations, we want to decide algorithmically whether or not an equation is a logical consequence of E. Recall that

$$E \models \forall X(t = t') \quad \text{iff} \quad t =_E t',$$

where $=_E$ is the fully invariant congruence on $\boldsymbol{T}_\Sigma(V)$ generated by E. Hence the validity problem for E can be reduced to the word problem of $=_E$. By Theorem 12 in Section 2.1.2,

$$t =_E t' \quad \text{iff} \quad t \leftrightarrow_E^* t',$$

where $\rightarrow_E$ is the fully invariant relation on $\boldsymbol{T}_\Sigma(V)$ generated by E. So, on the other hand, the word problem for $=_E$ can be transformed into the reduction problem for $\rightarrow_E$, which, in turn, can be treated by term rewriting.

Let us first consider the case where $\rightarrow_E$ is confluent. As usual, $\downarrow_E$ abbreviates $\rightarrow_E^* \cdot \leftarrow_E^*$ (see Section 2.1.1).

Theorem 30. *If E is a given set of equations such that $\rightarrow_E$ is confluent, then, for all equations $\forall X(t = t')$,*

$$E \models \forall X(t = t') \quad \textit{iff} \quad t \downarrow_E t'.$$

Proof. It remains to show that $=_E = \downarrow_E$. But this follows immediately from the Church-Rosser Theorem (Theorem 2 in Section 2.1.1) and Lemma 1 in Section 2.1.1. ∎

Besides confluence termination is also a necessary condition for the solvability of the word problem. Recall that, under the assumption that $\rightarrow_E$ is confluent and terminating, every term t has a unique normal form, denoted by $nf(t)$; often called its ***canonical normal form***.

Theorem 31. *If E is a given set of equations such that $\rightarrow_E$ is complete (i.e., confluent and terminating), then, for all equations $\forall X(t = t')$,*

$$E \models \forall X(t = t') \quad \textit{iff} \quad nf(t) = nf(t').$$

Proof. If $\rightarrow_E$ is supposed to be complete, then $t \downarrow_E t'$ iff $nf(t) = nf(t')$. Hence the assertion follows then from Theorem 30. ∎

This result shows the usefulness of canonical normal forms. When they are computable, a decision procedure for the validity problem of equational theories is achieved. The computation is performed with term rewriting. Canonical normal forms in certain finitely presented algebras are studied in, e.g., /Le Chenadec-86/.

Example 1. Consider a set E consisting of the associativity law $\forall x, y, z\ ((x \cdot y) \cdot z = x \cdot (y \cdot z))$ only. Either of the two orientations yields a complete TRS; take

$$(x \cdot y) \cdot z \to x \cdot (y \cdot z).$$

Termination may be proved by means of the polynomial interpretation method, for instance, $I^*(x \cdot y) = 2xy + x$ (see Example 2 in Section 2.2.3); and confluence is evident since there are no critical pairs.

For simplicity the canonical normal forms $(x_1 \cdot (\ldots (x_{n-1} \cdot x_n) \ldots))$ are identified with words $x_1 \ldots x_{n-1} x_n$.

Now an equation $\forall X(t = t')$ is a logical consequence of the associativity law iff both terms t and t', regarded as words, are equal. ∎

Here a word of caution is needed. The reader should not get confused with the famous unsolvability result of semigroups (see /Davis-58/). In the example above we have asked about the validity of equations in the free semigroup. Evidently, the word problem for free semigroups is solvable, whereas, however, the word problem for semigroups, that is the question whether or not an equation is valid in a given (finitely presented) semigroup, is unsolvable. In particular, the semigroup presented by the generators a, b, c, d, e and the relators (defining equations) $ac = ca$, $ad = da$, $bc = cb$, $bd = db$, $eca = ae$, $abae = abace$ has an unsolvable word problem.

As we know, the confluence of a terminating TRS can sometimes be forced by the KB-procedure.

Example 2. The completion of the group axioms by the KB-procedure (see Example 1 in Section 2.2.2) gives as the result the following rewrite rules:

(TG1) $(x \cdot y) \cdot z \to x \cdot (y \cdot z)$,

(TG2) $i(x) \cdot x \to e$,

(TG3) $e \cdot x \to x$,

(TG4) $i(x) \cdot (x \cdot z) \to z$,

(TG5) $y \cdot e \to y$,

(TG6) $i(i(y)) \to y$,

(TG7) $i(e) \to e$,

(TG8) $y \cdot i(y) \to e$,

(TG9) $y \cdot (i(y) \cdot x) \to x$,

(TG10) $i(x \cdot y) \to i(y) \cdot i(x)$.

For instance, to check whether

$$\forall x, y, z\ (((x \cdot y) \cdot i(x \cdot y)) \cdot (z \cdot e) = z)$$

is a logical consequence of the group axioms is the same as to ask whether the left-hand side of the equation is reducible to z.

There is the following reduction

$$\begin{aligned} ((x \cdot y) \cdot i(x \cdot y)) \cdot (z \cdot e) &\to ((x \cdot y) \cdot (i(y) \cdot i(x))) \cdot (z \cdot e) && \text{by (TG10)} \\ &\to (x \cdot (y \cdot (i(y) \cdot i(x)))) \cdot (z \cdot e) && \text{by (TG1)} \\ &\to (x \cdot i(x)) \cdot (z \cdot e) && \text{by (TG9)} \\ &\to e \cdot (z \cdot e) && \text{by (TG8)} \\ &\to z \cdot e && \text{by (TG3)} \\ &\to z && \text{by (TG5).} \end{aligned}$$ ■

Similarly as in the case of the word problem of semigroups we have to mention that, in spite of the solvable word problem of free groups, the word problem for groups is unsolvable. An overview of solvable and unsolvable word problems is given in /Pedersen-84/; see also /Boone-59, Evans-51/.

3.3 Implicationally Defined Classes of Algebras

By analogy with equationally defined classes of algebras, implicationally defined classes of algebras will be investigated here. First, implications must be introduced. In Section 3.3.1, we define implications whose premises and conclusions are term equations. Since an infinite number of premises is allowed, infinitely many variables may occur in an implication. Special cases are then implications with finitely many variables, called finitary implications, and implications with finitely many premises (and hence finitely many variables), called universal Horn clauses. Accordingly, three types of implicationally defined classes of algebras are considered: implicational classes, finitary implicational classes and universal Horn classes.

Free algebras were an important tool to achieve Birkhoff's Variety Theorem. In a certain sense, free algebras are the "greatest" images of term algebras. As a generalization, the greatest image of an algebra $\boldsymbol{A}$ in $\mathcal{K}$, if it exists, is said to be the sur-reflection of $\boldsymbol{A}$. Section 3.3.2 deals with such sur-reflections. The main result states that an algebra admits a sur-reflection in $\mathcal{K}$ iff $\mathcal{K}$ is an abstract class of algebras closed under subalgebras and direct products.

In Section 3.3.3, the algebraic characterization of implicational classes, finitary implicational classes and universal Horn classes in the sense of Birkhoff is exhibited:

(1) $\mathcal{K}$ is an implicational class iff $\mathcal{K}$ is closed under subalgebras and direct products.

(2) $\mathcal{K}$ is a finitary implicational class iff $\mathcal{K}$ is closed under directed unions, subalgebras and direct products.

(3) $\mathcal{K}$ is a universal Horn class iff $\mathcal{K}$ is closed under direct limits, subalgebras and direct products.

Section 3.3.4 presents implicational theories and implicational logic. Instead of fully invariant congruences, used for characterizing equational theories, we have to take fully invariant closure systems of congruences as a suitable algebraic counterpart of implicational theories.

Similarly, universal Horn theories and universal Horn logic are treated in Section 3.3.5. In addition, the fully invariant closure systems of congruences must be algebraic. Algebraicity can be thought of as an equivalent condition for the finiteness of the set of premises in a universal Horn clause.

Finally, in Section 3.3.6, conditional equational theories and conditional term rewriting systems are studied. Given a set H of universal Horn clauses, the set of all equations which are logical consequences of H is called the conditional equational theory of H. Under certain assumptions, conditional term rewriting provides an algorithmic tool to decide whether or not an equation is a logical consequence of H.

3.3.1 Implications, Finitary Implications and Universal Horn Clauses

In this section we generalize equations to implications. Although implications have more expressive power than equations, we should be aware that an implication, more precisely a universally quantified implication of term equations as it will be introduced subsequently, is still a simple kind of a logical formula. Nevertheless, implications are very useful and important for applications in theoretical computer science.

Let us consider two simple examples of algebras where special properties are expressed by implications. A semigroup $(A, \cdot)$ is said to be ***left-cancellative*** if, for all $a, b, c \in A$,

$$a \cdot b = a \cdot c \quad \text{implies} \quad b = c.$$

In a ***torsion-free*** commutative group $(A, +, -, 0)$ each of the following implications hold:

$$a + a = 0 \quad \text{implies} \quad a = 0;$$
$$a + a + a = 0 \quad \text{implies} \quad a = 0; \quad \text{etc.}$$

Observe that in both examples the premises and the conclusions of the implications are equations.

Definition 1. *Given a signature Σ, an* ***implication*** *(more precisely, Σ-implication), denoted by*

$$\forall X \left(\bigwedge_{m \in M} t_m = t'_m \Rightarrow t = t' \right),$$

is a 6-tuple $(X, M, (t_m | m \in M), (t'_m | m \in M), t, t')$ *with* X *and* M *sets,* $(t_m | m \in M)$ *and* $(t'_m | m \in M)$ *families of terms in* $T_\Sigma(X)$ *and* $t, t' \in T_\Sigma(X)$*. If* X *is empty, we speak of a* ***ground implication*** [3]*.*

For notational convenience, when referring to an implication we shall omit explicit mention of the index set M. The index set is always denoted by M. Furthermore, we shall use Φ as a short-hand notation for an arbitrary implication.

Observe that equations are special cases of implications. Therefore, we shall speak of a ***proper*** implication when M is not empty.

We are now going to generalize the notions of satisfaction and validation. Let $\boldsymbol{A}$ be any algebra. An assignment α from X to $\boldsymbol{A}$ ***satisfies*** $(\bigwedge t_m = t'_m \Rightarrow t = t')$ iff $\alpha^\sharp(t) = \alpha^\sharp(t')$ whenever $\alpha^\sharp(t_m) = \alpha^\sharp(t'_m)$ for all $m \in M$; and we write

$$(\boldsymbol{A}, \alpha) \models \left(\bigwedge_{m \in M} t_m = t'_m \Rightarrow t = t' \right).$$

Definition 2. *An implication* Φ *is* ***valid*** *in an algebra* $\boldsymbol{A}$*, in symbols*

$$\boldsymbol{A} \models \Phi,$$

if all assignments α *from* X *to* $\boldsymbol{A}$ *satisfy* Φ*.*

In the sequel we focus our attention on preservation properties.

Proposition 1. *Every implication valid in an algebra* $\boldsymbol{A}$ *is also valid in each subalgebra of* $\boldsymbol{A}$*.*

Proof. Let $\Phi = \forall X\, (\bigwedge t_m = t'_m \Rightarrow t = t')$ be an arbitrary implication. Without loss of generality we assume that Φ is proper; otherwise see Proposition 1 in Section 3.2.1. Let $\boldsymbol{A}$ be a given algebra. Consider any subalgebra of $\boldsymbol{B}$ of $\boldsymbol{A}$ and any assignment $\beta : X \to B$. Then $\alpha = \beta \cdot in_B$ is an assignment from X to $\boldsymbol{A}$, where in_B is the inclusion from $\boldsymbol{B}$ into $\boldsymbol{A}$. By the assumption $\boldsymbol{A} \models \Phi$, $\alpha^\sharp(t_m) = \alpha^\sharp(t'_m)$ for all $m \in M$ implies $\alpha^\sharp(t) = \alpha^\sharp(t')$. Since $\alpha^\sharp = \beta^\sharp \cdot in_B$, we have $\beta^\sharp(t) = \beta^\sharp(t')$ provided $\beta^\sharp(t_m) = \beta^\sharp(t'_m)$ for all $m \in M$. Note that in_B is injective. Hence, $(\boldsymbol{B}, \beta) \models \Phi$ for any β. That is, Φ is valid in $\boldsymbol{B}$. ■

In contrast to equations, implications are not preserved under images, as the following example indicates.

Example 1. Consider the multiplicative monoid $(\mathbb{Z}, \cdot, 1)$ of integers, which is left-cancellative:

$$\forall x, y, z\, (x \cdot y = x \cdot z \Rightarrow y = z)$$

is valid.

---

[3] As for ground equations we shall use "$\forall\emptyset$" as quantification.

Now fix any natural number n and construct the quotient of $\mathbb{Z}$ modulo n: $a \sim b$ iff $a \equiv b \pmod{n}$. Put $Z_n = \mathbb{Z}/\sim$. Then

$$Z_n = \{[0], [1], \ldots, [n-1]\}.$$

For $n \geq 4$, the image Z_n of $\mathbb{Z}$ does not satisfy the implication above. For instance, if $n = 4$, then

$$[2] \cdot [0] = [2] \cdot [2] \quad \text{but} \quad [0] \neq [2].$$ ■

As an easy exercise the reader may verify that the implications are preserved under direct products.

Proposition 2. *Let $(\boldsymbol{A}_i | i \in I)$ be a family of algebras. Every implication valid in each $\boldsymbol{A}_i$, $i \in I$, is also valid in the direct product $\prod(\boldsymbol{A}_i | i \in I)$.* ■

Together with Proposition 1 we obtain:

Proposition 3. *Let $(\boldsymbol{A}_i | i \in I)$ be a family of algebras. Every implication valid in each $\boldsymbol{A}_i$, $i \in I$, is also valid in any subdirect product of $(\boldsymbol{A}_i | i \in I)$.* ■

Therefore, implications are preserved under the formation of subalgebras, direct products and subdirect products.

The next example demonstrates that implications are not preserved under direct unions.

Example 2 (after /Burmeister-88/). Consider a signature consisting of a single unary operation symbol σ. Let Φ be the implication

$$\forall X \left(\bigwedge_{m \in \mathbb{N}} \sigma(\sigma(x_{m+1})) = \sigma(x_m) \Rightarrow \sigma(\sigma(x_0)) = \sigma(x_0) \right),$$

where $X = \{x_m | m \in \mathbb{N}\}$. We define an ω-chain of algebras

$$\boldsymbol{A}_0 \subseteq \boldsymbol{A}_1 \subseteq \boldsymbol{A}_2 \ldots$$

as follows

$$A_n = \{0, 1, a_0, a_1, \ldots, a_n, b_0, b_1, \ldots, b_n\}$$

and the realization σ_n of σ in $\boldsymbol{A}_n$ is given by

$$\sigma_n(0) = 0, \quad \sigma_n(1) = 0, \quad \sigma_n(a_i) = b_i \text{ for } i = 0, 1, \ldots, n$$

$$\sigma_n(b_i) = \begin{cases} 1 & \text{if } i = 0, \\ b_{i-1} & \text{if } 0 < i \leq n. \end{cases}$$

The algebra $\boldsymbol{A}_n$ may be depicted as in Fig. 3.11.

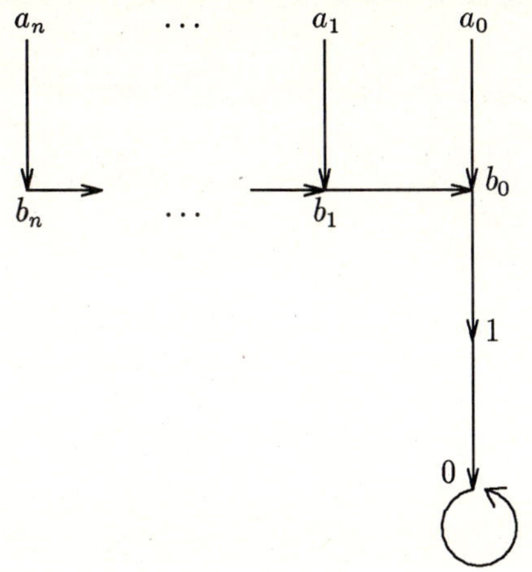

The arrows indicate the application of the operation σ_n

Fig. 3.11

Certainly, $\boldsymbol{A}_n$ is a subalgebra of $\boldsymbol{A}_{n+1}$ for every n. Since any ω-chain is especially directed we can construct the directed union

$$\boldsymbol{A} = \bigcup\{\boldsymbol{A}_n | n \in I\!N\}.$$

It is easily seen that the implication from above is not valid in $\boldsymbol{A}$: If we take that assignment α from X to $\boldsymbol{A}$ defined by $\alpha(x_m) = a_m$ for all $m \in I\!N$, then the premises hold but the conclusion does not.

Now we claim that each algebra $\boldsymbol{A}_n$ of the chain validates the implication. Assume indirectly that there is an assignment α from X to $\boldsymbol{A}_n$ such that

$$\sigma_n(\sigma_n(\alpha(x_{m+1}))) = \sigma_n(\alpha(x_m)) \text{ for all } m \in I\!N, \text{ but } \sigma_n(\sigma_n(\alpha(x_0))) \neq \sigma_n(\alpha(x_0)).$$

Then $\alpha(x_0)$ must be different from 0 and 1. Hence, $\alpha(x_0) = a_i$ or $\alpha(x_0) = b_i$ for some $i \in I\!N$.

First suppose that $\alpha(x_0) = a_i$ for some i. Then $\alpha(x_1) = a_{i+1}$ or $\alpha(x_1) = b_{i+2}$. Without loss of generality we assume that $\alpha(x_1) = a_{i+1}$. If we proceed in this manner, then there is a variable, say x_k, with $\alpha(x_k) = a_n$. But this leads to a contradiction:

$$\sigma_n(\sigma_n(\alpha(x_{k+1}))) = \sigma_n(a_n) = b_n.$$

So it remains to examine the second case where $\alpha(x_0) = b_i$ for some i. Then $\alpha(x_1) = a_i$ or $\alpha(x_1) = b_{i+1}$. Without loss of generality we assume that $\alpha(x_1) = b_{i+1}$. As in the case above, there exists a variable, say x_k, such that $\alpha(x_k) = b_n$. But then $\alpha(x_{k+1}) = a_n$ leads to a contradiction, as above.

Hence, all assignments α from X to $\boldsymbol{A}_n$ satisfy Φ. That is, Φ is valid in A_n.

Therefore, implications are generally not preserved under directed unions. ■

Definition 3. *An implication* $\forall X\,(\bigwedge t_m = t'_m \Rightarrow t = t')$ *is called* ***finitary*** *if* X *is finite, say* $X = \{x_1, \ldots, x_n\}$*; we also write*

$$\forall x_1, \ldots, x_n \left(\bigwedge t_m = t'_m \Rightarrow t = t'\right).$$

The restriction to a finite number of variables forces a further preservation property.

Proposition 4. *Let* $(\boldsymbol{A}_i | i \in I)$ *be a directed family of algebras. Every finitary implication valid in each* $\boldsymbol{A}_i$*,* $i \in I$*, is also valid in the directed union* $\bigcup(\boldsymbol{A}_i | i \in I)$*.*

Proof. Let $\Phi = \forall X\,(\bigwedge t_m = t'_m \Rightarrow t = t')$ be any finitary implication. Without loss of generality we assume that Φ is proper; otherwise see Proposition 4 in Section 3.2.1. Let $\boldsymbol{A}$ be the directed union over all $\boldsymbol{A}_i$.

Suppose, by way of contradiction, that Φ is valid in all $\boldsymbol{A}_i$, $i \in I$, but Φ is not valid in $\boldsymbol{A}$. Then, by definition, there exists an assignment $\alpha : X \to A$ such that α does not satisfy Φ.

Since X is assumed to be finite, α factorizes through some component of $\boldsymbol{A}$, say $\boldsymbol{A}_k$, that is, $\alpha = \alpha_k \cdot in_k$ for some assignment $\alpha_k : X \to A_k$, where $in_k : \boldsymbol{A}_k \to \boldsymbol{A}$ is the inclusion of $\boldsymbol{A}_k$ into $\boldsymbol{A}$. Then $\alpha^\sharp = \alpha_k^\sharp \cdot in_k$. Hence α satisfies Φ since α_k does so. But this is a contradiction. ■

Finitary implications are hence preserved under the formation of subalgebras, direct products, subdirect products and directed unions. The example below shows that finitary implications are generally not preserved under direct limits.

Example 3. Let $A = \{0\} \cup \{a_n | n \in I\!N\}$ be a countably infinite set. Considering all elements of A as nullary operation symbols and adding one unary operation symbol σ we fix a signature.

First, a family $(\boldsymbol{A}_i | i \in I\!N)$ of algebras is introduced by

(1) $A_i = A \cup \{b_n | n \geq i\}$, where the countably infinitely many new elements b_n are not in A;

(2) Each nullary operation symbol is realized as a constant by itself;

(3) The realization of σ, denoted by σ_i, is given by

$$\sigma_i(0) = 0;$$
$$\sigma_i(a_n) = \begin{cases} 0 & \text{if } n < i, \\ b_n & \text{if } n \geq i; \end{cases}$$
$$\sigma_i(b_n) = 0 \quad \text{for } n \geq i.$$

$\boldsymbol{A}_i$ may be depicted as in Fig. 3.12.

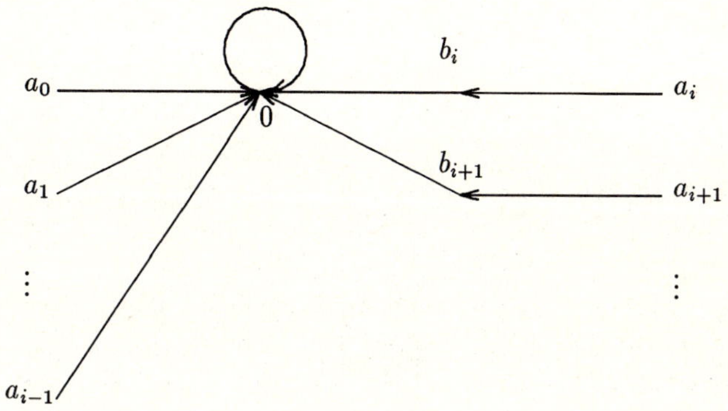

The arrows indicate the application of the operation σ_i.

Fig. 3.12

It is easily seen that every algebra $\boldsymbol{A}_i$ validates the following ground implication

$$\Phi = \forall\, \emptyset \left(\bigwedge_{m \in \mathbb{N}} \sigma(a_m) = 0 \Rightarrow a_0 = 0 \right).$$

Our aim is to show that the direct limit of all $\boldsymbol{A}_i$ does not validate Φ. For that purpose a direct family $(h_{ij} : \boldsymbol{A}_i \to \boldsymbol{A}_j)$ must be introduced:

$$h_{ij}(0) = 0;$$
$$h_{ij}(a_n) = a_n \quad \text{for all } n \in \mathbb{N};$$
$$h_{ij}(b_n) = \begin{cases} 0 & \text{if } i \leq n < j, \\ b_n & \text{if } n \geq j. \end{cases}$$

Observe that

$$h_{ii} = id_{A_i} \quad \text{for all } i \in I; \text{ and}$$
$$h_{ij} \cdot h_{jk} = h_{ik} \quad \text{for all } i \leq j \leq k.$$

Now the direct limit can be defined. Letting $\boldsymbol{A}$ be the algebra with carrier set A, each nullary operation symbol is realized as a constant by itself and the realization of σ, denoted by σ, too, is given by $\sigma(0) = 0$ and $\sigma(a_n) = 0$. $\boldsymbol{A}$ may be depicted as in Fig. 3.13.

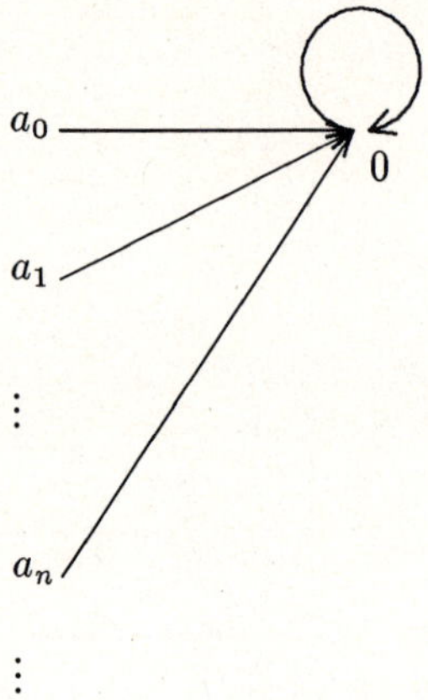

Fig. 3.13

Since $\sigma(a_m) = 0$ for all $m \in \mathbb{N}$, but $a_0 \neq 0$, Φ is not valid in $\boldsymbol{A}$.

Claim: $\boldsymbol{A}$ is the direct limit of $(h_{ij} : \boldsymbol{A}_i \to \boldsymbol{A}_j)$ with the limit cone $(h_i : \boldsymbol{A}_i \to \boldsymbol{A})$ defined by $h_i(0) = 0$, $h_i(a_n) = a_n$ for all $n \in \mathbb{N}$ and $h_i(b_n) = 0$ for all $n \geq i$.

Evidently, every h_i is a homomorphism and

$$h_i = h_{ij} \cdot h_j \quad \text{for all } i \leq j.$$

As an exercise the reader may show that the family $(h_i : \boldsymbol{A}_i \to \boldsymbol{A})$ fulfills the universal property (L) and so, by Proposition 6 in Section 3.1.2, $\boldsymbol{A}$ is in fact the direct limit. ■

In order to derive a closure property for implications, where the number of premises is restricted to be finite, we need a technical lemma which expresses validation in algebraic terms. With any implication

$$\Phi = \forall X \left(\bigwedge t_m = t'_m \Rightarrow t = t'\right)$$

two congruences on $\boldsymbol{T}_\Sigma(X)$ are associated as follows:

$$P = con(\{(t_m, t'_m) | \, m \in M\})$$

and

$$Q = con(\{(t_m, t'_m) | \, m \in M\} \cup \{(t, t')\});$$

P is the congruence generated by the premises of Φ, while Q is the congruence generated by the premises together with the conclusion of Φ. Since $P \subseteq Q$, we can define a homomorphism $h_\Phi : \boldsymbol{T}_\Sigma(X)/P \to \boldsymbol{T}_\Sigma(X)/Q$ as follows:

$$h_\Phi\left([t]_P\right) = [t]_Q \quad \text{for all } t \in \boldsymbol{T}_\Sigma(X).$$

We say that an algebra $\boldsymbol{A}$ is ***injective with respect to*** Φ if, for every homomorphism f from $\boldsymbol{T}_\Sigma(X)/P$ to $\boldsymbol{A}$, there exists a homomorphism g from $\boldsymbol{T}_\Sigma(X)/Q$ to $\boldsymbol{A}$ such that $f = h_\Phi \cdot g$ (see Fig. 3.14).

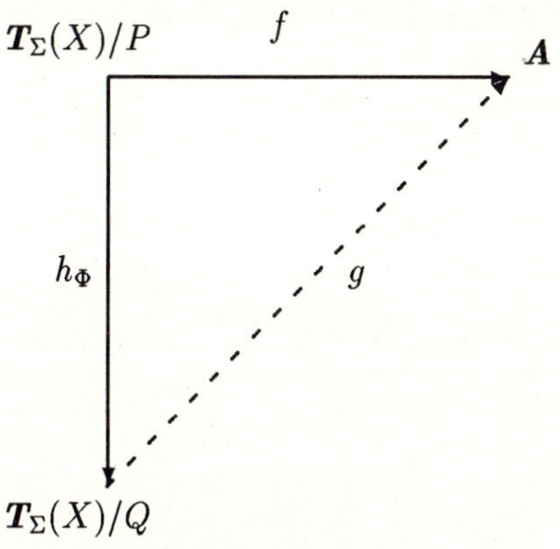

Fig. 3.14

Consider the special case where Φ is an equation, i.e., $\Phi = \forall X(t = t')$. Then P is the trivial congruence on $\boldsymbol{T}_\Sigma(X)$ and Q is the congruence generated by $\{(t, t')\}$. Furthermore, h_Φ is the natural homomorphism from $\boldsymbol{T}_\Sigma(X)$ to $\boldsymbol{T}_\Sigma(X)/Q$. It is easily seen that $\boldsymbol{A}$ is injective with respect to Φ iff Φ is valid in $\boldsymbol{A}$. But this holds also true for any implication.

Lemma 5 (Banaschewski-Herrlich Criterion). *An implication Φ is valid in an algebra $\boldsymbol{A}$ iff $\boldsymbol{A}$ is injective with respect to Φ.*

Proof. Let $\Phi = \forall\, X\, (\bigwedge t_m = t'_m \Rightarrow t = t')$ be an arbitrary implication.

For the "if-part" assume that Φ is valid in a given algebra $\boldsymbol{A}$. Observe that we can associate with any homomorphism f from $\boldsymbol{T}_\Sigma(X)/P$ to $\boldsymbol{A}$ an assignment $\alpha : X \to A$ by the rule

$$\alpha(x) = f([x]_P) \quad \text{for all } x \in X.$$

Then $\alpha^\sharp = nat_P \cdot f$, where nat_P is the natural homomorphism from $\boldsymbol{T}_\Sigma(X)$ to $\boldsymbol{T}_\Sigma(X)/P$. By the assumption that Φ is valid in $\boldsymbol{A}$, we derive $f([t]_P) = f([t']_P)$ whenever $f([t_m]_P) = f([t'_m]_P)$ for all $m \in M$. Therefore a homomorphism g from $\boldsymbol{T}_\Sigma(X)/Q$ to $\boldsymbol{A}$ can be defined by

$$g([t]_Q) = f([t]_P) \quad \text{for all } t \in \boldsymbol{T}_\Sigma(X),$$

which fulfills the condition $f = h_\Phi \cdot g$, by definition. Thus $\boldsymbol{A}$ is injective with respect to Φ.

For the "only if-part" assume that $\boldsymbol{A}$ is injective with respect to Φ. Let α be an arbitrary assignment from X to $\boldsymbol{A}$ such that $\alpha^\sharp(t_m) = \alpha^\sharp(t'_m)$ for all $m \in M$. By assumption, $\alpha^\sharp$ factorizes through $\boldsymbol{T}_\Sigma(X)/P$:

$$\alpha^\sharp = nat_P \cdot f$$

for some homomorphism $f : \boldsymbol{T}_\Sigma(X)/P \to \boldsymbol{A}$. Hence, by the injectivity of $\boldsymbol{A}$, there exists a homomorphism $g : \boldsymbol{T}_\Sigma(X)/Q \to \boldsymbol{A}$ with $f = h_\Phi \cdot g$. Thus, $\alpha^\sharp = nat_P \cdot h_\Phi \cdot g = nat_Q \cdot g$, whence $\alpha^\sharp(t) = g([t]_Q) = g([t']_Q) = \alpha^\sharp(t')$. That is, α satisfies Φ, and so Φ is valid in $\boldsymbol{A}$ since α is arbitrary. ■

Finitary implications with a finite number of premises are given a name.

Definition 4. *A finitary implication* $\forall X\, (\bigwedge t_m = t'_m \Rightarrow t = t')$ *is called* ***universal Horn clause*** [4] *if* M *is finite, say* $M = \{1, \ldots, k\}$*, and we also write*

$$\forall\, X\, (t_1 = t'_1 \wedge \ldots \wedge t_k = t'_k \Rightarrow t = t')$$

or

$$\forall\, x_1, \ldots, x_n\ (t_1 = t'_1 \wedge \ldots \wedge t_k = t'_k \Rightarrow t = t')$$

if $X = \{x_1, \ldots, x_n\}$.

For universal Horn clauses we are able to prove the closure under direct limits.

Proposition 6. *Let* $(h_{ij} : \boldsymbol{A}_i \to \boldsymbol{A}_j)$ *be a direct family of algebras. Every universal Horn clause valid in each* $\boldsymbol{A}_i$, $i \in I$*, is also valid in the direct limit* $\lim(\boldsymbol{A}_i | i \in I)$.

Proof. Let $\boldsymbol{A}$ be the direct limit of $(h_{ij} : \boldsymbol{A}_i \to \boldsymbol{A}_j)$ with the limit cone $(h_i : \boldsymbol{A}_i \to \boldsymbol{A})$. Assume that Φ is valid in each $\boldsymbol{A}_i$, $i \in I$. Then $\boldsymbol{A}_i$ is injective with respect to Φ, by Lemma 5. We have to show that also $\boldsymbol{A}$ is injective with respect to Φ.

Consider an arbitrary homomorphism $f : \boldsymbol{T}_\Sigma(X)/P \to \boldsymbol{A}$. Since $\boldsymbol{T}_\Sigma(X)/P$ is finitely presented, f factorizes through some component, say $\boldsymbol{A}_k$, by Proposition 8 in Section 3.1.2. That is, $f = f_k \cdot h_k$ for some homomorphism $f_k : \boldsymbol{T}_\Sigma(X)/P \to \boldsymbol{A}_k$. Now, since $\boldsymbol{A}_k$ is injective with respect to Φ, there exists a homomorphism $g_k : \boldsymbol{T}_\Sigma(X)/Q \to \boldsymbol{A}_k$ such that $f_k = h_\Phi \cdot g_k$. Hence, $f = h_\Phi \cdot (g_k \cdot h_k)$, which means that $\boldsymbol{A}$ is injective with respect to Φ. ■

Recall that $\mathbf{P}_{red} \leq \mathbf{LP}$ (see Proposition 15 in Section 3.1.4). Reduced products can be constructed by means of direct limits and direct products. Together with Proposition 2 we conclude from Proposition 6 the following fact.

Proposition 7. *Let* $(\boldsymbol{A}_i | i \in I)$ *be a family of algebras and let* F *be a filter over* I*. Every universal Horn clause valid in each* $\boldsymbol{A}_i$, $i \in I$*, is also valid in the reduced product* $\prod(\boldsymbol{A}_i | i \in I)/F$. ■

---

[4] More precisely, $\forall X\ \left(\bigwedge t_m = t'_m \Rightarrow t = t'\right)$ is called positive universal Horn clause if M is finite (see Appendix 2).

Altogether we have that universal Horn clauses are preserved under the formation of subalgebras, direct products, subdirect products, directed unions, direct limits and reduced products.

The notion of a model is generalized in a straightforward way. Given a set I of implications, the model class of I, also denoted by $Mod\ I$, consists of all algebras which validate each implication of I.

Definition 5. *An abstract class $\mathcal{K}$ of algebras is called an* ***implicational class*** *(or* ***implicationally definable****) if $\mathcal{K}$ is the model class of some set of implications.*

The closure properties of an implicational class follow from Propositions 1 – 3.

Theorem 8. *Every implicational class is closed under subalgebras, direct products and subdirect products.* ∎

By finiteness restrictions of implications, special subclasses can be defined.

Definition 6. *An abstract class $\mathcal{K}$ of algebras is called a* ***finitary implicational class*** *(or* ***finitary implicationally definable****) if $\mathcal{K}$ is the model class of some set of finitary implications.*

Finitary implicational classes are additionally closed under directed unions, as we can conclude from Proposition 4.

Theorem 9. *Every finitary implicational class is closed under subalgebras, direct products, subdirect products, and directed unions.* ∎

Using universal Horn clauses we are led to the following concept.

Definition 7. *An abstract class $\mathcal{K}$ of algebras is called* ***(strict) universal Horn class***[5] *if $\mathcal{K}$ is the model class of some set of universal Horn clauses.*

From Theorem 9 together with Propositions 6 and 7 we obtain the result below.

Theorem 10. *Every universal Horn class is closed under subalgebras, direct products, subdirect products, directed unions, direct limits and reduced products.* ∎

The difference between universal Horn classes and equational classes lies in the fact that equational classes are closed under images, whereas universal Horn classes are not.

---

[5] Here we will simply speak of universal Horn classes. In Appendix 2, the difference between strict and nonstrict universal Horn classes is explained.

3.3.2 Sur-Reflections

Free algebras may be generalized to obtain a suitable method for characterizing implicational classes similar to that for equational classes.

Definition 8. *Let $\mathcal{K}$ be an abstract class of algebras. A homomorphism r from an algebra $\boldsymbol{A}$ to an algebra $\boldsymbol{R}$ in $\mathcal{K}$ is called a **reflection** of $\boldsymbol{A}$ in $\mathcal{K}$ if, for every homomorphism h from $\boldsymbol{A}$ to any algebra $\boldsymbol{B}$ in $\mathcal{K}$, there exists exactly one homomorphism $h^* : \boldsymbol{R} \to \boldsymbol{B}$ such that $h = r \cdot h^*$ (see Fig. 3.15). A **sur-reflection** of $\boldsymbol{A}$ in $\mathcal{K}$ is a reflection $r : \boldsymbol{A} \to \boldsymbol{R}$ of $\boldsymbol{A}$ in $\mathcal{K}$ such that r is a surjective homomorphism.*

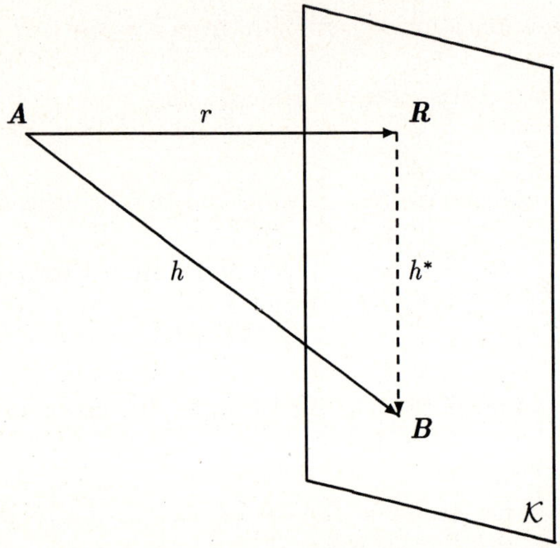

Fig. 3.15

When $r : \boldsymbol{A} \to \boldsymbol{R}$ is a reflection (sur-reflection) of $\boldsymbol{A}$ in $\mathcal{K}$, often $\boldsymbol{R}$ is simply said to be a reflection (sur-reflection) of $\boldsymbol{A}$ in $\mathcal{K}$. Note that $\boldsymbol{R}$ is uniquely determined up to isomorphism. Therefore we will speak of the reflection (sur-reflection) of $\boldsymbol{A}$ in $\mathcal{K}$, written $\boldsymbol{R}_{\mathcal{K}}(\boldsymbol{A})$. The related (surjective) homomorphism from $\boldsymbol{A}$ to $\boldsymbol{R}_{\mathcal{K}}(\boldsymbol{A})$ is always denoted by r, or sometimes by r_A.

In a certain sense the sur-reflection of an algebra $\boldsymbol{A}$ in $\mathcal{K}$ is the "greatest" image of $\boldsymbol{A}$ in $\mathcal{K}$. Consider images $\boldsymbol{B}$ and $\boldsymbol{C}$ of $\boldsymbol{A}$ with $f : \boldsymbol{A} \to \boldsymbol{B}$ and $g : \boldsymbol{A} \to \boldsymbol{C}$ surjective homomorphisms. We put $\boldsymbol{C} \lesssim \boldsymbol{B}$ iff there exists a homomorphism $h : \boldsymbol{B} \to \boldsymbol{C}$ such that $g = f \cdot h$. If h exists, it is unique by the surjectivity of f. Evidently, $\lesssim$ is a quasi-order (reflexive and transitive). Moreover, if $\boldsymbol{B} \lesssim \boldsymbol{C}$ and $\boldsymbol{C} \lesssim \boldsymbol{B}$, then $\boldsymbol{B}$ and $\boldsymbol{C}$ are isomorphic. For $\boldsymbol{B} \lesssim \boldsymbol{C}$ and $\boldsymbol{C} \lesssim \boldsymbol{B}$ imply that there are uniquely homomorphisms $h : \boldsymbol{B} \to \boldsymbol{C}$ and $h' : \boldsymbol{C} \to \boldsymbol{B}$ with $g = f \cdot h$ and $f = g \cdot h'$, respectively. Hence $g = g \cdot (h' \cdot h)$ and so $h' \cdot h = id_C$, whence h' is an injection. Since h' is also surjective, by the surjectivity of f, h is actually a bijective homomorphism. That is, $\boldsymbol{B}$ and $\boldsymbol{C}$ are isomorphic. Indeed, we have a partial order on classes of isomorphic algebras.

Lemma 11. *Assume $\mathcal{K}$ is an abstract class of algebras such that $\mathcal{K}$ is closed under subalgebras. Then $\boldsymbol{R}$ is the sur-reflection of any given algebra $\boldsymbol{A}$ in $\mathcal{K}$ iff $\boldsymbol{R}$ is the greatest image of $\boldsymbol{A}$ in $\mathcal{K}$.*

Proof. If $\boldsymbol{R}$ is the sur-reflection of $\boldsymbol{A}$ in $\mathcal{K}$, then $\boldsymbol{R}$ is the greatest image of $\boldsymbol{A}$ in $\mathcal{K}$, by definition.

Conversely, assume that $\boldsymbol{R}$ is the greatest image of $\boldsymbol{A}$ in $\mathcal{K}$ with $r : \boldsymbol{A} \to \boldsymbol{R}$ as related surjective homomorphism. Let h be a homomorphism from $\boldsymbol{A}$ to any algebra $\boldsymbol{B}$ in $\mathcal{K}$. By Proposition 3 in Section 3.1.2, h factorizes uniquely as follows: $h = f \cdot g$, where $f : \boldsymbol{A} \to \boldsymbol{C}$ is a surjective homomorphism and $g : \boldsymbol{C} \to \boldsymbol{B}$ is an injective homomorphism. Since $\mathcal{K}$ is supposed to be closed under subalgebras, $\boldsymbol{C}$ belongs to $\mathcal{K}$. Now, by the assumption that $\boldsymbol{R}$ is the greatest image in $\mathcal{K}$, there is a homomorphism from $\boldsymbol{R}$ to $\boldsymbol{C}$, say $f^* : \boldsymbol{R} \to \boldsymbol{C}$, such that $f = r \cdot f^*$. Keep in mind that f^* is unique. Put $h^* = f^* \cdot g$. Then $h = r \cdot h^*$ is the unique factorization required. Hence $\boldsymbol{R}$ is the sur-reflection of $\boldsymbol{A}$ in $\mathcal{K}$. ■

It is obvious that free algebras are special sur-reflections.

Proposition 12. *Let $\mathcal{K}$ be an abstract class of algebras. If the free algebra $\boldsymbol{F}_{\mathcal{K}}(X)$ over a given set X exists in $\mathcal{K}$, then $\boldsymbol{F}_{\mathcal{K}}(X)$ is the sur-reflection of the absolutely free algebra $\boldsymbol{T}_{\Sigma}(X)$ in $\mathcal{K}$.* ■

Definition 9. *An abstract class $\mathcal{K}$ of algebras is called* ***sur-reflective*** *if any algebra admits a sur-reflection in $\mathcal{K}$.*

As a main result we have the following characterization.

Theorem 13. *An abstract class of algebras is sur-reflective if and only if it is closed under subalgebras and direct products.*

Proof. Let $\mathcal{K}$ be an abstract class of algebras.

(1) Necessity: Assume that $\mathcal{K}$ is sur-reflective. First, we show that $\mathcal{K}$ is closed under subalgebras. Therefore we consider a subalgebra $\boldsymbol{B}$ of any algebra $\boldsymbol{A}$ in $\mathcal{K}$. Denote by $h : \boldsymbol{B} \to \boldsymbol{A}$ the inclusion of $\boldsymbol{B}$ into $\boldsymbol{A}$. That is, h is an injective homomorphism. Now, by definition, there exists exactly one homomorphism $h^* : \boldsymbol{R}_{\mathcal{K}}(\boldsymbol{B}) \to \boldsymbol{A}$ such that $h = r \cdot h^*$. Since h is injective, r is injective, too. Together with the surjectivity of r, we obtain that r is an isomorphism. Hence $\boldsymbol{B}$ belongs to $\mathcal{K}$.

Second, we are going to prove that $\mathcal{K}$ is closed under direct products. Recall that the direct product of the empty family of algebras is the trivial algebra $\boldsymbol{A}$ with a singleton as its carrier. Evidently, $\boldsymbol{A}$ belongs to $\mathcal{K}$. Therefore, let us suppose that $(\boldsymbol{A}_i | i \in I)$ is a nonempty family of algebras in $\mathcal{K}$. Denote by $\boldsymbol{A}$ the direct product of $(\boldsymbol{A}_i | i \in I)$. Since $\mathcal{K}$ is sur-reflective $\boldsymbol{A}$ admits a sur-reflection in $\mathcal{K}$ such that $r : \boldsymbol{A} \to \boldsymbol{R}_{\mathcal{K}}(\boldsymbol{A})$ is a surjective homomorphism. Now, by definition, each projection $pr_i : \boldsymbol{A} \to \boldsymbol{A}_i$ factorizes uniquely through the sur-reflection of $\boldsymbol{A}$, i.e., $pr_i = r \cdot p_i$ for all $i \in I$, where $p_i : \boldsymbol{R}_{\mathcal{K}}(\boldsymbol{A}) \to \boldsymbol{A}_i$. Using the universal property (P) of a direct product (see Lemma 9 in Section 3.1.3), we have a homomorphism $p = \prod(p_i \mid i \in I)$ from $\boldsymbol{R}_{\mathcal{K}}(\boldsymbol{A})$ to $\boldsymbol{A}$ such that $p \cdot pr_i = p_i$ for all $i \in I$. Hence $(r \cdot p) \cdot pr_i = pr_i$ for all $i \in I$, which implies $r \cdot p = id_A$. Thus r is an injection. Together with the surjectivity of r we obtain that r is indeed an isomorphism. Hence $\boldsymbol{A}$ belongs to $\mathcal{K}$.

(2) Sufficiency: Assume that $\mathcal{K}$ is closed under subalgebras and direct products. Consider an arbitrary algebra $\boldsymbol{A}$. The construction of the sur-reflection of $\boldsymbol{A}$ in $\mathcal{K}$ is visualized in Fig. 3.16.

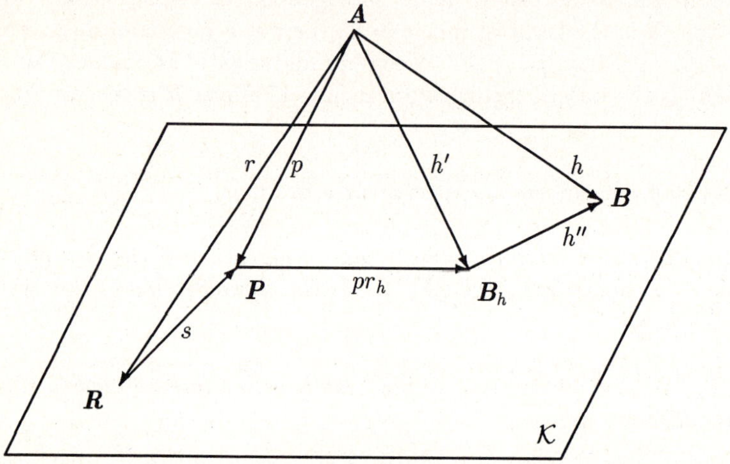

Fig. 3.16

Let $Hom(\boldsymbol{A}, \mathcal{K})$ denote the class of all homomorphisms from $\boldsymbol{A}$ to any algebra $\boldsymbol{B}$ in $\mathcal{K}$. Since $\mathcal{K}$ is supposed to be closed under direct products, $\mathcal{K}$ is not empty and so $Hom(\boldsymbol{A}, \mathcal{K})$ is nonempty. By Proposition 3 in Section 3.1.2, each $h : \boldsymbol{A} \to \boldsymbol{B}$ of $Hom(\boldsymbol{A}, \mathcal{K})$ can be uniquely factorized: $h = h' \cdot h''$ with $h' : \boldsymbol{A} \to \boldsymbol{B}_h$ a surjective homomorphism and $h'' : \boldsymbol{B}_h \to \boldsymbol{B}$ an injective homomorphism. Since $\mathcal{K}$ is supposed to be closed under subalgebras, $\boldsymbol{B}_h$ belongs to $\mathcal{K}$. Observe, however, that $\{\boldsymbol{B}_h \mid h \in Hom(\boldsymbol{A}, \mathcal{K})\}$ is a proper class. Using the Homomorphism Theorem (Theorem 2 in Section 3.1.2), we can choose a set of representatives, say $\{\boldsymbol{B}_h \mid h \in H\}$ with $H \subseteq Hom(\boldsymbol{A}, \mathcal{K})$, where H is a set.

Let $\boldsymbol{P}$ denote the direct product over all these representatives: $\boldsymbol{P} = \prod(\boldsymbol{B}_h \mid h \in H)$. Since $\mathcal{K}$ is supposed to be closed under direct products, $\boldsymbol{P}$ belongs to $\mathcal{K}$. By Lemma 9 in Section 3.1.3, there exists a unique homomorphism $p = \prod(h' \mid h \in H)$ from $\boldsymbol{A}$ to $\boldsymbol{P}$ such that $p \cdot pr_h = h'$ for all $h \in H$.

Now factorize p in a unique way: $p = r \cdot s$ with $r : \boldsymbol{A} \to \boldsymbol{R}$ a surjective homomorphism and $s : \boldsymbol{R} \to \boldsymbol{P}$ an injective homomorphism. Since $\mathcal{K}$ is supposed to be closed under subalgebras, $\boldsymbol{R}$ belongs to $\mathcal{K}$.

Claim: $\boldsymbol{R}$ is the sur-reflection of $\boldsymbol{A}$ in $\mathcal{K}$.

By definition, $r : \boldsymbol{A} \to \boldsymbol{R}$ is a surjective homomorphism. Let h be a homomorphism from $\boldsymbol{A}$ to any algebra $\boldsymbol{B}$ in $\mathcal{K}$. Then h factorizes uniquely through $\boldsymbol{R} : h = r \cdot h^*$ with $h^* = s \cdot pr_h \cdot h''$. Hence, by definition, $\boldsymbol{R}$ is the sur-reflection of $\boldsymbol{A}$ in $\mathcal{K}$.

Thus we have proved that $\mathcal{K}$ is sur-reflective whenever $\mathcal{K}$ is closed under subalgebras and direct products. ■

As a direct consequence we get that every nontrivial abstract class $\mathcal{K}$ of algebras admits free algebras over any set whenever $\mathcal{K}$ is closed under subalgebras and direct products. However, the proof of Theorem 15 in Section 3.2.3 presents, in fact, a construction of free algebras.

3.3.3 Sur-Reflective Classes, Semivarieties and Quasivarieties

In this section, the logical notions of implicational class, finitary implicational class and universal Horn class are characterized algebraically in terms of closure operators.

Theorem 14 (Banaschewski-Herrlich Theorem). *Let $\mathcal{K}$ be an abstract class of algebras. Then $\mathcal{K}$ is an implicational class if and only if $\mathcal{K}$ is a sur-reflective class.*

Proof. If $\mathcal{K}$ is an implicational class, then $\mathcal{K}$ is sur-reflective by Theorem 13 in Section 3.3.2 and Theorem 8 in Section 3.3.1.

To prove the converse we assume that $\mathcal{K}$ is a sur-reflective class. By definition, any algebra $\boldsymbol{A}$ admits a sur-reflection $r_A : \boldsymbol{A} \to \boldsymbol{R}_{\mathcal{K}}(\boldsymbol{A})$ in $\mathcal{K}$.

Consider the term algebra $\boldsymbol{T}_\Sigma(A)$ over the carrier of $\boldsymbol{A}$. The identity mapping id_A on A has a unique homomorphic extension $id_A^\sharp : \boldsymbol{T}_\Sigma(A) \to \boldsymbol{A}$. Let $\{(t_m, t'_m) | m \in M\}$ be the kernel of $id_A^\sharp$ and put

$$I(\boldsymbol{A}) = \Big\{\Phi | \Phi = \forall A \left(\bigwedge t_m = t'_m \Rightarrow t = t'\right) \quad \text{for some terms } t, t' \text{ of } \boldsymbol{T}_\Sigma(A) \\ \text{such that } r_A(id_A^\sharp(t)) = r_A(id_A^\sharp(t'))\Big\}.$$

By $I(\mathcal{K})$ we denote the union over all $I(\boldsymbol{A})$, where $\boldsymbol{A}$ ranges over all algebras.

Claim 1: $\mathcal{K} \subseteq Mod\ I(\mathcal{K})$.

We have to show $\mathcal{K} \subseteq Mod\ I(\boldsymbol{A})$ for all algebras $\boldsymbol{A}$. Let $\boldsymbol{B}$ be an arbitrary algebra of $\mathcal{K}$ and take any assignment $\beta : A \to B$. Using Proposition 3 in Section 3.1.2 we factorize $\beta^\sharp$ as follows: $\beta^\sharp = f \cdot g$ with $f : \boldsymbol{T}_\Sigma(A) \to \boldsymbol{C}$ a surjective and $g : \boldsymbol{C} \to \boldsymbol{B}$ an injective homomorphism (see Fig. 3.17).

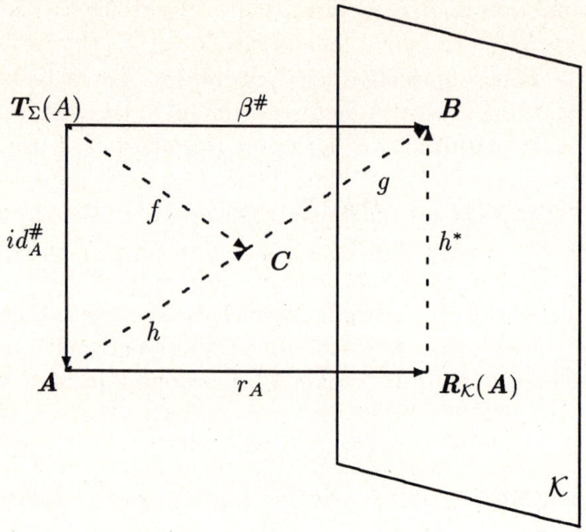

Fig. 3.17

Now assume that $\beta^\sharp(t_m) = \beta^\sharp(t'_m)$ for all $m \in M$, hence $ker\ id^\sharp_A \subseteq ker\ \beta^\sharp \subseteq ker\ f$; and so $f = id^\sharp_A \cdot h$ for some homomorphism $h : \boldsymbol{A} \to \boldsymbol{C}$. Notice that f, g and h are uniquely determined.

By the definition of sur-reflection, the composed homomorphism $h \cdot g$ from $\boldsymbol{A}$ to $\boldsymbol{B}$ factorizes through $\boldsymbol{R}_\mathcal{K}(\boldsymbol{A})$, i.e., there exists a unique homomorphism $h^* : \boldsymbol{R}_\mathcal{K}(\boldsymbol{A}) \to \boldsymbol{B}$ such that $h \cdot g = r_A \cdot h^*$. Thus, $\beta^\sharp = f \cdot g = id^\sharp_A \cdot h \cdot g = id^\sharp_A \cdot r_A \cdot h^*$, whence $ker\ (id^\sharp_A \cdot r_A) \subseteq ker\ \beta^\sharp$. That is, β satisfies $\forall\, A\, (\bigwedge t_m = t'_m \Rightarrow t = t')$ of $I(\boldsymbol{A})$, which proves Claim 1.

Claim 2: $Mod\ I(\mathcal{K}) \subseteq \mathcal{K}$:

It suffices to show that, for each $\boldsymbol{A}$ of $Mod\ I(\mathcal{K})$, the surjective reflection homomorphism $r_A : \boldsymbol{A} \to \boldsymbol{R}_\mathcal{K}(\boldsymbol{A})$ is also injective, since then $\boldsymbol{A}$ is isomorphic to $\boldsymbol{R}_\mathcal{K}(\boldsymbol{A})$ in $\mathcal{K}$. Let $\boldsymbol{A} \in Mod\ I(\mathcal{K})$. Then, in particular, $\boldsymbol{A} \in Mod\ I(\boldsymbol{A})$. Thus, for every assignment $\alpha : A \to A$, $ker\ id^\sharp_A \subseteq ker\ \alpha^\sharp$ implies $ker\ (id^\sharp_A \cdot r_A) \subseteq ker\ \alpha^\sharp$. Take $\alpha = id_A$. Then it follows that $ker\ (id^\sharp_A \cdot r_A) \subseteq ker\ id^\sharp_A$, which means that r_A is injective. ∎

Some clarifying remarks about the Banaschewski-Herrlich Theorem are necessary. Inspecting the "only if-part" of its proof carefully we have to note that, in fact, the following sufficient condition is proved: If $\mathcal{K}$ is a sur-reflective class, then there exists a proper class of implications, viz. $I(\mathcal{K})$, such that an algebra $\boldsymbol{A}$ belongs to $\mathcal{K}$ iff $\boldsymbol{A}$ is a model of $I(\mathcal{K})$. Here even the notion of model has to be generalized in that way that $\boldsymbol{A}$ validates each implication of the proper class. But this is not the problem. Recall that the definition of an implicational class requires a set of implications. Strictly speaking, a sur-reflective class is, therefore, not implicational in our sense. Recently Adamek /Adamek-88/ has shown, however, that under some mild set theoretic assumption every sur-reflective class $\mathcal{K}$ is a model class for some set of implications. In other words, the Banaschewski-Herrlich Theorem is true under Adamek's assumption, which will be supposed tacitly here and in the sequel.

Given an abstract class $\mathcal{K}$ of algebras, an implication is said to be valid in $\mathcal{K}$ if it is valid in each algebra of $\mathcal{K}$. By $Imp\ \mathcal{K}$ we denote the set of all implications $\forall X\ (\bigwedge t_m = t'_m \Rightarrow t = t')$, which are valid in $\mathcal{K}$, such that X is a subset of a large enough set, say Z. By the foregoing observation we can always choose, without loss of generality, such a set Z. $Imp\ \mathcal{K}$ is called the ***implicational theory*** of $\mathcal{K}$. When referring to $Imp\ \mathcal{K}$, the set of all variables will not be mentioned explicitly.

Let us summarize the different characterizations of an implicational class.

Corollary. *For any abstract class $\mathcal{K}$ of algebras the following are equivalent:*

(1) $\mathcal{K}$ is an implicational class.

(2) $\mathcal{K}$ is a sur-reflective class.

(3) $\mathcal{K}$ is closed under **S** *and* **P**.

(4) $\mathcal{K} = Mod\ Imp\ \mathcal{K}$.

(5) $\mathcal{K} = Mod\ Imp\ \mathcal{K}'$ for some abstract class $\mathcal{K}'$.

(6) $\mathcal{K} = \mathbf{SP}\mathcal{K}$.

(7) $\mathcal{K} = \mathbf{SP}\mathcal{K}'$ for some abstract class $\mathcal{K}'$. ■

The proof of the equivalences is based on the Banaschewski-Herrlich Theorem and Theorem 13.

As in the equational case, Mod and Imp form a Galois connection so that $Mod\ Imp$ and $Imp\ Mod$ are closure operators. The $Mod\ Imp$-closed classes of algebras are just the sur-reflective classes. In particular, $Mod\ Imp = \mathbf{SP}$ since $\mathbf{SP}$ is the closure operator related to sur-reflective classes.

Our next aim is the algebraic characterization of finitary implicational classes.

Definition 10. *A sur-reflective class $\mathcal{K}$ of algebras is called a* ***semivariety*** *if $\mathcal{K}$ is closed under direct unions.*

The first problem to be investigated in this context concerns the closure operator associated with semivarieties. To solve this problem we need the following fact.

Lemma 15. *Let $\mathcal{K}$ be an abstract class of algebras. An arbitrary algebra $\boldsymbol{A}$ belongs to $\mathbf{US}\mathcal{K}$ iff all finitely generated subalgebras of $\boldsymbol{A}$ are in $\mathbf{S}\mathcal{K}$.*

Proof. Assume that $\boldsymbol{A}$ is an algebra in $\mathbf{US}\mathcal{K}$. By definition, $\boldsymbol{A} = \bigcup(\boldsymbol{A}_i | i \in I)$ for some directed family of algebras $\boldsymbol{A}_i \in \mathbf{S}\mathcal{K}$, $i \in I$. Consider any subalgebra $\boldsymbol{B}$ of $\boldsymbol{A}$, which is generated by a finite set X. We have to show that $\boldsymbol{B}$ belongs to $\mathbf{S}\mathcal{K}$. Since X is finite, $\boldsymbol{B}$ is a subalgebra of some component $\boldsymbol{A}_k$, by the assumption that $(\boldsymbol{A}_i | i \in I)$ is directed. But now $\boldsymbol{B} \in \mathbf{SS}\mathcal{K}$; hence $\boldsymbol{B} \in \mathbf{S}\mathcal{K}$.

The converse implication follows directly from Theorem 1 in Section 3.1.1. ■

Using Lemma 15 we can show that **US** is a closure operator.

Lemma 16. **US** *is a closure operator on abstract classes of algebras.*

Proof. Obviously, **US** is extensive and monotone. Therefore, it remains to prove that **US** is idempotent.

Claim 1: $\mathbf{SU} \leq \mathbf{US}$.

If $\boldsymbol{B} \in \mathbf{SU}\mathcal{K}$, then $\boldsymbol{B}$ is a subalgebra of an algebra $\boldsymbol{A}$, which is the directed union, $\boldsymbol{A} = \bigcup(\boldsymbol{A}_i | i \in I)$, of a directed family $(\boldsymbol{A}_i | i \in I)$ of algebras $\boldsymbol{A}_i \in \mathcal{K}$. Define a new direct family $(\boldsymbol{B}_i | i \in I)$ as follows: $B_i = B \cap A_i$ for all $i \in I$. Then $\boldsymbol{B} = \bigcup(\boldsymbol{B}_i | i \in I)$, where $\boldsymbol{B}_i \in \mathbf{S}\mathcal{K}$; hence $\boldsymbol{B} \in \mathbf{US}\mathcal{K}$.

Claim 2: $\mathbf{UUS} \leq \mathbf{US}$.

If $\boldsymbol{A} \in \mathbf{UUS}\mathcal{K}$, then $\boldsymbol{A} = \bigcup(\boldsymbol{A}_i | i \in I)$, where $(\boldsymbol{A}_i | i \in I)$ is a directed family of algebras $\boldsymbol{A}_i \in \mathbf{US}\mathcal{K}$. By Lemma 15, all finitely generated subalgebras of $\boldsymbol{A}_i$ are in $\mathbf{S}\mathcal{K}$. We have to show, by Lemma 15 again, that each finitely generated subalgebra $\boldsymbol{B}$ of $\boldsymbol{A}$ is contained in $\mathbf{S}\mathcal{K}$. But notice that $\boldsymbol{B}$ is then, in particular, a subalgebra of some component $\boldsymbol{A}_k$; and hence $\boldsymbol{B} \in \mathbf{S}\mathcal{K}$.

Now idempotency follows readily:

$$\mathbf{USUS} \leq \mathbf{UUS} \leq \mathbf{US}.$$

■

To continue, a further property is required.

Lemma 17. $\mathbf{PU} \leq \mathbf{UP}$.

Proof. If $\boldsymbol{A} \in \mathbf{PU}\mathcal{K}$, then $\boldsymbol{A} = \prod(\boldsymbol{A}_i | i \in I)$ for a family of algebras $\boldsymbol{A}_i \in \mathbf{U}\mathcal{K}$, $i \in I$. Thus, $\boldsymbol{A}_i = \bigcup(\boldsymbol{A}_{i,m} | m \in M_i)$, where $(\boldsymbol{A}_{i,m} | m \in M_i)$ is some directed family of algebras. Observe that the direct product of all directed index sets M_i, $M = \prod(M_i | i \in I)$, is directed, too, under coordinatewise ordering. Now define algebras $\boldsymbol{B}_m$ as follows: $\boldsymbol{B}_m = \prod(\boldsymbol{A}_{i,m_i} | i \in I)$ for all $m = (m_i | i \in I)$. Of course, $\boldsymbol{B}_m \in \mathbf{P}\mathcal{K}$.

Since $\boldsymbol{A} = \bigcup(\boldsymbol{B}_m | m \in M)$, we have $\boldsymbol{A} \in \mathbf{UP}\mathcal{K}$. ■

Corollary. **USP** *is a closure operator on abstract classes of algebras.*

Proof. Since **P** and **US** are closure operators, it is enough to prove **PUS** $\leq$ **USP**. But this follows easily by Lemma 17. ■

According to our terminology we say that a semivariety $\mathcal{V}$ is ***generated*** by a given abstract class $\mathcal{K}$ of algebras if $\mathcal{V}$ is the least semivariety such that $\mathcal{K} \subseteq \mathcal{V}$. Similarly to varieties and sur-reflective classes as well, the semivariety generated by $\mathcal{K}$ can be constructed in a single step.

Theorem 18. *If $\mathcal{K}$ is any abstract class of algebras, then* **USP**$\mathcal{K}$ *is the semivariety generated by $\mathcal{K}$.* ■

To axiomatize semivarieties by finitary implications we can always require, without loss of generality, that all variables involved in any finitary implication belong to a fixed countably infinite set of variables, say V. Given an abstract class $\mathcal{K}$ of algebras, we denote by $Imp_\omega\mathcal{K}$ the set of all finitary implications $\forall X\,(\bigwedge t_m = t'_m \Rightarrow t = t')$, valid in $\mathcal{K}$. $Imp_\omega\mathcal{K}$ is called the ***finitary implicational theory*** of $\mathcal{K}$.

Proposition 19. *If $\mathcal{K}$ is a semivariety, then $\mathcal{K} = Mod\ Imp_\omega\mathcal{K}$.*

Proof. Assume that $\mathcal{K}$ is a semivariety. Then, $\mathcal{K} = Mod\ Imp\,\mathcal{K}$. Because of $Imp_\omega\mathcal{K} \subseteq Imp\,\mathcal{K}$, we derive

$$\mathcal{K} \subseteq Mod\ Imp_\omega\mathcal{K}.$$

Claim: $Mod\ Imp_\omega\mathcal{K} \subseteq \mathcal{K}$.

Since $\mathcal{K}$ is assumed to be closed under **U**, it suffices to show that any finitely generated algebra $\boldsymbol{B}$ of $Mod\ Imp_\omega\mathcal{K}$ belongs to $\mathcal{K}$. Consider the sur-reflection of $\boldsymbol{B}$ in $\mathcal{K}$

$$r_B : \boldsymbol{B} \to \boldsymbol{R}_\mathcal{K}(\boldsymbol{B}).$$

Now it remains to prove that r_B is injective. Let us indirectly assume that there are two distinct elements, say b and b', of B such that $r_B(b) = r_B(b')$. Since $\boldsymbol{B}$ is supposed to be finitely generated there is a surjective homomorphism $h : \boldsymbol{T}_\Sigma(X) \to \boldsymbol{B}$ for a suitable finite set X.

Let $\{(t_m, t'_m) | m \in M\}$ be the kernel of h. We define a finitary implication

$$\Phi = \forall X \left(\bigwedge t_m = t'_m \Rightarrow t = t' \right)$$

where t and t' are the inverse images of b and b', respectively, i.e., $h(t) = b$ and $h(t') = b'$. It is obvious that Φ is not valid in $\boldsymbol{B}$ and so Φ is not in $Imp_\omega\mathcal{K}$. Hence, there exists an algebra $\boldsymbol{A}$ in $\mathcal{K}$ such that Φ is not valid in $\boldsymbol{A}$. It follows, by definition that there exists an assignment α from X to A such that $ker\ h \subseteq ker\ \alpha^\sharp$ but $(t, t') \notin ker\ \alpha^\sharp$.

Because of $ker\ h \subseteq ker\ \alpha^\sharp$, $\alpha^\sharp$ factorizes through $\boldsymbol{B} : \alpha^\sharp = h \cdot g$ for some homomorphism $g : \boldsymbol{B} \to \boldsymbol{A}$. Hence, there is a homomorphism $g^* : \boldsymbol{R}_{\mathcal{K}}(\boldsymbol{B}) \to \boldsymbol{A}$ such that $g = r_B \cdot g^*$, by the definition of sur-reflection. But this leads to a contradiction:

$$\alpha^\sharp(t) = g^*(r_B(h(t))) = g^*(r_B(b)) = g^*(r_B(b')) = g^*(r_B(h(t'))) = \alpha^\sharp(t').$$

Thus, r_B is injective and so r_B is a bijection. Hence, $\boldsymbol{B}$ is isomorphic to $\boldsymbol{R}_{\mathcal{K}}(\boldsymbol{B})$ in $\mathcal{K}$. That is, $\boldsymbol{B} \in \mathcal{K}$. ■

Together with Theorem 9 in Section 3.3.1, we immediately derive our desired characterization.

Theorem 20 (Semivariety Theorem). *Let $\mathcal{K}$ be an abstract class of algebras. Then $\mathcal{K}$ is a finitary implicational class if and only if $\mathcal{K}$ is a semivariety.* ■

As previously, we sum up the different characterizations of finitary implicational classes.

Corollary. *For any abstract class $\mathcal{K}$ of algebras the following are equivalent:*

(1) $\mathcal{K}$ is a finitary implicational class.

(2) $\mathcal{K}$ is a semivariety.

(3) $\mathcal{K}$ is closed under **S**, **P** *and* **U**.

(4) $\mathcal{K} = Mod\ Imp_\omega\mathcal{K}$.

(5) $\mathcal{K} = Mod\ Imp_\omega\mathcal{K}'$ for some abstract class $\mathcal{K}'$.

(6) $\mathcal{K} = \mathbf{USP}\mathcal{K}$.

(7) $\mathcal{K} = \mathbf{USP}\mathcal{K}'$ for some abstract class $\mathcal{K}'$. ■

The proof of the equivalences follows from the Semivariety Theorem, Proposition 19 and Theorem 18.

Semivarieties are the closed classes with respect to the closure operator $Mod\ Imp_\omega$. By Theorem 18, we obtain

$$Mod\ Imp_\omega = \mathbf{USP}.$$

Now we turn to universal Horn classes. For their algebraic characterization we introduce the following concept.

Definition 11. *A sur-reflective class $\mathcal{K}$ of algebras is called a* ***quasivariety*** *if $\mathcal{K}$ is closed under direct limits.*

Searching for the associated closure operator we need the following fact.

Lemma 21. *Let $\mathcal{K}$ be an abstract class of algebras. An arbitrary algebra $\boldsymbol{A}$ belongs to* **LSP**$\mathcal{K}$ *iff $\boldsymbol{A}$ fulfills the condition (Q) below.*

> *(Q) Every homomorphism f from any finitely presented algebra $\boldsymbol{B}$ to $\boldsymbol{A}$ factorizes through the sur-reflection of $\boldsymbol{B}$ in* **SP**$\mathcal{K}$.

Proof. Let $\mathcal{K}$ be an abstract class of algebras.

(1) Necessity: If we assume that an arbitrary algebra $\boldsymbol{A}$ belongs to **LSP**$\mathcal{K}$, then $\boldsymbol{A}$ is the direct limit, $\boldsymbol{A} = \lim(\boldsymbol{A}_i | i \in I)$, of some direct family $(h_{ij} : \boldsymbol{A}_i \to \boldsymbol{A}_j)$ of algebras $\boldsymbol{A}_i$ in **SP**$\mathcal{K}$.

Consider a homomorphism f from any finitely presented algebra $\boldsymbol{B}$ into $\boldsymbol{A}$. Using Proposition 8 in Section 3.1.2, we factorize f through some component $\boldsymbol{A}_k : f = g \cdot h_k$ with $g : \boldsymbol{B} \to \boldsymbol{A}_k$ and $h_k : \boldsymbol{A}_k \to \boldsymbol{A}$ belongs to the associated limit cone $(h_i : \boldsymbol{A}_i \to \boldsymbol{A})$ (see Fig. 3.18).

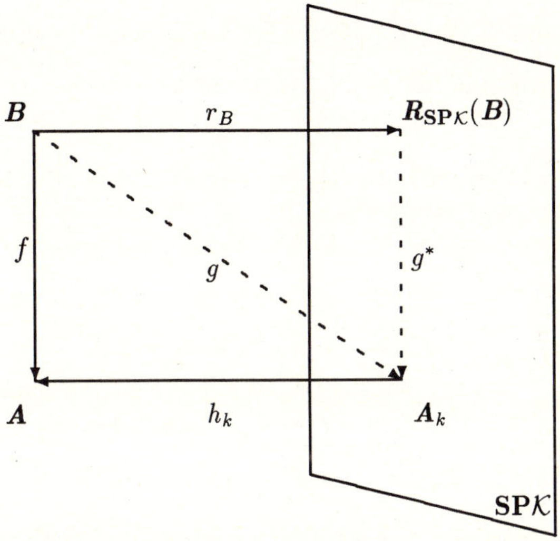

Fig. 3.18

Since $\boldsymbol{A}_k$ is in **SP**$\mathcal{K}$, by the definition of sur-reflection, g factorizes through $\boldsymbol{R}_{\mathbf{SP}\mathcal{K}}(\boldsymbol{B})$. That is, $g = r_B \cdot g^*$, where $r_B : \boldsymbol{B} \to \boldsymbol{R}_{\mathbf{SP}\mathcal{K}}(\boldsymbol{B})$ is the sur-reflection and $g^* : \boldsymbol{R}_{\mathbf{SP}\mathcal{K}}(\boldsymbol{B}) \to \boldsymbol{A}_k$. Hence we get $f = r_B \cdot (g^* \cdot h_k)$ as required.

(2) Sufficiency: Assume that $\boldsymbol{A}$ is an arbitrary algebra satisfying condition (Q). By Theorem 7 in Section 3.1.2, $\boldsymbol{A}$ is isomorphic to a direct limit of finitely presented algebras. For simplicity we put $\boldsymbol{A} = \lim(\boldsymbol{A}_i | i \in I)$, where $(h_{ij} : \boldsymbol{A}_i \to \boldsymbol{A}_j)$ is a direct family of finitely presented algebras. Let $(h_i : \boldsymbol{A}_i \to \boldsymbol{A})$ be the associated limit cone.

Denote by $\boldsymbol{R}_i$ the sur-reflection of $\boldsymbol{A}_i$ in **SP**$\mathcal{K}$ with $r_i : \boldsymbol{A}_i \to \boldsymbol{R}_i$ as the related surjective homomorphism $(i \in I)$. By the definition of sur-reflection, $(h_{ij} : \boldsymbol{A}_i \to \boldsymbol{A}_j)$ induces another direct family $(g_{ij} : \boldsymbol{R}_i \to \boldsymbol{R}_j)$ such that

$$r_i \cdot g_{ij} = h_{ij} \cdot r_j \quad \text{for all } i \le j$$

(see Fig. 3.19).

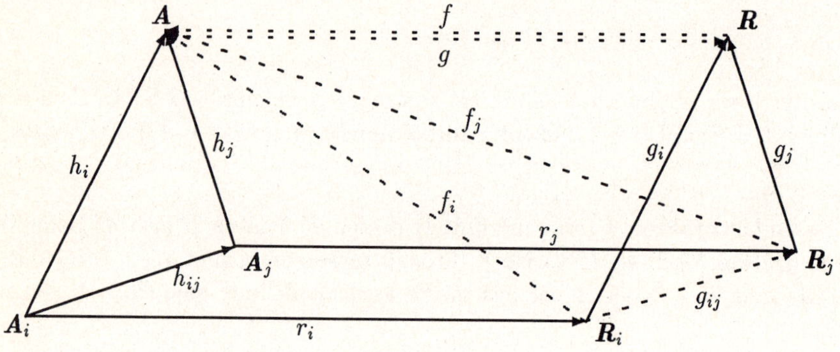

Fig. 3.19

Let $\boldsymbol{R}$ be the direct limit of $(g_{ij} : \boldsymbol{R}_i \to \boldsymbol{R}_j)$ with the associated limit cone $(g_i : \boldsymbol{R}_i \to \boldsymbol{R})$. By definition, $\boldsymbol{R}$ is in $\mathbf{LSP}\mathcal{K}$. So it suffices to show that $\boldsymbol{A}$ is isomorphic to $\boldsymbol{R}$.

By Lemma 5 in Section 3.1.2, there is exactly one homomorphism $g : \boldsymbol{A} \to \boldsymbol{R}$ such that

$$r_i \cdot g_i = h_i \cdot g \quad \text{for all } i \in I$$

since $(r_i \cdot g_i | i \in I)$ is a cone, i.e., $h_{ij} \cdot (r_j \cdot g_j) = (h_{ij} \cdot r_j) \cdot g_j = r_i \cdot g_{ij} \cdot g_j = r_i \cdot g_i$ for all $i \le j$.

By the condition (Q), each h_i factorizes through $\boldsymbol{R}_i$: $h_i = r_i \cdot f_i$ for some homomorphism $f_i : \boldsymbol{R}_i \to \boldsymbol{A}$. Note that $(f_i | i \in I)$ is a cone since $g_{ij} \cdot f_j = f_i$, because

$$r_i \cdot (g_{ij} \cdot f_j) = h_{ij} \cdot (r_j \cdot f_j) = h_{ij} \cdot h_j = h_i = r_i \cdot f_i \quad \text{implies} \quad g_{ij} \cdot f_j = f_i,$$

by the surjectivity of r_i. Hence, by Lemma 5 in Section 3.1.2, there is exactly one homomorphism $f : \boldsymbol{R} \to \boldsymbol{A}$ such that

$$f_i = g_i \cdot f \quad \text{for all } i \in I.$$

It holds that $h_i \cdot (g \cdot f) = r_i \cdot g_i \cdot f = r_i \cdot f_i = h_i$ for all $i \in I$. Since $(h_i \mid i \in I)$ is a cone we get

(i) $g \cdot f = id_A$.

Note that $(r_i \cdot g_i) \cdot (f \cdot g) = r_i \cdot f_i \cdot g = h_i \cdot g = r_i \cdot g_i$ implies $g_i \cdot (f \cdot g) = g_i$, by the surjectivity of r_i, for all $i \in I$. Since $(g_i \mid i \in I)$ is a cone we get

(ii) $f \cdot g = id_R$.

Thus, f and g are bijections; hence $\boldsymbol{A}$ is isomorphic to $\boldsymbol{R}$. ■

We are now able to prove that **LSP** is a closure operator.

Lemma 22. **LSP** *is a closure operator on abstract classes of algebras.*

Proof. Clearly, **LSP** is extensive and monotone. Therefore, we have only to show that **LSP** is idempotent. This will be done in three steps.

Claim 1: **PLSP** $\leq$ **LSP**.

If an algebra $\boldsymbol{A}$ belongs to $\mathbf{PLSP}\mathcal{K}$, then $\boldsymbol{A} = \prod(\boldsymbol{A}_i | i \in I)$ for some family of algebras $\boldsymbol{A}_i$ in $\mathbf{LSP}\mathcal{K}$, $i \in I$. Using Lemma 21, we have to show that $\boldsymbol{A}$ satisfies the condition (Q). Consider a homomorphism f from any finitely presented algebra $\boldsymbol{B}$ to $\boldsymbol{A}$; put $f_i = f \cdot pr_i$ for $i \in I$. Since $\boldsymbol{A}_i \in \mathbf{LSP}\mathcal{K}$, f_i factorizes through $\boldsymbol{R}_{\mathbf{SP}\mathcal{K}}(\boldsymbol{B})$, by (Q). That is, $f_i = r_B \cdot g_i$, where $r_B : \boldsymbol{B} \to \boldsymbol{R}_{\mathbf{SP}\mathcal{K}}(\boldsymbol{B})$ is the surjective reflection homomorphism and $g_i : \boldsymbol{R}_{\mathbf{SP}\mathcal{K}}(\boldsymbol{B}) \to \boldsymbol{A}_i$ (see Fig. 3.20).

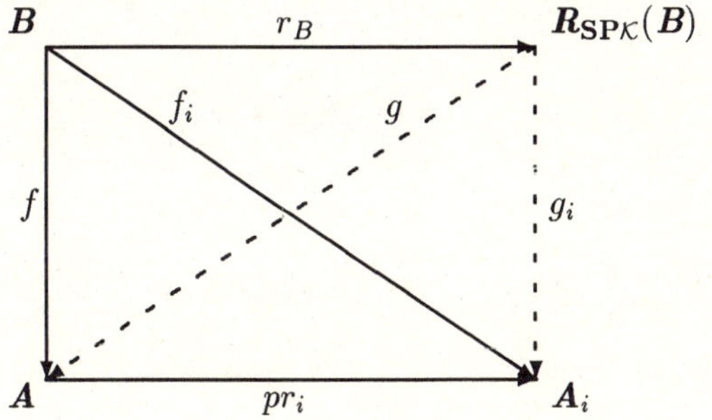

Fig. 3.20

By Lemma 9 in Section 3.1.3, the family $(g_i | i \in I)$ uniquely determines a homomorphism $g : \boldsymbol{R}_{\mathbf{SP}\mathcal{K}}(\boldsymbol{B}) \to \boldsymbol{A}$ such that $g \cdot pr_i = g_i$ for all $i \in I$. Now we derive $r_B \cdot g_i = r_B \cdot g \cdot pr_i = f \cdot pr_i$, which implies $f = r_B \cdot g$. Hence, $\boldsymbol{A}$ satisfies (Q) and consequently, $\boldsymbol{A} \in \mathbf{LSP}\mathcal{K}$.

Claim 2: **SLSP** $\leq$ **LSP**.

If an algebra $\boldsymbol{A}$ belongs to $\mathbf{SLSP}\mathcal{K}$, then $\boldsymbol{A}$ is a subalgebra of some algebra $\boldsymbol{C} \in \mathbf{LSP}\mathcal{K}$. Using Lemma 21, we have to show that $\boldsymbol{A}$ satisfies the condition (Q). Consider a homomorphism f from any finitely presented algebra $\boldsymbol{B}$ to $\boldsymbol{A}$. Put $g = f \cdot in_A$, where in_A is the inclusion of $\boldsymbol{A}$ in $\boldsymbol{C}$. By (Q), there exists a unique homomorphism $g^* : \boldsymbol{R}_{\mathbf{SP}\mathcal{K}}(\boldsymbol{B}) \to \boldsymbol{C}$ such that $f \cdot in_A = r_B \cdot g^*$ (see Fig. 3.21).

By Proposition 3 in Section 3.1.2, we factorize f and g^*:

$$f = f' \cdot f'' \quad \text{with} \quad f' : \boldsymbol{B} \to \boldsymbol{D} \quad \text{and} \quad f'' : \boldsymbol{D} \to \boldsymbol{A}$$

and

$$g^* = g' \cdot g'' \quad \text{with} \quad g' : \boldsymbol{R}_{\mathbf{SP}\mathcal{K}}(\boldsymbol{B}) \to \boldsymbol{D}' \quad \text{and} \quad g'' : \boldsymbol{D}' \to \boldsymbol{C},$$

where f' and g' are injective and f'' and g'' are surjective homomorphisms. Now we get two factorizations for g:

$$g = f' \cdot (f'' \cdot in_A) = (r_B \cdot g') \cdot g''.$$

Since image factorization is unique up to isomorphism, there is a diagonal fill-in $d : \boldsymbol{D}' \to \boldsymbol{D}$ such that $f' = r_B \cdot g' \cdot d$ and $g'' = d \cdot f'' \cdot in_A$. Thus, $f = f' \cdot f'' = r_B \cdot (g' \cdot d \cdot f'')$ and consequently, $\boldsymbol{A}$ satisfies (Q). By Lemma 21, $\boldsymbol{A} \in \mathbf{LSP}\mathcal{K}$.

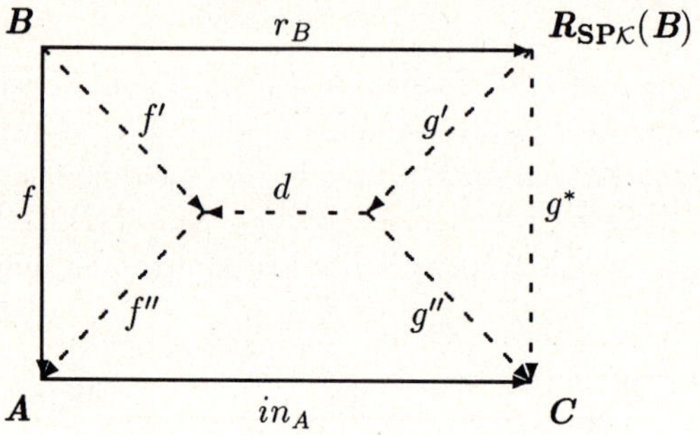

Fig. 3.21

Claim 3: **LLSP** $\leq$ **LSP**.

If an algebra $\boldsymbol{A}$ belongs to $\mathbf{LLSP}\mathcal{K}$, then $\boldsymbol{A} = \lim(\boldsymbol{A}_i | i \in I)$ for some direct family $(h_{ij} : \boldsymbol{A}_i \to \boldsymbol{A}_j)$ of algebras $\boldsymbol{A}_i$ in $\mathbf{LSP}\mathcal{K}$, $i \in I$. Using Lemma 21, we have to show that $\boldsymbol{A}$ satisfies (Q). Consider a homomorphism f from any finitely presented algebra $\boldsymbol{B}$ to $\boldsymbol{A}$. By Proposition 8 in Section 3.1.2, f factorizes through some component, say $\boldsymbol{A}_k$. That is, $f = g \cdot h_k$ for some homomorphism $g : \boldsymbol{B} \to \boldsymbol{A}_k$ and $h_k : \boldsymbol{A}_k \to \boldsymbol{A}$ belongs to the associated limit cone (see Fig. 3.22).

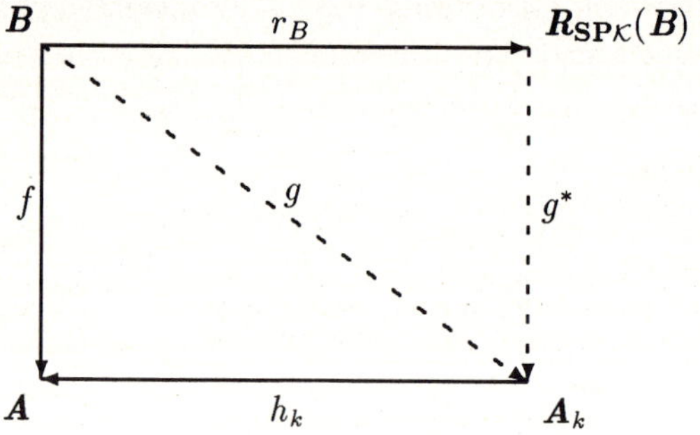

Fig. 3.22

Since $\boldsymbol{A}_k \in \mathbf{LSP}\mathcal{K}$, g factorizes through $\boldsymbol{R}_{\mathbf{SP}\mathcal{K}}(\boldsymbol{B})$, by (Q), i.e., $g = r_B \cdot g^*$. But now $f = r_B \cdot (g^* \cdot h_k)$. Hence, $\boldsymbol{A}$ satisfies (Q) and so $\boldsymbol{A} \in \mathbf{LSP}\mathcal{K}$.

Now idempotency follows easily:

$$\mathbf{LSPLSP} \leq \mathbf{LSLSP} \leq \mathbf{LLSP} \leq \mathbf{LSP}. \qquad \blacksquare$$

As a direct consequence we obtain:

Theorem 23 (Fujiwara's Theorem). *If $\mathcal{K}$ is an abstract class of algebras, then* **LSP**$\mathcal{K}$ *is the quasivariety generated by $\mathcal{K}$.* ■

Given an abstract class $\mathcal{K}$ of algebras, $Horn\ \mathcal{K}$ denotes the set of all universal Horn clauses (with variables from V), valid in $\mathcal{K}$. $Horn\ \mathcal{K}$ is called the ***universal Horn theory*** of $\mathcal{K}$.

Proposition 24. *If $\mathcal{K}$ is a quasivariety, then $\mathcal{K} = Mod\ Horn\ \mathcal{K}$.*

Proof. Assume that $\mathcal{K}$ is a quasivariety. Since $\mathcal{K} \subseteq Mod\ Horn\ \mathcal{K}$ holds trivially, we have only to prove the converse inclusion. Let $\boldsymbol{A}$ be an algebra in $Mod\ Horn\ \mathcal{K}$. By Theorem 7 in Section 3.1.2, $\boldsymbol{A}$ is isomorphic to a direct limit of finitely presented algebras $\boldsymbol{A}_i$, $i \in I$. It is easily seen that each $\boldsymbol{A}_i$ is a model of $Horn\ \mathcal{K}$, too. Since $\mathcal{K}$ is assumed to be closed under direct limits, it suffices to show that every finitely presented algebra of $Mod\ Horn\ \mathcal{K}$ belongs to $\mathcal{K}$.

Let $\boldsymbol{B}$ be a finitely presented algebra from $Mod\ Horn\ \mathcal{K}$. Then there is a surjective homomorphism h from the term algebra $\boldsymbol{T}_\Sigma(X)$ to $\boldsymbol{B}$, where X is a suitable finite set and the kernel of h is finitely generated as a congruence. Let $\{(t_m, t'_m) | \, m \in M\}$ be the finite generating system of $ker\ h$.

Now we are going to prove that the surjective homomorphism $r_B : \boldsymbol{B} \to \boldsymbol{R}_{\mathcal{K}}(\boldsymbol{B})$ is injective and, consequently, bijective, which implies that $\boldsymbol{B}$ belongs to $\mathcal{K}$.

We indirectly assume that there are two distinct elements b and b' of B such that $r_B(b) = r_B(b')$. Consider the universal Horn clause

$$\Phi = \forall X \left(\bigwedge_{m \in M} t_m = t'_m \Rightarrow t = t' \right),$$

where $\{(t_m, t'_m) | m \in M\}$ is the kernel of r_B and t and t' are inverse images of b and b', respectively. It is obvious that Φ is not valid in $\boldsymbol{B}$ and hence Φ is not in $Horn\ \mathcal{K}$. That is, there exists an algebra $\boldsymbol{A}$ in $\mathcal{K}$ and an assignment α from X to $\boldsymbol{A}$ with

$$ker\ h \subseteq ker\ \alpha^\sharp \quad \text{but} \quad (t, t') \notin ker\ \alpha^\sharp.$$

Because $ker\ h \subseteq ker\ \alpha^\sharp$, $\alpha^\sharp$ factorizes through $\boldsymbol{B}$, i.e., $\alpha^\sharp = h \cdot g$ for some homomorphism $g : \boldsymbol{B} \to \boldsymbol{A}$. Thus, there exists a homomorphism $g^* : \boldsymbol{R}_{\mathcal{K}}(\boldsymbol{B}) \to \boldsymbol{A}$ with $g = r_B \cdot g^*$. But this yields a contradiction:

$$\alpha^\sharp(t) = g^*(r_B(h(t))) = g^*(r_B(b)) = g^*(r_B(b')) = g^*(r_B(h(t'))) = \alpha^\sharp(t').$$

Therefore, r_B is an isomorphism and $\boldsymbol{B}$ is isomorphic to $\boldsymbol{R}_{\mathcal{K}}(\boldsymbol{B})$. Hence $\boldsymbol{B}$ belongs to $\mathcal{K}$. ■

Together with Theorem 10 in Section 3.3.1 we derive our first main result about universal Horn classes.

Theorem 25 (First Quasivariety Theorem). *Let $\mathcal{K}$ be an abstract class of algebras. Then $\mathcal{K}$ is an universal Horn class if and only if $\mathcal{K}$ is a quasivariety.* ■

In the literature, universal Horn classes are usually characterized by closure under reduced products.

Lemma 26. *Let $\mathcal{K}$ be an abstract class of algebras. If $\mathcal{K}$ is closed under subalgebras and reduced products, then $\mathcal{K} = Mod\ Horn\,\mathcal{K}$.*

Proof. Let $\mathcal{K}$ be an abstract class of algebras. Assume $\mathcal{K}$ is closed under subalgebras and reduced products. In particular, $\mathcal{K}$ is a sur-reflective class and, hence, $\mathcal{K} = Mod\ Imp\,\mathcal{K}$. Since $Horn\,\mathcal{K}$ is included in $Imp\,\mathcal{K}$ we get $Mod\ Imp\,\mathcal{K} \subseteq Mod\ Horn\,\mathcal{K}$.

To prove the converse inclusion we indirectly assume there is an algebra, say $\boldsymbol{A}$, such that $\boldsymbol{A} \in Mod\ Horn\,\mathcal{K}$ but $\boldsymbol{A} \notin Mod\ Imp\,\mathcal{K}$. Observe that $\boldsymbol{A} \notin Mod\ Imp\,\mathcal{K}$ means $\boldsymbol{A}$ does not validate each implication valid in $\mathcal{K}$. Suppose

$$\Phi = \forall X \left(\bigwedge_{m \in M} t_m = t'_m \Rightarrow t = t' \right)$$

is such an implication with $\boldsymbol{A} \not\models \Phi$ and $\mathcal{K} \models \Phi$. Now, Φ induces a family of universal Horn clauses by selecting finite subsets of premises. Formally, let I denote the set of all finite subsets of M. For each i of I we define a universal Horn clause Φ_i as follows:

$$\Phi_i = \forall X_i \left(\bigwedge_{m \in i} t_m = t'_m \Rightarrow t = t' \right),$$

where X_i is a finite subset of X such that $t_m, t'_m \in T_\Sigma(X_i)$ for all $m \in i$ and $t, t' \in T_\Sigma(X_i)$. Of course, no Φ_i is valid in $\boldsymbol{A}$ and so, by the assumption $\boldsymbol{A} \in Mod\ Horn\,\mathcal{K}$, no Φ_i is in $Horn\,\mathcal{K}$. Hence, there exists for every $i \in I$ an algebra $\boldsymbol{B}_i \in \mathcal{K}$ such that $\boldsymbol{B}_i$ does not validate Φ_i for each i of I.

We intend to construct a reduced product of $(\boldsymbol{B}_i | i \in I)$ so that Φ is not valid in it. This then leads to a contradiction. First, we have to define a filter over I. With each m of M we associate the set $\hat{m}$ of all those finite subsets of M that contain m: $\hat{m} = \{i \in I | m \in i\}$. Let F be the filter over I generated by $\hat{M} = \{\hat{m} | m \in M\}$ (see Example 3 in Section 3.1.4). The reduced product $\prod(\boldsymbol{B}_i | i \in I)/F$ will be abbreviated by $\boldsymbol{B}$. Note that $\boldsymbol{B}$ belongs to $\mathcal{K}$ since $\mathcal{K}$ is assumed to be closed under reduced products and each $\boldsymbol{B}_i, i \in I$, is in $\mathcal{K}$.

It remains to show that Φ is not valid in $\boldsymbol{B}$. Therefore, we have to find an assignment, say β, from X to $\prod(\boldsymbol{B}_i | i \in I)$ so that $\beta^\sharp(t_m) =_F \beta^\sharp(t'_m)$ for all $m \in M$ and $\beta^\sharp(t) \neq_F \beta^\sharp(t')$.

Keep in mind that $\boldsymbol{B}_i$ does not validate Φ_i for each i of I. That is, there is an assigment β_i from X_i to $\boldsymbol{B}_i$ with

$$\beta_i^\sharp(t_m) = \beta_i^\sharp(t'_m) \text{ for all } m \in i \text{ and } \beta_i^\sharp(t) \neq \beta_i^\sharp(t'). \qquad (*)$$

Without loss of generality each β_i can be considered as a mapping from X to $\boldsymbol{B}_i$ (set $\beta_i(x) = x$ for all $x \in X - X_i$). We claim that the induced assignment $\beta = \prod(\beta_i | i \in I)$ does not satisfy Φ in $\boldsymbol{B}$. Since $\hat{m} \in F$ we conclude

$$\{i \in I | \, \beta_i^\sharp(t_m) = \beta_i^\sharp(t'_m)\} \in F$$

because $\{i \in I | \, \beta_i^\sharp(t_m) = \beta_i^\sharp(t'_m)\} = \{i \in I | \, m \in i\} = \hat{m}$ by $(*)$. Thus

$$\beta^\sharp(t_m) =_F \beta^\sharp(t'_m) \quad \text{for all } m \in M.$$

On the other hand, $\beta_i^\sharp(t) \neq \beta_i^\sharp(t')$ for all $i \in I$ by $(*)$ implies

$$\{i \in I | \, \beta_i^\sharp(t) = \beta_i^\sharp(t')\} = \emptyset.$$

Because F is a proper filter (cf. Example 3 in Section 3.1.4) $\emptyset$ is not in F. That is,

$$\beta^\sharp(t) \neq_F \beta^\sharp(t').$$

Hence Φ is not valid in $\boldsymbol{B}$. But $\boldsymbol{B} \in \mathcal{K}$ means Φ is not valid in $\mathcal{K}$, which contradicts the assumption $\mathcal{K} \models \Phi$. Therefore, $Mod\,Imp\,\mathcal{K} = Mod\,Horn\,\mathcal{K}$ and so $\mathcal{K} = Mod\,Horn\,\mathcal{K}$. ■

Using Proposition 7 of Section 3.3.1 we immediately derive from Theorem 25 and Lemma 26 our second main result concerning quasivarieties.

Theorem 27 (Second Quasivariety Theorem). *An abstract class $\mathcal{K}$ of algebras is a quasivariety if and only if $\mathcal{K}$ is closed under subalgebras and reduced products.* ■

We already know that $\mathbf{P}_{red} \leq \mathbf{LP}$ and now, by Theorem 27,

$$\mathbf{SP}_{red} = \mathbf{LSP}$$

since $\mathbf{SP}_{red}$ is a closure operator. Furthermore, $\mathbf{P}_{red} \leq \mathbf{SPP}_u$ as shown, e.g., in /Burris-Sankappanavar-81/. Hence, $\mathbf{SP}_{red} \leq \mathbf{SPP}_u \leq \mathbf{SP}_{red}$ and so

$$\mathbf{SP}_{red} = \mathbf{SPP}_u,$$

which was first proved by Grätzer and Lakser /Grätzer-Lakser-70/. The following equations are shown in /Kashiwagi-65/:

$$\mathbf{SPP}_u = \mathbf{SP}_u\mathbf{P} = \mathbf{SP}_{sub}\mathbf{P}_u.$$

As in the other cases we summarize all different characterizations of strict universal Horn classes derived above.

Corollary. *For any abstract class $\mathcal{K}$ of algebras the following are equivalent:*

(1) $\mathcal{K}$ is a universal Horn class.

(2) $\mathcal{K}$ is a quasivariety.

(3) $\mathcal{K}$ is closed under $\mathbf{S}, \mathbf{P}$ and $\mathbf{L}$.

(4) $\mathcal{K}$ is closed under $\mathbf{S}$ and $\mathbf{P}_{red}$.

(5) $\mathcal{K}$ is closed under $\mathbf{S}, \mathbf{P}$ and $\mathbf{P}_u$.

(6) $\mathcal{K} = Mod\ Horn\ \mathcal{K}$.

(7) $\mathcal{K} = Mod\ Horn\ \mathcal{K}'$ for some abstract class $\mathcal{K}'$.

(8) $\mathcal{K} = \mathbf{LSP}\mathcal{K}$.

(9) $\mathcal{K} = \mathbf{LSP}\mathcal{K}'$ for some abstract class $\mathcal{K}'$.

(10) $\mathcal{K} = \mathbf{SP}_{red}\mathcal{K}$.

(11) $\mathcal{K} = \mathbf{SP}_{red}\mathcal{K}'$ for some abstract class $\mathcal{K}'$.

(12) $\mathcal{K} = \mathbf{SPP}_u\mathcal{K}$.

(13) $\mathcal{K} = \mathbf{SPP}_u\mathcal{K}'$ for some abstract class $\mathcal{K}'$. ■

Quasivarieties, semivarieties and sur-reflective classes are stepwise generalizations of the variety concept.

Proposition 28. *The following hold:*

(1) Every variety is a quasivariety.

(2) Every quasivariety is a semivariety.

(3) Every semivariety is a sur-reflective class.

Proof. (1) By Proposition 22 in Section 3.2.3, every variety is closed under direct limits, and hence, by definition, it is a quasivariety.

(2) Since directed unions can be regarded as special cases of direct limits, every quasivariety is a semivariety. Another argument is the following. If $\mathcal{K}$ is a quasivariety, then $\mathcal{K} = Mod\ Horn\ \mathcal{K}$, by Proposition 24. Since $Horn\ \mathcal{K}$ is, in particular, a set of finitary implications, $\mathcal{K}$ is a finitary implicational class and, by Theorem 20, $\mathcal{K}$ is a semivariety.

(3) Every semivariety is a sur-reflective class, by definition. ■

This yields a hierarchy of abstract classes of algebras as depicted in Fig. 3.23.

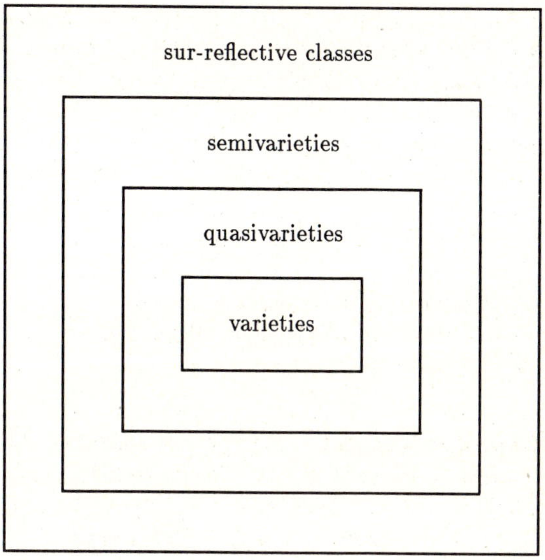

Fig. 3.23

Although we already know that the hierarchy is strict from the examples of Section 3.3.1, some further examples serve to demonstrate the strictness.

Example 1. Let G be the class of all finite abelian groups. We consider the sur-reflective class $\mathcal{K} = \mathbf{SP}G$ and the semivariety $\mathcal{K}' = \mathbf{USP}G$. Now we search for an abelian group $\boldsymbol{A}$ in $\mathcal{K}'$ but not in $\mathcal{K}$. To guarantee that $\boldsymbol{A}$ is in $\mathcal{K}'$, all finitely generated subgroups of $\boldsymbol{A}$ must be in $\mathcal{K}$. Take the abelian group introduced in Example 2 in Section 3.1.1:

$$A = \{x \in \mathbb{Q} \mid 0 \leq x < 1\}$$

with 0 as constant and addition defined by

$$x * y = \begin{cases} x + y & \text{if } x + y < 1, \\ x + y - 1 & \text{if } x + y \geq 1. \end{cases}$$

Recall that the (additive) inverse of x is defined by $i(x) = 1 - x$.

It was shown that all finitely generated subgroups of $\boldsymbol{A}$ are finite. So, $\boldsymbol{A}$ belongs to $\mathbf{U}G$ and, therefore, $\boldsymbol{A} \in \mathcal{K}'$. Specifically, $\boldsymbol{A}$ is the directed union over all cyclic groups $\boldsymbol{Z}_n$ of order n, where n ranges over all natural numbers.

On the other hand, any homomorphic image of $\boldsymbol{A}$ is either trivial or an infinite abelian group. There are no nontrivial finite abelian groups, which are images. Hence, the sur-reflection of $\boldsymbol{A}$ in $\mathcal{K}$ is the trivial group $\{0\}$.

Claim: $\boldsymbol{A}$ is not in $\mathcal{K}$.

From the indirect assumption that $\boldsymbol{A}$ is a subgroup of a direct product $\prod(\boldsymbol{A}_i | i \in I)$ in G follows that each $\boldsymbol{A}_i$ must be an image of the sur-reflection in $\mathcal{K}$. Thus, $\boldsymbol{A}_i = \{0\}$ for all $i \in I$ and, consequently, $\prod(\boldsymbol{A}_i | i \in I) = \{0\}$ which is a contradiction.

This example shows that there are sur-reflective classes which are not semivarieties. ■

Example 2. In this example, which is due to /Bloom-Wright-82/, we let Σ be a signature consisting only of nullary operation symbols 0, 1 and a_n, b_n for all natural numbers n. Consider the ground implication

$$\Phi = \forall \emptyset \left(\bigwedge_{n \in \mathbb{N}} a_n = b_n \Rightarrow 0 = 1 \right)$$

and denote by $\mathcal{K}$ the model class of Φ. By the Semivariety Theorem (Theorem 20), $\mathcal{K}$ is a semivariety.

Claim: $\mathcal{K}$ is not a quasivariety.

Take the sur-reflection of the ground term algebra in $\mathcal{K}$, this is the initial algebra $\boldsymbol{F}_{\mathcal{K}}$ in $\mathcal{K}$. We intend to define a direct family. For that purpose a family of congruences R_i on $\boldsymbol{F}_{\mathcal{K}}$ is introduced: R_i is the congruence generated by $\{(a_n, b_n) | n < i\}$ for all natural numbers i. Let $\boldsymbol{A}_i$ abbreviate the quotient $\boldsymbol{F}_{\mathcal{K}}/R_i$. The unique homomorphism h_i from $\boldsymbol{F}_{\mathcal{K}}$ to $\boldsymbol{A}_i$ has the property:

$$h_i(a_n) = h_i(b_n) \quad \text{for } n < i; \text{ and}$$

$$h_i(a_n) \neq h_i(b_n) \quad \text{for } n \geq i.$$

Hence, $h_i(a_n) = h_i(b_n)$ for all $n \in \mathbb{N}$ implies $0 = 1$ is a true statement, which means that

$$\boldsymbol{A}_i \models \Phi \quad \text{for all } i \in \mathbb{N}.$$

Now we are going to define a direct family of homomorphisms. If $i \leq j$, then a homomorphism h_{ij} from $\boldsymbol{A}_i$ into $\boldsymbol{A}_j$ is determined as follows:

$$h_{ij}([t]_{R_i}) = [t]_{R_j} \quad \text{for } t \in F_{\mathcal{K}}.$$

Indeed, (h_{ij}) is a direct family. Let $\boldsymbol{A}$ denote its direct limit. It is easily seen that $\boldsymbol{A}$ is isomorphic to the quotient of $\boldsymbol{F}_{\mathcal{K}}$ modulo the congruence generated by $\{(a_n, b_n) | n \in \mathbb{N}\}$. Then the unique homomorphism h from $\boldsymbol{F}_{\mathcal{K}}$ to $\boldsymbol{A}$ fulfills the premises of Φ:

$$h(a_n) = h(b_n) \quad \text{for all } n \in \mathbb{N},$$

but $h(0) \neq h(1)$, which means that Φ is not valid in $\boldsymbol{A}$.

This example indicates that there are semivarieties which are not quasivarieties. ■

Example 3. Consider the class $\mathcal{K}$ of all left-cancellative monoids, which is certainly a quasivariety. In Example 1 in Section 3.3.1, we have shown that $\mathcal{K}$ is not closed under images. So $\mathcal{K}$ cannot be a variety.

Hence, there are quasivarieties which are not varieties. ■

We close the section with a further example to show that not every semivariety is a quasivariety.

Example 4. Given a countably infinite set $A = \{0\} \bigcup \{a_n | n \in \mathbb{N}\}$, we fix a signature as in Example 3 in Section 3.3.1 by regarding all elements of A as nullary operation symbols and adding one unary operation symbol σ. Consider the ground implication

$$\Phi = \forall \emptyset \left(\bigwedge_{m \in \mathbb{N}} \sigma(a_m) = 0 \Rightarrow a_0 = 0 \right).$$

By $\mathcal{K}$ we denote the model class of Φ, which is a semivariety by Theorem 20.

In order to show that $\mathcal{K}$ is not a quasivariety we first define a family $(\boldsymbol{A}_i | i \in \mathbb{N})$ of algebras. The carrier set of each $\boldsymbol{A}_i$ is A, each nullary operation symbol is realized as a constant by itself and the realization of σ, denoted by σ_i, is given by

$$\sigma_i(x) = \begin{cases} a_i & \text{if } x = a_i, \\ 0 & \text{if } x \neq a_i. \end{cases}$$

It is evident that

$$\boldsymbol{A}_i \models \Phi \quad \text{for all } i \in \mathbb{N}.$$

Let F be the Fréchet filter over $\mathbb{N}$, i.e., $F = \{J | J \subseteq \mathbb{N} \text{ and } \mathbb{N} - J \text{ is a finite set}\}$. The reduced product of $(\boldsymbol{A}_i | i \in \mathbb{N})$ modulo F is abbreviated by $\boldsymbol{A}$. Recall that for any two sequences $x = (x_i | i \in \mathbb{N})$ and $y = (y_i | i \in \mathbb{N})$

$$\begin{aligned} x =_F y \quad &\text{iff} \quad \{i \in \mathbb{N} | x_i = y_i\} \in F \\ &\text{iff} \quad \{i \in \mathbb{N} | x_i \neq y_i\} \text{ is finite.} \end{aligned}$$

Hence, $\sigma(a_m) =_F 0$ for all $m \in \mathbb{N}$, but $a_0 \neq_F 0$, and so Φ is not valid in $\boldsymbol{A}$. In other terms, $\mathcal{K}$ is not closed under reduced products and, consequently, $\mathcal{K}$ is not a quasivariety by Theorem 27. ■

3.3.4 Implicational Theories

In this section, implicational theories are studied along the same lines as equational theories.

Definition 12. *A set I of implications is called an* ***implicational theory*** *if I is the implicational theory of some abstract class of algebras.*

Using the fact that Imp and Mod form a Galois connection we have $Imp\ Mod\ Imp\ \mathcal{K} = Imp\ \mathcal{K}$. Thus, I is an implicational theory iff

$$I = Imp\ Mod\ I.$$

The notion of logical consequence is extended in a straightforward manner. An implication Φ is said to be a ***logical consequence*** of a given set I of implications, in symbols $I \models \Phi$, if Φ is valid in all models of I (cf. Definition 7 in Section 3.2.4). Note that $I \models \Phi$ iff $\Phi \in Imp\ Mod\ I$. Hence we conclude that implicational theories are closed under logical consequence.

Proposition 29. *A set I of implications is an implicational theory if and only if an implication Φ belongs to I whenever Φ is a logical consequence of I.* ■

It will turn out that closure systems of congruences are the algebraic counterpart of implicational theories. To introduce them, "closed congruences" or, more generally, "closed relations" must be defined. Informally speaking, a relation P is closed with respect to a given set I of implications if every pair of terms t and t' belongs to P provided that the implication with premises P and conclusion $t = t'$ is a logical consequence of I.

For notational simplicity we adopt the following convention. When $P = \{(t_m, t'_m) | \, m \in M\}$ is a relation on $T_\Sigma(Z)$, we will write

$$P \Rightarrow t = t'$$

instead of the implication $\forall X \left(\bigwedge_{m \in M} t_m = t'_m \Rightarrow t = t' \right)$ where X is the set of all variables occurring in $t_m, t'_m, (m \in M)$ t and t'. If P is empty, we simply write equations without quantification.

As noted above (in the remarks on the Banaschewski-Herrlich Theorem) an arbitrary but fixed set Z may always be given such that all variables occuring in any implication belong to Z.

Definition 13. *Given a set I of implications, a relation P on $T_\Sigma(Z)$ is called I-**closed** if, for all pairs of terms t and t' in $T_\Sigma(Z)$,*

$$I \models P \Rightarrow t = t' \quad \textit{implies} \quad (t, t') \in P.$$

As an easy exercise the reader may prove that any I-closed relation on $T_\Sigma(Z)$ is a congruence.

Given a set I of implications, the set of all I-closed congruences is abbreviated by $\mathcal{C}(I)$.

Lemma 30. *For any set I of implications, $\mathcal{C}(I)$ is a closure system.*

Proof. Evidently, $T_\Sigma(Z) \times T_\Sigma(Z)$ is I-closed. Consider a nonempty set $\mathcal{P}$ of I-closed congruences on $\boldsymbol{T}_\Sigma(Z)$. It is easily seen that

$$I \models \bigcap \mathcal{P} \Rightarrow t = t' \text{ implies } I \models P \Rightarrow t = t' \text{ for each } P \text{ of } \mathcal{P}.$$

Now assume that $I \models \bigcap \mathcal{P} \Rightarrow t = t'$. Then, $(t, t') \in P$ for each P of $\mathcal{P}$, by the I-closedness of P. Hence $(t, t') \in \bigcap \mathcal{P}$ and so $\bigcap \mathcal{P}$ is I-closed. Moreover, $\bigcap \mathcal{P}$ is a congruence. ■

So far, we have a hint that the algebraic counterpart of an implicational theory could be a closure system of congruences. Recall that equational theories are characterizable by fully invariant congruences. Therefore, we try to generalize the notion of full invariance. If h is an endomorphism of $\boldsymbol{T}_\Sigma(Z)$ and P is a relation on $T_\Sigma(Z)$, then put $h(P) = \{(h(t), h(t')) | (t, t') \in P\}$ and $h^{-1}(P) = \{(t, t') | (h(t), h(t')) \in P\}$. The following definition is due to H.J. Hoehnke.

Definition 14. *A closure system $\mathcal{C}$ of congruences on $\boldsymbol{T}_\Sigma(Z)$ is called **fully invariant** if, for all endomorphisms h of $\boldsymbol{T}_\Sigma(Z)$ and all relations P on $T_\Sigma(Z)$, $h^{-1}(P)$ belongs to $\mathcal{C}$ whenever $P \in \mathcal{C}$.*

Full invariance is also characterizable via closure operators.

Proposition 31. *A closure system $\mathcal{C}$ of congruences on $\boldsymbol{T}_\Sigma(Z)$ is fully invariant if and only if its corresponding closure operator $cl_\mathcal{C}$ fulfills the condition*

$$h(cl_\mathcal{C}(P)) \subseteq cl_\mathcal{C}(h(P))$$

for all relations P on $T_\Sigma(Z)$ and all endomorphisms h of $\boldsymbol{T}_\Sigma(Z)$.

Proof. Let $\mathcal{C}$ be a closure system of congruences on $\boldsymbol{T}_\Sigma(Z)$. Given any relation P on $T_\Sigma(Z)$,

$$cl_\mathcal{C}(P) = \bigcap \{C | C \in \mathcal{C} \text{ and } P \subseteq C\},$$

by definition.

(1) Necessity: Assume that $\mathcal{C}$ is fully invariant. For an arbitrary endomorphism h of $\boldsymbol{T}_\Sigma(Z)$ we derive $h(cl_\mathcal{C}(P)) = \bigcap \{h(C) | C \in \mathcal{C} \text{ and } P \subseteq C\}$. Put $D = h(C)$; then $C \subseteq h^{-1}(D)$. This yields

$$h(cl_\mathcal{C}(P)) = \bigcap \{D | h^{-1}(D) \in \mathcal{C} \text{ and } P \subseteq h^{-1}(D)\}.$$

By the assumption that $\mathcal{C}$ is fully invariant, $\{D|\, D \in \mathcal{C}$ and $h(P) \subseteq D\}$ is a subset of $\{D|\, h^{-1}(D) \in \mathcal{C}$ and $P \subseteq h^{-1}(D)\}$. Hence the intersection of the latter one is included in the intersection of the first one, which coincides with $cl_{\mathcal{C}}(h(P))$. Thus

$$h(cl_{\mathcal{C}}(P)) \subseteq cl_{\mathcal{C}}(h(P)).$$

(2) Sufficiency: Assume that $h(cl_{\mathcal{C}}(P)) \subseteq cl_{\mathcal{C}}(h(P))$ for all relations P on $T_\Sigma(Z)$ and all endomorphisms h of $\boldsymbol{T}_\Sigma(Z)$. Consider an arbitrary congruence $C \in \mathcal{C}$. For $P = h^{-1}(C)$ we obtain $h(cl_{\mathcal{C}}(h^{-1}(C))) \subseteq cl_{\mathcal{C}}(h(h^{-1}(C))) \subseteq cl_{\mathcal{C}}(C) = C$. That is,

$$cl_{\mathcal{C}}(h^{-1}(C)) \subseteq h^{-1}(C).$$

Hence $h^{-1}(C) \in \mathcal{C}$, which means that $\mathcal{C}$ is fully invariant. ∎

Consider a fully invariant closure system $\mathcal{C}$. Then, in particular, $h(cl_{\mathcal{C}}(\emptyset)) \subseteq cl_{\mathcal{C}}(\emptyset)$. That is, $cl_{\mathcal{C}}(\emptyset)$ is a fully invariant congruence. In other terms, the least element of any fully invariant closure system of congruences is a fully invariant congruence. Conversely, if C_0 is a fully invariant congruence on $\boldsymbol{T}_\Sigma(Z)$, we can build a fully invariant closure system of congruences such that C_0 is its least element: $\mathcal{C} = \{C|\, C_0 \subseteq C$ and C is a congruence on $\boldsymbol{T}_\Sigma(Z)\}$.

The closure operator associated with the closure system $\mathcal{C}(I)$ of all I-closed congruences on $\boldsymbol{T}_\Sigma(Z)$ can be described explicitely. Let us first define a mapping, denoted by $cons_I$, from the set of all relations on $T_\Sigma(Z)$ into itself as follows:

$$cons_I(P) = \{(t, t')| I \models P \Rightarrow t = t'\}$$

for all relations P on $T_\Sigma(Z)$.

Lemma 32. *Given a set I of implications, $cons_I$ is the closure operator associated with $\mathcal{C}(I)$.*

Proof. We have to show that $cons_I(P)$ is the least I-closed relation including P.

(1) $P \subseteq cons_I(P)$ since $I \models P \Rightarrow t = t'$ for each $(t, t') \in P$.

(2) $cons_I(P)$ is I-closed: Let $Q = \{(t_m, t'_m)|\, m \in M\}$ be any nonempty relation on $T_\Sigma(Z)$. The logical consequence fulfills the following transitivity law: If $I \models P \Rightarrow t_m = t'_m$ for all $m \in M$ and $I \models Q \Rightarrow t = t'$, then $I \models P \Rightarrow t = t'$ for any pair of terms $t, t' \in T_\Sigma(Z)$.

Assume $I \models cons_I(P) \Rightarrow t = t'$. We have to show $(t, t') \in cons_I(P)$. If $cons_I(P) = \{(t_m, t'_m)|\, m \in M\}$, then $I \models P \Rightarrow t_m = t'_m$ for all $m \in M$, by definition. Hence $I \models P \Rightarrow t = t'$ and so $(t, t') \in cons_I(P)$.

(3) Assume that C is any I-closed relation on $T_\Sigma(Z)$ such that $P \subseteq C$. Then $I \models C \Rightarrow t_m = t'_m$ for all $m \in M$, where $\{(t_m, t'_m)|\, m \in M\} = P$. If $(t, t') \in cons_I(P)$, then

$I \models P \Rightarrow t = t'$. Thus $I \models C \Rightarrow t = t'$ and, consequently, $(t, t') \in C$ since C is assumed to be I-closed. Hence $cons_I(P) \subseteq C$. That is, $cons_I(P)$ is the least I-closed relation containing P. ■

A necessary condition for the algebraic characterization of implicational theories will be based on the following proposition.

Proposition 33. *If I is a set of implications, then $\mathcal{C}(I)$ is a fully invariant closure system of congruences.*

Proof. By Lemma 30, it remains to prove that $\mathcal{C}(I)$ is fully invariant. Let P be any relation on $T_\Sigma(Z)$ and let h be an arbitrary endomorphism of $\boldsymbol{T}_\Sigma(Z)$. Consider any pair (t, t') of terms $t, t' \in T_\Sigma(Z)$. If $(t, t') \in h(cons_I(P))$, then $t = h(t_0)$ and $t' = h(t'_0)$ for some terms $t_0, t'_0 \in T_\Sigma(Z)$ such that

$$I \models P \Rightarrow t_0 = t'_0.$$

It follows that

$$I \models h(P) \Rightarrow h(t_0) = h(t'_0).$$

Hence $(t, t') \in cons_I(h(P))$ and so

$$h(cons_I(P)) \subseteq cons_I(h(P)).$$

That is, $\mathcal{C}(I)$ is fully invariant by Proposition 31. ■

In order to derive a sufficient condition of the algebraic characterization mentioned above we must also associate conversely a set of implications with any closure system $\mathcal{C}$ of congruences on $\boldsymbol{T}_\Sigma(Z)$:

$$Imp\, \mathcal{C} = \{P \Rightarrow t = t' \,|\, P \subseteq T_\Sigma(Z) \times T_\Sigma(Z) \text{ and } (t, t') \in cl_{\mathcal{C}}(P)\}.$$

The following lemma is crucial for the subsequent development.

Lemma 34. *If $\mathcal{C}$ is a fully invariant closure system of congruences on $\boldsymbol{T}_\Sigma(Z)$, then*

$$C \in \mathcal{C} \quad \textit{iff} \quad \boldsymbol{T}_\Sigma(Z)/C \in Mod\; Imp\, \mathcal{C}.$$

Proof. Let $\mathcal{C}$ be a fully invariant closure system of congruences on $\boldsymbol{T}_\Sigma(Z)$. First, we derive a criterion for the validation of an implication $P \Rightarrow t = t'$ in $\boldsymbol{T}_\Sigma(Z)/C$.

Claim: $\boldsymbol{T}_\Sigma(Z)/C \models P \Rightarrow t = t'$ iff, for all endomorphisms h of $\boldsymbol{T}_\Sigma(Z)$, $(t, t') \in h^{-1}(C)$ whenever $P \subseteq h^{-1}(C)$.

Consider any assigment α from Z to $\boldsymbol{T}_\Sigma(Z)/C$. By the Axiom of Choice, there is an assignment β from Z to $\boldsymbol{T}_\Sigma(Z)$ determined by the rule: $\beta(z) = t$ iff $\alpha(z) = [t]_C$ for all z in Z and all t in $T_\Sigma(Z)$. It is easily seen that $\alpha^\sharp = \beta^\sharp \cdot nat_C$, where nat_C is the natural homomorphism from $\boldsymbol{T}_\Sigma(Z)$ to $\boldsymbol{T}_\Sigma(Z)/C$ defined by $nat_C(t) = [t]_C$ for $t \in T_\Sigma(Z)$. Specifically, $\beta^\sharp$ is an endomorphism of $\boldsymbol{T}_\Sigma(Z)$. On the other hand, every endomorphism h of $\boldsymbol{T}_\Sigma(Z)$ determines an assignment α from Z to $\boldsymbol{T}_\Sigma(Z)/C$ such that $\alpha^\sharp = h \cdot nat_C$. Thus, $P \Rightarrow t = t'$ is valid in $\boldsymbol{T}_\Sigma(Z)/C$ iff $P \subseteq ker(h \cdot nat_C)$ implies $(t,t') \in ker(h \cdot nat_C)$ for all endomorphisms h. Now, it is important to observe that $P \subseteq ker(h \cdot nat_C)$ iff $P \subseteq h^{-1}(C)$. Hence, $\boldsymbol{T}_\Sigma(Z)/C$ validates $P \Rightarrow t = t'$ iff, for all endomorphisms h, $P \subseteq h^{-1}(C)$ implies $(t,t') \in h^{-1}(C)$, which proves the claim.

Assume that $C \in \mathcal{C}$. Then, by the full invariance of $\mathcal{C}$, $h^{-1}(C)$ is in $\mathcal{C}$, too. So, $P \subseteq h^{-1}(C)$ implies $cl_\mathcal{C}(P) \subseteq h^{-1}(C)$. By definition, $P \Rightarrow t = t'$ belongs to $Imp\,\mathcal{C}$ iff $(t,t') \in cl_\mathcal{C}(P)$. Thus, each implication of $Imp\,\mathcal{C}$ is valid in $\boldsymbol{T}_\Sigma(Z)/C$.

Conversely, assume that $\boldsymbol{T}_\Sigma(Z)/C$ validates each implication of $Imp\ \mathcal{C}$. We have to show that $cl_\mathcal{C}(C) \subseteq C$. Consider the implication $C \Rightarrow t = t'$, where t and t' are arbitrary terms. By definition, $(C \Rightarrow t = t') \in Imp\ \mathcal{C}$ iff $(t,t') \in cl_\mathcal{C}(C)$. Since, by assumption, $\boldsymbol{T}_\Sigma(Z)/C \models C \Rightarrow t = t'$ iff $(t,t') \in cl_\mathcal{C}(C)$, we get $(t,t') \in C$ whenever $(t,t') \in cl_\mathcal{C}(C)$. That is, $cl_\mathcal{C}(C) \subseteq C$. Hence, $C \in \mathcal{C}$. ■

Corollary. *If $\mathcal{C}_1$ and $\mathcal{C}_2$ are fully invariant closure systems of congruences on $\boldsymbol{T}_\Sigma(Z)$, then $\mathcal{C}_1 \subseteq \mathcal{C}_2$ iff $Mod\ Imp\,\mathcal{C}_1 \subseteq Mod\ Imp\,\mathcal{C}_2$.* ■

We cannot expect that a given set I of implications equals the set $Imp\,\mathcal{C}(I)$ of implications assigned to $\mathcal{C}(I)$, but I is obviously a subset of $Imp\,\mathcal{C}(I)$. Hence $Mod\ Imp\,\mathcal{C}(I) \subseteq Mod\ I$. In fact, however, both model classes coincide.

Lemma 35. *For any set I of implications,*

$$Mod\ Imp\,\mathcal{C}(I) = Mod\ I.$$

Proof. We indirectly assume that $Mod\ I$ is not included in $Mod\ Imp\ \mathcal{C}(I)$. Then there is an algebra $\boldsymbol{A} \in Mod\ I$ such that $\boldsymbol{A}$ is not in $Mod\ Imp\ \mathcal{C}(I)$. Therefore, by definition, $\boldsymbol{A}$ does not validate all implications in $Imp\,\mathcal{C}(I)$. Suppose that $\boldsymbol{A}$ does not validate, say, $P \Rightarrow t = t'$ of $Imp\ \mathcal{C}(I)$. By definition, $(t,t') \in cons_I(P)$ since $cons_I$ is the closure operator associated with $\mathcal{C}(I)$ as shown in Lemma 32. Hence $I \models P \Rightarrow t = t'$ and, consequently, $\boldsymbol{A}$ validates $P \Rightarrow t = t'$, which is a contradiction. ■

Corollary. *If I is a set of implications, then*

$$C \in \mathcal{C}(I) \quad \textit{iff} \quad \boldsymbol{T}_\Sigma(Z)/C \in Mod\ I.$$ ■

Our next aim is the generation of the closure operator $cons_I$. For that purpose we must generally ask the question whether the set of all fully invariant closure operators itself forms a closure system.

We introduce a partial order on the set of all mappings from the set of all relations on $T_\Sigma(Z)$ into itself. Let cl and cl' be arbitrarily given mappings from $Rel(T_\Sigma(Z))$ into itself:

$$cl \leq cl' \quad \text{iff} \quad cl(P) \subseteq cl'(P) \text{ for all } P \in Rel(T_\Sigma(Z)).$$

In fact, $\leq$ is a partial order with greatest element d defined by $d(P) = T_\Sigma(Z) \times T_\Sigma(Z)$ for all $P \in Rel(T_\Sigma(Z))$. It is easily checked that d is even a fully invariant closure operator such that $d(P)$ is a congruence for each relation P on $T_\Sigma(Z)$. Now the question arises whether all fully invariant closure operators $cl : Rel(T_\Sigma(Z)) \to Con(\boldsymbol{T}_\Sigma(Z))$, where $Con(\boldsymbol{T}_\Sigma(Z))$ is the set of all congruences on $\boldsymbol{T}_\Sigma(Z)$, themselves form a closure system. Only if the answer is affirmative can we generate the fully invariant closure operators.

Lemma 36. *The set of all fully invariant closure operators* $cl : Rel(T_\Sigma(Z)) \to Con(\boldsymbol{T}_\Sigma(Z))$ *is a closure system.*

Proof. We have only to show that the intersection of a nonempty set $\{cl_j | j \in J\}$ of fully invariant closure operators $cl_j : Rel(T_\Sigma(Z)) \to Con(\boldsymbol{T}_\Sigma(Z))$ is also a fully invariant closure operator. Put $cl = \bigcap\{cl_j | j \in J\}$. Then $cl(P) = \bigcap\{cl_j(P) | j \in J\}$ and, of course, $cl(P)$ is a congruence for any relation P on $T_\Sigma(Z)$.

(1) cl is extensive:

Since $P \subseteq cl_j(P)$ for all $j \in J$ we get $P \subseteq \bigcap\{cl_j(P) | j \in J\}$ and hence $P \subseteq cl(P)$.

(2) cl is idempotent:

$$\begin{aligned} cl(cl(P)) &= \bigcap \left\{ cl_j \left(\bigcap\{cl_k(P) | k \in J\} \right) | j \in J \right\} \\ &\subseteq \bigcap \{cl_j(cl_j(P)) | j \in J\} \\ &\subseteq cl(P). \end{aligned}$$

(3) cl is monotone:

If $Q \subseteq P$, then $cl_j(Q) \subseteq cl_j(P)$ for all $j \in J$ and so $cl(Q) \subseteq cl(P)$.

(4) cl is fully invariant:

For an arbitrary endomorphism h of $\boldsymbol{T}_\Sigma(Z)$ we derive

$$\begin{aligned} h(cl(P)) = h\left(\bigcap\{cl_j(P) | j \in J\}\right) &\subseteq \bigcap\{h(cl_j(P)) | j \in J\} \\ &\subseteq \{cl_j(h(P)) | j \in J\} = cl(h(P)). \end{aligned}$$

■

To any set I of implications we associate a mapping c_I from $Rel(T_\Sigma(Z))$ into itself by

$$c_I(P) = \{(t, t') | (P \Rightarrow t = t') \in I\}$$

for each relation P on $T_\Sigma(Z)$. In case c_I is a closure operator we abbreviate the corresponding closure system $\mathcal{C}_{c_I}$ by $\overline{I}$.

If I is an implicational theory, then $\overline{I} = \mathcal{C}(I)$ and hence $\overline{I}$ is a fully invariant closure system of congruences on $\boldsymbol{T}_\Sigma(Z)$, by Proposition 33.

Proposition 37. *Given a set I of implications, $cons_I$ is the fully invariant closure operator from $Rel(T_\Sigma(Z))$ to $Con(\boldsymbol{T}_\Sigma(Z))$ generated by c_I.*

Proof. Evidently, $c_I(P) \subseteq cons_I(P)$ for all $P \in Rel(T_\Sigma(Z))$. Therefore we have to show that $cons_I$ is the least fully invariant closure operator from $Rel(T_\Sigma(Z))$ to $Con(\boldsymbol{T}_\Sigma(Z))$, which includes c_I.

Assume that $cl : Rel(T_\Sigma(Z)) \to Con(\boldsymbol{T}_\Sigma(Z))$ is a fully invariant closure operator with $c_I \le cl$. Then $I \subseteq Imp\ \mathcal{C}_{cl}$, where $\mathcal{C}_{cl}$ is the closure system related to cl. Since, by Lemma 35, $Mod\ I = Mod\ Imp\ \mathcal{C}(I)$ we obtain $Mod\ Imp\ \mathcal{C}_{cl} \subseteq Mod\ Imp\ \mathcal{C}(I)$ and, consequently, $\mathcal{C}_{cl} \subseteq \mathcal{C}(I)$, whence $cons_I \le c_I$. ■

A sufficient condition for the algebraic characterization of implicational theories will be derived from the proposition below.

Proposition 38. *If I is a set of implications such that $\overline{I}$ is a fully invariant closure system of congruences on $\boldsymbol{T}_\Sigma(Z)$, then $I = Imp\ Mod\ I$.*

Proof. Assume I is a set of implications such that $\overline{I}$ is a fully invariant closure system of congruences on $\boldsymbol{T}_\Sigma(Z)$. If we put $J = Imp\ Mod\ I$, then $Mod\ J = Mod\ Imp\ Mod\ I = Mod\ I$. Now, by the corollary to Lemma 35, $\mathcal{C}(J) = \mathcal{C}(I)$. Since J is an implicational theory we have $\overline{J} = \mathcal{C}(J)$. On the other hand, $\overline{I} = \mathcal{C}(I)$ follows from Proposition 37. Hence $\overline{J} = \overline{I}$ and so $c_J(P) = c_I(P)$ for all relations P on $T_\Sigma(Z)$. That is, $(P \Rightarrow t = t') \in J$ iff $(P \Rightarrow t = t') \in I$. Thus $\overline{J} = \overline{I}$ implies $J = I$. So we get $I = Imp\ Mod\ I$. ■

Now we obtain our main result.

Theorem 39 (Criterion for Implicational Theories). *Let I be a set of implications. Then I is an implicational theory if and only if $\overline{I}$ is a fully invariant closure system of congruences on $\boldsymbol{T}_\Sigma(Z)$.* ■

This result can be thought of as an algebraic characterization of logical consequence, which is a semantical notion. Its counterpart, the syntactical notion of deducibility, is hence somehow coded in a fully invariant closure system of congruences. Hence, there is an inference rule to each defining property of a fully invariant closure system of congruences.

The first group of inference rules determines the elements of fully invariant closure systems, namely congruences.

(I) Rules of congruence

$$(IL1) \quad P \Rightarrow t = t;$$

$$(IL2) \quad \frac{P \Rightarrow t = t'}{P \Rightarrow t' = t};$$

$$(IL3) \quad \frac{P \Rightarrow t = t', P \Rightarrow t' = t''}{P \Rightarrow t = t''};$$

$$(IL4) \quad \frac{P \Rightarrow t_1 = t_1', \ldots, P \Rightarrow t_n = t_n'}{P \Rightarrow \sigma\, t_1 \ldots t_n = \sigma\, t_1' \ldots t_n'} \quad \text{for every } n\text{-ary operation symbol } \sigma.$$

To establish the inference rules of the second group in a concise form the defining properties of the closure operator associated with a fully invariant closure system of congruences on $\boldsymbol{T}_\Sigma(Z)$ must be exploited. By Proposition 31, $\mathcal{C}$ is a fully invariant closure system of congruences on $\boldsymbol{T}_\Sigma(Z)$ iff, for all relations P and Q on $T_\Sigma(Z)$ and all endomorphisms h of $\boldsymbol{T}_\Sigma(Z)$, the conditions (1) – (3) below are fulfilled:

(1) $P \subseteq cl_{\mathcal{C}}(P)$;

(2) $Q \subseteq cl_{\mathcal{C}}(P)$ implies $cl_{\mathcal{C}}(Q) \subseteq cl_{\mathcal{C}}(P)$; and

(3) $h(cl_{\mathcal{C}}(P)) \subseteq cl_{\mathcal{C}}(h(P))$.

Observe that condition (2) expresses idempotency as well as monotonicity. Indeed, $P \subseteq cl_{\mathcal{C}}(P)$ implies $cl_{\mathcal{C}}(cl_{\mathcal{C}}(P)) \subseteq cl_{\mathcal{C}}(P)$, so $cl_{\mathcal{C}}$ is idempotent; and $Q \subseteq P$ implies $Q \subseteq cl_{\mathcal{C}}(P)$, by (1), which, in turn, implies $cl_{\mathcal{C}}(Q) \subseteq cl_{\mathcal{C}}(P)$, so $cl_{\mathcal{C}}$ is monotone.

In an elementwise description we obtain

(1) $(t, t') \in cl_{\mathcal{C}}(P)$ for each pair (t, t') of P;

(2) Case 1: $Q = \emptyset$.

If $(t, t') \in cl_{\mathcal{C}}(\emptyset)$, then $(t, t') \in cl_{\mathcal{C}}(P)$.

Case 2: Let $Q = \{(t_m, t_m') \mid m \in M\}$ be nonempty.

If $(t_m, t_m') \in cl_{\mathcal{C}}(P)$ for all $m \in M$ and if $(t, t') \in cl_{\mathcal{C}}(Q)$, then $(t, t') \in cl_{\mathcal{C}}(P)$.

(3) If $(t, t') \in cl_{\mathcal{C}}(P)$, then $(h(t), h(t')) \in cl_{\mathcal{C}}(h(P))$.

These conditions can now easily be transformed into inference rules.

(II) Rule of extensitivity

$$(IL5) \quad P \Rightarrow t = t' \quad \text{if } (t,t') \in P.$$

(III) Rules of idempotency and monotonicity

$$(IL6) \quad \frac{t = t'}{P \Rightarrow t = t'};$$

$$(IL7) \quad \frac{\{P \Rightarrow t_m = t'_m \mid m \in M\}, \{(t_m, t'_m) \mid m \in M\} \Rightarrow t = t'}{P \Rightarrow t = t'}.$$

(IV) Rule of full invariance

$$(IL8) \quad \frac{P \Rightarrow t = t'}{h(P) \Rightarrow h(t) = h(t')} \quad \text{for all endomorphisms } h \text{ of } \boldsymbol{T}_\Sigma(Z).$$

It is important to notice, however, that $(IL7)$ is not an inference rule in our sense (cf. Section 1.2.4) since it may posses infinitely many premises. By allowing such generalized inference rules we are forced to extend the notion of formal proofs.

To explain this generalization we use a tree representation of formal proofs. Let $\mathcal{R}$ be any set of inference rules over S. Recall that an element p is provable from a given subset X of S using $\mathcal{R}$ iff there is a finite sequence $p_1, \ldots, p_k$ of elements of S such that p_k is p and, for each $i = 1, \ldots, k$, either $p_i \in X$ or there is an n-ary inference rule R in $\mathcal{R}$ (for some $n \geq 0$) and there are $j_1, \ldots, j_n < i$ such that $(p_{j_1}, \ldots, p_{j_n}, p_i) \in R$.

The linear notation of a formal proof $p_1, \ldots, p_k$ does not show explicitly how the inference rules have been used. Therefore, we will assign a finite tree labelled by the elements occuring in $p_1, \ldots, p_k$ in such a way that the labels of the leaves are either elements from X or axioms (i.e., elements of a nullary inference rule) and the label of any other node is obtained from the labels of its immediate successors using some inference rule. Note that the root is labelled by p_k.

Formally, the tree assigned to a formal proof has to be defined inductively.

(1) Any formal proof p of length 1 is represented by the trivial tree consisting of the root only, which is labelled by p.

(2) Assume that all formal proofs of length less than k are already represented by labelled trees. Consider a formal proof $p_1, \ldots, p_k$ of length k such that $(p_{j_1}, \ldots, p_{j_n}, p_k) \in R$ for some n-ary inference rule R in $\mathcal{R}$ and indices $j_1, \ldots, j_n < i$. By induction hypothesis, there are trees, say $t_1, \ldots, t_n$, representing the formal proofs of $p_{j_1}, \ldots, p_{j_n}$, respectively.

Now we assign a labelled tree t to $p_1, \ldots, p_k$ so that $t/i = t_i$ for $i = 1, \ldots, n$ and the root of t is labelled by p_k.

Every inference rule

$$\frac{p_1, \ldots, p_n}{p},$$

which is expressible as follows $\{p_1, \ldots, p_n\} \vdash p$, can also be represented by a labelled tree

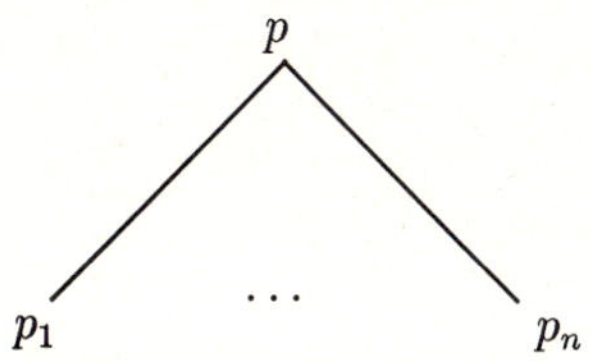

where $p_1, \ldots, p_n, p$ is the formal proof of p from $\{p_1, \ldots, p_n\}$.

A formal proof can now generally be thought of as a labelled finite tree. In the presence of infinitary inference rules, such as $(IL7)$ with infinitely many premises, such a tree becomes, however, infinitely branching. But we require that a ***generalized formal proof*** is a tree of finite level (i.e., all branches have finite length), which is labelled by elements of S in a way similar to usual formal proofs. When p can be deduced from X by a generalized formal proof we will write

$$X \Vdash_R p$$

or simply $X \Vdash p$.

The set of inference rules $(IL1)$ to $(IL7)$ from above (together with the generalized notion $\Vdash_{IL}$ of deducibility) is called ***implicational logic***.

First, the soundness of implicational logic will be studied. By analogy with equational logic, this problem reduces to the question whether each inference rule is sound. Here we have to use the Principle of Tree Induction instead of the Principle of Finite Induction.

For example, let us investigate the soundness of $(IL7)$, which is the only infinitary inference rule. Given an arbitrary set I of implications, we assume that $I \models P \Rightarrow t_m = t'_m$ for all $m \in M$ and $I \models \{(t_m, t'_m) | \, m \in M\} \Rightarrow t = t'$. By definition, every model $\boldsymbol{A}$ of I validates each implication $P \Rightarrow t_m = t'_m$, $m \in M$, as well as $\{(t_m, t'_m) | \, m \in M\} \Rightarrow t = t'$. Hence, for any $\alpha : Z \to A$, $\alpha^\sharp(P) \subseteq ker\ \alpha^\sharp$ implies $\{(t_m, t'_m) | \, m \in M\} \subseteq ker\ \alpha^\sharp$ and, on the other hand, $\{(t_m, t'_m) | \, m \in M\} \subseteq ker\ \alpha^\sharp$ implies $(t, t') \in ker\ \alpha^\sharp$. That is, $\alpha^\sharp(P) \subseteq ker\ \alpha^\sharp$ implies $(t, t') \in ker\ \alpha^\sharp$. Thus $\boldsymbol{A} \models P \Rightarrow t = t'$ for any model $\boldsymbol{A}$ of I, i.e., $I \models P \Rightarrow t = t'$. Therefore, $(IL7)$ is sound.

The soundness of the remaining inference rules can be verified analogously.

To prove completeness we need the following closure operator ded_I defined by

$$ded_I(P) = \{(t, t') | \, I \Vdash_{IL} P \Rightarrow t = t'\}$$

for all relations P on $T_\Sigma(Z)$.

Lemma 40. *ded_I is a fully invariant closure operator from the set of all relations on $T_\Sigma(Z)$ to the set of all congruences on $\mathbf{T}_\Sigma(Z)$.* ■

The straightforward proof is omitted.

By the soundness of implicational logic, we have $ded_I(P) \subseteq cons_I(P)$ for all relations P on $T_\Sigma(Z)$; while completeness means $cons_I(P) \subseteq ded_I(P)$ for all relations P on $T_\Sigma(Z)$. To prove completeness we are going to use the statement of Proposition 37 that $cons_I$ is the least fully invariant closure operator which includes c_I. Hence, by Lemma 40, it is enough to show that $c_I \leq ded_I$.

Indeed, $\overline{I}(P) \subseteq ded_I(P)$ for all relations P on $T_\Sigma(Z)$ because $I \Vdash P \Rightarrow t = t'$ whenever $P \Rightarrow t = t'$ belongs to I. This leads to the completeness result.

Theorem 41 (Completeness of Implicational Logic). *Let I be a set of implications. An arbitrary implication $P \Rightarrow t = t'$ is a logical consequence of I if and only if $P \Rightarrow t = t'$ is deducible from I (by a generalized formal proof). Formally,*

$$I \models P \Rightarrow t = t' \quad \text{iff} \quad I \Vdash_{IL} P \Rightarrow t = t'.$$ ■

The different characterizations of implicational theories will now be summarized.

Corollary. *For any set I of implications the following are equivalent:*

(1) I is an implicational theory.

(2) $\overline{I}$ is a fully invariant closure system of congruences on $\mathbf{T}_\Sigma(Z)$.

(3) $I = Imp\ Mod\ I$.

(4) $I = Imp\ Mod\ I'$ for some set I' of implications.

(5) If $I \models P \Rightarrow t = t'$, then $(P \Rightarrow t = t') \in I$.

(6) If $I \Vdash_{IL} P \Rightarrow t = t'$, then $(P \Rightarrow t = t') \in I$.

Proof. The equivalence of (1) and (2) is the assertion of Theorem 39. Evidently, (1) and (3) are equivalent. The implication (3) $\Rightarrow$ (4) is trivial, while, by definition, (4) implies (1). The equivalence of (3) and (5) is obvious since $I \models P \Rightarrow t = t'$ iff $(P \Rightarrow t = t') \in Imp\ Mod\ I$. By Theorem 41, (5) and (6) are equivalent. ■

Here *Mod* and *Imp* define a Galois connection so that *Mod Imp* and *Imp Mod* are closure operators. We already know that the *Mod Imp*-closed classes are the sur-reflective classes of algebras, while the *Imp Mod*-closed sets are the implicational theories.

It is easily seen that there is a bijection from the set of all implicational theories to the set of all fully invariant closure operators $cl : Rel(T_\Sigma(Z)) \rightarrow Con(\mathbf{T}_\Sigma(Z))$ which assigns $cons_I$ to any implicational theory I. Hence the lattice of all implicational theories is isomorphic to the lattice of all fully invariant closure operators since $I \subseteq J$ iff $cons_I \leq cons_J$ for all implicational theories I and J. Neumann's correspondence for the equational case can now be generalized: The lattice of all fully invariant closure operators from $Rel(T_\Sigma(Z))$ to $Con(\boldsymbol{T}_\Sigma(Z))$ is anti-isomorphic to the lattice of all sur-reflective classes of algebras.

3.3.5 Universal Horn Theories

Let $\mathcal{K}$ be an abstract class of algebras. Recall that $Horn\ \mathcal{K}$ is the set of all universal Horn clauses valid in $\mathcal{K}$. $Horn\ \mathcal{K}$ was called the ***universal Horn theory*** of $\mathcal{K}$. As we know, when dealing with universal Horn clauses we can fix a countably infinite set, say V, of variables.

Definition 15. *A set H of universal Horn clauses is called a* ***universal Horn theory*** *if H is the universal Horn theory for some abstract class of algebras.*

We immediately get that H is a universal Horn theory iff

$$H = Horn\ Mod\ H$$

iff H is closed under logical consequences. That is, H is a universal Horn theory iff a universal Horn clause Φ belongs to H whenever Φ is a logical consequence of H.

Definition 16. *Given a set H of universal Horn clauses, a relation P on $T_\Sigma(V)$ is called H-**closed** if, for all pairs of terms t and t' in $T_\Sigma(V)$, $(t, t') \in P$ whenever there is a finite subset Q of P such that $H \models Q \Rightarrow t = t'$.*

By analogy with I-closedness we get

Lemma 42. *Any H-closed relation on $T_\Sigma(V)$ is a congruence.*

Proof. Let H be a set of universal Horn clauses. Assume that P is an H-closed relation on $T_\Sigma(V)$.

(1) P is reflexive. Evidently, $(t, t) \in P$ for all t in $T_\Sigma(V)$ since $H \models Q \Rightarrow t = t$ for each finite subset Q of P.

(2) P is symmetric. If we suppose that $(t, t') \in P$, then $H \models Q \Rightarrow t = t'$ for some finite subset Q of P. But, of course, $H \models Q \Rightarrow t' = t$, i.e., $(t', t) \in P$.

(3) P is transitive. Suppose that $(t, t') \in P$ and $(t', t'') \in P$. Trivially, there are finite subsets P' and P'' of P such that $H \models P' \Rightarrow t = t'$ and $H \models P'' \Rightarrow t' = t''$. Putting $Q = P' \cup P''$ we obviously get $H \models Q \Rightarrow t = t'$ and $H \models Q \Rightarrow t' = t''$. But then we have $H \models Q \Rightarrow t = t''$, i.e., $(t, t'') \in P$ since Q is, of course, a finite subset of P.

(4) P is compatible. Let σ be any n-ary operation symbol. If $(t_i, t'_i) \in P$ for $i = 1, \ldots, n$, then there are finite subsets P_i of P such that $H \models P_i \Rightarrow t_i = t'_i$. Putting $Q = P_1 \cup \ldots \cup P_n$ we derive $H \models Q \Rightarrow t_i = t'_i$ for $i = 1, \ldots, n$. Consequently, $H \models Q \Rightarrow \sigma\, t_1 \ldots t_n = \sigma\, t'_1 \ldots t'_n$ and so $(\sigma\, t_1 \ldots t_n, \sigma\, t'_1 \ldots t'_n)$ is in P. ■

Given a set H of universal Horn clauses, to any finite relation P on $T_\Sigma(V)$ we assign

$$cons_H(P) = \{(t, t') \mid H \models P \Rightarrow t = t'\}.$$

Let $\mathcal{C}(H)$ denote the set of all H-closed congruences on $\boldsymbol{T}_\Sigma(V)$. It is easily seen that the associated closure operator has the property

$$cl_{\mathcal{C}(H)}(P) = \bigcup\{cons_H(P') \mid P' \subseteq P,\ P' \text{ finite}\}. \qquad (*)$$

Lemma 43. *If H is a set of universal Horn clauses, then for all finite relations P and Q on $T_\Sigma(V)$ and all endomorphisms h of $\boldsymbol{T}_\Sigma(V)$,*

(1) $P \subseteq cons_H(P)$;

(2) $Q \subseteq cons_H(P)$ implies $cons_H(Q) \subseteq cons_H(P)$; and

(3) $h(cons_H(P)) \subseteq cons_H(h(P))$.

Proof. Let P and Q be finite relations on $T_\Sigma(V)$.

(1) $P \subseteq cons_H(P)$ since $H \models P \Rightarrow t = t'$ for each (t, t') of P.

(2) First consider the case where Q is empty. We have to show $cons_H(\emptyset) \subseteq cons_H(P)$. But, for any pair (t, t') of terms in $T_\Sigma(V)$ such that $H \models t = t'$ it follows that $H \models P \Rightarrow t = t'$. Thus $(t, t') \in cons_H(P)$ and so $cons_H(\emptyset) \subseteq cons_H(P)$.

Second, assume that $Q = \{(t_1, t'_1), \ldots, (t_k, t'_k)\}$ is a nonempty finite relation on $T_\Sigma(V)$. If $Q \subseteq cons_H(P)$, then, by definition, $H \models P \Rightarrow t_i = t'_i$ for $i = 1, \ldots, k$. Consider an arbitrarily given pair (t, t') of terms in $T_\Sigma(V)$. If we suppose that $H \models Q \Rightarrow t = t'$, then $H \models P \Rightarrow t = t'$. Thus $(t, t') \in cons_H(P)$ for all $(t, t') \in cons_H(Q)$. That is, $cons_H(Q) \subseteq cons_H(P)$.

(3) Assume that $(t, t') \in cons_H(P)$. Then, by definition, $H \models P \Rightarrow t = t'$. Now, for every endomorphism h of $\boldsymbol{T}_\Sigma(V)$, $H \models h(P) \Rightarrow h(t) = h(t')$ which implies $(h(t), h(t')) \in cons_H(h(P))$ and, consequently, $h(cons_H(P)) \subseteq cons_H(h(P))$. ■

Corollary. *$cl_{\mathcal{C}(H)}$ is an algebraic, fully invariant closure operator.*

Proof. Using the property $(*)$ we conclude

(1) $P \subseteq cl_{\mathcal{C}(H)}(P)$;

(2) $Q \subseteq cl_{\mathcal{C}(H)}(P)$ implies $cl_{\mathcal{C}(H)}(Q) \subseteq cl_{\mathcal{C}(H)}(P)$; and

(3) $h(cl_{\mathcal{C}(H)}(P)) \subseteq cl_{\mathcal{C}(H)}(h(P))$

for all relations P and Q on $T_\Sigma(V)$ and all endomorphisms h of $\boldsymbol{T}_\Sigma(V)$. Thus, $cl_{\mathcal{C}(H)}$ is a fully invariant closure operator. Furthermore, we get

(4) $cl_{\mathcal{C}(H)}(P) = \bigcup\{cl_{\mathcal{C}(H)}(P') \mid P' \subseteq P,\ P' \text{ finite}\}$

because $cl_{\mathcal{C}(H)}(P') = cons_H(P')$ for any finite relation P' on $T_\Sigma(V)$. Hence, by the Birkhoff-Frink Theorem (Lemma 5 in Section 1.2.4), $cl_{\mathcal{C}(H)}$ is algebraic. ■

Since $cl_{\mathcal{C}(H)}$ is uniquely determined by $cons_H$ we shall write $cons_H$ instead of $cl_{\mathcal{C}(H)}$. In other words, $cons_H$ is extended to arbitrary relations as follows

$$cons_H(P) = \bigcup\{cons_H(P') \mid P' \subseteq P,\ P' \text{ finite}\}$$

for each relation P on $T_\Sigma(V)$.

We are now going to study the generation of $cons_H$. The reader may prove as an exercise that all algebraic, fully invariant closure operators from $Rel(T_\Sigma(V))$ to $Con(\boldsymbol{T}_\Sigma(V))$ form a closure system so that we can generate them by mappings from $Rel(T_\Sigma(V))$ into itself. Let H be a set of universal Horn clauses. A mapping $c_H : Rel(T_\Sigma(V)) \to Rel(T_\Sigma(V))$ is associated with H as follows:

$$c_H(P) = \{(t,t') \mid (P' \Rightarrow t = t') \in H \text{ for some finite subset } P' \text{ of } P\}.$$

Using Proposition 37 and the algebraicity of $cons_H$ we get

Proposition 44. *Given a set H of universal Horn clauses, $cons_H$ is the algebraic, fully invariant closure operator from $Rel(T_\Sigma(V))$ to $Con(\boldsymbol{T}_\Sigma(V))$ generated by c_H.* ■

In case c_H is a closure operator the corresponding closure system $\mathcal{C}_{c_H}$ is abbreviated by $\overline{H}$. If H is a universal Horn theory, then $c_H = cons_H$, by Proposition 44, and so $\overline{H} = \mathcal{C}(H)$. Thus $\overline{H}$ is an algebraic, fully invariant closure system of congruences on $\boldsymbol{T}_\Sigma(V)$ whenever H is a universal Horn theory.

Similarly as for implications, a set of universal Horn clauses, denoted as $Horn\ \mathcal{C}$, is assigned to any closure system $\mathcal{C}$ of congruences on $\boldsymbol{T}_\Sigma(V)$:

$$Horn\ \mathcal{C} = \{P \Rightarrow t = t' \mid P \text{ is a finite relation on } T_\Sigma(V) \text{ and } (t,t') \in cl_{\mathcal{C}}(P)\}.$$

Lemma 45. *If $\mathcal{C}$ is an algebraic, fully invariant closure system of congruences on $\boldsymbol{T}_\Sigma(V)$, then*

$$C \in \mathcal{C} \quad \text{iff} \quad \boldsymbol{T}_\Sigma(V)/C \in Mod\ Horn\ \mathcal{C}.$$

Proof. Let $\mathcal{C}$ be an algebraic, fully invariant closure system of congruences on $\boldsymbol{T}_\Sigma(V)$. Consider an arbitrary universal Horn clause $P \Rightarrow t = t'$. From the proof of Lemma 34 we know that, for all congruences C on $\boldsymbol{T}_\Sigma(V)$, $\boldsymbol{T}_\Sigma(V)/C \models P \Rightarrow t = t'$ iff $P \subseteq h^{-1}(C)$ implies $(t, t') \in h^{-1}(C)$ for all endomorphisms h of $\boldsymbol{T}_\Sigma(V)$.

If $C \in \mathcal{C}$, then $h^{-1}(C) \in \mathcal{C}$, by the full invariance of $\mathcal{C}$, and if $(P \Rightarrow t = t') \in Horn\ \mathcal{C}$, then $cl_\mathcal{C}(P) \subseteq h^{-1}(C)$ implies $(t, t') \in h^{-1}(C)$ for all endomorphisms h of $\boldsymbol{T}_\Sigma(V)$. Thus $\boldsymbol{T}_\Sigma(V)/C \in Mod\ Horn\ \mathcal{C}$.

Conversely, assume that $\boldsymbol{T}_\Sigma(V)/C \in Mod\ Horn\ \mathcal{C}$. We have to show that $cl_\mathcal{C}(C) \subseteq C$. Since $\mathcal{C}$ is algebraic,

$$cl_\mathcal{C}(C) = \bigcup\{cl_\mathcal{C}(P) \mid P \subseteq C,\ P \text{ finite}\}.$$

Therefore, it suffices to prove $cl_\mathcal{C}(P) \subseteq C$ for each finite subset P of C. By assumption, $\boldsymbol{T}_\Sigma(V)/C \models P \Rightarrow t = t'$ for all $(P \Rightarrow t = t') \in Horn\ \mathcal{C}$. In particular, $P \subseteq C$ implies $(t, t') \in C$ for all $(P \Rightarrow t = t') \in Horn\ \mathcal{C}$. Now we have for all finite relations P on $T_\Sigma(V)$ and all $(t, t') \in cl_\mathcal{C}(P)$, $P \subseteq C$ implies $(t, t') \in C$. That is, $cl_\mathcal{C}(P) \subseteq C$ for all finite subsets P of C. ∎

As a corollary we obtain: If H is a set of universal Horn clauses, then $C \in \mathcal{C}(H)$ iff $\boldsymbol{T}_\Sigma(V)/C \in Mod\ H$. Since $Mod\ H = Mod\ Horn\ Mod\ H$, $Mod\ H = Mod\ H'$ for $H' = Horn\ Mod\ H$ and hence $\mathcal{C}(H) = \mathcal{C}(H')$, where H' is a universal Horn theory by definition. Thus $\mathcal{C}(H') = \overline{H}'$. If we assume that $\overline{H}$ is an algebraic, fully invariant closure system of congruences on $\boldsymbol{T}_\Sigma(V)$, then $\overline{H} = \mathcal{C}(H)$ and so $\overline{H} = \overline{H}'$. This proves the following statement.

Proposition 46. *If H is a set of universal Horn clauses such that $\overline{H}$ is an algebraic, fully invariant closure system of congruences on $\boldsymbol{T}_\Sigma(V)$, then $H = Horn\ Mod\ H$.* ∎

Now we are in a position to derive the algebraic characterization of universal Horn theories.

Theorem 47 (Hoehnke's Criterion for Universal Horn Theories). *Let H be a set of universal Horn clauses. Then H is a universal Horn theory if and only if $\overline{H}$ is an algebraic, fully invariant closure system of congruences on $\boldsymbol{T}_\Sigma(V)$.* ∎

In contrast to implicational theories, the generalized inference rule $(IL7)$ can now be replaced by a normal one with finitely many premises only, because of condition (2) of Lemma 43. Moreover, it is even expressible in a more convenient form

$$\frac{P \Rightarrow t_0 = t_0',\ \{(t_0, t_0')\} \cup Q \Rightarrow t = t'}{P \cup Q \Rightarrow t = t'},$$

called the ***cut rule*** in the literature.

In principle, the inference rules exhibited previously together with the cut rule instead of $(IL7)$ constitute a formal proof system for universal Horn theories. However, we prefer to write universal Horn clauses as logical sentences. According to our definition

$$\forall X(t_1 = t_1' \wedge \ldots \wedge t_k = t_k' \Rightarrow t = t'),$$

where X is the finite set of all variables occurring in t_i, t'_i ($i = 1, \ldots, k$) and t, t', is written instead of $P \Rightarrow t = t'$ with $P = \{(t_1, t'_1), \ldots, (t_k, t'_k)\}$.

As a matter of fact, all short-hand notations in the inference rules above must be decoded, so to speak. For that purpose new inference rules have to be added so that the translation of a set P into a (formal) conjunction of equations is determined and, on the other hand, the universal quantification of the finitely many variables in any universal Horn clause is regulated. Considering conjunction as an operation, we have to require that $\wedge$ is associative, commutative and idempotent. Similarly as in equational logic, rules of abstraction or concretion have to be considered.

Definition 17. *The set of inference rules ($HL1$) to ($HL18$) given below is called* ***universal Horn logic****:*

(I) Rules of congruence

($HL1$) $\forall X(t = t)$;

($HL2$) $\forall X(t = t' \Rightarrow t' = t)$;

($HL3$) $\forall X(t = t' \wedge t' = t'' \Rightarrow t = t'')$;

($HL4$) $\forall X(t_1 = t'_1 \wedge \ldots \wedge t_n = t'_n \Rightarrow \sigma t_1 \ldots t_n = \sigma t'_1 \ldots t'_n)$
for every n-ary operation symbol σ.

(II) Rules of closure

($HL5$) $\forall X(t_1 = t'_1 \wedge \ldots \wedge t_k = t'_k \Rightarrow t_1 = t'_1)$;

($HL6$) $$\frac{\forall X(t = t')}{\forall X(t_1 = t'_1 \wedge \ldots \wedge t_k = t'_k \Rightarrow t = t')};$$

($HL7$) $$\frac{\forall X(t_0 = t'_0), \forall X(t_0 = t'_0 \Rightarrow t = t')}{\forall X(t = t')};$$

($HL8$) $$\frac{\forall X(t_1 = t'_1 \wedge \ldots \wedge t_k = t'_k \Rightarrow t_0 = t'_0), \forall X(t_0 = t'_0 \Rightarrow t = t')}{\forall X(t_1 = t'_1 \wedge \ldots \wedge t_k = t'_k \Rightarrow t = t')};$$

($HL9$) $$\frac{\begin{array}{l}\forall X(t_1 = t'_1 \wedge \ldots \wedge t_k = t'_k \Rightarrow t_0 = t'_0),\\ \qquad \forall X(t_0 = t'_0 \wedge t_{k+1} = t'_{k+1} \wedge \ldots \wedge t_{k+n} = t'_{k+n} \Rightarrow t = t')\end{array}}{\forall X(t_1 = t'_1 \wedge \ldots \wedge t_k = t'_k \wedge t_{k+1} = t'_{k+1} \wedge \ldots \wedge t_{k+n} = t'_{k+n} \Rightarrow t = t')}.$$

(III) Rules of full invariance

($HL10$) $$\frac{\forall X(t = t')}{\forall Y(s^\sharp(t) = s^\sharp(t'))}$$

for every substitution $s : X \to T_\Sigma(V)$, and
$Y = \bigcup\{var(s(x)) | x \in X\}$;

(HL11) $$\frac{\forall X(t_1 = t'_1 \wedge \ldots \wedge t_k = t'_k \Rightarrow t = t')}{\forall Y(s^\sharp(t_1) = s^\sharp(t'_1) \wedge \ldots \wedge s^\sharp(t_k) = s^\sharp(t'_k) \Rightarrow s^\sharp(t) = s^\sharp(t'))}$$
for every substitution $s : X \to T_\Sigma(V)$, and
$Y = \bigcup\{var(s(x)) | x \in X\}$.

(IV) Rules of conjunction

(HL12) $$\frac{\forall X(t_1 = t'_1 \wedge t_1 = t'_1 \Rightarrow t = t')}{\forall X(t_1 = t'_1 \Rightarrow t = t')};$$

(HL13) $$\frac{\forall X(t_1 = t'_1 \wedge t_1 = t'_1 \wedge t_2 = t'_2 \wedge \ldots \wedge t_k = t'_k \Rightarrow t = t')}{\forall X(t_1 = t'_1 \wedge \ldots \wedge t_k = t'_k \Rightarrow t = t')};$$

(HL14) $$\frac{\forall X(t_1 = t'_1 \wedge \ldots \wedge t_k = t'_k \Rightarrow t = t')}{\forall X(t_{\pi(1)} = t'_{\pi(1)} \wedge \ldots \wedge t_{\pi(k)} = t'_{\pi(k)} \Rightarrow t = t')}$$
for every permutation π of $\{1, \ldots, k\}$.

(V) Rules of abstraction

(HL15) $$\frac{\forall X(t = t')}{\forall Y(t = t')}$$
where $Y = X \cup \{y\}$ for some $y \in V - X$;

(HL16) $$\frac{\forall X(t_1 = t'_1 \wedge \ldots \wedge t_k = t'_k \Rightarrow t = t')}{\forall Y(t_1 = t'_1 \wedge \ldots \wedge t_k = t'_k \Rightarrow t = t')}$$
where $Y = X \cup \{y\}$ for some $y \in V - X$.

(VI) Rules of concretion

(HL17) $$\frac{\forall X(t = t')}{\forall Y(t = t')}$$
where $Y = X - \{x\}$ for some x that does not occur as a variable in t or t';

(HL18) $$\frac{\forall X(t_1 = t'_1 \wedge \ldots \wedge t_k = t'_k \Rightarrow t = t')}{\forall Y(t_1 = t'_1 \wedge \ldots \wedge t_k = t'_k \Rightarrow t = t')}$$
where $Y = X - \{x\}$ for some x that does not occur as a variable
in t_i, t'_i $(i = 1, \ldots, k)$ or t, t'.

It is intuitively clear that the rules of congruence, namely reflexivity $(HL1)$, symmetry $(HL2)$, transitivity $(HL3)$ and compatibility $(HL4)$ need only to be stated for empty sets of premises. This could already have been done for implicational logic because of $(IL6)$ and $(IL7)$. The second group, $(HL5)$ to $(HL9)$, consists of the decoded inference rules $(IL5)$ to $(IL7)$; they guarantee the extensitivity, idempotency and monotonicity of the closure operator in question. $(IL5)$ is directly transformed into $(HL5)$ and $(IL6)$ into $(HL6)$. Decoding the cut rule yields three new rules $(HL7)$ to $(HL9)$ according to the three cases: (1) P and Q are empty; (2) P is nonempty and Q is empty; and (3) P and Q are nonempty. The third group contains the two inference rules $(HL10)$ and $(HL11)$ of full invariance derived from $(IL8)$, where endomorphisms are replaced by substitutions. Our additional inference rules for conjunction, $(HL12)$ to $(HL14)$, are packed together into the fourth group. Finally, the last two groups contain the inference rules $(HL15)$ to $(HL18)$ responsible for universal quantification.

Remark. Our formal proof system for universal Horn logic is quite similar to that proposed by A. Selman /Selman-72/. Since in Selman's calculus universal quantification is not explicitly mentioned, the related rules of abstraction and concretion are omitted. In calculi where conjunctions of premises are merely treated as sets, the rules $(HL12)$ to $(HL14)$ are redundant, the rules of full invariance can be expressed by a single inference rule, called the ***substitution rule***, and, furthermore, rules $(HL7)$ to $(HL9)$ reduce to the cut rule. ■

Deductions are finite sequences of universal Horn clauses called ***formal proofs*** leading from a given set H of universal Horn clauses, the premises of the deduction, to another universal Horn clause $\forall X(t_1 = t_1' \wedge \ldots \wedge t_k = t_k' \Rightarrow t = t')$, the conclusion of the deduction. Universal Horn clauses occurring in a formal proof are either in H or else can be inferred from earlier ones of the sequence by one of the inference rules $(HL1)$ to $(HL18)$. We say that $\forall X(t_1 = t_1' \wedge \ldots \wedge t_k = t_k' \Rightarrow t = t')$ is ***deducible*** from H if there is a deduction from H whose last universal Horn clause is $\forall X(t_1 = t_1' \wedge \ldots \wedge t_k = t_k' \Rightarrow t = t')$. In this case we write

$$H \vdash_{HL} \forall X(t_1 = t_1' \wedge \ldots \wedge t_k = t_k' \Rightarrow t = t').$$

To prove the soundness of universal Horn logic is, as usual, an easy task. Since formal proofs are defined to be finite sequences, where in each step an inference rule may be applied, it is enough to prove the soundness of each inference rule. Then, by the Principle of Finite Induction, the soundness of the formal proof system is verified.

Consider, for example, the inference rule $(HL8)$. If we assume that

$$H \models \forall X(t_1 = t_1' \wedge \ldots \wedge t_k = t_k' \Rightarrow t_0 = t_0')$$

and

$$H \models \forall X(t_0 = t_0' \Rightarrow t = t'),$$

then, for an arbitrary model $\boldsymbol{A}$ for H and all assignments α from X to A, we have:

(1) $\alpha^\sharp(t_0) = \alpha^\sharp(t_0')$ whenever $\alpha^\sharp(t_i) = \alpha^\sharp(t_i')$ for all $i = 1, \ldots, k$; and

(2) $\alpha^\sharp(t_0) = \alpha^\sharp(t_0')$ implies $\alpha^\sharp(t) = \alpha^\sharp(t')$.

Hence $(\boldsymbol{A}, \alpha) \models \forall X(t_1 = t_1' \wedge \ldots \wedge t_k = t_k' \Rightarrow t = t')$. By definition, $H \models \forall X(t_1 = t_1' \wedge \ldots \wedge t_k = t_k' \Rightarrow t = t')$ and thus $(HL8)$ is sound.

In the same way the other inference rules may be proved to be sound.

Proposition 48 (Soundness of Universal Horn Logic). *If H is a given set of universal Horn clauses, then every universal Horn clause deducible from H is a logical consequence of H.* ■

To prove completeness we first introduce the counterpart of $cons_H$.
Recall that $cons_H(P) = \{(t,t')|\, H \models P \Rightarrow t = t'\}$ for any finite relation P on $T_\Sigma(V)$. Therefore, we define $ded_H(P) = \{(t,t')|\, H \vdash_{HL} P \Rightarrow t = t'\}$. In particular,

$$ded_H(\emptyset) = \{(t,t')|\, H \vdash_{HL} \forall X(t = t')\}.$$

If $P = \{(t_1,t_1'),\ldots,(t_k,t_k')\}$ is a nonempty finite relation on $T_\Sigma(V)$, then

$$ded_H(P) = \{(t,t')|\, H \vdash_{HL} \forall X(t_1 = t_1' \wedge \ldots \wedge t_k = t_k' \Rightarrow t = t')\}.$$

Soundness is now expressible as

$$ded_H(P) \subseteq cons_H(P)$$

for all finite relations P on $T_\Sigma(V)$, while completeness means just the opposite inclusion. By Proposition 44, it is enough to show

(1) $ded_H(P)$ is a congruence;

(2) ded_H fulfills the same properties as $cons_H$ stated in Lemma 43; and

(3) $c_H(P) \subseteq ded_H(P)$.

Lemma 49. *If H is a set of universal Horn clauses, then $ded_H(P)$ is a congruence on $\mathbf{T}_\Sigma(V)$ for all finite relations P on $T_\Sigma(V)$.*

Proof. Evidently, $ded_H(\emptyset)$ is a congruence by $(HL1)$ to $(HL4)$. Assume that $P = \{(t_1,t_1'),\ldots,(t_k,t_k')\}$ is a nonempty finite relation on $T_\Sigma(V)$.

(1) $ded_H(P)$ is reflexive. For all terms t in $T_\Sigma(V)$, $H \vdash_{HL} \forall X(t = t)$, by $(HL1)$. Suppose that X' is the set of all variables occuring in t_i, t_i' $(i = 1,\ldots,k)$. If we put $Y = X \cup X'$, then

$$H \vdash_{HL} \forall Y(t = t)$$

by $(HL15)$. Using $(HL6)$ we infer

$$H \vdash_{HL} \forall Y(t_1 = t_1' \wedge \ldots \wedge t_k = t_k' \Rightarrow t = t).$$

Hence, by definition, $(t,t) \in ded_H(P)$ for all $t \in T_\Sigma(V)$.

(2) $ded_H(P)$ is symmetric. Suppose that $(t, t') \in ded_H(P)$ for any terms t, t' in $T_\Sigma(V)$. By definition,

$$H \vdash_{HL} \forall X(t_1 = t'_1 \wedge \ldots \wedge t_k = t'_k \Rightarrow t = t').$$

Together with $H \vdash_{HL} \forall X(t = t' \Rightarrow t' = t)$, which follows from $(HL2)$ by $(HL16)$, we infer

$$H \vdash_{HL} \forall X(t_1 = t'_1 \wedge \ldots \wedge t_k = t'_k \Rightarrow t' = t)$$

according to $(HL8)$. Thus, by definition, $(t', t) \in ded_H(P)$.

(3) $ded_H(P)$ is transitive. Suppose that $(t, t') \in ded_H(P)$ and $(t', t'') \in ded_H(P)$ for any terms $t, t', t'' \in T_\Sigma(V)$. Then

$$H \vdash_{HL} \forall X'(t_1 = t'_1 \wedge \ldots \wedge t_k = t'_k \Rightarrow t = t') \qquad (*)$$

and

$$H \vdash_{HL} \forall X''(t_1 = t'_1 \wedge \ldots \wedge t_k = t'_k \Rightarrow t' = t'') \qquad (**)$$

by definition. Take $(HL3)$ $H \vdash_{HL} \forall X(t = t' \wedge t' = t'' \Rightarrow t = t'')$.

Using $(HL9)$ and $(HL16)$ we deduce from $(*)$ and $(HL3)$

$$H \vdash_{HL} \forall Y'(t_1 = t'_1 \wedge \ldots \wedge t_k = t'_k \wedge t' = t'' \Rightarrow t = t''),$$

where $Y' = X' \cup X$. The premises can be permuted with the help of $(HL14)$:

$$H \vdash_{HL} \forall Y'(t' = t'' \wedge t_1 = t'_1 \wedge \ldots \wedge t_k = t'_k \Rightarrow t = t'').$$

Similarly we get from $(**)$

$$H \vdash_{HL} \forall Y''(t_1 = t'_1 \wedge \ldots \wedge t_k = t'_k \wedge t_1 = t'_1 \wedge \ldots \wedge t_k = t'_k \Rightarrow t = t''),$$

where $Y'' = Y' \cup X''$. The rules of conjunction allow the premises to be simplified:

$$H \vdash_{HL} \forall Y''(t_1 = t'_1 \wedge \ldots \wedge t_k = t'_k \Rightarrow t = t'').$$

Finally, by $(HL16)$,

$$H \vdash_{HL} \forall Y(t_1 = t'_1 \wedge \ldots \wedge t_k = t'_k \Rightarrow t = t''),$$

where Y is the set of all variables occuring in t, t'' and t_i, t'_i $(i = 1, \ldots, k)$. Hence, by definition, $(t, t'') \in ded_H(P)$.

(4) $ded_H(P)$ is compatible: similar to (3). ■

Lemma 50. *If H is a set of universal Horn clauses, then for all finite relations P and Q on $T_\Sigma(V)$ and all endomorphisms h on $\boldsymbol{T}_\Sigma(V)$*

(1) $P \subseteq ded_H(P)$;

(2) $Q \subseteq ded_H(P)$ *implies* $ded_H(Q) \subseteq ded_H(P)$; *and*

(3) $h(ded_H(P)) \subseteq ded_H(h(P))$.

Proof. Let H be a set of universal Horn clauses.

(1) $P \subseteq ded_H(P)$. Without loss of generality we assume that P is a nonempty finite relation on $T_\Sigma(V)$, say $P = \{(t_1, t_1'), \ldots, (t_k, t_k')\}$. By $(HL5)$ and $(HL14)$, we get

$$H \vdash_{HL} \forall X(t_1 = t_1' \wedge \ldots \wedge t_k = t_k' \Rightarrow t_i = t_i')$$

for $i = 1, \ldots, k$. Hence, by definition, $(t_i, t_i') \in ded_H(P)$ for $i = 1, \ldots, k$.

(2) $Q \subseteq ded_H(P)$ implies $ded_H(Q) \subseteq ded_H(P)$.

Case 1: $Q = \emptyset$ and $P = \{(t_1, t_1'), \ldots, (t_k, t_k')\}$ is a nonempty finite relation on $T_\Sigma(V)$.

We have to show that

$$ded_H(\emptyset) = \{(t, t') \mid H \vdash_{HL} \forall X(t = t')\}$$

is a subset of $ded_H(P)$. Assume that Y is the set of all variables occuring in t_i, t_i' $(i = 1, \ldots, k)$ and t, t'. By $(HL15)$, $H \vdash_{HL} \forall Y(t = t')$.

Now using $(HL6)$ we infer

$$H \vdash_{HL} \forall Y(t_1 = t_1' \wedge \ldots \wedge t_k = t_k' \Rightarrow t = t'),$$

i.e., $(t, t') \in ded_H(P)$. Thus $ded_H(\emptyset) \subseteq ded_H(P)$.

Case 2: $P = \emptyset$ and $Q = \{(t_1, t_1'), \ldots, (t_k, t_k')\}$ is a nonempty finite relation on $T_\Sigma(V)$.

If we assume that $Q \subseteq ded_H(\emptyset)$, then $H \vdash_{HL} \forall X_i(t_i = t_i')$ for $i = 1, \ldots, k$. Consider an arbitrary pair (t, t') of $ded_H(Q)$. By definition,

$$H \vdash_{HL} \forall X(t_1 = t_1' \wedge \ldots \wedge t_k = t_k' \Rightarrow t = t').$$

First, by $(HL15)$, we infer $H \vdash_{HL} \forall X(t_i = t_i')$ for $i = 1, \ldots, k$.

Subcase 2a: $k = 1$. Using $(HL7)$ we deduce $H \vdash_{HL} \forall X(t = t')$ and so, by $(HL17)$, $H \vdash_{HL} \forall Y(t = t')$, where $Y = var(t) \cup var(t')$. Hence, by definition, $(t, t') \in ded_H(\emptyset)$, which proves $ded_H(Q) \subseteq ded_H(\emptyset)$.

Subcase 2b: $k > 1$. From the assumption we derive, in particular,

$$H \vdash_{HL} \forall X'(t_1 = t_1' \Rightarrow t_k = t_k')$$

by $(HL6)$, where $X' = X_1 \cup X_k$. This yields

$$H \vdash_{HL} \forall X(t_1 = t'_1 \Rightarrow t_k = t'_k)$$

by $(HL15)$. Applying $(HL9)$ and $(HL14)$ we obtain

$$H \vdash_{HL} \forall X(t_1 = t'_1 \wedge \ldots \wedge t_{k-1} = t'_{k-1} \Rightarrow t = t').$$

The procedure is repeated until Subcase 2a is reached.

Case 3: $P = \{(t_1, t'_1), \ldots, (t_k, t'_k)\}$ and $Q = \{(t_{k+1}, t'_{k+1}), \ldots, (t_{k+n}, t'_{k+n})\}$ are non-empty finite relations on $T_\Sigma(V)$.

If we assume that $Q \subseteq ded_H(P)$, then, by definition,

$$H \vdash_{HL} \forall X_j(t_1 = t'_1 \wedge \ldots \wedge t_k = t'_k \Rightarrow t_{k+j} = t'_{k+j})$$

for $j = 1, \ldots, n$. Consider an arbitrary pair (t, t') of $ded_H(Q)$. Then

$$H \vdash_{HL} \forall X(t_{k+1} = t'_{k+1} \wedge \ldots \wedge t_{k+n} = t'_{k+n} \Rightarrow t = t'). \qquad (*)$$

From the assumption we infer, by $(HL15)$,

$$H \vdash_{HL} \forall X(t_1 = t'_1 \wedge \ldots \wedge t_k = t'_k \Rightarrow t_{k+j} = t'_{k+j})$$

for $j = 1, \ldots, n$.

Subcase 3a: $n = 1$. Using $(HL8)$ one gets

$$H \vdash_{HL} \forall X(t_1 = t'_1 \wedge \ldots \wedge t_k = t'_k \Rightarrow t = t')$$

and, by $(HL18)$,

$$H \vdash_{HL} \forall Y(t_1 = t'_1 \wedge \ldots \wedge t_k = t'_k \Rightarrow t = t'),$$

where Y is the set of all variables occuring in t_i, t'_i $(i = 1, \ldots, k)$ and t, t'. Thus, $(t, t') \in ded_H(P)$ and, consequently, $ded_H(Q) \subseteq ded_H(P)$.

Subcase 3b: $n > 1$. If we apply $(HL9)$ on

$$H \vdash_{HL} \forall X(t_1 = t'_1 \wedge \ldots \wedge t_k = t'_k \Rightarrow t_{k+n} = t'_{k+n}),$$

which holds by assumption, and

$$H \vdash_{HL} \forall X(t_{k+n} = t'_{k+n} \wedge t_{k+1} = t'_{k+1} \wedge \ldots \wedge t_{k+n-1} = t'_{k+n-1} \Rightarrow t = t'),$$

which follows from $(*)$ by $(HL14)$, then

$$H \vdash_{HL} \forall X(t_1 = t'_1 \wedge \ldots \wedge t_{k+n-1} = t'_{k+n-1} \Rightarrow t = t').$$

The procedure is repeated until Subcase 3a is reached.

(3) $h(ded_H(P)) \subseteq ded_H(h(P))$.

Case 1: $P = \emptyset$. We have to show that $h(ded_H(\emptyset)) \subseteq ded_H(\emptyset)$. If (t, t') belongs to $h(ded_H(\emptyset))$, then $t = h(t_0)$ and $t' = h(t'_0)$ for some t_0 and t'_0 such that $H \vdash_{HL} \forall X(t_0 = t'_0)$.

By $(HL10)$, we deduce $H \vdash_{HL} \forall\, Y(s^\sharp(t_0) = s^\sharp(t'_0))$ for every substitution s, where $Y = \bigcup\{var(s(x)) | x \in X\}$. Now choose s as follows: $s(x) = h(x)$ for all x in X. Evidently, $s^\sharp = h$ and hence

$$H \vdash_{HL} \forall\, Y(t = t'),$$

which means $(t, t') \in ded_H(\emptyset)$. Thus $h(ded_H(\emptyset)) \subseteq ded_H(\emptyset)$.

Case 2: $P = \{(t_1, t'_1), \ldots, (t_k, t'_k)\}$ is a nonempty finite relation on $T_\Sigma(V)$.

Let (t, t') be an arbitrarily given element of $h(ded_H(P))$. Then there are terms t_0 and t'_0 such that $t = h(t_0)$, $t' = h(t'_0)$ and

$$H \vdash_{HL} \forall X(t_1 = t'_1 \wedge \ldots \wedge t_k = t'_k \Rightarrow t_0 = t'_0).$$

Using $(HL11)$ we get

$$H \vdash_{HL} \forall\, Y(s^\sharp(t_1) = s^\sharp(t'_1) \wedge \ldots \wedge s^\sharp(t_k) = s^\sharp(t'_k) \Rightarrow s^\sharp(t_0) = s^\sharp(t'_0))$$

for every substitution s, where $Y = \bigcup\{var(s(x)) | x \in X\}$. Again we choose s as in Case 1: $s(x) = h(x)$ for all x in X. Therefore, we derive

$$H \vdash_{HL} \forall\, Y(h(t_1) = h(t'_1) \wedge \ldots \wedge h(t_k) = h(t'_k) \Rightarrow t = t').$$

Hence, by definition, $(t, t') \in ded_H(h(P))$ and, consequently,

$$h(ded_H(P)) \subseteq ded_H(h(P)). \qquad \blacksquare$$

Now it follows immediately that ded_H determines an algebraic, fully invariant closure operator from $Rel(T_\Sigma(V))$ to $Con(\boldsymbol{T}_\Sigma(V))$. Moreover, $c_H(P) \subseteq ded_H(P)$ for all finite relations P on $T_\Sigma(V)$, since, by the definition of formal proofs, every universal Horn clause belonging to H is also deducible from H. But $cons_H$ is the least algebraic, fully invariant closure operator from $Rel(T_\Sigma(V))$ to $Con(\boldsymbol{T}_\Sigma(V))$, which contains $\overline{H}$, as we have shown in Proposition 44. Hence

$$cons_H(P) \subseteq ded_H(P)$$

for all finite relations P on $T_\Sigma(V)$.

Theorem 51 (Completeness of Universal Horn Logic). *Let H be a set of universal Horn clauses. An arbitrary universal Horn clause is a logical consequence of H if and only if it is deducible from H. Formally,*

$$H \models \forall X(t_1 = t'_1 \wedge \ldots \wedge t_k = t'_k \Rightarrow t = t') \text{ iff}$$

$$H \vdash_{HL} \forall X(t_1 = t_1' \wedge \ldots \wedge t_k = t_k' \Rightarrow t = t').$$

Proof. By Proposition 48, $H \models \forall X(t_1 = t_1' \wedge \ldots \wedge t_k = t_k' \Rightarrow t = t')$, whenever $H \vdash_{HL} \forall X(t_1 = t_1' \wedge \ldots \wedge t_k = t_k' \Rightarrow t = t')$. To prove the converse implication we assume that

$$H \models \forall X(t_1 = t_1' \wedge \ldots \wedge t_k = t_k' \Rightarrow t = t').$$

Hence, $(t,t') \in cons_H(\{(t_1,t_1'),\ldots,(t_k,t_k')\})$. Because of $cons_H \leq ded_H$, it follows $(t,t') \in ded_H(\{(t_1,t_1'),\ldots,(t_k,t_k')\})$. That is,

$$H \vdash_{HL} \forall X(t_1 = t_1' \wedge \ldots \wedge t_k = t_k' \Rightarrow t = t'). \qquad \blacksquare$$

Similarly to implicational theories we get the following list of equivalent characterizations of universal Horn theories.

Corollary. *For any set H of universal Horn clauses the following are equivalent:*

(1) H is a universal Horn theory.

(2) $\overline{H}$ is an algebraic, fully invariant closure system of congruences on $\mathbf{T}_\Sigma(V)$.

(3) $H = Horn\ Mod\ H$.

(4) $H = Horn\ Mod\ H'$ for some set H' of universal Horn clauses.

(5) If $H \models \forall X(t_1 = t_1' \wedge \ldots \wedge t_k = t_k' \Rightarrow t = t')$, then $\forall X(t_1 = t_1' \wedge \ldots \wedge t_k = t_k' \Rightarrow t = t') \in H$.

(6) If $H \vdash_{HL} \forall X(t_1 = t_1' \wedge \ldots \wedge t_k = t_k' \Rightarrow t = t')$, then $\forall X(t_1 = t_1' \wedge \ldots \wedge t_k = t_k' \Rightarrow t = t') \in H$. ■

As a generalization of Neumann's correspondence we get the following one (cf. /Hoehnke-83/): The lattice of all algebraic, fully invariant closure operators from $Rel(T_\Sigma(V))$ to $Con(\mathbf{T}_\Sigma(V))$ is anti-isomorphic to the lattices of all quasivarieties.

3.3.6 Conditional Equational Theories and Conditional Term Rewriting

The aim of this section is to characterize the set of all equations that are logical consequences of a given set of universal Horn clauses. Let us fix a set H of universal Horn clauses throughout the sequel.

Definition 18. *The* ***conditional equational theory*** *of H is the set of all equations which are logical consequences of H, i.e., $E = Eq\ Mod\ H$.*

Let $P \Rightarrow t = t'$ be an arbitrary universal Horn clause. For simplicity we shall write $H \models P$ to mean that each equation (premise) of P is a logical consequence of H. Since

Eq Mod H is uniquely determined by $cons_H(\emptyset)$, where $cons_H$ is the closure operator associated with H, we immediately derive:

Lemma 52. *Let $P \Rightarrow t = t'$ be an arbitrary universal Horn clause. If $H \models P \Rightarrow t = t'$ and $H \models P$, then $H \models t = t'$.* ■

This yields a necessary condition for our intended characterization: If E is the conditional equational theory of H, then $\overline{E}$ is a fully invariant congruence on $\boldsymbol{T}_\Sigma(V)$ (i.e., E is an equational theory) such that $(t, t') \in \overline{E}$ whenever there is a universal Horn clause $P \Rightarrow t = t'$ in H with $P \subseteq \overline{E}$.

Definition 19. *A relation R on $\boldsymbol{T}_\Sigma(V)$ is called H-**admissible** if, for all terms t and t' in $T_\Sigma(V)$, $(t, t') \in R$ whenever there is a universal Horn clause $P \Rightarrow t = t'$ in H such that P is included in the equivalence relation generated by R.*

Observe that a congruence R on $\boldsymbol{T}_\Sigma(V)$ is H-admissible iff, for all universal Horn clauses $P \Rightarrow t = t'$ in H, $P \subseteq R$ implies $(t, t') \in R$. If R is additionally fully invariant, then R is H-admissible iff, for all universal Horn clauses $P \Rightarrow t = t'$ in H and all endomorphisms h, $P \subseteq h^{-1}(R)$ implies $(t, t') \in h^{-1}(R)$. By analogy with the proof of Lemma 34 in Section 3.3.4 one derives directly the following result.

Lemma 53. *If R is a fully invariant congruence on $\boldsymbol{T}_\Sigma(V)$, then R is H-admissible iff $\boldsymbol{T}_\Sigma(V)/R \models H$.* ■

Now we are in a position to present a criterion for conditional equational theories.

Theorem 54 (Criterion for Conditional Equational Theories). *A set E of equations is the conditional equational theory of H if and only if $\overline{E}$ is the least H-admissible fully invariant congruence on $\boldsymbol{T}_\Sigma(V)$.*

Proof. Suppose E is the conditional equational theory of H. Then $\overline{E} = cons_H(\emptyset)$ and hence $\overline{E}$ is an H-admissible fully invariant congruence on $\boldsymbol{T}_\Sigma(V)$.

Conversely, assume that E is a set of equations such that $\overline{E}$ is an H-admissible fully invariant congruence on $\boldsymbol{T}_\Sigma(V)$. Then, by Lemma 53, $\boldsymbol{T}_\Sigma(V)/\overline{E} \models H$. That is, $E \models P \Rightarrow t = t'$ for all universal Horn clauses $P \Rightarrow t = t'$ in H. In particular, $E \models t = t'$ for all equations $t = t'$ in H, i.e., $\overline{E} \subseteq cons_H(\emptyset)$.

Therefore, it remains to show that $cons_H(\emptyset)$ is also included in $\overline{E}$ or, in other words, $cons_H(\emptyset)$ is the least H-admissible fully invariant congruence on $\boldsymbol{T}_\Sigma(V)$. So, suppose C is any H-admissible fully invariant congruence on $\boldsymbol{T}_\Sigma(V)$. By Lemma 53, $\boldsymbol{T}_\Sigma(V)/C$ is a model of H and hence, by Lemma 34 in Section 3.3.4, C belongs to $\mathcal{C}(H)$, where we use the fact that $Mod\ H = Mod\ Horn\ \mathcal{C}(H)$. But, then $cons_H(\emptyset) \subseteq C$.

Thus $\overline{E} = cons_H(\emptyset)$ and, consequently, E is the conditional equational theory of H. ■

Let us only mention that adjoining the following two inference rules of H-admissibility:

$$\forall X(t = t') \quad \text{if} \quad \forall X(t = t') \in H; \text{ and}$$

$$\frac{\forall X_1(t_1 = t_1'), \ldots, \forall X_k(t_k = t_k')}{\forall X(t = t')} \quad \text{if} \quad \forall Y(t_1 = t_1' \wedge \ldots \wedge t_k = t_k' \Rightarrow t = t') \in H,$$

where $Y = X_1 \cup \ldots \cup X_k \cup X$

to equational logic yields a sound and complete ***conditional equational logic*** (cf. /Hussmann-85/).

In order to reduce the validity problem for conditional equational theories to a reduction problem similarly as we did with equational theories (see Section 3.2.5), an appropriate generation principle for H-admissible fully invariant congruences would be needed. Then we would know how to generalize term reduction. However, this step will be skipped here. Following Kaplan /Kaplan-84/ we say that $(P, t \to t')$ is a ***conditional reduction rule*** if $P = \{(t_i, t_i') | \, i = 1, \ldots, k\}$ is a finite relation on $T_\Sigma(V)$ and $t, t' \in T_\Sigma(V)$ such that

(1) $var(t') \subseteq var(t)$; and

(2) $var(t_i) \cup var(t_i') \subseteq var(t)$ for all $i = 1, \ldots, k$.

A finite set R of such conditional reduction rules is called a ***conditional term rewriting system*** (hereafter abbreviated $CTRS$). Its associated (conditional) term reduction on $T_\Sigma(V)$, denoted by $\to_R$, is defined as follows: $t \to_R t'$ iff there are: a conditional rewrite rule $(P, t_0 \to t_0')$ with $P = \{(t_i, t_i') | \; i = 1, \ldots, k\}$ in R, a substitution $s : V \to T_\Sigma(V)$ and an address u of t such that $t/u = s^\sharp(t_0)$, $t' = t[u/s^\sharp(t_0')]$ and $s^\sharp(t_i) \downarrow_R s^\sharp(t_i')$ for $i = 1, \ldots, k$, where $\downarrow_R = \to_R^* \cdot \leftarrow_R^*$.

Any set H of universal Horn clauses determines a $CTRS$, also denoted by H, if each $P \Rightarrow t = t'$ in H is regarded as a conditional rewrite rule $(P, t \to t')$ provided the variable restrictions are fulfilled.

Theorem 55. *If H is a given set of universal Horn clauses such that $\to_H$ is confluent, then, for all equations $\forall X(t = t')$,*

$$H \models \forall X(t = t') \quad \textit{iff} \quad t \downarrow_H t'. \qquad \blacksquare$$

For a proof the reader is referred to /Kaplan-84/.

When $\to_H$ is confluent and terminating, the validity problem for conditional equational theories becomes solvable.

4 Applications

In the last few years the applications of universal algebra in theoretical computer science have increased more and more. Most of them deal with formal semantics. By splitting the syntactic and semantic part of a data type, a program or any other object of interest, universal algebra provides methods to define and argue about semantics in a suitable formal framework. The basic idea is simple. All operation symbols involved in the syntactic description of our objects are interpreted as operations in an algebra. Semantics is then definable as a model class. However, the crucial point is that such model classes only become manageable if we are able to select "standard models". As we shall see, free or initial algebras play this role.

In Section 4.1, we are concerned with the algebraic specification of abstract data types. By a data type we mean a collection of data items of different sorts, like lists, booleans, numbers, etc., and operations manipulating with them. For an appropriate formal description of data types the concept of an algebra has to be generalized. Given a set S of sorts, an S-sorted or many-sorted algebra consists of an S-tuple of carrier sets and operations with declarations such that the argument sorts of the input and the output sort are determined. First, we develop the theory of many-sorted algebras. Then the fundamental ideas of algebraic specification methods, especially initial semantics, are motivated and presented.

Section 4.2 deals with the algebraic semantics of recursive program schemes. To deal properly with recursion we use fixpoint techniques. For that purpose, algebras have to be equipped with an ω-complete order. The main part of this section is devoted to the development of ω-complete ordered algebras. We close this section with the study of recursive program schemes without parameters. Only basic concepts and results of the algebraic semantics of recursive program schemes are presented.

4.1 Algebraic Specification of Abstract Data Types

Algebraic specification of abstract data types is based on the representation of data types by many-sorted algebras. A specification is then simply a many-sorted signature together with axioms for the operations. Such a specification determines a model class consisting of all many-sorted algebras subject to the given axioms.

Section 4.1.1 presents the theory of many-sorted algebras. The generalization of the necessary concepts is more or less a matter of an appropriate notation; there are only a few subtle differences from the one-sorted case.

In Section 4.1.2, specifications with equations as axioms are considered. By means of initial algebras we define initial semantics. Using the example of natural numbers we motivate the view that initiality describes "abstractness".

Finally, Section 4.1.3 deals with the operational semantics based on term rewriting.

4.1.1 Many-Sorted Algebras

The aim of this section is to provide an algebraic framework suitable for specification of data types by using algebras with more than one carrier set. Such so-called ***many-sorted algebras*** were first introduced by Higgins /Higgens-63/ and later by Birkhoff and Lipson /Birkhoff-Lipson-70/. For simplicity we will focus our attention on equational classes and theories of many-sorted algebras. In other words, many-sorted equations are the only formulas we will consider in the sequel. The generalization of the necessary concepts is, roughly speaking, more or less a matter of an appropriate notation; there are only a few subtle differences from the one-sorted case studied in Section 3.2. These differences will be explained in a detailed manner, whereas all other generalizations are mentioned quickly by pointing out their analogy with the known case. Here we mainly follow Goguen and Meseguer's approach (see, e.g., /Meseguer-Goguen-85/, /Goguen-Meseguer-86/).

Let S be a set (of ***sorts***). To emphazise our intention of "sorting", an S-indexed family of sets is therefore called an ***S-sorted set***. An S-sorted set $A = (A_s \mid s \in S)$ is said to be ***finite*** if the disjoint union over all its components is finite, i.e., $\bigcup(A_s \mid s \in S)$ is finite and, in addition, A_s is nonempty for only finitely many indices s of S. Instead of $x \in A_s$ we often write simply $x \in A$ when s is clear from the context; or we say x is an element of A with sort s, denoted as $x : s$. Hence a finite S-sorted set may be written as $\{x_1 : s_1, \ldots, x_n : s_n\}$. Given S-sorted sets A and B, A is called an ***(S-sorted) subset*** of B if $A_s \subseteq B_s$ for all s in S.

Correspondingly, all set theoretic notions can be transformed into S-sorted ones in this way. So we shall speak of S-sorted mappings, S-sorted relations, etc. For instance, if A and B are S-sorted sets, an ***S-sorted mapping*** f from A to B, also denoted by $f : A \to B$, is just a family $(f_s \mid s \in S)$ of mappings $f_s : A_s \to B_s$. Frequently, the attribute "S-sorted" will be omitted since a mapping from one S-sorted set to another is only meaningful when understood as S-sorted. For simplicity we often write $f(x)$ instead of $f_s(x)$ when no confusion about the index s may arise. Of course, an S-sorted mapping is called injective, surjective or bijective if all its components have the respective properties.

An ***S-sorted relation*** R on an S-sorted set A is a family $R = (R_s \mid s \in S)$ of relations R_s on A_s. Again, the attribute "S-sorted" may be omitted, and instead of xR_sy we often simply write xRy if the index s is clear from the context. R is called an equivalence if all R_s are equivalences.

All set theoretic operations, like union, intersection, direct product, etc., are defined componentwise. For instance, the union of two S-sorted sets A and B is the S-sorted set $(A_s \cup B_s \mid s \in S)$.

The usual power notation is generalized as follows. To any S-sorted set $A = (A_s \mid s \in S)$ a $W(S)$-sorted set $A^* = (A^w \mid w \in W(S))$ is assigned by $A^e = \{\emptyset\}$ and $A^{sw} = A_s \times A^w$ for all $s \in S$, $w \in W(S)$. As usual, $A_s \times \{\emptyset\}$ is identified with A_s. Recall that $W(S)$ is the word monoid over S with e (the empty word) as unit. Observe that $W(S)$ can be regarded as the set of natural numbers if S is a singleton (one-sorted case). Then, in this case, A^* consists of the usual powers A^n, $n \in I\!N$.

Similarly, any S-sorted mapping $f = (f_s \mid s \in S)$ from A to B induces a $W(S)$-sorted mapping $f^* = (f_w \mid w \in W(S))$ from A^* to B^* as follows: $f_e(\emptyset) = \emptyset$ and $f_{sw}(x,\boldsymbol{x}) = (f_s(x), f_w(\boldsymbol{x}))$ for all $s \in S$, $w \in W(S)$, $x \in A_s$ and $\boldsymbol{x} \in A^w$.

An S-***sorted signature*** is a set Σ, whose elements are called operation symbols, together with an arity function ar from Σ to $W(S) \times S$, which assigns to each operation symbol σ of Σ an ordered pair (w, s) with its first component w a word over S, called the ***arity*** (or ***domain***) of σ, and its second component s an element of S, called the ***sort*** (or ***range***) of σ. The arity expresses what sorts of data σ expects to see as inputs and in what order; and the sort of σ expresses the sort of data it returns. Instead of $ar(\sigma) = (w, s)$ we often write $\sigma : w \to s$; and call $w \to s$ the ***declaration*** of σ. When σ and τ have the same declaration, we simply write $\sigma, \tau : w \to s$. For any nullary operation symbol σ of sort s we prefer to declare $\sigma :\to s$ or even $\sigma : s$, without explicit mention of the empty word as arity. Any S-sorted signature is uniquely determined by the induced $W(S) \times S$-sorted set $(\Sigma_{w,s} \mid (w, s) \in W(S) \times S)$, where $\Sigma_{w,s}$ contains all operation symbols of Σ with the same declaration $w \to s$.

There is a convenient and easily readable representation of many-sorted signatures: the sorts are listed after the key word "sorts" and the operation symbols after "opns" with the arrow notation for their declarations.

Example 1. Consider the stack signature (see Section 2.1.1).

stack = sorts: *alphabet*
stack

opns: $a_1, \ldots, a_n$: *alphabet*
nil: *stack*
pop: *stack* $\to$ *stack*
push: *alphabet stack* $\to$ *stack*.

According to our notation, S is a two-element set,

$$S = \{alphabet, stack\},$$

and the set of operation symbols is determined by

$$\Sigma_{e,alphabet} = \{a_1, \ldots, a_n\},$$

$\Sigma_{e,stack} = \{nil\}$,

$\Sigma_{stack,stack} = \{pop\}$,

$\Sigma_{alphabet\ stack,stack} = \{push\}$,

$\Sigma_{w,s} = \emptyset$ otherwise. ■

Sometimes a graphical representation as depicted in Fig. 4.1 is quite useful.

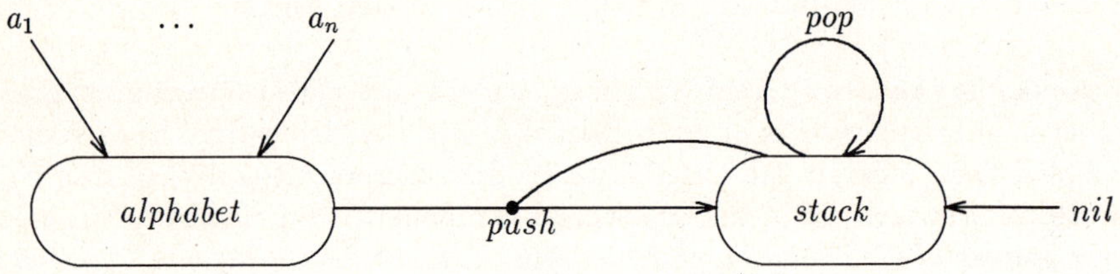

Fig. 4.1

Example 2. The group signature has the following representation:

group = sorts: *group*

opns: e: *group*
i: *group* → *group*
·: *group group* → *group* ■

A Σ-***algebra A*** consists of an S-sorted set A and a family of operations such that each operation symbol $\sigma : w \to s$ of Σ is realized as an operation $\sigma^A : A^w \to A_s$. When Σ is unspecified or unemphazised, we speak of a (***many-sorted***) ***algebra***.

As usual, structure-preserving mappings are called homomorphisms. Specifically, an S-sorted mapping h from a Σ-algebra $\boldsymbol{A}$ to a Σ-algebra $\boldsymbol{B}$ is a ***homomorphism*** or, more precisely, a Σ-homomorphism if $h_s(\sigma^A(\boldsymbol{x})) = \sigma^B(h_w(\boldsymbol{x}))$ for all operation symbols $\sigma : w \to s$ in Σ and all $\boldsymbol{x} \in A^w$. Notation: $h : \boldsymbol{A} \to \boldsymbol{B}$.

Next we introduce varieties of many-sorted algebras. Given Σ-algebras $\boldsymbol{A}$ and $\boldsymbol{B}$, $\boldsymbol{A}$ is a ***subalgebra*** of $\boldsymbol{B}$ if A is a subset of B and the inclusion $in_A : A \to B$ is an (injective) homomorphism; while $\boldsymbol{B}$ is called an ***image***[1)] of $\boldsymbol{A}$ if there is a surjective homomorphism from $\boldsymbol{A}$ onto $\boldsymbol{B}$. The ***direct product*** $\prod(\boldsymbol{A}_i \mid i \in I)$ of a family $(\boldsymbol{A}_i \mid i \in I)$ of Σ-algebras is a Σ-algebra with carrier $\prod(A_i \mid i \in I)$ and operations defined coordinatewise. Now an abstract class of many-sorted algebras is called a ***variety*** if it is closed under subalgebras, images and direct products.

---

1) As in Chap. 3, we agree to speak of an image instead of a homomorphic image.

The logical characterization of varieties in the sense of Birkhoff requires a generalized notion of equation. For that purpose many-sorted terms have to be defined first. Fix an S-sorted signature Σ. Given an S-sorted set X disjoint from Σ, let us think of the elements of X_s as variables of sort s. The S-sorted set of all Σ-***terms*** over X, denoted by $T_\Sigma(X)$, is defined as follows. Let $T_\Sigma(X) = (T_\Sigma(X)_s \mid s \in S)$. Each set $T_\Sigma(X)_s$ of Σ-terms over X of sort s is the least set of words over $\Sigma \cup X_s$ such that $X_s \subseteq T_\Sigma(X)_s$ and, for all operation symbols $\sigma : w \to s$ in Σ and all $(t_1, \ldots, t_n)$ in $T_\Sigma(X)^w$, $\sigma t_1 \ldots t_n$ belongs to $T_\Sigma(X)_s$.

Evidently, $T_\Sigma(X)$ carries the structure of a Σ-algebra if each operation symbol $\sigma : w \to s$ of Σ is realised as follows: $\sigma^{T_\Sigma(X)}(t_1, \ldots, t_n) = \sigma t_1 \ldots t_n$ for all $(t_1, \ldots, t_n)$ in $T_\Sigma(X)^w$. As usually $\boldsymbol{T}_\Sigma(X)$ denotes the term algebra over X.

The ***Principle of Finitary Algebraic Recursion*** can be generalized in a straightforward manner: Every S-sorted mapping α from X to any Σ-algebras $\boldsymbol{A}$ admits a unique homomorphic extension $\alpha^\# : \boldsymbol{T}_\Sigma(X) \to \boldsymbol{A}$.

A Σ-equation or, for short, an ***equation*** (of sort s) is a triple (X, t, t'), denoted

$$\forall X(t = t'),$$

where X is a finite S-sorted set of variables and $t, t' \in T_\Sigma(X)_s$. To make the variables explicit, we will also write

$$\forall x_1 : s_1, \ldots, x_m : s_m(t = t'),$$

instead of $\forall X(t = t')$, where $X = \{x_1 : s_1, \ldots, x_m : s_m\}$.

Let $\boldsymbol{A}$ be a Σ-algebra. A Σ-equation $\forall X(t = t')$ is ***valid*** in $\boldsymbol{A}$, in symbols

$$\boldsymbol{A} \models \forall X(t = t'),$$

if $\alpha^\#(t) = \alpha^\#(t')$ for all assignments $\alpha : X \to A$. Given a set E of Σ-equations, we say that E is valid in $\boldsymbol{A}$ if $\boldsymbol{A}$ validates each equation of E. Notation: $\boldsymbol{A} \models E$.

Now we reach the point of a serious difference between one-sorted and many-sorted algebras with respect to validation. For a normal (one-sorted) equation $\forall X(t = t')$ it seems superfluous to mention explicitly the quantification over X since any pair (t, t') of terms (over a fixed standard alphabet of variables) determines a finite set, namely the set of all variables occuring in both terms. Let us say for the moment that $\forall X(t = t')$ is in normal form if $X = var(t) \cup var(t')$. In this case we could simply write $t = t'$. Then, it is easily seen that an arbitrary equation $\forall X(t = t')$ is valid in an algebra $\boldsymbol{A}$ iff $t = t'$ is valid in $\boldsymbol{A}$. (This is also the reason why any set of equations can be thought of as a relation on terms).

The difference mentioned above shall now be illustrated by an example. Take a two-sorted signature and consider the equation

$$\forall x : s_1, y : s_1, z : s_2(x = y).$$

Any algebra $\boldsymbol{A}$ with $A_{s_1} = \{a,b\}$ and $A_{s_2} = \emptyset$ validates this equation since there is no assignment α from $(\{x,y\},\{z\})$ to $\boldsymbol{A}$, and in particular there is no mapping $\alpha_{s_2} : \{z\} \to \emptyset$, where $\alpha = (\alpha_{s_1}, \alpha_{s_2})$. But, of course,

$$\forall x : s_1, y : s_1(x = y)$$

is not valid in $\boldsymbol{A}$ because $\alpha_{s_1}(x) \neq \alpha_{s_1}(y)$ for an assignment α with $\alpha_{s_1}(x) = a$, $\alpha_{s_1}(y) = b$ and α_{s_2} the empty mapping.

Goguen and Meseguer /Goguen-Meseguer-85/ first recognized the important model-theoretic consequence of quantification in many-sorted equations. They demonstrated it by the following example.

Example 3. Consider the signature:

sig = sorts: *fool*
bool

opns: $0, 1 : bool$
$f : fool \to bool$
$\neg : bool \to bool$
$\vee, \wedge : bool\ bool \to bool.$

As the set of equations (without quantification) take

$$E = \{\neg 0 = 1,\ \neg 1 = 0,\ x \vee \neg x = 1,\ x \wedge \neg x = 0,\ x \vee x = x,\ x \wedge x = x,\ \neg f(x) = f(x)\}.$$

Then one could deduce in an ordinary way:

$$\begin{aligned} 0 &= f(x) \wedge \neg f(x) = f(x) \wedge f(x) = f(x) \\ &= f(x) \vee f(x) = f(x) \vee \neg f(x) = 1. \end{aligned}$$

But, there is an algebra A with $A_{fool} = \emptyset$ and $A_{bool} = \{0,1\}$ that does not validate E. Hence the deduction above is unsound. In fact, the equation

$$\forall x : fool(0 = 1)$$

has been deduced as we will see later. This equation is, however, valid in $\boldsymbol{A}$. Here, we observe once more the effect of different quantifications: $\forall x : fool(0 = 1)$ is valid in $\boldsymbol{A}$, but $\forall \emptyset (0 = 1)$ is not. ■

Given a set E of equations, we denote by $Mod\ E$ the class of all algebras which validate E; $Mod\ E$ is called the ***model class*** of E and a class $\mathcal{K}$ of algebras is said to be an ***equational class*** if $\mathcal{K} = Mod\ E$ for some set E of equations.

Birkhoff's Variety Theorem can be transferred directly to the many-sorted case: An abstract class of many-sorted algebras is a variety if and only if it is an equational class.

Another difference compared to the one-sorted case appears now in dealing with equational theories. By Birkhoff's Criterion, equational theories are characterizable as fully invariant congruences. But, in the many-sorted case, the congruence concept is not quite suitable. We have to search for a finer description. Fix a "standard alphabet" $V = (V_s \mid s \in S)$ of variables, where all V_s are countably infinite sets.

A family $R = (R(X) \mid X$ is a finite subset of $V)$ is called a ***clone congruence*** on $\boldsymbol{T}_\Sigma(V)$ if the following conditions are fulfilled:

(1) $R(X) = (R(X)_s \mid s \in S)$ is an S-sorted equivalence relation on $T_\Sigma(X)$;

(2) If $\sigma : s_1 \ldots s_n \to s$ is an operation symbol in Σ, then $t_i R(X_i)_{s_i} t'_i$ for $i = 1, \ldots, n$ implies $\sigma t_1 \ldots t_n R(X)_s \sigma t'_1 \ldots t'_n$, where $X = \bigcup(X_i \mid i = 1, \ldots, n)$;

(3) For every homomorphism $h : \boldsymbol{T}_\Sigma(X) \to \boldsymbol{T}_\Sigma(Y)$, $tR(X)_s t'$ implies $h(t)\ R(Y)_s\ h(t')$; and

(4) If $Y \subseteq X$, then $tR(X)_s t'$ implies $tR(Y)_s t'$ provided $t, t' \in T_\Sigma(Y)_s$ and $T_\Sigma(Y)_s \neq \emptyset$ whenever $X_s \neq \emptyset$.

Remark. In the literature (see, e.g., /Goguen-Meseguer-85/), clone congruences are defined in a slightly different way. Observe that any subset $X = \{x_1 : s_1, \ldots, x_n : s_n\}$ of V can be represented by the word $w = s_1 \ldots s_n$ over S; and hence $T_\Sigma(w)$ is written instead of $T_\Sigma(X)$. The empty set corresponds to the empty word, i.e., $T_\Sigma(e) = T_\Sigma(\emptyset) = T_\Sigma$. Now a clone congruence is regarded as a $W(S) \times S$-sorted relation $R = (R_{w,s} \mid (w, s) \in W(S) \times S)$ with $R_{w,s}$ a relation on $T_\Sigma(w)_s$ satisfying conditions which are quite similar to those given above. ■

Any set E of equation (with variables from V) can be thought of as a family $\overline{E} = (E(X) \mid X$ is a finite subset of $V)$ where $E(X) = (E(X)_s \mid s \in S)$ is an S-sorted relation such that $E(X)_s = \{(t, t') \mid \forall X(t = t')$ is an equation of sort s in $E\}$.

Given an abstract class $\mathcal{K}$ of algebras. The equational theory of $\mathcal{K}$ means the set of all equations valid in all algebras in $\mathcal{K}$, denoted as $Eq\ \mathcal{K}$. A set E of equations is said to be an ***equational theory*** if $E = Eq\ \mathcal{K}$ for some abstract class $\mathcal{K}$ of algebras.

As second main result we have the generalized **Birkhoff Criterion for Equational Theories**: A set E of equations is an equational theory if and only if $\overline{E}$ is a clone congruence.

We say that an equation $\forall X(t = t')$ is a ***logical consequence*** of a given set E of equations, in symbols

$$E \models \forall X(t = t'),$$

if $\forall X(t = t')$ is valid in all models of E, i.e., $\boldsymbol{A} \models \forall X(t = t')$ for all $\boldsymbol{A} \in Mod\ E$. Logical consequence is characterizable as follows: $E \models \forall X(t = t')$ iff (t, t') belongs to the clone congruence generated by $\overline{E}$.

Using this characterization of equational theories we know how to derive inference rules for a ***many-sorted equational logic***, namely by translating the defining properties of a clone congruence. But, because of the close similarities to those of fully invariant congruence, the algebraic counterpart of equational theories in the one sorted-case, we obtain the same inference rules (EL1) to (EL7) as in Section 3.2.4 with some minor modifications. For instance, the concretion rule (EL7) reads in the many-sorted case as follows: From $\forall X(t = t')$ we infer $\forall Y(t = t')$ with $Y = X - \{x\}$ if $x : s$ does not appear in either t or t', and if s is a nonempty sort, where a sort s is called ***empty*** in Σ if $\Sigma_{e,s} = \emptyset$ and there is no operation symbol $\sigma : s_1 \dots s_n \to s$ in Σ with all $s_1, \dots, s_n$ nonempty in Σ. As usual, we write $E \vdash_{EL} \forall X(t = t')$ if $\forall X(t = t')$ is deducible from a given set E of equations using (EL1) to (EL7).

Example 4. Let us reconsider Goguen and Meseguer's example from above (see Example 3), where E consists of the following (quantified) equations:

(E1) $\forall\emptyset(\neg 0 = 1)$,

(E2) $\forall\emptyset(\neg 1 = 0)$,

(E3) $\forall x : bool(x \vee \neg x = 1)$,

(E4) $\forall x : bool(x \wedge \neg x = 0)$,

(E5) $\forall x : bool(x \vee x = x)$,

(E6) $\forall x : bool(x \wedge x = x)$,

(E7) $\forall x : fool(\neg f(x) = f(x))$.

For instance, the equation $\forall x : fool(0 = 1)$ is deducible from E by the following formal proof:

(1) $\forall x : fool(f(x) = f(x))$	by (EL1),
(2) $\forall x : fool(f(x) \wedge \neg f(x) = f(x) \wedge f(x))$	by (EL4) from (1) and (E7),
(3) $\forall x : fool(f(x) \wedge \neg f(x) = 0)$	by (EL5) from (E4) substituting $x : bool$ by $f(x)$ with $x : fool$,
(4) $\forall x : fool(0 = f(x) \wedge \neg f(x))$	by (EL2) from (3),
(5) $\forall x : fool(0 = f(x) \wedge f(x))$	by (EL3) from (4) and (2),
(6) $\forall x : fool(f(x) \wedge f(x) = f(x))$	by (EL5) from (E6) substituting $x : bool$ by $f(x)$ with $x : fool$,
(7) $\forall x : fool(0 = f(x))$	by (EL3) from (5) and (6),
(8) $\forall x : fool(f(x) = 1)$	similarly to (1)-(7),
(9) $\forall x : fool(0 = 1)$	by (EL3) from (7) and (8).

Since $fool$ is an empty sort, the concretion rule is not applicable on (9). Hence $\forall\emptyset(0 = 1)$ is not deducible from E. ■

Many-sorted equational logic is sound and complete: For any set E of equations and every equation $\forall X(t = t')$,

$$E \models \forall X(t = t') \text{ iff } E \vdash_{EL} \forall X(t = t').$$

Summarizing, we can say that almost all generalizations of one-sorted concepts and results to the many-sorted versions are basically straightforward. The few exceptions mentioned earlier result from the fact that a many-sorted algebra can have carriers of some sorts empty and others nonempty, an impossibility for one-sorted algebras.

4.1.2 Initial Semantics of Equational Specifications

In this section we concentrate on a well-developed but relatively simple method of data specification. Mainly basic ideas and concepts are presented. Generally speaking, a specification consists of a signature and a set of formulas, often called axioms of the specification. In the pioneering papers /ADJ-76, Guttag-75/, many-sorted signatures and many-sorted equations are used, and hence many-sorted equational logic is the underlying logical framework. Nowadays, however, more expressive logical systems are applied such as universal Horn logic, first-order and higher-order logic, infinitary logic and many others, where all these logics may be considered with or without predicates, admitting partial operations or not. Some thoughts on those specification techniques can be found in /Sannella-Tarlecki-84/.

For a more detailed introduction to the initial semantics of equational specifications the reader is referred to the literature (see, e.g., /Ehrich-Gogolla-Lipeck-89/, /Ehrig-Mahr-85/, /Ehrig-Mahr-90/, /Klaeren-83/).

Definition 1. *An (**equational) specification** is a pair (Σ, E) consisting of an S-sorted signature Σ and a set E of Σ-equations.*

The representation for signatures can be enlarged so that even specifications are expressible in the same way by using the key word "eqns" and listing all equations of E after it.

Example 1. A specification of stacks is given below:

stack = sorts: *alphabet*
stack

opns: $a_1, \ldots, a_n$: *alphabet*
nil: *stack*
pop: *stack* $\rightarrow$ *stack*
push: *alphabet stack* $\rightarrow$ *stack*

eqns: $\forall\emptyset(pop(nil) = nil)$
$\forall x : alphabet, s : stack(pop(push(x, s)) = s)$.

We have to mention that our specification is a very simplified version of what is usually understood by a stack. Only the second equation is generally accepted as a meaningful requirement for the stack principle, whereas the first one is problematic since *pop* of *nil* could be considered as undefined or an error. For analogous reasons the top operation is suppressed to avoid all kinds of "exception" or "error" handling. We omit all these pecularities and try to demonstrate the idea of specifications in principle. The interested reader is referred to the literature, e.g., /Bergstra-Tucker-88/ where a detailed explanation of a wide variety of stack specifications is presented. ■

A quite natural approach to semantics is the following. Given a specification (Σ, E), the class $Mod\ E$ of all models of E is called the ***loose semantics*** of (Σ, E). Of course, we assume tacitly that $Mod\ E$ is not empty, that is to say E is consistent. Otherwise, when $Mod\ E = \emptyset$, the specification (Σ, E) is incorrect.

In this context a model $\boldsymbol{A}$ of E is said to be a (concrete) data type for the specification (Σ, E). Often, however, one requires additionally that $\boldsymbol{A}$ is ***minimal*** in the sense that $\boldsymbol{A}$ has no proper subalgebras. Observe that an arbitrary algebra is minimal iff it is generated by the empty set. So, any minimal algebra is finitely generated but not vice versa. Therefore, it is misleading to call minimal algebras finitely generated as sometimes is done in the literature on data specification; other acceptable notations for minimal algebras are ***reachable*** or ***simple***.

Lemma 1. *Let Σ be an S-sorted signature. A Σ-algebra $\boldsymbol{A}$ is minimal iff $\boldsymbol{A}$ is an image of the ground term algebra $\boldsymbol{T}_\Sigma$. In particular, $\boldsymbol{T}_\Sigma$ is minimal.* ■

Hence, any element a of a minimal algebra $\boldsymbol{A}$ is denoted by a ground term, i.e., $a = h_A(t)$ for some $t \in T_\Sigma$, where h_A is the unique (surjective) homomorphism from $\boldsymbol{T}_\Sigma$ to $\boldsymbol{A}$. That is why elements of a minimal algebra can be thought of as computable using only operation symbols of the underlying signature.

Let us first consider a specification without equations (sometimes called a specification by a signature). For instance,

nat = sorts: *nat*

opns: $zero : nat$
$succ : nat \rightarrow nat$

is such a specification for the natural numbers. As "standard" algebra we take $NAT = (I\!N, 0, s)$ with $I\!N$ as carrier (of sort *nat*), 0 as constant realizing *zero* and $s : I\!N \rightarrow I\!N$, defined by $s(n) = n + 1$ for all $n \in I\!N$, as realization of *succ*. Formally, $0 = zero^{I\!N}$ and $s = succ^{I\!N}$.

In the following we exhibit the relationship between NAT and the ***Peano Axioms*** (see Appendix 1) by which natural numbers are defined:

(P1) 0 is a natural number.

(P2) Every natural number has a uniquely determined successor.

(P3) The successor of any natural number is different from 0.

(P4) If the successors of any two natural numbers are equal, then so are the natural numbers themselves.

(P5) Any set of natural numbers which contains 0 and is closed under successors includes all natural numbers.

Commonly, (P5) is called the ***induction axiom***. It is just another formulation for the Principle of Finite Induction.

In our terminology, axioms (P1) and (P2) express nothing else than the fact that $\mathbb{N}$ equipped with 0 and s is a **nat**-algebra NAT, while (P5) is equivalent to the minimality of NAT. An interpretation of (P3) and (P4) will be a postponed for a while. No nontrivial equation is valid in NAT, which is to say, NAT is typical.

If we limit our investigations to minimal **nat**-algebras, we have to exclude for example the **nat**-algebras $(\mathbb{Z}, 0, s)$ of all integers endowed with 0 as constant and the common successor function s because NAT is obviously a proper subalgebra. With respect to our intention of data type **nat**, $\mathbb{Z}$ has redundant elements, namely all negative integers. Informally speaking, an algebra which is not a minimal model contains "junk".

It is easily seen that any minimal **nat**-algebra $\boldsymbol{A} = (A, a_0, f)$ has an at most countably infinite carrier A. For if A were infinite, but not countably infinite, then $\{f^n(a_0) \mid n \in \mathbb{N}\}$ would form a proper subalgebra, in contradiction to the assumption that $\boldsymbol{A}$ is minimal. But observe, however, that minimality does not exclude finite **nat**-algebras. What conditions should be added to achieve this ?

Suppose $\boldsymbol{A} = (A, a_0, f)$ is a finite **nat**-algebra. Then at least two distinct natural numbers m and n exist such that $f^m(a_0) = f^n(a_0)$. That is, $\boldsymbol{A}$ validates a ground equation $\forall\emptyset(succ^m(zero) = succ^n(zero))$ which is not deducible from the **nat**-specification; that is, not deducible from the empty set (of equations). In this sense, $\boldsymbol{A}$ is not (ground) typical for **nat** since there are "confusions".

We say generally that an algebra $\boldsymbol{A}$ is ground typical, or ***typical*** for short, for a given specification (Σ, E) if a ground equation is valid in $\boldsymbol{A}$ iff it is deducible from E.

Lemma 2. *Let Σ be an S-sorted signature. A Σ-algebra $\boldsymbol{A}$ is typical for $(\Sigma, \emptyset)$ iff the unique homomorphism h_A from $\boldsymbol{T}_\Sigma$ to $\boldsymbol{A}$ is injective.*

Proof. Assume that $\boldsymbol{A}$ is Σ-algebra typical for $(\Sigma, \emptyset)$. By definition, for all ground equations $\forall\emptyset(t = t')$, $\boldsymbol{A} \models \forall\emptyset(t = t')$ iff $\emptyset \vdash_{EL} \forall\emptyset(t = t')$. Note that $\emptyset \vdash_{EL} \forall\emptyset(t = t')$ iff $\boldsymbol{T}_\Sigma \models \forall\emptyset(t = t')$ and hence $\boldsymbol{A} \models \forall\emptyset(t = t')$ iff $\boldsymbol{T}_\Sigma \models \forall\emptyset(t = t')$. If the unique homomorphism $h_A : \boldsymbol{T}_\Sigma \to \boldsymbol{A}$ is not injective, then there are two different terms t and

t' in T_Σ such that $h_A(t) = h_A(t')$. This leads to a contradiction since $\forall\emptyset(t = t')$ is valid in $\boldsymbol{A}$ but not in $\boldsymbol{T}_\Sigma$.

Conversely, we assume that the unique homomorphism h_A is injective. If $\boldsymbol{A}$ is not typical for $(\Sigma, \emptyset)$, then there is a ground equation, say $\forall\emptyset(t = t')$, valid in $\boldsymbol{A}$ but not deducible from the empty set of equations or, in other words, not valid in $\boldsymbol{T}_\Sigma$. That is, $h_A(t) = h_A(t')$ but $t \neq t'$, which contradicts injectivity. ■

As a corollary we get that a Σ-algebra $\boldsymbol{A}$ is minimal and typical for a specification $(\Sigma, \emptyset)$ without equations iff $\boldsymbol{A}$ is isomorphic to $\boldsymbol{T}_\Sigma$. Recall that the ground term algebra $\boldsymbol{T}_\Sigma$ is initial in the class of all Σ-algebras and, moreover, any two initial algebras are isomorphic. On the other hand, if a Σ-algebra $\boldsymbol{A}$ is initial in the class of all Σ-algebras, then $\boldsymbol{A}$ is minimal and typical for $(\Sigma, \emptyset)$. So, initiality represents the two principles stated above.

Proposition 3. *NAT is initial in the class of all* **nat***-algebras.*

Proof. Given an arbitrary **nat**-algebra $\boldsymbol{A} = (A, a_0, f)$, we have to show there is exactly one homomorphism h_A from NAT to $\boldsymbol{A}$. Define a family $(a_n \mid n \in \mathbb{N})$ in A starting with the constant a_0 and putting $a_n = f(a_{n-1})$ for all $n \geq 1$. Of course, this family is nothing but a mapping, say h_A, from $\mathbb{N}$ to A, defined by $h_A(n) = a_n$ for all $n \in \mathbb{N}$. Since $h_A(0) = a_0$ and $h_A(s(n)) = f(h_A(n))$ for all $n \geq 1$, h_A is a homomorphism.

By induction we are going to prove that h_A is unique. For if $g : \mathbb{N} \to \boldsymbol{A}$ is another homomorphism, then $g(0) = a_0 = h_A(0)$ (i.e., the induction basis is valid) and $g(n) = h_A(n)$ (induction hypothesis) implies $g(n+1) = g(s(n)) = f(g(n)) = f(h_A(n)) = h_A(s(n)) = h_A(n+1)$ (i.e., the induction step is valid); hence $g = h_A$. ■

By the above observation NAT is isomorphic to the ground **nat**-term algebra $\boldsymbol{T}_{\mathbf{nat}}$, which is independent of any representation. It is already determined by the signature. This is what we will understand by an abstract data type.

In our example the initiality characterizes the natural numbers more simply but more abstractly than Peano's Axioms.

Let us give an intuitive motivation, due to /Burstall-Goguen-82/, for using initiality to describe "abstractness". Assume we have a concrete data type and that we can tell whether or not two concrete data items in it represent the same abstract data item; call the two concrete data items equivalent in that case. Now a data representation is said to be ***standard*** if the following conditions are satisfied:

(1) No junk: Every data item can be constructed using only operation symbols; a data item that cannot be so constructed was called junk.

(2) No confusion: Two data items are equivalent iff they can be proved so from the given equations.

Formalizing both principles we get the following notion.

Definition 2. *Given a specification (Σ, E), a Σ-algebra $\boldsymbol{A}$ is called a (Σ, E)-**Peano algebra** if*

(1) $\boldsymbol{A}$ is minimal; and

(2) $\boldsymbol{A}$ is typical for (Σ, E).

To generalize the logical equivalence between initiality and the two (formalized) principles, we first recall that a Σ-algebra $\boldsymbol{A}$ is initial in a class $\mathcal{K}$ of Σ-algebras iff $\boldsymbol{A}$ belongs to $\mathcal{K}$ and there is exactly one homomorphism from $\boldsymbol{A}$ to any algebra in $\mathcal{K}$.

Theorem 4. *Let (Σ, E) be a specification and let $\boldsymbol{A}$ be a Σ-algebra. Then $\boldsymbol{A}$ is a (Σ, E)-Peano algebra if and only if $\boldsymbol{A}$ is initial in $Mod\ E$.*

Proof. Assume that $\boldsymbol{A}$ is a (Σ, E)-Peano algebra. By the minimality of $\boldsymbol{A}$, the unique homomorphism $h_A : \boldsymbol{T}_\Sigma \to \boldsymbol{A}$ is surjective. Now consider the sur-reflection of $\boldsymbol{T}_\Sigma$ in $Mod\ E$, say $\boldsymbol{R}$. By definition, there is a surjective homomorphism $r : \boldsymbol{T}_\Sigma \to \boldsymbol{R}$. That is, $\boldsymbol{R}$ is initial in $Mod\ E$ since there is a unique homomorphism from $\boldsymbol{R}$ to any other algebra in $Mod\ E$. We claim that $\boldsymbol{A}$ is isomorphic to $\boldsymbol{R}$. For that it suffices to show that, for all ground terms t and t' of T_Σ, $h_A(t) = h_A(t')$ iff $r(t) = r(t')$. But this is just another formulation for the typicality of $\boldsymbol{A}$ for (Σ, E). Hence $\boldsymbol{A}$ is initial in $Mod\ E$. Conversely, any initial algebra in $Mod\ E$ is a (Σ, E)-Peano algebra. ■

Definition 3. *Let (Σ, E) be a specification. The **initial semantics** of (Σ, E) is the class*

$$ADT(\Sigma, E) = \{\boldsymbol{A} \mid \boldsymbol{A} \text{ is initial in } Mod\ E\}.$$

*$ADT(\Sigma, E)$ is also called the **(initial) abstract data type** defined by (Σ, E). Given a Σ-algebra $\boldsymbol{A}$ of $Mod\ E$, the specification (Σ, E) is called **(initially) correct** with respect to $\boldsymbol{A}$ if $\boldsymbol{A}$ belongs to $ADT(\Sigma, E)$.*

Initial semantics pursues the philosophy that the equivalence of data items has to be specified explicitly. As a method available we have deductions in many-sorted equational logic, which makes initial semantics executable in most cases; an important property for designing specifications and prototyping.

Let $\mathcal{K}$ be a class of Σ-algebras. We denote by $GEq\mathcal{K}$ the set of all ground equations valid in all $\boldsymbol{A} \in \mathcal{K}$. As in the one-sorted case we have

$$GEq\ ADT(\Sigma, E) \ = \ GEq\ Mod\ E.$$

Since minimal models are images of initial algebras it follows that

$$Eq\ ADT(\Sigma, E) \ = \ Eq\{\boldsymbol{A} \in Mod\ E \mid \boldsymbol{A} \text{ minimal}\}.$$

Hence, any ground equation, which is valid in $ADT(\Sigma, E)$, and consequently valid in all minimal models, is deducible from E and vice versa.

Again, specifications without equations will be studied first. From the observation above we derive

$$ADT(\Sigma, \emptyset) = \{\boldsymbol{A} \mid \boldsymbol{A} \text{ is isomorphic to } \boldsymbol{T}_\Sigma\}.$$

Example 2. Consider a specification of strings:

string = sorts: *alphabet*
string

opns: $a_1, \ldots, a_n$: *alphabet*
empty : *string*
insert : *alphabet string* → *string*

Now we have to compute the ground term algebra $\boldsymbol{T}_{\mathbf{string}}$. Evidently,

$$\boldsymbol{T}_{\mathbf{string},\mathbf{alphabet}} = \{a_1, \ldots, a_n\}.$$

The **string**-terms of sort *string* are the following:

$$\begin{array}{l} empty,\ insert(a_1, empty), \ldots, insert(a_n, empty), \\ insert(a_1, insert(a_1, empty)), \ldots, insert(a_i, insert(a_j(empty)), \ldots, \\ insert(a_i, insert(a_j, \ldots, insert(a_k, empty) \ldots), \ldots . \end{array}$$

They are obviously identifiable with words over $\{a_1, \ldots, a_n\}$, where the empty word corresponds to *empty*.

Let us define a **string**-algebra $STRING = (A, W(A), a_1, \ldots, a_n, e, i)$, where $A = \{a_1, \ldots, a_n\}$ is the carrier of sort *alphabet*, $W(A)$ is the carrier of sort *string*, $a_1, \ldots, a_n$ are constants of sort alphabet (realizing themselves), the empty word e over A realizes *empty* and i is the realization of *insert* defined by $i(a, w) = aw$ for all $a \in A$ and $w \in W(A)$.

It is easily seen that $STRING$ is isomorphic to $\boldsymbol{T}_{\mathbf{string}}$. So, by definition, the specification **string** is correct with respect to $STRING$. In other words, our intention regarding strings, expressed in the definition of $STRING$, is correctly specified by **string**. ■

By what follows we are going to study the initial semantics of specifications (Σ, E) with equations by constructing a distinguished initial algebra in $Mod\ E$. Of course, initial algebras exist in $Mod\ E$ since $Mod\ E$ is closed under subalgebras and direct products; $Mod\ E$ is even a variety. As we know (cf. Lemma 11 in Section 3.3.2), such an initial algebra is obtained as the sur-reflection of the ground term algebra $\boldsymbol{T}_\Sigma$ in $Mod\ E$. By analogy with the one-sorted case, the sur-reflection of $\boldsymbol{T}_\Sigma$ in $Mod\ E$ is the greatest image of $\boldsymbol{T}_\Sigma$ in $Mod\ E$. Furthermore, any image of $\boldsymbol{T}_\Sigma$ is isomorphic to a quotient algebra of $\boldsymbol{T}_\Sigma$. Therefore we search for the least congruence R on $\boldsymbol{T}_\Sigma$ such that $\boldsymbol{T}_\Sigma / R \models E$.

Clearly, a congruence on $\boldsymbol{T}_\Sigma$ is an S-sorted equivalence relation $R = (R_s \mid s \in S)$ such that, for all operation symbols $\sigma : s_1 \ldots s_n \to s$ in Σ and all $t_i, t_i' \in T_{\Sigma,s_i}$ $(i = 1, \ldots, n)$, $t_i R_{s_i} t_i'$ for $i = 1, \ldots, n$ implies $\sigma t_1 \ldots t_n R_s \sigma t_1' \ldots t_n'$. If R is a congruence on $\boldsymbol{T}_\Sigma$, then $\boldsymbol{T}_\Sigma/R$ has the carrier $T_\Sigma/R = (T_{\Sigma,s}/R_s \mid s \in S)$ and operations defined as follows: $\sigma^{T_\Sigma/R}([t_1], \ldots, [t_n]) = [\sigma t_1 \ldots t_n]$ for each operation symbol $\sigma : s_1 \ldots s_n \to s$ of Σ and all $t_i \in T_{\Sigma,s_i}$ $(i = 1, \ldots, n)$.

Given set E of Σ-equations, we define an S-sorted relation $G(E) = (G(E)_s \mid s \in S)$ on T_Σ by $G(E)_s = \{(g^\#(t), g^\#(t')) \mid \forall X(t = t')$ is a Σ-equation of sort s in E and $g : X \to T_\Sigma$ is a ground substitution $\}$.

Lemma 5. *For any congruence on* $\boldsymbol{T}_\Sigma$,

$$\boldsymbol{T}_\Sigma/R \models E \quad \textit{iff} \quad G(E) \subseteq R.$$

Proof. Suppose R is a congruence on $\boldsymbol{T}_\Sigma$ such that $\boldsymbol{T}_\Sigma/R \models E$. Then all equations $\forall X(t = t')$ in E are valid in $\boldsymbol{T}_\Sigma/R$. That is, $\alpha^\#(t) = \alpha^\#(t')$ for every assignment $\alpha : X \to T_\Sigma/R$. Now consider an arbitrary ground substitution $g : X \to T_\Sigma$. Let $nat_R : \boldsymbol{T} \to \boldsymbol{T}_\Sigma/R$ be the natural homomorphism defined by $nat_R(t) = [t]_R$. It is easily seen that, for the assignment $\alpha = g \cdot nat_R$, $\alpha^\# = g^\# \cdot nat_R$ holds and so $[g^\#(t)] = [g^\#(t')]$, i.e., $(g^\#(t), g^\#(t')) \in R$, for all $\forall X(t = t')$ in E and all ground substitutions $g : X \to T_\Sigma$. Hence $G(E) \subseteq R$.

Conversely, assume that $G(E)$ is included in a given congruence R on $\boldsymbol{T}_\Sigma$. Then $nat_R(g^\#(t)) = nat_R(g^\#(t'))$ for all $\forall X(t = t')$ in E and all ground substitutions $g : X \to T_\Sigma$. Let $\alpha : X \to T_\Sigma/R$ be an arbitrary assignment. By the surjectivity of nat_R, there is a mapping $f : T_\Sigma/R \to T_\Sigma$ with $f \cdot nat_R = id_{T_\Sigma/R}$. For $g = \alpha \cdot f$ we get $g \cdot nat_R = \alpha$ and hence $\alpha^\# = g^\# \cdot nat_R$. Therefore, $\alpha^\#(t) = \alpha^\#(t')$, which means that $\boldsymbol{T}_\Sigma/R \models \forall X(t = t')$ for all equations $\forall X(t = t')$ in E. That is, $\boldsymbol{T}_\Sigma/R \models E$. ∎

Let $=_{G(E)}$ denote the congruence on $\boldsymbol{T}_\Sigma$ generated by $G(E)$; it is sometimes called the ***ground equational theory*** of E. Instead of $\boldsymbol{T}_\Sigma/ =_{G(E)}$ we will write $\boldsymbol{T}_{(\Sigma,E)}$. $\boldsymbol{T}_{(\Sigma,E)}$ can be characterized as follows:

$$E \models \forall\emptyset(t = t') \quad \text{iff} \quad \boldsymbol{T}_{(\Sigma,E)} \models \forall\emptyset(t = t').$$

As an immediate consequence we derive our main result.

Theorem 6. *If* (Σ, E) *is a specification, then*

$$ADT(\Sigma, E) \;=\; \{\boldsymbol{A} \mid \boldsymbol{A} \textit{ is isomorphic to } \boldsymbol{T}_{(\Sigma,E)}\}. \qquad ∎$$

The definition of the initial semantics of a specification (Σ, E) is therefore reduced to constructing $\boldsymbol{T}_{(\Sigma,E)}$.

Example 3. Let **stack** be the stack specification introduced in Example 1. We want to construct $\boldsymbol{T}_{\mathbf{stack}}$. First, we have to exhibit the set of ground terms, where T_a and T_s abbreviate $T_{\mathbf{stack},alphabet}$ and $T_{\mathbf{stack},stack}$. It is obvious that $T_a = \{a_1, \ldots a_n\}$. T_s is recursively defined by $T_s = \{nil\} \cup \{pop(t) \mid t \in T_s\} \cup \{push(a,t) \mid a \in T_a, t \in T_s\}$. Next, the ground equational theory of the defining equations must be determined. Let $=_a$ and $=_s$ be its components of sort *alphabet* and *stack*, respectively. Evidently, $=_a$ is the identity on T_a; and each term of T_s is congruent either to *nil* or to a term of the form $push(a_{i_1}, push(a_{i_2}, \ldots, push(a_{i_n}, nil) \ldots)$.

Define a **stack**-algebra $STACK = (A; A(W), a_1, \ldots, a_n, e, pop, push)$, where $A = \{a_1, \ldots, a_n\}$ is the carrier of sort *alphabet* and the word monoid $W(A)$ over A is the carrier of sort *stack*, $a_1, \ldots, a_n$ are constants of sort *alphabet* (realizing themselves), the empty word e is the constant of sort *stack* realizing *nil*, while *pop* and *push* (as realizations of *pop* and *push*) are defined as follows:

$$pop(w) = \begin{cases} v & \text{if } w = av \text{ for some } a \in A, v \in W(A), \\ e & \text{if } w = e; \end{cases}$$

and

$$push(a, w) = aw \quad \text{for all } a \in A,\ w \in W(A).$$

It is easily seen that $STACK$ is isomorphic to $\boldsymbol{T}_{\mathbf{stack}}$. Hence the stack specification **stack** is correct with respect to $STACK$. ■

Example 4. Natural numbers are to be endowed with equality. We use the following specification:

nateq = sorts: *nat*
bool

opns: $zero:\ nat$
$succ:\ nat \to nat$
$true,\ false:\ bool$
$eq:\ nat\ nat \to bool$

eqns: $\forall\emptyset(eq(zero, zero) = true)$
$\forall x : nat(eq(zero, succ(x)) = false)$
$\forall x : nat(eq(succ(x), zero) = false)$
$\forall x : nat, y : nat(eq(succ(x), succ(y)) = eq(x, y))$.

Let us abbreviate $T_{\mathbf{nateq},nat}$ and $T_{\mathbf{nateq},bool}$ by T_n and T_b, respectively. Then

$$T_n = \{succ^n(zero) \mid n \in I\!N\}$$

and

$$T_b = \{true, false\} \cup \{eq(succ^m(zero), succ^n(zero)) \mid m, n \in I\!N\},$$

where $succ^0(zero) = zero$ and $succ^n(zero) = succ(succ^{n-1}(zero))$ for $n \geq 1$. The two components of the related ground equational theory will be denoted by $=_n$ and $=_b$

respectively. Of course, $=_n$ is the identity relation on T_n. By induction over m and n one may prove

$$eq(succ^m(zero), succ^n(zero)) =_b \begin{cases} true & \text{if } m = n. \\ false & \text{if } m \neq n. \end{cases}$$

Hence $T_{\mathbf{nateq},bool} = \{[true], [false]\}$.

Define a **nateq**-algebra $NATEQ = (\mathbb{N}, \{tt, ff\}, 0, s, tt, ff, =)$ with $\mathbb{N}$ as the carrier of sort *nat*, $\{tt, ff\}$ as the carrier of sort *bool*, 0 as constant of sort *nat* realizing *zero*, $s : \mathbb{N} \to \mathbb{N}$ with $s(n) = n + 1$ as the realization of *succ*, *tt* and *ff* as constants of sort *bool* realizing *true* and *false*, respectively, and $=$ is regarded as a binary operation from $\mathbb{N} \times \mathbb{N}$ to $\{tt, ff\}$ defined by

$$= (m, n) \ = \begin{cases} tt & \text{if } m = n, \\ ff & \text{if } m \neq n. \end{cases}$$

Since $NATEQ$ is isomorphic to $\boldsymbol{T}_{\mathbf{nateq}}$, the specification **nateq** is correct with respect to $NATEQ$. ■

As we already know, induction is a proof method in minimal models and hence in $ADT(\Sigma, E)$.

Example 5. A specification of natural numbers with addition is given below:

natplus = sorts: *nat*

opns: $zero : \ nat$
$succ : \ nat \to nat$
$+ : nat \ nat \to nat$

eqns: $\forall x : nat(zero + x = x)$
$\forall x : nat, y : nat(succ(x) + y = succ(x + y))$.

We want to show inductively that addition is commutative in $\boldsymbol{T}_{\mathbf{natplus}}$ and hence in all minimal **natplus**-algebras.

Let $=_{nat}$ denote the ground equational theory associated with the specification **natplus**. First we claim that every ground **natplus**-term t is congruent modulo $=_{nat}$ to a ground **nat**-term (in which no "+" occurs). If t does not contain $+$, then t is a ground **nat**-term. Now assume that t has a subterm of the form $succ^n(zero) + t'$. If $n = 0$, then $zero+t' =_{nat} t'$. Otherwise, $succ^n(zero)+t' =_{nat} succ(succ^{n-1}(zero))+t' =_{nat} \cdots =_{nat} succ^n(zero + t') =_{nat} succ^n(t')$. Replacing the subterm $succ^n(zero) + t'$ by $succ^n(t')$ in t yields a new ground **natplus**-term, say t'', and t'' has one $+$ less than t. By induction on the number of the operation symbol $+$ in t one shows that $t =_{nat} succ^n(zero)$ for some $n \in \mathbb{N}$.

Observe that

$$\boldsymbol{T}_{\mathbf{natplus}} \models \forall x : nat, y : nat(x + y = y + x)$$

iff $t + t' =_{nat} t' + t$ for all $t, t' \in T_{\mathbf{natplus}}$. Indeed, we have to prove

$$succ^m(zero) + succ^n(zero) =_{nat} succ^n(zero) + succ^m(zero). \qquad (*)$$

If $m = n = 0$, then $(*)$ holds trivially. If $m = 0$ and n is positive, then

$$zero + succ^n(zero) =_{nat} succ^n(zero) =_{nat}$$

$$succ(succ^{n-1}(zero) + zero) =_{nat} succ^n(zero) + zero.$$

Similarly, if m is positive and $n = 0$, then $(*)$ holds. Now suppose m and n are positive. Then we derive

$$succ^m(zero) + succ^n(zero) =_{nat}$$

$$succ(succ^{m-1}(zero) + succ^n(zero)) =_{nat} \cdots =_{nat}$$

$$succ^m(zero + succ^n(zero)) =_{nat} succ^{m+n}(zero) =_{nat}$$

$$succ^n(zero + succ^m(zero)) =_{nat} \cdots =_{nat}$$

$$succ^n(zero) + succ^m(zero).$$ ■

Although additional equations may be proved valid in initial algebras, we already mentioned in a remark on Birkhoff's Completeness Theorem for Equational Logic (in Section 3.2.4) that there is no sound and complete logic for the so-called inductive theory; even enlarging equational logic by structural induction is not enough.

4.1.3 Operational Semantics

The initial semantics of a specification (Σ, E) is basically determined by the quotient term algebra $\boldsymbol{T}_{(\Sigma,E)}$. As we know, computations in a quotient algebra are done using representatives of its congruence classes. However, their choice is not always constructive; otherwise the related word problem would be solvable. To circumvent this problem we search for a distinguished algebra in $ADT(\Sigma, E)$ consisting just of ground terms. Under certain assumptions, operational semantics provides a method to construct such an algebra.

Let us, more generally, consider a minimal algebra $\boldsymbol{A}$. Then, by Lemma 1, the unique homomorphism $h_A : \boldsymbol{T}_\Sigma \to \boldsymbol{A}$ is surjective. Hence, there is, by the Axiom of Choice, a choice function $f : A \to T_\Sigma$ such that $f \cdot h_A = id_A$. Observe that f is injective. For if $f(a) = f(a')$, then $a = h_A(f(a)) = h_A(f(a')) = a'$. Now define an algebra $\boldsymbol{B}$ with carrier $B = f(A)$ and operations:

$$\sigma^B(b_1, \ldots, b_n) = f(\sigma^A(a_1, \ldots, a_n)) \text{ iff } f(a_i) = b_i \text{ for } i = 1, \ldots, n;$$

for all $\sigma : w \to s$ in Σ and all $(b_1, \ldots b_n) \in B^w$. It is easily seen that f cut down to B, also denoted by f, is the unique isomorphism with $h_B = h_A \cdot f$, where $h_B : \boldsymbol{T}_\Sigma \to$

$\boldsymbol{B}$ is the unique homomorphism, and furthermore, for all $t \in T_\Sigma$, $h_B(t) = t$ iff $t \in B$. Of course, if $h_B(t) = t$, then $t \in B$. Conversely, assume $t \in B$. Then $t = f(h_A(t'))$ for some $t' \in T_\Sigma$ and so $h_B(t) = h_B(f(h_A(t'))) = f(h_A(f(h_A(t')))) = f(h_A(t')) = t$ since $h_A(f(h_A(t'))) = h_A(t')$.

Definition 4. *A minimal algebra $\boldsymbol{A}$ is called a* ***canonical term algebra*** *if the following conditions are fulfilled:*

(1) $A \subseteq T_\Sigma$;

(2) For all $t \in T_\Sigma$, $h_A(t) = t$ *iff* $t \in A$;

(3) For all $\sigma : w \to s$ *in* Σ *and all* $(t_1, \ldots, t_n) \in T_\Sigma^w$, $\sigma t_1 \ldots t_n \in A_s$ *implies* $(t_1, \ldots, t_n) \in A^w$.

Up to isomorphism, any minimal algebra satisfies conditions (1) and (2), whereas condition (3), which expresses closure under subterms, is not so obvious. It requires a suitable choice function.

Recall that every set can be well-ordered by the Principle of Well-Ordering (which is logically equivalent to the Axiom of Choice, see Section 1.3.5). Given a well-order $\leq$ on Σ, its lexical extension to T_Σ, denoted by $\sqsubseteq$, becomes a well-order, too. If $t = \sigma t_1 \ldots t_m$ and $t' = \sigma' t'_1 \ldots t'_n$, then put $t \sqsubset t'$ iff either (1) $|\, t \,|<|\, t' \,|$ or (2) $|\, t \,|=|\, t' \,|$ and either (i) $\sigma < \sigma'$ or (ii) $\sigma = \sigma'$ and $t_1 = t'_1, \ldots, t'_{i-1} = t'_{i-1}$, $t_i \sqsubset t'_i$ for some i with $(1 \leq i \leq m)$; where $|\, t \,|$ is the length of t (i.e., the number of operation symbols in t). Observe that $\sqsubseteq$ is invariant. Therefore we can always assume that there is an invariant well-order on $\boldsymbol{T}_\Sigma$.

Proposition 7. *Every minimal algebra is isomorphic to a canonical term algebra.*

Proof. Let $\boldsymbol{A}$ be a minimal Σ-algebra. Then the unique homomorphism $h_A : \boldsymbol{T}_\Sigma \to \boldsymbol{A}$ is surjective. Given an invariant well-order $\leq$ on $\boldsymbol{T}_\Sigma$, a choice function $f : A \to T_\Sigma$ is defined by the rule: $f(a)$ is the least element of $\{t \in T_\Sigma \mid h_A(t) = a\}$. Of course, $f \cdot h_A = id_A$ and f is injective. Hence $\boldsymbol{A}$ is isomorphic to a minimal Σ-algebra $\boldsymbol{B}$ with $B = f(A)$ such that (1) $B \subseteq T_\Sigma$; and (2) for all $t \in T_\Sigma$, $h_B(t) = t$ iff $t \in B$, by the observation above.

Claim: For all $\sigma : w \to s$ in Σ and all $(t_1, \ldots, t_n) \in T_\Sigma^w$, $h_B(\sigma t_1 \ldots t_n) = \sigma t_1 \ldots t_n$ implies $h_B(t_i) = t_i$ for $i = 1, \ldots, n$.

Assume the contrary, that $h_B(\sigma t_1 \ldots t_n) = \sigma t_1 \ldots t_n$ and $h_B(t_j) < t_j$ for some j. Note that $h_B(t) \neq t$ iff $h_B(t) < t$. Then $\sigma t_1 \ldots h_B(t_j) \ldots t_n < \sigma t_1 \ldots t_j \ldots t_n$, by the invariance of $<$. Since

$$\begin{aligned} h_A(\sigma t_1 \ldots h_B(t_j) \ldots t_n) &= \sigma^A(h_A(t_1), \ldots, h_A(h_B(t_j)), \ldots, h_A(t_n)) \\ &= \sigma^A(h_A(t_1), \ldots, h_A(t_j), \ldots, h_A(t_n)) \\ &= h_A(\sigma t_1 \ldots t_j \ldots t_n) \end{aligned}$$

we derive a contradiction: $h_B(\sigma t_1 \ldots t_n) < \sigma t_1 \ldots t_n$. Now, by (2), condition (3) follows directly. ■

Combining this with Theorem 6 we derive the following conclusion.

Corollary. *Every specification* (Σ, E) *possesses a canonical term algebra in* $ADT(\Sigma, E)$. ■

So, in principle, correctness proofs for initial semantics can be carried out via symbolic calculations in canonical term algebras.

Our next aim is to construct canonical term algebras by means of term rewriting.

Example 1. Consider the specification **natplus** from Example 5 in Section 4.1.2. The **natplus**-algebra $\boldsymbol{A}$ with carrier $A = \{succ^n(zero) \mid n \in \mathbb{N}\}$ and operations, defined by

$$zero^A = zero,$$

$$succ^A(succ^n(zero)) = succ^{n+1}(zero) \text{ for all } n \in \mathbb{N}, \text{ and}$$

$$succ^m(zero) +^A succ^n(zero) = succ^{m+n}(zero) \text{ for all } m, n \in \mathbb{N},$$

is a canonical term algebra.

The unique homomorphism h_A maps a ground **natplus**-term t to $succ^n(zero)$ iff t contains n times $succ$.

The specification **natplus** determines a (one-sorted) term rewriting system R consisting of the reduction rules:

$$zero + x \to x.$$

$$succ(x) + y \to succ(x + y).$$

R is terminating, as one may prove using the following polynomial interpretation (see Section 2.2.4):

$$I(zero) = 2,$$

$$I(succ(x)) = 2x,$$

$$I(x + y) = x^2 y.$$

R is locally confluent since there is no critical pair. Hence R is confluent.

Every **natplus**-term t has a normal form, say $nf_R(t)$. It is easily seen that $succ^n(zero)$, $n \in I\!N$, are the normal forms of ground **natplus**-terms. That is, $h_A(t) = nf_R(t)$ for all $t \in T_{natplus}$ and $A = \{nf_R(t) \mid t \in T_{\mathbf{natplus}}\}$. ■

A (many-sorted) ***term rewriting system*** (TRS) R is given by $R = (R(X) \mid X$ is a finite subset of $V)$ with $R(X) = (R(X)_s \mid s \in S)$ an S-sorted relation on $T_\Sigma(X)$. The elements of $R(X)_s$ are called ***reduction rules*** (of sort s with variable declaration X). Instead of $(t, t') \in R(X)_s$ we shall write $(X, t \to t')_s$ or, $(X, t \to t')$ for short. The associated ***term reduction***, denoted by $\to_R$, is defined as follows: $\to_R = (\to_{R(X)} \mid X$ is a finite subset of $V)$ with $\to_{R(X)} = (\to_{R(X),s} \mid s \in S)$ and, for all $t, t' \in T_\Sigma(X)_s$, $t \to_{R(X),s} t'$ iff there exists a substitution $f : Y \to T_\Sigma(X)$, an address u of t and a reduction rule $(Y, t_1 \to t_2)$ in R such that $t/u = f^\#(t_1)$ and $t' = t[u/f^\#(t_2)]$.

For notational simplicity we shall write $(X, t \to_R t')_s$ or even $(X, t \to_R t')$ instead of $t \to_{R(X),s} t'$.

Example 2. Let us be given a signature

$$
\begin{aligned}
\textbf{sig} = \ & \text{sorts: } fool \\
& \qquad\quad\ \ bool \\
\\
& \text{opns: } 0, 1 : bool \\
& \qquad\quad\ \ f : fool \to bool \\
& \qquad\quad\ \ \neg : bool \to bool \\
& \qquad\quad\ \ \vee, \wedge : bool\ bool \to bool.
\end{aligned}
$$

Consider the TRS R consisting of the reduction rules (R1) to (R7):

(R1) $(\emptyset, \neg 0 \to 1)$,

(R2) $(\emptyset, \neg 1 \to 0)$,

(R3) $(x : bool, x \vee \neg x \to 1)$,

(R4) $(x : bool, x \wedge \neg x \to 0)$,

(R5) $(x : bool, x \vee x \to x)$,

(R6) $(x : bool, x \wedge x \to x)$,

(R7) $(x : fool, \neg f(x) \to f(x))$.

Then, for instance, we obtain

(1) $(x : fool, f(x) \wedge \neg f(x) \to_R^* f(x))$,

(2) $(x : fool, f(x) \wedge \neg f(x) \to_R^* 0)$,

(3) $(x : fool, f(x) \vee \neg f(x) \to_R^* f(x))$,

(4) $(x : fool, f(x) \vee \neg f(x) \rightarrow^*_R 1)$

and hence $(x : fool, 0 \leftrightarrow^*_R 1)$. ■

Let R be a complete TRS. By $nf_R(t)$ we denote the normal form of t. R determines an algebra $\boldsymbol{A}$ with carrier $A = \{nf_R(t) \mid t \in T_\Sigma\}$ and operations:

$$\sigma^A(t_1, \ldots, t_n) = nf_R(\sigma t_1 \ldots t_n)$$

for all $\sigma : w \to s$ in Σ and all $(t_1, \ldots t_n) \in A^w$. Evidently, $\boldsymbol{A}$ is a canonical term algebra, often called the ***normal form algebra*** of R.

By analogy with the one-sorted case, any set E of equations can be thought of as a TRS $\overline{E}$ such that

$$(X, t \to t') \in \overline{E} \text{ iff } \forall X(t = t') \in E.$$

Definition 5. *Given a specification (Σ, E), the related TRS $\overline{E}$ is called the* ***operational semantics*** *of (Σ, E).*

If the operational semantics $\overline{E}$ of a specification (Σ, E) is complete, the normal form algebra of $\overline{E}$ will be denoted by $NFA(\Sigma, E)$.

Theorem 8. *Let (Σ, E) be a specification. If the operational semantics of (Σ, E) is complete, then the normal form algebra $NFA(\Sigma, E)$ of (Σ, E) is isomorphic to $\boldsymbol{T}_{(\Sigma,E)}$. That is, $NFA(\Sigma, E)$ belongs to $ADT(\Sigma, E)$.*

Proof. Assume that the operational semantics $\overline{E}$ of (Σ, E) is complete. Let h be the unique homomorphism from $\boldsymbol{T}_\Sigma$ to $NFA(\Sigma, E)$. Recall that $h(t) = nf_{\overline{E}}(t)$ for all $t \in T_\Sigma$. Now it is important to observe that $NFA(\Sigma, E)$ is isomorphic to $\boldsymbol{T}_{(\Sigma,E)}$ whenever, for all $t, t' \in T_\Sigma$, $t =_{G(E)} t'$ iff $nf_{\overline{E}}(t) = nf_{\overline{E}}(t')$. Since $\overline{E}$ is assumed to be complete, $nf_{\overline{E}}(t) = nf_{\overline{E}}(t')$ iff $(\emptyset, t \leftrightarrow^*_{\overline{E}} t')$ for all $t, t' \in T_\Sigma$. But, by definition, $\leftrightarrow^*_{\overline{E}(\emptyset)}$ coincides with $=_{G(E)}$, which completes the proof. ■

Operational semantics serves as a method for implementing a specification by interpreting it as a term rewriting system (where a direction to equations may be imposed automatically). If the operational semantics of a specification (Σ, E) is complete or can be completed, for instance, by the Knuth-Bendix Procedure, ground terms are executable in the normal form algebra $NFA(\Sigma, E)$. Such an interpretation is a useful tool for early prototyping (see, e.g., /Drosten-89/).

4.2 Algebraic Semantics of Recursive Program Schemes

In order to define semantics of recursive program schemes we need ω-complete ordered algebras. The development of their theory is divided into three steps.

In Section 4.2.1, we introduce ordered algebras. Classes of ordered algebras definable by inequalities are characterized as order varieties generalizing Birkhoff's Variety Theorem. The existence of free ordered algebras is investigated and, finally, a completeness result of the logic of inequalities is derived.

Section 4.2.2 is concerned with the role of a least element in ordered algebras.

Section 4.2.3 deals with ω-complete ordered algebras. A variety result and an existence criterion for free ω-complete ordered algebras are obtained; but no related logic is available.

In the last Section 4.2.4, we study the semantics of recursive program schemes without parameters by means of fixpoint techniques.

4.2.1 Ordered Algebras

In this section, Birkhoff's theory is generalized to (one-sorted) ordered algebras, which are algebras equipped with a partial order such that all operations are order-preserving. It should be intuitively clear that equations as basic formulas have to be replaced by inequalities. Hence, more precisely speaking, the following two fundamental problems for ordered algebras will be solved. First, abstract classes of ordered algebras defined by sets of inequalities will be characterized in terms of closure operators similarly as in Birkhoff's Variety Theorem; and, second, an algebraic criterion for theories of inequalities will be derived.

Let us recall some basic notions for convenience. A partial order on a set A is a reflexive, transitive and antisymmetric relation on A, while a quasi-order on A is a reflexive and transitive relation on A. A set together with a partial order on it is said to be a poset. Given posets A and B, a mapping $f : A \to B$ is called monotone (order-preserving) if, for all $x, y \in A$, $x \leq y$ implies $f(x) \leq f(y)$. We say that f is a full monotone mapping if $x \leq y$ iff $f(x) \leq f(y)$ for all $x, y \in A$. Note that any full monotone mapping is an injection. In what follows a (one-sorted) signature Σ will be fixed; and we will simply speak of an algebra instead of a Σ-algebra.

Definition 1. *An algebra is called an* ***ordered algebra*** *if its carrier is a poset and all its operations are monotone in each argument.*

A partial order $\leq$ on A extends coordinatewise to each finite power A^n. If $(x_1, \ldots, x_n)$ and $(y_1, \ldots, y_n)$ are in A^n, then $(x_1, \ldots, x_n) \leq (y_1, \ldots, y_n)$ iff $x_i \leq y_i$ for all $i = 1, \ldots, n$. Hence, each n-ary operation in an ordered algebra is a monotone mapping from A^n to A.

The partial order in an ordered algebra will always be denoted by $\leq$ when the context makes it clear which algebra is being discussed; otherwise superscripts will be used to avoid confusion so that, e.g., $\leq^A$ is the partial order in $\boldsymbol{A}$.

Example 1. Every algebra $\boldsymbol{A}$ can be thought of as an ordered algebra if the identity relation of A is taken as the partial order. Then we say that $\boldsymbol{A}$ is ***trivially ordered*** or that $\boldsymbol{A}$ is a ***discrete algebra.*** ■

Example 2. Any lattice $(A; \vee, \wedge)$ is an ordered algebra under the induced partial order: $x \leq y$ iff $x \wedge y = x$ for all $x, y \in A$. ■

Example 3. The semiring of natural numbers is an ordered algebra with respect to the usual order on $\mathbb{N}$. ■

Definition 2. *Given two ordered algebras* $\boldsymbol{A}$ *and* $\boldsymbol{B}$, *a (full) monotone homomorphism from* $\boldsymbol{A}$ *to* $\boldsymbol{B}$ *is called* ***(full) morphism*** [2].

Two ordered algebras $\boldsymbol{A}$ and $\boldsymbol{B}$ are said to be ***isomorphic*** if there is a bijection h from A to B such that h and h^{-1} are morphisms; h is then called an ***isomorphism.*** Note that a surjective morphism h is an isomorphism iff h is a full morphism.

If $\boldsymbol{B}$ is an ordered algebra, then each subalgebra $\boldsymbol{A}$ of $\boldsymbol{B}$ is ordered, when the partial order in $\boldsymbol{A}$ is the restriction of the partial order in $\boldsymbol{B}$ (i.e., for all $x, y \in A$, $x \leq^A y$ iff $x \leq^B y$). The embedding of $\boldsymbol{A}$ into $\boldsymbol{B}$ is obviously a full morphism.

Let $\boldsymbol{A}$ and $\boldsymbol{B}$ be ordered algebras, $\boldsymbol{B}$ is called an ***ordered image*** [3] of $\boldsymbol{A}$ if there is a surjective morphism from $\boldsymbol{A}$ to $\boldsymbol{B}$.

Given an abstract class $\mathcal{K}$ of ordered algebras, $\mathbf{S}\mathcal{K}$ and $\mathbf{H}_0\mathcal{K}$ denote the abstract class of all subalgebras of algebras in $\mathcal{K}$ and all ordered images of algebras in $\mathcal{K}$, respectively. Note that an ordered algebra $\boldsymbol{A}$ belongs to $\mathbf{S}\mathcal{K}$ iff there is a full morphism from $\boldsymbol{A}$ to some algebra in $\mathcal{K}$; while $\boldsymbol{A} \in \mathbf{H}_0\mathcal{K}$ iff there is a surjective morphism from $\boldsymbol{A}$ to some algebra in $\mathcal{K}$.

Example 4. Consider the abstract class $\mathcal{K}$ of all ordered algebras with a least element. $\mathcal{K}$ is closed neither under subalgebras nor under ordered images. ■

Example 5. The abstract class of all ordered semirings is closed under subalgebras and ordered images. ■

In order to prevent set theoretic difficulties when dealing with ordered images we must make sure that all ordered images of a given ordered algebra form a set, not a proper class. As for ordinary algebras, ordered images are internally describable by quotients.

Definition 3. *Let* $\boldsymbol{A}$ *be an ordered algebra. An admissible quasi-order* $\lesssim$ *on* A *is called a* ***quasi-congruence*** *if all operations in* $\boldsymbol{A}$ *are also monotone with respect to* $\lesssim$.

---

[2] The notion of a "morphism" is borrowed from category theory.

[3] Again, we simply speak of an ordered image instead of an ordered homomorphic image.

That is, for all n-nary operation symbols σ in Σ and all $(x_1, \ldots, x_n)$, $(y_1, \ldots, y_n)$ in A^n, $(x_1, \ldots, x_n) \lesssim (y_1, \ldots, y_n)$ implies $\sigma^A(x_1, \ldots, x_n) \lesssim \sigma^A(y_1, \ldots, y_n)$.

It is easily seen that any quasi-congruence $\lesssim$ on $\boldsymbol{A}$ induces a congruence $\sim = \lesssim \cap \gtrsim$, and hence the quotient poset $A/\lesssim$ is actually an algebra. This leads to the following definition.

Definition 4. *Let $\boldsymbol{A}$ be an ordered algebra. If $\lesssim$ is a quasi-congruence on $\boldsymbol{A}$, then $\boldsymbol{A}/\lesssim$ is called an* ***ordered quotient algebra*** *of $\boldsymbol{A}$ modulo $\lesssim$.*

Of course, all ordered quotient algebras of $\boldsymbol{A}$ form a set since there is only a set of quasi-congruences on $\boldsymbol{A}$.

If $\mathcal{K}$ is an abstract class of ordered algebras, then $\mathbf{Q}_0\mathcal{K}$ denotes the abstract class of all ordered quotient algebras of algebras in $\mathcal{K}$. Note that $\mathbf{Q}_0\mathcal{K} \subseteq \mathbf{H}_0\mathcal{K}$ since any ordered quotient algebra $\boldsymbol{A}/\lesssim$ of $\boldsymbol{A}$ is an ordered image of $\boldsymbol{A}$; indeed, $nat : \boldsymbol{A} \to \boldsymbol{A}/\lesssim$ is a surjective morphism.

To show the opposite inclusion we generalize the Homomorphism Theorem (Theorem 2 in Section 3.1.2). For that purpose ordered kernels are used. Let $\boldsymbol{A}$ and $\boldsymbol{B}$ be ordered algebras. If h is a morphism from $\boldsymbol{A}$ to $\boldsymbol{B}$, then $ker_{\leq}h = \{(x,y) \in A \times A \mid h(x) \leq h(y)\}$ is a quasi-congruence on $\boldsymbol{A}$.

Proposition 1. *Let $\boldsymbol{A}$ and $\boldsymbol{B}$ be ordered algebras. If $h : \boldsymbol{A} \to \boldsymbol{B}$ is a surjective morphism, then $\boldsymbol{B}$ is isomorphic to $\boldsymbol{A}/ker_{\leq}h$.* ■

Hence $\mathbf{H}_0\mathcal{K} \subseteq \mathbf{Q}_0\mathcal{K}$ for any abstract class $\mathcal{K}$ of ordered algebras which yields $\mathbf{H}_0\mathcal{K} = \mathbf{Q}_0\mathcal{K}$ and gives a solution to the set theoretic problem mentioned above.

For our approach we need later the unique factorization of morphisms similar to the image factorization of ordinary algebras.

Proposition 2 (Ordered Image Factorization). *Every morphism h admits a factorization $h = f \cdot g$, where f is a surjective morphism and g is a full morphism. This factorization is unique in the following sense. If $h = f' \cdot g'$ is another factorization with f' a surjective morphism and g' a full morphism, then there exists a unique morphism d such that $f \cdot d = f'$ and $d \cdot g' = g$.*

Proof. Let $\boldsymbol{A}$ and $\boldsymbol{B}$ be ordered algebras. Any morphism h from $\boldsymbol{A}$ to $\boldsymbol{B}$ factorizes through the quotient algebra $\boldsymbol{A}/ker_{\leq}h$. That is, $h = nat \cdot g$ with $g : \boldsymbol{A}/ker_{\leq}h \to \boldsymbol{B}$ defined as follows: $g([x]) = h(x)$ for all $x \in A$. Note that g is well-defined. For if $[x] = [y]$, then $(x,y) \in ker_{\leq}h$ and $(y,x) \in ker_{\leq}h$, i.e., $h(x) \leq h(y)$ and $h(y) \leq h(x)$, hence $h(x) = h(y)$. Conversely, $h(x) = h(y)$ implies $[x] = [y]$. Thus g is, indeed, a full monotone mapping. Evidently, g is a homomorphism since h is so. Hence h admits a factorization into a surjective morphism followed by a full morphism.

Now it remains to show the uniqueness of such factorizations. Therefore suppose $f : \boldsymbol{A} \to \boldsymbol{C}$, $f' : \boldsymbol{A} \to \boldsymbol{C}'$ are surjective morphisms and $g : \boldsymbol{C} \to \boldsymbol{B}$, $g' : \boldsymbol{C}' \to \boldsymbol{B}$ are full morphisms such that $f \cdot g = f' \cdot g'$. Since f is assumed to be surjective we can define a mapping $d : C \to C'$ by $d(c) = f'(a)$ for all $c \in C$ such that $f(a) = c$ for some $a \in A$. It is easily seen that d is a morphism with $f \cdot d = f'$ and $d \cdot g' = g$. Furthermore, d is uniquely determined by the surjectivity of f (or the injectivity of g'). ■

Given a family $(\boldsymbol{A}_i \mid i \in I)$ of ordered algebras, the direct product $\prod(\boldsymbol{A}_i \mid i \in I)$ is again an ordered algebra under coordinatewise order. That is, $(x_i \mid i \in I) \leq (y_i \mid i \in I)$ iff $x_i \leq y_i$ for all $i \in I$.

If $\mathcal{K}$ is an abstract class of ordered algebras, $\mathbf{P}\mathcal{K}$ denotes the abstract class of all (ordered) direct products of families of algebras in $\mathcal{K}$.

Definition 5. *An abstract class $\mathcal{K}$ of ordered algebras is called an* ***order variety*** *if $\mathcal{K}$ is closed under subalgebras, ordered images and direct products.*

Now we have to introduce our basic formulas by which a model theoretic characterization of order varieties can be obtained.

Definition 6. *An* ***inequality*** *is a triple (X, t, t') consisting of a finite set X and terms $t, t' \in T_\Sigma(X)$, usually written*

$$\forall X(t \leq t')$$

or $\forall x_1, \ldots, x_n(t \leq t')$ if $X = \{x_1, \ldots, x_n\}$.

An inequality $\forall X(t \leq t')$ is ***valid*** in an ordered algebra $\boldsymbol{A}$, in symbols

$$\boldsymbol{A} \models \forall X(t \leq t'),$$

if $\alpha^{\#}(t) \leq \alpha^{\#}(t')$ for all assignements α from X to $\boldsymbol{A}$. If $\mathcal{K}$ is an abstract class of ordered algebras, $\mathcal{K} \models \forall X(t \leq t')$ means that $\boldsymbol{A} \models \forall X(t \leq t')$ for all $\boldsymbol{A}$ in $\mathcal{K}$.

Let E be a set of inequalities. An ordered algebra $\boldsymbol{A}$ validates E, denoted $\boldsymbol{A} \models E$, if each inequality of E is valid in $\boldsymbol{A}$. In this case we say that $\boldsymbol{A}$ is an ***ordered model*** of E. $Mod_0 E$ denotes the abstract class of all ordered algebras which are ordered models of E. An abstract class $\mathcal{K}$ of ordered algebras is said to be ***definable by inequalties*** if $\mathcal{K} = Mod_0 E$ for some set E of inequalities.

Example 6. The abstract class $\mathcal{K}$ of all lattices, considered as ordered algebras, is definable as the model class of the following six inequalities:

(L1) $\forall x(x \vee x \leq x)$,

(L2) $\forall x, y(x \leq x \vee y)$,

(L3) $\forall x, y(x \vee y \leq y \vee x)$,

(L4) $\forall x(x \leq x \wedge x)$,

(L5) $\forall x, y(x \wedge y \leq x)$,

(L6) $\forall x, y(x \wedge y \leq y \wedge x)$.

It suffices to show that in any model $\boldsymbol{A}$ of the inequalities (L1) to (L6), $a \vee b$ is the supremum of $\{a, b\}$ and $a \wedge b$ is the infimum of $\{a, b\}$ for all $a, b \in A$. We prove only $a \vee b = \sup\{a, b\}$. By (L2) and (L3), $a \vee b$ is an upper bound of $\{a, b\}$ since $a \leq a \vee b$ and $b \leq b \vee a \leq a \vee b$. If c is another upper bound of $\{a, b\}$, i.e., $a \leq c$ and $b \leq c$, then $a \vee b \leq c \vee c$, by the assumption that $\boldsymbol{A}$ is an ordered algebra. Now, by (L1), $a \vee b \leq c$. Thus $a \vee b$ is the least upper bound of $\{a, b\}$. ■

Proposition 3. *If E is a set of inequalities, then $Mod_0 E$ is an order variety.*

Proof. Let E be a set of inequalities. We have to show that $Mod_0 E$ is closed under subalgebras, ordered images and direct products. The proofs of closure under subalgebras and direct products are omitted; they are similar to the usual case.

Proving that $Mod_0 E$ is closed under ordered images is the same as proving that $Mod_0 E$ is closed under ordered quotient algebras. Let $\boldsymbol{A}$ be an ordered model of E and assume that $\lesssim$ is a quasi-congruence on $\boldsymbol{A}$. For each inequality $\forall X(t \leq t')$ of E, we have to verify $\boldsymbol{A}/\lesssim \models \forall X(t \leq t')$. If β is any assignmnet from X to $\boldsymbol{A}/\lesssim$, then there is an assignment α from X to $\boldsymbol{A}$ such that $\beta = \alpha \cdot nat$ since the natural morphism $nat : \boldsymbol{A} \to \boldsymbol{A}/\lesssim$ is a surjection. Because $\beta^{\#} = \alpha^{\#} \cdot nat$, $\beta^{\#}(t) \lesssim \beta^{\#}(t')$ iff $nat(\alpha^{\#}(t)) \lesssim nat(\alpha^{\#}(t'))$ iff $\alpha^{\#}(t) \lesssim \alpha^{\#}(t')$. By the assumption $\boldsymbol{A} \models \forall X(t \leq t')$, $\alpha^{\#}(t) \leq \alpha^{\#}(t')$ holds and hence $\alpha^{\#}(t) \lesssim \alpha^{\#}(t')$ since $\lesssim$ is admissible for $\leq$, which proves $\boldsymbol{A}/\lesssim \models \forall X(t \leq t')$. ■

Our next aim is to prove the converse implication. Free algebras are used.

Let $\mathcal{K}$ be any abstract class of ordered algebras. We say that an ordered algebra $\boldsymbol{F}$ is ***free in*** $\mathcal{K}$ over a set X if (1) $\boldsymbol{F}$ belongs to $\mathcal{K}$; (2) X is a subset of F (possibly under a suitable identification); and (3) every mapping α from X to any ordered algebra $\boldsymbol{A}$ in $\mathcal{K}$ admits a unique extension to a morphism $\alpha^* : \boldsymbol{F} \to \boldsymbol{A}$. If a free ordered algebra over X exists in $\mathcal{K}$, it is unique up to isomorphism; and will be denoted by $\boldsymbol{F}_{\mathcal{K}}(X)_0$. We call $\boldsymbol{F}_{\mathcal{K}}(X)_0$ the ***absolutely free ordered algebra*** over X if $\mathcal{K}$ is the class of all ordered algebras.

Theorem 4. *The discrete term algebras are the absolutely free ordered algebras.* ■

The simple proof is omitted. It follows directly from the fact that $\boldsymbol{T}_{\Sigma}(X)$ is the absolutely free algebra over X in conjunction with the observation that any homomorphism from a discrete algebra to an ordered one is always a morphism.

As in the ordinary case sur-reflections will be used to guarantee the existence of free ordered algebras under suitable conditions. Let $\mathcal{K}$ be an abstract class of ordered algebras. An algebra $\boldsymbol{A}$ admits a ***sur-reflection*** in $\mathcal{K}$ when every morphism h from $\boldsymbol{A}$ to any algebra $\boldsymbol{B}$ in $\mathcal{K}$ factorizes uniquely through an ordered image $\boldsymbol{R}$ of $\boldsymbol{A}$ in $\mathcal{K}$: $h = r \cdot h^*$ where $r : \boldsymbol{A} \to \boldsymbol{R}$ is the surjective morphism related to the ordered image $\boldsymbol{R}$ of $\boldsymbol{A}$ and $h^* : \boldsymbol{R} \to \boldsymbol{B}$ is a morphism, which exists uniquely. The sur-reflection of $\boldsymbol{A}$ in $\mathcal{K}$, if it exists, is denoted by $\boldsymbol{R}_{\mathcal{K}}(\boldsymbol{A})$. Note that $\boldsymbol{R}_{\mathcal{K}}(\boldsymbol{A})$ is uniquely determined up to isomorphism. $\mathcal{K}$ is called ***sur-reflective*** if any algebra admits a sur-reflection in $\mathcal{K}$. In a straightforward manner we are able to generalize the characterization of sur-reflective classes of algebras (see Theorem 13 in Section 3.3.2): An abstract class $\mathcal{K}$ of ordered algebras is sur-reflective iff $\mathcal{K}$ is closed under subalgebras and direct products.

Theorem 5 (Existence of Free Ordered Algebras). *Let $\mathcal{K}$ be a nontrivial abstract class of ordered algebras. If $\mathcal{K}$ is closed under subalgebras and direct products, then free ordered algebras exist in $\mathcal{K}$.*

Proof. Assume $\mathcal{K}$ is a nontrivial abstract class of ordered algebras closed under subalgebras and direct products. If $\mathcal{K}$ is the class of all ordered algebras, then $\boldsymbol{T}_\Sigma(X)$ is the free ordered algebra in $\mathcal{K}$ over any set X, by Theorem 4. Now, let $\mathcal{K}$ be any subclass with the properties required above. Consider the sur-reflection of $\boldsymbol{T}_\Sigma(X)$ in $\mathcal{K}$, $r : \boldsymbol{T}_\Sigma(X) \to \boldsymbol{R}_{\mathcal{K}}(\boldsymbol{T}_\Sigma(X))$.

Claim: $\boldsymbol{R}_{\mathcal{K}}(\boldsymbol{T}_\Sigma(X))$ is the free ordered algebra over X in $\mathcal{K}$.

We have to verify the three defining conditions stated earlier. By definition, $\boldsymbol{R}_{\mathcal{K}}(\boldsymbol{T}_\Sigma(X))$ belongs to $\mathcal{K}$; hence condition (1) of a free ordered algebra X is satisfied.

Denote by $\varphi : X \to \boldsymbol{R}_{\mathcal{K}}(\boldsymbol{T}_\Sigma(X))$ the restriction of r to X. We must show that φ is injective. By assumption, $\mathcal{K}$ contains a nontrivial ordered algebra, say $\boldsymbol{A}$, with at least two different elements. If φ were not injective, then $\varphi(x) = \varphi(y)$ for two elements x, y of X such that $x \neq y$. Take a mapping α from X to A with $\alpha(x) \neq \alpha(y)$, which is possible because A has two different elements. The homomorphic extension $\alpha^\# : \boldsymbol{T}_\Sigma(X) \to \boldsymbol{A}$ of α, which is, indeed, a morphism, factorizes through the sur-reflection of $\boldsymbol{A}$: $\alpha^\# = r \cdot \alpha^*$ where $\alpha^* : \boldsymbol{R}_{\mathcal{K}}(\boldsymbol{T}_\Sigma(X)) \to \boldsymbol{A}$. Hence $\alpha = in_X \cdot r \cdot \alpha^* = \varphi \cdot \alpha^*$, where in_X is the inclusion of X in $T_\Sigma(X)$. This yields a contradiction: $\alpha(x) = \alpha^*(\varphi(x)) = \alpha^*(\varphi(y)) = \alpha(y)$. Thus φ is an injection and X can be regarded as a subset of $\boldsymbol{R}_{\mathcal{K}}(\boldsymbol{T}_\Sigma(X))$. That is, condition (2) of a free ordered algebra is satisfied.

It remains to prove that condition (3) of a free ordered algebra is also fulfilled. Let α be a mapping from X to any algebra $\boldsymbol{A}$ in $\mathcal{K}$. As shown above, α admits a unique homomorphic extension $\alpha^\# : \boldsymbol{T}_\Sigma(X) \to \boldsymbol{A}$ such that $\alpha = in_X \cdot \alpha^\#$, In fact, $\alpha^\#$ is a morphism since $\boldsymbol{T}_\Sigma(X)$ is trivially ordered. Now, by the definition of sur-reflection, $\alpha^\#$ has a unique factorization $\alpha^\# = r \cdot \alpha^*$ with $\alpha^* : \boldsymbol{R}_{\mathcal{K}}(\boldsymbol{T}_\Sigma(X)) \to \boldsymbol{A}$, which results in $\alpha = in_X \cdot r \cdot \alpha^* = \varphi \cdot \alpha^*$. ■

We are now going to solve our first main problem mentioned at the beginning. Therefore we still have to show that every order variety is definable by inequalities. Since in any inequality only finitely many variables are involved, a countably infinite set of variables, say V, is sufficient. Let $\mathcal{K}$ be an abstract class of ordered algebras. The set of all inequalities $\forall X(t \leq t')$ with $X \subseteq V$, which are valid in $\mathcal{K}$ is denoted by $Ineq\mathcal{K}$. It is obvious that $Ineq$ and Mod_0 form a Galois connection. That is,

(1a) $\mathcal{K} \subseteq Mod_0 Ineq\mathcal{K}$ for any abstract class $\mathcal{K}$ or ordered algebras;

(1b) $E \subseteq IneqMod_0 E$ for any set of inequalities;

(2a) For any pair of abstract classes $\mathcal{K}$ and $\mathcal{K}'$ of ordered algebras, $Mod_0\mathcal{K} \subseteq Mod_0\mathcal{K}'$ whenever $\mathcal{K}' \subseteq \mathcal{K}$;

(2b) For any pair of of sets E and E' of inequalities, $IneqE \subseteq IneqE'$ whenever $E' \subseteq E$.

Theorem 6 (Bloom's Order Variety Theorem). *Let $\mathcal{K}$ be an abstract class of ordered algebras. Then $\mathcal{K}$ is definable by inequalities if and only if $\mathcal{K}$ is an order variety.*

Proof. By Proposition 3, we have only to show that any order variety $\mathcal{K}$ is definable by inequalities. Let E be the set of all inequalities valid in $\mathcal{K}$, i.e., $E = Ineq\mathcal{K}$. Evidently, $\mathcal{K}$ is a subclass of $Mod_0 E$. We want, however, to prove $\mathcal{K} = Mod_0 E$ since then, by definition, $\mathcal{K}$ is definable by inequalities.

To verify the remaining inclusion, $Mod_0 E \subseteq \mathcal{K}$, assume that $\boldsymbol{A}$ is an ordered model of E. There is a surjective morphism from $\boldsymbol{T}_\Sigma(A)$ to $\boldsymbol{A}$, namely $id_A^\# : \boldsymbol{T}_\Sigma(A) \to \boldsymbol{A}$, the extension of the identity mapping $id_A : A \to A$. By Theorem 5, the free ordered algebra $\boldsymbol{F}_\mathcal{K}(A)_0$ exists in $\mathcal{K}$ with $r : \boldsymbol{T}_\Sigma(A) \to \boldsymbol{F}_\mathcal{K}(A)_0$ the related surjective reflection morphism.

It suffices to establish a factorization of $id_A^\#$ through $\boldsymbol{F}_\mathcal{K}(A)_0$, say $id_A^\# = r \cdot h$ with $h : \boldsymbol{F}_\mathcal{K}(A)_0 \to \boldsymbol{A}$. Since h is then surjective, $\boldsymbol{A}$ is an ordered image of $\boldsymbol{F}_\mathcal{K}(A)_0$; hence $\boldsymbol{A}$ belongs to $\mathcal{K}$.

It is easily seen that h exists iff $ker_{\leq} r \subseteq ker_{\leq} id_A^\#$. Let $t, t' \in T_\Sigma(X)$ with $X = var(t) \cup var(t')$. Suppose $(t, t') \in ker_{\leq} r$. Then $r(t) \leq r(t')$. Hence $\forall X(t \leq t')$ is valid in $\boldsymbol{F}_\mathcal{K}(A)_0$ and, consequently, valid in $\mathcal{K}$. By assumption, $\boldsymbol{A}$ validates $\forall X(t \leq t')$, too, which implies $id_A^\#(t) \leq id_A^\#(t')$ and therefore $(t, t') \in ker_{\leq} id_A^\#$. Thus $Mod_0 E$ is included in $\mathcal{K}$, which completes the proof. ■

Our next aim is the algebraic characterization of theories of inequalities. Let E be a set of inequalities. We call an inequality $\forall X(t \leq t')$ a ***logical consequence*** of E, in symbols $E \models_0 \forall X(t \leq t')$, if $Mod_0 E \models \forall X(t \leq t')$.

Definition 7. *A set E of inequalities is called an* ***order theory*** *if E is closed under logical consequences, i.e., $\forall X(t \leq t') \in E$ whenever $E \models_0 \forall X(t \leq t')$ for any inequality $\forall X(t \leq t')$.*

The analogy with theories studied so far is presented in the following lemma.

Lemma 7. *A set of inequalities is an order theory iff $E = Ineq\mathcal{K}$ for some abstract class $\mathcal{K}$ of ordered algebras.*

Proof. If E is an order theory, then $IneqMod_0 E \subseteq E$ by definition. Combining this with the converse inclusion, $E \subseteq IneqMod_0 E$, which holds for any set E of inequalities, we derive $E = IneqMod_0 E$.

Conversely, if $E = Ineq\mathcal{K}$ for some abstract class $\mathcal{K}$ of ordered algebras, then $E = IneqMod_0 E$ since $E = Ineq\mathcal{K} = IneqMod_0 Ineq\mathcal{K}$; hence E is an order theory. ■

To characterize order theories we will use quasi-congruences. Similar to congruences, a quasi-congruence $\lesssim$ on an ordered algebra $\boldsymbol{A}$ is fully invariant iff $\lesssim$ is stable. That is, for all $x, y \in A$ and all morphisms $h : \boldsymbol{A} \to \boldsymbol{A}$, $x \lesssim y$ implies $h(x) \lesssim h(y)$. The set of all fully invariant quasi-congruences on an ordered algebra forms a closure system. Therefore, fully invariant quasi-congruences can be generated by arbitrary relations.

Any set E of inequalities can be thought of as a relation $\overline{E}$ on $T_\Sigma(V)$, where $\overline{E} = \{(t, t') \mid \forall X(t \leq t') \in E\}$. Let $\lesssim_E$ denote the fully invariant quasi-congruence on $\boldsymbol{T}_\Sigma(V)$ generated by $\overline{E}$.

Proposition 8. *If E is an order theory of inequalities, then $\overline{E}$ is a fully invariant quasi-congruence on $\boldsymbol{T}_\Sigma(V)$. That is, $\lesssim_E = \overline{E}$.*

Proof. Let E be an order theory of inequalities.

(1) $\overline{E}$ is an admissible quasi-order:

The admissibililty of $\overline{E}$ is obvious since $\boldsymbol{T}_\Sigma(V)$ is trivially ordered. Evidently, $\overline{E}$ is reflexive because $E \models \forall X(t \leq t)$ for all $t \in T_\Sigma(V)$, where $X = var(t)$, hence $(t, t) \in \overline{E}$ by the assumption that E is an order theory. To show that $\overline{E}$ is transitive we assume $(t, t') \in \overline{E}$ and $(t', t'') \in \overline{E}$, i.e., $\forall X(t \leq t') \in E$ and $\forall Y(t' \leq t'') \in E$, where $X = var(t) \cup var(t')$ and $Y = var(t') \cup var(t'')$. Now it suffices to prove that $\forall Z(t \leq t'')$ is a logical consequence of E, where $Z = var(t) \cup var(t'')$. Let $\boldsymbol{A}$ be any ordered model of E. Consider an arbitrary assignment $\alpha : V \to A$. Then, by assumption, $\alpha^\#(t) \leq \alpha^\#(t')$ and $\alpha^\#(t') \leq \alpha^\#(t'')$ and hence $\alpha^\#(t) \leq \alpha^\#(t'')$. That is, $\boldsymbol{A} \models \forall Z(t \leq t'')$ and consequently $Mod_0 E \models \forall Z(t \leq t'')$. Thus $\forall Z(t \leq t'')$ is a logical consequence of E and so $(t, t'') \in \overline{E}$, by the assumption that E is an order theory.

(2) $\overline{E}$ is compatible with the operations:

Let σ be any n-ary operation symbol and suppose $(t_i, t_i') \in \overline{E}$ for $i = 1, \ldots, n$. Then, by definition, $\forall X_i(t_i \leq t_i') \in E$ for $i = 1, \ldots, n$, where $X_i = var(t_i) \cup var(t_i')$. Now consider any model $\boldsymbol{A}$ of E. If $\alpha : V \to A$ is an arbitrary assignment, then $\alpha^\#(t_i) \leq \alpha^\#(t_i')$ for $i = 1, \ldots, n$; hence $\alpha^\#(\sigma t_1 \ldots t_n) \leq \alpha^\#(\sigma t_1' \ldots t_n')$. That is, $A \models \forall X(\sigma t_1 \ldots t_n \leq \sigma t_1' \ldots t_n')$ with $X = \bigcup(X_i \mid i = 1, \ldots, n)$ and consequently

$Mod_0E \models \forall X(\sigma t_1 \dots t_n \leq \sigma t'_1 \dots t'_n)$. Thus $\forall X(\sigma t_1 \dots t_n \leq \sigma t'_1 \dots t'_n)$ is a logical consequence of E and so $(\sigma t_1 \dots t_n, \sigma t'_1 \dots t'_n) \in \overline{E}$, by the assumption that E is an order theory

(3) $\overline{E}$ is fully invariant:

Let $(t, t') \in \overline{E}$. By definition, $\forall X(t \leq t') \in E$ with $X = var(t) \cup var(t')$. Consider any ordered model $\boldsymbol{A}$ of E and suppose $\alpha : V \to A$ is an arbitrary assignment. Every morphism $h : \boldsymbol{T}_\Sigma(V) \to \boldsymbol{T}_\Sigma(V)$ determines a new assignment $\beta : V \to A$ by $\beta(x) = \alpha(h(x))$ for all $x \in V$. Because $\beta^\# = h \cdot \alpha^\#$ and $\beta^\#(t) \leq \beta^\#(t')$, we obtain $\alpha^\#(h(t)) \leq \alpha^\#(h(t')))$. That is, $\boldsymbol{A} \models \forall Y(h(t) \leq h(t'))$, where $Y = h(X)$, and consequently, $\forall Y(h(t) \leq h(t'))$ is a logical consequence of E. Thus $(h(t), h(t')) \in \overline{E}$, by the assumption that E is an order theory. ■

Let us say that a set E of inequalities is ***nontrivial*** if E does not contain $\forall x, y(x \leq y)$ for any pair of different variables x and y in V.

Proposition 9. *If E is a nontrivial set of inequalities, then $\boldsymbol{T}_\Sigma(V)/\lesssim_E$ is the free ordered algebra over V in Mod_0E.*

Proof. Let E be a nontrivial set of inequalities.

First, note that an arbitrary inequality $\forall X(t \leq t')$ is valid in $\boldsymbol{T}_\Sigma(V)/\lesssim_E$ iff $t \lesssim_E t'$. Hence $\boldsymbol{T}_\Sigma(V)/\lesssim_E$ is an ordered model of E. That is, condition (1) for free ordered algebras is satisfied.

Second, we have to show that the mapping $\varphi : V \to \boldsymbol{T}_\Sigma(V)/\lesssim_E$ which is the restriction to V of the natural homomorphism from $\boldsymbol{T}_\Sigma(V)$ to $\boldsymbol{T}_\Sigma(V)/\lesssim_E$, is an injection. Suppose the contrary, that $\varphi(x) = \varphi(y)$ for some pair of different variables x and y in V. Then $x \lesssim_E y$ and hence $\forall x, y(x \leq y)$ is valid in $\boldsymbol{T}_\Sigma(V)/\lesssim_E$, i.e., $\forall x, y(x \leq y) \in E$ is a contradiction. Thus φ is, indeed, injective and condition (2) of free ordered algebras is also satisfied.

Third, consider an arbitrary assignment α from V to any model $\boldsymbol{A}$ of E. Its extension $\alpha^\# : \boldsymbol{T}_\Sigma(V) \to \boldsymbol{A}$ factorizes through $\boldsymbol{T}_\Sigma(V)/\lesssim_E$ since $\lesssim_E$ is included in $ker_\leq \alpha^\#$. Take into consideration that $ker_\leq \alpha^\#$ is a fully invariant quasi-congruence including $\overline{E}$. Hence $\alpha^\# = nat \cdot \alpha^*$ for a unique morphism α^* from $\boldsymbol{T}_\Sigma(V)/\lesssim_E$ to $\boldsymbol{A}$. Because $\alpha = in_V \cdot \alpha^\#$, we get $\alpha = in_V \cdot nat \cdot \alpha^* = \varphi \cdot \alpha^*$. Hence condition (3) of free ordered algebras is satisfied. ■

Our second main result is now derivable.

Theorem 10 (Criterion for Order Theories of Inequalities). *Let E be a set of inequalities. Then E is an order theory if and only if $\overline{E}$ is a fully invariant quasi-congruence on $\boldsymbol{T}_\Sigma(V)$.*

Proof. If E is an order theory of inequalities, then $\overline{E}$ is a fully invariant quasi-congruence on $\boldsymbol{T}_\Sigma(V)$ by Proposition 8.

Assume E is a set of inequalities such that $\overline{E}$ is a fully invariant quasi-congruence on $\boldsymbol{T}_\Sigma(V)$. If E contains $\forall x, y(x \leq y)$, then $\overline{E}$ is obviously the entire relation $T_\Sigma(V) \times T_\Sigma(V)$, which is, in fact, a fully invariant quasi-congruence on $\boldsymbol{T}_\Sigma(V)$. Therefore suppose additionally that E is nontrivial. By Proposition 9, $\boldsymbol{T}_\Sigma(V)/\lesssim_E$ is the free ordered algebra over V in $Mod_0 E$. Observe that $\forall X(t \leq t')$ is a logical consequence of E iff $\forall X(t \leq t')$ is valid in $\boldsymbol{T}_\Sigma(V)/\lesssim_E$. On the other hand, $\boldsymbol{T}_\Sigma(V)/\lesssim_E \models \forall X(t \leq t')$ iff $\forall X(t \leq t') \in E$. Hence E is closed under logical consequence. That is, E is an order theory. ■

As usual, the defining properties of the algebraic counterpart of theories, namely fully invariant quasi-congruences in case of inequalities, can be transformed directly into inference rules. Therefore the ***Logic of Inequalities*** consists of the following inference rules (IEL1) to (IEL6):

(I) Rules of quasi-congruence

$$(IEL1)\quad \forall X(t \leq t');$$

$$(IEL2)\quad \frac{\forall X(t \leq t'), \forall X(t' \leq t'')}{\forall X(t \leq t'')};$$

$$(IEL3)\quad \frac{\forall X_1(t_1 \leq t'_1), \ldots, \forall X_n(t_n \leq t'_n)}{\forall X(\sigma t_1 \ldots t_n \leq \sigma t'_1 \ldots t'_n)}$$

for every n-ary operation symbol σ, where $X = X_1 \cup \ldots \cup X_n$.

(II) Rule of full invariance

$$(IEL4)\quad \frac{\forall X(t \leq t')}{\forall Y(s^{\#}(t) \leq s^{\#}(t'))}$$

for all substitutions $s : X \to T_\Sigma(V)$, where $Y = \bigcup\{var(s(x)) \mid x \in X\}$.

(III) Rule of abstraction

$$(IEL5)\quad \frac{\forall X(t \leq t')}{\forall Y(t \leq t')}$$

where $Y = X \cup \{y\}$ for some $y \in V - X$.

(IV) Rule of concretion

$$(IEL6)\quad \frac{\forall X(t \leq t')}{\forall Y(t \leq t')}$$

where $Y = X - \{x\}$ for some $x \in V - (var(t) \cup var(t'))$.

Deductions are finite sequences of inequalities called ***formal proofs*** leading from a given set E of inequalities, the premises of the deduction, to another inequality $\forall X(t \leq t')$, the conclusion of the deduction. Inequalities occurring in a formal proof are either in E or else can be inferred from earlier inequalities of the sequence by one of the inference rules (IEL1) to (IEL6). We say that $\forall X(t \leq t')$ is ***deducible*** from E if there is a formal proof from E whose last inequality is $\forall X(t \leq t')$. In this case we write

$$E \vdash_{IEL} \forall X(t \leq t').$$

Bloom /Bloom-76/ first proved that the Logic of Inequalities is sound and complete. Given a set E of inequalities, an arbitrary inequality $\forall X(t \leq t')$ is a logical consequence of E if and only if $\forall X(t \leq t')$ is deducible from E. Formally,

$$E \models_0 \forall X(t \leq t') \quad \text{iff} \quad E \vdash_{IEL} \forall X(t \leq t').$$

4.2.2 Strict Ordered Algebras

In this section, we study the role of a least element in ordered algebras. The existence of a least element is a necessary condition for computing least fixpoints in the semantics of recursive program schemes defined later.

Recall that a poset is strict if it has a least element, usually denoted by $\perp$. Let A and B be strict posets. A mapping f from A to B is called ***strict*** if f preserves least elements, i.e., $f(\perp) = \perp$. Again we fix a (one-sorted) signature Σ .

Definition 8. *An ordered algebra is called* ***strict*** *if its carrier is a strict poset.*

Two strict ordered algebras $\boldsymbol{A}$ and $\boldsymbol{B}$ are said to be ***isomorphic*** if there is a bijection h from A to B such that h and h^{-1} are strict morphisms; h is called an ***isomorphism***.

Example 1. Any trivial algebra with a singleton as carrier is a strict ordered algebra. ■

Example 2. The ordered multiplicative monoid of natural numbers is a strict ordered algebra. ■

Now we are going to introduce the strict ordered algebra of trees. Let X be any set disjoint from the signature Σ. Recall that a (partial) Σ-tree over X is a mapping from $W(I\!N_+)$ to $\Sigma \cup X$ such that $Dom(T)$ is prefix-closed, and for all w in $Dom(T)$, $T(w) \in \Sigma_0 \cup X$ if w is a leaf (i.e., $w \in Dom(T)$ but $w.k \notin Dom(T)$ for all $k \in I\!N_+$), and $T(w) \in \Sigma_n$, $n \geq 1$, if $w.k \in Dom(T)$ for some $k \leq n$ (see Definition 2 in Section 1.4.2).

$Tr_\Sigma(X)$ denotes the set of all Σ-trees over X, while $FTr_\Sigma(X)$ is the subset of all finite Σ-trees over X, where T in $Tr_\Sigma(X)$ is finite if $Dom(T)$ is finite. By Lemma 3 in

Section 1.4.2, $Tr_\Sigma(X)$ is a strict poset with respect to the so-called syntactic order $\sqsubseteq$, defined by: $T \sqsubseteq T'$ iff $Dom(T) \subseteq Dom(T')$ and $T(w) = T'(w)$ for all $w \in Dom(T)$.

In a natural way, each n-ary operation symbol σ can be realized as an n-ary operation on $Tr_\Sigma(X)$, namely joining n trees $T_1, \ldots, T_n \in Tr_\Sigma(X)$ by σ; formally $\sigma^{Tr_\Sigma(X)}(T_1, \ldots, T_n)$ is a Σ-tree over X defined by $Dom(\sigma^{Tr_\Sigma(X)}(T_1, \ldots, T_n)) = \{e\} \cup \{w \mid w = k.v$ and $v \in Dom(T_k)$ for all $k = 1.\ldots, n\}$ and

$$(\sigma^{Tr_\Sigma(X)}(T_1, \ldots, T_n))(w) = \begin{cases} \sigma & \text{if } w = e \\ T_k(v) & \text{if } w = k.v,\ v \in Dom(T_k) \text{ and } 1 \leq k \leq n. \end{cases}$$

Hence, $Tr_\Sigma(X)$ becomes a Σ-algebra, called the Σ-tree algebra over X or the ***tree algebra***, for short.

Proposition 11. *Any tree algebra is a strict ordered algebra.*

Proof. By Lemma 3 in Section 1.4.2, $Tr_\Sigma(X)$ is a strict poset with respect to syntactic order. So, it remains to show that all operations are monotone.

Let σ be any n-ary operation symbol, and let $T_i, T_i' \in Tr_\Sigma(X)$ for $i = 1, \ldots, n$. We set $T = \sigma^{Tr_\Sigma(X)}(T_1, \ldots, T_n)$ and $T' = \sigma^{Tr_\Sigma(X)}(T_1', \ldots, T_n')$. Assume that $T_i \sqsubseteq T_i'$ for $i = 1, \ldots, n$. Then, by definition, $Dom(T_i) \subseteq Dom(T_i')$ and $T_i(w) = T_i'(w)$ for all $w \in Dom(T_i)$, $i = 1, \ldots, n$. Now it follows easily that $Dom(T) \subseteq Dom(T')$ and $T(w) = T'(w)$ for all $w \in Dom(T)$, hence $T \sqsubseteq T'$. That is, $\sigma^{Tr_\Sigma(X)}$ is monotone. ■

Notice that the operations in $Tr_\Sigma(X)$ are not strict.

Let $\boldsymbol{A}$ be a subalgebra of a strict ordered algebra $\boldsymbol{B}$. We call $\boldsymbol{A}$ a ***strict subalgebra*** of $\boldsymbol{B}$ if $\boldsymbol{A}$ contains the least element of $\boldsymbol{B}$.

Example 3. $\boldsymbol{FTr}_\Sigma(X)$ is a strict subalgebra of $\boldsymbol{Tr}_\Sigma(X)$. ■

Example 4. Consider the ordered multiplicative monoid $(\mathbb{N}, \cdot, 1, \leq)$ of natural numbers from Example 2. Obviously, the submonoid of all positive natural numbers is not a strict monoid. But $(\mathbb{N}, \cdot, 1, \leq)$ possesses strict subalgebras; for instance, $(\{0,1\}, \cdot, 1, \leq)$ which is, moreover, the smallest strict subalgebra of $(\mathbb{N}, \cdot, 1, \leq)$. ■

Let $\mathcal{K}$ be an abstract class of strict ordered algebras. Then $\mathbf{S}_\perp\mathcal{K}$ denotes the abstract class of all strict subalgebras of algebras in $\mathcal{K}$. Note that $\boldsymbol{A} \in \mathbf{S}_\perp\mathcal{K}$ iff there is a strict morphism from $\boldsymbol{A}$ to some algebra in $\mathcal{K}$.

Given strict ordered algebras $\boldsymbol{A}$ and $\boldsymbol{B}$, $\boldsymbol{B}$ is called a ***strict ordered image*** of $\boldsymbol{A}$ if there is a surjective strict morphism from $\boldsymbol{A}$ onto $\boldsymbol{B}$.

Again, the question arises whether strict ordered images are isomorphic to ordered quotients. Let $\boldsymbol{A}$ be a strict ordered algebra. We call a quasi-order $\lesssim$ on A ***strict*** if, for all a in A, $\bot \lesssim a$ holds. Observe that the ordered kernel of any strict morphism is a strict quasi-congruence. Given a strict quasi-congruence $\lesssim$ on a strict ordered algebra $\boldsymbol{A}$, the ordered quotient algebra $\boldsymbol{A}/\lesssim$ has also a least element, namely $[\bot]$. Now the Homomorphism Theorem for Ordered Algebras can be generalized in a straightforward manner: If h is a surjective strict morphism from a strict ordered algebra $\boldsymbol{A}$ onto a strict ordered algebra $\boldsymbol{B}$, then $\boldsymbol{B}$ is isomorphic to the strict ordered quotient algebra $\boldsymbol{A}/\ker_{\leq} h$. Hence, any strict ordered image is isomorphic to a strict ordered quotient algebra.

Let $\mathcal{K}$ be an abstract class of strict ordered algebras. Then $\mathbf{H}_{\bot}\mathcal{K}$ denotes the abstract class of all strict ordered images of algebras in $\mathcal{K}$, while $\mathbf{Q}_{\bot}\mathcal{K}$ denotes all strict ordered quotient algebras of algebras in $\mathcal{K}$. Note that $\mathbf{H}_{\bot}\mathcal{K} = \mathbf{Q}_{\bot}\mathcal{K}$.

It is easily seen that the class of all strict ordered algebras is closed under direct product.

Definition 9. *An abstract class of strict ordered algebras is called* ***strict order variety*** *if it is closed under strict subalgebras, strict ordered images, and direct products.*

It is intuitively clear that any strict order variety is definable by inequalities. Let E be a set of inequalities. $Mod_{\bot}E$ denotes the ***strict ordered model class*** of E. That is, $\boldsymbol{A}$ belongs to $Mod_{\bot}E$ iff $\boldsymbol{A}$ is a strict ordered algebra that validates E. An abstract class of strict ordered algebras is said to be ***definable by inequalities*** if $\mathcal{K} = Mod_{\bot}E$ for some set E of inequalities.

Proposition 12. *If E is a set if inequalities, then $Mod_{\bot}E$ is a strict order variety.*

Proof. This follows directly from Proposition 3 in Section 4.2.1. ∎

To prove that any strict order variety is definable by inequalities we will use free algebras. Let $\mathcal{K}$ be any abstract class of strict ordered algebras. We say that a strict ordered algebra $\boldsymbol{F}$ is ***free in*** $\mathcal{K}$ over a set X if (1) $\boldsymbol{F}$ belongs to $\mathcal{K}$; (2) X is a subset of F (possibly under a suitable identification); and (3) every mapping α from X to any strict ordered algebra in $\mathcal{K}$ admits a unique extension to a strict morphism $\alpha^* : \boldsymbol{F} \to \boldsymbol{A}$. If a free strict ordered algebra over X exists in $\mathcal{K}$, it is unique up to isomorphism, and will be denoted by $\boldsymbol{F}_{\mathcal{K}}(X)_{\bot}$. When $\mathcal{K}$ is the class of all strict ordered algebras $\boldsymbol{F}_{\mathcal{K}}(X)_{\bot}$ is called the ***absolutely free strict ordered algebra*** over X.

Proposition 13. *$\boldsymbol{FTr}_{\Sigma}(X)$ is the absolutely free strict ordered algebra over X.*

Proof. Since $\boldsymbol{FTr}_{\Sigma}(X)$ is a strict ordered algebra including X, we have only to show that every mapping α from X to any strict ordered algebra $\boldsymbol{A}$ admits a unique extension. Define a mapping $\alpha^* : FTr_{\Sigma}(X) \to A$ as follows

(1) $\alpha^*(\bot) = \bot$;

(2) $\alpha^*(x) = \alpha(x)$ for all $x \in X$; and

(3) $\alpha^*(\sigma^{FTr_\Sigma(X)}(T_1, \ldots T_n)) = \sigma^A(\alpha^*(T_1), \ldots, \alpha^*(T_n))$ for all $\sigma \in \Sigma_n$ and all $T_1, \ldots, T_n \in FTr_\Sigma(X)$.

Obviously, α^* is well-defined and a strict morphism which extends α.

Therefore, it remains to prove that α^* is unique. Suppose $f : \boldsymbol{FTr}_\Sigma(X) \to \boldsymbol{A}$ is another strict morphism with $f(x) = \alpha(x)$ for all x in X. Using the Principle of Tree Induction we are going to verify $f = \alpha^*$. For that purpose a property $\mathcal{P}$ is defined so that for each T of $FTr_\Sigma(X)$, $\mathcal{P}(T)$ means $f(T) = \alpha^*(T)$. Induction basis: $\mathcal{P}$ holds for all trees of level 0 since (i) $f(\bot) = \bot = \alpha^*(\bot)$; (ii) $f(x) = \alpha(x) = \alpha^*(x)$ for all $x \in X$; and (iii) $f(\sigma) = \sigma^A = \alpha^*(\sigma)$ for all $\sigma \in \Sigma_0$. Induction step: Assume $\mathcal{P}$ holds for $T_1, \ldots, T_n$ (induction hypothesis). Then we derive

$$\begin{aligned} f(\sigma^{FTr_\Sigma(X)}(T_1, \ldots, T_n)) &= \sigma^A(f(T_1), \ldots, f(T_n)) && f \text{ is a morphism} \\ &= \sigma^A(\alpha^*(T_1), \ldots, \alpha^*(T_n)) && \text{induction hypothesis} \\ &= \alpha^*(\sigma^{FTr_\Sigma(X)}(T_1, \ldots, T_n)) && \alpha^* \text{ is a morphism.} \end{aligned}$$

Hence $\mathcal{P}$ holds for $T = \sigma^{FTr_\Sigma(X)}(T_1, \ldots, T_n)$, whence $f = \alpha^*$. ■

Our next aim is to describe the absolutely free strict ordered algebra as a term algebra. In other words, we search for a strict ordered term algebra which is isomorphic to the finite tree algebra $\boldsymbol{FTr}_\Sigma(X)$. The main problem is to find a suitable order on a term algebra. Let us start with the flat poset $X_\bot$, where $\bot$ is a new element associated with X, i.e., $X_\bot = X \cup \{\bot\}$, such that $\bot \le x$ for all $x \in X$. Now we extend $\le$ to an order on $T_\Sigma(X_\bot)$. First, an auxilary relation is introduced: for arbitrary terms t_1 and t_2 from $T_\Sigma(X_\bot)$ we put $t_1 \to t_2$ if any proper subterm of t_1 is replaced by $\bot$. Formally, $t_1 \to t_2$ iff there is an adress u of t_1 such that $t_1/u \neq \bot$ and $t_2 = t_1[u/\bot]$. It is easily seen that $\to$ is invariant. That is, $t_1 \to t_2$ implies $t[v/t_1] \to t[v/t_2]$ for all terms $t \in T_\Sigma(X_\bot)$ and all addresses v of t. Hence, the reflexive and transitive closure of $\to$ is a quasi-congruence on $T_\Sigma(X_\bot)$. We denote $\xrightarrow{*}$ by $\sqsupseteq$.

Consider the ordered quotient algebra $\boldsymbol{T}_\Sigma(X_\bot)/\sqsubseteq$. The congruence associated with $\sqsubseteq$ is the identity since $\sqsubseteq$ is obviously antisymmetric. Thus $T_\Sigma(X_\bot)/\sqsubseteq$ will be identified with $T_\Sigma(X_\bot)$ such that $T_\Sigma(X_\bot)$ becomes a strict poset with respect to $\sqsubseteq$. All operations are monotone since $\sqsubseteq$ is a quasi-congruence. This justifies the following definition.

Definition 10. *$\boldsymbol{T}_\Sigma(X_\bot)$ is called the strict ordered Σ-term algebra over X or, for short, the* ***strict ordered term algebra****.*

By definition, $\boldsymbol{T}_\Sigma(X_\bot)$ and $\boldsymbol{FTr}_\Sigma(X)$ are isomorphic as strict ordered algebras. As a consequence of Proposition 13 we get

Theorem 14. *The strict ordered term algebras are absolutely free strict ordered algebras.* ■

Given a mapping α from X to any strict ordered algebra A, $\alpha_\perp : X_\perp \to A$ will denote its strict extension defined by $\alpha_\perp(\perp) = \perp$ and $\alpha_\perp(x) = \alpha(x)$ for all x in X. Now the Principle of Finitary Algebraic Recursion can be modified: Every mapping α from X to any strict ordered algebra $\boldsymbol{A}$ extends uniquely to a strict morphism $\alpha^\S : \boldsymbol{T}_\Sigma(X_\perp) \to \boldsymbol{A}$ such that $\alpha^\S(x) = \alpha(x)$ for all x in X (see Fig. 4.2). Note that $\alpha^\S = (\alpha_\perp)^\sharp$.

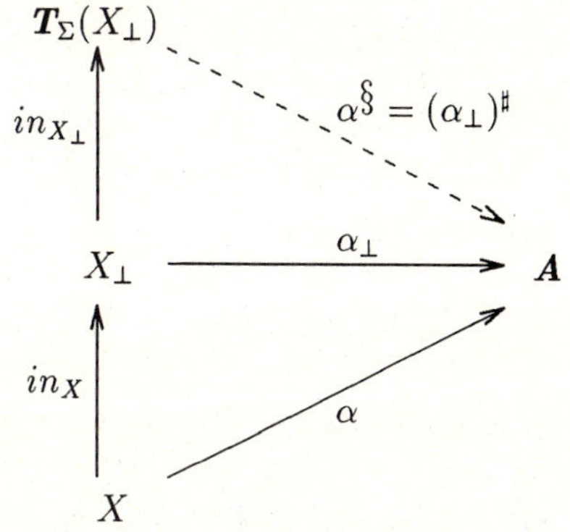

Fig. 4.2

This modified Principle of Finitary Algebraic Recursion can also be regarded as a reformulation of Theorem 14.

The existence of free strict ordered algebras can now be guaranteed under certain conditions.

Theorem 15 (Existence of Free Strict Ordered Algebras). *Let $\mathcal{K}$ be a nontrivial abstract class of strict ordered algebras. If $\mathcal{K}$ is closed under strict subalgebras and direct products, then free strict ordered algebras exist in $\mathcal{K}$.*

Proof sketch. Let $\mathcal{K}$ be a nontrivial abstract class of strict ordered algebras which is closed under strict subalgebras and direct products. First, consider the class $\mathcal{K}$ of all strict ordered algebras. Then $\boldsymbol{T}_\Sigma(X_\perp)$ is the absolutely free strict ordered algebra over any set X, by Theorem 14. Now, let $\mathcal{K}$ be any subclass with the properties assumed above. It is easily seen that $\boldsymbol{T}_\Sigma(X_\perp)$ admits a strict sur-reflection in $\mathcal{K}$, say $\boldsymbol{R}$. That is, $\boldsymbol{R}$ is a strict ordered image of $\boldsymbol{T}_\Sigma(X_\perp)$ and $r : \boldsymbol{T}_\Sigma(X_\perp) \to \boldsymbol{R}$ is a surjective strict morphism such that every strict morphism h from $\boldsymbol{T}_\Sigma(X_\perp)$ to any algebra $\boldsymbol{A}$ in $\mathcal{K}$ factorizes uniquely through R: $h = r \cdot h^*$ where $h^* : \boldsymbol{R} \to \boldsymbol{A}$ is a strict morphism, which exists uniquely. By definition, $\boldsymbol{R}$ is the free strict ordered algebra over X in $\mathcal{K}$. ∎

If E is a given set of inequalities, then

$$Mod_\perp E = Mod_0(E \cup \{\forall x(\perp \le x)\}).$$

Hence, by Proposition 9, $\boldsymbol{T}_\Sigma(X_\perp)/\lesssim_{E,\perp}$ is the free strict ordered algebra in $Mod_\perp E$, where $\lesssim_{E,\perp}$ is the strict fully invariant quasi-congruence on $\boldsymbol{T}_\Sigma(X_\perp)$ generated by $\overline{E} \cup \{(\perp, x) \mid x \in X\}$.

Theorem 16 (Strict Order Variety Theorem). *Let $\mathcal{K}$ be an abstract class of strict ordered algebras. Then $\mathcal{K}$ is definable by inequalities if and only if $\mathcal{K}$ is a strict order variety.*

Proof. Let $\mathcal{K}$ be an abstract class of strict ordered algebras. If $\mathcal{K}$ is definable by inequalities, then $\mathcal{K}$ is a strict order variety by Proposition 12.

Conversely, assume that $\mathcal{K}$ is a strict order variety. Define E to be the set of all inequalities valid in $\mathcal{K}$, i.e., $E = \mathit{Ineq}\,\mathcal{K}$. Then $\mathcal{K} \subseteq \mathit{Mod}_\perp E$. So, it remains to verify the opposite inclusion in order to get $\mathcal{K} = \mathit{Mod}_\perp E$, yielding that $\mathcal{K}$ is definable by inequalities.

Let $\boldsymbol{A} \in \mathit{Mod}_\perp E$. Evidently, $\boldsymbol{A}$ is a strict ordered image of $\boldsymbol{T}_\Sigma(A_\perp)$ with $id_A^\S : \boldsymbol{T}_\Sigma(A_\perp) \to \boldsymbol{A}$ the related surjective strict morphism. By Theorem 15, the free strict ordered algebra over A exists in $\mathcal{K}$. Let $r : \boldsymbol{T}_\Sigma(A_\perp) \to \boldsymbol{F}_\mathcal{K}(A)_\perp$ be the surjective strict morphism related to the strict sur-reflection of $\boldsymbol{T}_\Sigma(A_\perp)$ in $\mathcal{K}$. Now it suffices to show that $id_A^\S$ factorizes through $\boldsymbol{F}_\mathcal{K}(A)_\perp$: $id_A^\S = r \cdot h$ for some surjective strict morphism h from $\boldsymbol{F}_\mathcal{K}(A)_\perp$ to $\boldsymbol{A}$. Then $\boldsymbol{A}$ is a strict image of an algebra in $\mathcal{K}$; hence $\boldsymbol{A}$ is in $\mathcal{K}$, too.

We know that h exists iff $\mathit{ker}_\leq r \subseteq \mathit{ker}_\leq id_A^\S$. Let $t, t' \in \boldsymbol{T}_\Sigma(A_\perp)$ with $X = \mathit{var}(t) \cup \mathit{var}(t')$. Suppose $(t, t') \in \mathit{ker}_\leq r$. Then $r(t) \leq r(t')$ and so $\forall X(t \leq t')$ is valid in $\mathcal{K}$. That is, $\forall X(t \leq t')$ belongs to E. By assumption, $\boldsymbol{A}$ validates $\forall X(t \leq t')$. Hence $id_A^\S(t) \leq id_A^\S(t')$ and consequently, $(t, t') \in \mathit{ker}_\leq id_A^\S$. Thus h exists and $\boldsymbol{A}$ is a strict ordered image of $\boldsymbol{F}_\mathcal{K}(A)_\perp$, which proves $\mathit{Mod}_\perp E \subseteq \mathcal{K}$. ∎

We say that a set E of inequalities is a ***strict order theory*** if an inequality $\forall X(t \leq t')$ belongs to E whenever $E \models_\perp \forall X(t \leq t')$, where $E \models_\perp \forall X(t \leq t')$ means $\mathit{Mod}_\perp E \models \forall X(t \leq t')$.

We get immediately the following criterion: E is a strict order theory of inequalities iff $\overline{E}$ is a strict fully invariant quasi-congruence on $\boldsymbol{T}_\Sigma(X_\perp)$.

If we add the inference rule

(IEL0) $\quad \forall x(\perp \leq x)$

to the Logic of Inequalities and write $E \vdash_{IEL_\perp} \forall X(t \leq t')$ if $\forall X(t \leq t')$ is deducible from E using (IEL0) to (IEL6), then

$$E \models_\perp \forall X(t \leq t') \text{ iff } E \vdash_{IEL_\perp} \forall X(t \leq t').$$

The simple proof of this completeness result is left to the reader.

4.2.3 ω-Complete Ordered Algebras

Our intention to use ordered algebras in semantics of recursive program schemes requires fixpoint methods, and therefore ordered algebras must have ω-complete carriers and ω-continuous operations.

For convenience we recall some more basic notions. A poset A is said to be ω-complete if every countable chain (directed subset) in A has a supremum (for equivalent definitions see Proposition 3 in Section 1.5.1). Note that every ω-complete poset has a least element. Given posets A and B, that a mapping $f : A \to B$ is ω-continuous means that for every nonempty countable chain (directed subset) X in A with a supremum, $f(X)$ has a supremum in B and $f(\sup X) = \sup f(X)$. An ω-continuous mapping is always monotone but not necessarily strict. We fix a (one-sorted) signature Σ in the sequel.

Definition 11. *An ordered algebra is called* ***ω-complete*** [4] *if its carrier is an ω-complete poset and all operations are ω-continuous in each argument.*

Since any ω-complete ordered algebra $\boldsymbol{A}$ is strict we will always assume henceforth that the underlying signature contains a distinguished nullary operation symbol, denoted by $\perp$, which is realized as the least element in $\boldsymbol{A}$. As usual we shall simply write $\perp$ instead of $\perp^A$. So, the least elements in all ω-complete ordered algebras and the nullary operation symbol $\perp$ are notationally identified.

If $\boldsymbol{A}$ is an ω-complete poset, then so is each finite power A^n (with respect to the coordinatewise order). Hence, in any ω-complete algebra $\boldsymbol{A}$ we have

$$\sigma^A(\sup X_1, \ldots, \sup X_n) = \sup\{\sigma^A(x_1, \ldots, x_n) \mid x_1 \in X_1, \ldots, x_n \in X_n\}$$

for all n-ary operation symbols σ in Σ and all nonempty countable directed subsets $X_1, \ldots, X_n$ in A. Note that $\{\sigma^A(x_1, \ldots, x_n) \mid x_1 \in X_1, \ldots, x_n \in X_n\}$ is a nonempty countable directed subset in A if $X_1, \ldots, X_n$ are so.

Example 1. Any flat ordered algebra is ω-complete, whereas a discrete algebra $\boldsymbol{A}$ is ω-complete iff A is a singleton; otherwise A does not have a least element. ■

Now we have to specialize the concept of morphism to preserve not only operations and order but also suprema of countable chains. In particular, the least element must be preserved. This leads to the following definition.

Definition 12. *Let $\boldsymbol{A}$ and $\boldsymbol{B}$ be strict ordered algebras. A strict ω-continuous morphism from $\boldsymbol{A}$ to $\boldsymbol{B}$ is called an* ***ω-morphism****. Specifically, a* ***full ω-morphism*** *means a strict ω-continuous full morphism.*

Two ω-complete ordered algebras $\boldsymbol{A}$ and $\boldsymbol{B}$ are said to be ***isomorphic*** if there is a bijection h from A to B such that h as well as h^{-1} are ω-morphisms; h is then called an ***isomorphism***.

---

[4] In the literature, ω-complete ordered algebras are also called ω-continuous.

To achieve our goal of characterizing abstract classes of ω-complete algebras that are defined by inequalities we have to study the corresponding closure operators.

We start with subalgebras. It is obvious that a subalgebra of a given ω-complete ordered algebra $\boldsymbol{A}$ need not be ω-complete. But since the set of all ω-complete ordered subalgebras of $\boldsymbol{A}$ is a closure system, we can generate them. If X is any subset of A, $\langle X\rangle_\omega$ denotes the ω-complete ordered subalgebra of $\boldsymbol{A}$ generated by X. Given an abstract class $\mathcal{K}$ of ω-complete ordered algebras, $\mathbf{S}_\omega\mathcal{K}$ denotes the abstract class of all ω-complete ordered subalgebras of algebras in $\mathcal{K}$. An ω-complete ordered algebra $\boldsymbol{A}$ belongs to $\mathbf{S}_\omega\mathcal{K}$ iff there is a full ω-morphism from $\boldsymbol{A}$ to some algebra in $\mathcal{K}$.

Next we turn to images. Let $\boldsymbol{A}$ and $\boldsymbol{B}$ be ω-complete ordered algebras. $\boldsymbol{B}$ is called an ***ω-complete ordered image*** of $\boldsymbol{A}$ if there is a surjective ω-morphism from $\boldsymbol{A}$ onto $\boldsymbol{B}$. Given an abstract class $\mathcal{K}$ of ω-complete ordered algebras, $\mathbf{H}_\omega\mathcal{K}$ denotes the abstract class of all ω-complete ordered images of algebras in $\mathcal{K}$.

When dealing with images we are always confronted with a set theoretic problem; all ω-complete ordered images of a given ω-complete ordered algebra form a proper class. However, there is no possibility to find a set of nonisomorphic representatives. That is why we introduce a more general version of an image. To do that we have to enlarge the class of surjective ω-morphisms.

Definition 13. *Let $\boldsymbol{A}$ and $\boldsymbol{B}$ be ω-complete ordered algebras. An ω-morphism h from $\boldsymbol{A}$ to $\boldsymbol{B}$ is called **dense** if $\boldsymbol{B}$ is generated by the ordered image $h(\boldsymbol{A})$, i.e., $\boldsymbol{B} = \langle h(\boldsymbol{A})\rangle_\omega$.*

The composition of two dense ω-morphisms is again a dense ω-morphism. The proof is left to the reader. The main point is to verify that for every ω-morphism $h : \boldsymbol{A} \to \boldsymbol{B}$ and all subsets X of A, $\langle h(\langle X\rangle_\omega)\rangle_\omega = \langle h(X)\rangle_\omega$ holds (cf. /Meseguer-78/).

Every surjective ω-morphism is dense but not vice versa, as the following example illustrates.

Example 2. Consider a signature consisting of one unary operation symbol, say σ. Define two ω-complete ordered algebras $\boldsymbol{A}$ and $\boldsymbol{B}$ as follows: $A = \mathbb{N} \cup \{\bot\}$ is a flat poset with $\bot$ as least element, and $B = \mathbb{N} \cup \{\top\}$ is the chain $0 < 1 < 2 < \ldots < \top$ with $\top$ as greatest element. The operations are defined by

$$\sigma^A(\bot) = 0,\ \sigma^A(n) = n+1 \text{ for all } n \in \mathbb{N}; \text{ and}$$

$$\sigma^B(n) = n+1 \text{ for all } n \in \mathbb{N},\ \sigma^B(\top) = \top.$$

The mapping $h : A \to B$, determined by $h(\bot) = 0$ and $h(n) = n+1$ for all $n \in \mathbb{N}$, is an ω-morphism. Evidently, h is dense but not surjective. ■

Let $\boldsymbol{A}$ and $\boldsymbol{B}$ be ω-complete ordered algebras. $\boldsymbol{B}$ is called a ***dense image*** of $\boldsymbol{A}$ if there is a dense ω-morphism from $\boldsymbol{A}$ to $\boldsymbol{B}$. If $\mathcal{K}$ is an abstract class of ω-complete ordered algebras, $\mathbf{H}_d\mathcal{K}$ denotes the abstract class of all dense images of algebras in $\mathcal{K}$. Notice that $\mathbf{H}_\omega\mathcal{K} \subseteq \mathbf{H}_d\mathcal{K}$.

Now we shall answer the question whether all nonisomorphic dense images of a given ω-complete ordered algebra $\boldsymbol{A}$ form a set. Of course, there is only a set of nonisomorphic ordered images $h(\boldsymbol{A})$, where h varies over all ω-morphisms from $\boldsymbol{A}$ to any ω-complete ordered algebra. Specifically, the cardinality of this set is bounded by $2^{card(A)}$ since all quasi-congruences on $\boldsymbol{A}$ are a subset of the power set $\wp(A \times A)$, and $card(\wp(A \times A)) = 2^{card(A)}$. Next, we have to show that there is only a set of nonisomorphic completions of $h(\boldsymbol{A})$ to an ω-complete ordered subalgebra of some ω-complete ordered algebra. It suffices to study the generation process for posets only. Let X be a subset of an ω-complete poset A. Suppose X is infinite. To generate the least ω-complete subposet containing X we have to adjoin successively the suprema of all possible countable chains: $X_0 = X$, $X_{\alpha+1} = X_\alpha \cup \{a \in A \mid \text{there is a countable chain } C \text{ in } X_\alpha \text{ such that } a = \sup C \text{ in } A\}$, and for β a limit ordinal, $X_\beta = \bigcup\{X_\alpha \mid \alpha < \beta\}$. The process stops for an ordinal γ such that $card(\gamma) \leq 2^{card(A)}$. By the Principle of Transfinite Induction, one may prove that $card(X_\alpha) \leq 2^{card(X)}$ for all $\alpha < \gamma$. Hence, the cardinality of all possible completions is bounded by $2^{card(A)}$, and consequently the set of all nonisomorphic ω-complete subposets is bounded by $2^{2^{card(A)}}$. This is also an upper bound for the cardinality of the set of all nonisomorphic dense images of $\boldsymbol{A}$.

Proposition 17 (Dense Image Factorization). *Let $\boldsymbol{A}$ and $\boldsymbol{B}$ be ω-complete ordered algebras. Every ω-morphism h from $\boldsymbol{A}$ to $\boldsymbol{B}$ admits a factorization $h = f \cdot g$, where f is a dense and g is a full ω-morphism. This factorization is unique in the following sense. If $h = f' \cdot g'$ is another factorization with f' a dense and g' a full ω-morphism, then there is a unique ω-morphism d such that $f' = f \cdot d$ and $g = d \cdot g'$.* ∎

The proof is omitted since it can easily be adapted from other image factorization proofs.

Based on dense image factorization and the fact that all nonisomorphic dense images of any ω-complete ordered algebra form a set, every ω-complete ordered algebra $\boldsymbol{A}$ has a dense reflection in $\mathcal{K}$ provided $\mathcal{K}$ is an abstract class of ω-complete ordered algebras closed under ω-complete subalgebras and direct products. We call a dense image of $\boldsymbol{A}$, say $\boldsymbol{R}$ in $\mathcal{K}$, a ***dense reflection*** of $\boldsymbol{A}$ if every ω-morphism from $\boldsymbol{A}$ to any ω-complete ordered algebra in $\mathcal{K}$ factorizes uniquely through $\boldsymbol{R}$.

Before we introduce free ω-complete ordered algebras the problem of completing a given strict ordered algebra will be studied. As we know (see Section 1.5.3) any strict poset has a free ω-completion with a certain universal property. Generalizing this property we are led to the following definition.

Definition 14. *Let $\boldsymbol{A}$ be a strict ordered algebra. An ω-complete ordered algebra $\boldsymbol{A}_\omega$ is called a **free ω-completion** of $\boldsymbol{A}$ if there is a strict full morphism $m : \boldsymbol{A} \to \boldsymbol{A}_\omega$ with the following universal property:*

> *(C) Every strict morphism h from $\boldsymbol{A}$ to any ω-complete ordered algebra $\boldsymbol{B}$ admits a unique ω-morphism $h_\omega : \boldsymbol{A}_\omega \to \boldsymbol{B}$ with $h = m \cdot h_\omega$ (see Fig. 4.3).*

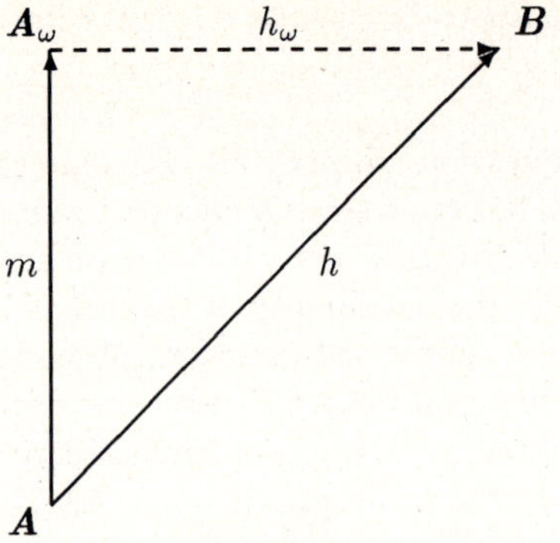

Fig. 4.3

Note that the free ω-completion of a given strict ordered algebra $\boldsymbol{A}$, if it exists, is uniquely determined up to isomorphism. We denote it by $\mathbf{C}_\omega(\boldsymbol{A})$.

Theorem 18 (Existence of Free ω-Completion). *For any strict ordered algebra the free ω-completion exists.*

Proof. Let $\boldsymbol{A}$ be a strict ordered algebra. By definition, its carrier A is a strict poset, which has a free ω-completion $A_\omega = \{(D] \mid D \in \mathcal{D}_\omega(A)\}$, where $\mathcal{D}_\omega(A)$ is the set of all nonempty countable directed subsets of A. Recall that $(D]$ is an ideal in A. Operations on A_ω are definable as follows. For any n-ary operation symbol σ and all $X_1, \ldots, X_n$ in $\mathcal{D}_\omega(A)$

$$\sigma^{A_\omega}((X_1], \ldots, (X_n]) = (\sigma^A(X_1, \ldots, X_n)] \qquad (*)$$

where $\sigma^A(X_1, \ldots, X_n) = \{\sigma^A(x_1, \ldots, x_n) \mid x_i \in X_i \text{ for } i = 1, \ldots, n\}$.

It is not very complicated to check that operations are ω-continuous in each argument. Take into account that the supremum of any countable directed subset D of A is its union $\bigcup D$.

Evidently, the embedding $m : A \to A_\omega$, defined by $m(x) = (x]$ for all x in A, is a strict full morphism.

Now consider any ω-complete ordered algebra $\boldsymbol{B}$. With every strict morphism h from $\boldsymbol{A}$ to $\boldsymbol{B}$ we associate a mapping $h_\omega : A_\omega \to B$ defined so that $h_\omega((X]) = \sup h(X)$ for all X in $\mathcal{D}_\omega(A)$. By Theorem 15 in Section 1.5.3, h_ω is the unique strict ω-continuous mapping such that $h = m \cdot h_\omega$. We have still to show that h_ω is a homomorphism. For each n-ary operation symbol σ of Σ and all $X_1, \ldots, X_n$ in $\mathcal{D}_\omega(A)$, we derive

$$\begin{aligned}
h_\omega(\sigma^{A_\omega}((X_1], \ldots, (X_n])) &= h_\omega((\sigma^A(X_1, \ldots, X_n)]) && \text{by } (*)\\
&= \sup h(\sigma^A(X_1, \ldots, X_n)) && \text{by the definition of } h_\omega\\
&= \sup \sigma^B(h(X_1), \ldots, h(X_n)) && \text{since } h \text{ is a strict morphism}\\
&= \sigma^B(\sup h(X_1), \ldots, \sup h(X_n)) && \text{since } \sigma^B \text{ is } \omega\text{-continuous}\\
&= \sigma^B(h_\omega(X_1), \ldots, h_\omega(X_n)) && \text{by the definition of } h_\omega.
\end{aligned}$$

Hence $\boldsymbol{A}_\omega$ has the universal property (C). ■

Let $\boldsymbol{A}$ and $\boldsymbol{B}$ be strict ordered algebras. If $h : \boldsymbol{A} \to \boldsymbol{B}$ is a strict morphism, then there is a unique strict ω-morphism from $\mathrm{C}_\omega(\boldsymbol{A})$ to $\mathrm{C}_\omega(\boldsymbol{B})$, denoted by $\mathrm{C}_\omega(h)$, such that the following diagram (Fig. 4.4) commutes.

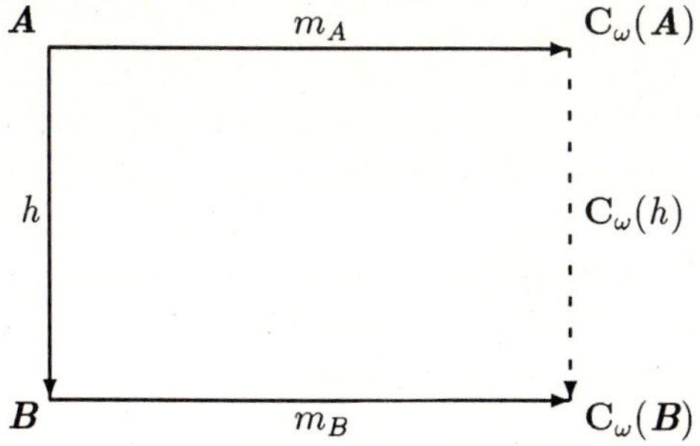

Fig. 4.4

It is important to observe that C_ω preserves fullness of morphisms.

Lemma 19. *If* $h : \boldsymbol{A} \to \boldsymbol{B}$ *is a strict full morphism, then* $\mathrm{C}_\omega(h) : \mathrm{C}_\omega(\boldsymbol{A}) \to \mathrm{C}_\omega(\boldsymbol{B})$ *is a strict full morphism, too.*

Proof. Let $h : \boldsymbol{A} \to \boldsymbol{B}$ be a strict full morphism. Keep in mind that the members of $\mathrm{C}_\omega(\boldsymbol{A})$ are ideals $(X]$ with $X \in \mathcal{D}_\omega(A)$. By definition, $\mathrm{C}_\omega(h)$ assigns $(h(X)]$ to each $(X]$ with $X \in \mathcal{D}_\omega(A)$. If we suppose $(h(X)] \subseteq (h(Y)]$, then $(X] \subseteq (Y]$ since h is full monotone. That is, $\mathrm{C}_\omega(h)$ is full monotone. ∎

Corollary. *If* $\boldsymbol{A}$ *is a strict ordered subalgebra of* $\boldsymbol{B}$, *then* $\mathrm{C}_\omega(\boldsymbol{A})$ *is an* ω*-complete ordered subalgebra of* $\mathrm{C}_\omega(\boldsymbol{B})$. ∎

Example 3. Consider the strict ordered semiring of natural numbers equipped with the usual order. Let $\mathcal{N} = \mathbb{N} \cup \{\top\}$ with $x \leq \top$ for all x in $\mathcal{N}$. Then $\mathcal{N}$ becomes an ω-complete ordered semiring if addition and multiplication are extended to $\mathcal{N}$ as follows:

$$x + \top = \top + x = \top \text{ for all } x \text{ in } \mathcal{N}; \text{ and}$$

$$x \cdot \top = \top \cdot x = \top \qquad \text{for all } x \text{ in } \mathcal{N}.$$

The inclusion $in_\mathcal{N} : \mathbb{N} \to \mathcal{N}$ is certainly a strict full morphism that embeds $\mathbb{N}$ into $\mathcal{N}$. If $\boldsymbol{B}$ is any ω-complete ordered semiring and $h : \mathbb{N} \to \boldsymbol{B}$ is a strict semiring morphism, then define a mapping $h^* : \mathcal{N} \to B$ by $h^*(x) = h(x)$ for all x in $\mathbb{N}$, and $h^*(\top) = \sup h(\mathbb{N})$. Indeed, h^* is a semiring ω-morphism. We claim that h^* is unique as extension. Suppose $g : \mathcal{N} \to \boldsymbol{B}$ is another semiring ω-morphism g with $g(x) = h(x)$ for x in $\mathbb{N}$. Then $g(\top) = g(\sup \mathbb{N}) = \sup g(\mathbb{N}) = \sup h(\mathbb{N}) = h^*(\top)$ and $g = h^*$. Hence $\mathcal{N}$ is the free ω-completion of $\mathbb{N}$. ∎

Now we are going to introduce free ω-complete ordered algebras. Let $\mathcal{K}$ be an abstract class of ω-complete ordered algebras. We say that an ω-complete ordered algebra $\boldsymbol{F}$ is ***free in*** $\mathcal{K}$ over a set X in $\mathcal{K}$ if (1) $\boldsymbol{F}$ belongs to $\mathcal{K}$; (2) X is a subset of F (possibly under a suitable identification); and (3) every mapping α from X to any ω-complete ordered algebra $\boldsymbol{A}$ in $\mathcal{K}$ admits a unique extension to an ω-morphism $\alpha^* : \boldsymbol{F} \to \boldsymbol{A}$. If a free

ω-complete ordered algebra over X exists in $\mathcal{K}$, it is unique up to isomorphism; and is denoted by $\boldsymbol{F}_{\mathcal{K}}(X)_\omega$. When $\mathcal{K}$ is the class of all ω-complete ordered algebras, $\boldsymbol{F}_{\mathcal{K}}(X)_\omega$ is also called the ***absolutely free*** ***ω-complete ordered algebra*** over X.

Theorem 20. *The tree algebras are the absolutely free ω-complete ordered algebras.*

Proof. For any set X the Σ-tree algebra over X is isomorphic to the free ω-completion of $T_\Sigma(X_\perp)$. Therefore, it suffices to show that $\mathbf{C}_\omega(T_\Sigma(X_\perp))$ is the absolutely free ω-complete ordered algebra over X. Consider an arbitrary mapping α from X to any ω-complete ordered algebra A. First, α extends uniquely to a strict morphism $\alpha^\S : T_\Sigma(X_\perp) \to A$ such that $\alpha^\S(x) = \alpha(x)$ for all x in X. Now $\alpha^\S$ admits a unique extension to an ω-morphism, namely $(\alpha^\S)_\omega : \mathbf{C}_\omega(T_\Sigma(X_\perp)) \to A$, such that $(\alpha^\S)_\omega(x) = \alpha(x)$ for all x in X, which completes the proof. ■

This result generalizes the Principle of Finitary Algebraic Recursion. It is visualized in Fig. 4.5, where the unique extension of a mapping α from X to an ω-complete ordered algebra A is denoted by $\alpha^\$$.

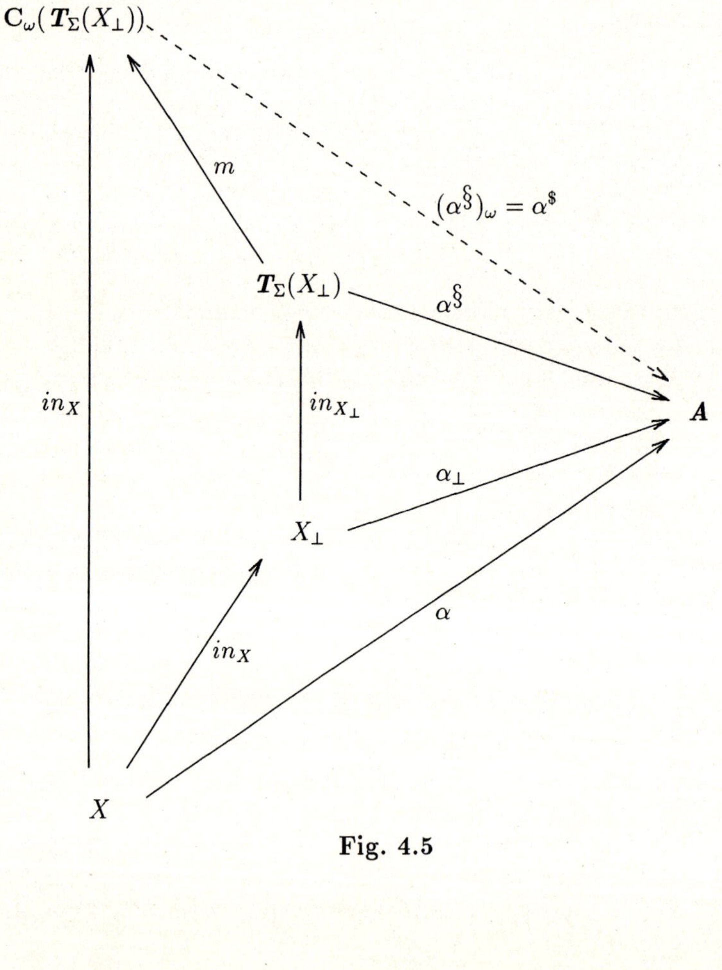

Fig. 4.5

Using dense reflections we are able to ensure the existence of free ω-complete ordered algebras.

Theorem 21 (Existence of Free ω-Complete Ordered Algebras). *Let $\mathcal{K}$ be a nontrivial abstract class of ω-complete ordered algebras. If $\mathcal{K}$ is closed under ω-complete subalgebras and direct products, then free ω-complete ordered algebras exist in $\mathcal{K}$.* ■

The proof is entirely analogous to the other existence proofs and is therefore omitted.

Example 4. An ω-complete ordered semilattice $(A+, \leq)$ is defined as follows:

(1) $(A, +)$ is a semilattice (i.e., $+$ is associative, commutative and idempotent);

(2) $(A, \leq)$ is an ω-complete poset; and

(3) For all a in A and all nonempty countable chains C in A, $a + \sup C = \sup\{a + c \mid c \in C\}$.

Since the abstract class of all ω-complete ordered semilattices is closed under ω-complete ordered subalgebras and direct products, free ω-complete ordered semilattices over any set X exist. But there is even an explicit description for them (cf. /Adamek-Nelson-Reitermann-86/). Consider the set $F(X)$ of all countable subsets Y of $X \cup \{\perp\}$ such that $\perp$ is in Y whenever Y is infinite. $F(X)$ becomes an ω-complete ordered semilattices if union is taken as a binary operation and partial order is defined by: $Y \leq_P Y'$ iff $Y = Y'$ or ($\perp \in Y$ and $Y - \{\perp\} \subseteq Y'$). This partial order was first introduced by Plotkin in his "power domain" construction /Plotkin-76/. It is easy to see that $\boldsymbol{F}(X)$ is the free ω-complete ordered semilattice over X. ■

For our further development of ω-complete ordered algebras we have to study free ω-completion as a new operator. Let $\mathcal{K}$ be an abstract class of strict ordered algebras. $\mathbf{C}_\omega\mathcal{K}$ denotes the class of all free ω-completions of algebras in $\mathcal{K}$. Naturally, a first question concerns the preservation of inequalities. To answer this question affirmatively the following lemma will be used. Its proof is straightforward and is therefore omitted. If $\boldsymbol{A}$ is any strict ordered algebra, we shall always identify $\boldsymbol{A}$ with the strict subalgebra of its free ω-completion $\mathbf{C}_\omega(\boldsymbol{A})$ that consists of all principal ideals of $\boldsymbol{A}$. For simplicity, $\boldsymbol{A}$ is identified with $m(\boldsymbol{A})$, where $m : \boldsymbol{A} \to \mathbf{C}_\omega(\boldsymbol{A})$ is the embedding of $\boldsymbol{A}$ into $\mathbf{C}_\omega(\boldsymbol{A})$. After identification, embedding becomes inclusion and we shall write $in_A : \boldsymbol{A} \to \mathbf{C}_\omega(\boldsymbol{A})$ instead of $m : \boldsymbol{A} \to \mathbf{C}_\omega(\boldsymbol{A})$.

Lemma 22. *Let $\boldsymbol{A}$ be a strict ordered algebra, and let $\boldsymbol{B}$ be an ω-complete ordered subalgebra of its free ω-completion $\mathbf{C}_\omega(\boldsymbol{A})$. If $\boldsymbol{A}$ is (isomorphic to) a strict subalgebra of $\boldsymbol{B}$, then $\boldsymbol{B}$ equals $\mathbf{C}_\omega(\boldsymbol{A})$.* ■

Let t be any term in free variables $x_1, \ldots, x_n$. Then t^A is an n-ary operation in a given algebra $\boldsymbol{A}$, called a ***derived operation***, which is defined by $t^A(a_1, \ldots, a_n) = \alpha^{\#}(t)$ if α is an assignment from $\{x_1, \ldots, x_n\}$ to $\boldsymbol{A}$ with $\alpha(x_i) = a_i$ for $i = 1, \ldots, n$. It is easy to check that t^A is even a homomorphism from $\boldsymbol{A}^n$ to $\boldsymbol{A}$. When $\boldsymbol{A}$ is an ordered algebra, t^A is a morphism; and in case $\boldsymbol{A}$ is an ω-complete ordered algebra, t^A is an ω-continuous morphism, not necessarily strict.

Now consider an inequality $\forall x(t_1 \leq t_2)$ with terms t_1 and t_2 having only one free variable. Suppose $\forall x(t_1 \leq t_2)$ is valid in a given strict ordered algebra $\boldsymbol{A}$. We claim that its free ω-completion $\mathbf{C}_\omega(\boldsymbol{A})$ validates $\forall x(t_1 \leq t_2)$, too. To prove this assertion we are going to use Lemma 22. Keep in mind that $\boldsymbol{A}$ is regarded as a strict subalgebra of $\mathbf{C}_\omega(\boldsymbol{A})$. Thus, $t_1^{\mathbf{C}_\omega(A)}(a) \leq^{\mathbf{C}_\omega(A)} t_2^{\mathbf{C}_\omega(A)}(a)$ for all a in A. Next, define a subset B of $\mathbf{C}_\omega(\boldsymbol{A})$ by $B = \{b \in \mathbf{C}_\omega(\boldsymbol{A}) \mid t_1^{\mathbf{C}_\omega(A)}(b) \leq^{\mathbf{C}_\omega(A)} t_2^{\mathbf{C}_\omega(A)}(b)\}$. Clearly, A is a subset of B and, in particular, the least element is in B. Since the derived operations in $\mathbf{C}_\omega(\boldsymbol{A})$ are ω-continuous morphisms, B is actually the carrier of an ω-complete subalgebra of $\mathbf{C}_\omega(\boldsymbol{A})$ including $\boldsymbol{A}$ as a strict subalgebra. By Lemma 22, $\boldsymbol{B}$ equals $\mathbf{C}_\omega(\boldsymbol{A})$ and hence $t_1^{\mathbf{C}_\omega(A)}(b) \leq^{\mathbf{C}_\omega(A)} t_2^{\mathbf{C}_\omega(A)}(b)$ for all b in $\mathbf{C}_\omega(\boldsymbol{A})$, that is $\mathbf{C}_\omega(\boldsymbol{A}) \models \forall x(t_1 \leq t_2)$ provided $\boldsymbol{A} \models \forall x(t_1 \leq t_2)$.

By finite induction, we may derive the following preservation result from the observation above.

Proposition 23. *Let $\boldsymbol{A}$ be any strict ordered algebra. Every inequality valid in $\boldsymbol{A}$ is also valid in its free ω-completion $\mathbf{C}_\omega(\boldsymbol{A})$.* ■

We are now in a position to choose a suitable variety concept.

Definition 15. *An abstract class $\mathcal{K}$ of ω-complete ordered algebras is called an **ω-complete order variety** if $\mathcal{K}$ is closed under ω-complete ordered subalgebras, ω-complete ordered images, direct products, and free ω-completion.*

Let E be a set of inequalities, $Mod_\omega E$ denotes the class of all ***ω-complete ordered models*** of E, i.e., $Mod_\omega E = \{\boldsymbol{A} \in Mod_0 E \mid \boldsymbol{A}$ is an ω-complete ordered algebra$\}$. An abstract class $\mathcal{K}$ of ω-complete ordered algebras is called ***definable by inequalities*** if $\mathcal{K} = Mod_\omega E$ for some set E of inequalities.

Proposition 24. *If E is a set of inequalities, then $Mod_\omega E$ is an ω-complete order variety.*

The proof follows directly from Proposition 23 in conjunction with Proposition 3 in Section 4.2.1. ■

Theorem 25 (Meseguer's ω-Complete Order Variety Theorem). *Let $\mathcal{K}$ be an abstract class of ω-complete ordered algebras. Then $\mathcal{K}$ is an ω-complete order variety if and only if $\mathcal{K}$ is definable by inequalities.*

Proof. If an abstract class of ω-complete ordered algebras is definable by inequalities, then it is an ω-complete order variety by Proposition 24.

To prove the converse we assume that $\mathcal{K}$ is an ω-complete order variety of ω-complete ordered algebras. Define $E = Ineq\mathcal{K}$. We want to show that $\mathcal{K} = Mod_\omega E$. Evidently, $\mathcal{K}$ is a subclass of $Mod_\omega E$. So it remains to verify that each ω-complete ordered model of E belongs to $\mathcal{K}$.

Let $A \in Mod_\omega E$. First, we have a surjective strict morphism from the strict ordered term algebra over A to $\boldsymbol{A}$, namely $id_A^\S : \boldsymbol{T}_\Sigma(A_\perp) \to \boldsymbol{A}$, extending the identity mapping id_A. Now, consider the free ω-completion $\mathbf{C}_\omega(\boldsymbol{T}_\Sigma(A_\perp))$ of $\boldsymbol{T}_\Sigma(A_\perp)$, which is isomorphic to $\boldsymbol{Tr}_\Sigma(A)$. The dense reflection of $\boldsymbol{Tr}_\Sigma(A)$ in $\mathcal{K}$ yields the free ω-complete ordered algebra in $\mathcal{K}$, where $r : \boldsymbol{Tr}_\Sigma(A) \to \boldsymbol{F}_\mathcal{K}(A)_\omega$ is the related dense ω-morphism. Set $\boldsymbol{R} = r(\boldsymbol{T}_\Sigma(A_\perp))$ and let r' and f denote, respectively, the strict morphism from $\boldsymbol{T}_\Sigma(A_\perp)$ to $\boldsymbol{R}$ and the full ω-morphism from $\boldsymbol{R}$ to $\boldsymbol{F}_\mathcal{K}(A)_\omega$. Then we get the factorization $in_T \cdot r = r' \cdot f$, where in_T is the inclusion of $\boldsymbol{T}_\Sigma(A_\perp)$ into $\boldsymbol{Tr}_\Sigma(A)$.

Claim: There exists a morphism $h : \boldsymbol{R} \to \boldsymbol{A}$ such that $id_A^\S = r' \cdot h$.

It suffices to show that $ker_\le r' \subseteq ker_\le id_A^\S$. Note that $ker_\le r' = ker_\le r$. Let $t, t' \in T_\Sigma(A_\perp)$ with $X = var(t) \cup var(t')$. Suppose $(t, t') \in ker_\le r$. Then $r(t) \le r(t')$ and $\forall X(t \le t')$ is valid in $\boldsymbol{F}_\mathcal{K}(A)_\omega$; hence it is valid in $\mathcal{K}$. By assumption, $\boldsymbol{A}$ validates $\forall X(t \le t')$. That is, $id_A^\S(t) \le id_A^\S(t')$ and so $(t, t') \in ker_\le id_A^\S$. Thus h exists. In fact, h is a surjective strict morphism.

Second, consider the free ω-completion of $\boldsymbol{R}$. By definition, there is a unique ω-morphism $h_\omega : \mathbf{C}_\omega(\boldsymbol{R}) \to \boldsymbol{A}$ such that $h = m_R \cdot h_\omega$. Since h is surjective, so is h_ω. Thus $\boldsymbol{A}$ is an ω-complete ordered image of $\mathbf{C}_\omega(\boldsymbol{R})$.

On the other hand, $\mathbf{C}_\omega(\boldsymbol{R})$ is an ω-complete subalgebra of $\mathbf{C}_\omega(\boldsymbol{F}_\mathcal{K}(A)_\omega)$ because $\boldsymbol{R}$ is a strict ordered subalgebra of $\boldsymbol{F}_\mathcal{K}(A)_\omega$. By the assumption that $\mathcal{K}$ is closed under free ω-completions, $\mathbf{C}_\omega(\boldsymbol{F}_\mathcal{K}(A)_\omega)$ belongs to $\mathcal{K}$. Hence $\mathbf{C}_\omega(\boldsymbol{R})$ is in $\mathcal{K}$ since $\mathcal{K}$ is closed under ω-complete ordered subalgebras. Moreover, $\boldsymbol{A}$ is in $\mathcal{K}$ by the fact that $\mathcal{K}$ is closed under ω-complete ordered images. This proves that $Mod_\omega E$ is included in $\mathcal{K}$. ■

This result shows that, in principle, we are unable to express properties about suprema by inequalities (between terms) since such properties are not preserved under free ω-completions. On the contrary, each supremum of a countable chain in an ω-complete ordered algebra is destroyed in its free ω-completion. Therefore, a more general kind of formula is needed where trees are used instead of terms. If T and T' are trees over X, we call $\forall X(T \le T')$ an ***inequality between trees***. An ω-complete ordered algebra A validates $\forall X(T \le T')$ if $\alpha^\$(T) \le \alpha^\$(T')$ for all assignments α from X to A. A related variety result for abstract classes of ω-complete ordered algebras definable by inequalities between trees is derived in /Adamek-Nelson-88/, where the free ω-completion is replaced by the so-called absolute ω-completion.

4.2.4 Recursive Program Schemes

This section presents a short survey about the algebraic semantics of recursive program schemes; for a detailed investigation the interested reader is referred to /Guessarian-81/, /Nivat-Reynolds-85/.

As we already know (see Section 1.5.2), a recursive program can be considered as a finite set of recursive definitions for unknown functions.

Example 1. Let us consider the recursive definition of the faculty function

$$fac(x) = \textbf{\textit{if}}\ x = 0\ \textbf{\textit{then}}\ 1\ \textbf{\textit{else}}\ x * fac(x-1).$$

We introduce the following functions on natural numbers: f and m as binary functions and s as a unary function determined by $f(0, y) = 1$ and $f(x, y) = y$ iff $x \neq 0; m(x, y) = x * y$; and $s(x) = x - 1$ for all natural numbers x, y. Then we get

$$fac(x) = t^{\mathbb{N}}(x),$$

where $t^{\mathbb{N}}(x)$ is a function derived from the term $t = f(x, m(x, fac(s(x))))$ which is built up by the known function (symbols) f, m and s and the unknown function (symbol) fac. ■

In general, for the definition of a recursive program scheme we need two different signatures. Let us denote them by Σ and Φ, respectively. We prefer to call the elements of Σ ***function symbols***, while the elements of Φ are said to be ***function variables***. A combined signature, denoted by $\Sigma + \Phi$, is defined as follows: $(\Sigma + \Phi)_n = \Sigma_n \cup \Phi_n$ for all natural numbers n, where Σ and Φ are assumed to be disjoint. Furthermore, we suppose that both signatures are finite.

Example 2. Let Σ be a signature consisting of two binary function symbols f and m and a unary function symbol s and let Φ be a signature consisting of a single unary function variable F. Then

$$t = f(x, m(x, F(s(x))))$$

is a $(\Sigma + \Phi)$-term over $\{x\}$. ■

Given two signatures Σ and Φ of function symbols and function variables, respectively, a ***recursive program scheme***, ***RPS*** for short, is a system of equations

$$F_i(v_1, \ldots, v_{n_i}) = t_i \text{ for } i = 1, \ldots, m,$$

where t_i is a $(\Sigma + \Phi)$-term over $\{v_1, \ldots, v_{n_i}\}$ and n_i is the arity of F_i.

Example 3. Let Σ and Φ be two given signatures with a binary function symbol f, two unary function symbols g and h, and a nullary function symbol a in Σ, and a unary function variable F and a nullary function variable G in Φ. Then

$$\begin{aligned} F(v) &= f(g(v), G) \\ G &= f(a, h(F(a))). \end{aligned}$$

is a recursive program scheme. ■

In the sequel we will restrict ourselves to the special case where all function variables in any recursive program scheme are nullary. That is, $\Phi = \Phi_0$. Observe that a nullary function variable can be treated as an ordinary variable. Therefore, we shall write $\Phi_0 = \{x_1, \ldots, x_m\}$ and we shall agree to identify ground $(\Sigma + \Phi_0)$-terms with Σ-terms over Φ_0. Fix an countably infinite set $X = \{x_n \mid n \geq 1\}$ of variables. Then we define $X_0 = \emptyset$ and $X_m = \{x_1, \ldots, x_m\}$ for $m \geq 1$.

Now such a restricted recursive program scheme is a system of equations

$$x_i = t_i \text{ for } i = 1, \ldots, m,$$

where t_i is a Σ-term over X_m.

It is more convenient to write systems of term equations as mappings, which leads to the following definition.

Definition 16. *Let Σ be a signature. A* ***regular recursive program scheme*** *over Σ is a mapping*

$$S : X_m \to T_\Sigma(X_m)$$

for some natural number m.

When we present a regular RPS, we mostly do it in equational form. Instead of $S : X_m \to T_\Sigma(X_m)$ we write

$$x_i = t_i \text{ with } t_i = S(x_i) \text{ for } i = 1, \ldots, m.$$

Our aim is to interpret a regular RPS S over Σ in an ω-complete ordered Σ-algebra $\boldsymbol{A}$. Let $S : X_m \to T_\Sigma(X_m)$. First, a mapping S^A from A^m into itself is defined by the rule

$$S^A(a_1, \ldots, a_m) = (t_1^A(a_1, \ldots, a_m), \ldots, t_m^A(a_1, \ldots, a_m))$$

for all $a_1, \ldots, a_m$ in A, where t_i^A is the operation derived from t_i. S^A is said to be the ***realization*** of S in $\boldsymbol{A}$.

Lemma 26. *Let $S : X_m \to T_\Sigma(X_m)$ be a regular RPS and let $\boldsymbol{A}$ be an ω-complete ordered algebra. The realization of S in $\boldsymbol{A}$ is an ω-continuous mapping from A^m into itself.*

Proof. It suffices to show that any derived operation in the ω-complete ordered algebra $\boldsymbol{A}$ is ω-continuous. Derived operations are compositions of operations. By definition, each operation in $\boldsymbol{A}$ is ω-continuous. Therefore, it remains to show the following claim. If $f, g_1, \ldots, g_n$ are ω-continuous mapping such that f is n-ary and $g_1, \ldots, g_n$ are m-ary, then the composition $f(g_1, \ldots, g_n)$ is also ω-continuous, where $f(g_1, \ldots, g_n)$ is defined by $f(g_1, \ldots, g_n)(a_1, \ldots, a_m) = f(g_1(a_1, \ldots, a_m), \ldots, g_n(a_1, \ldots, a_m))$ for all $a_1, \ldots, a_m$ in A. Let $g = g_1 \times \ldots \times g_n$ and put $a = (a_1, \ldots, a_m)$. Then $f(g_1, \ldots, g_n)(a_1, \ldots, a_m) =$

$f(g(a))$. Since the composition of any two ω-continuous mappings is again an ω-continuous mapping, we have proved the claim. ■

This result enables us to use the Fixpoint Theorem (Theorem 7 in Section 1.5.2). If $S : X_m \to T_\Sigma(X_m)$ is a regular RPS, then its realization S^A in any ω-complete ordered algebra $\boldsymbol{A}$ has a least fixpoint:

$$fix(S^A) = \sup((S^A)^n(\perp^A, \ldots, \perp^A) \mid n \in I\!N),$$

where $\perp^A$ is the least element of $\boldsymbol{A}$. Note that $fix(S^A)$ is an m-tuple $(a_1, \ldots, a_m)$ of elements from A.

The first component a_1, denoted by $Val_A(S)$, will be given a name. We think of the first equation in any (regular) RPS as the "main recursive definition (procedure)".

Definition 17. *Let S be a regular RPS and let $\boldsymbol{A}$ be an ω-complete ordered algebra. The first component of the least fixpoint of the realization of S in $\boldsymbol{A}$, $Val_A(S)$, is called the* ***computed value*** *of S in $\boldsymbol{A}$.*

Now we are going to find a purely syntactic solution of a regular RPS. As we know (Theorem 20 in Section 4.2.3), the tree algebra over X is the absolutely free ω-complete ordered algebra. In particular, the ground tree algebra $\boldsymbol{Tr}_\Sigma$ is initial in the class of all ω-complete ordered algebras. By definition, there exists exactly one ω-morphism from $\boldsymbol{Tr}_\Sigma$ to any ω-complete ordered algebra $\boldsymbol{A}$, say $h_A : \boldsymbol{Tr}_\Sigma \to \boldsymbol{A}$, defined by the following conditions:

(1) $h_A(\perp) = \perp^A$ and $h_A(\sigma) = \sigma^A$ for all $\sigma \in \Sigma_0$.

(2) $h_A(\sigma^{Tr_\Sigma}(T_1, \ldots, T_n)) = \sigma^A(h_A(T_1), \ldots, h_A(T_n))$ for all $\sigma \in \Sigma_n$ and all $T_1, \ldots, T_n$ in Tr_Σ.

As a direct consequence we get that derived operations are compatible with the unique ω-morphism. Let t be a Σ-term over X_m. Then

$$h_A(t^{Tr_\Sigma}(T_1, \ldots, T_m)) = t^A(h_A(T_1), \ldots, h_A(T_m))$$

for all $T_1, \ldots, T_m$ in Tr_Σ.

Example 4. Let a signature Σ be given by a binary function symbol f, a unary function symbol g and a nullary function symbol c. Consider the regular RPS S defined by

$$x = f(g(x), c).$$

The computed value of S in $\boldsymbol{Tr}_\Sigma$ is the ground tree T with $Dom(T) = \{1^n \mid n \in I\!N\} \cup \{1^{2n}.2 \mid n \in I\!N\}$ and

$$T(w) = \begin{cases} f & \text{if } w = 1^{2n}, n \in I\!N, \\ g & \text{if } w = 1^{2n}.1, n \in I\!N, \\ c & \text{if } w = 1^{2n}.2, n \in I\!N, \end{cases}$$

(see Section 1.4.2). The (infinite) tree T can be regarded as a purely syntactic solution, and no interpretation of f, g and c is needed.

Now, take any ω-complete ordered algebra $\boldsymbol{A}$. If we map T into $\boldsymbol{A}$, we get

$$h_A(T) = f^A(g^A(h_A(T)), c^A).$$

Put $h_A(T) = a$. This yields $a = f^A(g^A(a), c^A)$. By the ω-continuity of h_A, a is the least solution of this equation. Hence

$$h_A(T) = Val_A(S).$$

The computed value of S in $\boldsymbol{A}$ is the image of T under h_A. ■

Definition 18. *Let S be a regular RPS. The computed value of S in the ground tree algebra is called the* ***symbolic solution*** *of S; it is denoted by $T(S)$.*

The symbolic solution contains all information about the computed values in any ω-complete ordered algebra.

Theorem 27 (Mezei-Wright Theorem). *Let S be a regular RPS. The computed value of S in any ω-complete ordered algebra $\boldsymbol{A}$ is the image of the symbolic solution under the unique ω-morphism h_A. Formally,*

$$Val_A(S) = h_A(T(S)).$$

Proof. Let $S : X_m \to T_\Sigma(X_m)$ be a regular RPS and let $\boldsymbol{A}$ be an ω-complete ordered algebra. Consider the realization of S in $\boldsymbol{A}$ and $\boldsymbol{Tr}_\Sigma$, S^A and S^{Tr_Σ}, respectively. Both realizations are ω-continuous by Lemma 26. Hence the last fixpoints $fix(S^A)$ and $fix(S^{Tr_\Sigma})$ exist.

Now, by the observation above that all derived operations are compatible with h_A, we get

$$H_A(S^{Tr_\Sigma}(T_1, \ldots, T_m)) = S^A(h_A(T_1), \ldots, h_A(T_m))$$

for all $T_1, \ldots, T_m$ in Tr_Σ, where $H_A = h_A \times \ldots \times h_A$ (m times). Note that H_A is an ω-morphism from $\boldsymbol{Tr}_\Sigma^m$ to $\boldsymbol{A}^m$. This yields

$$\begin{aligned} H_A((S^{Tr_\Sigma})^n(\bot, \ldots, \bot)) &= (S^A)^n(h_A(\bot), \ldots, h_A(\bot)) \\ &= (S^A)^n(\bot^A, \ldots, \bot^A) \end{aligned}$$

for all natural numbers n. Hence

$$\begin{aligned} H_A(fix(S^{Tr_\Sigma})) &= H_A(\sup((S^{Tr_\Sigma})^n(\bot, \ldots, \bot) \mid n \in \mathbb{N})) \\ &= \sup(H_A((S^A)^n(\bot^A, \ldots, \bot^A)) \mid n \in \mathbb{N}) \\ &= \sup((S^A)^n(\bot^A, \ldots, \bot^A) \mid n \in \mathbb{N}) \\ &= fix(S^A). \end{aligned}$$

In particular, the first component of $fix(S^{Tr_\Sigma})$ is mapped onto the first component of $fix(S^A)$ under h_A. That is,

$$h_A(T(S)) = Val_A(S). \qquad \blacksquare$$

The symbolic solution can also be computed in an ***operational*** way. To each regular RPS $S : X_m \to T_\Sigma(X_m)$ we assign a term rewriting systems $R(S)$ as follows

$$R(S) = \{x_i \to \bot \mid i = 1, \ldots, m\} \cup \{x_i \to t_i \mid i = 1, \ldots, m\}.$$

Terms over $\{\bot\}$ will be identified with finite ground trees. Now, consider the set of all finite ground trees t which can be rewritten from x_1, i.e., $\{t \in FTr_\Sigma \mid x_1 \Rightarrow^*_{R(S)} t\}$. Each such t is a compact element of Tr_Σ (cf. Proposition 16 in Section 1.5.3) with the property $t \sqsubseteq T(S)$ and, vice versa, every compact element t of Tr_Σ with $t \sqsubseteq T(S)$ can be rewritten from x_1. Hence, $Fin(T(S)) = \{t \in FTr_\Sigma \mid x_1 \Rightarrow^*_{R(S)} t\}$ and, consequently,

$$T(S) = \sup\{t \in FTr_\Sigma \mid x_1 \Rightarrow^*_{R(S)} t\},$$

by Lemma 17 in Section 1.5.3 in connection with Theorem 22 in Section 1.5.3.

Example 5. Consider the regular RPS given in Example 3:

$$x = f(g(x), c).$$

The associated TRS consists of the two reduction rules

$$x \to \bot \text{ and } x \to f(g(x), c).$$

The following finite ground trees can be rewritten: $\bot$, $f(g(\bot), c)$, $f(g(f(g(\bot), c)), c)$, $f(g(f(g(f(g(\bot), c)), c)), c), \ldots$ It is easily seen that these are just the finite cuts of the symbolic solution (see Example 3). $\blacksquare$

We close the section with a simple semantical consideration of regular RPSs. First, a quasi-order $\lesssim$ on all regular RPSs is introduced. Let S_1 and S_2 be regular RPSs. We define $S_1 \lesssim S_2$ if $Val_A(S_1) \leq Val_A(S_2)$ for all ω-complete ordered algebras $\boldsymbol{A}$. When $S_1 \sim S_2$, i.e., $S_1 \lesssim S_2$ and $S_2 \lesssim S_1$, we say that S_1 and S_2 are ***semantically equal.***

Semantical equality can be reduced to the syntactic equality of the symbolic solutions, as we shall prove below. That is to say, semantics can be reduced to syntax.

Theorem 28. *For any two regular RPSs S_1 and S_2, we have*

$$S_1 \lesssim S_2 \textit{ iff } T(S_1) \sqsubseteq T(S_2).$$

Proof. Let S_1 and S_2 be regular RPSs. If $S_1 \lesssim S_2$, then $Val_A(S_1) \leq Val_A(S_2)$ and hence $Val_{Tr_\Sigma}(S_1) \leq Val_{Tr_\Sigma}(S_2)$, i.e., $T(S_1) \sqsubseteq T(S_2)$. Conversely, assume that $T(S_1) \sqsubseteq T(S_2)$. Then $h_A(S_1) \leq h_A(S_2)$ for all ω-complete ordered algebras $\boldsymbol{A}$, by the monotonicity of h_A. Thus $Val_A(S_1) \leq Val_A(S_2)$, by the Mezei-Wright Theorem. Now, by definition, $S_1 \lesssim S_2$. ■

In a more general setting we would fix a class $\mathcal{K}$ of ω-complete ordered algebras and define $S_1 \lesssim_{\mathcal{K}} S_2$ if $Val_A(S_1) \leq Val_A(S_2)$ for all $\boldsymbol{A}$ in $\mathcal{K}$. To use the symbolic solution above, we must require that the initial ω-complete ordered algebra exists in $\mathcal{K}$. Let $T_{\mathcal{K}}(S)$ denote the computed value of any regular RPS S in the initial ω-complete ordered algebra in $\mathcal{K}$. Then we obtain

$$S_1 \lesssim_{\mathcal{K}} S_2 \text{ iff } T_{\mathcal{K}}(S_1) \sqsubseteq T_{\mathcal{K}}(S_2)$$

as a generalization of the result obtained above.

Now, the question arises whether it is possible to derive inequalities of (infinite) trees syntactically by an appropriate formal proof system. As we know, this question is closely connected with the construction of the initial ω-complete ordered algebra in $\mathcal{K}$. The related problems were already mentioned in the previous sections. Let $\boldsymbol{F}_{\mathcal{K},\omega}$ denote the initial ω-complete ordered algebra in $\mathcal{K}$. $\boldsymbol{F}_{\mathcal{K},\omega}$ is isomorphic to the free ω-completion of the initial strict ordered algebra in $\mathcal{K}$, denoted by $\boldsymbol{F}_{\mathcal{K},\perp}$. For the sake of simplicity we shall identify both algebras. That is $\boldsymbol{F}_{\mathcal{K},\omega} = \mathbf{C}_\omega(\boldsymbol{F}_{\mathcal{K},\perp})$. Observe that $\boldsymbol{F}_{\mathcal{K},\perp}$ can be represented as a quotient algebra of $\boldsymbol{FTr}_\Sigma$ modulo an admissible quasi-congruence $\lesssim$.

From the logical point of view the algebraic properties of $\lesssim$ correspond to the inference rules (IEL0) to (IEL6) presented in Sections 4.2.1 and 4.2.2. Note that the rule of full invariance, (IEL4), is superfluous for the ground case. The crucial point is now the "syntactic description" of the free ω-completion. Given a strict ordered algebra $\boldsymbol{A}$, the carrier of its free ω-completion, $\mathbf{C}_\omega(\boldsymbol{A})$, is denoted by A_ω. In Section 1.5.3 we have shown that A_ω consists of all ideals $(X]$, where $X \in \mathcal{D}_\omega(A)$. $\mathcal{D}_\omega(A)$ denotes the set of all nonempty countable directed subsets of A. The ordering in A_ω is defined as follows: $(X] \leq (Y]$ iff X is cofinal in Y. X is cofinal in Y, in symbols $X \sqsubseteq Y$, iff $\forall x \in X \, \exists y \in Y (x \leq y)$.

Now, it is important to observe that A_ω is isomorphic to the quotient poset $\mathcal{D}_\omega(A)/\sqsubseteq$. That is to say, free ω-completion is essentially described by cofinality, which is expressible as a generalized inference rule:

$$\frac{\forall i \in I\!N \, \exists j \in I\!N (t_i \leq t'_j)}{\sup(t_n \mid n \in I\!N) \leq \sup(t'_n \mid n \in I\!N)}$$

where $(t_n \mid n \in I\!N)$ and $(t'_n \mid n \in I\!N)$ are supposed to be ω-chains of finite ground trees. Keep in mind that every (ground) tree is the supremum of an ω-chain of finite (ground) trees.

Together with the modified inference rules (IEL0) to (IEL6), without (IEL4), where (possibly infinite) trees are used instead of terms, we obtain a complete and sound logic for inequalities of trees (cf. /Guessarian-85/).

References

LNCS abbreviates Lecture Notes in Computer Science.

/Adamek-88/
Adamek, J.: How many variables does a quasi-variety need? *Algebra Universalis* **27**, 44-48 (1990)

/Adamek-Nelson-88/
Adamek, J.; Nelson, E.: Absolutely definable varieties of continuous algebras. *Algebra Universalis* **24**, 267-278 (1987)

/Adamek-Nelson-Reiterman-86/
Adamek, J.; Nelson, E.; Reiterman, J.: Continuous semilattices. *Theoretical Computer Science* **43**, 293-313 (1986)

/ADJ-76/
Goguen, J.; Thatcher, J.; Wagner, E.: An initial algebra approach to the specification, correctness and implementation of abstract data types. *Technical Report* RC 6487, IBM T.J. Watson Research Center, Oct. 1976
Reprinted in: Yeh, R. (ed.): *Current Trends in Programming Methodology IV.* Prentice-Hall 1978, pp. 80-149

/Bachmair-Plaisted-85/
Bachmair, L.; Plaisted, D.A.: Associative path ordering. *J. Symbolic Computation* **1**, 329-349 (1985)

/Banaschewski-Herrlich-76/
Banaschewski, B.; Herrlich, H.: Subcategories defined by implications. *Houston J. Math.* **2**, 149-171 (1976)

/Banaschewski-Nelson-82/
Banaschewski, B.; Nelson, E.: Completion of partially ordered sets. *SIAM J. Comput.* **11**, 521-528 (1982)

/Ben-Cherifa-Lescanne-86/
Ben-Cherifa, A.; Lescanne, P.: An actual implementation of a procedure that mechanically proves termination of rewriting systems based on inequalities between polynomial interpretations. *LNCS* **230**, Springer 1986, pp. 42-51

/Benninghofen-Kemmerich-Richter-87/
Benninghofen, B.; Kemmerich, S.; Richter, M.M.: *Systems of Reductions. LNCS* **277**, Springer 1987

/Bergstra-Tucker-88/
Bergstra, J.; Tucker, J.V.: The inescapable stack: an exercise in algebraic specification with total functions. *Report* P8804, University of Amsterdam, Dept. of Mathematics and Computer Science, Feb. 1988

/Birkhoff-35/
Birkhoff, G.: On the structure of abstract algebras. *Proc. Cambridge Phil. Soc.* **31**, 433-454 (1935)

/Birkhoff-44/
Birkhoff, G.: Subdirect unions in universal algebra. *Amer. Math. Soc.* **50**, 764-768 (1944)

/Birkhoff-48/
Birkhoff, G.: *Lattice Theory*, New York: AMS, rev. ed., 1948

/Birkhoff-Frink-48/
Birkhoff, G.; Frink, O.: Representation of lattices by sets. *Trans. Amer. Math. Soc.* **64**, 299-316 (1948)

/Birkhoff-Lipson-70/
Birkhoff, G.; Lipson, J.D.: Heterogeneous algebras. *J. Comb. Theory* **8**, 115-133 (1970)

/Bloom-76/
Bloom, S.L.: Varieties of ordered algebras. *J. Computer and System Science* **13**, 200-212 (1976)

/Bloom-Wright-82/
Bloom, S.L., Wright, J.B.: Finitary quasi varieties. *J. Pure and Appl. Algebra* **25**, 121-154 (1982)

/Boone-59/
Boone, W.N.: The word problem. *Ann. Math.* **70**, 207-265 (1959)

/Buchberger-87/
Buchberger, B.: History and basic features of the critical-pair/completion procedure. *J. Symbolic Computation* **3**, 3-38 (1987)

/Burmeister-88/
Burmeister, P.: private communication, 1988

/Burris-Sankappanavar-81/
Burris, S.; Sankappanavar, H.P.: *A Course in Universal Algebra*. Springer 1981

/Burstall-Goguen-82/
Burstall, R.M.; Goguen, J.: Algebras, theories and freeness: An introduction for computer scientists. Proc. Intern. Summer School *Theoretical Foundations of Programming Methodology*, Marktoberdorf 1981, Dordrecht: Reidel 1982

/Davis-58/
Davis, M.: *Computability and Unsolvability*. New York: McGraw-Hill, 1958

/Davis-Matijasevic-Robinson-76/
Davis, M; Matijasevic, Y.V.; Robinson, J.: Hilbert's tenth problem. Diophantine equations: positive aspects of a negative solution. *Proc. Symposia in Pure Math. AMS* **28**, 323-378 (1976)

/Dershowitz-79/
Dershowitz, N.: A note on simplification orderings. *Inform. Processing Letters* **9**, 212-215 (1979)

/Dershowitz-82/
Dershowitz, N.: Orderings for term-rewriting systems. *Theoretical Computer Science* **17**, 279-301 (1982)

/Dershowitz-87/
Dershowitz, N.: Termination of rewriting. *J. Symbolic Computation* **3**, 69-116 (1987)

/Dershowitz-Jouannaud-90/
Dershowitz, N.; Jouannand, J.P.: Rewrite systems. In: van Leeuwen, J. (ed.): *Handbook of Theoretical Computer Science*, vol. B. Amsterdam: Elsevier 1990

/Dershowitz-Manna-79/
Dershowitz, N.; Manna, Z.: Proving termination with multiset orderings. *Commun. ACM* **22**, 465-476 (1979)

/Drosten-89/
Drosten, K.: *Termersetzungssysteme.* Informatik-Fachberichte 210. Springer 1989

/Ehrich-Gogolla-Lipeck-89/
Ehrich, H.-D.; Gogolla, M.; Lipeck, U.W.: *Algebraische Spezifikation abstrakter Datentypen.* Stuttgart: Teubner-Verlag 1989

/Ehrig-Mahr-85/
Ehrig, H.; Mahr, B.: *Fundamentals of Algebraic Specification 1.* Springer 1985

/Ehrig-Mahr-90/
Ehrig, H.; Mahr, B.: *Fundamentals of Algebraic Specification 2.* Springer 1990

/Evans-78/
Evans, T.: Word problems. *Bull. AMS* **84**, 789-802 (1978)

/Fujiwara-71/
Fujiwara, T.: On the construction of the least universal Horn class containing a given class. *Osaka J. Math.* **8**, 425-436 (1971)

/Goguen-Meseguer-85/
Goguen, J.; Meseguer, J.: Completeness of many-sorted logic. *Houston J. Math.* **11**, 307-334 (1985)

/Goguen-Meseguer-86/
Goguen, J.; Meseguer, J.: *Semantics of Computation.* Book manuscript 1986

/Grätzer-Lakser-70/
Grätzer, G.; Lakser, H.: Some new relations on operators in general for pseudocomplemented lattices in particular. *Notices of the ACM* **17**, 642-653 (1970)

/Guessarian-81/
Guessarian, I.: *Algebraic Semantics. LNCS* **99**, Springer 1981

/Guessarian-85/
Guessarian, I.: Survey on classes of interpretations and some of their applications. In: Nivat, M., Reynolds, J. C. (eds.): *Algebraic Methods of Semantics.* Cambridge: Cambridge University Press 1985, pp. 384-409

/Guttag-75/
Guttag, J.: The specification and application to programming of abstract data types. *PhD thesis*, University of Toronto, Computer Science Department, *Report* CSRG-59, 1975

/Halmos-74/
Halmos, P.: *Naive Set Theory*. Springer 1974

/Higgins-63/
Higgins, P.J.: Algebras with a scheme of operators. *Math. Nachrichten* **27**, 115-132 (1963)

/Higman-52/
Higman, G.: Orderings by divisibility in abstract algebras. *Proc. London Math. Soc.* **3**, 326-336 (1952)

/Hoehnke-83/
Hoehnke, H.-J.: Fully invariant closure systems of congruences and quasi varieties of algebras. *Coll. Math. Soc. J. Bolyai* vol. **43**, Lectures in Universal Algebra, Szeged (Hungary), 1983, pp. 189-207

/Huet-81/
Huet, G.: A complete proof of correctness of the Knuth-Bendix completion algorithm. *J. Computer and System Science* **23**, 11-21 (1981)

/Huet-Lankford-78/
Huet, G.; Lankford, D.S.: On the uniform halting problem for term rewriting systems. *Rapport* Laboria 283, INRIA, March 1978

/Huet-Oppen-80/
Huet, G.; Oppen, D.: Equations and rewrite rules: a survey. In: Book, R. (ed.): *Formal Languages: Perspectives and Open Problems.* New York, London: Academic Press 1980

/Hussmann-85/
Hussmann, H.: Unification in conditional-equational theories. *Technical Report* MIP-8502, University of Passau, Jan. 1985 (Corrigenda 1988)

/Jouannaud-Lescanne-87/
Jouannaud, J.-P.; Lescanne, P.: Rewriting systems. *Technology and Science of Informatics* **6**, 181-199 (1987)

/Jouannaud-Lescanne-Reinig-82/
Jouannaud, J.-P.; Lescanne, P.; Reinig, F.: Recursive decomposition ordering. *Proc. of the Second IFIP Workshop on Formal Description of Programming Concepts*, Garmisch-Partenkirchen 1982, pp. 331-348

/Kaplan-84/
Kaplan, S.: Conditional rewrite rules. *Theoretical Computer Science* **33**, 175-193 (1984)

/Kapur-Narendra-Sivakumar-85/
Kapur, D.; Narendra, P.; Sivakumar, G.: A path ordering for proving termination of term rewriting systems. *LNCS* **185**, Springer 1985, pp. 173-185

/Kashiwagi-65/
Kashiwagi, T.: On (m, A)-implicational classes. *Mathematica Japonicae* **17**, 253-272 (1965)

/Klaeren-83/
Klaeren, J.B.: *Algebraische Spezifikation. Eine Einführung.* Springer 1983

/Klop-87/
Klop, J.W.: Term rewriting systems: A tutorial. *Bull. EATCS* **32**, 143-182 (1987)

/Knuth-Bendix-70/
Knuth, D.F.; Bendix P.B.: Simple word problems in universal algebras. In: Leech, J. (ed.): *Computational Problems in Abstract Algebra.* Oxford: Pergamon Press 1970, pp. 263-297

/König-26/
König, D.: Sur les correspondences multivoques des ensembles. *Fund. Math.* **8**, 114-134 (1926)

/Kogalovskii-65/
Kogalovskii, S.R.: On a theorem of Birkhoff (Russian). *Uspehi Mat. Nauk.* **20**, 206-207 (1965)

/Kruse-67/
Kruse, A.H.: An abstract property P for groupoids such that locally locally P is weaker than locally P. *J. London Math. Soc.* **42**, 81-85 (1987)

/Kruskal-60/
Kruskal, J.B.: Well-quasi-ordering, the Tree theorem, and Vazsonyi's conjecture. *Trans. Amer. Math. Soc.* **95**, 210-225 (1960)

/Kruskal-72/
Kruskal, J.B.: The theory of well-quasi-ordering: A frequently discovered concept. *J. Comb. Theory Ser. A* **13**, 297-305 (1972)

/Lankford-79/
Lankford, D.S.: On proving term rewriting systems are Noetherian. *Memo* MTP-3, Mathematics Department, Louisiana Tech. University, Ruston 1979

/Lassez-Nguyen-Sonenberg-82/
Lassez, J.-L.; Nguyen, V.L.; Sonenberg, E.A.: Fixed point theorems and semantics: A folk tale. *Inform. Processing Letters* **14**, 112-116 (1982)

/Le Chenadec-86/
Le Chenadec, P.: *Canonical Forms in Finitely Presented Algebras.* New York, Toronto: John Wiley 1986

/Lescanne-84/
Lescanne, P.: Some properties of decomposition ordering, a simplification ordering to prove termination of rewriting systems. *RAIRO Theoretical Informatics* **16**, 331-347 (1984)

/Loeckx-Sieber-84/
Loeckx, J.; Sieber, K.: *The Foundations of Program Verification.* Stuttgart: Teubner-Verlag 1984

/Manna-Ness-70/
Manna, Z.; Ness, S.: Termination of Markov algorithms. *Proc. of the Third Hawaii International Conference on System Science*, Honolulu 1970, pp. 789-792

/Markowsky-76/
Markowsky, G.: Chain-complete posets and directed sets with applications. *Algebra Universalis* **6**, 53-68 (1976)

/Meseguer-78/
Meseguer, J.: Completions, factorizations and colimits for ω-posets. *Coll. Math. Soc. J. Bolyai*, vol. **26**, Mathematical Logic in Computer Science, Salgótarján (Hungary), 1978, pp. 509-545

/Meseguer-81/
Meseguer, J.: A Birkhoff-like theorem for algebraic classes of interpretations of program schemes. *LNCS* **107**, Springer 1981, pp. 152-168

/Meseguer-Goguen-85/
Meseguer, J.; Goguen, J.A.: Initiality, induction, and computability. In: Nivat, M.; Reynolds, J.C. (eds.): *Algebraic Methods in Semantics.* Cambridge: Cambridge University Press 1985

/Milner-79/
Milner, R.: LCF: a way of doing proofs with a machine. *LNCS* **92**, Springer 1979, pp. 146-159

/Nash-Williams-63/
Nash-Williams, C.St.J.A.: On well-quasi-ordering finite trees. *Proc. Cambridge Phil. Soc.* **59**, 833-835 (1963)

/Neumann-62/
Neumann, B.H.: *Special Topics in Algebra: Universal Algebra.* Lectures delivered in the Fall Semester 1961-62. Courant Institute of Math. Sciences, New York University, 1962

/Newman-42/
Newman, M.H.A.: On theories with a combinatorial definition of "equivalence". *Ann. Math.* **43**, 223-243 (1942)

/Nivat-Reynolds-85/
Nivat, M.; Reynolds, J. C. (eds.): *Algebraic Methods in Semantics.* Cambridge: Cambridge University Press 1985

/Nourani-81/
Nourani, F.: On induction for programming logic: syntax, semantics, and inductive closure. *Bull. EATCS* **13**, 51-64 (1981)

/Park-70/
Park, D.: Fixpoint induction and proofs of program properties. In: Meltzler, B.; Michie, D. (eds.): *Machine Intelligence 5.* Edinburgh: Edinburgh University Press, 1970, pp. 59-78

/Pedersen-84/
Pedersen, J.F.: Confluence methods and the word problem in universal algebra. *PhD thesis*, Department of Mathematics and Computer Science, Emory University, 1984

/Platt-71/
Platt, C.: Iterated limits of universal algebras. *Algebra Universalis* **1**, 167-181 (1971)

/Plotkin-76/
Plotkin, G.D.: A powerdomain construction. *SIAM J. Comput.* **5**, 452-487 (1976)

/Puel-76/
Puel, L.: Using unavoidable sets of trees to generalize Kruskal's theorem. *Rapport*-LITP, Paris 1965

/Raoult-88/
Raoult, J.-C.: Induction on open properties. *Rapport* INRIA, No. 813, March 1988, Le Chesnay

/Rusinowitch-87/
Rusinowitch, M.: Path of subterms ordering and recursive decomposition ordering revisited. *J. Symbolic Computation* **3**, 117-131 (1987)

/Sannella-Tarlecki-87/
Sannella, D.; Tarlecki, A.: Some thoughts on algebraic specification. *Report* ECS-LFCS-87-21, Department of Computer Science, University of Edinburgh, March 1987

/Selman-72/
Selman, A.: Completeness of calculi for axiomatically defined classes of algebras. *Algebra Universalis* **2**, 20-32 (1972)

/Simpson-85/
Simpson, S.G.: Nichtbeweisbarkeit von gewissen kombinatorischen Eigenschaften endlicher Bäume. *Archiv für Mathematik, Logik und Grundlagen* **25**, 45-65 (1985)

/Stoll-61/
Stoll, R.R.: *Set Theory and Logic.* San Francisco, London: W.H. Freeman 1961

/Scott-Strachey-71/
Scott, D.S.; Strachey, C.: Toward a mathematical semantics for computer languages. In: Fox, J. (ed.): *Proc. Symp. Computers and Automata.* Polytechnic Institute of Brooklyn Press, 1971, pp. 19-46

/Tarski-45/
Tarski, A.: A remark on functionally free algebras. *Ann. Math.* **47**, 163-165 (1947)

Appendix 1

Sets and Classes

The aim of this appendix is to present for an interested reader a more detailed introduction to set theory, which is not really necessary to understand universal algebra as developed in Chap. 3. It is assumed that nonformalized set theory is familiar to the reader.

The concept of a ***set*** is used intuitively as it was originally proposed by G. Cantor, the founder of set theory. According to his definition, a set is "any collection of definite and separate objects of our intuition or thought into a whole" [1]. The essential point is that a collection of objects is to be regarded as a single entity.

As usual, the membership relation is denoted by $\in$ and its negation by $\notin$. The ***equality of sets*** is defined by extensionality: two sets A and B are equal, in symbols $A = B$, whenever $x \in A$ iff $x \in B$ for all x. It should be noticed that the principle of extension is a nontrivial assumption about the membership relation. Following Halmos let us interpret, for instance, $x \in A$ as "x is an ancestor of (a human being) A". If $A = B$, then $x \in A$ iff $x \in B$ for all x, but the opposite implication is not true.

By the principle of extension a set is fully determined by its elements. Therefore we have two ways of specifying sets: a set may be given as a list of its elements or the elements of a set may be described by a property which characterizes them. The uniquely determined set whose elements are $x_1, x_2, \ldots, x_n$ will be written $\{x_1, x_2, \ldots, x_n\}$. The second possibility is based on the famous ***set-building principle*** due to G. Frege [2]:

$$\{x \mid \mathcal{P}(x)\}$$

where $\mathcal{P}$ is a property so that $a \in \{x \mid \mathcal{P}(x)\}$ iff a has the property $\mathcal{P}$. We will use predicative formulas (often in a rather informal way) to define such properties [3]. Various modifications of the basic brace notation for sets will be allowed (as $\{x \in A \mid \mathcal{P}(x)\}$, $\{f(x) \mid \mathcal{P}(x)\}$ and so on) where the meaning is clear from the context.

It is well known that an unrestricted use of set-building leads to contradictions. One example is Russell's paradox: If the collection of all sets that are not elements of themselves is a set, then this set has the property that it is an element of itself if and only if it is not an element of itself. Generally speaking, such contradictions arise from considering "very large" collections as sets. In principle, there are two alternatives to prevent

---

[1] Cantor,G.: Beiträge zur Begründung der transfiniten Mengenlehre. Math. Ann. **46** (1895), 418-512

[2] Frege, G.: Grundgesetze der Arithmetik, begriffsschriftlich abgeleitet. Bd. I. Jena 1893

[3] $\mathcal{P}(x)$ is technically expressed in terms of x, the membership relation, the equality of sets, and the logical connectives, including quantifications of sets.

those contradictions. Either we restrict set-building by permitting only a certain kind of properties or we must distinguish two types of collections: arbitrary collections that we call ***classes*** and certain special collections that we call sets. Here we prefer the second alternative. However, classes and sets will be treated only on an intuitive level[4]. Classes will be considered as collections generalizing sets in the following sense:

For each property $\mathcal{P}$ of sets we can form the class $\{X \mid \mathcal{P}(X)\}$.

In other words, $\{X \mid \mathcal{P}(X)\}$ represents the collection of all sets X such that X has the property $\mathcal{P}$, even if that collection is not a set. Of course, every set A is a class; for $A = \{X \mid X \in A\}$.

Note that we only allow to build up classes from sets and not classes from classes. For example, all sets form a class: $\{X \mid X = X\}$, called the ***universal class***. Another example is the Russell class $\mathcal{R} = \{X \mid X \notin X\}$. Now, Russell's paradox is resolved since $\mathcal{R}$ is not a set. Classes which are not sets are said to be ***proper***.

Taking into account that the elements of a class are always sets and that any set belongs to a class, we have the following criterion:

A is a set iff $A \in \mathcal{A}$ for some class $\mathcal{A}$.

Although it is necessary in axiomatic set theory to analyse each property $\mathcal{P}$ whether the class $\{X \mid \mathcal{P}(X)\}$ is, in particular, a set or not, we will simply treat such a class as a set if it is intuitively clear that $\{X \mid \mathcal{P}(X)\}$ is not "too large" [5].

Equality of classes is defined as for sets. Let $\mathcal{A}$ and $\mathcal{B}$ be classes. We say that $\mathcal{A}$ and $\mathcal{B}$ are ***equal***, in symbols $\mathcal{A} = \mathcal{B}$, if $X \in \mathcal{A}$ iff $X \in \mathcal{B}$ for all X. In an axiomatic approach we call this property of the membership relation the ***Axiom of Extensionality***. Given classes $\mathcal{A}$ and $\mathcal{B}$, $\mathcal{A}$ is called a ***subclass*** of $\mathcal{B}$, in symbols $\mathcal{A} \subseteq \mathcal{B}$, if all X of $\mathcal{A}$ belong to $\mathcal{B}$. It is intuitively clear that any subclass of a set is also a set.

The ***power class***, denoted by $\wp(\mathcal{A})$, of a given class $\mathcal{A}$ is the class of all subsets of $\mathcal{A}$, i.e., $\wp(\mathcal{A}) = \{X \mid X \subseteq \mathcal{A}\}$. In particular, if $\mathcal{A}$ is a set, then so is $\wp(\mathcal{A})$. (Then $\wp(\mathcal{A})$ is called the power set of $\mathcal{A}$.) In axiomatic set theory this property is stated as the ***Power Set Axiom***.

---

[4] For a clear discussion of axiomatic set theory and the definition of classes see Schoenfield, J.R.: Axioms of set theory. In: Barwise, J. (ed.): Handbook of Mathematical Logic (Part B). Amsterdam: North-Holland 1977

[5] Schoenfield says that "sets are intended to be those safe, comfortable classes which are used by mathematicians in their daily life and work, whereas proper classes are thought of as monstrously large collections which, if permitted to be sets, would engender contradictions".

Union and intersection can be defined for classes. Given a class $\mathcal{A}$, we put

$$\bigcup \mathcal{A} = \{X \mid X \in Y \text{ for some } Y \in \mathcal{A}\},$$
$$\bigcap \mathcal{A} = \{X \mid X \in Y \text{ for all } Y \in \mathcal{A}\}.$$

Here we have the next rule which says that $\bigcup \mathcal{A}$ is a set whenever $\mathcal{A}$ is a set. This property is called the ***Union Axiom*** in an axiomatic set theory.

By definition, $\bigcup \emptyset = \emptyset$ and $\bigcap \emptyset = \mathcal{U}$, where $\mathcal{U}$ is the universal class introduced above. Concerning intersection we can show that $\bigcap \mathcal{A}$ is a set provided that $\mathcal{A}$ is a nonempty set. Let us assume that $\mathcal{A}$ is a nonempty set. Then there is an element X of $\mathcal{A}$, which is certainly a set. Because of $\bigcap \mathcal{A} \subseteq X$, $\bigcap \mathcal{A}$ is a set, too.

To extend the notion of direct product to classes we have to generalize the concept of an ordered pair. In set theory this concept was used to express the following two properties: (1) for any two objects x and y there exists an object denoted by (x, y), called an ordered pair; (2) given two ordered pairs (x, y) and (u, v), then $(x, y) = (u, v)$ iff $x = u$ and $y = v$. It was Kuratowski's simple but excellent idea [6] to define (x, y) as set the $\{\{x\}, \{x, y\}\}$. It is easily seen that this definition satisfies conditions (1) and (2). Let us now start with two sets X and Y. Then $\{X\}$ and $\{X, Y\}$ are sets, too. In any formalized approach the requirement that for two sets X and Y, $\{X\}$ and $\{X, Y\}$ are sets, is called the ***Axiom of Pairing***. Therefore we can define an ordered pair of sets as follows:

$$(X, Y) = \{\{X\}, \{X, Y\}\}.$$

Given two classes $\mathcal{A}$ and $\mathcal{B}$, the ***direct product*** $\mathcal{A} \times \mathcal{B}$ is defined as usual:

$$\mathcal{A} \times \mathcal{B} = \{(X, Y) \mid X \in \mathcal{A} \text{ and } Y \in \mathcal{B}\}.$$

Take into consideration that X and Y are indeed sets since they are elements of classes $\mathcal{A}$ and $\mathcal{B}$, respectively.

By definition, $\mathcal{A} \times \mathcal{B}$ is a subclass of $\wp(\wp(\mathcal{A} \cup \mathcal{B}))$. Thus, if $\mathcal{A}$ and $\mathcal{B}$ are sets, then so is $\mathcal{A} \times \mathcal{B}$. Note that $\mathcal{A} \times \mathcal{B}$ is empty whenever $\mathcal{A}$ or $\mathcal{B}$ is empty. In case that neither $\mathcal{A}$ nor $\mathcal{B}$ is empty, $\mathcal{A} \times \mathcal{B}$ is a proper class if $\mathcal{A}$ or $\mathcal{B}$ is proper. To prove that fact we have to introduce the projections $pr_{\mathcal{A}} : \mathcal{A} \times \mathcal{B} \to \mathcal{A}$ and $pr_{\mathcal{B}} : \mathcal{A} \times \mathcal{B} \to \mathcal{B}$, defined by $pr_{\mathcal{A}}((X, Y)) = X$ and $pr_{\mathcal{B}}((X, Y)) = Y$, as class mappings. (Class mappings will be defined later generally.) Let $\mathcal{A}$ be a proper class and assume that $\mathcal{A} \times \mathcal{B}$ is a set. Since $\mathcal{A}$ is the image of $\mathcal{A} \times \mathcal{B}$ under $pr_{\mathcal{A}}$ and as we will see later that every image of a set even under a class mapping is again a set, we derive that $\mathcal{A}$ should be a set, which contradicts the assumption. Having the notion of direct product we are in a position to introduce relations. Given classes $\mathcal{A}$ and $\mathcal{B}$, a ***class relation*** $\mathcal{R}$ from $\mathcal{A}$ to $\mathcal{B}$ is just a

---

[6] Kuratowski, K.: Sur la notion de l'ordre dans le théorie des ensembles. Fund. Math. **2**, 161-171 (1921)

subclass of $\mathcal{A} \times \mathcal{B}$. Define the domain, denoted by $Dom(\mathcal{R})$, and the range, denoted by $Rg(\mathcal{R})$, of a class relation $\mathcal{R}$ as follows:

$$Dom(\mathcal{R}) = \{X \mid (X,Y) \in \mathcal{R} \text{ for some } Y \in \mathcal{B}\},$$
$$Rg(\mathcal{R}) = \{Y \mid (X,Y) \in \mathcal{R} \text{ for some } X \in \mathcal{A}\}.$$

By an easy calculation we get $Dom(\mathcal{R}) \subseteq \bigcup(\bigcup \mathcal{R})$. For any X of $Dom(\mathcal{R})$ there exists some set Y of $\mathcal{B}$ such that $(X,Y) \in \mathcal{R}$, by definition. Set $U = \{X,Y\}$. Now, $U \in V$ (put $V = \{\{X\},\{X,Y\}\}$) and $X \in U$, which means that $X \in \bigcup(\bigcup \mathcal{R})$. It should be mentioned that $Rg(\mathcal{R}) \subseteq \bigcup(\bigcup \mathcal{R})$ holds also true. But this fact will not be used later.

A ***class mapping*** $\mathcal{F}$ from a class $\mathcal{A}$ to a class $\mathcal{B}$, denoted by $\mathcal{F} : \mathcal{A} \to \mathcal{B}$, is a special class relation from $\mathcal{A}$ to $\mathcal{B}$ such that (1) $Dom(\mathcal{F}) = \mathcal{A}$ and (2) for all X, Y, Z, $(X,Y) \in \mathcal{F}$ and $(X,Z) \in \mathcal{F}$ imply $Y = Z$. As usual, we denote the image of $X \in \mathcal{A}$ under $\mathcal{F}$ by $\mathcal{F}(X)$. Since $\mathcal{F}(X) \in \mathcal{B}$, $\mathcal{F}(X)$ is always a set. Furthermore, the image of a subset A of $\mathcal{A}$ under $\mathcal{F}$, defined by $\mathcal{F}(A) = \bigcup\{Y \mid (X,Y) \in \mathcal{F} \text{ for some } X \in A\}$, is also a set, which is (axiomatically) required by the ***Replacement Axiom***.

For any class mapping $\mathcal{F}$ from $\mathcal{A}$ to $\mathcal{B}$ we have that $\mathcal{F}$ is a subclass of $\mathcal{A} \times \mathcal{F}(\mathcal{A})$. Hence a class mapping $\mathcal{F}$ from $\mathcal{A}$ to $\mathcal{B}$ is a set whenever $\mathcal{A}$ is a set. However, $\mathcal{F}$ is proper if $\mathcal{A}$ is so. Otherwise, a proper class would be a subclass of a set because of $\mathcal{A} \subseteq \bigcup(\bigcup \mathcal{F})$.

Given two classes $\mathcal{A}$ and $\mathcal{B}$, we denote by $\mathcal{B}^{\mathcal{A}}$ the class of all class mappings from $\mathcal{A}$ to $\mathcal{B}$, which are sets. If $\mathcal{A}$ and $\mathcal{B}$ are sets, then so is $\mathcal{B}^{\mathcal{A}}$. But if $\mathcal{A}$ is a proper class, all mappings from $\mathcal{A}$ to $\mathcal{B}$ are proper classes. Thus

$$\mathcal{B}^{\mathcal{A}} = \emptyset \qquad \text{if } \mathcal{A} \text{ is a proper class.}$$

By means of class mappings we could generalize the notion of a family to get a family of sets indexed by a class; but this notion is not as general as needed. Here we propose to define a ***family of classes indexed by a class*** $\mathcal{I}$ as a class relation $\mathcal{R}$ from $\mathcal{I}$ to the universal class $\mathcal{U}$. Setting $\mathcal{A}_i = \{X \mid (i,X) \in \mathcal{R}\}$, we will write $(\mathcal{A}_i \mid i \in \mathcal{I})$ instead of $\mathcal{R}$.

Union and intersection can be defined for any family $(\mathcal{A}_i \mid i \in \mathcal{I})$ of classes $\mathcal{A}_i$ indexed by a class $\mathcal{I}$ as follows:

$$\bigcup(\mathcal{A}_i \mid i \in \mathcal{I}) = \{X \mid X \in \mathcal{A}_i \text{ for some } i \in \mathcal{I}\},$$
$$\bigcap(\mathcal{A}_i \mid i \in \mathcal{I}) = \{X \mid X \in \mathcal{A}_i \text{ for all } i \in \mathcal{I}\}.$$

As a consequence of the fact that $\mathcal{B}^{\mathcal{A}}$ is empty for a proper class $\mathcal{A}$, the direct product of a family of classes or even sets indexed by a proper class would always be empty. Thus it does not make sense to introduce the direct product of such families. Given a family of classes $\mathcal{A}_i$ indexed by a set I, the ***direct product*** can defined as:

$$\prod(\mathcal{A}_i \mid i \in I) = \{X \mid X : I \to \bigcup(\mathcal{A}_i \mid i \in I) \text{ such that } X(i) \in \mathcal{A}_i \text{ for all } i \in I\}.$$

Evidently, the direct product of a family of sets indexed by a set is a set, too. But even when each member of the family is nonempty it cannot be shown in general that the direct product is also nonempty. For that conclusion we need a further assumption, which will be discussed subsequently.

* * *

One crucial point in criticism of set theory concerns the acceptance of the existence of (actual) infinity leading to some non-constructive tools. From the point of view of theoretical computer science, which may be thought of as a part of constructive mathematics, we should always be aware of any use of non-constructive arguments. Although we will tolerate them if it is absolutely necessary, we should indicate any use of them explicitly.

Ernst Zermelo has recognized the significance and role of the ***Axiom of Choice*** as a basis for reasoning about infinity. He was the first to formulate it precisely and, in fact, it was the first clearly stated axiom of set theory:

(AC) For any set A there exists a mapping f, called a ***choice function***, from the power set of A to A such that for every nonempty subset X of A the image $f(X)$ belongs to X [7].

In other words, to any set there exists at least one choice function by which an element of each nonempty subset can be selected. This, in general simultaneous, selection of infinitely many elements at one time is the critical point. The plausibility of (AC) rests on the fact that it is obvious for finite sets. But for infinite sets it may lead to some results violating our intuition.

In this context the question arises whether (AC) is derivable from the other generally accepted axioms of set theory or perhaps refutable by them. Kurt Gödel proved that (AC) is consistent with the other axioms provided that they are consistent with each another [8]. So, it is not possible to refute (AC) by the other axioms. On the other hand, Paul Cohen has shown the independence of (AC) from the other axioms [9]. Consequently, we may feel free to agree upon (AC) as a general principle of our (intuitive) set theory. But we are more or less forced to accept it for a twofold reason. First, set theory itself, specifically the theory of cardinals, is simplified by assuming (AC) and secondly, there are so many important theorems, the truth of which is often obvious, but which nevertheless have not been verified without using (AC).

---

[7] Zermelo, E.: Beweis, daß jede Menge wohlgeordnet werden kann. Math. Ann. **59**, 514-516 (1904)

[8] Gödel, K.: The consistency of the axiom of choice and the generalized continuum hypothesis. Proc. Nat. Acad. Sci. USA **24**, 556-557 (1938)

[9] Cohen, P.: The independence of the continuum hypothesis. Proc. Nat. Acad. Sci. USA **50**, 1143-1148 (1963)

The intensive discussion about (AC) over a long time has produced a large variety of equivalent versions. Most of them have been established to enable a better insight. Here we will only mention a few that are really used in our investigations. The interested reader may consult the literature [10].

A reformulation of (AC) using the notion of direct product reads as follows:

(AC_P) Let $(A_i \mid i \in I)$ be a family of sets indexed by a set I. If $A_i \neq \emptyset$ for all $i \in I$, then $\prod(A_i \mid i \in I) \neq \emptyset$.

It is easily seen that (AC) implies the following statement:

(AC_M) Let $f : A \to B$ be a mapping. If f is surjective, then there exists a mapping $g : B \to A$ such that $f \cdot g$ is the identity mapping on A, i.e., $g(f(x)) = x$ for all $x \in A$.

To prove the opposite implication we first show that (AC_M) implies (AC_R):

(AC_R) For every relation R there is a mapping f such that $f \subseteq R$.

Both formulations, (AC_M) and (AC_R), which will be shown to be equivalent, are due to P. Bernays [11].

Given a relation R, define an auxiliary mapping h from R to its domain $Dom(R)$ by the rule: $h((x, y)) = x$. Since h is surjective, there exists by (AC_M) a mapping g from $Dom(R)$ to R such that $g(h((x, y))) = (x, y)$. The required mapping f is now defined as follows: $f(x)$ is the second component of $g(x)$. Clearly, $f \subseteq R$. Hence, (AC_R) follows from (AC_M).

Our next step is the derivation of the following statement: For every mapping f there exists a mapping g with the same domain as f and for all x in domain of f, $g(x) \in f(x)$ if $f(x)$ is nonempty. Given an arbitrary mapping f, we define a relation R_f by the rule: $(x, y) \in R_f$ iff $y \in f(x)$. By (AC_R), there is a mapping g with $g \subseteq R_f$. Thus we get $g(x) \in f(x)$ whenever $f(x)$ is nonempty.

Let A be a given set. By the statement above, corresponding to the identity mapping from $\wp(A)$ into itself there exists a mapping f with domain $\wp(A)$ such that $f(X) \in X$ for each nonempty subset X of A. Hence, $f : \wp(A) \to A$ is a choice function. Thus (AC_R) implies (AC). That is, all formulations of the Axiom of Choice are equivalent.

* * *

[10] Jech, T.J.: About the Axiom of Choice. In: Barwise, J. (ed.): Handbook of Mathematical Logic (Part B). Amsterdam: North-Holland 1977

[11] Bernays, P.: A system of axiomatic set theory II. J. of Symbolic Logic **6**, 1-17 (1941)

This subsection is devoted to ordinal and cardinal numbers. Ordinal numbers make counting somehow possible even in the transfinite case. Similarly, cardinal numbers describe the number of elements in sets, not only in finite sets.

Here we need a further assumption, called the ***Axiom of Foundation***: every nonempty class $\mathcal{A}$ contains an element X such that $\mathcal{A} \cap X = \emptyset$. This axiom excludes "$\in$-loops". Consider a set $A = \{A_1, A_2, \ldots, A_n\}$ such that $A_1 \in A_2 \in \ldots \in A_n \in A_1$ (which is an $\in$-loop). Then $A \cap X \neq \emptyset$ for all $X \in A$.

A class $\mathcal{A}$ is said to be ***$\in$-transitive*** if for all X, $X \in \mathcal{A}$ implies $X \subseteq \mathcal{A}$. An $\in$-transitive set A is called an ***ordinal number*** (or simply an ***ordinal***) if each element of A is also $\in$-transitive. Observe that each element of an ordinal is an ordinal too.

Recall that the natural numbers may be represented as finite sets $0 = \emptyset$ and $n = \{0, 1, \ldots, n-1\}$ for $n \geq 1$. It follows directly from this representation that the finite ordinals are the natural numbers.

We are now going to extend the proper order on the set of natural numbers to all ordinals. Let Ord denote the class of all ordinals. As a rule we shall use lower case Greek letter for (infinite) ordinals. For numbers we have $m < n$ iff $m \in n$. Hence we put

$$\alpha < \beta \text{ iff } \alpha \in \beta$$

for all $\alpha, \beta \in Ord$. Evidently, $<$ is transitive by the definition of ordinals. Moreover, $<$ is irreflexive by the Axiom of Foundation. As usual, $\leq$ designates the reflexive closure of $<$. Our definition of ordinals is, of course, quite artifical. It is just a trick. The intuitive idea of an ordinal is not a set at all, but a type of well-ordering. This essential property will now be derived. First, we assert that $\leq$ is Noetherian. For if $\mathcal{A}$ is a nonempty subclass of Ord, then, by the Axiom of Foundation, there exists an element, say α, in $\mathcal{A}$ such that $\mathcal{A} \cap \alpha = \emptyset$. Because of $\alpha = \{\beta \mid \beta \in \alpha\} = \{\beta \mid \beta < \alpha\}$ we get $\mathcal{A} \cap \{\beta \mid \beta < \alpha\} = \emptyset$, which means that α is minimal in $\mathcal{A}$. Hence $\leq$ is Noetherian. Now it remains to show that Ord is a chain with respect to $\leq$. If we indirectly assume that there exist ordinals which are incomparable, then we can choose them to be minimal in the following sense: α is minimal with the property that there is at least one ordinal incomparable with α; β is minimal among all ordinals incomparable with α. We claim that β is a subset of α. Let γ be an element of β. Note that γ is an ordinal as an element of an ordinal. By the minimality of β, we get that γ is comparable with α since $\gamma < \beta$. Hence $\gamma < \alpha$ or $\gamma = \alpha$ or $\alpha < \gamma$. In order to show that $\gamma \in \alpha$ we have to exclude the latter two alternatives. Therefore assume, on the contrary, that $\gamma = \alpha$ or $\alpha < \gamma$. Because of $\gamma < \beta$, we obtain $\alpha < \beta$ by the transitivity of $<$. Since, by assumption, β is different from α, the complement $\alpha - \beta$ is nonempty. There must be an ordinal, say γ, such that $\gamma \in \alpha$ and $\gamma \notin \beta$. By the minimality of α, we derive that there is no ordinal incomparable with γ. In particular, γ has to be comparable with β. But $\gamma \notin \beta$ yields $\gamma = \beta$ or $\beta < \gamma$. Together with $\gamma < \alpha$ we get $\beta < \alpha$, which is a contradiction since α and β were assumed to be incomparable. Thus $\leq$ is a total order on Ord and, consequently, Ord is a well-order with respect to $\leq$. Hence an ordinal is a set α such that α is $\in$-transitive and α is well-ordered with respect to $\in$. Often in the literature this is taken as a definition of ordinals. To get the equivalence with our definition we have to show that each element β of an $\in$-transitive set α, which is well-ordered with respect to $\in$, is also $\in$-transitive. Let γ be an element of β. By the $\in$-transitivity of α, β is a subset of α. Hence γ is an element of α. Now we are going to prove that γ is a subset of β as required. Given an element δ of γ, then $\delta \in \alpha$ since α is $\in$-transitive. So we have $\delta \in \gamma$ and $\gamma \in \beta$ for $\beta, \gamma, \delta \in \alpha$. Thus, $\delta \in \beta$ by the assumption that α is well-ordered with respect to $\in$. Of course, we need only the fact that $\in$ is a transitive relation on α.

First Principle of Transfinite Induction: A property $\mathcal{P}$ holds for all ordinals α whenever $\mathcal{P}$ holds for all ordinals β with $\beta < \alpha$ (induction hypothesis).

Proof: We denote by $\mathcal{A}_\mathcal{P}$ the subclass of all ordinals with the property $\mathcal{P}$: $\mathcal{A}_\mathcal{P} = \{\alpha \in Ord \mid \mathcal{P}(\alpha)\}$. If we indirectly assume that $\mathcal{A}_\mathcal{P}$ is different from Ord, then the complement $\mathcal{B} = Ord - \mathcal{A}_\mathcal{P}$ is nonempty. Hence $\mathcal{B}$ has a least element, say β. Because of $\beta = \{\gamma \mid \gamma \in \beta\}$ we have $\mathcal{B} \cap \beta = \emptyset$ and, consequently, $\beta \subseteq \mathcal{A}_\mathcal{P}$, which means $\mathcal{P}(\gamma)$ for all ordinals γ with $\gamma \in \beta$ (induction hypothesis). Hence $\mathcal{P}$ holds for β, i.e., $\beta \in \mathcal{A}_\mathcal{P}$. But this is a contradiction to $\beta \notin \mathcal{A}_\mathcal{P}$. ■

An ordinal α is called a ***successor*** (ordinal) if $\alpha = \beta \cup \{\beta\}$ for some ordinal β , where $\beta \cup \{\beta\}$ is said to be the ***immediate successor*** of β. Observe that there is no ordinal between β and $\beta \cup \{\beta\}$ since, otherwise $\beta < \gamma$ and $\gamma < \beta \cup \{\beta\}$ would lead to an $\in$-loop $\beta \in \gamma \in \beta$. The immediate successor of β will also be denoted by $\beta + 1$. An ordinal different from 0, which is not a successor, is called a ***limit ordinal***. By $Sord$ and $Lord$ we denote the class of all successor ordinals including 0 and the class of all limit ordinals, respectively.

The finite ordinals are exactly the successor ordinals such that their elements are successors too. Hence the set $\mathbb{N}$ of all natural numbers equals the set $\{n \mid n \cup \{n\} \subseteq Sord\}$, which is denoted by ω. It is an easy matter to verify the ***Peano Axioms*** for ω [12]. Hence $\mathbb{N}$ and ω will be identified as sets.

(P1) $0 \in \omega$;

(P2) $n + 1 \in \omega$ whenever $n \in \omega$;

(P3) $n + 1 \neq 0$ for all n in ω;

(P4) $m = n$ whenever $m + 1 = n + 1$ for all m, n in ω;

(P5) A set A contains all natural numbers if $0 \in A$ and $n+1 \in A$ whenever $n \in A$.

Let us prove (P5), which is called the induction axiom. If we assume that A is a set such that $\omega - A \neq \emptyset$, then there is a least element, say n, in $\omega - A$. Since $0 \in A$, by

[12] It is important to mention that we are only able to prove that ω is an $\in$-transitive class such that all its elements are $\in$-transitive sets. The fact that ω should be a set must be required axiomatically (by the ***Axiom of Infinity***).

assumption, n is different from 0. Taking into account that n is a successor we have $n = \beta + 1$ for some β. But, of course, β belongs to ω. Because $\beta < n$, β is not in $\omega - A$, or equivalently $\beta \in A$. Thus $\beta + 1 \in A$ by assumption, which leads to a contradiction, namely $n \in A$. Therefore, $\omega \subseteq A$.

As a reformulation of (P5) we obtain the ***Principle of Finite Induction.*** To prove that a property $\mathcal{P}$ holds for all natural numbers it suffices to show the validity of (1) and (2) below:

(1) Induction basis: $\mathcal{P}$ holds for 0.

(2) Induction step: If $\mathcal{P}$ holds for n (induction hypothesis), then $\mathcal{P}$ holds for $n + 1$.

Generalizing this proof method to all ordinals we get the ***Second Principle of Transfinite Induction.*** To prove that a property $\mathcal{P}$ holds for all ordinals it suffices to show the validity of (1), (2) and (3) below:

(1) Induction basis: $\mathcal{P}$ holds for 0.

(2) Induction step 1: If $\mathcal{P}$ holds for α (induction hypothesis), then $\mathcal{P}$ holds for $\alpha + 1$.

(3) Induction step 2: If α is a limit ordinal and $\mathcal{P}$ holds for all β such that $\beta < \alpha$ (induction hypothesis), then $\mathcal{P}$ holds for α.

The proof follows from the First Principle of Transfinite Induction.

Let us mention that ω is the least limit ordinal. Since all finite ordinals are successors we have to show only that ω is a limit ordinal. If we indirectly assume that ω is a successor, then $\omega + 1 \subseteq Sord$ since $\omega \subseteq Sord$. But this yields $\omega \in \omega$, which contradicts the Axiom of Foundation.

Finally, we turn to cardinals, which were introduced as equivalence classes of sets modulo equipotency in Section 1.1.1. But assuming the Axiom of Choice there is a simpler way to define them. The (AC) is equivalent to the ***Principle of Counting***:

Every set is equipotent to an ordinal [13].

By this principle, to any set A a unique minimal ordinal α can be associated so that A and α are equipotent. This minimal ordinal is called the ***cardinal number*** of A denoted by $card(A)$. For any ordinal α we have $card(\alpha) \leq \alpha$. Therefore, α is a cardinal iff $\alpha = card(\alpha)$. All finite ordinals are cardinals. Also ω is a cardinal.

[13] The proof of the equivalence is based on the two facts that every set can be well-ordered and that every well-ordered set is equipotent to an ordinal.

Appendix 2

Ordered Algebras as First-Order Structures

In this appendix ordered algebras are treated as first-order structures to provide a better insight into the way they generalize ordinary algebras. For their definition two signatures, say Σ and P, are needed, where Σ consists of operation symbols and P contains relation symbols with positive arity only. A pair (Σ,P) is often called a ***first-order language***. It is called a ***language of algebras*** if $\mathsf{P}=\emptyset$ and a ***language of relational structures*** if $\Sigma=\emptyset$.

A (Σ,P)-***structure*** $\boldsymbol{A}$ is a triple $\boldsymbol{A}=(A,\Sigma^A,\mathsf{P}^A)$, where A is a set, called the ***carrier*** of $\boldsymbol{A}$, $\Sigma^A=(\sigma^A \mid \sigma\in\Sigma)$ and $\mathsf{P}^A=(\varrho^A \mid \varrho\in\mathsf{P})$ are families of operations and relations on A such that $\sigma^A : A^n \to A$ is the realization of each n-ary operation symbol σ of Σ, and $\varrho^A \subseteq A^n$ is the realization of each n-ary relation symbol ϱ of P. $\boldsymbol{A}$ is also called a ***first-order structure*** or a ***structure***, for short, when (Σ,P) is unspecified or unemphazised. If $\mathsf{P}=\emptyset$, then $\boldsymbol{A}$ is an algebra, while $\boldsymbol{A}$ is called a ***relational structure*** if $\Sigma=\emptyset$. In case both signatures are finite, say, $\Sigma=\{\sigma_1,\dots,\sigma_m\}$ and $\mathsf{P}=\{\varrho_1,\dots,\varrho_n\}$, we often write $\boldsymbol{A}=(A,\sigma_1^A,\dots,\sigma_m^A,\varrho_1^A,\dots,\varrho_n^A)$ instead of $\boldsymbol{A}=(A,\Sigma^A,\mathsf{P}^A)$ adopting the convention that operations as well as relations are listed with decreasing arity.

Example 1. Consider a first-order language with an arbitrary signature Σ of operation symbols and a single binary relation symbol, say $\le$. Then ordered algebras are structures $\boldsymbol{A}=(A,\Sigma^A,\le^A)$ such that $(A,\le^A)$ is a poset and all operations σ^A in Σ^A are monotone. ■

The basic concepts of universal algebra can be generalized for structures. We now briefly review them. Throughout the remainder of the appendix a first-order language (Σ,P) is fixed and all structures are tacitly understood as (Σ,P)-structures. If $\boldsymbol{A}$ is a structure, we say that (A,Σ^A) is the ***algebra part*** of $\boldsymbol{A}$ or the ***underlying algebra*** of $\boldsymbol{A}$.

Let $\boldsymbol{A}$ and $\boldsymbol{B}$ be structures. $\boldsymbol{A}$ is called a ***substructure*** of $\boldsymbol{B}$ if (A,Σ^A) is a subalgebra of (B,Σ^B) and, for all relation symbols ϱ in P, ϱ^A is the restriction of ϱ^B to A, i.e., $\varrho^A=\varrho^B\cap A^n$ if ϱ has arity n.

Example 2. Let $\boldsymbol{A}$ and $\boldsymbol{B}$ be ordered algebras considered as structures as in Example 1. $\boldsymbol{A}$ is a substructure of $\boldsymbol{B}$ iff $\boldsymbol{A}$ is a subalgebra of $\boldsymbol{B}$. ■

A mapping h from a structure $\boldsymbol{A}$ to a structure $\boldsymbol{B}$ is called a ***morphism*** if h is a homomorphism from (A,Σ^A) to (B,Σ^B) and, for all n-ary relation symbols ϱ in P and all $x_1,\dots,x_n$ in A,

$$(x_1,\dots x_n)\in\varrho^A \text{ implies } (h(x_1),\dots,h(x_n))\in\varrho^B.$$

We say that h is a ***full morphism*** if additionally

$$(x_1, \ldots, x_n) \in \varrho^A \text{ whenever } (h(x_1), \ldots, h(x_n)) \in \varrho^B.$$

Note that the composition of (full) morphisms is again a (full) morphism.

A bijective morphism h from $\boldsymbol{A}$ to $\boldsymbol{B}$ is called an ***isomorphism*** if h^{-1} is also a morphism. If $h : \boldsymbol{A} \to \boldsymbol{B}$ is an isomorphism, then $\boldsymbol{A}$ and $\boldsymbol{B}$ are called ***isomorphic***.

If $\boldsymbol{A}$ is a substructure of $\boldsymbol{B}$, the embedding $in_A : \boldsymbol{A} \to \boldsymbol{B}$ is an injective full morphism.

We call a structure $\boldsymbol{B}$ an ***image*** of a structure $\boldsymbol{A}$ if there is a surjective morphism from $\boldsymbol{A}$ to $\boldsymbol{B}$. In contrast to the case of algebras images are not now describable internally by quotients. With any morphism $h : \boldsymbol{A} \to \boldsymbol{B}$ we associate an equivalence: $x \sim y$ iff $h(x) = h(y)$, called the ***kernel*** of h and denoted $kerh$. Actually, $kerh$ is a congruence on the algebra part of $\boldsymbol{A}$. For any congruence $\sim$ on $\boldsymbol{A}$ (precisely, on the algebra part of $\boldsymbol{A}$) the quotient algebra $(A, \Sigma^A)/\sim$ can be enlarged to a structure if each n-ary relation symbol ϱ of P is realized as follows. For all $x_1, \ldots, x_n$ in A: $([x_1], \ldots, [x_n]) \in \varrho^{A/\sim}$ iff

$$(y_1, \ldots, y_n) \in \varrho^A \text{ for some } y_1, \ldots, y_n \in A \text{ with } x_i \sim y_i \text{ for } i = 1, \ldots, n.$$

The resulting structure is also called ***quotient structure*** of $\boldsymbol{A}$ modulo $\sim$, written $\boldsymbol{A}/\sim$. As usual, $nat : \boldsymbol{A} \to \boldsymbol{A}/\sim$ is the ***natural morphism***, defined by $nat(x) = [x]$ for each x of A. The Homomorphism Theorem (Theorem 2 in Section 3.1.2) is only extendable in the following way: If $h : \boldsymbol{A} \to \boldsymbol{B}$ is a surjective full morphism, then $\boldsymbol{A}/kerh$ is isomorphic to $\boldsymbol{B}$. Let us call $\boldsymbol{B}$ a ***full image*** of $\boldsymbol{A}$ in this case. That is, only full images are describable internally by quotients, not images in general.

The ***direct product*** $\boldsymbol{A}$ of a family $(\boldsymbol{A}_i \mid i \in I)$ of structures $\boldsymbol{A}_i$, denoted by $\prod(\boldsymbol{A}_i \mid i \in I)$, is defined by realising the operations and relations coordinatewise. Let $x_1, \ldots, x_n \in A$. For each n-ary operation symbol σ of Σ we have

$$pr_i(\sigma^A(x_1, \ldots, x_n)) = \sigma^{A_i}(pr_i(x_1), \ldots, pr_i(x_n))$$

for all $i \in I$; and for each n-ary relation symbol ϱ in P we have

$$(x_1, \ldots, x_n) \in \varrho^A \text{ iff } (pr_i(x_1), \ldots, pr_i(x_n)) \in \varrho^{A_i}$$

for all $i \in I$; where $pr_i : \boldsymbol{A} \to \boldsymbol{A}_i$ is the i-th projection, which is a surjective morphism.

Now we shall generalize direct unions.

Let I be a directed poset, and let $\boldsymbol{A}_i$, $i \in I$, be structures such that $(\boldsymbol{A}_i \mid i \in I)$ is a directed family, i.e., for all $i, j \in I$, $\boldsymbol{A}_i$ and $\boldsymbol{A}_j$ are substructures of $\boldsymbol{A}_k$ for some upper bound k of i, j. The ***directed union*** $\boldsymbol{A}$ of $(\boldsymbol{A}_i \mid i \in I)$, denoted by $\bigcup(\boldsymbol{A}_i \mid i \in I)$, is a structure defined on the union $A = \bigcup(A_i \mid i \in I)$ over all carriers and operation and relation symbols are realized as unions: $\sigma^A = \bigcup(\sigma^{A_i} \mid i \in I)$ for all $\sigma \in \Sigma$, and $\varrho^A = \bigcup(\varrho^{A_i} \mid i \in I)$ for all $\varrho \in \mathsf{P}$. The corresponding embedding of $\boldsymbol{A}_i$ into $\boldsymbol{A}$ is denoted by in_i.

Directed union is a special case of direct limit, which is defined similarly. Consider a direct family $(h_{ij} : \boldsymbol{A}_i \to \boldsymbol{A}_j)$ of morphisms, i.e., $(\boldsymbol{A}_i \mid i \in I)$ is a family of structures such that, for all $i \leq j$, h_{ij} is a morphism from $\boldsymbol{A}_i$ to $\boldsymbol{A}_j$ with the properties: (1) $h_{ii} = id_{A_i}$ for all $i \in I$; and (2) $h_{ij} \cdot h_{jk} = h_{ik}$ for all $i \leq j \leq k$. The ***direct limit*** of $(h_{ij} : \boldsymbol{A}_i \to \boldsymbol{A}_j)$, denoted by $\lim(\boldsymbol{A}_i \mid i \in I)$, is a structure $\boldsymbol{A}$ together with a family $(h_i : \boldsymbol{A}_i \to \boldsymbol{A})$ of morphisms such that $h_i \cdot h_{ij} = h_j$ for all $i \leq j$, called the ***cone*** of $\boldsymbol{A}$, satisfying the following universal property: (L) For every family $(f_i : \boldsymbol{A}_i \to \boldsymbol{B})$ of morphisms with $f_i = h_{ij} \cdot f_j$ for all $i \leq j$ there exists a unique morphism $f : \boldsymbol{A} \to \boldsymbol{B}$ such that $f_i = h_i \cdot f$ for all $i \in I$. Note that a direct limit, if it exists, is unique up to isomorphism. The existence follows from the fact that the direct limit, say (A, Σ^A), of the underlying algebras of $\boldsymbol{A}_i$ exists and each n-ary relation symbol ϱ of P can be realized in a natural way. Recall that $A = \bigcup(A_i \mid i \in I)/\sim$, where $\sim$ is the equivalence given by: $x \sim y$ iff $x \in A_i$, $y \in A_j$ and there exists $z \in A_k$ such that $i, j \leq k$ and $h_{ik}(x) = z = h_{jk}(y)$. Given n elements of A, say $[x_1], \ldots, [x_n]$, there are indices $i_1, \ldots, i_n$ of I such that $x_i \in A_{i_1}, \ldots, x_n \in A_{i_n}$. Now, by the definition of $\sim$, there are elements $y_1, \ldots, y_n \in A_k$ for some $k \in I$ with $x_i \sim y_i$ for $i = 1, \ldots, n$. We define ϱ^A by:

$$([x_1], \ldots, [x_n]) \in \varrho^A \text{ iff } (y_1, \ldots, y_n) \in \varrho^{A_k}.$$

Finally, the notion of reduced product has to be defined for structures. Let $(\boldsymbol{A}_i \mid i \in I)$ be a family of structures. Given any filter F over I, an equivalence $=_F$ on $\prod(A_i \mid i \in I)$ is defined by: $(x_i \mid i \in I) =_F (y_i \mid i \in I)$ iff $\{i \in I \mid x_i = y_i\} \in F$. In fact, $=_F$ is a congruence of the algebra part of the direct product $\boldsymbol{A} = \prod(\boldsymbol{A}_i \mid i \in I)$ so that $\boldsymbol{A}/{=_F}$ carries an algebra. In addition, each n-ary relation symbol ϱ of P can be realized as follows. Let $[x_1], \ldots, [x_n] \in A$.

$$([x_1], \ldots, [x_n]) \in \varrho^A \text{ iff } \{i \in I \mid (pr_i(x_1), \ldots, pr_i(x_n)) \in \varrho^{A_i}\} \in F.$$

We call $\boldsymbol{A}$ the ***reduced product*** of $(\boldsymbol{A}_i \mid i \in I)$ modulo F; written $\prod(\boldsymbol{A}_i \mid i \in I)/F$. In particular, $\prod(\boldsymbol{A}_i \mid i \in I)/F$ is called the ***ultraproduct*** of $(\boldsymbol{A}_i \mid i \in I)$ modulo F if F is an ultrafilter.

The closure operators

$$\mathbf{S},\ \mathbf{H},\ \mathbf{P},\ \mathbf{U},\ \mathbf{L},\ \mathbf{P}_{red},\ \mathbf{P}_{\mathrm{u}}$$

are defined for abstract classes of structures similarly as for abstract classes of algebras. If $\mathcal{K}$ is an abstract class of structures (i.e., $\mathcal{K}$ is closed under isomorphic structures), then $\boldsymbol{A} \in \mathbf{S}\mathcal{K}$ iff $\boldsymbol{A}$ is a substructure of a structure in $\mathcal{K}$; $\boldsymbol{A} \in \mathbf{H}\mathcal{K}$ iff A is an image of a structure in $\mathcal{K}$; $\boldsymbol{A} \in \mathbf{P}\mathcal{K}$ iff $\boldsymbol{A}$ is a direct product of a family of structures in $\mathcal{K}$; $\boldsymbol{A} \in \mathbf{U}\mathcal{K}$ iff $\boldsymbol{A}$ is a directed union of a directed family of structures in $\mathcal{K}$; $\boldsymbol{A} \in \mathbf{L}\mathcal{K}$ iff $\boldsymbol{A}$ is a direct limit of a direct family of structures in $\mathcal{K}$; $\boldsymbol{A} \in \mathbf{P}_{red}\mathcal{K}$ iff $\boldsymbol{A}$ is a reduced product of a family of structures in $\mathcal{K}$; and $\boldsymbol{A} \in \mathbf{P}_u\mathcal{K}$ iff $\boldsymbol{A}$ is an ultraproduct of a family of structures in $\mathcal{K}$. We use all the same conventions as for closure operators on abstract classes of algebras.

Example 3. Consider a language for relational structures consisting of a single binary relational symbol ϱ. A structure $\boldsymbol{A}$ is a pair (A, ϱ^A), where ϱ^A is a binary relation on A. Let $\mathcal{K}$ be the class of all structures with a reflexive relation. Then $\mathcal{K}$ is obviously closed under substructures, images and direct products. For instance, let $\boldsymbol{B} = (B, \varrho^B)$ be an image of $\boldsymbol{A} = (A, \varrho^A)$. By definition, there is a surjection $f : A \to B$ such that, for all $x, y \in A$, $(x, y) \in \varrho^A$ implies $(f(x), f(y)) \in \varrho^B$. Suppose ϱ^A is reflexive. Then ϱ^B is also reflexive. Let b be an arbitrary element of B. If a is an inverse image of b, that is, $b = f(a)$, then $(a, a) \in \varrho^A$ implies $(f(a), f(a)) \in \varrho^B$. Hence $(b, b) \in \varrho^B$. ■

Example 4. Take the same language for relational structures as in Example 3 and let $\mathcal{K}$ be the class of all quasi-ordered sets. It is easily seen that $\mathcal{K}$ is closed under substructures and direct products, but $\mathcal{K}$ is not closed under images. Consider two structures $\boldsymbol{A}$ and $\boldsymbol{B}$ with the same carrier $A = B = \{a, b, c\}$ and with relations $\varrho^A = \{(a, a), (b, b), (c, c)\}$ and $\varrho^B = \{(a, a), (a, b), (b, b), (b, c), (c, c)\}$. Clearly, $\boldsymbol{A}$ belongs to $\mathcal{K}$, however, $\boldsymbol{B}$ is not in $\mathcal{K}$ since ϱ^B is not transitive. $\boldsymbol{B}$ is an image of $\boldsymbol{A}$ because the identity mapping is a surjective morphism from $\boldsymbol{A}$ to $\boldsymbol{B}$. Hence $\mathcal{K}$ is not closed under images.

Observe that $\mathcal{K}$ is closed under direct limits. Let $(h_{ij} : \boldsymbol{A}_i \to \boldsymbol{A}_j)$ be a direct family of structures $\boldsymbol{A}_i$ in $\mathcal{K}$. For technical reasons we assume that the sets A_i, $i \in I$, are pairwise disjoint. Denote by ϱ_i the realization of ϱ in $\boldsymbol{A}_i$, i.e., $\varrho_i = \varrho^{A_i}$ for $i \in I$. By definition, the direct limit $\boldsymbol{A}$ of $(\boldsymbol{A}_i \mid i \in I)$ is determined by $A = \bigcup(A_i \mid i \in I)/\sim$, where $x \sim y$ iff $x \in A_i$, $y \in A_j$ and there exists $z \in A_k$ such that $i, j \leq k$ and $h_{ik}(x) = z = h_{jk}(y)$, and ϱ^A is defined by: $([x_1], [x_2]) \in \varrho^A$ iff $(y_1, y_2) \in \varrho_k$ for some $y_1, y_2 \in A_k$ with $x_1 \sim y_1$ and $x_2 \sim y_2$. The reflexivity of ϱ^A is obvious. To show transitivity we assume $([a], [b]) \in \varrho^A$ and $([b], [c]) \in \varrho^A$. If $a \in A_i$, $b \in A_j$ and $c \in A_k$, then there are $a', b' \in A_l$ with $i, j \leq l$ and $a \sim a'$, $b \sim b'$ as well as $b'', c'' \in A_m$ with $j, k \leq m$ and $b \sim b''$, $c \sim c''$. By assumption, $(a', b') \in \varrho_l$ and $(b'', c'') \in \varrho_m$. Suppose n is an upper bound of l and m. Then $(h_{ln}(a'), h_{ln}(b')) \in \varrho_n$ and $(h_{mn}(b''), h_{mn}(c'')) \in \varrho_n$ since h_{ln} and h_{mn} are morphisms for $l \leq m$ and $m \leq n$. Because of $b' \sim b''$ we derive $h_{ln}(b') = h_{mn}(b'')$ and so $(h_{ln}(a'), h_{mn}(c'')) \in \varrho_n$, by the transitivity of ϱ_n. This yields $(h_{in}(a), h_{kn}(c) \in \varrho_n$ since $h_{in} = h_{il} \cdot h_{ln}$ and $h_{kn} = h_{km} \cdot h_{mn}$ for $i \leq l \leq n$ and $k \leq m \leq n$, respectively. Hence, by definition, $([a], [c]) \in \varrho^A$. That is, ϱ^A is transitive. ■

Example 5. Similarly as in the case of quasi-ordered sets we may show that the class of all posets, considered as relational structures, is closed under substructures, direct products and direct limits. ■

Example 6. Consider the class $\mathcal{K}$ of all posets with a least element. $\mathcal{K}$ is closed under direct products but neither under substructures nor under direct limits. Let $\boldsymbol{A}$ be a flat poset with three elements. That is, $A = \{\perp, a, b\}$ and $\varrho^A = \{(\perp, \perp), (\perp, a), (\perp, b), (a, a), (b, b)\}$. Then the substructure of $\boldsymbol{A}$ with carrier $\{a, b\}$ has no least element.

We shall show that $\mathcal{K}$ is not even closed under directed unions; hence, in particular, $\mathcal{K}$ is also not closed under direct limits. For $n \in \mathbb{N}$, define posets $\boldsymbol{A}_n$ as follows: $A_n = \{0, 1, \ldots, n\}$ and the partial order on A_n is the converse of the common ordering: $0 > 1 > \ldots > n$. As a finite chain each $\boldsymbol{A}_n$ has a least element, namely n. The family $(\boldsymbol{A}_n \mid n \in \mathbb{N})$ is itself a chain. Therefore we can build the directed union $\boldsymbol{A} = \bigcup(\boldsymbol{A}_n \mid n \in \mathbb{N})$, which is, of course, a poset but without a least element. $\boldsymbol{A}$ is isomorphic with $\mathbb{N}$ equipped with the converse order.

$\mathcal{K}$ is, however, closed under reduced products. Let $(\boldsymbol{A}_i \mid i \in I)$ be a family of posets $\boldsymbol{A}_i = (A_i, \leq_i)$ with least element $\perp_i$ for all $i \in I$. If F is a filter over I, we have to show that the poset $\boldsymbol{A} = \prod(\boldsymbol{A}_i \mid i \in I)/F$ has a least element, too. By definition, for all elements $[x]$ and $[y]$ in A with $x = (x_i \mid i \in I)$ and $y = (y_i \mid i \in I)$, $[x] \leq [y]$ iff $\{i \in I \mid x_i \leq_i y_i\} \in F$. We set $\perp = [(\perp_i \mid i \in I)]$. Then $\perp \leq [x]$ for all $[x]$ in A since $\{i \in I \mid \perp_i \leq_i x_i\} = I$ and I belongs to any filter F over I. Thus, $\boldsymbol{A}$ is a poset with a least element. That is, $\mathcal{K}$ is closed under reduced products. ■

To axiomatize classes of structures we have to introduce first-order formulas. Let (Σ,P) be a first-order language and V be a countably infinite set. As customary, V is thought of as a "standard alphabet" of variables. For technical reasons V is supposed to be disjoint from Σ and P, respectively. Terms of type (Σ,P) over V are just Σ-terms over V. The ***atomic formulas*** of type (Σ,P) over V are either (unquantified) term equations

$t = t'$, where $t, t' \in T_\Sigma(V)$,

or expressions of the form

$\varrho(t_1, \ldots, t_n)$, where ϱ is any n-ary relational symbol of P and $t_1, \ldots, t_n \in T_\Sigma(V)$.

The set of all atomic formulas of type (Σ,P) over V is denoted by $At(\Sigma,\mathsf{P},V)$. We agreed to write terms in the most readable way, and so we do with atomic formulas. In particular, we write $x\varrho y$ instead of $\varrho(x, y)$ for any binary relation symbol ϱ.

Based on atomic formulas the set of all ***first-order formulas*** of (Σ,P) over V, denoted by $Fml(\Sigma,\mathsf{P},V)$, is defined using additional rules of formation which introduce negation $(\neg)$, conjunction $(\wedge)$, and universal quantification $(\forall)$. Formally, $Fml(\Sigma,\mathsf{P},V)$ is the least set of words over the alphabet $L(\Sigma,\mathsf{P},V)$, which is the union of Σ, P, V, $\{=, \neg, \wedge, \forall\}$ and $\{(,)\}$, such that $At(\Sigma,\mathsf{P},V) \subseteq Fml(\Sigma,\mathsf{P},V)$ and $Fml(\Sigma,\mathsf{P},V)$ is closed under the three rules:

(1) If $\Phi \in Fml(\Sigma,\mathsf{P},V)$, then $(\neg\Phi) \in Fml(\Sigma,\mathsf{P},V)$.

(2) If $\Phi_1, \Phi_2 \in Fml(\Sigma,\mathsf{P},V)$, then $(\Phi_1 \wedge \Phi_2) \in Fml(\Sigma,\mathsf{P},V)$.

(3) If $\Phi \in Fml(\Sigma,\mathsf{P},V)$ and $x \in V$, then $(\forall x(\Phi)) \in Fml(\Sigma,\mathsf{P},V)$.

Parentheses in formulas will be omitted whenever there is no danger of confusion. To avoid unnecessary parentheses we shall not write outermost pairs of parentheses. For instance, $\neg\Phi$ is our abbreviation for the formula $(\neg\Phi)$. We shall also adopt the common practice of omitting parentheses on the basis of a binding hierarchy of the connections. After we have introduced the remaining logical connectives, disjunction ($\vee$), implication ($\Rightarrow$) and (logical) equivalence ($\Leftrightarrow$), $\neg$ is considered more binding than $\wedge$ and $\vee$, which in turn are more binding than $\Leftarrow$ and $\Leftrightarrow$.

We use $\equiv$ to mean "is defined by". For any Φ_1, Φ_2, Φ in $Fml(\Sigma,\mathsf{P},V)$ and $x \in V$:

(4) $\Phi_1 \vee \Phi_2 \equiv \neg(\neg\Phi_1 \wedge \neg\Phi_2)$;

(5) $\Phi_1 \Rightarrow \Phi_2 \equiv \neg\Phi_1 \vee \Phi_2$;

(6) $\Phi_1 \Leftrightarrow \Phi_2 \equiv (\Phi_1 \Rightarrow \Phi_2) \wedge (\Phi_2 \Rightarrow \Phi_1)$;

(7) $\exists x(\Phi) \equiv \neg\forall x(\neg\Phi)$.

A formula Φ' is called a ***subformula*** of a formula Φ if there is a subword (a consecutive string of symbols from $L(\Sigma,\mathsf{P},V)$) in Φ which is precisely the formula Φ'.

A particular variable $x \in V$ may appear several times in the word over $L(\Sigma,\mathsf{P},V)$ which constitutes a formula Φ; each of these is called an ***occurrence*** of x. An occurrence x in Φ is said to be ***bound*** if it occurs in $(\forall x)$ or is within the scope of a quantifier $(\forall x)$, where Φ' is called the ***scope*** of $(\forall x)$ if $\forall x(\Phi')$ is a formula in $Flm(\Sigma,\mathsf{P},V)$. Otherwise, an occurrence of x is ***free*** in Φ. For a variable x to be ***free*** (***bound***) in Φ means that some occurrence of x is free (bound) in Φ. Observe that a variable can appear free and bound in a formula. We find it convenient to write $\Phi(x_1, \ldots, x_n)$ if all free variables of Φ are among $\{x_1, \ldots, x_n\}$. A ***sentence*** is a formula with no free variables.

We say that a formula is ***open*** if there is no quantifier (universal or existential) in it. A formula is said to be in the ***prenex normal form*** if it is of the form

$$Q_1 x_1 \ldots Q_n x_n \Phi,$$

where each Q_i is a quantifier and Φ is an open formula. $Q_1 x_1 \ldots Q_n x_n$ is called the ***prefix*** and Φ the ***matrix*** of the formula $Q_1 x_1 \ldots Q_n x_n \Phi$.

If a formula is in prenex normal form and all its quantifiers are universal, then it is called a ***universal formula***. In this case we simply write

$$\forall x_1, \ldots, x_n \Phi,$$

instead of $\forall x_1 \ldots \forall x_n \Phi$.

In Chap. 3 we already introduced special kinds of universal sentences (over a language of algebras), namely (universally quantified) equations

$$\forall x_1, \ldots, x_n (t_1 = t_2),$$

where $t_1, t_2 \in T_\Sigma(\{x_1, \ldots, x_n\})$, and so-called universal Horn clauses

$$\forall x_1, \ldots, x_n(t_1 = t_1' \wedge \ldots \wedge t_k = t_k' \Rightarrow t = t'),$$

where $t_1, t_1', \ldots, t_k, t_k', t, t' \in T_\Sigma(\{x_1, \ldots, x_n\})$.

However, it is important to observe that neither implications nor finitary implications are first-order formulas. In the first case, (universal) quantification over infinitely many variables and infinite conjunctions in the premises of implications are used, while finitary implications differ from first-order formulas in using infinitely many conjunctions.

Semantics are defined in what follows. Let $\boldsymbol{A}$ be an arbitrary structure and let $\alpha : V \to A$ be any assignment of variables in $\boldsymbol{A}$. First, consider atomic formulas. We write

$$(\boldsymbol{A}, \alpha) \models t = t' \text{ iff } \alpha^{\#}(t) = \alpha^{\#}(t'); \text{ and}$$

$$(\boldsymbol{A}, \alpha) \models \varrho(t_1, \ldots, t_n) \text{ iff } (\alpha^{\#}(t_1), \ldots, \alpha^{\#}(t_n)) \in \varrho^A.$$

Second, the relation $\models$ is extended to all first-order formulas according to the formation rules (1) – (3) above. For any Φ, Φ_1 and Φ_2 in $Fml(\Sigma, \mathsf{P}, V)$ we define

(1) $(\boldsymbol{A}, \alpha) \models \neg\Phi$ iff $(\boldsymbol{A}, \alpha) \models \Phi$ does not hold (which we abbreviate to $(\boldsymbol{A}, \alpha) \not\models \Phi$);

(2) $(\boldsymbol{A}, \alpha) \models \Phi_1 \wedge \Phi_2$ iff $(\boldsymbol{A}, \alpha) \models \Phi_1$ and $(\boldsymbol{A}, \alpha) \models \Phi_2$;

(3) $(\boldsymbol{A}, \alpha) \models \forall x(\Phi)$ iff $(\boldsymbol{A}, \beta) \models \Phi$ for all $\beta : V \to A$ such that $\beta(y) = \alpha(y)$ for every $y \in V - \{x\}$.

We say that a first-order formula Φ is ***satisfied by*** α ***in*** $\boldsymbol{A}$ if $(\boldsymbol{A}, \alpha) \models \Phi$ holds. In checking satisfaction we have to decompose Φ to the "pieces" it was built up from. Since in this process (when (3) is applied) the number of free variables may increase, it is not convenient to start with $\alpha : X \to A$, where X is the set of free variables in Φ. However, if the free variables in Φ are at most $x_1, \ldots, x_n$, then we can say that $(a_1, \ldots, a_n) \in A^n$ satisfies $\Phi(x_1, \ldots, x_n)$ iff there is an assignment α from $\{x_1, \ldots, x_n\}$ to $\boldsymbol{A}$ such that $\alpha(x_i) = a_i$ for $i = 1, \ldots, n$ and $(\boldsymbol{A}, \alpha) \models \Phi(x_1, \ldots, x_n)$. In this case, we will also write

$$\boldsymbol{A} \models \Phi(a_1, \ldots, a_n)$$

and say that $\Phi(a_1, \ldots, a_n)$ is ***valid*** in $\boldsymbol{A}$.

For any universal sentence we get

$$\boldsymbol{A} \models \forall x_1, \ldots, x_n \Phi$$

iff $(\boldsymbol{A}, \alpha) \models \Phi$ for all assignments α from $\{x_1, \ldots, x_n\}$ to $\boldsymbol{A}$. In particular, $\boldsymbol{A} \models \forall x_1, \ldots, x_n(t = t')$ iff $\alpha^{\#}(t) = \alpha^{\#}(t')$ for all assignments α from $\{x_1 \ldots, x_n\}$ to $\boldsymbol{A}$ (cf.

Definition 2 in Section 3.2.1). Similarly, we can show that $\boldsymbol{A} \models \forall x_1, \ldots, x_n(t_1 = t'_1 \wedge \ldots \wedge t_k = t'_k \Rightarrow t = t')$ iff $\alpha^{\#}(t_i) = \alpha^{\#}(t'_i)$ for $i = 1, \ldots, k$ implies $\alpha^{\#}(t) = \alpha^{\#}(t')$ (cf. Definition 2 in Section 3.3.1).

We are now going to generalize the notion of model. Let Γ be a set of sentences. A structure $\boldsymbol{A}$ is a ***model*** of Γ if $\boldsymbol{A} \models \Phi$ for all Φ in Γ. $Mod\ \Gamma$ denotes the class of all models of Γ.

A further concept is needed for the characterization of model classes. Two structures $\boldsymbol{A}$ and $\boldsymbol{B}$ are said to be ***elementarily equivalent*** if every sentence which is valid in $\boldsymbol{A}$ is valid in $\boldsymbol{B}$ as well. If $\boldsymbol{A}$ and $\boldsymbol{B}$ are isomorphic, then, of course, $\boldsymbol{A}$ and $\boldsymbol{B}$ are elementarily equivalent, but not vice versa. It is worthwhile to mention that elementarily equivalence can be described algebraically: Two structures are elementarily equivalent iff they have isomorphic ultrapowers [1)].

A class $\mathcal{K}$ of structures is called ***axiomatic*** if $\mathcal{K}$ is the model class of some set of sentences.

Theorem 1. *A class of structures is axiomatic if and only if it is closed under elementary equivalence and ultraproducts.* ■

A proof of this theorem and the following theorems can be found in, e.g., Burris, S.; Sankappanvar, H.P.: A course in universal algebra. Springer 1981.

In checking whether a given class of structures is closed under ultraproducts we often use the following result.

Proposition 2. *Let $(\boldsymbol{A}_i \mid i \in I)$ be a family of structures, and F be any ultrafilter over I. For every formula Φ with free variables among $\{x_1, \ldots, x_n\}$ and all $[a_1], \ldots, [a_n]$ in $\prod(\boldsymbol{A}_i \mid i \in I)/F$, the conditions (1) and (2) below are equivalent:*

(1) $\prod(\boldsymbol{A}_i \mid i \in I)/F \models \Phi([a_1], \ldots, [a_n])$; *and*

(2) $\{i \in I \mid \boldsymbol{A}_i \models \Phi(pr_i(a_1), \ldots, pr_i(a_n))\} \in F$.

Proof. We abbreviate $\boldsymbol{A} = \prod(\boldsymbol{A}_i \mid i \in I)/F$ and $X = \{x_1, \ldots, x_n\}$. By definition, $\boldsymbol{A} \models \Phi([a_1], \ldots, [a_n])$ iff $(\boldsymbol{A}, \alpha) \models \Phi$, where α is an assignment from X to $\boldsymbol{A}$ such that $\alpha(x_j) = [a_j]$ for $j = 1, \ldots, n$. Note that $\alpha = \beta \cdot nat_F$ with $\beta : X \to \prod(\boldsymbol{A}_i \mid i \in I)$ and $nat_F : \prod(\boldsymbol{A}_i \mid i \in I) \to \boldsymbol{A}$ such that $\beta(x_j) = a_j$ for $j = 1, \ldots, n$ and $nat_F(a) = [a]$ for all a in $\prod(\boldsymbol{A}_i \mid i \in I)$. Furthermore, we set $\beta_i = \beta \cdot pr_i$ for all $i \in I$, i.e., $\beta_i(x_j) = pr_i(a_j)$ for all $i \in I$, $j = 1, \ldots, n$.

First, let us consider atomic formulas. If $\Phi \equiv (t = t')$ with $t, t' \in T_\Sigma(X)$, then $(\boldsymbol{A}, \alpha) \models \Phi$ iff $\alpha^{\#}(t) = \alpha^{\#}(t')$. Since $\alpha^{\#}(t) = \alpha^{\#}(t')$ iff $\beta^{\#}(t) =_F \beta^{\#}(t')$ iff $\{i \in I \mid pr_i(\beta^{\#}(t)) =$

---

1) Cf. Shelah, S.: Every two elementarily equivalent models have isomorphic ultrapowers. Israel J. Math. **10**, 224-233 (1971).

$pr_i(\beta^{\#}(t'))\} \in F$ and, on the other hand, $pr_i(\beta^{\#}(t)) = pr_i(\beta^{\#}(t'))$ iff $(\boldsymbol{A}_i, \beta_i) \models \Phi$, we derive the equivalence of (1) and (2) for Φ. The other atomic case is entirely analogous.

Second, we perform an induction over the formation rules for building up formulas from basic ones.

(i) Let $\Phi \equiv \neg\Phi'$ and suppose conditions (1) and (2) are equivalent for Φ' (induction hypothesis). By definition, $\boldsymbol{A} \models \Phi([a_1], \ldots, [a_n])$ iff $\boldsymbol{A} \not\models \Phi'([a_1], \ldots, [a_n])$. Thus $\boldsymbol{A} \models \Phi([a_1], \ldots, [a_n])$ iff $\{i \in I \mid \boldsymbol{A}_i \models \Phi'(pr_i(a_1), \ldots, pr_i(a_n))\}$ is not in F. Now, it is important that F is assumed to be an ultrafilter. This yields $\{i \in I \mid \boldsymbol{A}_i \models \Phi'(pr_i(a_1), \ldots, pr_i(a_n))\} \notin F$ iff $\{i \in I \mid \boldsymbol{A}_i \not\models \Phi'(pr_i(a_1), \ldots, pr_i(a_n))\} \in F$. Hence $\boldsymbol{A} \models \Phi([a_1], \ldots, [a_n])$ is equivalent to $\{i \in I \mid \boldsymbol{A}_i \models \Phi(pr_i(a_1), \ldots, pr_i(a_n))\} \in F$.

(ii) If $\Phi \equiv \Phi_1 \wedge \Phi_2$ and Φ_1, Φ_2 fulfill the induction hypothesis, then conditions (1) and (2) are equivalent for Φ. Here we use the fact that any filter is closed under intersection.

(iii) Let $\Phi \equiv \forall x\Phi'$ and suppose Φ' fulfills the induction hypothesis. By assumption, Φ' may have x as an additional free variable; hence we write $\Phi'(x, x_1, \ldots, x_n)$. Then the following statements are equivalent: $\boldsymbol{A} \models \Phi([a_1], \ldots, [a_n])$ and $\boldsymbol{A} \models \Phi'([a], [a_1], \ldots, [a_n])$ for all $[a] \in A$, which in turn is equivalent to $\{i \in I \mid \boldsymbol{A}_i \models \Phi'(pr_i(a),\ pr_i(a_1), \ldots, pr_i(a_n))\} \in F$ for all $[a] \in A$, by induction hypothesis. Since $\Phi(pr_i(a_1), \ldots, pr_i(a_n))$ is valid in $\boldsymbol{A}_i$ iff $\Phi'(pr_i(a), pr_i(a_1), \ldots, pr_i(a_n))$ is valid in $\boldsymbol{A}_i$ for all $[a] \in A$, we obtain that $\{i \in I \mid \boldsymbol{A}_i \models \Phi(pr_i(a_i), \ldots, pr_i(a_n))\}$ includes $\{i \in I \mid \boldsymbol{A}_i \models \Phi'(pr_i(a), pr_i(a_1), \ldots, pr_i(a_n))\}$ for all $[a] \in A$. Hence $\{i \in I \mid \boldsymbol{A}_i \models \Phi(pr_i(a_1), \ldots, pr_i(a_n))\} \in F$ whenever $\{i \in I \mid \boldsymbol{A}_i \models \Phi'(pr_i(a), pr_i(a_1), \ldots, pr_i(a_n))\} \in F$ for all $[a]$ in A. Thus, conditions (1) and (2) are equivalent for Φ. ■

Example 7. Let $\mathcal{K}$ be the class of all ω-complete posets, considered as relational structures. It is intuitively clear that $\mathcal{K}$ is not an axiomatic class but we will prove it. For that purpose it suffices to show that $\mathcal{K}$ is not closed under ultraproducts.

For every natural number n, define an ω-complete poset $\boldsymbol{A}_n$ as an initial segment of $\mathbb{N}$: $A_n = \{0, 1, \ldots, n+1\}$ with the usual ordering $0 < 1 < \ldots < n < n+1$. Evidently, $\boldsymbol{A}_n$ is an ω-complete chain with the following properties: (1) $\boldsymbol{A}_n$ has a least and a greatest element; (2) Every element of $\boldsymbol{A}_n$, except the greatest element of $\boldsymbol{A}_n$, has an immediate successor; and (3) Every element of $\boldsymbol{A}_n$, except the least one, has an immediate predecessor.

Now, take any ultrafilter F over $\mathbb{N}$ which contains all cofinite subsets of $\mathbb{N}$. Keep in mind that such an ultrafilter exists.

Claim: $\prod(\boldsymbol{A}_n \mid n \in \mathbb{N})/F$ is a poset, which is not ω-complete.

We are going to show that $\prod(\boldsymbol{A}_n \mid n \in \mathbb{N})/F$ is isomorphic to the poset $\boldsymbol{A}$ defined as follows: $A = \{a_n \mid n \in \mathbb{N}\} \cup \{b_n \mid n \in \mathbb{N}\}$ and $a_0 < a_1 < \ldots < a_n < \ldots < b_n < b_{n-1} < \ldots < b_1 < b_0$. That is, $\boldsymbol{A}$ is an infinite chain, where a_0 is the least element, and b_0 is the greatest element. Furthermore, every element x of A with $x \neq b_0$ has an immediate successor, and every element x of A with $x \neq a_0$ has an immediate predecessor.

To prove the claim we introduce a formula d_m, for each $m \geq 2$, which expresses the existence of m pairwise distinct elements:

$$d_m = \exists x_1, \ldots, x_m(x_1 \neq x_2 \wedge \ldots \wedge x_1 \neq x_m \wedge x_2 \neq x_3 \wedge \ldots \wedge x_{m-1} \neq x_m),$$

where $x \neq y \equiv \neg(x = y)$. Obviously, $\{n \in I\!N \mid \boldsymbol{A}_n \models d_m\}$ is cofinite and hence belongs to F. By Proposition 2, $d_m(m \geq 2)$ is valid in $\prod(\boldsymbol{A}_n \mid n \in I\!N)/F$. Thus the ultraproduct $\prod(\boldsymbol{A}_n \mid n \in I\!N)/F$ is an infinite poset.

Now, the other properties mentioned above can be expressed by the following formulas:

$$least(x) \equiv \forall y(x \leq y),$$

$$greatest(x) \equiv \forall y(y \leq x),$$

$$comp(x, y) \equiv x \leq y \vee y \leq x,$$

$$succ(x) = \neg greatest(x) \Rightarrow \exists y(x < y \wedge \neg\exists z(x < z \wedge z < y)),$$

$$pred(x) = \neg least(x) \Rightarrow \exists y(y < x \wedge \neg\exists z(z < x \wedge y < z)),$$

where $x < y \equiv x \leq y \wedge x \neq y$.

Consider the following two sequences $\bot = (\bot_n \mid n \in I\!N)$ and $\top = (\top_n \mid n \in I\!N)$, defined by $\bot_n = 0$ and $\top_n = n + 1$ for all $n \in I\!N$. Then $least([\bot])$ is valid in the ultraproduct since $\{n \in I\!N \mid \boldsymbol{A}_n \models least(\bot_n)\} = I\!N$ and hence belongs to F. Similarly, $\prod(\boldsymbol{A}_n \mid n \in I\!N)/F \models greatest([\top])$. That is, $[\bot]$ is the least and $[\top]$ is the greatest element in $\prod(\boldsymbol{A}_n \mid n \in I\!N)/F$. Using the formula $comp(x, y)$, we may show that the ultraproduct is actually an infinite chain (with least and greatest element).

Let $x = (x_n \mid n \in I\!N)$ be an arbitrary sequence with $x_n \in A_n$ for all $n \in I\!N$. By Proposition 2, $\prod(\boldsymbol{A}_n \mid n \in I\!N)/F \models succ([x])$ iff $\{n \in I\!N \mid \boldsymbol{A}_n \models succ(x_n)\} \in F$. But $succ(x_n)$ is valid in every $\boldsymbol{A}_n$, $n \in I\!N$, so $succ([x])$ is valid in $\prod(\boldsymbol{A}_n \mid n \in I\!N)/F$. Analogously, $\prod(\boldsymbol{A}_n \mid n \in I\!N)/F \models pred([x])$. Thus, $\prod(\boldsymbol{A}_n \mid n \in I\!N)/F$ is isomorphic to $\boldsymbol{A}$.

It is easy to see that $\boldsymbol{A}$ is not ω-complete. Take the countably infinite chain $(a_n \mid n \in I\!N)$ of $\boldsymbol{A}$. Then each b_n is an upper bound of it but there is no least upper bound. Hence, the class of all ω-complete posets is not closed under ultraproducts. ■

A class $\mathcal{K}$ of structures is called a ***universal class*** if $\mathcal{K}$ is the model class for some set of universal sentences. It is easy to see that every universal class is closed under substructures and as a special axiomatic class, also under ultraproducts. Of course, it is closed under elementary equivalence, too. But this condition can be relaxed.

Theorem 3. *An abstract class of structures is universal if and only if it is closed under substructures and ultraproducts.* ■

Example 8. Consider the class $\mathcal{K}$ of all posets with a least element. From Example 6 we know that $\mathcal{K}$ is not closed under substructures but closed under reduced products, and hence closed under ultraproducts. Thus, $\mathcal{K}$ is an axiomatic class but not a universal one. In fact, $\mathcal{K}$ is the model class of the set of the following sentences:

(1) $\forall x(x \leq x)$;

(2) $\forall x, y(x \leq y \wedge y \leq x \Rightarrow x = y)$;

(3) $\forall x, y, z(x \leq y \wedge y \leq z \Rightarrow x \leq z)$;

(4) $\exists x \forall y(x \leq y)$.

Of course, the requirement of a least element cannot be expressed by a universal sentence. ■

Example 9. The class $\mathcal{K}$ of all posets is clearly a universal class. Indeed, $\mathcal{K}$ is the model class of the first three universal sentences (1) – (3) from Example 8. Hence, by Theorem 3, $\mathcal{K}$ is an abstract class closed under substructures and ultraproducts. In Example 5, it is claimed that $\mathcal{K}$ is closed under substructures, direct products and direct limits. As for algebras one can show that any abstract class of structures is closed under reduced products whenever it is closed under direct products and direct limits. ■

In the case of algebras we know already that (strict) universal Horn classes are an important specialization of universal classes. To define them for structures, we have to generalize the notion of a universal Horn clause. A first-order formula Φ is a ***basic Horn formula*** provided Φ is a disjunction of formulas, at most one of which is atomic and the remainder of which are negations of atomic formulas. A basic Horn formula is called a ***positive Horn clause*** if exactly one of its disjuncts is atomic, whereas a ***negative Horn clause*** is a disjunction of negated atomic formulas. A ***universal Horn sentence*** Φ is a universal sentence the matrix of which is a conjunction of basic Horn formulas. If all basic Horn formulas in Φ are positive, respectively, negative Horn clauses, we call Φ a ***positive***, respectively, ***negative universal Horn sentence.*** In particular, a ***positive*** or ***negative universal Horn clause*** means a universal sentence whose matrix consists just of one positive or negative Horn clause, respectively.

Consider a language for algebras. Any positive universal Horn clause is either a universally quantified equation, $\forall x_1, \ldots, x_n(t = t')$, or is of the form

$$\forall x_1, \ldots, x_n(t_1 = t'_1 \wedge \ldots \wedge t_k = t'_k \Rightarrow t = t'),$$

where t, t', t_i, t'_i are terms over $\{x_1, \ldots, x_n\}$ for $i = 1, \ldots, k$. In accordance with our notation in Chap. 3, positive (universal) Horn clauses are simply called (***universal***) ***Horn clauses.***

A class $\mathcal{K}$ of structures is called a ***universal Horn class*** if $\mathcal{K} = Mod\ \Gamma$ for some set Γ of universal Horn sentences. If Γ consists of positive universal Horn sentences, $\mathcal{K}$ is called a ***strict universal Horn class***.

For the characterization of universal classes by closure operators we have to restrict direct and reduced products. Let $\mathcal{K}$ be an abstract class of structures. $\mathbf{P}^*\mathcal{K}$ and $\mathbf{P}^*_{red}\mathcal{K}$ denote the abstract class of all direct or reduced products, respectively, of nonempty families of structures of $\mathcal{K}$.

There is only a slight difference between closure under direct or reduced products and their restricted versions. Observe that $\mathbf{P}\mathcal{K}$ and $\mathbf{P}_{red}K$ always contain trivial algebras with singleton carriers, whereas $\mathbf{P}^*\mathcal{K}$ and $\mathbf{P}^*_{red}\mathcal{K}$ do not necessarily contain such trivial algebras.

Example 10. Consider a language of relational structures with a single binary relational symbol, say $<$. Let Γ be the set of the following universal Horn sentences:

(1) $\forall x(x \not< x)$;

(2) $\forall x, y, z(x < y \wedge y < z \Rightarrow x < z)$.

The model class of Γ consists of all properly ordered sets. $Mod\ \Gamma$ is a universal Horn class but not a strict one. Observe that $Mod\ \Gamma$ does not contain any trivial structure with a singleton as carrier since there is no proper order on any singleton; specifically, irreflexivity (1) cannot be satisfied. ■

Theorem 4. *For any abstract class $\mathcal{K}$ of structures the following conditions are equivalent:*

(1) $\mathcal{K}$ is a universal Horn class;

(2) $\mathcal{K}$ is a universal class, and $\mathcal{K}$ is closed under nonempty direct products;

(3) $\mathcal{K}$ is closed under substructures and nonempty reduced products;

(4) $\mathcal{K}$ is closed under substructures, direct limits and nonempty direct products. ■

Generalizing our results about strict universal classes of algebras we get

Theorem 5. *For any abstract class of structures the following conditions are equivalent:*

(1) $\mathcal{K}$ is a strict universal Horn class;

(2) $\mathcal{K}$ is a universal Horn class, and $\mathcal{K}$ contains a trivial structures with a singleton as carrier;

(3) $\mathcal{K}$ is a universal class, and $\mathcal{K}$ is closed under direct products;

(4) $\mathcal{K}$ is closed under substructures and reduced products;

(5) $\mathcal{K}$ is closed under substructures, direct limits, and direct products. ∎

Example 11. Let $(\Sigma, \{\leq\})$ be a first-order language. Consider the set Γ_0 consisting of the following (positive) universal Horn clauses:

(1) $\forall x(x \leq x)$;

(2) $\forall x, y(x \leq y \wedge y \leq x \Rightarrow x = y)$;

(3) $\forall x, y, z(x \leq y \wedge y \leq z \Rightarrow x \leq z)$;

and for any n-ary operation symbol σ of Σ

$$(4_\sigma)\ \forall x_1, \ldots, x_n, y_1, \ldots, y_n(x_1 \leq y_1 \wedge \ldots \wedge x_n \leq y_n \Rightarrow \sigma x_1 \ldots x_n \leq \sigma y_1 \ldots y_n).$$

Obviously, *Mod* Γ_0 is the class of all orderd Σ-algebras, which is a strict universal Horn class. By Theorem 5, *Mod* Γ_0 is closed under substructures, direct limits, and direct products. That is, the class of all ordered Σ-algebras is closed under subalgebras, direct limits and direct products. ∎

In what follows, ordered algebras will always be regarded as structures, as presented in the example above.

Now we turn to the relative axiomatization of ordered algebras. Given a set Γ of sentences, we denote by $Mod_0\Gamma$ the class of all ordered algebras $\boldsymbol{A}$ such that $\boldsymbol{A} \models \Phi$ for each Φ of Γ. That is, $\boldsymbol{A} \in Mod_0\Gamma$ iff $\boldsymbol{A} \in Mod\ \Gamma$ and $\boldsymbol{A}$ is an ordered algebra. Let us denote by Γ_0 the set of (positive) universal Horn clauses (1) – (3) and (4_σ) for all operation symbols σ given in Example 11. Then

$$Mod_0\Gamma = Mod(\Gamma \cup \Gamma_0);$$

and we may say that an abstract class $\mathcal{K}$ of ordered algebras is ***relatively definable*** by Γ if $\mathcal{K} = Mod_0\Gamma$. Bloom's Order Variety Theorem (Theorem 6 in Section 4.2.1) states that an abstract class $\mathcal{K}$ of ordered algebras is relatively definable by inequalities iff $\mathcal{K}$ is an order variety.

If we assume that there is a distinguished nullary operation symbol, say $\perp$, then

$$Mod_\perp\Gamma = Mod(\Gamma \cup \Gamma_\perp),$$

where $\Gamma_\perp = \Gamma_0 \cup \{\forall x(\perp \leq x)\}$). Similarly, an abstract class $\mathcal{K}$ of strict ordered algebras is relatively definable by inequalities iff $\mathcal{K}$ is a strict order variety.

As we already know, there is no possibility to relatively axiomatize abstract classes of ω-complete ordered algebras since there is no way to describe ω-completeness and ω-continuity by first-order formulas. For that purpose, we would have to use a more general kind of formula such as inequalities between trees (which are infinitely long expressions).

Subject Index

EATCS Monographs on Theoretical Computer Science

Vol. 1: K. Mehlhorn
Data Structures and Algorithms 1:
Sorting and Searching

Vol.2: K. Mehlhorn
Data Structures and Algorithms 2:
Graph Algorithms and NP-Completeness

Vol.3: K. Mehlhorn
Data Structures and Algorithms 3:
Multidimensional Searching and Computational Geometry

Vol.4: W. Reisig
Petri Nets
An Introduction

Vol.5: W. Kuich, A. Salomaa
Semirings, Automata, Languages

Vol.6: H. Ehrig, B. Mahr
Fundamentals of Algebraic Specification 1
Equations and Initial Semantics

Vol. 7: F. Gécseg
Products of Automata

Vol. 8: F. Kröger
Temporal Logic of Programs

Vol. 9: K. Weihrauch
Computability

Vol. 10: H. Edelsbrunner
Algorithms in Combinatorial Geometry

Vol. 11: J. L. Balcázar, J. Díaz, J. Gabarró
Structural Complexity I

Vol. 12: J. Berstel, C. Reutenauer
Rational Series and Their Languages

Vol. 13: E. Best, C. Fernàndez C.
Nonsequential Processes
A Petri Net View

Vol. 14: M. Jantzen
Confluent String Rewriting

Vol. 15: S. Sippu, E. Soisalon-Soininen
Parsing Theory
Volume I: Languages and Parsing

Vol. 16: P. Padawitz
Computing in Horn Clause Theories

Vol. 17: J. Paredaens, P. De Bra, M. Gyssens, D. Van Gucht
The Structure of the Relational Database Model

Vol. 18: J. Dassow, G. Păun
Regulated Rewriting in Formal Language Theory

Vol. 19: M. Tofte
Compiler Generators
What they can do, what they might do, and what they will probably never do

Vol. 20: S. Sippu, E. Soisalon-Soininen
Parsing Theory
Volume II: LR(k) and LL(k) Parsing

Vol. 21: H. Ehrig, B. Mahr
Fundamentals of Algebraic Specification 2
Module Specifications and Constraints

Vol. 22: J. L. Balcázar, J. Díaz, J. Gabarró
Structural Complexity II

Vol. 23: A. Salomaa
Public-Key Cryptography

Vol. 24: T. Gergely, L. Úry
First-Order Programming Theories

Vol. 25: W. Wechler
Universal Algebra for Computer Scientists